NEW YORK REVIEW B
CLASSICS

MEMOIRS FROM BEYOND THE GRAVE

FRANÇOIS-RENÉ DE CHATEAUBRIAND (1768–1848) was born in Saint-Malo, on the northern coast of Brittany, the youngest son of an aristocratic family. After an isolated adolescence, spent largely in his father's castle, he moved to Paris not long before the Revolution began. In 1791, he sailed for America but quickly returned to Europe, where he enrolled in the counterrevolutionary army, was wounded, and emigrated to England. The novellas *Atala* and *René*, published shortly after his return to France in 1800, made him a literary celebrity. Long recognized as one of the first French Romantics, Chateaubriand was also a historian, a diplomat, and a staunch defender of the freedom of the press. Today he is best remembered for his posthumously published *Memoirs from Beyond the Grave*.

ALEX ANDRIESSE was born in Cedar Rapids, Iowa, in 1985. In addition to *Memoirs from Beyond the Grave*, he has translated the work of Roberto Bazlen, Italo Calvino, and Marcel Schwob. He is the editor of *The Uncollected Essays of Elizabeth Hardwick* (published by NYRB Classics) and an associate editor at New York Review Books.

JULIEN GRACQ (1910–2007) was born Louis Poirier in Saint-Florent-le-Vieil, a small village in western France. His first book, *The Castle of Argol* (1938), was praised by André Breton as the first surrealist novel. Opposed to publicity and self-promotion, he refused the Prix Goncourt when he was awarded it for his 1951 novel, *The Opposing Shore*. His novel *Balcony in the Forest* (1958) is published by NYRB Classics.

MEMOIRS FROM BEYOND THE GRAVE

1800–1815

FRANÇOIS-RENÉ DE CHATEAUBRIAND

Translated from the French by
ALEX ANDRIESSE

Afterword by
JULIEN GRACQ

NEW YORK REVIEW BOOKS

New York

THIS IS A NEW YORK REVIEW BOOK
PUBLISHED BY THE NEW YORK REVIEW OF BOOKS
435 Hudson Street, New York, NY 10014
www.nyrb.com

Library of Congress Cataloging-in-Publication Data
Names: Chateaubriand, François-René, vicomte de, 1768–1848 author. |
  Andriesse, Alex translator.
Title: Memoirs from beyond the grave: 1768–1800 / by François-René de
  Chateaubriand ; introduction by Anka Muhlstein ; translation by Alex
  Andriesse.
Description: New York: New York Review Books, 2018.
Identifiers: LCCN 2017025073 (print) | LCCN 2017028760 (ebook) |
  ISBN 9781681376189 (epub) | ISBN 9781681376172 (alk. paper)
Subjects: LCSH: France—History—Consulate and First Empire, 1799–1815. |
  Napoleon I, Emperor of the French, 1769–1821—Contemporaries.
Classification: LCC DC255.C4 (ebook) | LCC DC255.C4 A3 2017 (print) |
  DDC 944.04—dc23
LC record available at https://lccn.loc.gov/2017025073

ISBN 978-1-68137-617-2
Available as an electronic book; ISBN 978-1-68137-618-9

Printed in the United States of America on acid-free paper.
10 9 8 7 6 5 4 3 2 1

CONTENTS

BOOK TWENTY-THREE

MEMOIRS FROM BEYOND THE GRAVE

BOOK THIRTEEN

I.

SOJOURN IN DIEPPE—TWO SOCIETIES

Dieppe, 1836; Revised in December 1846

YOU KNOW that I have moved from place to place many times while writing these *Memoirs*, that I have often described these places, spoken of the feelings they inspired in me, and retraced my memories, mingling the stories of my restless thoughts and sojourns with the story of my life.

You see where I am living now. This morning, out walking on the cliffs behind the Château de Dieppe, I gazed at the archway that leads to those cliffs by means of a bridge thrown over a moat. Through that same archway, Madame de Longueville escaped from Queen Anne of Austria. Stealing away on a ship that set sail from Le Havre, she landed in Rotterdam and rendezvoused in Stenay with Marshal de Turenne. The great captain's laurels had by then been sullied, and the exiled tease treated him none too well.[1]

Madame de Longueville, who did honor to the Hôtel de Rambouillet, the throne of Versailles, and the city of Paris, fell in love with the author of the *Maxims*[2] and tried her best to be faithful to him. The latter lives on thanks less to his "thoughts" than to the friendship of Madame de La Fayette and Madame de Sévigné, the poetry of La Fontaine, and the love of Madame de Longueville. So you see the value of having famous friends.

The Princesse de Condé on her deathbed said to Madame de Brienne, "My dear friend, write to that poor wretch in Stenay and acquaint her with the state in which you see me, so that she may learn how to die." Fine words—but the princess was forgetting that she had once been courted by Henri IV, and that, when her husband took her to Brussels, she yearned to find her way back to the Béarnese, "to climb out a window at night and ride thirty or forty leagues on horseback." She was at that time a "poor wretch" of seventeen.

At the foot of the cliff, I found myself on the high road to Paris. This road rises steeply as it leaves Dieppe. To the right, on the ascendant line of an embankment, stands a cemetery wall; along this wall is a wheel for winding rope. Two rope-makers, walking backward side by side, swinging their weight from one leg to the other, were singing together in low voices. I pricked up my ears. They had come to these two lines in "Le Vieux Caporal," that fine poetic lie which has led us where we are today:

> *Qui là-bas sanglote et regarde?*
> *Eh! c'est la veuve du tambour.*[3]

The two men sang the refrain, *Conscrits, au pas; ne pleurez pas…* *Marchez au pas, au pas*, in such manly and melancholy voices that tears welled in my eyes. As they kept in step and wound their hemp, they seemed to be spinning out the old corporal's dying moments. I cannot say what share of this glory, so forlornly disclosed by two sailors singing of a soldier's death in plain view of the sea, belonged to Béranger.

The cliff had put me in mind of monarchical grandeur, the road of plebeian celebrity, and I now compared the men at these two ends of society. I asked myself to which of these epochs I would prefer to belong. When the present has vanished like the past, which of these two forms of fame will most attract the attention of posterity?

And yet if facts were everything, if in history the value of names did not counterweigh the value of events, what a difference between my days and the days that passed between the deaths of Henry IV and Mazarin! What are the troubles of 1648 compared to the Revolution that has devoured the old world, of which it will die perhaps, leaving behind neither an old nor a new society. The scenes I have described in my *Memoirs*—are they not incomparably more important than those recounted by the Duc de La Rochefoucauld? Even here in Dieppe, what is the blithe and voluptuous idol of seduced, insurgent Paris set beside Madame la Duchesse de Berry?[4] The cannon fire that announced the royal widow to the sea sounds no longer; those blandishments of powder and smoke have left nothing on shore except the moaning waves.

The two Bourbon daughters, Anne-Geneviève and Marie-Caroline, are nowhere to be found; the two sailors singing the song of the plebeian poet will sink into obscurity; Dieppe is void of me. It was another "I," an "I" of early days long gone who lived in these places, and that "I" has already succumbed, for our days die before us. Here, you have seen me as a sublieutenant in the Navarre Regiment exercising recruits on the shale. Here, you have seen me exiled by Bonaparte. Here, you will see me once more, when the days of July take me by surprise. Here I am again, and here I take up my pen one more time to continue my Confessions.

So that we understand each other, it will be useful to take a look around at the current state of my *Memoirs*.

2.

THE STATE OF MY *MEMOIRS*

WHAT HAS happened to me is what happens to every contractor working on a large scale. To begin with, I built the outer wings, then—shifting and reshifting my scaffolding—raised the stone and mortar of the structures in between. It took many centuries to complete the Gothic cathedrals. If heaven permits me to go on living, this monument of mine will be finished in the course of my years; the architect, still one and the same, will have changed only in age. Still, it is taxing to keep one's intellectual being intact, imprisoned in its weather-beaten shell. Saint Augustine, feeling his clay crumbling, said unto God, "Be Thou a tabernacle unto my soul." And to men he said, "When you find me in these books of mine, pray for me."

Thirty-six years divide the events that set my *Memoirs* in motion from those that occupy me today. How can I resume, with any real intensity, the narration of a subject that once filled me with fire and passion, now that there are no longer any living people with whom I can speak of these things; now that it is a matter of reviving frozen effigies from the depths of Eternity and descending into a burial vault to play at life? Am I not already half dead myself? Have my opinions not changed? Can I still see things from the same point of view? The prodigious public events that accompanied or followed those private events that so perturbed me—has their importance not dwindled in the eyes of the world, as it has in my own? Anyone who prolongs his career on earth feels a chill descending on his days; he no longer finds tomorrow as interesting as he found it yesterday. When I rack my brains, there are names, and even people, that escape me, no matter how much they once may have caused my heart to pound. Oh, the vanity of man forgetting and forgotten! It is not enough to say to our dreams, our loves, "Wake up!" for them to come to life again. The realm of the shades can only be opened with the golden bough,[5] and a young hand is needed to pull it down.

3.

1800—VIEW OF FRANCE—I ARRIVE IN PARIS

Dieppe, 1836

Aucuns venants des Lares patries.
(Rabelais)[6]

SHUT AWAY in Great Britain for eight years, I had seen nothing outside the English world, so different, especially then, from the rest of the European world. In the spring of 1800, as the Dover packet-boat approached Calais, my eyes preceded me ashore. I was struck by the forsaken look of the country. Only a scant few masts could be seen in the harbor. A throng of people in carmagnole jackets and cotton caps came down the jetty to meet us: the conquerors of the continent were announced to me by the sound of their wooden shoes. When we came alongside the pier, the gendarmes and customs officers jumped on deck and inspected our baggage and passports. In France, a man is always suspect, and the first thing to be seen in our matters of business and pleasure alike is a tricorn hat or a bayonet.

Madame Lindsay was waiting for us at the inn. The next day we left for Paris: I, Madame Lindsay, Madame d'Aguesseau, and the latter's young kinswoman.[7] We saw almost no men on the road. Weathered, sun-darkened women, barefoot, with their heads uncovered or wrapped in kerchiefs, were tilling the fields: one might have thought them slaves. I should instead have been struck by the independence and virility of that land where the women were wielding the mattock while the men were off wielding the musket. It looked as though a fire had swept through the villages; they were wretched and half-razed. Everywhere was mud and dust, muck and rubble.

On both sides of the road there were houses demolished. Nothing remained of their felled groves except a few squared stumps, where children played. We saw broken enclosure walls, deserted churches from which the dead had been expelled, belfries without bells, cemeteries without crosses, beheaded saints stoned in their niches. The walls were stained with already-antiquated Republican slogans: LIBERTÉ, ÉGALITÉ, FRATERNITÉ OU LA MORT.[8] At times someone had tried to erase the word *mort*, but the black or red letters were resurfacing now from beneath the coat of lime. This nation, which seemed on the point of dissolution, was beginning a world anew, like those nations emerging from the barbarian, ruinous night of the Dark Ages.

Approaching the capital, between Écouen and Paris, I saw the elms had not yet been felled. I was struck by those handsome itinerary avenues[9] unknown on English soil. France was now as new to me as the American forests had been. Saint-Denis lay bare, its windows broken; the rain poured down on its weedy naves, and all the tombstones were gone. I have, since, seen Louis XVI's bones, the Cossacks, the Duc de Berry's coffin, and Louis XVIII's catafalque within those walls.

Auguste de Lamoignon came to visit Madame Lindsay: his elegant carriage made quite a contrast with the bulky carts and filthy, dilapidated diligences drawn by rope-harnessed nags that I had been seeing on the road from Calais. Madame Lindsay was then living in Les Thernes.[10] I was dropped off on the Chemin de la Révolte[11] and made my way across fields to my hostess's house. There I stayed for twenty-four hours and talked with a tall fat man called Monsieur Lasalle, who helped Madame Lindsay arrange the émigrés' affairs. She sent word of my arrival to M. de Fontanes, and after forty-eight hours he came to fetch me from the depths of the little room Madame Lindsay had rented me at an inn close by.

It was a Sunday. Around three o'clock in the afternoon, we entered

Paris on foot through the Barrière de l'Étoile. We have no idea today of the impression the excesses of the Revolution had made on European minds, and above all on men who had not been in France during the Terror. It seemed to me that I was literally about to descend into Hell. I had been a witness, it's true, to the first stirrings of the Revolution; but the great crimes had not yet been committed, and I had endured the yoke of the deeds that followed as they were related to me in peaceable, orderly England.

Proceeding under my false name and convinced I was compromising my friend Fontanes, I was astonished, on entering the Champs-Élysées, to hear the sounds of violins, horns, clarinets, and drums. I saw open-air halls where men and women were dancing. Farther down, the Tuileries Palace loomed in the hollow between its two great stands of chestnuts. As for the Place Louis XV,[12] it was bare; it had the dilapidation, the melancholy and deserted air of an old amphitheater, and we crossed it quickly. I was surprised to hear no sounds of moaning. I feared stepping in the blood not a trace of which remained. I could not tear my gaze from the empty space where the deadly instrument had stood. I imagined I could see my brother and sister-in-law shirted and bound beside the blood-smeared machine. That, I thought, was the place where Louis XVI's head had fallen. Despite the cheerful mood in the streets, the church towers stood silent. I felt as though I'd returned on Good Friday, the day of infinite sorrow.

M. de Fontanes was living on the rue Saint-Honoré, near Saint-Roch. He brought me to his home, introduced me to his wife, and afterward took me to his friend M. Joubert,[13] who gave me temporary shelter. I was received like a traveler of whom one has heard tell.

The next day I went to the police, under the name Lassagne, to give up my foreign passport in exchange for a permit to remain in Paris which would be renewed from month to month. Within a few days, I had rented an entresol on the rue de Lille, near the rue des Saints-Pères.

I had brought with me *The Genius of Christianity* and the first proofs of that work, which had been printed in London. I was directed to M. Migneret, a good man, who agreed to finish the interrupted printing and to advance me something to live on. Not a soul had heard of my *Essai historique sur les révolutions*, despite what M. Lemière had written me.[14] I disinterred the old philosopher Delisle de Sales, who had just published his *Mémoire en faveur de Dieu*, and went to pay a visit to Ginguené.[15] The latter was lodging in the rue de Grenelle-Saint-Germain, near the Hôtel du Bon La Fontaine. His porter's box still read: "Here we honor each other with the title of citizen and say *tu*, not *vous*. Close the door behind you, please." I climbed the stairs. M. Ginguené, who hardly acknowledged me, spoke from the heights of the grandeur of all that he was and all that he had been. I went away humbly and did not seek to renew such disproportionate relations.

In my heart of hearts, I was still nurturing English regrets and memories. I had lived so long in England I had adopted its habits. I could not reconcile myself to the dirtiness of our houses, staircases, and tables, to our impropriety, our noisiness, our familiarity, to the indiscretion of our gossip. I was English in manners, taste, and, to a certain degree, in thought, for if, as has been claimed, Lord Byron drew some inspiration from *René* in *Childe Harold*, it is also true to say that eight years' residence in England, preceded by a voyage in America, and my habit of talking, writing, and even thinking in English, had necessarily influenced the turn and expression of my ideas. But gradually I came to savor the sociability that distinguishes us—that charming, simple, rapid exchange of intelligence, that absence of all stiffness and prejudice, that disregard of great fortunes and names, that natural leveling of all ranks, and that equality of minds which makes French society unlike any other, and which redeems our faults. After a few months' residence among us, a man feels that he can no longer live except in Paris.

4.

1800—MY LIFE IN PARIS

Paris, 1837

I LOCKED myself up in my entresol and gave myself over completely to my work. During intervals of rest, I went to survey various sections of the city. In the middle of the Palais-Royal, the Circus had been leveled.[16] Camille Desmoulins no longer held forth in the open air. There was no trace of those bands of prostitutes, virginal companions of the goddess Reason, marching to the drum of David, their costumier and Corybant.[17] In the galleries at the end of every passageway, one found men advertising curiosities: shadow theaters, *vues d'optique*, wonder rooms, exotic animals. So many heads had rolled, and yet the rabble remained. From the depths of the cellars of the Palais-Marchand came bursts of music and the rumble of big drums. Perhaps this was the dwelling place of those giants I was looking for, which such immense events must by rights have produced? I descended. A subterranean ball was in full swing; onlookers sat along the edges, drinking beer. A little hunchback perched on a table was playing the violin and singing a hymn to Bonaparte which ended with the lines:

> *Par ses vertus, par ses attraits,*
> *Il méritait d'être leur père!*[18]

He was given a sou for this refrain. Such is the basis of that human society which bore Alexander and which in those days was bearing Napoleon.

I revisited the places where I had led my youthful dreams. In the old convents, the club members had been chased out just as surely as the monks before them. Strolling behind the Luxembourg, my footsteps led me to the Charterhouse. Its demolition was almost complete.[19]

The Place des Victoires and the Place de Vendôme mourned the missing statues of the great king; the community of Capuchins had been sacked: the cloister within was being used as a sanctuary for Robertson's phantasmagoria.[20] At the Cordeliers, I asked in vain after the Gothic nave where I had seen Marat and Danton in their prime. On the Quai des Théatins, the church of that order had become a café and a rope-dancing hall. On the door a colored poster depicted dancers on a tightrope and, in large letters, bore the words ADMISSION FREE. I plunged with the crowd into that perfidious lair and was not quite seated when the waiters came in with napkins in their hands, shouting like madmen, "Eat up, messieurs! Eat up!" I did not have to be told twice, and I made my piteous escape to the mocking laughter of everyone there, for I had no money to "eat up."

5.
SOCIETY'S CHANGES

THE REVOLUTION has been divided into three parts that have nothing in common: the Republic, the Empire, and the Restoration. These three distinct worlds, each as complete unto itself as the others, seem centuries apart. Each one had a fixed principle: the principle of the Republic was equality; of the Empire, power; of the Restoration, liberty. The Republican era is the most original and the most deeply etched because it was unique in history. No one had ever seen, and no one will ever see again, physical order produced by moral disorder, unity issuing from government by the multitude, the scaffold substituted for the rule of law and obeyed in the name of humanity.

I was present, in 1801, at the second social transformation. The turmoil was bizarre. By an agreed-upon travesty, a horde of individuals had become persons they were not: each wore his assumed or borrowed name hung around his neck, as the Venetians at Carnival carry a little mask in their hands to make it clear they are "masked." One was supposed to be Italian or Spanish, another Prussian or Dutch. I was Swiss. Mothers passed for aunts, fathers for uncles; the owner of an estate became its steward. These actions reminded me, with the direction reversed, of the events of 1789, when the monks and nuns departed their cloisters and the old society was invaded by the new. The latter, having taken the place of the former, were now being replaced in turn.

Yet the orderly world was beginning to reassert itself. Men left the cafés and returned to their houses; they gathered what was left of

their families; they recomposed their inheritances by culling together
the scraps, as when, after a battle, the roll is called and the losses are
tallied. The churches, or what remained of them, were reopened: I
had the good fortune to sound the trumpet at the temple gate. The
old Republican generations were fading and the imperial generations
coming to the fore. Penniless, requisitioned generals, rude-tongued
and stern-faced, who had brought home nothing from all their cam-
paigning but wounds and ragged coats, crossed paths with officers
agleam with the gold bars of the consular army. The returning émigré
chatted peaceably with the murderers of a few of his relations. All
the porters, great partisans of Robespierre, lamented the spectacles
of the Place Louis XV, where they cut off the heads of women whose
necks—my own concierge in the rue de Lille told me—"were as white
as chicken flesh." The Septembriseurs,[21] having changed their names
and neighborhoods, now sold baked potatoes on street corners; but
they were often obliged to take to their heels when people recognized
them and overturned their carts, out for blood. Revolutionaries who
had struck it rich began to move into the huge mansions of the Faubourg Saint-Germain. The Jacobins, on their way to becoming barons
and counts, spoke only of the horrors of 1793, the necessity of punish-
ing the proletarians and repressing the excesses of the populace.
Bonaparte, finding positions for the Brutuses and Scaevolas[22] on his
police force, was getting ready to bedeck them with ribbons, befoul
them with titles, force them to betray their opinions and dishonor
their crimes. Amidst all this, a vigorous generation was growing up,
sown in blood, but raised to spill only the blood of foreigners. Day
by day, the transformation of republicans into imperialists—and from
the tyranny of all into the despotism of one—was coming to pass.

6.

WHILE I was busy cutting, crowding, and changing the sheets of *The Genius of Christianity*, necessity forced me to pursue other projects. At the time, M. de Fontanes was editing the *Mercure de France* and proposed I write something for the paper. These sorties into print were not without danger: one could not touch the political world except through the written word, and it was well understood that nothing escaped the eyes of Bonaparte's police. Some unusual circumstances, by preventing me from sleeping, lengthened my days and gave me more time. I had bought two turtledoves, and they cooed constantly. In vain I tried shutting them up at night in my little traveling trunk, which only made them coo louder. In one of the many moments of insanity they caused me, I made up my mind to write a letter to Madame de Staël for the *Mercure*. This riposte brought me abruptly out of the shadows. A few pages in a newspaper accomplished what two fat volumes on revolutions had not. My head had emerged ever so slightly above the level of utter obscurity.

This first success seemed to herald the one that followed. I was in the midst of revising the proofs of *Atala* (a self-contained episode, like *René*, in *The Genius of Christianity*) when I noticed that some pages were missing. Fear gripped me: I was sure that my novel had been stolen. It was a rather unfounded fear to entertain, to be certain, since no one would have thought it worth the trouble of thieving. Be that as it may, I decided to publish *Atala* separately, and I announced my decision in a letter addressed to the *Journal des Débats* and the *Publiciste*.

Before risking the work out in the open, I showed it to M. de Fontanes, who had already read fragments of the manuscript in London. When he came to Father Aubry's speech at Atala's deathbed, he said to me brusquely, in a rough voice:

"That's not right. It's no good. You must redo it!"

I left the room devastated; I didn't feel capable of doing better. I wanted to throw the whole thing in the fire. From eight until eleven o'clock that night, I sat at the table in my entresol with my forehead resting on the backs of my hands, palms spread across the paper. I was as frustrated with myself as I was with Fontanes. I didn't even try to write, I felt so hopeless. Around midnight, I heard the voices of my turtledoves, muffled by distance and made all the more plaintive by the prison in which I kept them. Inspiration found me. In a trance, I traced the missionary's speech without adding or striking through a single word, just as it would remain and does remain to this day. The next morning, my heart pounding, I took it to Fontanes, who exclaimed:

"This is it, this is it! I told you you could do better!"

Whatever noise I have made in this world dates from the publication of *Atala*. It was at that point that I ceased to live for myself alone and began my public career. After so many military successes, a literary success seemed a miracle: the crowd was hungry for it, and the strangeness of the work only added to their surprise. *Atala*, tumbling out among the literature of the Empire—a literature of that painted-lady classical school, the very sight of which inspired boredom—was a new production of an unforeseen sort. No one knew whether to class it among the "monstrosities" or the "beauties." Was it a Gorgon or a Venus? The academicians in their meetings learnedly discoursed upon its sex and nature, just as they would *The Genius of Christianity*. The old century rejected it, and the new one welcomed it.

Atala became so popular that she went to swell, with Madame de Brinvilliers,[23] the Curtius waxworks. Roadside inns were decorated with lithographs in red, green, and blue depicting Chactas, Father Aubry, and Simaghan's daughter. In the wooden boxes on the quais, they displayed my characters molded in wax, as images of the Virgin and the saints are displayed at fairs. At a street theater, I once saw my savage girl coiffed in cockerel feathers, talking about the "soul of solitude" to another savage of her tribe in such a way that I sweated with embarrassment. At the Variétés,[24] they put on a play in which a girl and a boy, leaving their lodgings, went by coach to be married in their little village. Once there, they rambled on vaguely about alligators, storks, and forests, to the point that their parents thought they'd gone insane. Parodies, caricatures, and mockeries oppressed me. To confound me, Abbé Morellet made his servant girl sit on his lap to demonstrate it was impossible to hold the young virgin's feet in his hands as Chactas held Atala's feet during the storm. If the Chactas of the rue d'Anjou had also painted himself up like the original, I would have forgiven him this criticism.

The whole train of events added to the commotion surrounding my appearance. I became all the rage. My head was turned. I was unacquainted with the pleasures of self-importance, and I was intoxicated by them: I loved fame like a woman or, rather, like a first love. Yet, coward that I was, my fear was equal to my passion: a conscript, I conducted myself poorly under fire. My inborn unsociability, the doubt I have always harbored about my talent, made me humble amid my triumphs, and I shrunk from my conspicuous success. I went for walks by myself, trying to douse the brilliant halo with which my head had been crowned. In the evenings, with my hat pulled down over my eyes for fear someone might recognize *the great man*, I went to the café to surreptitiously read my praises sung in one or another unknown little paper. Alone together with my reputation, I extended my strolls as far as the Chaillot fire pump, along the same stretch where I'd suffered on my way to the royal Court.

I was no more at ease with my new honors. When His Highness dined for thirty sous in the Latin Quarter, the food went down the wrong pipe, he was so bothered by the gazes he believed were trained upon him. I contemplated myself, and declared: "Even you—you extraordinary creature—eat like an ordinary man!" There was a café on the Champs-Élysées I liked on account of the nightingales that inhabited a cage suspended all round the perimeter of the room. Madame Rousseau, the proprietress of the place, knew me by sight without knowing who I was. Around ten o'clock every evening she would bring me a cup of coffee, and I would look for *Atala* in the *Petites Affiches*, to the songs of five or six Philomelas. Alas, I was soon to see poor Madame Rousseau die. Our little world of nightingales and the Indian girl who sang, "Sweet habit of love, so necessary to life," lasted only a moment.

If success could not prolong this idiotic engorgement of my vanity or pervert my reason, it did hold some dangers of another sort. These dangers increased with the appearance of *The Genius of Christianity* and my resignation over the death of the Duc d'Enghien. Then there came pressing in around me, together with the crowd of young women who weep at novels, a crowd of Christians, and those other noble enthusiasts whose hearts beat faster at an honorable act. Ephebes of thirteen or fourteen were the most dangerous: not knowing what they want or what they want of you, they mix up their image of you with a beguiling world of fables, ribbons, and flowers. Jean-Jacques Rousseau speaks of the declarations he received on the publication of *The New Héloïse* and the conquests offered him: I don't know if empires would have been likewise delivered unto me, but I do know that I was buried deep beneath a pile of perfumed notes. If these notes were not today notes from grandmothers, I would be embarrassed to recount, with appropriate modesty, how they would fight with each other for a word from my hand, how they would pick up an envelope signed by me and, blushing, hide it from sight, bowing their heads beneath the tumbling veils of their long locks. If I was not spoiled by all this, I must really have a good nature.

Out of genuine politeness or frail curiosity, I sometimes even let myself believe I was obliged to go in person and thank these unknown ladies who had sent me their names along with their compliments. One day, in a fourth-floor apartment, I found a ravishing creature, kept under her mother's wing, whose house I never set foot in again.

A Polish woman received me in silk-lined rooms; part odalisque and part Valkyrie, she looked like a snowflake with white petals, or one of those elegant heathers that take the place of the other daughters of Flora before their season has arrived, or after their season has passed. This choir of women of all different ages and beauties was my old sylph made flesh. The effect on my vanity and feelings might have been even more perilous considering that, up to then, apart from one serious attachment, I had neither been sought after nor picked out from the crowd. Yet I must say this: easy as it would have been for me to abuse some passing delusion, the prospect of a love affair lit by the chaste fires of religion revolted me. To be loved for *The Genius of Christianity*, loved for "Extreme Unction"—for "The Dance of Death"! I could never have been such a shameful Tartuffe.

I once knew a Provençal man of medicine called Doctor Vigaroux. Having arrived at the age where every pleasure deducts a day, "he had no regrets," he said, regarding the way he'd squandered his time. Without bothering about whether he'd given as much joy as he'd received, he was going down to death, which he hoped to make his "final delectation." Yet I was witness to his sad tears at the end. He could not conceal his suffering from me. He was out of time. His white hairs were not long enough to hide or wipe away his tears. There is no real unhappiness in leaving this world except for the unbeliever: for the man without faith, existence has something dreadful about it, which bespeaks nothingness; if a man were never born, he could never experience the horror of no longer being. An atheist's life is a horrible lightning strike that serves only to show him the abyss.

Great and merciful God, you have not hurled us down to earth for petty pains and miserable pleasures! Our inevitable disenchantment warns us that our destinies lie somewhere more sublime. Whatever our errors have been, if we have retained a serious soul and thought of you in the midst of our weakness, we shall be transported, when your goodness delivers us, to that realm where all bonds are eternal.

7.

MADAME DE BEAUMONT AND HER CIRCLE

Paris, 1837

I DID NOT have to wait long to be punished for my authorial vanity—the most detestable, if not the most hideous, of all. I had thought I would be able to savor *in petto* the satisfaction of being a sublime genius, not by sporting a beard and unusual clothes as nowadays, but by remaining accoutered in the same fashion as ordinary people, set apart only by my excellence. Vain hope! My pride was bound to be chastised, and the chastisement came by way of the political men I was obliged to get to know. The profits of fame are charged to the soul.

M. de Fontanes was Madame Baciocchi's friend. He introduced me to this sister of Bonaparte and soon after to the First Consul's brother Lucien. The latter had a country house near Senlis (le Plessis), where I was coerced to go and dine. This château had belonged to Cardinal de Bernis. In the garden was the tomb of Lucien's first wife, a half-German, half-Spanish lady, and the memory of the poet-cardinal. The nourishing nymph of a stream dug out by the spade was a mule, who drew water from a well: that was the springhead of all the rivers Bonaparte was to set flowing in his Empire. Steps were being taken toward striking my name off the blacklist; I was already being called and openly calling myself Chateaubriand, forgetting I was supposed to be Lassagne. Émigrés were coming to see me—among others, M. de Bonald and M. Chênedollé. Christian de Lamoignon, my fellow exile in London, took me to Madame Récamier's house. The curtain between her and me was abruptly lowered.

But the person who occupied the greatest place in my life on my return from the Emigration was Madame la Comtesse de Beaumont. She lived for part of the year at the Château de Passy, near Villeneuve-sur-Yonne, where M. Joubert summered. When Madame de Beaumont returned to Paris, she asked to meet me.

So that my life might be one long chain of regrets, Providence willed that the first person who treated me with kindness at the start of my public career was also the first to vanish: Madame de Beaumont heads the funeral procession of women who have passed away before me. My earliest memories rest on ashes, and they have continued to fall from coffin to coffin; like the Indian pandit, I recite prayers for the dead until the flowers of my rosary have faded.

Madame de Beaumont was the daughter of Armand Marc de Saint-Herem, Comte de Montmorin, French ambassador to Madrid, commandant in Brittany, member of the Assembly of Notables in 1787, and entrusted with the business of foreign affairs under Louis XVI, by whom he was well liked: he perished on the scaffold, where he was followed by other members of his family.

Madame de Beaumont, whose features were more wan than fair, bore a strong resemblance to the portrait done by Madame Lebrun. Her face was pale and drawn; her almond-shaped eyes would perhaps have been too bright had an extraordinary sweetness not dimmed them, making them glimmer languidly, like a ray of light dampened by its passage through crystalline waters. Her character had a sort of inflexibility and impatience which arose from the force of her feelings and the physical pains she suffered. She was a lofty soul, courageous, born for the world, from which her mind had retreated by choice and bad fortune; but when a friendly voice called that solitary intelligence out into the open, it came and spoke to you in the most heavenly words. Madame de Beaumont's extreme frailty caused her to speak slowly, and that slowness was touching. I knew this afflicted woman only in the moments before she took flight; she was already death-stricken, and her sufferings became the center of my existence. I had taken lodgings on the rue Saint-Honoré at the Hôtel d'Étampes, near the rue Neuve-du-Luxembourg, where Madame de Beaumont lived in an apartment with a view of the gardens of the Ministry of Justice.

Every evening I went there with our mutual friends, M. Joubert, M. de Fontanes, M. de Bonald, M. Molé, M. Pasquier, M. Chênedollé—men who have played a role in literature and public affairs.

Full to the brim with crazes and originality, M. Joubert will forever be missed by those who knew him. He exercised an extraordinary hold on the mind and heart, and once he had taken possession of you his image was there like a fact, like a fixed idea, like an obsession you could not shake. His great pretension was to tranquility—and yet no one could have been more anxious. He kept an eye on himself, hoping to guard against those soulful emotions he believed harmful to his health; but his friends were always disrupting the precautions he took to stay well, for he could not help being moved by their sadness or joy: he was an egotist who occupied himself exclusively with others. To regain his strength, he deemed it necessary to close his eyes as often as possible and to go without speaking for hours at a stretch: God knows what noise and activity went on inside him during these periods of self-prescribed silence! M. Joubert also changed his diet and his regimen from one moment to the next, so that one day he might be living on milk, and the next on ground beef; one day he might go bounding at a great trot over the roughest roads, and the next he would be dawdling with tiny steps on freshly paved avenues. When he read a book, he would tear out the pages that displeased him and consequently came to possess a library fit only for his personal use, composed of expurgated works bound in overlarge covers.

A profound metaphysician, his philosophy, following an elaboration all its own, became like painting or poetry. A Plato with the heart of a La Fontaine, he had adopted an idea of perfection that prevented him from finishing anything. In the manuscripts discovered after his death, he says: "I am like an aeolian harp that makes beautiful sounds and plays no tune." Madame Victoirine de Chastenay claimed: "he had the look of a soul that has encountered a body by chance and was muddling through as best it could." A true and charming statement.

Joubert and I laughed at M. de Fontanes's enemies, who wanted to pass him off as a secret politician. He was, quite simply, an irascible poet, blunt to the point of bluster, a spirit whom contrariness pushed to extremes, and who could no more hide his opinion than he could espouse someone else's. The literary principles of his friend Joubert were alien to him. While Joubert found something good everywhere and in every writer, Fontanes, on the contrary, had a horror of this or that doctrine and could not bear even to hear the *names* of certain authors mentioned. He was the sworn enemy of the principles of modern composition. To lay out physical happenings before the reader's eyes—the crime in its particulars, or the gibbet with its rope—seemed to him an enormity. He claimed that no one should ever have to behold an object except in a poetical milieu, as beneath a crystal globe. Suffering being paraded mechanically about he considered something like a "sensation," suited only to the Circus or the Grève.[25] He did not understand the tragic sensibility that ennobled suffering through admiration and, through the work of art, found in it a "charming pity."[26] I brought up the example of Greek vases. In their arabesques, the body of Hector is seen being dragged by Achilles's chariot, while a tiny figure flying in the air represents the shade of Patroclus, consoled by this act of vengeance committed by the son of Thetis.

"Well then, Joubert!" Fontanes said. "What do you make of this transformation of the nude? How those Greeks bodied forth the soul!"

Joubert felt he was under attack and set Fontanes in contradiction with himself, reproaching him for his indulgence toward me.

These arguments, which were often quite comical, never came to an end. One night at half past eleven, when I was living on Place Louis XV in Madame de Coislin's attic, Fontanes came trudging up my eighty-four steps to vent his fury, knocking at my door with the end of his cane and finishing the argument he'd broken off earlier in the evening. It concerned Picard, whom at that time he ranked high above Molière. But even he would have hesitated to write down a single word of what he said: Fontanes talking and Fontanes with pen in hand were two different men.

It was M. de Fontanes, I love to recount, who encouraged my first attempts; it was he who heralded *The Genius of Christianity*; it was his Muse full of awestruck faith that directed mine toward the new paths she was hastening to take. He taught me to conceal the ugliness of objects by my manner of lighting them and to put, to the extent I was able, classical language in the mouths of my romantic characters. Once there were men who served as guardians of taste, like those dragons that guarded the golden apples in the garden of the Hesperides: they did not allow the young to enter until they could handle the fruit without spoiling it.

My friend's writings set you on a happy course. Your mind is filled with a feeling of well-being and finds itself in a harmonious landscape where everything is beautiful and nothing hurts. M. de Fontanes revised his works endlessly. No one was ever so convinced of the truth of the maxim "Hasten slowly." What would he say today, when, in matters moral and material alike, everyone is striving to blaze the trail and no one thinks it can ever be done quickly enough? M. de Fontanes preferred to travel at a pleasant pace. You have already seen what I said of him when I met him in London, and the regrets I expressed then I must repeat now. Life obliges us to mourn continually, in anticipation or in remembrance.

M. de Bonald had a fine mind. Some mistook his cleverness for genius. He had conceived his philosophical politics in Condé's army, in the Black Forest, like those professors of Jena and Göttingen who have since led their students on the march and got themselves killed for German liberty. Although he had been a musketeer under Louis XVI, he was an innovator and regarded the ancients as children in matters of politics and literature. He was among the first to make use of the fatuousness of the new language, claiming that the Grand Master of the University was "not yet advanced enough to understand it."[27]

Chênedollé, whose knowledge and talent were not natural but learned, was so melancholy that he was nicknamed the Crow. He marauded my works. We drew up a treaty: I relinquished to him my skies, mists, and clouds, but it was agreed that he would leave me my breezes, waves, and woods.

I am speaking now only of my literary friends. As regards my political friends, I don't think I ought to discuss them with you.[28] Principles and speeches have dug great gulfs between us.

Madame de Vintimille and Madame Hocquart often came to gatherings at the rue Neuve-du-Luxembourg. Madame de Vintimille, a woman of an earlier time, the like of which few remain, circulated in society and reported back to us what transpired there; I asked her whether people were "still building cities." The petty scandals she described with piquant but inoffensive mockery made us all the more appreciative of the cautions we took. Madame de Vintimille and her sister had been celebrated in verse by M. La Harpe. Her language was circumspect, her character restrained, her wit acquired. She had breathed the same air as Mesdames de Chevreuse, de Longueville, de La Vallière, and de Maintenon—with Madame Geoffrin and Madame du Deffant. She moved easily in those circles whose charm derived from the differences between minds and in the combination of their various qualities.

Madame Hocquart, for her part, was well beloved by Madame de Beaumont's brother, who dwelled on "the lady of his thoughts" even on the scaffold, like Aubiac, who went to the gallows kissing a sleeve of crushed blue velvet generously given to him by Marguerite de Valois.[29] Never again will there be a place where so many distinguished people belonging to different ranks and destinies come together under the same roof, able to chat on equal terms about the most ordinary or lofty things: a simplicity of speech that did not derive from indigence but from conscious choice. These were perhaps the last gatherings at which the wit of the old regime made its appearance. Among the new generations one no longer finds this urbanity—a fruit born of education and transformed by long use into an attribute of character. What has become of those men and women? Make your plans, gather your friends together, and in that way prepare yourself for eternal grief! Madame de Beaumont is no more. Joubert is no more. Chênedollé is no more. Madame de Vintimille is no more.

In the old days, during the grape harvest, I used to visit M. Joubert at Villeneuve. I used to walk with him along the banks of the Yonne.

He would go gathering Caesar's mushrooms in the copses while I went picking crocuses in the meadows. We would talk of everything under the sun then, but especially of our friend Madame de Beaumont, gone away forever. We would conjure up the memories of our old hopes. At night we would return to Villeneuve, a village circled by crumbling walls from the days of Philip Augustus and by half-ruined towers above which the smoke once plumed from the grape pickers' hearths. Off in the distance, on a hill, Joubert would point out to me a sandy path through the woods that he had taken when he used to go and see his neighbor, who had hidden in the Château de Passy all through the Terror.

Since the death of my dear host, I have traveled through the Sens four or five times. From the highway, I have gazed at the hillsides where Joubert walks no more. I recognized the trees, the fields, the vineyards, and the low heaps of stone where we used to sit and take our ease. Passing through Villeneuve, I have shot a glance at the deserted street and the shuttered house where my friend once lived. The last time I was there, I was on my way to the embassy in Rome. Ah! If he had only been at his fireside, I would have taken him with me to Madame de Beaumont's grave. It pleased God to reveal to M. Joubert a celestial Rome, far better suited to his Platonic soul, turned Christian. I will not be seeing him down here again. "I shall go to him, but he shall not return to me."[30]

8.

SUMMER IN SAVIGNY

THE SUCCESS of *Atala* prompted me to begin work again on *The Genius of Christianity*, whose first two volumes had already been printed. Madame de Beaumont offered me a room in the country, in a house she had just rented in Savigny. I spent six months at that hideaway of hers, with M. Joubert and our other friends.

The house stood at the entrance to the village, on the Paris side, near an old highway known in that part of the world as the Chemin de Henri IV. It leaned against a vine-clad slope and looked across to the Parc de Savigny, bounded by a wood and traversed by the little river Orge. To the left, the plain of Viry extended as far as the Juvisy fountains. All around, the countryside was creased with valleys where we used to go every evening in search of new walks.

In the mornings we would breakfast together. After breakfast, I withdrew to my work. Madame de Beaumont was kind enough to copy the quotations I marked for her. This noble woman offered me sanctuary at a time when I had none. Without the peace she gave me, I would probably never have finished the work I had been unable to complete in my poverty.

I will remember forever some of the evenings I spent in that companionable place. After we returned from our walks, we would sit together by a pool of fresh water on a lawn in the garden. Madame Joubert, Madame de Beaumont, and I took our seats on a bench as Madame Joubert's son rolled in the grass at our feet. (This young man has already passed away.) Meanwhile, M. Joubert would go off alone to walk on some sandy path. Two dogs and a cat sported about us, and the pigeons cooed at the edge of the roof. What happiness this was for a man only recently disembarked from exile, who had spent eight years in deep desolation, except for a few fleeting days! It was on those evenings that my friends urged me to tell the tales of my travels: I cannot imagine I have ever described the wilderness of the New World so well as I did then. At night, with the windows of our rustic sitting room thrown open, Madame de Beaumont pointed out the constellations to me, saying one day I would remember it was she who had taught me them. Since I have lost her, in the depths of the countryside, not far from her tomb in Rome, I have many times searched the firmament for the stars whose names she told me; I have watched them shining above the Sabine Hills, with their long light-rays glancing off the surface of the Tiber. The place where I saw them over the woods of Savigny, the places where I have seen them since, the inconstancy of my fate, this sign that a woman left me in the sky as a memento of her—all of it has broken my heart. By what miracle does man consent to do all he does on this earth, he who is destined to die?

One evening in our sanctuary, we saw someone stealthily slipping through one window and leaving by another. This was M. Laborie, escaping Bonaparte's claws.

Shortly after, we were visited by one of those souls in pain that are of a different species from other souls, and that, in their passage, merge their private woe with the common sufferings of the human race. This was Lucile, my sister.

Following my arrival in France, I had written my family to inform them of my return. My eldest sister, Madame la Comtesse de Marigny, was the first to come seek me out, but she mixed up the street and met five different Monsieur Lassagnes—the last of whom climbed up from a cobbler's hatch at the sound of his name. Madame de Chateaubriand came in her turn: she was charming and replete with all the qualities necessary to give me the happiness I have found with her ever since we were reunited.[31] Madame la Comtesse de Caud, Lucile, was the next to present herself. M. Joubert and Madame de Beaumont treated her with heartfelt affection and tender pity. A correspondence sprang up between them that ended only with the deaths of these two women, who were inclined toward each other like two flowers of the same nature, very soon to wither. When Madame Lucile stopped at Versailles on September 30, 1801, I received this note: "I am writing to beg you to thank Madame de Beaumont on my behalf for her invitation to Savigny. I intend to enjoy this pleasure in about two weeks, at least if, on Madame de Beaumont's side, there are no impediments." Madame de Caud would indeed come to Savigny as promised.

I have told you that, when she was young, my sister, a canoness in the Chapter of L'Argentière destined for Remiremont, had been attracted to M. de Malfilâtre, councillor at the high court of Brittany—an attraction that, locked away in her breast, had exacerbated her inborn melancholy. During the Revolution, she married Monsieur le Comte de Caud only to lose him after fifteen months of marriage. The death of Madame la Comtesse de Farcy, her beloved sister, deepened Madame de Caud's melancholy. She then attached herself to Madame de Chateaubriand, my wife, and held sway over her to a degree that became difficult to bear, for Lucile was violent, imperious, unreasonable, and Madame de Chateaubriand, bending to her will, hid from her so that she might more effectively render the services that a richer friend can give to a susceptible and less fortunate one.

Lucile's spirit and character had brought her to the brink of the madness of Jean-Jacques Rousseau. She believed secret enemies were out to get her; she gave me, Madame de Beaumont, and M. Joubert false mailing addresses; she examined the seals on her letters to make sure they had not been broken; she wandered from house to house, unable to stay either with my sisters or my wife. She developed an antipathy toward them, and Madame de Chateaubriand, after being devoted to her beyond all imagining, was finally overwhelmed by the burden of such a cruel attachment.

Then another blow struck Lucile: M. Chênedollé, who then lived

Tancrède or Coucy, or, at least, he transformed them into heroes of a Middle Ages all his own: Othello lurked beneath the flesh of his Vendôme.[32]

What sort of man was Talma then? He was a creature of his century and of ancient times. His passion for love and country went deep and burst from his breast explosively. His inspirations were macabre and his genius was chaotic, like the Revolution through which he had passed. The terrible scenes that had surrounded him echoed, in his brilliance, with the doleful, distant accents of the choruses of Sophocles and Euripides. His grace, which was not at all conventional grace, overcame you like an illness. Black ambition, remorse, jealousy, spiritual melancholy, physical pain, the insanity sent down by the gods and brought on by adversity, human grief: that was what he knew. His mere entrance into a scene, the mere sound of his voice, was powerfully tragic. Suffering and thought wrinkled his brow and breathed life into his stillness, postures, gestures, paces. "Greek," he came, panting and deathlike, from the ruins of Argos, immortal Orestes, tormented as he was for three thousand years by the Erinyes; "French," he emerged from the solitudes of Saint-Denis, where the Fates of 1793 had snipped the thread of the funerary life of the kings. Sad beyond sadness, awaiting some unknown thing decreed by an unjust Heaven, he carried on, enslaved by destiny, inexorably enchained between terror and fate.

The times cast an inevitable shadow on the old theatrical masterpieces; their darkness changed the brightest Raphael into a Rembrandt. Without Talma, many of the marvels of Corneille and Racine would never have been brought to light. A talent for the stage is a torch; it lends its flame to other torches, half extinguished, and revitalizes ghosts, who delight you with their newfound splendor.

To Talma, we owe the perfection of the actor's costume. But are theatrical accuracy and authenticity of dress really as necessary to the art as is supposed? Racine's characters gain nothing from the cut of their clothes. In the pictures of the old masters, the backgrounds are neglected and the outfits inexact. Orestes pursued by the Furies or the prophecy of Joad, read in a salon by Talma in a tailcoat, would have been just as affecting if he had declaimed them in a Greek cloak or a Jewish robe. Iphigenia was dressed like Madame de Sévigné when Boileau addressed these lovely verses to his friend:

> *Jamais Iphigénie en Aulide immolée*
> *N'a coûté tant de pleurs à la Grèce assemblée,*
> *Que, dans l'heureux spectacle à nos yeux étalé*
> *En a fait, sous son nom, verser la Champmeslé.*[33]

Accuracy in the representation of inanimate objects is the spirit of the arts in our times. It heralds high poetry and true drama's decline into decadence. We content ourselves with insignificant beauties when we are powerless to create great ones; we imitate armchairs and velvet cushions to trick the eye when we are no longer able to depict the person seated on those cushions and chairs. Yet now that we have descended to this realism of material forms, we find ourselves forced to reproduce it. For the public, who have become materialists themselves, demand it.

10.

1802 AND 1803—*THE GENIUS OF CHRISTIANITY*—
FORECAST FAILURE—CAUSE OF ULTIMATE SUCCESS

MEANWHILE, I was finishing *The Genius of Christianity*. Lucien[34] asked to see a few proofs, and I sent them along; he scribbled some rather unremarkable notes in the margins.

Although the success of my big book was just as explosive as that of little *Atala*, it was much more contested. It was a serious work, in which I was no longer content to combat the principles of the old literature and philosophy with fiction, but attacked them instead with arguments and facts. The Voltairean contingent raised a cry and rushed to arms. Madame de Staël, for one, was quite wrong about what lay in store for my religious studies. She was sent the work before it was cut. Sticking her fingers in between the pages at random, she stumbled on the chapter about virginity and said to M. Adrien de Montmorency, who happened to be beside her: "Oh, my God! Our poor Chateaubriand! This will fall flat on its face!" Abbé Boullogne, who had seen a few chapters of my work before it went to press, told a publisher who asked his opinion: "If you want to ruin yourself, go ahead and print it." Yet the abbé later wrote a much too magnificent piece in praise of my book.

Everything in fact seemed to forecast my failure. What hope was there for a nameless young man to undo the influence of Voltaire, in ascendance for more than half a century; Voltaire, who had raised the enormous edifice completed by the Encyclopedists and fortified by every famous man in Europe? Didn't Diderot and d'Alembert, Duclos and Dupuis, Helvétius and Condorcet, have the last word?

Was the world supposed to return to the Golden Legend, renouncing the acclaim it had learned to give to the masterworks of science and reason? How could I hope to win a cause that wrathful Rome and its powerful priesthood could not save—a cause defended in vain by the archbishop of Paris, Christophe de Beaumont, who had the backing of parliamentary decrees, the strength of arms, and the name of the king? Was it not both ridiculous and impudent for an obscure man to oppose himself to a philosophical movement so irresistible it had produced the Revolution? How curious it was to see a pygmy "flexing his little arms"[35] to hold back the progress of the age, put a halt to civilization, and set the human race going in reverse. By the grace of God, a single word would be enough to pulverize this madman: M. Ginguené, lambasting *The Genius of Christianity* in *La Décade*, declared that the review came too late; my bloviation was already well forgotten. He said this five or six months after the publication of a work that the entire Académie française, attacking it on the occasion of the decennial prize, could not make die.

It was among the ruins of our temples that I published *The Genius of Christianity*. The faithful believed themselves saved. At that time, there was a need for faith, a craving for religious consolations which came of being so long deprived of them. What supernatural powers were needed to suffer so many adversities! How many mutilated families had looked to the Heavenly Father for the children they had lost! How many broken hearts and forsaken souls called out for a divine hand to heal them! People hastened to the house of God as they hasten to the doctor's house during a plague. The victims of our troubles (and what an array of victims there were) threw themselves on the altar like shipwrecked men, clinging to the rock on which they seek their salvation.

Bonaparte, who was then attempting to build his power upon society's earliest foundation, had recently made arrangements with the See of Rome. He did not, to begin with, stand in the way of the publication of a work useful to popularizing his plans. He had done battle with the men around him and with the declared enemies of the faith, and he was therefore happy to be defended from the outside by someone expressing the opinions *The Genius of Christianity* expressed. Later, he would repent of his mistake. Ideas of legitimate monarchy came in with those religious ideas.

An episode from *The Genius of Christianity*, which caused less of a stir than *Atala*, came to define one of the characters of modern literature; but I should say that, if *René* did not already exist, I would not write it today. If it were possible for me to destroy it, I would: the brood of René poets and René prosateurs have run riot. Every sentence now is deplorable and disjointed, as if there were no longer anything but winds and storms, and secret words delivered to the clouds and the night. There is no scribbler fresh from school who hasn't imagined himself the unhappiest of men; no stripling of sixteen who hasn't grown weary of life, who hasn't believed himself tormented by his genius; who, in the abyss of his brain, hasn't given himself over to the "wave of his passions"; who hasn't struck his pale, disheveled brow, astonishing the dumbstruck men around him with a misery that neither he nor they can name.

In *René*, I had laid bare one of the sicknesses of my era, but it was another form of madness altogether for novelists to universalize such exceptional afflictions. The common feelings that compose the foundation of mankind—paternal and maternal affection, filial piety, friendship, and love—are inexhaustible, but particular ways of feeling, idiosyncrasies of mind and character, cannot be spun out and multiplied in tapestry after tapestry. The little undiscovered corners of the human heart are a narrow field: there is nothing left to gather there after the first hand has reaped it. A sickness of the soul is not a permanent or natural state. One cannot reproduce it, or make a literature of it, or make use of it like a common passion, endlessly modified by the artist who shapes it and changes its form.

Be that as it may, literature was dyed with the colors of my religious tableaux, as public affairs have retained the phraseology of my writings on society. *The Monarchy According to the Charter* has been crucial to our representative government, and my article for the *Conservateur* on "Moral and Material Interests" has bequeathed those two terms to politics.

Writers did me the honor of imitating *Atala* and *René* in the same way that priests borrowed my tales of the missions and good works of Christianity. The passages where I demonstrated that, by chasing the pagan gods from the woods, our broadened faith restored nature to its solitude; the paragraphs where I discuss the influence of our religion on our ways of seeing and painting, where I examine the changes wrought in poetry and eloquence; the chapters I devote to the foreign feelings ascribed to classical characters in modern plays, contain the germ of the new criticism. Racine's characters, as I put it, are both Greek and not Greek; they are Christian: that is what no one had understood.

If the effect of *The Genius of Christianity* had only been a reaction against the doctrines to which the Revolutionary misdeeds were attributed, that effect would have disappeared with its cause. It would not have persisted up to the very moment I write. But the influence of *The Genius of Christianity* on public opinion was not confined to the momentary resurrection of a religion that was supposed to be dead in its grave. A more lasting transformation took place. If the work represented an innovation of literary style, it also represented a change of doctrine; not only the manner but the matter was different. Atheism and materialism were no longer the basis of belief or unbelief in young minds. The idea of God and the immortality of the soul again came into ascendance, and the chain of ideas, linked one to the other, was altered. A person was no longer nailed in place by anti-religious prejudice; he no longer felt himself obliged to remain a mummy of nullity bound in the bandages of philosophy. He was free to examine any system, however absurd it seemed to him, *even if it were Christian*.

The various abstract schemes only replace the Christian mystery with mysteries even more incomprehensible. Pantheism, which in any case takes many forms, and which it has become fashionable to attribute to enlightened minds, is the most absurd of Oriental reveries, brought back into the light by Spinoza: on this subject, one need only read the article by the skeptical Bayle. The trenchant tone with which some people talk of all these things would be revolting if it weren't the fault of poor education. They are taken in by words they don't understand and imagine they are the words of transcendent geniuses. There is no question that Abelard, Saint Bernard, Saint Thomas Aquinas, and so on, came to metaphysics with a superior understanding we cannot now approach; that the Saint-Simonian, Phalansterian, Fourierist, and Humanist systems were long ago discovered and practiced by all sorts of heretics; that what is supposed to pass for progress and novel discoveries is so much old lumber hawked about for fifteen centuries in the schools of Greece and the colleges of the Middle Ages. The trouble is the first sectarians could not manage to establish their Neoplatonist republic in the days when Gallienus agreed to let Plotinus give it a try in Campania. Later, people committed the reprehensible crime of burning the sectarians when they wanted to establish communal property, and pronounced prostitution sacred, asserting that a woman could not, without sin, refuse a man who asked her for a passing union in the name of Jesus Christ.[36] The only thing needed to accomplish this union, they said, was to annihilate the soul and let it rest a moment in the bosom of God.

The shock *The Genius of Christianity* delivered to men's minds thrust the eighteenth century out of its rut and put it off the road for good. People once again began—or rather they began for the first time—to study the sources of Christianity. Rereading the Fathers of the Church (supposing that they had ever read them in the first place), they were amazed to find so many curious facts, so much philosophical knowledge, so many stylistic beauties of every type, so many ideas that, by a more or less perceptible gradation, paved the way for the transition from ancient to modern society: a unique and memorable human era, when Heaven communicated with earth through the souls housed in men of genius.

Long ago, in the crumbling pagan world, there arose, as though outside society, another world, a spectator of those great spectacles, poor and retiring, solitary, taking no part in the business of life except when there was some need for its teachings or its assistance. It must have been a marvelous thing to behold those first bishops, almost all of them honored by the name of saint or martyr, those simple priests watching over the relics and graveyards, those monks and hermits in their convents or caves, laying down laws of peace, morality, and charity, when everything was war, corruption, and barbarism, going between the tyrants of Rome and the chiefs of the Tartars and Goths, trying to quell the injustice of the former and the cruelty of the latter, stopping armies in their tracks with a wooden cross and a peaceable word: the weakest of men, protecting the world from Attila, placed between two universes to serve as a link between them, to console a dying society in its last moments and support an infant society in its first steps.

II.

GENIUS OF CHRISTIANITY, CONTINUED—FAULTS OF THE WORK

IT WAS inevitable that the truths elaborated in *The Genius of Christianity* should contribute to the changing of ideas. The current taste for medieval buildings can be dated to the appearance of this work. I am the one who provoked the young century to admire the old temples. If my opinion has been taken too far; if it is not true that our cathedrals approach the beauty of the Parthenon; if it is false that these churches teach us, in their documents of stone, facts forgotten; if it is madness to maintain that these memories in granite reveal to us things that escaped the Benedictine scholars; if everyone is bored to death of hearing about the Gothic, it is not my fault. I know the shortcomings of *The Genius of Christianity* when it comes to the arts. That portion of the work is deficient because, in 1800, I did not understand the arts: I had not yet visited Italy, Greece, or Egypt. I also did not make enough use of the lives of the saints or of legends, though they offered me marvelous tales. If I had selected them tastefully, I might have reaped a plentiful harvest. This rich field of medieval imagination is more fertile even than Ovid's *Metamorphoses* or the Milesian tales. There are, moreover, a few narrow-minded or false judgments, such as the one I leveled against Dante, to whom I have since paid resounding homage.

In truth, I completed *The Genius of Christianity* in my *Études historiques*—one of the least discussed and most plundered of my writings.

The success of *Atala* had enchanted me because my soul was still fresh. The success of *The Genius of Christianity* annoyed me. I was obliged to sacrifice my time to more or less pointless correspondence and foreign courtesies. So-called admiration was no recompense for the horrors that attend a man whose name is retained by the crowd. What reward can take the place of the peace you lose by admitting the public into your private life? Add to this the anxieties the Muses love to inflict on those devoted to their cult, the confusion of an even-keeled nature, an ineptitude for happiness, loss of leisure, moodiness, keen affections, unreasonable melancholy, groundless joys. Given the choice, who would want to purchase, on these conditions, the uncertain advantages of a reputation, which you are never sure you have achieved, which will be contested as long as you live, which posterity will not uphold, and from which your death will estrange you forever?

The literary controversy over stylistic novelties aroused by *Atala* started up again with the publication of *The Genius of Christianity*.

One characteristic trait of the imperial school, and indeed of the Republican school, should be noted: while society advanced, for better or worse, literature stagnated. A stranger to the change in ideas, it did not belong to its own time. In comedy, the village squires, the Colins, the Babets, or the obsolete intrigues of salons were staged (as I have remarked already) for coarse and bloodthirsty men busy destroying the way of life depicted for their pleasure. In tragedy, an audience of commoners were held spellbound by noble families and kings.

Two things kept literature bogged down in the eighteenth century: the impiety of Voltaire and the Revolution, and the bullying despotism of Bonaparte. The head of state saw merit in that subordinate literature that he had put into barracks; that presented arms to him; that answered to the cry of "To your posts!"; marched in rank and file; and maneuvered like soldiers. Any sort of independence was taken as a rebellion against his power. He would suffer a riot of words and ideas no sooner than he would suffer an insurrection. He suspended habeas corpus in matters of thought as well as individual freedom. Let us also acknowledge that the public, weary of anarchy, was glad to submit again to the yoke of law and order.

The literature expressive of the new era did not begin its reign until forty or fifty years after the time whose idiom it adopted. During that half century, it was employed only by the opposition. Madame de Staël, Benjamin Constant, Lemercier, Bonard, and I were the first to have spoken this language. The transformation of letters in the nineteenth century came about as a result of emigration and exile. It was M. de Fontanes who brooded those birds of a different species, for, in going back to the seventeenth century, he had acquired the strength of that fruitful age and sloughed off the sterility of the century that followed. Only one part of the human mind—that taken up with transcendent matters—advances in pace with civilization. Unfortunately, the glory of science was not unsullied: the Laplaces, the Lagranges, the Monges, the Chaptals, the Berthollets, all of these prodigies, once proud democrats, became Napoleon's most obsequious servants. Let it be said, to the honor of letters, that the new literature was free where science was servile. Character was no match for genius, and these men whose research had soared to the loftiest heavens could not raise their souls above Bonaparte's boots. They pretended to have no need of God, and that is why they had need of a tyrant.

The Napoleonic classic was the spirit of the nineteenth century coiffed in a Louis XIV wig or curled à la Louis XV. Bonaparte did not like the men of the Revolution to appear at Court except in full regalia, wearing swords at their side. Contemporary France was nowhere to be seen; there was no order, there was only discipline. And nothing could have been more boring than the resurrection of old-fashioned literary modes. These cold tracings and barren anachronisms vanished the moment the new literature raucously erupted with *The Genius of Christianity*. The Duc d'Enghien's death, by casting me out, allowed me to follow my private inspiration in solitude and kept me from enlisting in the Parnassian infantry. I owed my moral freedom to my intellectual freedom.

In the last chapter of *The Genius of Christianity*, I examine what would have become of the world had faith not been preached when the barbarians invaded; in another passage, I mention an important work to be undertaken on the changes that Christianity introduced into the laws after Constantine's conversion.

Assuming religious thought were still much as it is at the present moment, and *The Genius of Christianity* were yet to be written, I would compose it quite differently. Instead of recalling the benefits and institution of our religion in the past, I would show that Christianity is the thought of the future and of human liberty; that this redemptive and messianic thought is the only basis for social equality; that it alone can establish it, because it balances that equality with the sense of duty which corrects and regulates the democratic impulse. Legality is not sufficient restraint, because it is impermanent; it derives its power from the law, and the law is the work of mortal and various men. A law is not always obligatory; it can always be changed by another law: unlike morality, which is permanent and derives its power from within, because it springs from the immutable order. It alone can endure.

I would also show that wherever Christianity has prevailed, it has changed minds, rectified notions of justice and injustice, substituted affirmation for doubt, embraced the whole human race with its doctrines and precepts. I would try to divine the distance we still have to travel before we fulfill the Gospels by calculating the number of evils destroyed and ameliorations accomplished in the eighteen centuries run down on this side of the Cross. Christianity acts slowly because it acts everywhere. It is not attached to the reform of one particular society; it works upon society as a whole. Its philanthropy extends to all the sons of Adam. That is what it expresses with such wonderful simplicity in its commonest orations and daily prayers, when it says to the crowd in the temple: "Let us pray for all who suffer on earth." What religion has ever spoken this way? The Word was not made flesh in a man of pleasure; it was incarnated in a man of sorrow, so that every soul would be set free—so that there would be universal brotherhood and boundless salvation.

If only *The Genius of Christianity* had given birth to such investigations, I might congratulate myself on having published it. Who knows whether, at the time the book appeared, another *Genius of*

Christianity, constructed along the lines that I have just barely sketched, would have met with the same success? In 1803, when the old religion was ignored and scorned, when no one knew the first thing about it, what good would it have done for someone to speak of the future's liberty descending from Calvary, at a time when people were still bruised from the excesses of the liberty of the passions? Would Bonaparte have permitted such a work to appear? Perhaps it was useful to stir up regrets, to interest the imagination in such a neglected cause, to call attention to the despised object and point out its charms, before showing how serious it was, how powerful and salutary.

Now, supposing my name leaves any trace behind, I will owe it to *The Genius of Christianity*. Though I have no illusions about the work's intrinsic value, I recognize it had an accidental value; it arrived at just the right moment. For that reason, it caused me to take my place in one of those historical periods which, involving the individual in the general run of things, compels him to be remembered. If the influence of my work is not limited to the change it has wrought among the living generations these last forty years; if, among the latecomers, it continues to revive a spark of the civilized truths of the earth; if the slight symptoms of life that may be perceived in it are sustained in generations to come, I will go to my grave filled with hope for divine mercy. Oh, reconciled Christian, do not forget me in your prayers when I am gone. My transgressions may detain me at those gates where my charity cried out on your behalf: "Lift ye up, everlasting doors!" *Elevamini, portae aeternales!*[37]

BOOK FOURTEEN

I.

1802–1803—CHÂTEAUX—MADAME DE CUSTINE—M. DE SAINT-MARTIN—MADAME D'HOUDETOT AND SAINT-LAMBERT

Paris, 1837; Revised in December 1846

My LIFE became chaotic the moment it ceased to be mine. I acquired a horde of acquaintances outside my usual circle and was invited to one restored château after another. As soon as they were able, people returned to these half-furnished manors, and the old armchairs were set down next to the new ones. A few of these houses were still intact, such as Le Marais, which had been demised to Madame La Briche, an excellent woman who could never be divested of her good cheer. I remember that I, the immortal genius, once went to the rue Saint-Dominique-d'Enfer to take a seat in a grim rented carriage bound for Le Marais in the company of Madame de Vintimille and Madame de Fezensac. At Champlâtreux, M. Molé was having some little rooms on the second floor redone. His father, who had been killed in the Revolutionary style, was replaced—in a huge, dilapidated parlor—by a painting in which Mathieu Molé[1] was shown putting down a riot with his square cap: an image that made clear how thoroughly times had changed. A superb *patte d'oie* of lindens had been felled, but one of the three avenues survived, in all the magnificence of its ancient shade. New plantings had been mixed with the old. We are now living through an age of poplars.[2]

When the Emigration was over, there was no returned exile, however poor, who did not make plans to lay the winding paths of an English garden in the ten feet of ground or courtyard he'd regained. Did I myself not plant the Vallée-aux-Loups? Was it not among those trees that I began these *Memoirs*? Did I not continue them in the park at Montboissier, where they were then trying to breathe new life into a landscape disfigured by neglect? Did I not go on writing them in the park at Maintenon, only recently rebuilt, and now fresh prey for the new wave of democracy? The houses burned down in 1789 should have served as a warning to those that remain hidden in their ruins; but the towers of the swallowed villages that break through the lava of Vesuvius do not prevent new churches and hamlets being planted on that same ground.

Among the bees then busy building their hives was the Marquise de Custine, inheritress of the long locks of Marguerite de Provence, wife of Saint Louis, whose blood flowed in her veins. I was there when she took possession of Fervaques, and I had the honor of sleeping in the Béarnais's bed—just as I had slept in Queen Christina's bed at Combourg many years before. It was no small affair, that journey. Into the carriage were crowded her son Astolphe de Custine, the tutor M. Berstecher, an old Alsatian maid who spoke only German, Jenny the chambermaid, and Trim, the famous dog who ate up all our provisions for the journey. Wouldn't it have seemed as though this colony was returning to Fervaques for good? And yet the house was not finished being furnished before the signal to retreat was given. I saw that woman who faced the scaffold with such great courage; I saw her, whiter than one of the Fates, dressed in black, her figure wasted by death, her head adorned only by her silken hair; I saw her smile at me with her pale lips and lovely teeth as she was leaving Sécherons, near Geneva, to breathe her last in Bex, at the gateway to the Valais; I heard her coffin going by at night through the lonely streets of Lausanne to its eternal resting-place at Fervaques. She was hastening to go to ground in a patch of land she had possessed but for a moment, like her life. On a corner of the hearth in that house, I had read one of those mean rhymes attributed to Gabrielle's lover:[3]

The Lady of Fervaques
Merits bold attacks.

The soldier-king had said as much to many others. Oh, the momentary declarations of men, so quickly effaced and passed from beauty to beauty, down to Madame de Custine! Fervaques has since been sold.

I was reintroduced to the Duchesse de Châtillon, who, when I was away during the Hundred Days, decorated my valley in Aulnay. Madame Lindsay, whom I'd continued to see, introduced me to Julie Talma. Madame de Clermont-Tonnerre coaxed me to her estate. We had a grandmother in common and she was quite pleased to call me her cousin. Widowed by the Comte de Clermont-Tonnerre, she later married the Marquis de Talaru. In prison, she had converted M. La Harpe. It was through her that I got to know the painter Neveu, who had been enlisted as one of her chaperones. Neveu put me momentarily in touch with Saint-Martin.

M. de Saint-Martin believed he had discovered some sort of secret language in *Atala*, which baffled me, but which to him proved that our beliefs were in harmony. Desiring to bring two brothers together, Neveu invited us to dine in the room where he lived, at the top of one of the buildings near the Palais-Bourbon. When I arrived at the rendezvous at six o'clock, the heavenly philosopher was already at his post. At seven, a servant very discreetly set a tureen of soup on the table, withdrew, and closed the door. We sat and began to eat in silence. M. de Martin, who, incidentally, had very fine manners, uttered only a few oracular phrases. Neveu replied with exclamations, accompanied by painterly grimaces and gestures. I did not say a word.

After half an hour, the necromancer returned, removed the soup, and placed another dish on the table. The courses succeeded each other one by one, at long intervals. M. de Saint-Martin, gradually warming to his subject, began talking like an archangel. The more he spoke, the more obscure his language became. Neveu had insinuated to me, while shaking my hand, that we would see extraordinary things and hear noises. For six mortal hours I listened and heard nothing. At midnight, the visionary abruptly rose to his feet. I thought that the spirit of darkness or the heavenly spirit might be descending, that bells would echo from mysterious corridors; but M. de Saint-Martin announced that he was exhausted and that we would have to resume our conversation some other time. He put on his hat and left. Unfortunately for him, he was stopped at the door and obliged to return by an unexpected visitor. Nevertheless, he did not take his time disappearing. I never saw him again. He rushed off to die in the garden of M. Lenoir-Laroche, my neighbor in Aulnay.

I am a rebellious subject for Swedenborgianism. Abbé Furia, during a dinner at Madame de Custine's, bragged that he could kill a canary by hypnotizing it. The canary proved to be the stronger of the two, and the abbé, beside himself, had to leave the party, for fear of being killed by the bird. As a Christian, I suppose my mere presence had rendered the oracle powerless.

Another time, the famous Gall—again at Madame de Custine's—dined beside me not knowing who I was, misjudged my facial angle, took me for a frog,[4] and wanted, when he learned my identity, to patch up his science in a way that made me embarrassed for him. The shape of the head may help in distinguishing an individual's sex or in indicating what belongs to the beast, to the animal passions, but as for the intellectual faculties, phrenology will be forever ignorant of them. If it were possible to collect the skulls of all the great men who have died since the beginning of time and to lay them out under the eyes of the phrenologists without telling them whose they were, not a single brain would be sent to the right address. The study of *bumps* would produce the most laughable errors.

But I am seized by remorse: I have spoken a bit mockingly of M. de Saint-Martin, and I repent of it. This impulse to mock that I am constantly suppressing, and that continually comes over me, gives me great pain, for I hate satirical wit; it is the pettiest, the commonest, and the easiest of all. I am not, of course, impugning high comedy. In the final analysis, M. de Saint Martin was a man of great merit with a noble and independent spirit. When his ideas were explicable, they were lofty and of the highest kind. Perhaps I ought to sacrifice the last two pages to the generous and much too flattering declarations of the author of *A Self-Portrait of M. de Saint-Martin*? I would not hesitate to cross them out if what I said could do the least bit of harm to M. de Saint-Martin's solemn renown or the esteem that will eternally cling to his name. Besides, I am pleased to see my memory has not deceived me. M. de Saint-Martin may not have had quite the same experience of the dinner I mentioned, but you will see that I have not invented the scene and that, in large part, M. de Saint-Martin's account resembles my own:

"On January 27, 1803, during a dinner arranged for the purpose," he says, "I chatted with M. de Chateaubriand at M. Neveu's rooms in the École Polytechnique. It would have been a great boon to have gotten to know him earlier: he is the only honest man of letters I've ever met in my life, and yet I only had the pleasure of his conversation for the length of the meal, for soon after a visitor arrived who rendered him mute for the rest of the evening; and who knows whether there will be an occasion to see him again? The ruler of this world has taken great pains to put a spoke in the wheel of my cart. But what need have I of anyone but God?"

M. de Saint-Martin is worth a thousand of me: the dignity of that last sentence of his squashes my harmless teasing with the weight of a serious soul.

At Le Marais, I had caught a glimpse of Monsieur de Saint-Lambert and Madame d'Houdetot, both representing the opinions and the freedom of bygone days carefully packed and preserved: here was the eighteenth century dead and married, in its own peculiar fashion. If you can only stay alive long enough, illegitimacies become legitimate; immorality inspires boundless esteem simply because it hasn't ceased to be, and because time has decorated it with wrinkles. In truth the two virtuous spouses who were not spouses, and who stayed together out of mutual human respect, suffered somewhat from their venerable state; they bored and detested each other cordially with all the ill humor of age. That is God's justice.

Cursed be they that Heaven grants long years![5]

It became difficult to make sense of certain pages of the *Confessions* once you had seen the object of Rousseau's transports. Had Madame d'Houdetot kept the letters Jean-Jacques wrote her, which he said were more ardent than those of *The New Héloïse*? It is believed she sacrificed them for the sake of Saint-Lambert.

Nearing eighty, Madame d'Houdetot still cried out, in charming verse:

> And love consoles me!
> Nothing can ever console me for him.

She never went to bed without striking the floor three times with her slipper, saying to the dear departed author of *Les Saisons* "Goodnight, my friend!" That was what, in 1803, the philosophy of the eighteenth century was reduced to.

The society of Madame d'Houdetot, Diderot, Saint-Lambert, Rousseau, Grimm, and Madame d'Épinay made the valley of Montmorency hard to bear, and though, out of historical interest, I might have been delighted to gaze upon a relic of the Voltairean age with my own eyes, I have no nostalgia for that age. In Sannois, not long ago, I paid another visit to the house where Madame d'Houdetot lived. It is just an empty shell, reduced to four bare walls. An abandoned fireplace is always interesting; but what does a hearth say when no beauty or motherly tenderness or faith has ever tarried there? What does a hearth say whose ashes, if they had not been scattered, would only cast the mind back to days that knew nothing but destruction?

2.

VOYAGE TO THE MIDI

Paris, 1838

IN THE month of October 1802, an edition of *The Genius of Christianity* pirated in Avignon called me to the South of France. I was familiar only with my poor Brittany and the provinces of the north I had traveled through when I left my country. Now I was going to see the Provençal sun, and that sky which would give me a foretaste of Italy and Greece, toward which my instinct and my muse propelled me. I was in a happy frame of mind; my reputation had made life easy. A man dreams many dreams in the first inebriating flush of fame, and at the outset his eyes are filled with the dawning light; but when this light goes down, it leaves you in the dark. If it lingers, you grow so used to it, you soon cease to notice it is there.

Lyon was a great pleasure for me. I renewed my acquaintance with those Roman works I hadn't seen since the day, in the amphitheater at Trèves, I read aloud a few pages from *Atala* rustled out of my rucksack. The sailcloth boats ferried from one bank of the Saône to the other, bearing lights on board once darkness fell. They were steered by women. A sailor girl of eighteen took me on, reaching up to read-just, with each stroke of the oar, a bouquet of flowers pinned unevenly to her hat. In the morning, I woke to the sound of church bells; the monasteries hung upon the hillsides seemed to have recovered their hermits. The son of M. Ballanche, who, after M. Migneret, owned the rights to *The Genius of Christianity*, was my host: he became my friend. Who today does not know the Christian philosopher whose writings burn with that peaceful brightness on which we are happy to affix our gaze as on the beam of a friendly star in the heavens?

On October 27, the mail boat taking me to Avignon had to stop in Tain because of bad weather. I was able to imagine I was in America again: the Rhône reminded me of the big, wild rivers I had known there. I nested in a little inn beside the waters. A soldier was standing by the hearth; he had a haversack on his back and was on his way to join the Army of Italy; I was writing, using the chimney bellows as a desk, across from the innkeeper who sat in silence before me, and who, out of respect for the traveler, kept the dog and cat from making noise.

What I wrote was an article—which was almost done by the time I'd descended the Rhône—regarding Monsieur de Bonald's *Législation Primitive*. I predicted what has since come to pass. "The face of French literature," I said, "is going to change; with the Revolution, other thoughts, other views of things and men, will be born. It is easy to foresee that writers will be divided. Some will endeavor to follow the old paths; others will try to follow classical models but by presenting them in the new light. It is quite probable that the latter will end up triumphing over their adversaries, because by relying on the great traditions and the great men, they will have more dependable guides and more fecund sources."

The lines that concluded my nomadic criticism were historic; from that moment on, my mind walked in step with my century. "The author of this article," I said, "cannot deny himself an image furnished to him by the situation in which he finds himself. At the very moment he writes these words, he is traveling down one of the mightiest rivers in France. On the two mountains opposite are two ruined towers; at the top of these towers are little bells, which the mountain folk toll as we pass. This river, these mountains, these sounds, these Gothic monuments, momentarily catch the onlooker's eye; but no one stops to go where the bell invites him. So it is that the men who preach morality and religion today vainly give the signal from their lofty ruins to those dragged along by the torrent of the age. The traveler is amazed by the grandeur of the ruins, the sweetness of the sounds that issue, the majesty of the memories that rise from them; but he does not interrupt his course, and at the first bend in the river, it is all forgotten."

Arriving in Avignon on All Hallows' Eve, a child hawking books held them out for me to see: straight off, I bought three different pirated editions of a slim novel called *Atala*. By going from bookshop to bookshop, I disinterred the counterfeiter (who didn't know me by sight). He sold me the four volumes of *The Genius of Christianity* at the reasonable price of nine francs per copy, singing the praises of the work and the author. He lived in a handsome mansion, between a courtyard and a garden. At first I thought I'd struck gold, but within twenty-four hours I'd grown bored with the idea of running after money and came to terms with the thief for next to nothing.

I paid a visit to Madame de Janson, a white-haired, strong-willed, lean little woman, who, on her property, fought with the Rhône, traded gunshots with the river rats, and did battle with the years.

Avignon put me in mind of my countryman. Du Guesclin was easily the equal of Bonaparte, seeing that he wrested France from conquest. When he arrived in this City of Popes with the adventurers that his glory trailed after him to Spain, he said to the provost sent before him by the pontiff, "'Friar, do not dissemble: where does this money come from? Has the pope taken it from his own treasury?' And the friar answered him no, saying that the common people of Avignon had each paid their share. 'Then,' said Bertrand, 'I promise you we would never in our lives take one denier of it, and I would ask that all the money taken up be returned to those who paid it, and be sure to tell the pope he must give it to them; for if I hear anything to the contrary, it will weigh upon me; and, even if I be across the sea, I would still sail back to these shores.' Thereupon Bertrand was paid in the pope's money, and his men were absolved again, and the aforementioned absolution confirmed again."

Journeys over the Alps used to begin in Avignon. It was the gateway to Italy. The geographies say: "The Rhône belongs to the king, but the city of Avignon is watered by a branch of the river called the Sorgue, which belongs to the pope." Is the pope really so certain he holds rights to the Tiber for such a long stretch?

Travelers also used to visit the Celestine monastery. Good King René, who lowered taxes whenever the tramontane blew, had a skeleton painted in one of the monastery's rooms: it was the skeleton of a great beauty he had loved.

In the Church of the Cordeliers is the tomb of Madonna Laura.[6] François I ordered it opened and saluted her immortalized ashes. The victor of Marignan left behind this epitaph for the new tomb he had erected:

> *En petit lieu compris vous pouvez voir*
> *Ce qui comprend beaucoup par renommée:*
> *... O gentille âme, estant tant estimée,*
> *Qui te pourra louer qu'en se taisant?*
> *Car la parole est tousjours réprimée,*
> *Quand le sujet surmont le disant.*[7]

Whatever else may be said of him, the "father of literature," the friend of Benvenuto Cellini, Leonardo da Vinci, and Primaticcio, the king to whom we owe Diana, sister of the Apollo Belvedere, and Raphael's *Holy Family*; the eulogist of Laura, the admirer of Petrarch, has been given everlasting life by the fine arts, in gratitude.

I went to Vaucluse to pick some sprigs of sweet-smelling heather and the first olive borne by a young olive tree by the side of the spring:

> *Chiara Fontana, in quell medesmo bosco,*
> *Sorgea d'un sasso; ed acque fresche e dolci*
> *Spargea soavemente, mormorando.*
> *Al bel seggio riposte, ombroso e fosco*
> *Ne pastori appressavan, ne bifolci;*
> *Ma nimfe e muse a quell tenor cantando.*[8]

Petrarch recalled how he came upon this valley. "I was inquiring," he says, "about a hidden spot where I might retreat, as though into a haven, when I found a small, secluded valley, Vaucluse, a quite solitary place, where the wellspring of the Sorgue bubbles up, the queen of all springs. There I settled, there I composed my poems in the common tongue, and there I described the travails of my youth."

It was also in Vaucluse that he heard, as could still be heard when I was passing through, the clash of arms reverberant from Italy. He exclaimed:

> *Italia mia . . .*
> *O diluvio raccolto*
> *Di che deserti strain*
> *Per inondar I nostril dolci campi!*
> *. . . Non è questo ;l terren ch' io toccai pria?*
> *Non è questo 'l mio nido,*
> *Ove nudrito fui si dolcemente?*
> *Non è questa la patria, in ch' io mi fido,*
> *Madre benigna e pia*
> *Chi copre l'uno et l'altro mio parente?*[9]

Later, the lover of Laura invited Urban V to transport himself to Rome. "What will you say to Saint Peter," as he so eloquently phrased it, "when he asks you: 'What's the news from Rome? In what state is my temple, my tomb, my people? Do you have nothing to say? Where are you coming from? You've been living on the banks of the Rhône? You were born there, you say: and I, was I not born in Galilee?'"

What a lush, young, deep-feeling era, which stirs the heart to admiration—an age that obeyed a great poet's lyre as though it were a legislator's law! It is to Petrarch that we owe the sovereign pontiff's return to the Vatican; it is his voice that produced Raphael and raised Michelangelo's dome!

On returning to Avignon, I looked for the Palace of the Popes and was shown La Glacière. The Revolution had laid claim to the famous sites. Memories of the past are obliged to sprout and turn green again over a layer of bones. Alas, the screams of the victims die away soon after them; they have scarcely managed to make the echo that keeps them alive for a moment when the voice that raised them is already stamped out. But while the death cries faded on the banks of the Rhône, the distant sounds of Petrarch's lute could still be heard—a lonely *canzone* escaping the tomb and still lending Vaucluse the charm of immortal melancholy, and of love pains from long ago.

Alain Chartier had come from Bayeux to be buried at Avignon, in the Church of Saint Anthony. He had written *La Belle Dame sans Mercy*, and the kiss bestowed upon him by Margaret of Scotland gave him life.

From Avignon, I made my way to Marseille. What more can be said of a city to which Cicero addressed these words, whose oratorical turn Bossuet imitated: "Nor do I pass over you, Marseille, whose might is so eminent that most nations must yield to you, and to whom not even Greece can compare." (*Pro L. Flacco*.)[10] Tacitus, in the *Agricola*, likewise praises Marseille, for combining Greek civility with Latin thrift. Daughter of Hellenism, teacher of Gaul, celebrated by Cicero, and seized by Caesar—isn't this more than enough glory? I was eager to climb up to Notre-Dame de la Garde and admire the sea that touches the happy shores and the ruins of all the famous countries of antiquity. That almost tideless sea is the wellspring of mythology, as the ocean, which rises twice each day, is the abyss to which Jehovah said: "You shall go no further."

In this very year of 1838, I climbed to those heights again, and again looked out over that sea I now know so well, on whose far side the cross and the grave rose up in victory. The mistral was blowing. I went into the fort built by François I, where a lone veteran of the Egyptian Army stood guard, and a conscript, bound for Algeria, stood obscured beneath the shadowy vaults. Silence reigned in the restored chapel, though the wind moaned out of doors. The Breton sailors' hymn to Notre-Dame de Bon-Secours came back into my mind. You know when and under what circumstances I have already recalled this lament from my earliest oceanic days:

> *Je mets ma confiance,*
> *Vierge, en votre secours…*

How many events it took to bring me back to the feet of the Star of the Seas, to whom I had been vowed in my childhood! When I contemplated those ex-votos, those paintings of shipwrecks hung all around me, I felt I was reading the story of my life. Beneath the Carthaginian porticoes, Virgil places a Trojan moved to tears by the sight of a picture representing the burning of Troy,[11] and the bard of Hamlet took a lesson from the bard of Dido.[12]

Down below this rock, once lush with a forest praised by Lucan,[13] I did not recognize Marseille. In its straight streets, long and wide, I could no longer lose my way; the port was choked with ships. Thirty-six years ago, I would have been at pains to find a single *nave* captained by the progeny of Pytheas[14] to take me from Cyprus to Joinville. Time rejuvenates cities—exactly the opposite of men. But I preferred the old Marseille with its memories of Bérenger, the Duc d'Anjou, King René, Guise, and Épernon, its monuments to Louis XIV and the virtuous Bishop Belzunce. I liked the wrinkles on its brow. Perhaps, in regretting the years she had shed, I was only lamenting the years I have put on. Marseille gave me a gracious welcome, it's true, but the emulator of Athens has grown too young for me.

If Alfieri's *Memoirs* had been published in 1803, I would not have left Marseille without visiting the rock where the poet used to bathe. This rough-mannered man did sometimes find charming words for charming reveries:

"After the theater," he writes, "one of my pastimes in Marseille was to bathe in the sea almost every evening. I had found a quite agreeable little spot on a spit of land to the right of the port where, sitting on the sand, with my back against a small rock—a position which kept me invisible from land—I had nothing before me but sky and sea. Between these two immensities beautified by the rays of the setting sun, I spent a few delectable hours lost in dreams. In that spot, I might have become a poet—if only I'd been able to put it all into words."[15]

I returned to Paris by way of Languedoc and Gascony. In Nîmes, the Arena and the Maison Carrée had not yet been excavated: this year of 1838, I have seen them exhumed. I have also sought out Jean Reboul. In general I'm a bit wary of worker poets, who are typically neither poets nor workers, but M. Reboul is an exception. I found him in his bakery and unwittingly addressed him, as I was unable to tell him apart from his fellow servants of Ceres. He took my name and told me he would go and see whether the person I wanted was at home. A few minutes later, he returned and introduced himself. He led me into his storeroom, where we wended our way through a labyrinth of flour sacks and climbed up a sort of ladder into a closet a little like the upper room of a windmill. There we sat and talked. I was as happy as I'd been in my garret in London, and happier than I am in my ministerial armchair in Paris. Monsieur Reboul pulled out a manuscript from a chest of drawers and read me a few energetic lines from a poem he was writing about the Last Judgment. I complimented him on his faith and his talent. Then I took leave of my host, but not before wishing him the gardens of Horace. I would have preferred to see him dreaming beside the waterfalls of Tivoli rather than gathering up wheat milled by a wheel far above that cascade—even if it's true that Sophocles may have been a blacksmith in Athens, and that Plautus, in Rome, was a harbinger of Rebours in Nîmes.

Between Nîmes and Montpellier, to my left, I saw Aigues-Mortes, which I visited again in 1838. This town, with its high outer walls and towers, remains untouched, stranded like a high-sided ship on the sands where Saint Louis, time, and the sea have left it. The saintly king gave the town of Aigues-Mortes its statutes and its "usages": "He wills that the prison be such that it serve not for the extermination of the person, but for his protection; that no legal action be taken against injurious remarks; that adultery not be investigated, except in certain cases; and that he who violates a virgin, *volente vel nolente*, not be deprived of his life nor any of his members, *sed alio modo puniatur*."[16]

In Montpellier, I gazed again at the sea, which I gladly would have called, as the Most Christian King did the Swiss Federation, "my faithful ally and great friend." This city, which Scaliger would have liked to make "the nest of his old age,"[17] derived its name from two virgin saints, *Mons puellarum*:[18] hence the beauty of its women. Falling before Cardinal Richelieu, it witnessed the death of the aristocratic constitution of France.[19]

On the road from Montpellier to Narbonne, I reverted to my natural state and suffered an attack of dreaminess. I might have forgotten this attack if, like so many sick men of fiction, I had not recorded my crisis right then and there on a scrap of paper—the only note from that time I have found to aid my memory. It was, on that occasion, a dry stretch of land thick with foxglove that made me forget the world: my vision soared over that sea of purplish stalks and was halted only by the distant bluish chain of the Cantal massif. In nature, apart from the sky, and the ocean, and the sun, the large things do not inspire me; they only fill me with a sense of grandeur, which lays me low, in all my smallness, my distress and despair, at the feet of God. But a flower that I pick, a trickle of water that steals among the rushes, a bird that darts and perches before me, carries me away into a world of dreams. Is it not better to be moved without knowing why than to go through life seeking charms grown stale from replication and repetition? Nowadays, everything is worn down—even misery.

In Narbonne, I saw the Canal des Deux-Mers. Corneille, praising this work, lends his greatness to that of Louis XIV:

> *La Garonne et le Tarn, en leurs grottes profondes,*
> *Soupiraient dès longtemps pour marier leurs ondes,*
> *Et faire ainsi couler par un heureux penchant*
> *Les trésors de l'aurore aux rives du couchant.*
> *Mais à des voeux si doux, à des flammes si belles*
> *La nature, attachée à des lois éternelles,*
> *Pour obstacle invincible opposait fièrement*
> *Des monts et des rochers l'affreux enchaînement.*
> *France, ton grand roi parle, et ces roches se fendent,*
> *La terre ouvre son sein, les pluts hauts monts descendent.*
> *Tout cède.*[20]

In Toulouse, from the Garonne bridge, I glimpsed the line of the Pyrenees, which four years later I was going to cross: horizons succeed one another, like our days. Someone offered to take me to a vault to see the desiccated body of La Belle Paule; but blessed are those who believe without seeing! Montmorency had been beheaded in the courtyard of the Hôtel de Ville—a severed head of great importance apparently, since people were still going on about it after so many other heads had rolled. I doubt whether there is another eyewitness deposition in the history of criminal trials that better testifies to a man's identity:

"The fire and smoke around him," said Guitaut, "at first made it difficult to pick him out; but seeing a man who, after breaking through six of our ranks, still went on to kill several soldiers in the seventh, I judged that it could be none other than M. de Montmorenci; I knew for certain it was he when I saw him knocked to the ground beneath his dead horse."[21]

The architecture of the abandoned Church of Saint-Sernin impressed me. This church is connected with the history of the Albigensians, which the poem, so well translated by M. Fauriel, brings to life before our eyes:

The valiant young count, his father's heir and the light of his life, with cross and sword, enters through one of the doors. In the rooms, on the landings, not one maiden remains; the inhabitants of the town, great and small, all come to gaze at the count as at a bloom on a rosebush.[22]

It was in the days of Simon de Montfort that the loss of langue d'oc began: "Simon, seeing himself lord of so many lands, allocated them among the gentlemen, both French and foreign, *atque loci loges dedimus*," say the eight signatory archbishops and bishops.

In Toulouse, I would have liked to have had time to inquire after one of my great admirations, Cujas, writing, lying flat on his stomach with his books spread about him. I do not know if people still remember Suzanne, his daughter, who married twice. She had no great liking for constancy and attached little importance to it; but she kept one of her husbands alive with the infidelities that had killed the other. Cujas was protected by the daughter of François I, Pibrac by the daughter of Henry II, two Marguerites of Valois blood, true blood of the Muses. Pibrac is particularly remembered for his quatrains, which were translated into Persian. (I may have stayed the night in his father's house.) "Good Monsieur de Pibrac," says Montaigne, "had such a noble mind, such sound opinions, such a gentle character; his soul was so out of tune and proportion with our corruption and tempests!"[23] Pibrac also wrote an apology for the Saint Bartholomew's Day Massacres.

I hurried on, unable to stop. Fate sent me back in 1838 to admire the city of Raymond de Saint-Gilles in detail, and to talk with the new acquaintances I made there: M. de Lavergne, a man of talent, wit, and sense, and Mademoiselle Honorine Gasc, the Malibran of the future.[24] This woman reminded me, in my new position as a servant of Clémence Isaure,[25] of those verses that Chapelle and Bachaumont wrote on the island of Aubijoux, near Toulouse:

> *Hélas! que l'on seroit heureux*
> *Dans ce beau lieu digne d'envie,*
> *Si, toujours aimé de Sylvie,*
> *On pouvait, toujours amoureux,*
> *Avec elle passer sa vie!*[26]

May Mademoiselle Honorine be on guard against her beautiful voice! Talent is "gold from Toulouse":[27] it brings misfortune.

Bordeaux, when I saw it in 1802, had scarcely rid itself of its scaffolds and its spineless Girondins. All the towns I saw had the look of beautiful women only recently recuperated from a violent illness just beginning to breathe easily again. In Bordeaux, Louis XIV had once ordered the pillars of the Temple of the Tutelary Spirits torn down to make way for the Château Trompette, whereupon Charles Spon and the friends of antiquity groaned:

> Why do they demolish these pillars of the gods,
> The work of the Caesars, a tutelary shrine?

Today, only a few fragments of the Arena remain. But were we to mourn for all things that fall, there would be no end to our weeping.

I embarked from Bordeaux for Blaye. I saw that castle—at that time unknown to me—to which I would address these words in 1833: "O captive of Blaye! I regret I can do nothing to change your present destinies!"[28] I made my way to Rochefort and arrived in Nantes, by way of the Vendée.

The country there, like an old warrior, bore the mutilations and scars of its valor. I saw bones blanched by time and ruins blackened by fire. When the Vendeans prepared to attack the enemy, they got down on their knees and received the blessing of a priest: this prayer intoned in arms was not considered weakness, for the Vendean who raised his sword to the heavens was praying for victory and not for life.

The coach in which I found myself interred was filled with travelers who told tales of the rapes and murders with which they'd glorified their lives during the Vendean wars. My heart pounded when, crossing the Loire in Nantes, I entered Brittany. I rode past the walls of the Collège de Rennes that witnessed the last years of my childhood. I was able to stay with my wife and sisters for only twenty-four hours before returning to Paris.

3.

1802–1803—MONSIEUR LA HARPE: HIS DEATH

Paris, 1838

I ARRIVED in time to witness the death of a man who belonged to those superior, second-rank names of the eighteenth century—one of those men who, forming a solid rear guard in society, gave that society fullness and consistency.

I had gotten to know Monsieur La Harpe in 1789. Like Flins, he had been smitten with a great passion for my sister, Madame la Comtesse de Farcy. He used to come to the house with three fat volumes of his own works tucked under his tiny arms, and he was quite surprised to discover his fame did not conquer the most rebellious of hearts. With his booming voice and animated gestures, he would thunder against every abuse, making do with an omelet at the ministers' houses where he didn't like the food, eating with his fingers, trailing his sleeves through the dishes, talking philosophical scurrilities to the most influential lords, who reveled in his insolence; but on the whole he had an enlightened and right-thinking mind, impartial despite its passion, capable of sensing talent, of admiring it, of weeping at beautiful verses or a beautiful deed, and possessing a foundation sturdy enough to support repentance. He did not falter at the end; I saw him die a courageous Christian, his taste enlarged by faith, having retained disdain only for impiety, and hatred only for "revolutionary language."

On my return from the Emigration, religion had inclined him favorably toward my books. The illness that attacked him did not prevent him from working. He recited me some passages from a poem he was composing on the Revolution. There were a few energetic lines that railed against the crimes of the age and the "good men" who had permitted them:

> But if they dared do everything, it was at your say:
> The viler the oppressor, the viler the slave.

Forgetting he was ill, dressed in a wadded spencer and a white nightcap, he declaimed at the top of his lungs; then, letting his notebook fall from his hand, said in a voice scarcely audible:

"I can't go on—it's as if there's an iron claw digging in my side."

And if, by some misfortune, a maid walked past the door, he would again shout at the top of his lungs:

"Away with you! Get away! Shut the door!"

I said to him one day:

"You will live for the sake of religion."

"Ah, yes," he replied, "it would indeed be for God; but He does not wish it, and I will die in a matter of days."

Falling back into his armchair and pulling his nightcap down over his ears, he expiated his pride with his resignation and humility.

During a dinner at Migneret's house, I had heard him speak of himself with the greatest modesty, saying he'd done nothing out of the ordinary, though he believed that art and language had not degenerated in his hands.

Monsieur La Harpe left this world on February 11, 1803. He was buried on February 12 in the cemetery at the Barrière de Vaugirard. The coffin having been placed beside the grave, atop the little mound of earth that was soon to cover it, Monsieur de Fontanes gave a speech. The scene was lugubrious: whirlwinds of snow fell from the sky and whitened the mortuary sheet, which the wind lifted, so that the last words of friendship might reach the ears of the deceased. The cemetery has since been destroyed and Monsieur La Harpe exhumed: almost nothing remained of his existence but a meager handful of ashes. Married under the Directory, Monsieur La Harpe had not been happy with his beautiful wife; she had loathed the sight of him, and refused to accord him any rights.[29]

In any case, Monsieur La Harpe had shrunk, like everything else, in the ever-growing shadow of the Revolution. Reputations hastened to retreat before this Revolution's representative, just as dangers lost their power before him.

4.

1802–1803—ENCOUNTER WITH BONAPARTE

WHILE we were busy with the petty matters of living and dying, the world was taking a gigantic step; the Man of his times took his seat at the head of the table of the human race. Amid these colossal stirrings—precursors of the widespread displacement to come—I had stepped off the ship in Calais to take part in the action, like any other foot soldier. I arrived, in the first year of the century, at the camp where Bonaparte was calling fate to arms. He was soon to become First Consul.

After the adoption of the Concordat by the Corps Législatif in 1802, Lucien, Minister of the Interior, gave a reception for his brother. I had been invited because I had rallied the Christian forces and led them back into the fray. When Napoleon came in, I was in the gallery; he made a favorable impression on me; I had never seen him except from afar. His smile was warm and handsome; his eyes were marvels to behold, especially the way they were set beneath his temples and framed by his eyebrows. There was still nothing of the charlatan in his gaze, nothing theatrical or affected. *The Genius of Christianity*, which was then causing no small stir, had struck a chord with Napoleon. A prodigious imagination animated that coldly calculating politician: he would not have been what he was if the Muse had not been with him. Reason effectuated a poet's ideas. All these men who lead great lives are a compound of two natures, for they must be capable of both inspiration and action: one man conceives the plan, and the other executes it.

Bonaparte saw and recognized me, I do not know how. As he made his way toward me, no one knew whom he was seeking; the ranks opened, one after another, everyone hoping that the Consul would stop and speak to him. He seemed to exhibit a certain impatience with these misunderstandings. I hid behind my neighbors. Suddenly, Bonaparte raised his voice and said, "Monsieur de Chateaubriand!" I was then left standing by myself, for the crowd drew back and quickly reassembled in a circle around the two of us. Bonaparte addressed me unpretentiously. Without paying me any compliments, without any pointless questions, without any preamble, he started talking to me about Egypt and the Arabs, as if I had long been a close friend of his and he were merely continuing a conversation we had already begun.

"I was always quite struck," he said, "when I saw the sheikhs fall to their knees in the middle of the desert, turn toward the east, and touch their brows to the sand. I thought, What is this strange thing they're worshipping in the east?"

Bonaparte interrupted himself and went on to another subject without transition:

"Christianity! Haven't the ideologues tried to make an astronomical system of it? If that's the case, how do they expect me to believe Christianity is a trifle? If Christianity is an allegory of the motion of the spheres and the geometry of the stars, the freethinkers have done well, since in spite of themselves they've still granted 'the loathsome thing' a certain grandeur!"[30]

Bonaparte then walked away without a word.

Like Job, in my darkness, "a spirit passed before me; the hair of my flesh stood up: a face unknown to me appeared to my eyes, and I heard a voice like a faint wind blowing."[31]

My days have been but a series of visions. Hell and Heaven have been cracked open again and again beneath my feet or over my head, but I haven't had time to sound their shadows or their lights. Just once, on the shore between the two worlds, did I meet Washington, the man of the last century, and Napoleon, the man of the new. I exchanged a few words with each of them, and both sent me back into solitude—the first with a kindly wish, the second with a crime.

I noticed that, as he moved through the crowd, Bonaparte looked at me more closely than he had while he was speaking to me. I, too, followed him with my eyes:

> *Chi è quel grande, che non par che curi*
> *L'incendio?*
> (DANTE)[32]

5.

1803—I AM NAMED FIRST SECRETARY OF THE EMBASSY IN ROME

Paris, 1837

As a result of this encounter, Bonaparte thought of me for Rome. He had decided at a glance where and how I could be useful to him. It mattered little to him that I had no experience in politics and didn't know the first thing about practical diplomacy; he believed that some minds grasp everything and have no need of apprenticeship. He was a great discoverer of men; but he wanted them to put their talents to work only for him, and on the condition that these talents were not too much discussed. Jealous of every reputation, he regarded them as usurpations of his own. There was to be no one but Napoleon in the universe.

Fontanes and Madame Baciocchi spoke to me of the satisfaction the Consul had derived from "my conversation." I had not so much as opened my mouth—which suggested that Bonaparte was rather satisfied with himself. They pressed me to take advantage of fortune, but the idea of being something had never occurred to me. I flatly refused. Then they sent an authority I found it hard to resist.

Abbé Emery, the superior at the seminary of Saint-Sulpice, came to beseech me, in the name of the clergy and for the sake of religion, to accept the position of first secretary to the ambassador, to which post Bonaparte was going to appoint his uncle, Cardinal Fesch. He had me understand that the cardinal's mind was not very remarkable and that I would soon find myself in charge of things. An unusual coincidence made me feel close to Abbé Emery: I had gone to the United States with Abbé Nagot and a number of seminarians, as you know. The memory of my obscurity, my youth, and my life as a wanderer, now being mirrored in my public life, captured my heart and imagination. Abbé Emery, esteemed by Bonaparte, was made slight by nature, by his robe, and by the Revolution; but this triple slightness was all to the benefit of his true merit. Circumspect in his words and deeds, it would have been superfluous to bend Abbé Emery to your will, for he always put himself entirely at your service, all the while holding fast to his own will, which he refused to yield. His strength was always ahead of you, seated on his tomb.

In his first attempt he failed, but he came charging back, and his perseverance made up my mind. I accepted the post he'd been tasked with offering me, though I wasn't in the least convinced I would be of use in the position: I am worth nothing in the second line. Indeed, I might still have turned it down had the thought of Madame de Beaumont not entered into my considerations. The daughter of M. de Montmorin was dying. She had been told the Italian climate would be favorable to her health. Seeing that I was going to Rome, she resolved to cross the Alps. In hope of saving her, I sacrificed myself. Madame de Chateaubriand prepared to join me,[33] M. Joubert spoke of accompanying me, and Madame de Beaumont departed for Mont d'Or, en route to her cure by the Tiber.

M. de Talleyrand was then Minister of Foreign Affairs and sent me my nomination. I dined at his house. He has remained in my mind just as he lodged himself there during our first encounter. His fine manners contrasted with those of the boors of his entourage, and his wiles took on unimaginable importance: in the eyes of a brute nest of hornets, corrupted morals looked like genius and trivial wit like profundity. The Revolution was too modest. It did not fully appreciate its superiority. It is not the same thing to be above crimes as to be beneath them.

I met the ecclesiastics attached to the cardinal and singled out the cheerful Abbé de Bonnevie. He had formerly been a chaplain in the Army of Princes and took part in the retreat from Verdun. He had also been vicar general of the Bishop of Châlon, M. de Clermont-

Tonnerre, who set out behind us to claim a pension from the Holy See, in his capacity as a Chiaramonti.[34]

No sooner were the preparations for my journey finished than I went on my way: I was supposed to be in Rome before Napoleon's uncle arrived.

6.

1803—JOURNEY FROM PARIS TO THE ALPS OF SAVOY

Paris, 1838

IN LYON, I saw my friend M. Ballanche again and attended the renascent feast of Corpus Christi. I felt I had played some part in those bouquets of flowers and that heavenly joy I had summoned back upon the globe.

I continued on my way and a cordial welcome followed me, for my name was associated with the reestablishment of the altars. The profoundest pleasure I've experienced is to have felt myself honored both in France and abroad with signs of serious interest. Sometimes it has happened, stopping off at a village inn, I have seen a father and mother come in with their son, telling me they are bringing their child to thank me. Was it self-regard that, in such moments, gave me the pleasure I describe? How could it tickle my vanity when good people I did not know gave voice to their gratitude along the roadside, in a place where no one else could hear them? What has touched me—at least I venture to think so—is the thought that I have done some little good, that I have consoled a few distressed souls, that I have revived in a mother's breast the hope of raising a Christian child, which is to say a submissive, respectful child, attached to his parents. Would I have tasted this pure joy if I had written a book that morals and religion would have had reason to bewail?

The road leaving Lyon is rather melancholy: from La Tour-du-Pin to Le Pont-de-Beauvoisin, it is cool and overhung with woods. In Chambéry, where the chivalrous soul of Bayard showed itself so fine,

a man was welcomed by a woman, and in exchange for the hospitality he received believed himself philosophically obliged to dishonor
her.[35] Such is the danger of literature: our desire to make a splash gets
the better of our generous feelings. If Rousseau had not become a
famous writer, he would have concealed the frailties of the woman
who had kept him alive in the valleys of Savoie; he would have sacrificed for her; he would have comforted her in her old age instead of
being satisfied to give her a snuffbox and then run off. Oh, may the
voice of friendship betrayed never be raised against our tomb!

Once past Chambéry, the waters of the Isère appear. Everywhere
in these valleys, one sees wayside crosses and Madonnas in the trunks
of pines. The little churches, surrounded by trees, stand in touching
contrast to the tall mountains. When the winter storms sweep down
from these summits overburdened with ice, the Savoyard takes shelter in his rustic temple and prays.

The valleys above Montmélian are bordered by hills of every shape,
some half bare, some clothed in woods. Aiguebelle seems to bring
the Alps to a close, but on rounding a lonely rock, fallen in the road,
you see still more valleys following the course of the Arc. The hills
on both sides stand tall; their slopes grow perpendicular, and their
barren summits begin to display a few glaciers. Mountain streams
tumble down these slopes to swell the Arc, which runs wildly on.
Amid this tumult of waters, you may distinguish a slender cascade
falling with infinite grace, behind a curtain of willows.

Having passed through Saint-Jean-de-Maurienne and arrived with
the setting sun in Saint-Michel, I found no horses. Forced to stop, I
went for a walk outside the village. The air was glassy over the mountain peaks, whose serration was outlined with utmost clarity, and
meanwhile a great darkness was rising up, from trough to crest. The
voice of the nightingale sounded below and the cry of the eagle above;
the checker tree bloomed in the valley and in the white snow on the
mountain. A castle—the work of the Carthaginians, according to
popular legend—was visible on the sheer-cut ledge. Embodied in that
rock was one man's hatred, more powerful than all the obstacles in

his path. The vengeance of the human race bore down upon a free people, who could not establish their greatness except through slavery and the rest of the world's blood.[36]

I left at daybreak and, at two in the afternoon, rode into Lans-le-Bourg, at the foot of Mont Cenis. Entering this village, I saw a peasant gripping a baby eagle by the talons. A pitiless throng hit at the young king, abused in his youthful frailty and fallen majesty. The father and mother of the noble orphan had been killed. He was offered to me for sale, but died of the mistreatment he had suffered before I could rescue him. I thought then of poor little Louis XVII; I think today of Henri V. How swiftly downfall and misfortune come!

At this point the traveler begins to climb Mont Cenis and leaves behind the little river Arc, which leads you to the mountain. On the other side of Mont Cenis, the Doria opens the gate to Italy. The rivers are not only "great, moving roads," as Pascal called them;[37] they also show men the way.

When I found myself on the crest of the Alps for the first time, I was overcome by a strange emotion. I was like the lark that crossed the icy plateau along with me and, after singing its little song of the plain, fell down dead in the snow, never reaching the harvests. The stanzas these mountains inspired in me in 1822 fairly represent the feelings that stirred in me in 1803:

> *Alpes, vous n'avez point subi mes destinées!*
> *Le temps ne vous peut rien;*
> *Vos fronts légèrement ont porté les années*
> *Qui pèsent sur le mien.*
>
> *Pour la première fois, quand, rempli d'espérance,*
> *Je franchis vos remparts,*
> *Ainsi que l'horizon, un avenir immense*
> *S'ouvrait à mes regards.*
>
> *L'italie à mes pieds, et devant moi le monde!*[38]

But did I ever really make it into that world? Christopher Columbus had a vision that showed him the land of his dreams before he
discovered it. In his travels, Vasco da Gama came face-to-face with
the colossus of the storms.[39] Which of these two great men prefigured
my future? The thing I would have liked above all would have been
a life whose glory derived from a brilliant discovery destined for
obscurity. Do you know the first European ashes to lie in American
ground? They belonged to Bjorn the Scandinavian, who died on his
way to Vinland and was buried on a hill by his companions. Who
remembers that? Who knows anything about the man whose sail
preceded the Genoese captain's ship to the New World? Bjorn sleeps
at the end of a forgotten headland, and for a thousand years his name
has come down to us only through the sagas of the poets, in a language
that no one now speaks.

7.

FROM MONT CENIS TO ROME—MILAN AND ROME

I HAD BEGUN my travels in the opposite direction of other travelers. The ancient forests of America were revealed to me before the ancient cities of Europe. I found my way into these cities just as they were being rejuvenated, and dying, in a new revolution. Milan was occupied by our troops. The castle, witness to the wars of the Middle Ages, had been demolished.

The French army had settled, like a military colony, on the plains of Lombardy. Guarded here and there by fellow soldiers on sentry, these foreigners from Gaul, wearing police caps and carrying sabers instead of sickles over their round jackets, looked like bright and eager farmhands. They shifted stones, rolled cannon, drove wagons, and built sheds and huts out of brushwood. Horses pranced, turned about, and reared in the crowd like dogs playing with their masters. Italian women sold fruit from stalls in the marketplace of this armed fairground. Our soldiers made them presents of their pipes and flints, saying to them, as their forefathers the ancient barbarians had said to their beloveds: "I, Fotrad, son of Eupert, of the race of the Franks, give to you, Helgine, my dear wife, in honor of your beauty (*in honore pulchritudinis tuae*), my house in the district of Les Pins."[40]

We make curious enemies. At first we are found a bit insolent, and too cheerful, too restless. But no sooner have we turned on our heels than we are missed. Lively, witty, intelligent, the French soldier involves himself in the doings of the people he lives among. He draws water from the well, like Moses for the daughters of Midian.[41] He waves off the shepherds and leads the lambs to the washing place, chops wood, makes fires, watches the pot, carries the child in his arms or rocks it to sleep in its cradle. His good humor and energy bring everything to life. He comes to be regarded as a member of the family. And when the drum sounds? The soldier runs for his musket, leaves his host's daughters weeping at the door, and goes out of the cottage, never to think of it again, until, perhaps, he is admitted to the Invalides.

When I was passing through Milan, a great people awoke for a moment and opened its eyes. Italy was emerging from its slumber and recalling her spirit as if it were a heavenly dream. Advantageous to our own renascence, she brought to the shabbiness of our poverty the magnificence of the transalpine nature, nourished as Ausonia[42] was by artistic masterpieces and the lofty recollections of a famous fatherland. Now Austria has come. She has again laid her leaden cloak over the Italians. She has forced them back into their coffin. Rome has sunk back into her ruins, Venice into her sea. Venice has slumped, beautifying the sky with her last smile; she has lain down in her waves, like a star that will never rise again.

General Murat was then commander-in-chief at Milan. I was carrying a letter for him from Madame Baciocchi. I spent the day with the aides-de-camp, who were not as poor as my comrades near Thionville. French civility reappeared among the ranks, as though the soldiers wished to prove they were still living in the days of Lautrec.

On the 23rd of June, I dined at a grand gala given by M. de Melzi on the occasion of the baptism of one of General Murat's sons. M. de Melzi, the vice president of the Cisalpine Republic, had known my brother. His manners were beautiful, and his house was like that of a prince who would always be a prince: he treated me politely and coldly. He found my disposition quite similar to his.

I arrived at my destination on the evening of June 27, two days before the Feast of Saint Peter: the prince of the Apostles awaited me, as my own poor patron would later welcome me to Jerusalem.[43] On June 28, I rushed around all day. I cast a first glance at the Colosseum, the Pantheon, Trajan's Column, and Castel Sant'Angelo. That night, M. Artaud took me to a ball at a house near Saint Peter's Square. You could see the gleam of Michelangelo's dome in between the swirling of the waltzers who spun before the open windows; the fireworks launched from Hadrian's mausoleum blossomed in brightness at Sant'Onofrio, over Tasso's tomb. Silence, solitude, and night lay upon the Roman countryside.

The next day I attended Mass at Saint Peter's. Pale, sad, and reverent, Pius VII was truly the pontiff of tribulations. Two days later I was presented to His Holiness. He invited me to sit next to him. A volume of *The Genius of Christianity* lay obligingly open on his table. Cardinal Consalvi, flexible and firm, gently and politely resistant, was the very embodiment of the ancient Roman politician, minus the faith of those times and plus the tolerance of the age.

Walking through the Vatican, I paused to contemplate those staircases that might be climbed on the back of a mule; those ascending galleries folded one into another and hung with masterpieces, where the popes of old used to pass in their pomp; those loggias adorned by so many immortal artists and admired by so many illustrious men (Petrarch, Tasso, Ariosto, Montaigne, Milton, Montesquieu); and then the queens and kings, mighty or fallen; and finally the multitude of pilgrims pouring in from the four corners of the earth: all of it now stilled and silenced, a theater where the deserted tiers, gaping in solitude, are scarcely visited by a ray of sun.

I had been advised to take a walk in the moonlight. From the top of the Trinità dei Monti, the distant buildings looked like a painter's sketches, or like a smoky coastline seen from the sea, from the side of a ship. The star of the night—that globe imagined to be an extinct world—shed its pale desert light over the deserts of Rome, illuminating uninhabited streets, yards, and squares, gardens where no one went, monasteries where the monks' voices had fallen silent, cloisters as mute and unpeopled as the porticoes of the Colosseum.

What was happening, eighteen centuries earlier, at that same hour, in that very place? What men had here passed through the shadow of those obelisks, after that shadow had ceased to fall on the sands of Egypt? Not only is ancient Italy gone, medieval Italy has vanished.

Yet the trace of these two Italys is still visible in the Eternal City. If modern Rome reveals Saint Peter's and its masterworks, ancient Rome counters with the Pantheon and its ruins. If the consuls came down from the Capitol, so the pontiffs come down from the Vatican. The Tiber separates these two glories. Planted in the same dust, pagan Rome subsides deeper and deeper into its tombs, while Christian Rome is descending again, little by little, into its catacombs.

8.

CARDINAL FESCH'S PALACE—MY OCCUPATIONS

CARDINAL Fesch had rented the Lancelotti Palace, very near the Tiber, which I saw again in 1827 when I visited Princess Lancelotti. In 1803, I was given the run of the palace's top floor. Upon entering, such a huge quantity of fleas leaped upon my legs that my white pants were turned quite black; the Abbé de Bonnevie and I tried, as best we could, to clean our quarters. I felt I had been transported back to my hovel on New Road in London—a not unpleasant reminder of my poverty.

Having settled into that diplomatic cubbyhole, I started doling out passports and keeping myself busy with other similarly important tasks. My handwriting was an obstacle to my talents, however, and Cardinal Fesch shrugged his shoulders whenever he saw my signature. I had almost nothing to do in my aerial chamber except stare out across the rooftops, into a neighboring house, at the washerwomen, who waved to me. An aspiring opera singer, training her voice, tormented me with her eternal scales. Blessed were the days when some funeral or other came to relieve me of my boredom! From the height of my window, in the chasm of the street, I saw a young mother's cortège: she was being carried, her face uncovered, between two lines of pilgrims in white; her newborn, also dead and crowned with flowers, was laid out at her feet.

I committed a great faux pas. Naively, I thought I might visit a few worthies and went to pay my respects to the dethroned king of Sardinia. A horrible scandal resulted from this inconceivable course of action, and all the diplomats tied themselves up in knots. "It's all over for him!" whispered the trainbearers and the attachés, with the charitable pleasure people take in a man's misadventures, whoever the man may be. Not one diplomatic halfwit, in the heights of his idiocy, failed to feel superior to me. They were hoping I would fall, though I was nobody and counted for nothing. No matter. *Somebody* was about to fall, and that is always enjoyable. In my simplicity, I had no idea of my crime, and as always, I didn't give a straw for anyone's position. Kings, to whom (it was supposed) I attached such great significance, were in my eyes significant in misfortune only. My shocking blunders were bandied about from Rome to Paris. Luckily, I had had dealings with Napoleon. What should have been my ruin was my salvation.

All the same, if at first glance and in a single bound to become first secretary of the embassy under a prince of the Church, an uncle of Napoleon, seemed quite something, it was in most respects as though I'd been hired as a shipping clerk in a customhouse. I managed to keep myself busy with the little problems that cropped up, but I was not initiated into any mysteries. I was perfectly resigned to doing chancellery paperwork, though I wondered: what was the point of wasting my time on details within the grasp of any scrivener?

Coming back to the office after my long, mooning walks along the Tiber, all I found to keep me occupied was the closefisted quibbling of the cardinal, the snobbish boasting of the Bishop of Châlon,[44] and the outlandish fibbing of the future Bishop of Morocco. Abbé Guillon, exploiting a similarity in sound between two names, staked the claim that, after miraculously escaping from the Carmelite Convent, he had given absolution to Madame de Lamballe in La Force prison. He also bragged that he was the author of Robespierre's speech on the Supreme Being. I bet, one day, that I could make him tell me he had been to Russia. He did not quite go along with it, but he did humbly admit to having spent a few months in Saint Petersburg.

M. de La Maisonfort, a man of intelligence who was then in hiding, applied to me for assistance, and M. Bertin the Elder, who owned the *Débats*, acted as a friend to me under sorrowful circumstances.

Exiled to the isle of Elba by the man who, returning from Elba himself, would later force him to Ghent, M. Bertin had, in 1803, obtained permission from the Republican M. Briot, an acquaintance of mine, to live out his exile in Italy. With him, I visited the ruins of Rome and saw Madame de Beaumont die—two things that have bound his life to mine. A critic of great taste, like his brother, he gave me excellent advice on my work; he would have shown a real talent for oratory had he been called to the podium. A Legitimist of long standing, who underwent the trial of imprisonment at the Temple and exile on Elba, his principles have, at bottom, remained the same. I will forever be faithful to my companion in misfortune. All the political opinions in the world would not be worth the sacrifice of one hour of true friendship. Suffice it to say that I remain as invariable in my opinions as I remain attached to my memories.

Somewhere in the middle of my stay in Rome, Princess Borghèse arrived. I was put in charge of delivering her some shoes from Paris. I was presented to her; she shod herself in my presence. The new and pretty slippers she put on her feet were to tread this old earth only for a moment.

Sorrow finally came to fill my days: it is a resource on which one can always rely.

BOOK FIFTEEN

I.

1803—MADAME DE BEAUMONT—THE LETTERS OF MADAME DE CAUD

Paris, 1838; Revised February 22, 1845

WHEN I left France, we were in the dark about Madame de Beaumont's condition. She wept often, and her will made it clear she knew that she was going to die. But her friends, without letting fall a word about their fears, tried to reassure each other; they put their faith in the miracles of the waters and the Italian sun; down different roads, they went their separate ways. Their rendezvous was Rome.

A few fragments written in Paris, Mont d'Or, and Rome, by Madame de Beaumont, found among her papers, reveal the state of her soul:

Paris

For several years, I have felt my health declining. Symptoms I believe to be the signal to depart have arisen, but I have not been quite ready to go. Delusions redouble hand in hand with the disease. I have seen many examples of this bizarre weakness, and I am well aware that they will do me no good. Already I am submitting to treatments as tedious as they are ineffectual, and no doubt I shall soon lack the strength to shield myself from those cruel cures with which they never fail to martyr people dying of lung ailments. Like others, I will surrender to hope. Hope! Why should I even want to live? My life up to now has been a series of misfortunes, my life at present is full of turmoil and distress. Peace of mind has fled from me forever.

My death would be a momentary pain for some, a small blessing for others, and the greatest of blessings for me.

This 21st of Floréal, May 10, marks the anniversary of the death of my mother and brother:

Je péris la dernière et la plus misérable![1]

Oh, why don't I have the courage to die? My illness, which I have almost had the weakness to fear, has subsided, and perhaps I am condemned to live a long time. It seems to me, however, that I would die gladly:

Mes jours ne valent pas qu'il m'en coûte un soupir.[2]

No one has a greater right than I to complain of nature. By refusing me everything, she has made me sensible of all I lack. Not a moment goes by I don't feel the weight of the total mediocrity to which I am condemned. I know that self-satisfaction and happiness are often the result of this mediocrity I so bitterly lament, but by withholding the gift of illusion, nature has turned it into a torture. I'm like a fallen creature who cannot forget what it has lost and lacks the strength to regain. This absolute absence of illusion, and thus of enthusiasm, has in many ways been my ruin. I judge myself as a stranger might judge me and see my friends just as they are. My one good quality is my kindness, which is not active enough to be appreciated or truly useful, and which is robbed of all its charm by my impatience: it makes me suffer the misfortunes of others much more than it gives me the means to ameliorate them. Yet I owe it the few real joys I have had in my life; I owe it especially my ignorance of envy, the usual prerogative of the self-aware mediocrity.

Mont d'Or

I had planned to put down a few details about myself, but boredom makes the pen drop from my fingers.

Everything painful and upsetting in my situation would be transformed into happiness if I were sure I would be out of this life in a few months' time.

Even if I had the strength to bring myself to put an end to my sorrows in the only possible way, I would not exert it: it would go against my intentions, revealing the extent of my sufferings and inflicting too grievous a wound on the soul I have deemed worthy of supporting me in my miseries.

I "implore myself in tears" to steel myself. Charlotte Corday claims that "there is no act of self-sacrifice that does not confer more pleasure than pain." But she was going to die, and I may live a long time yet. What will become of me? Where can I go to ground? How can I fend off hope? What power will wall up the door?

To go away in silence, let myself be forgotten, entomb myself forever—that is the duty laid upon me, a duty I hope to have the courage to fulfill. If the cup is too bitter, nothing, once I am forgotten, will force me to empty it to the dregs, and perhaps my life may, after all, not be so long as I fear.

If I knew where I was going to go to ground, I feel I would be calmer, but the difficulty of the moments compounds the difficulties born of my weakness, and it requires something supernatural to act against oneself with force, to treat oneself as harshly as a cruel and violent enemy might do.

Rome, October 28

For the past ten months, I have been suffering without cease. For the past six, all the symptoms of consumption, and some in their final stage. Now the only thing I lack are illusions, though perhaps I still have a few.

Joubert, alarmed by this desire for death that was tormenting Madame de Beaumont, addressed these words to her in his *Pensées*:

"Love life, and respect it, if not for its own sake, at least for the sake of your friends. In whatever state you may find yourself, I would always prefer to know that you were busy piecing things together rather than ripping them apart."

My sister, too, used to write to Madame de Beaumont. I am in possession of this correspondence, which death delivered me. The poetry of the ancients represents some Nereid or other as a flower floating over the abyss: Lucile was that flower. Bringing the fragments above together with Lucile's letters, one is struck by the similarity of the sadness expressed by the different tongues of these two ill-fated angels. When I think that I have lived in the company of such minds, I marvel at how insignificant I am. My eyes never light on these pages by two superior women, gone from the earth a short distance apart, without my feeling cruelly beset.

Lascardais, July 30

I was so charmed, Madame, to receive a letter from you at last that I did not give myself time to take pleasure in reading it from start to finish: I interrupted my reading to go tell everyone in this house I'd just received news from you, without stopping to think that, here, my happiness hardly matters, since almost no one knows I have been in correspondence with you. Seeing myself surrounded by cold expressions, I went back to my room and made up my mind to be happy by myself. I sat down to finish reading your letter, and, though I have reread it several times, to tell you the truth, Madame, I still could not say for certain everything it relates. The joy I always feel, seeing one of your longed-for letters, has kept me from giving it the attention it deserves.

But am I right you are going away, Madame? Please, do not neglect your health when you reach Mont d'Or; give it all your attention, I beg you—with all the finest and most tender feelings of my heart. My brother has told me that he hopes to see you in Italy. Destiny, like nature, was pleased to distinguish him from me in a very favorable manner. But at least I will not yield to my brother the happiness of loving you. I will share it with him all my life. My God, Madame, how my heart aches and pounds! You don't know how much your letters mean to me, how they make me disdain my own troubles! The very idea that I am in your thoughts, that I interest you, plucks up my courage enormously. Write to me then, Madame, please, so that I might hold onto this idea that has become quite necessary to my well-being.

Lucile

Lascardais, September 2

What you write me, Madame, of your health, alarms and saddens me; yet I reassure myself by thinking of your youth and recalling that, though you are quite delicate, you are full of life.

I am sorry that you find yourself in a country you do not like: I would prefer to see you surrounded by things that distract and delight you. I hope that, with the return of your health, you will become reconciled to Auvergne: there is hardly any place that cannot offer *some* beauty to eyes such as yours. I am now living in Rennes and find I am rather happy in my seclusion. As you know, I have moved more times than anyone can count. I seem to have been made for displacement. In truth, it's no passing fancy if I regard myself as one of the earth's superfluous creations. I believe, Madame, you spoke of my sorrows and agitations. All that is over for the moment, and I am enjoying an inner peace no one can take from me. Despite my age, having led—by chance and by taste—a life that has almost always been solitary, I have gotten to know nothing of the world. I have at last made that disagreeable acquaintance. Fortunately, a few thoughts came to rescue me. I asked myself what was so formidable about this world and where its worth lay— this world that can never be anything, in its good or evil, but an object of pity. Is it not true, Madame, that man's judgment is as bounded as the rest of his being, and as changeable and unbelieving as it is ignorant? All these thoughts, fine or foul, have made it easier for me to toss aside the bizarre robe I had pulled around me. I have found myself full of sincerity and strength. Nothing more can trouble me. I am working with all my might to recover possession of my life, to put it entirely under my control.

Remember, too, Madame, that I am not too much to be pitied, since my brother, the better part of myself, is in such an agreeable position, since I still have eyes to admire the wonders of nature, God for support, and, for refuge, a heart filled with peace and beautiful memories. If you have the goodness, Madame, to go on writing to me, that will bring me even greater happiness.

The mystery of style, a mystery palpable everywhere and present nowhere; the revelation of a painfully favored nature; the naivety of a girl one might imagine to be in her early youth, and the humble simplicity of an unselfconscious genius shine through these letters. Did Madame de Sévigné write with more appreciative affection to Madame de Grignan than Madame de Caud to Madame de Beaumont? "Their tender feelings might have strolled side by side, and hand in hand." My sister loved my friend with all the passion of the grave, for she sensed that she was going to die. Lucile almost never left the country around Des Rochers;[3] but she was the daughter of her era. She was the Sévigné of solitude.

2.

MADAME DE BEAUMONT ARRIVES IN ROME

Paris, 1837

A LETTER from M. Ballanche, dated the 30th of Fructidor, let me know that Madame de Beaumont had arrived in Lyon and was on her way to Italy. He told me to put the calamity I was dreading out of my mind; the patient's health appeared to be improving. In Milan, Madame de Beaumont met M. Bertin, who was kind enough to attend to the poor traveler and ride with her to Florence, where I had gone to wait for her. When I saw her, I was terrified; she barely had the strength to smile. After a few days' rest, we got on the road to Rome, riding at a walking pace to avoid the worst of the bumps. Madame de Beaumont was generously cared for everywhere she went. You were charmed by something about this warmhearted woman, so forlorn and so long-suffering, the last surviving member of her family; at the roadside inns, even the serving girls could not help but be overcome by gentle commiseration.

What I was feeling might be surmised. You have taken friends to their graves—but they were mute, and no breath of inexplicable hope came to fan the fires of your pain. My eyes no longer saw the beautiful countryside we were passing through. We had taken the Perugia road. But what did I care about Italy? Whatever the weather did, I found it too harsh. The wind blew, and the gentlest breezes seemed to me like gales.

In Terni, Madame de Beaumont spoke of going to see the waterfall. After making an effort to walk leaning on my arm, she sat down again and said to me, "We'll have to let the waters fall without us." I had rented a house for her in Rome, near the Piazza di Spagna, below the Pincian Hill. There was a little garden with espaliered orange trees and a courtyard planted with a fig. That was where I lodged the dying woman. I had had a good deal of trouble procuring this retreat, for there was a prejudice in Rome against lung ailments, which were thought to be contagious.

In those days when the social order was being revived, everything that belonged to the old monarchy was sought after. The pope sent for news of M. de Montmorin's daughter, and Cardinal Consalvi and the members of the Sacred College followed His Holiness's suit. Cardinal Fesch himself showed Madame de Beaumont marks of deference and respect that I would not have expected of him and that made me forget the miserable schisms of my first days in Rome. I had written to Joubert of the anxieties that had plagued me before Madame de Beaumont's arrival: "Our friend writes me letters from Mont d'Or," I told him, "which break my heart. She says she 'feels there is no more oil in the lamp.' She speaks of the 'final beats of her heart.' Why has she been left to undertake this voyage alone? Why haven't you written to her? What will become of us if we lose her? Who could console us? We only sense how important our friends are when we are threatened with losing them. We are even deluded enough, when all is well, to think we can part from them with impunity—but the heavens punish us. They are taken from us, and we are appalled at the empty space they leave around us. Pardon me, my dear Joubert; today I feel as though my heart were twenty years old. Sorrow is my element: I'm only myself when I'm unhappy. My friends are now such a rare species that the mere thought of being robbed of one of them chills my blood. Please forgive my complaints. I'm sure you are just as unhappy as I am. Write to me, and write also to that other unfortunate, in Brittany."

At first Madame de Beaumont felt slightly better, and the sick woman herself began regaining her faith in life. I was satisfied to think that at least Madame de Beaumont would not be leaving me again: in the spring, I was planning to take her to Naples, and from there to send my resignation to the Ministry of Foreign Affairs.

M. d'Agincourt, that true philosopher, came to see the little bird of passage who had alighted in Rome before flying on to unknown lands, and M. Boguet, already the doyen of French painters, also came to visit. These bolsters of hope fortified the sick woman and comforted her with an illusion that, deep down, she could no longer maintain. Letters painful to read arrived from every quarter, speaking to me of fears and hopes. On October 4, Lucile wrote to me from Rennes:

> I had started a letter to you the other day and have just gone pointlessly searching for it. I was writing to you of Madame de Beaumont and complained of her silence toward me. My friend, what a sad, strange life I have been leading these last few months! The words of the prophet keep coming back to me: "The Lord will crown thee with sorrows and toss thee like a ball." But let us put my troubles aside and speak of your worries. I cannot persuade myself that they are justified: I always see Madame de Beaumont full of life and youth, and almost incorporeal; no dark thoughts can trouble me in this regard. Heaven, which knows our feelings for her, will keep her alive for our sake, without a doubt. My friend, we will not lose her, I am certain of it. I like to think that, by the time you receive this letter, your worries will be dispelled. Tell her for me what a true and tender interest I take in her; tell her that my memory of her is one of the most beautiful things I have in this world. Keep your promise and do not fail to send me news as often as you can. My God! How long it will take to receive a reply to this letter! Distance really is a cruel thing! Why did you tell me you might come back to France? You're trying to be kind to me, but you're deceiving me! Still, amid all my troubles, I am struck by a sweet thought—and that is the thought of your friendship, the thought that I exist in your memory exactly as it pleased God to make me. My friend, the earth is no longer as safe a place for me as your heart is. Farewell, my poor brother—will I see you again? I cannot quite imagine when or how. If we do see each other again, I'm afraid you'll find me quite insane. Farewell, you

whom I owe so much! Farewell, unadulterated bliss! Oh, memories of my good days, can you not now shed a little light on my melancholy hours?

I am not one of those people who exhaust their despondency at the moment of parting. Every day adds to the sorrow I feel at your absence, and were you to stay in Rome for a hundred years you would never exhaust that sorrow. To fool myself into feeling you are close, I read a few pages of your work each day: I make every effort to imagine I hear you speaking. The friendship I feel for you is quite natural; since our childhood, you have been my defender and friend. You have never made me shed a tear and never made a friend who has not also become mine. My beloved brother, Heaven, which is pleased to make sport with all my other sources of happiness, wills that I find my happiness wholly in you, that I put my faith in your heart. Give me news, as soon as you can, of Madame de Beaumont. Send your letters to Mademoiselle Lamotte's house, although I am not sure how long I can stay there. Since our last separation I have been, in relation to my dwelling place, like the shifting sands. It's quite true that for people unacquainted me, I must seem inexplicable; however, I vary only in form, for the substance remains constantly the same.

The song of the swan, getting ready to die, was transmitted, through me, to the dying swan: I was the echo of those last, ineffable concerts.

3.

LETTER FROM MADAME DE KRÜDENER

ANOTHER letter, quite different from Lucile's, written by a woman who has played an extraordinary role in the world, demonstrates the sway that Madame de Beaumont—without the powers of beauty, fame, or wealth—exercised over people's spirits and minds.[4]

Paris, November 24, 1803

I learned the day before yesterday from M. Michaud, who has just returned from Lyon, that Madame de Beaumont was in Rome and very, very ill: this is what he told me. I was deeply saddened to hear this; my nerves were affected, and I thought a great deal about this charming woman, whom I have not seen for a long time but whom I truly love. How many times have I wished her happiness! How many times have I wished she would cross the Alps and discover the sweet, deep emotions I myself experienced beneath Italian skies! Alas! She has come to that charming country only to suffer and be exposed to dangers! Forgive me, if I have been so absorbed with her I have not yet spoken to you about yourself, my dear Chateaubriand; you must know my sincere attachment to you, and that by expressing the very real affection I have for Madame de Beaumont, I am able to express my affection for you better than I could have done by speaking directly of you. I have the sad spectacle before my eyes; I know the secret of pain, and my heart is wrenched by those souls nature has endowed with the power to suffer more than others. I have been hoping Madame de Beaumont might enjoy the privilege she deserves, to be happier; I have been hoping she might recover a bit of her health under the Italian sun, with the added happiness of your presence. Ah! Reassure me, write to me; tell her that I love her sincerely and wish her well. Did she get my letter in reply to hers at Clermont? Address your answer to Michaud: I ask you only for a note, my dear Chateaubriand, for I know how sensitive you are and how much you suffer. I thought she was better; I did not write to her; I have been overwhelmed with business; but I thought of how happy she would be to see you again and could just picture it. Tell me a little about your own health; trust in my friendship, in the affection I shall always have for you, and do not forget me.

B. Krüdener

4.

DEATH OF MADAME DE BEAUMONT

Paris, 1838

THE GOOD the Roman air did Madame de Beaumont's health was not to last. The symptoms of imminent collapse had disappeared, it's true, but it seems the final moment always delays, to give us false hope. On two or three occasions I had tried taking the patient for a carriage ride, doing my best to distract her by showing her the countryside and the sky, but nothing interested her any longer. One day I took her to the Colosseum. It was one of those October days such as one never sees except in Rome. She managed to get out of the carriage and went to sit on a stone facing one of the altars along the edge of the building. She raised her eyes and let them wander slowly over the porticoes which had themselves been dead for so many years, and which had been witness to so much dying. The ruins were decorated with brambles and columbine, turned the color of saffron by the autumn air, and suffused with light. The dying woman then lowered her gaze, tier by tier, abandoning the sun and descending to the level of the arena. She rested her eyes on the altar cross and said to me:

"Let's go; I'm cold."

I took her home. She went to bed, and never rose again.*

---

*I had, by this point, gotten in touch with the Comte de la Luzerne. By each courier, I sent him another bulletin on his sister's health. When, years earlier, he had been sent on a diplomatic mission to London by Louis XVI, he took my brother with him: André Chénier was also a member of that embassy.

The doctors I had called, after the experimental drive, told me only a miracle could save Madame de Beaumont. She was obsessed by the idea that she would not live past November 2, the Day of the Dead. Then she recalled that one of her relatives—I don't know which—had died on November 4. I told her her mind was confused and she would soon see her fears were groundless. To console me, she replied:

"Oh, yes, no doubt I will, later on."

When she caught sight of some tears I was trying to hide from her, she reached out her hand to me and said:

"You are such a child. What did you expect to happen?"

On the eve of her death, Thursday, November 3, she seemed calmer. She spoke to me of the disposal of her fortune and told me, regarding her will, that everything was settled, but that everything still remained to be done, and that she would be glad to have just two hours to "see to it all." That night the doctor told me he felt obliged to warn the patient that the time had come to put her house in order. I had a moment of weakness. The fear of precipitating, with death's paperwork, the few instants that Madame de Beaumont still had to live overwhelmed me. I lost my temper with the doctor, then begged him to wait at least until the next day.

It was a harrowing night for me, with this secret locked away in my heart. The patient did not permit me to come into her room. I remained outside, trembling at every noise I heard. When the door was opened partway, I saw the weak flame of a night-light fizzling out.

On Friday, November 4, I went in, followed by the doctor. Madame de Beaumont saw that I was upset and said to me:

"What's wrong? I have had a good night."

The doctor then affected to tell me quite audibly that he wanted to speak to me in the next room. I went out: when I returned, I no longer knew whether I was alive or dead. Madame de Beaumont asked me what the doctor had wanted to tell me. I flung myself down by her bed, dissolving into tears. She lay for a moment not speaking, then looked at me and said in a firm voice, as if she wanted to give me strength:

"I wouldn't have thought it was going to be so quick. Well. The time has come to say goodbye. Call the Abbé de Bonnevie."

The Abbé de Bonnevie, having obtained the necessary powers, came to see Madame de Beaumont. She told him that she had always been deeply faithful at heart but that the unthinkable horrors that had befallen her during the Revolution had, for a time, made her doubt the justice of Providence; that she was prepared to confess her transgressions and to put herself at the mercy of God; but that she hoped the sorrows she had suffered in this world would curtail her expiation in the other. She gestured at me to leave and remained alone with her confessor.

I saw him come back an hour later, wiping his eyes and saying he had never heard more beautiful language nor seen such heroism. The parish priest was summoned to administer the sacraments. I returned to Madame de Beaumont's bedside. When she saw me, she asked:

"Well, are you pleased with me?"

She was moved by what she deigned to call "my kindness" to her. Oh, if at that moment I had been able to buy back a single one of her days in exchange for all of mine, I would have done so gladly! Madame de Beaumont's other friends, who were not there to see her then, at least had to weep but once. Standing beside that bed of sorrows where man hears the tolling of his final hour, every one of the sick woman's smiles restored me to life and then, fading, tore it away from me again. An awful realization played havoc with my mind: I came to understand that, to her last breath, Madame de Beaumont had doubted my affection for her: she kept showing her surprise, and she seemed to die desperate and happy. She had thought she was a burden to me, and she had wanted to go away and set me free.

The priest arrived at eleven o'clock; the room filled up with that crowd of curious and indifferent onlookers that cannot be kept from following a priest around Rome. Madame de Beaumont faced the dreadful solemnity without the slightest sign of fear. We knelt, and the sick woman received both Communion and Extreme Unction. When everyone had gone, she bade me sit on the edge of her bed and spoke to me for half an hour of my affairs and intentions with the greatest loftiness of mind and the tenderest affection. She urged me above all to live with Madame de Chateaubriand and M. Joubert. But was M. Joubert to go on living?

She begged me to open the window, she felt so breathless. A ray of sunshine lit her bed and seemed to cheer her. She started talking then about the plans to go live hidden away in the country we had sometimes discussed, and she burst into tears.

Sometime between two and three in the afternoon, Madame de Beaumont asked Madame Saint-Germain, the old Spanish chambermaid who served her with an affection befitting such a good mistress, to move her to another bed. The doctor forbade this, fearing Madame de Beaumont might die as she was being transported. She told me then that she could feel the last agonies approaching. Suddenly, she threw back her blanket, reached out for me with her hand, and held tightly to mine. Her eyes were wandering. With her free hand, she gestured at someone she saw at the foot of her bed; then bringing this hand back to her chest, she said, "It's there!" Unnerved, I asked her if she recognized me. The beginnings of a smile appeared in the midst of her confusion. She gave me a slight nod, yes. Her voice was already gone from this world. The convulsions lasted only a few minutes. We held her in our arms, the doctor, the watchman, and I. One of my hands was pressed against her heart, which could be felt beneath her frail bones. It was beating fast like a watch winding off its broken chain. Oh—moment of horror and fear—I felt it stop! We tilted her gently back onto her pillow, at rest. Her head drooped. A few curls, uncoiled, lay loose on her brow. Her eyes were closed, eternal night had fallen. The doctor brought a mirror and a candle to the stranger's mouth: the mirror was untarnished by the breath of life and the candle was still. It was all over.

5.
OBSEQUIES

Paris, 1838

USUALLY those who grieve are allowed to indulge their tears in peace while others see to the last rites of religion. As I was representing France on behalf of the cardinal-minister, who was away at the time, and as I was M. de Montmorin's daughter's only friend in Rome, and therefore responsible to her family, I found myself obliged to attend to everything. I had to choose the burial site, specify the depth and breadth of the grave, arrange for the delivery of the shroud, and give the undertaker the measurements for the coffin.

Two clergymen sat vigil beside this coffin soon to be taken to San Luigi dei Francesi. One of these fathers was from Auvergne and was a native of Montmorin itself. Madame de Beaumont had wished to be buried in a piece of cloth that her brother Auguste, the only one who escaped the scaffold, had sent her from Mauritius. This cloth was not in Rome, however, and all that we could find was a strip of it that she carried with her everywhere. Madame Saint-Germain fastened this belt around the body with a carnelian containing a lock of M. de Montmorin's hair. The French ecclesiastics were invited; Princess Borghèse lent her family's hearse; Cardinal Fesch had left orders, in the event of an all too foreseeable calamity, to send his livery and his carriages. On Saturday, November 5, at seven o'clock in the evening, by the light of torches and amid a great crowd, Madame de Beaumont went the way that we all must go. On Sunday, November 6, the funeral Mass was celebrated. The obsequies would have been less French in Paris than they were in Rome. That religious architecture, which bears in its ornamentations the blazons and inscriptions of our ancient homeland; those tombstones where the names of some of the most historic families of our annals are inscribed; that church, under the protection of a great saint, a great king, and a great man—none of it consoled, but it honored grief. I hoped that the last scion of a high-ranking family would find at least some support in my humble affection, and that friendship would not fail it as fortune had done.

The Roman people, accustomed to foreigners, treat them as brothers and sisters. On that ground so hospitable to the dead, Madame de Beaumont left a pious memory behind her. She is still remembered there. I have seen Leo XII praying at her tomb. In 1827, I paid a visit to the monument of this woman who was the very soul of a vanishing society. The noise of my footsteps around that mute monument, in a lonely church, were like an admonition: "I will love you always," the Greek epitaph says, "but you, down among the dead, drink not, I beg you, from that cup that makes you forget your old friends."[5]

6.

1803—LETTERS FROM M. CHÊNEDOLLÉ, M. DE FONTANES, M. NECKER, AND MADAME DE STAËL

Paris, 1838

IF I WERE to measure a private life's calamities against the weight of public events, these calamities would hardly warrant a word in my *Memoirs*. Who has not lost a friend? Who has not watched him die? Who could not recall a comparable scene of mourning? The observation is just, yet no one has ever chided himself for telling his own tales. Sailors, aboard the ship that transports them, have a family on land who are important to them and whose stories they tell each other. Every man has inside him a world apart—foreign to the general laws and destinies of the centuries. It is, anyway, a mistake to believe that revolutions, famous happenings, and momentous catastrophes are all there is of human greatness. We all, one by one, labor on the chain of history, and it is all of these individual existences that compose the human universe in the eyes of God.

I collect these letters mourning the loss of Madame de Beaumont simply as a way of leaving on her grave the garlands that were intended for her.[6]

LETTER FROM M. CHÊNEDOLLÉ

November 23, 1803

Have no doubt, my dear, unhappy friend, how much I share in your affliction. My sorrow is not as great as yours because that would be impossible, but I am profoundly afflicted by this loss, and it casts a still darker shadow on this life which, for a long time now, has been nothing but suffering for me. Everything good passes away and vanishes from the face of the earth. My poor friend, hurry back to France. Come seek some small consolation from your old friend. You know how much I love you: come.

I have been extremely worried about you. Three months have gone by since I've heard from you, and three of my letters have gone unanswered. Have you received them? Madame de Caud suddenly stopped writing me two months ago. This cut me to the quick, and yet I cannot imagine what I have done to offend her. But whatever she may do, she can never dispel the tender and respectful friendship I will always feel for her. Fontanes and Joubert have also stopped writing me. So it seems everyone I love is conspiring to forget me simultaneously! Please, do not forget me, my good friend! Let there still be one heart on whom I can rely in this vale of tears! Farewell! I embrace you, weeping. Be sure, my friend, that I feel your loss as it ought to be be felt.

LETTER FROM M. DE FONTANES

I share all your sorrows, my dear friend: I feel the painfulness of the position you are in. To die so young, and after outliving her entire family! But at least that interesting and unhappy woman did not lack the support and remembrance of friendship. Her memory will survive in hearts worthy of her. I have forwarded to M. de La Luzerne the moving account that was intended for him. The aged Saint-Germain, your friend's servant, took charge of delivering it. That good man made me weep when he spoke of his mistress. I told him that he had a bequest of ten thousand francs, but he did not give it a second thought. If it were possible to speak of money matters in such lugubrious circumstances, I would tell you it would be quite natural to give you at least the usufruct of a fortune which will go to distant and almost unknown collaterals.* I approve of your conduct; I know your discretion; but I cannot be as disinterested toward my friend as he is toward himself. I confess that this oversight surprises and pains me. Madame de Beaumont on her deathbed spoke to you, with the eloquence of the last farewell, of the future and what will become of you. Her voice must have had greater strength than mine. But did she advise you to renounce a salary of eight or ten thousand francs at a time when your path has barely been cleared of its first thorns? Why be so rash, my dear friend, in taking such a step? You have no doubt of the great pleasure it will give me to see you again. If I were only concerned with my own happiness, I would say to you: Come at once. But your interests are as dear to me as my own and I can see no resources for you that will compensate for the advantages you are voluntarily giving up. I know that your talent, your name, and your work will never leave you at the mercy of the barest necessity; but in all that I see more fame than fortune. Your upbringing and your habits require some small expenditure. Reputation alone is not enough for the things of life, and the miserable science of "bread and meat" takes charge if you want to live independent and at ease. I still hope that nothing will persuade you to seek your fortune among foreigners. Ah, my friend, be sure that after the first caresses they prove themselves even more worthless than your fellow countrymen. If your dying friend thought over all these things, her last moments must have been a bit disturbed; but I hope that, at the foot of her tomb, you will find lessons and insights superior to those your still-living friends might give you. That kind woman loved you; she shall advise you well. Her memory and your heart shall guide you safely: there is no more need for

*M. de Fontanes's friendship goes too far: Madame de Beaumont knew me better. She no doubt thought that, had she left me her fortune, I would not have accepted it.

me to worry if you heed them both. Farewell, my dear friend,
I embrace you tenderly.

M. Necker wrote me the only letter I ever received from him. I
had been a witness to the Court's cheers at the dismissal of this
minister whose honest opinions contributed to the toppling of the
monarchy. He, who had been a colleague of M. de Montmorin, was
soon to die in the place from which his letter was posted. As Madame
de Staël was not then with him, he shed tears for his daughter's friend:

LETTER FROM M. NECKER

Coppet, November 27, 1803

My daughter, monsieur, when setting off for Germany, asked
me to open any large parcels addressed to her, in order to decide
whether they were worth the trouble of forwarding by post.
This is how I came to learn the news of Madame de Beaumont's
death before she has. I forwarded your letter to her, monsieur,
in Frankfurt, but it will probably have to be forwarded farther,
perhaps to Weimar or Berlin. Do not therefore be surprised,
monsieur, if you do not receive a reply from Madame de Staël
as quickly as you have the right to expect. You must be assured,
monsieur, of the grief which Madame de Staël will feel on
hearing of the loss of a friend of whom I have always heard her
speak with profound affection. I share her sorrow, and yours,
too, monsieur—and I have my own private sorrow when I think
of the unhappy fate of my friend M. de Montmorin's family.

I see, monsieur, that you are on the verge of leaving Rome
to return to France. I hope that you will take the road through
Geneva, where I will be spending the winter. I would be very
eager to do you the honor of introducing you to a town where
you are already well known by reputation. But where are you
not known, monsieur? Your last work, sparkling with incomparable beauties, is in the hands of all those who love to read.

I have the honor of presenting you, monsieur, the assurances and the homage of my most distinguished sentiments.

Necker

LETTER FROM MADAME DE STAËL

Frankfurt, December 3, 1803

Ah, my God, my dear Francis, what sadness swept over me as I read your letter! Already, yesterday, the papers deluged me with dreadful news, and now your heart-rending account comes to engrave it forever in letters of blood upon my heart. How can you speak to me of our differing opinions on religion and on the priests? Can there be two opinions where feeling is one and the same? I have read your account only through the most sorrowful tears. My dear Francis, remember the days when you felt the greatest friendship for me; do not forget, especially, when my whole heart went out to you, and please know that these feelings, more tender and more profound than ever, are still what I feel for you at the bottom of my soul. I loved and admired Madame de Beaumont's character: I have never known anyone more generous, more grateful, more passionately sensitive. Ever since I first entered society, I have never broken ties with her and always felt, in spite of certain differences, that, at bottom, we were united. My dear Francis, give me a place in your life. I admire you, I love you, I loved the woman you mourn. I am a devoted friend, I will be a sister to you. More than ever, I must respect your opinions: Matthieu,[7] who has them, has been an angel to me in this latest sorrow I have experienced. Give me a new reason to make room for them: let me be useful or agreeable to you in some way. Are you aware I have been banished to a distance of no fewer than forty leagues from Paris? I have taken the opportunity to travel around Germany; but, in the spring, I will be back in Paris itself, if my exile is over, or else near Paris, or in Geneva. Let us meet somehow.

Do you not feel that my mind and my soul understand yours, and do you not feel how much we are alike despite our differences? Humboldt[8] wrote me a letter a few days ago in which he spoke of your work with an admiration that must flatter you, coming from a man of his stature and opinion. But why speak to you of your successes at such a moment? Yet she *loved* these successes of yours, and bound her glory to them. Continue to make illustrious the man she so adored. Farewell, my dear François. I will write you from Weimar in Saxony. Reply to me there, care of the bankers Desport. What heartrending words your story contains! And this resolution to keep on poor Saint-Germain: you must bring him to my house one day.

Farewell affectionately: sorrowfully farewell.

N. de Staël

This hasty letter, affectionately brisk, written by an illustrious woman, intensified my emotions twofold. Madame de Beaumont would have been very happy at that moment, had Heaven allowed her to be reborn, but our fond expressions, which may be heard by the dead, have no power to deliver them. When Lazarus was raised from the tomb, his feet and hands were bound with winding bands and his face was covered with a cloth. Now, friendship cannot say, as Christ did to Martha and Mary:

"Loose him, and let him go."[9]

Those who wrote to console me have passed away in their turn, and demand of me the tears I shed for another.

7.

1803 AND 1804—FIRST IDEA OF MY MEMOIRS—I AM NAMED AMBASSADOR TO THE REPUBLIC OF VALAIS— LEAVING ROME

Paris, 1838

I HAD MADE up my mind to abandon this career in which personal tragedy had now become inextricable from the meaninglessness of the work and the trifling annoyances of politics. You have not experienced desolation of the heart if you have never lingered on alone, wandering in places lately inhabited by a person who made your life worthwhile. You look for her and no longer find her. She speaks to you, smiles at you, walks beside you. Everything she wore or touched recalls her image. There is nothing between you and her but a transparent curtain, but so heavy you cannot lift it. The memory of the first friend who has left you along the way is cruel, for if you live a long time, you are bound to lose others. The dead that follow recall the first to die, and you find yourself mourning at once for a single person and for every person you have ever lost.

While I was making arrangements, prolonged by my remoteness from France, I remained, forsaken, on the ruins of Rome. On my first walk, everything looked different to me. I did not recognize the trees or the buildings or the sky. I lost myself in the countryside among the waterfalls and aqueducts as I had once lost myself beneath the cradling woods of the New World. I went back into the Eternal City, which had now added to its multitude of vanished existences one more extinguished life. Roving the lonely spaces along the Tiber, they engraved themselves so deeply in my memory I reproduced them with some precision in my letter to M. de Fontanes: "If the traveler is miserable," I said, "if he has mingled a beloved woman's bones with the bones of so many illustrious people gone down before her, how can he not be spellbound when he goes from the tomb of Caecilia Metella to the coffin of a woman doomed?"[10]

It was also in Rome that I first conceived the idea of writing the *Memoirs of My Life*. I find a few lines jotted down at random, among which I can decipher only a few words: "Having wandered the earth, passed the finest years of my youth far from my country, and suffered almost everything that a man can suffer, even starvation, I came back to Paris in 1800."

In a letter to M. Joubert, I sketched out my plan as follows:

"My only happiness is to steal away for a few hours and occupy myself with the one work capable of mollifying my grief: these are the *Memoirs of My Life*. Rome will enter into them. From now on, I can only speak of Rome in this way. Rest easy, though: these will not be confessions painful to my friends. If I am 'someone' in the future, my friends' names will be remembered there with love and respect; nor will I supply posterity with details of my weaknesses. I will say nothing of myself not in keeping with my dignity as a man and, I daresay, with the exaltation of my heart. One should show the world only what is beautiful. It is not lying in the eyes of God if we reveal only those parts of our life that will encourage noble and generous feelings in our fellow man. Of course it's not that, deep down, I have anything to hide; I've never had a servant girl dismissed over a stolen ribbon, or left my friend dying in the street, or dishonored the woman who took me in, or dropped off my bastard children at the Foundling Hospital;[11] but I have had my moments of weakness and despondency. A groan about myself should be enough to give the world an idea of these commonplace miseries, which are meant to be left behind the veil. What would society gain by reopening these wounds that can be found anywhere and everywhere? There's no shortage of examples if one wants to see poor human nature trounced."

In this plan I was making for myself, I forgot my family, my child-hood, my youth, my travels, and my exile. These are, however, the stories that have given me the most pleasure to tell.

But I was like a happy slave. Accustomed to putting his shoulder to the wheel, he no longer knows what to do with his freedom. Whenever I tried to set myself to work, a figure came to sit before me, and I could not tear my eyes away: religion alone commanded my attention with its seriousness and the loftier considerations it suggested to me. Yet, by occupying myself with the idea of writing my *Memoirs*, I thought I understood the importance the ancients attached to the value of their name. There is perhaps a touching reality in this perpetuation of memories that might otherwise be left on the wayside. Perhaps, among the great men of antiquity, this idea of an immortal human life took the place of the immortality of the soul, which for them remained a riddle. If fame is trivial, since it concerns only us, it must nevertheless be admitted that it is a fine privilege, attached to the goodwill of the genius, to give imperishable life to all he has loved.

I undertook a commentary on a few books of the Bible, beginning with *Genesis*. In the verse "And the Lord God said, Behold, the man is become as one of us, to know good and evil; and now, lest he put forth his hand, and take also of the tree of life, and eat and live for ever," I noted the Creator's formidable irony. Why shouldn't Adam "put forth his hand" now that he "is become as one of us"? Because he has tasted the fruit of knowledge and knows good from evil; he is now oppressed by misery. He should therefore not live forever. What a gift from God is death!

I began writing prayers, some for "the inquietudes of the soul," others to "shield against the prosperity of the wicked." I was trying to bring my thoughts, which had wandered far from me, back to a center of repose.

As God did not wish to end my life then and there—preserving it for lengthier trials—the storms that had been stirred up now subsided. Suddenly, the cardinal-ambassador changed in his dealings with me. I had a conversation with him and made it clear I had decided to resign. He was against this, claiming my resignation at that moment would carry an air of disgrace, that I would play into my enemies' hands and rankle the First Consul, who would keep me from living at peace in the places where I wished to hide. He suggested I go spend a few weeks or a month in Naples.

At this same time, Russia was sounding me out to see whether I would accept the position of tutor to a grand duke: this would have been something like if I had wished to sacrifice the last years of my life to Henry V.[12]

While I vacillated among a thousand possibilities, I received news that the First Consul had appointed me Minister to the Valais. He had at first flown into a rage over some denunciations, but, returning to his senses, he recognized that I was of that race which is no good except at the forefront and that I mustn't be mixed with others or I'd be no use to him at all. There was no position vacant, and so he created one. In keeping with my instinct for solitude and independence, he chose to post me in the Alps. He gave me a Catholic republic with a host of waterfalls: the Rhône and our soldiers would cross paths at my feet, the one flowing down toward France, the others coursing back toward Italy, with the Simplon Pass vividly opening before me. The Consul granted me as many leaves of absence as I wished, in order to travel around Italy, and Madame Baciocchi sent me word, by way of Fontanes, that the first important embassy to become available was mine. Thus I won this first diplomatic victory, neither expecting nor especially wanting to do so. The truth is that the brilliant mind at the head of the state had no wish to bury in bureaucratic intrigue another mind, which was all too disposed to keep its distance from power.

There is even more truth to this remark if we consider that M. le Cardinal Fesch, to whom I do justice in these *Memoirs* in a way he might not have expected, had sent two malevolent dispatches to Paris, around the same time his manners toward me had become more obliging, after the death of Madame de Beaumont. Were his true thoughts expressed in his conversation, when he permitted me to go to Naples, or in his diplomatic missives? The conversations and missives have the same date, and are contradictory. It would have been easy for me to set the cardinal in line with himself by eliminating all traces of the reports relating to me; when I was Minister of Foreign Affairs, it would only have been a matter of removing the ambassador's asinine written ravings: I would have done no more than what M. de

Talleyrand did in regard to his correspondence with the emperor. But I did not think I had the right to use my power to my advantage. If by chance someone were to go looking for these documents, he would find them in their place. Such a course of action may be taken under false pretenses, I admit; but so that I don't seem to be pretending to possess a virtue I lack, you must understand that this respect for the correspondence of my detractors is more the result of my contempt than my generosity. In archives relating to the Berlin embassy, I have also come across offensive letters about me written by M. le Marquis de Bonnay: far from sparing my own feelings, I am going to make these letters public.

M. le Cardinal Fesch was no more reticent regarding the poor Abbé Guillon (the Bishop of Morocco): he was described as a "Russian agent." Bonaparte called M. Lainé an "English agent." This was the sort of back-fence gossip that the great man had gotten into the habit of repeating from police reports. But wasn't there anything to say against M. Fesch himself? What did his own family make of him? Cardinal de Clermont-Tonnerre was also in Rome in 1803. There was not much he neglected to say about Napoleon's uncle! I have the letters.

But who cares about these contentions buried for forty years in worm-eaten bundles? Of the many actors of that epoch, only one remains: Bonaparte. All of us who are pretending to be alive are dead already. Can the insect's name be read by the feeble light it sometimes drags with it as it creeps along?

When M. le Cardinal Fesch met me again, I was ambassador to Leo XII. He gave me tokens of his esteem, and I, for my part, insisted on preempting him and paying him homage. Anyway, it is natural that I have been judged with a severity I do not spare myself. All of this is so far in the past! I would rather not even recognize the handwriting of the people who, in 1803, served as official or unofficial secretaries to the cardinal.

I left for Naples. That is how a year without Madame de Beaumont began—a year of absence, like so many others to follow. I have never seen Naples since, except in 1828, when I found myself at the gates of

the city, which I had promised to visit with Madame de Chateaubri-
and. The orange trees were laden with their fruits and the myrtles
with their flowers; Baiae, the Campi Elisi, and the sea were enchant-
ments I could no longer share with anyone. I climbed Vesuvius and
went down into its crater. I was plagiarizing myself: I was acting out
a scene from *René*.

In Pompeii, I was shown a skeleton in chains and some garbled
Latin words scribbled on the walls by soldiers. I returned to Rome.
Canova allowed me to visit his studio, where he was at work on a
statue of a nymph. In another part of the room, the marble models
of the tomb I had commissioned had already become quite expressive.
I went to pray over the remains at San Luigi and left for Paris on
January 21, 1804, another calamitous day.[13]

Such enormous misery! Thirty-five years have gone by since these
events took place. Was I not flattering myself, in the grief of those
now distant days, when I imagined the bond just broken would be
my last? And yet how quickly did I not forget, but replace, what was
precious to me! Man stumbles from one mistake to the next. When
he is young and drives his life before him, he still has a shadow of an
excuse, but when he is yoked to his life and drags it painfully behind
him, what excuses him then? The indigence of our nature is so profound that, in our faithless frailty, to express our freshest affections,
we have no choice but to use words we have already worn thin in our
previous relations. There are some words, however, that ought to be
used but once: we profane them by repeating them. Our betrayed
and abandoned friendships reproach us for the new company we keep.
Our days accuse each other. Our life is a perpetual blush, for it is a
neverending blunder.

BOOK SIXTEEN

I.

1804—THE REPUBLIC OF VALAIS—VISIT TO THE TUILERIES—HÔTEL DE MONTMORIN—I HEAR OF THE DEATH OF THE DUC D'ENGHIEN—I SUBMIT MY RESIGNATION

Paris, 1838; Revised February 22, 1845

As I HAD no intention of remaining in Paris, I stayed at the Hôtel de France on the rue de Beaune, where Madame de Chateaubriand was planning to join me before we set off for the Valais.[1] My old coterie, already half scattered to the winds, had lost the tie that bound it.

Bonaparte was marching toward empire, his genius growing to keep up with the greatness of events. He had the capacity, like gunpowder expanding, to blow the world away. His powers, which were by then already immense—however restricted he found them—tormented him. When I arrived in Paris, he was dealing with Pichegru and Moreau. Pettiness had led him to treat them as rivals. Moreau, Pichegru, and Georges Cadoudal, who was by far their superior, were arrested.[2]

This vulgar train of conspiracies such as we find in all walks of life held no appeal for me, and I was glad to be escaping to the mountains.

The city council of Sion wrote me a dispatch "from a religious people" so pure-hearted I cherish it still. My way into politics was through religion. *The Genius of Christianity* had thrown open the gates:

REPUBLIC OF VALAIS
February 20, 1804
Council of the City of Sion
To M. Chateaubriand, Secretary of the Legation of the French Republic at Rome

Sir, we have learned, from an official letter sent by our high bailiff, that you have been appointed Ambassador of France to our Republic. We hasten to express to you the absolute joy this choice gives us. We see in this appointment a precious pledge of benevolence on the part of the First Consul toward our Republic, and we congratulate ourselves on the honor of having you within our walls; we believe this bodes very well for our country and our city. As a token of our feelings, we would be honored to offer you temporary accommodation worthy of your person, provided with furniture and effects suitable for your use, to the extent that the locality and our circumstances allow, until you have been able to make your own arrangements.

Please, sir, accept this offer as a token of our sincere wish to honor the French government through its envoy, whose selection is particularly pleasing for a religious people such as ourselves. We entreat you to let us know when you expect to arrive in the city.

Accept, sir, the assurances of our respectful consideration.

De Riedmatten, President of the Council of the City of Sion
De Torrenté, Secretary of the Council of the City of Sion

Two days before March 21, I dressed to go and take my leave of Bonaparte at the Tuileries. I had not seen him since he spoke to me at Lucien's. The gallery in which he was receiving was full. He was accompanied by Murat and a principal aide-de-camp. He walked along almost without stopping. As he approached me, I was struck by the change in his face. His cheeks were sunken and livid, his eyes harsh, his complexion pale and blotchy, his expression fierce and dark. The fascination that he had previously exerted on me had dissolved. Instead of remaining in his path, I moved aside to avoid him. He shot me a glance as if trying to place me, took a few steps toward me, then turned around and walked away. Did I seem an omen to him? His aide-de-camp noticed me. While the crowd concealed me, this aide-de-camp kept trying to catch sight of me between the people who were blocking his view, dragging the Consul in my direction. This game continued for nearly a quarter of an hour, with me always retreating and Napoleon always following me unaware. I have never been sure what struck the aide-de-camp. Did he take me for a suspicious character he had never seen before? If he knew who I was, did he want to force Bonaparte to talk with me? Whatever the case might have been, Napoleon went on into another room. Satisfied at having done my duty by presenting myself at the Tuileries, I decamped. Given the joy I always feel whenever I am leaving palaces, it is evident I was not made to enter them.

Back at the Hôtel de France, I said to several of my friends:

"There must be something strange going on we don't know about, for Bonaparte cannot have changed this much—unless he is ill."

M. Bourrienne took note of my unusual foresight, although he is confused about the dates:

"When he came back from seeing the First Consul, M. de Chateaubriand told his friends that he had noticed a great change in Bonaparte and that there was something sinister in his eyes."

Yes, I noticed it: a superior mind does not bring forth evil painlessly, for it is not its natural fruit, and it should not bear it.

Two days later, on March 21, I rose early to honor a memory that is sad and dear to me. At the corner of rue Plumet, on the new Boulevard des Invalides, M. de Montmorin had a house. In the garden of this house, which was sold during the Revolution, Madame de Beaumont, when she was still a girl, had planted a cypress tree that she had several times taken pleasure in pointing out to me as we passed. It was to this cypress, whose origin and history was known to me alone, that I was going to say my goodbyes. It still exists, but it is languishing and barely rises to the height of the window beneath which a vanished hand once loved to tend to it. I can distinguish this tree among three or four others of the same species. It seems to know me and to rejoice at my approach. Melancholy breezes bend its yellowed head very slightly toward me as it murmurs at the window of the empty room. There is a mysterious understanding between us, which will cease only when one or the other of us falls.

Having paid my pious tribute, I went down the boulevard and the esplanade des Invalides, crossed the Pont Louis XVI and the Tuileries Garden, which I exited near the Pavillon de Marsan through the gate that now opens on the rue de Rivoli. There, sometime between eleven and noon, I heard a man and a woman who were crying the news. Passersby were stopping, turned instantly to stone by the words:

"The special military commission convened at Vincennes has sentenced to death THE MAN NAMED LOUIS-ANTOINE HENRI DE BOURBON, BORN AUGUST 2, 1772, IN CHANTILLY."

This cry struck me like a bolt. It changed my life, as it changed Napoleon's. I went home and said to Madame de Chateaubriand, "The Duc d'Enghien is about to be shot." I sat at a table and began writing my letter of resignation. Madame de Chateaubriand did not object and bravely watched me as I wrote. She was not unaware of the dangers. General Moreau and Georges Cadoudal were being brought to trial. The lion had tasted blood, and this was not a moment to irritate him.

At this juncture, M. Clausel de Coussergues arrived. He too had gotten wind of the sentence. He found me pen in hand. My letter, from which he made me delete, out of pity for Madame de Chateaubriand, a few angry phrases, went on its way to the Minister of Foreign Affairs. The wording did not much matter: my opinion and crime lay in the fact of my resignation. Bonaparte made no mistake about that. Madame Baciocchi began to scream at the top of her lungs when she learned of what she called my "defection." She sent for me and treated me to the sharpest reproofs. M. de Fontanes was almost crazed with fear at first: he considered me dead already, along with every person attached to me. For several days, my friends lived in fear of seeing me taken away by the police, who hourly appeared outside my door, always trembling as they passed the porter's lodge. The day after my resignation M. Pasquier came to embrace me, saying it was a blessing to have a friend such as I. He remained honorably moderate for quite a considerable time, far removed from position and power.[3]

Nevertheless, this sympathetic impulse, which leads us to praise a selfless action, was soon exhausted. I had accepted, with religion in mind, a position outside of France, a position conferred on me by a powerful genius, a vanquisher of anarchy, a leader sprung from the people, the *consul* of a *republic*, and not a king, the successor to a *monarchy* that had been usurped. At the time I was alone in feeling as I did, because I was consistent in my conduct; I withdrew as soon as the conditions to which I could subscribe had altered. But no sooner had the hero transformed into a murderer than the whole world converged on his antechambers. Six months after March 21, you might have thought that all high society was of the same opinion, except for a few snide remarks behind closed doors. "Fallen" people claimed to have been "forced," and only those with great names or importance were "forced" (so they said), and thus everyone, in order to prove his importance or his quarterings, contrived to be "forced" by force of appeals.

Those who had applauded me loudest retreated. My presence was a reproach to them. Prudent people find anyone who cedes to honor imprudent. There are times when loftiness of soul is a veritable infirmity. No one understands it; it passes for a kind of closed-mindedness, a prejudice, an obtuse ingrained habit, a caprice, a foible that prevents you from seeing things as they are. It is perhaps an honorable imbecility, people say, but also stupid helotry. What good is it to shut your eyes, to remain a stranger to the march of the age, the movement of ideas, the transformation of mores, the progress of society? Isn't it a regrettable error to assign events more importance than they have? Barricaded behind your parochial principles, your mind as blinkered as your judgment, you are like a man living at the back of a house looking out only on a narrow courtyard, oblivious to what is going on in the street or the noises to be heard outside. That is what a little independence reduces you to—an object of pity for the mediocre. As for the powerful, with their loving pride and haughty eyes, *oculos sublimes*,[4] they pardon you with merciful disdain because they know that you "cannot hear."⁵ So I slunk humbly back to my literary pursuits: a poor Pindar destined to sing "the excellence of water" in my first Olympic, leaving wine to the blessed.

Friendship made M. de Fontanes bold, and Madame Baciocchi interposed her benevolence between her brother's anger and my resolve. M. de Talleyrand, through indifference or calculation, held onto my resignation for several days before breathing a word of it: when he announced it to Bonaparte, the latter had already had time to reflect. Receiving from me the sole direct sign of blame given by an honest man unafraid to stand up to him, he uttered only these two words:

"Very well."

Later he said to his sister:

"You were quite afraid for your friend."

A long time after, talking with M. de Fontanes, Bonaparte admitted to him that my resignation was one of the things that had most impressed him.

M. de Talleyrand had an official letter sent to me in which he graciously reproached me for depriving his department of my talents and services. I returned the preliminary fee that had been paid me and everything was settled, so it seemed. But by daring to turn my back on Bonaparte, I had put myself on his level, and he was compelled to oppose me with all his treachery, as I opposed him with all my loyalty. Until the day of his downfall, he held the sword suspended above my head. From time to time, he came back around to me by a natural inclination and sought to drown me in his lethal milk and honey. Occasionally I was drawn to him by the admiration he inspired in me—by the idea that I was witnessing a social transformation, not a simple change of dynasty; but our two natures, opposite in so many respects, always reared their heads again, and if he would gladly have had me shot, killing him wouldn't have weighed too heavily on my conscience.

Death makes or unmakes a great man. It stops him on the step he was about to descend or the one he was about to climb. His destiny has been fulfilled or it has not. In the first case, we are reduced to examining what was; in the second, to conjecturing about what might have been.

If I had done my duty with distant views of ambition, I would have been deluding myself. Charles X only learned in Prague what I had done in 1804.[6]

"Chateaubriand," he asked me at Hradschin Castle, "you served Bonaparte?"

"Yes, sire."

"And you submitted your resignation upon the death of M. le Duc d'Enghien?"

"Yes, sire."

Misfortune instructs or restores the memory. I have told you how, one day in London, when I sheltered in an alley with M. de Fontanes during a downpour, M. le Duc de Bourbon happened to come take cover under that same roof. In France, he and his gallant father, who so politely thanked whoever wrote the funeral oration for M. le Duc d'Enghien, didn't give me a thought. Probably they, too, were unaware of what I had done. It is true I never mentioned it to them.

2.

DEATH OF THE DUC D'ENGHIEN

Chantilly, November 1838

LIKE THE migratory birds, I am taken by a restlessness in the month of October that would oblige me to change my clime if I still had strength in my wings and time to spare: the clouds scudding across the sky make me want to flee. To cheat this impulse, I have come to Chantilly. I have wandered on the lawn where old guardsmen dawdle along the edge of the woods. A few crows flying before me over the broom, the copses, and the clearings led me to the ponds of Commelles. Death has breathed on the friends who used to stroll with me to Queen Blanche's castle: the sites of these solitudes were but a sad horizon, half opening for a moment on the landscapes of my past. In the days of René, I would have found the mysteries of life in the stream called the Thève: it hides its course among the horsetails and mosses; reeds veil it; it dies out in those ponds it feeds with its youth, expiring ceaselessly and ceaselessly renewed. Such ripples of water used to bewitch me when I bore a desert within me, a desert populated by phantoms who smiled at me, in spite of their melancholy, and whom I decked with flowers.

Walking back along the hedges, which have vanished almost without a trace, I was surprised by the rain. I sheltered beneath a beech. Its last leaves were falling like my years and its top was growing bare, like my skull. There was a red circle marked on its trunk, indicating it was to be felled, like myself. Now that I have returned to my inn, with a harvest of autumn plants and in a mood indisposed to cheer, I will recount for you the death of M. le Duc d'Enghien as I stare out over the ruins of Chantilly.

At first this death froze all hearts with terror. Everyone was dreading a return of Robespierre's reign. Paris thought it was witnessing the recurrence of one of those days that no man sees more than once: the day of the execution of Louis XVI. Bonaparte's servants, friends, and relatives were dismayed. Abroad, popular feeling may have been stifled by the language of diplomacy, but it stirred nonetheless in the guts of the crowd. Among the exiled members of the Bourbon family, the blow struck home. Louis XVIII returned the insignia of the Order of the Golden Fleece, with which Bonaparte had just been decorated, to the King of Spain. Along with it was this letter, which does honor to the royal soul:

> MONSIEUR AND DEAR COUSIN, There can be nothing in common between me and the great criminal whom audacity and fortune have placed on the throne that he has had the barbarity to soil with the pure blood of a Bourbon, the Duc d'Enghien. Religion might make me pardon a murderer, but the tyrant of my people must always be my enemy. Providence, for inexplicable reasons, may condemn me to live out my days in exile, but neither my contemporaries nor posterity should ever be able to say that in times of adversity I showed myself unworthy of occupying my ancestors' throne.

We must not forget another name associated with the Duc d'Enghien: Gustav IV Adolf of Sweden, dethroned and banished, was the only king then reigning who dared to raise his voice in defense of the young French prince. He sent an aide-de-camp from Karlsruhe bearing a letter for Bonaparte. The letter arrived too late. The last of the Condés was gone. Gustav returned the ribbon of the Black Eagle to the King of Prussia for the same reason Louis XVIII sent the insignia of the Order of the Golden Fleece back to the King of Spain. Gustav declared to the heir of Frederick the Great that "according to the *laws of chivalry*, he could not consent to be the brother in arms of the murderer of the Duc d'Enghien." There is an unspeakably bitter irony in these almost insane tokens of chivalry—extinct everywhere except in the heart of an ill-fated king, remembering a murdered friend. Noble sympathies of misfortune, surviving in isolation, misunderstood, in a world ignored by men!

Alas, we had gone through too many different forms of despotism. Our characters, tamed by a chain of miseries and oppressions, no longer had the energy to let our grief wear mourning for the young Condé very long. Gradually, the tears dried up. Fear spluttered congratulations on the dangers the First Consul had just escaped; fear wept with gratitude at having been saved by such a holy sacrifice. Nero, at Seneca's dictation, wrote the Senate a letter explaining away the murder of Agrippina, and the delighted senators heaped benedictions on the magnanimous son who hadn't been afraid to rip out his own heart with such a salutary matricide.[7] Society rapidly returned to its pleasures, for it was afraid of its grief. After the Terror, the spared victims danced, tried hard to look happy, and, scared lest they be suspected of the crime of memory, carried on with the same good cheer they had shown on their way to the scaffold.

It was not on the spur of the moment, without forethought, that the Duc d'Enghien was arrested. Bonaparte had been made aware of the number of Bourbons in Europe. At a council to which M. de Talleyrand and M. Fouché were called, it was acknowledged that the Duc d'Angoulême was in Warsaw with Louis XVIII, and that the Comte d'Artois and the Duc de Berry were in London with the Prince de Condé and Prince de Bourbon. The youngest of the Condés[8] was in Ettenheim, in the duchy of Baden. It was in this borderland that Mr. Taylor and Mr. Drake, two English agents, had entered into intrigues. In a note of June 16, 1803, posted from London, and which still exists, the Duc de Bourbon warned his son of the possibility of arrest. Bonaparte summoned his two colleagues the consuls and bitterly reproached M. Réal for having left him in ignorance of what was being plotted against him. He listened patiently to their objections: it was Cambacérès who expressed himself most vigorously.

Bonaparte thanked him for what he said and moved on. (This is what I read in Cambacérès's memoirs, which one of his nephews allowed me to consult, an act of courteousness I shall never forget.) The bomb, once launched, does not return; it goes where the engineer flings it, and falls. To execute Bonaparte's orders, German territory had to be violated, and this territory was violated without second thoughts. The Duc d'Enghien was arrested in Ettenheim. Instead of General Dumouriez, only the Marquis de Thumery and a few other émigrés of small renown were discovered in his company. That should have warned them a mistake had been made. The Duc d'Enghien was carted off to Strasbourg. The beginning of the catastrophe of Vincennes has been recounted for us by the prince himself: he left behind a little travel journal kept from Ettenheim to Strasbourg. The hero of the tragedy takes center stage to pronounce the prologue.

JOURNAL OF THE DUC D'ENGHIEN

On Tuesday, March 15, in Ettenheim, my house surrounded by a detachment of dragoons and pickets of gendarmes; in total, about two hundred men, two generals, Colonel Charlot of the Strasbourg gendarmerie, at five o'clock (in the morning). At half past five the doors broken down, taken to Le Moulin near La Tuilerie. My papers confiscated, sealed. Driven in a cart, between two lines of riflemen, to the Rhine. Embarked for Rheinau. Disembarked and marched on foot to Pfortzheim. Breakfast at the inn. Climbed into a carriage with Colonel Charlot, the sergeant of the gendarmerie, a gendarme on the box, and Grunstein. Arrived in Strasbourg, at Colonel Charlot's house, about half past five. Transferred half an hour later in a fiacre to the citadel ... Sunday, March 18, they came to take me away at half past one in the morning. I was barely given time to dress. I embraced my unfortunate companions, my servants. I left by myself with two officers of the gendarmerie and two gendarmes. Colonel Charlot announced to me that we were going to the divisional general, who had received orders from

Paris. Instead of this, I find a carriage with six post-horses waiting on the Place de l'Église. Lieutenant Petermann climbs up beside me, Sergeant Blitersdorff on the box, two gendarmes inside, another outside.

Here, the shipwrecked man, about to be engulfed, interrupts his logbook.

Arriving at about four o'clock in the evening at one of the gates of the capital, at the end of the Strasbourg road, the carriage, instead of entering Paris, followed the outer boulevard and stopped at the Château de Vincennes. The prince stepped down from the carriage into the inner courtyard, was led to a room in the fortress, was locked in there, and went to sleep. As the prince drew closer and closer to Paris, Bonaparte had affected an unnatural calm. On March 18, he left for Malmaison. It was Palm Sunday. Madame Bonaparte, who, like everyone else in her family, was aware of the prince's arrest, spoke to him about it. Bonaparte told her, "You understand nothing of politics." Colonel Savary had become one of Bonaparte's closest companions. Why? Because he had seen the First Consul weeping at Marengo. Exceptional men should be careful of their tears, which put them under the yoke of the vulgar. Tears are one of those signs of weakness that a witness can use to make himself the master of a great man's decisions.

It has been claimed that the First Consul wrote all the orders for Vincennes. In one of those orders, it was stated that if the expected sentence was a death sentence, it was to be executed on the spot. I believe this version of events, although I cannot confirm it since the orders have gone missing. Madame de Rémusat, who on the evening of March 20 was playing chess with the First Consul at Malmaison, heard him murmur a few sentences about the clemency of Augustus. She thought Bonaparte had returned to his senses and that the prince was saved. No. Destiny had declared its oracle. When Savary reappeared at Malmaison, Madame Bonaparte divined the whole sad affair. The First Consul shut himself up alone for several hours. And then the breeze blew, and it was all over.

MILITARY COMMISSION APPOINTED

An order issued by Bonaparte on Ventôse 28, Year XII, had decreed that a military commission, composed of seven members appointed by the governor-general of Paris (Murat), would meet at Vincennes to pass judgment on "the former duc d'Enghien, accused of having borne arms against the Republic," etc.

In executing this decree, on Ventôse 29, Joachim Murat appointed seven officers to form the aforementioned commission, namely:

General Hulin, commanding the consular guard, chairman;

Colonel Guitton, commanding the First Regiment of Cuirassiers;

Colonel Bazancourt, commanding the Fourth Regiment of Light infantry;

Colonel Ravier, commanding the Eighteenth Regiment of Line Infantry;

Colonel Barrois, commanding the Ninety-Sixth Regiment of Line Infantry;

Colonel Rabbe, commanding the Second Regiment of the Municipal Guard of Paris;

Citizen d'Autancourt, major of the select legion, who would fulfill the role of the *capitaine rapporteur*.[9]

INTERROGATION BY THE CAPITAINE RAPPORTEUR

Citizen d'Autancourt, accompanied by Jacquin, the squadron leader of the select legion, two gendarmes of the same corps named Lerva and Tharsis, as well as Citizen Noirot, a select legion lieutenant, go to the Duc d'Enghien's room and wake him. He had only four hours to wait before getting back to sleep. The capitaine rapporteur, assisted by Citizen Molin, the captain of the Eighteenth Regiment, whom he has chosen as his clerk, interrogates the prince.

Asked: his name, surname, age, and birthplace.

Answered: that his name is Louis-Antoine-Henri de Bourbon, Duc d'Enghien, born August 2, 1772, in Chantilly.

Asked: in what places has he resided since he left France.

Answered: that after leaving with his family, the Condé corps was formed, and that he served throughout the whole war, and before that he had been through the campaign of 1792 in Brabant with the Bourbon corps.

Asked: whether he had ever been to England, and whether that power still paid him a pension.

Answered: that he had never gone there, and that this power paid him a pension, and that this was all he had to live on.

Asked: what rank he held in the army of Condé.

Answer: commander of the advance guard since 1796, before which he had been a volunteer at his grandfather's headquarters, but always, since 1796, commander of the advance guard.

Asked: whether he knew General Pichegru, and whether he had had any relations with him.

Answered: "I have, as far I know, never seen him. I have never had any relations with him. I know that he wished to see me. I congratulate myself on never having known him in light of the vile means you say he wanted to employ, if what you say is true."

Asked: whether he knew the ex-general Dumouriez, and whether he had any connection with him.

Answered: "No, not with him either."

The document on which all of this is recorded is signed by the Duc d'Enghien, Jacquin, Noirot, the two gendarmes, and the capitaine rapporteur. Before signing these minutes, the Duc d'Enghien said:

"I earnestly request to have a private audience with the First Consul. My name, my rank, the turn of my mind, and the horror of my situation induce me to hope that he will not refuse my request."

HEARING AND SENTENCING

At two o'clock in the morning on March 21, the Duc d'Enghien was led into the room where the commission was sitting and repeated what he had said during the capitaine rapporteur's interrogation. He persisted in his declaration. He added that he was ready to make war and that he wanted to be of service in England's latest war against France.

"Asked whether there was anything else he wanted to say in his defense, he replied that he had nothing more to say.

"The chairman ordered the accused be taken out of the room. The council deliberated behind closed doors; the chairman collected the votes, beginning with the most junior in rank and giving his own verdict last. The Duc d'Enghien was unanimously found guilty, and the article ... of the law ... thus worded ... was applied to him, and in consequence condemned him to the pain of death. The capitaine rapporteur ordered that this sentence should be executed at once, after being read to the condemned, in the presence of the various detachments of the corps of the garrison.

"Case heard, tried, and closed in an unbroken session at Vincennes on the days, month, and year abovementioned, as witness our hands ... "

The grave being *dug, filled,* and *sealed,* ten years of forgetfulness, general assent, and inconceivable glory were laid upon it. The grass grew to the sound of salvos proclaiming victory, beneath the illuminations that lighted the papal coronation, the wedding of the daughter of the Caesars, and the birth of the King of Rome.[10] Only a few rare mourners wandering in the woods ventured a furtive look down into the moat at the deplorable spot, while a few prisoners glimpsed it from the heights of the keep where they were locked up. Then the Restoration came: the earth of the grave was disturbed, and, with it, consciences. Each man sought to explain himself. M. Dupin the Elder published his account. M. Hulin, the chairman of the military commission, spoke up. M. le Duc de Rovigo entered the fray by accusing M. de Talleyrand. A third party replied on M. de Talleyrand's behalf, and Napoleon raised his mighty voice from the rock of Saint Helena.

These documents must be reproduced and studied in order to

assign each player his proper part in the drama. It is night, and we are in Chantilly. It was night when the Duc d'Enghien was at Vincennes.

3.

DUPIN

Chantilly, November 1838

WHEN M. Dupin published his pamphlet, he sent it to me with this letter:

Paris, November 10, 1823

Monsieur le vicomte,

Please accept a copy of my publication regarding the murder of the Duc d'Enghien.

It would have appeared long ago, had I not wanted, above all, to respect the wishes of His Lordship the Duc de Bourbon, who, having been made aware of my work, had informed me of his desire never to have this deplorable business exhumed.

But Providence having permitted others to take the initiative, it has become necessary to make the truth known, and after assuring myself that my silence was no longer insisted upon, I have spoken with frankness and sincerity.

I have the honor of being, with profound respect,

Your Excellency's most humble and obedient servant,

Dupin

M. Dupin, whom I congratulated and thanked, reveals in his cover letter a rare and moving concern for the noble and clement virtues of the victim's father. He begins his pamphlet thus:

The death of the ill-fated Duc d'Enghien is one of the events that has most afflicted the French nation: it dishonored the consular government.

A young prince, in the prime of life, taken treacherously by surprise on foreign soil, where he slept in peace under the protection of the law of nations; dragged violently away to France; brought before so-called judges who, in any case, were in no position to be his judges; accused of imaginary crimes; denied the assistance of counsel; interrogated and condemned behind closed doors; put to death at night in the moat of the fortress-castle that was used as a state prison. So many virtues ignored, so many fond hopes destroyed, make this catastrophe one of the most revolting acts ever committed by an absolute government!

If no formalities were respected; if the judges were unqualified to judge; if they failed even to take the trouble to include in their decision the date and text of the laws on which they claimed to base their condemnation; if the unfortunate Duc d'Enghien was gunned down because of a sentence *unsigned* ... and only legalized after the fact, then it is no longer merely a question of judicial error; the thing deserves its rightful name: it is a hateful murder.

This eloquent exordium leads M. Dupin to examine the documents. First he shows that the arrest was illegal. The Duc d'Enghien was not arrested in France; he was not a prisoner of war, since he was unarmed when he was taken; and he was not a prisoner in the civil sense, for no extradition had been demanded. It was a violent abduction comparable to the captures made by the pirates of Tunisia and Algeria, a thieves' errand, *incursio latronum*.

The jurist goes on to say that the military commission was unfit for its task, seeing that alleged plots hatched against the state have never been under the jurisdiction of military commissions. He then analyzes the sentence:

The interrogation took place on Ventôse 29 at midnight. On Ventôse 30, at two o'clock in the morning, the Duc d'Enghien was brought before the military commission.

In the formal sentence, we read: "Today, Ventôse 30 of Year XII of the Republic, at two o'clock in the morning." These words, "at two o'clock in the morning," which were only inserted because it was in fact that time of night, have been erased from the document and were not replaced by any other indication.

Not a single witness was heard or produced against the accused.

The accused was "declared guilty," but guilty of what? The sentence does not say.

Every ruling handing down a sentence must contain the citation of the law on the basis of which the sentence is being applied.

Well, here, none of these formalities has been followed. Nothing in the official report substantiates that the commissioners had a "copy of the law" before them; nothing demonstrates that the chairman "read the text" of the law before applying it. Far from it: the sentence as written proves that the commissioners condemned the accused without knowing either the date or the substance of the law; for, in the formal sentence, they have *left blank* the date of the law, the number of the article, and the place reserved for the quotation of its text. And yet it was on a sentence in this state of imperfection that the noblest blood was spilled by executioners!

The deliberation must be secret, but the decision must be announced in public: this is, again, what is dictated by the law. Now, the sentence of Ventôse 30 certainly says the council deliberated "behind closed doors," but it does not mention reopening the doors or announcing the result of the deliberation in a public session. Even had it said so, who would believe it? A public session, at two o'clock in the morning, in the keep of Vincennes, when all the entrances to the castle were guarded by officers of the select legion! But in the end they did not even take the precaution of resorting to a lie; the sentence passes over this point in silence.

This document is signed by the chairman and the six other commissioners, including the rapporteur, but it is worth noting that the minutes *are not signed by the court clerk*, whose assent is necessary in order to affirm their authenticity.

The sentence concludes with these terrible words: "Shall be executed AT ONCE, at the behest of the capitaine rapporteur."

AT ONCE! Desperate words, and the work of the judges! AT ONCE! When there is a law—that of Brumaire 15, year VI —which granted the right of appeal against any military sentence!

M. Dupin, moving on to the execution, continues:

Interrogated at night, tried at night, the Duc d'Enghien was killed at night. This horrible sacrifice was to be consummated in darkness, so that it might be said that every law had been violated—every one, including those requiring that executions take place in public.

The jurist says of the illegalities of the investigation:

Article 19 of the law of Brumaire 13, year V, states that, after he has finished his interrogation, the rapporteur shall tell the defendant to "choose a friend as his defender." The prisoner shall have "the power to choose this defender" from every class of citizen present on the premises; if he declares that he cannot make this choice, the rapporteur shall make it for him.

Ah, there is no doubt that the prince had no "friends"[11] among those who surrounded him; the cruel declaration was made clear to him by one of the abettors of that horrible crime! Alas! Why weren't we present? Why wasn't the prince permitted to make an appeal to the Bar of Paris? There, he would have found men friendly to his situation, defenders of his misfortune. It is with an eye toward making this sentence presentable to the public that a new version seems to have been prepared at leisure. The belated substitution of a second version, to all appearances more legal than the first (although equally unjust), in no way detracts from the heinousness of having put the Duc d'Enghien to death on the basis of a cursory sentence, hastily signed, and without the proper copies having been made.

Such is M. Dupin's illuminating pamphlet. Yet, with an act of the type that the author is examining, I am not sure whether a greater or lesser degree of legality is of much importance. If the Duc d'Enghien had been strangled in a post chaise on his way from Strasbourg to Paris instead of being killed in the woods of Vincennes, it would make no difference. But is it not providential to see some men, after so many years, demonstrating the illegality of a murder in which they took no part, and others come running, without having been asked, to give their testimony? What have they heard? What voice from on high has summoned them to bear witness?

4.
GENERAL HULIN

Chantilly, November 1838

FOLLOWING the great jurist, here comes a blind veteran. He has commanded the grenadiers of the Old Guard—which speaks volumes to the brave. His last wound he received from Mallet, whose powerless lead has remained lodged in a face that never once turned away from a bullet. "Blinded, withdrawn from the world, with his family as his only consolation" (these are his own words), the judge of the Duc d'Enghien seems to emerge from his tomb at the summons of the sovereign Judge; he pleads his case with no illusions and without making excuses for himself:

> Let there be no mistake about my intentions. I do not write out of fear, since I am under the protection of laws emanating from the throne itself, and since under the government of a just king I need not fear violence or lawlessness. I write to tell the truth, even as regards what may be against my own interests. I do not wish to justify either the form or the basis of the sentence, but I do wish to show under what influence and circumstances that sentence was passed; I wish to remove myself and my colleagues from the suspicion of having acted as partisan men. If we are still to be blamed, I want it also to be said of us: "They were in a very difficult position!"

General Hulin maintains that when he was appointed chairman

of a military commission, he did not know its purpose; that when he arrived at Vincennes, he was still in the dark; that the other members of the commission were in the dark as well; that the commander of the fortress, M. Harel, when questioned, told him he himself didn't know anything, adding:

"What do you want? I'm nobody here at the moment. Everything is being done without my orders or involvement. Someone else has been put in charge."

It was ten o'clock at night when General Hulin was relieved of his uncertainty by the disclosure of certain documents. The hearing was begun at midnight, once the examination of the prisoner by the capitaine rapporteur was finished.

> The reading of the documents gave rise to an incident. We noticed that at the end of the minutes submitted by the capitaine rapporteur the prince, before signing his name, *had written with his own hand a few lines in which he expressed his wish to have a conversation with the First Consul*. One member proposed to transmit this request to the government. The commission agreed, but at that same moment the general, who had come and posted himself behind my chair, pointed out to us that this request was "inopportune." Besides, we found no provision in the law authorizing us to delay. The commission therefore proceeded, reserving the right to satisfy the defendant's wishes after the deliberations were done.

This is according to General Hulin. Now, in the Duc de Rovigo's pamphlet we read the following: "There were so many people I found it difficult, when I arrived among the last, to shoulder my way behind the chairman's seat, where I positioned myself." Was it then the Duc de Rovigo who had posted himself behind Hulin's chair? But did he, or anyone else who was not part of the commission, have the right to intervene in the deliberations and point out that a request was "inopportune"?

Let us listen to the commander of the grenadiers of the Old Guard speak of the courage of the young son of the Condés. He was well versed in such things:

I proceeded to interrogate the defendant; I must say that he stood before us with noble self-assurance, dismissing out of hand the accusation that he had been directly or indirectly involved in a conspiracy to assassinate the First Consul, though he also admitted that he had borne arms against France, saying with a courage and pride that did not allow us, in his own interest, to make him change his way of addressing this point, that he had "upheld the rights of his family" and that "a Condé could never reenter France without a weapon in his hand." "My birth and my opinions," he added, "make me the sworn enemy of your government."

The firmness of his convictions drove his judges to despair. Ten times we put him on the road to revising his statements, and he always persisted unshakably: "I can see," he would say now and then, "the honorable intentions of the members of the commission, but I cannot avail myself of the terms they offer me." And on being warned that military commissions judged without appeal: "I know that," he replied, "and I am under no illusions about the risk I am running; I only wish to have an audience with the First Consul."

Is there a sadder page in all our history? The new France passing judgment on the old France, paying her homage, presenting arms to her, saluting her colors even as it condemns her; the tribunal set up in the fortress where the great Condé, held prisoner, used to water his flowers; the general of the grenadiers of Bonaparte's Guard sitting face-to-face with the last descendent of the victor of Rocroi, feeling himself moved to admiration before a man accused and undefended, alone on the earth, being interrogated while the noise of the gravedigger shoveling out the soil for the young soldier's grave mingles with his unwavering replies. A few days after the execution, General Hulin exclaimed, "Oh, the brave young man! What courage! I would like to die as he did!"

General Hulin, after speaking of the "minutes" and the "second version" of the sentence, says:

> As for the second version, the only true one, as it did not contain the order to "execute at once," but only to "read at once," the judgment being passed on the condemned man, the order to "execute at once" could not be the work of the commission, but only of those who found it incumbent upon them to hurry along this fated execution.

> Alas, we had other things on our minds! Hardly had the sentence been signed than I began to write a letter in which, with the unanimous support of the commission, I made the First Consul aware of the prince's wish to have an audience with him, and also to implore him to postpone a sentence that our difficult position did not allow us to avoid.

> At that moment a man, who had never left the deliberation room, and whom I would name in an instant if I did not take into consideration that, even when defending myself, it is best not to point fingers, approached me and asked:

> "What are you doing there?"

> "I am writing to the First Consul," I replied, "to inform him of the wishes of the council and the condemned man."

> "Your business here is done," he said, taking the quill from my hand. "Now it is up to me."

> I confess that, like several of my colleagues, I thought he meant "It is up to me to inform the First Consul." The reply, understood in this sense, allowed us to hope that the request would still be passed on. And how could it have occurred to us that anyone among us *had orders to neglect the formalities required by law*?

The whole secret of this gloomy catastrophe is contained in this deposition. The veteran, whose perpetual nearness to death on the battlefield had taught him the language of truth, concludes with these words:

> In the hallway outside the deliberation room, I was discussing what had just taken place; several separate conversations going on. I was waiting for my carriage, which, like those of the other members, had not been allowed to enter the inner courtyard, delaying my departure and theirs. We were ourselves locked up, and no one could communicate with the outside, when we heard an explosion: a terrible noise that echoed in the depths of our souls and froze them with terror and dread.
>
> Yes, I swear in the name of all my colleagues that we never authorized this execution. Our judgment stated that copies would be mailed to the Minister of War, the Minister of Justice, and the Governor of Paris.
>
> The order for execution could legally be given only by the latter; the copies were not yet sent; they could not be finished before some portion of the day had passed. Returning to Paris, I might have got hold of the governor, the First Consul—who knows? And all of a sudden there is a horrible noise that leaves no doubt that the prince is no longer among the living!
>
> We are ignorant as to whether the person who so cruelly precipitated this mournful execution *had orders: if he did not, he alone is responsible; if he did, the commission, uninformed of these orders, the commission, unlawfully kept under lock and key,* the commission, whose last wish was for the prince's salvation, was unable either to foresee or forestall the result. It cannot be held responsible.
>
> Twenty years gone by have not sweetened the bitterness of my regrets. Let me be accused of ignorance and error: I accept that. Let me be reproached for an obedience that, in similar circumstances today, I would be better able to evade; for my attachment to a man I thought destined to bring happiness to my country; for my loyalty to a government I then thought legitimate and had sworn to defend. But, when judging me and

my colleagues, let the disastrous circumstances in which we were summoned to make our decision also be taken into account.

The defense is weak, but you repent, general: peace be with you! Even if your decision gave the last Condé his marching orders, you will go and join that last conscript of our ancient homeland in the advance guard of the dead. The young soldier will be glad to share his resting place with the grenadier of the Old Guard. The France of Freiburg and the France of Marengo[12] will slumber together.

5.
DUC DE ROVIGO

Chantilly, November 1838

M. LE DUC de Rovigo, beating his breast, takes his place in the procession that comes to confess at the tomb. I had long been under the power of the Minister of Police; he fell under the influence that he supposed had been restored to me with the return of the Legitimacy, and he shared with me a part of his memoirs. Men in his position speak of what they have done with marvelous candor; they have no conception that what they are saying condemns them. Implicating themselves unawares, they do not suspect the existence of an opinion other than their own regarding the duties they have fulfilled and the actions they have taken. If they have been disloyal, they do not believe they have broken their vows; if they have taken on roles repugnant to other men, they think they have done a great service. Their naivety does not justify them, but it does excuse them.

M. le Duc de Rovigo consulted me about the chapters in which he speaks of the death of the Duc d'Enghien. He wanted to know what I thought, precisely because he knew what I had done. I was grateful to him for this token of esteem and, repaying frankness with frankness, advised him to publish none of it. I told him:

"Let all of this die. In France, you don't have to wait long for forgetfulness to come and swallow things up. You think you will clear Napoleon and cast the blame on M. de Talleyrand, but you do not sufficiently account for the former and you do not hold the latter sufficiently responsible. You leave yourself wide open to attack, and your enemies will not hesitate to answer you. Why should you remind the public that you commanded the select legion at Vincennes? They are not aware of the direct part you played in this miserable affair, and you are going to reveal it to them. General, throw the manuscript in the fire: I am telling you this for your own sake."

Full of the governmental maxims of the Empire, the Duc de Rovigo believed these maxims would serve just as well under the Legitimacy. He was convinced his pamphlet would reopen the doors of the Tuileries to him.

It is partly by the light of this pamphlet that posterity will see the phantoms of sorrow take shape. I volunteered to hide the guilty man who had come to ask me for shelter in the night, but he did not accept the protection I offered him.

M. de Rovigo tells the story of the departure of M. de Caulaincourt, whom he does not name; he speaks of the abduction in Ettenheim, the prisoner's passage through Strasbourg, and his arrival at Vincennes. Following an expedition on the coast of Normandy, General Savary had come back to the Malmaison. He is summoned at five o'clock in the evening on March 20, 1804, to the office of the First Consul, who hands him a sealed letter to be taken to General Murat, the governor of Paris. He flies to the general, crosses paths with the Minister of Foreign Affairs, receives the order to take the select legion and go to Vincennes. He arrives there at eight o'clock at night and sees the members of the commission coming in. He later makes his way into the room where the prince is being tried, at one o'clock in the morning, and he goes and sits down behind the president. He reports the Duc d'Enghien's replies more or less as they are reported in the minutes of the session. In person, he told me how the prince, after offering his final explanations, briskly removed his cap, set it on the table, and, like a man who is laying down his life, said to the chairman:

"Monsieur, I have nothing more to say."

M. de Rovigo insists that this session was in no way secret. "The doors to the room," he claims, "were open to anyone who cared to attend *at that hour*." M. Dupin had already remarked on this deranged explanation. On this point, M. Achille Roche, who seems to write on M. de Talleyrand's behalf, exclaims:

"The session was in no way secret! At midnight! Held in the inhabited part of the castle; in the inhabited part of a prison! Who is going to attend such a session? Jailers, soldiers, hangmen?"

No one could give more exact details about the time and place of the Duc d'Enghien's death than M. le Duc de Rovigo. Let us hear what he has to say:

> After the sentence had been pronounced, I withdrew with the officers of my corps who, like me, had been present at the proceedings, and I went to join the troops who were on the esplanade of the castle. The officer in charge of the infantry of my legion came to tell me, with great emotion, that he had been asked for a firing squad to carry out the military commission's sentence.
>
> "Then supply it," I replied.
>
> "But where should I post it?"
>
> "Where you can't hurt anyone."
>
> For the roads were already filled with the inhabitants of the busy outskirts of Paris, on their way to the markets.
>
> After carefully examining the grounds, the officer chose the moat as the surest place to avoid wounding any bystanders. M. le Duc d'Enghien was led there, down the staircase of the entrance tower on the park side, and there heard the reading of the sentence, which was then executed.

Beneath this paragraph, we find a note by the author of the memoir:

"Between the sentence and its execution, they had dug a grave: this is what gave rise to the report that it had been dug prior to the trial."

Unfortunately, the errors here are deplorable. "M. de Rovigo claims," says M. de Talleyrand's apologist, M. Achille Roche, "that he has followed orders! Who ordered him to carry out the execution? It seems this is a man named M. Delga, who was killed in Wagram. But whether or not it was M. Delga, if M. Savary is mistaken when he names M. Delga, doubtless no one today is going to step up to claim the distinction he confers upon this officer. M. de Rovigo is accused of having hastened the execution; he says he did not: a man who is dead told him that *he* had been given orders to hasten it."

The Duc de Rovigo is not very good on the subject of the execution, which he recounts as having taken place in daylight. This does not, in any case, change anything about the act, and would do no more than remove a torch from this scene of suffering.

"At sunrise, in the open air," the general says, "who would need a lantern to see a man *six paces away*? This is not to say that the sun," he adds, "was bright and clear. As a fine rain had been falling all night, there was still a thick mist that deferred its appearance. The execution took place at six o'clock in the morning: the fact is attested by *indisputable documents*."

But the general does not provide these documents or indicate where they can be found. The record of the trial demonstrates that the Duc d'Enghien was judged at two o'clock in the morning and gunned down at once. These words, "at two o'clock in the morning," originally written on the first minutes of the sentence, were later blotted out from these minutes. And besides, the official report of the exhumation proves, according to the depositions of three witnesses, Madame Bon, M. Godard, and M. Bounelet (who had helped dig the grave), that the execution was carried out at night. M. Dupin the Elder recalls that a lantern was fastened over the Duc d'Enghien's heart, to serve as a target, or held, for the same purpose, in one of the prince's own fists. There has been talk of a large stone retrieved from the grave which was used to crush the prisoner's head. Lastly, the Duc de Rovigo must have boasted of possessing a few spoils from the sacrifice: I myself believed these rumors, but the legal documents prove they were unfounded.

In the official report, dated Wednesday, March 20, 1816, drawn up by the doctors and surgeons who examined the corpse, it was confirmed that the skull was broken, that the "upper jaw, completely separated from the bones of the face, contained twelve teeth; that the lower jaw, fractured in its middle part, was broken in two, and only retained three teeth." The body was laid flat on its stomach, the head lower than the feet, and the vertebrae of the neck were wrapped round with a gold chain.

The second official exhumation report (also dated March 20, 1816), the "general report," states that together with the remains of the skeleton were found a purse of Morocco leather, containing eleven gold coins, seventy gold coins contained in sealed packets, bits of hair, shreds of clothing, and pieces of the prince's cap bearing the mark of the bullets that had pierced it.

Thus M. de Rovigo took no spoils. The earth that enclosed them restored them and thereby bore witness to the general's probity. No lantern was fastened over the prince's heart: its fragments would have been found, like those of the bullet-riddled cap. No large stone was retrieved from the grave. The lead of the squadron *six paces away* would have been enough to shatter the skull and "separate the upper jaw from the bones of the face," etc.

All that needs to be added to this mockery of human vanities is the immolation of Murat, the governor of Paris, Bonaparte's death in captivity, and this inscription engraved on the coffin of the Duc d'Enghien: "Here lies the *body* of the high and mighty Prince of the Blood, Peer of France, *died* at Vincennes, March 21, 1804; aged 31 years, 7 months, 19 days." The "body" consisted of a few bare bones smashed to bits; the "high and mighty prince" of the broken fragments of a soldier's carcass. Not a word to recall the tragedy, not a word of blame or sorrow in this epitaph carved by a grieving family—a staggering result of the respect the age shows to the deeds and sensitive subjects of the Revolution! No time was likewise lost removing all traces of the Duc de Berry's mortuary chapel.

What nullity! You Bourbons, who have pointlessly returned to your palaces, have done nothing but conduct exhumations and funerals. Your time of life is past. God has willed it. The ancient glory of France perished beneath the eyes of the great Condé, in a moat at Vincennes, perhaps at the very place where Louis IX, to whom men went as to a holy man, used to "lean against an oak tree, and where all those who had matters to be dealt with came and talked to him, without the interference of the ushers or anyone else; and when he saw something to correct in the discourse of those who were judging, he himself would speak up and decide on what would be the fairest outcome." (Joinville.)[13]

The Duc d'Enghien asked to speak to Bonaparte; he "had matters to be dealt with"; he was not heard. Who, from the edge of the ravelin, looking down into the depths of the moat, saw those rifles, those soldiers scarcely lit by a lantern in the shadows and the mist, as in night everlasting? Where was the lantern positioned? Did the Duc d'Enghien stand before his open grave? Was he obliged to step over it to put the six paces mentioned by the Duc de Rovigo between him and his executioners?

A letter has come down to us from the nine-year-old Duc d'Enghien to his father, the Duc de Bourbon. He writes to him:

"All the *Enguiens* are *lucky*; the one in the Battle of Cerizoles, the one who won the Battle of Rocroi: I hope to be so too."

Is it true that the victim was refused a priest? Is it true that he had great difficulty finding someone to take a last token of affection to a woman he loved? What was pity or tenderness to the executioners? They were there to kill, and the Duc d'Enghien was there to die.

The Duc d'Enghien had been secretly married, by a priest, to Princess Charlotte de Rohan. In those days, when the homeland was on the move, a man, precisely because of his rank, was hindered by a thousand political snares and traps. To enjoy what society grants to one and all, he had no choice but to live his life in hiding. This legitimate marriage, which is a secret no more, only adds to the luster of a tragic end; for heavenly mercy, it substitutes heavenly glory. Religion perpetuates the pomp of misfortune, after the disaster is over, when the cross is raised on the deserted spot.

6.

M. DE TALLEYRAND

Chantilly, November 1838

M. DE TALLEYRAND, according to M. de Rovigo's pamphlet, presented an explanatory memorandum to Louis XVIII. This memorandum, which I have never seen and which was supposed to clarify everything, clarified nothing. In 1820, having been named ambassador to Berlin, I unearthed, in the archives of the embassy, a letter from Citizen Laforest written to Citizen Talleyrand on the subject of M. le Duc d'Enghien. This vigorous letter is all the more honorable for its author when we consider that he was unafraid to compromise his career, even realizing he would not be rewarded by public opinion, since the step he was taking would remain unknown—a noble self-sacrifice on the part of a man who, through his own obscurity, had destined the good he had done to obscurity as well.

M. de Talleyrand learned his lesson and held his tongue. At least I found nothing from him in those same archives concerning the prince's death. The Minister of Foreign Affairs had, however, on the 2nd of Ventôse, written the Minister of the Electorate of Baden, saying that "the First Consul had thought it necessary to order some detachments to Offenburg and Ettenheim in order to capture the instigators of the unthinkable conspiracies that, by their nature, place all those who have provably taken part in them outside the law of nations."

A passage written by General Gourgaud, General Montholon, and Doctor Ward brings Bonaparte onto the stage:

"My minister," Bonaparte said, "told me in no uncertain terms that we needed to capture the Duc d'Enghien, even if he was in neutral territory. Still, I hesitated, and the Prince de Bénévent twice brought the arrest order for me to sign. It was, however, only after I had been convinced of the urgency of such an action that I decided to sign the order."

According to the *Memorial of Saint Helena*, these words are said to have fallen from Bonaparte's lips:

"The Duc d'Enghien behaved very bravely before the tribunal. When he arrived in Strasbourg, he wrote me a letter: this letter was given to Talleyrand, who kept it until after the execution."

I don't much believe in the existence of this letter. Napoleon must have transformed the Duc d'Enghien's request into a letter, or rather the few lines expressing this request that, before signing the minutes of the interrogation conducted by the capitaine rapporteur, the prince had written with his own hand. Still, the fact that this letter has not been found should not lead us to conclude definitively that it was never written. "I know," said the Duc de Rovigo, "that in the early days of the Restoration, in 1814, one of M. de Talleyrand's secretaries was ceaselessly combing the archives under the Museum gallery. I have this on the word of the man who received the order to let him in there. The same was done at the Ministry of War for the trial documents pertaining to M. le Duc d'Enghien, where all that remained was the sentence."

This much is true: all the diplomatic papers, and notably M. de Talleyrand's correspondence with the emperor and First Consul, were taken from the archives of the Museum to his house on rue Saint-Florentin. Some were destroyed. The rest were entombed in a stove where someone forgot to set fire to them: the prudence of a minister could only do so much to counterbalance the carelessness of a prince. The unburned documents were rediscovered, and someone thought them worth preserving. I held in my hands and read with my eyes a letter from M. de Talleyrand, dated March 8, 1804, and relating to the arrest, not yet carried out, of M. le Duc d'Enghien. In it, the minister invites the First Consul to crack down on his enemies. I was not permitted to keep this letter, and I retain only these two passages in my memory: "If justice obliges us to punish rigorously, politics demands us to punish without exception" and "I will point the First Consul to M. de Caulaincourt, to whom he might give these orders, and who would execute them both discreetly and loyally."

Will the Prince de Talleyrand's report appear someday in its entirety? I cannot say, but I know for certain that it was still in existence two years ago. There was a deliberation of the council concerning the arrest of the Duc d'Enghien. Cambacérès, in his unpublished memoirs, claims—and I believe him—that he opposed the arrest, but while he tells us what *he* said, he does not say what was said to him in reply.

Otherwise, *The Memorial of Saint Helena* gives the lie to any petitions for mercy Bonaparte might have received. The alleged scene of Josephine begging on her knees for the salvation of the Duc d'Engien, clinging to the tail of her husband's coat and being dragged along by that inexorable man, is one of those melodramatic inventions with which our fabulists nowadays compose "true history." Josephine had no idea, on the evening of March 19, that the Duc d'Enghien was going to be sentenced; she knew only that he had been arrested. She had promised Madame de Rémusat she would take an interest in the prince's fate. When Madame de Rémusat returned to Malmaison with Josephine, on the evening of March 19, it was observed that the future empress, far from being singly preoccupied with the perils of the prisoner of Vincennes, often popped her head out the door of her carriage to look at the general melee of her entourage: a woman's coquetry prevailed in the mind that might have saved the life of the Duc d'Enghien. It was not until March 21 that Bonaparte told his wife, "The Duc d'Enghien has been executed."

The memoirs of Madame de Rémusat, which I have read, are extremely intriguing when they come to the internal affairs of the imperial Court. The author burned these memoirs during the Hundred Days and then rewrote them: thus they are no more than memories reproduced from memory; their color is bleached; but Bonaparte is always shown there nakedly, and judged impartially.

Men attached to Napoleon said he was not aware of the death of the Duc d'Enghien until after the prince's execution. This version of events would seem to be given some validity by the anecdote the Duc de Rovigo reports about Réal going to Vincennes, if this anecdote were true. Once death had been brought about by the intrigues of the revolutionary party, Bonaparte recognized the deed was done, and he did not want to antagonize men whom he thought powerful. Such an ingenious explanation is not to be believed.

7.
EACH MAN'S ROLE

Now, ROUNDING up the facts, here is what they prove to me:

Bonaparte wanted the Duc d'Enghien dead, but no one had made this death a condition of his assuming the throne. This purported condition is one of those political insinuations that feign to find hidden causes for everything. —Yet it *is* probable that certain compromised men would not have been unhappy to see the First Consul permanently parted from the Bourbons. The judgment at Vincennes was the result of Bonaparte's violent temperament, a fit of cold rage fed by his minister's reports.

M. de Caulaincourt is guilty only of having executed the arrest order.

Murat has nothing to answer for except having communicated general orders and for not having had the strength to withdraw: he was not even at Vincennes during the trial.

The Duc de Rovigo found himself responsible for the execution. He probably had secret orders, as General Hulin insinuates. What man would have dared to execute a death sentence "at once" against the Duc d'Enghien, if he was not acting according to a mandate?

As for M. de Talleyrand, priest and gentleman, he inspired and prepared the murder by insistently working Bonaparte up: he feared the return of the Legitimacy. It would be possible, by bringing what Napoleon said on Saint Helena together with the letters that the Bishop of Autun wrote, to prove that the latter played a very significant part in the death of the Duc d'Enghien. It would be objected,

vainly, that the nonchalance, character, and education of the minister would make him a stranger to violence, and that corruption would
be a drag on his energy. It would nevertheless remain the case that
he prodded the First Consul toward the fatal arrest. The arrest of the
Duc d'Enghien on March 15 was not unknown to M. de Talleyrand:
he was in daily contact with Bonaparte and conferred with him.
During the interval that passed between the arrest and the execution,
did M. de Talleyrand, the instigating minister, repent; did he say a
single word to the First Consul in favor of the unfortunate prince?
It is quite natural to imagine him applauding the execution of the
sentence.

The military commission pronounced judgment on the Duc
d'Enghien, but with sadness and repentance.

Such is, speaking conscientiously, impartially, and strictly, each
man's role. My fate is too bound up with this catastrophe for me to
try to shed light on its darker reaches and expose the details. If
Bonaparte had not killed the Duc d'Enghien, if he had grown closer
and closer with him (and his fondness was carrying him in that direction), what would have been the result for me? My literary career was
over; fully launched on a political career, where I have proven what
I might have been able to do through the war in Spain, I would have
become rich and powerful. France may have gained something from
my alliance with the emperor, but I would have lost something.
Perhaps I would have succeeded in preserving a few ideas of liberty
and moderation in the great man's head; but my life, classed among
those called "happy," would have been deprived of what has given it
character and honor: poverty, struggle, and independence.

8.

BONAPARTE: HIS SOPHISMS AND HIS REGRETS
Chantilly, November 1838

THE FIRST to be accused comes last of all; he brings up the rear of the procession of bloodstained penitents. Imagine if a judge had summoned the "man named Bonaparte" before him, as the capitaine rapporteur had summoned the "man named d'Enghien." Imagine if we still had the minutes of the latter interrogation copied over the former, which remains to us. Read and compare:

Asked: his name and surname.

Answered: Napoleon Bonaparte.

Asked: where he has resided since he left France.

Answered: the Pyramids, Madrid, Berlin, Vienna, Moscow, and Saint Helena.

Asked: what rank he occupied in the army.

Answered: Commander of the advance guard in the armies of God. No other reply issues from the defendant's lips.

The various actors in the tragedy have all accused each other; Bonaparte alone did not cast blame on anyone else. He preserves his greatness beneath the weight of malediction. He does not turn his face away and stands straight and strong. He exclaims, like the Stoic, "Pain, I shall never admit that you are an evil!" But what, in his pride, he will not admit to the living, he is compelled to confess to the dead. This Prometheus with the vulture at his breast, stealer of celestial fire, believed himself superior to everyone, and he is forced to answer to the Duc d'Enghien, whom he turned into dust before his time.

The skeleton, the trophy over which he fell, questions him and over-masters him by heavenly necessity.

The domestic service and the military, the antechamber and the tent—all had their representatives on Saint Helena. A servant, esti-mable for his loyalty to the master he had chosen, had come to posi-tion himself near Napoleon like an echo at his service.[14] Simplicity repeated the fable and gave it a tone of sincerity. Bonaparte was "Destiny," and like destiny he *superficially* fooled fascinated minds; but, beneath his impostures, this inexorable truth was heard to re-sound: "I am!" And the world felt the weight of it.

The author of the most accredited book about the Saint Helena years expounds the theory that Napoleon invented for the murderers' benefit. The voluntary exile accepts as gospel truth an abundance of homicidal chatter with pretensions to profundity, which explains the life of Napoleon only as he wished it to be remembered and believed it ought to be written. He gave instructions to his neophytes which M. le Comte de Las Cases took without even being aware of it. The stupendous captive, wandering his solitary paths, hauled his credulous adulator behind him with a rope of lies, as Hercules once hung men from his mouth by golden chains.[15]

"The first time," says the honest chamberlain, "I heard Napoleon speak the Duc d'Enghien's name, I turned red with embarrassment. Happily, I was walking behind him on a narrow path, or he would not have failed to notice this. In any case, when, for the first time, the emperor elaborated on the entirety of this event, its details and incidentals; when he expounded on its various motives with his close, luminous, captivating reasoning, I must confess the affair gradually seemed to assume a different appearance.... The emperor would often circle back to this subject, which gave me the opportunity to observe certain very pronounced nuances in his character. On such occasions, I was very distinctly able to see in him the private man at odds with the public man, and the natural feelings of his heart at odds with those of his pride and the dignity of his position. In private, he showed himself far from indifferent to the fate of the hapless prince; but as soon as the public entered into it, it was quite another thing. One day, after speaking with me of the fate and youth of the unfortunate man, he finished by saying: 'And I learned later, my dear friend, that he was favorable to me; I was assured that he did not speak of me without some admiration. There you see what passes for distributive justice here below!' And these last words he spoke with such an expression, all the features of his face were in such harmony with them, that if the man Napoleon was lamenting had at that moment been in his power, I am quite sure that, whatever his intentions or his actions may have been, he would have been vigorously pardoned.... The emperor was in the habit of considering this affair from two very distinct points of view: that of common law or the established rules of justice, and that of natural law or deviations of violence.

"Between us and in private, the emperor used to say that that the blame in France might be assigned to an excess of zeal in those around him, or to dark intrigues or private views. He said that he had been unexpectedly urged on in this affair; that men had, so to speak, taken him by surprise; and that his measures had been accelerated, their outcome expedited. 'Rest assured,' he said, 'if I had been informed in time of certain circumstances concerning the opinions of the prince and his disposition; if, above all, I had seen the letter that he wrote me, and that, God knows for what reason, was only delivered to me after his death, I would certainly have pardoned him.' And it was easy for us to perceive that the emperor's words were dictated by his heart and by nature, and that they were only intended for us; for he would have felt greatly humiliated had he supposed anyone might think for a moment he endeavored to shift the blame upon some other person, or that he condescended to justify himself. His fear in this regard, or his sensitivity, was so great that when speaking to strangers or dictating on this subject for public purposes, he restricted himself to saying that, if he had been made aware of the prince's letter, perhaps he would have pardoned him, given the great political advantages he would have accrued. Writing his last thoughts in his own hand, which he supposes will be enshrined by his contemporaries and reach posterity, he again pronounces on this subject, which he regards as one of the most delicate regarding his memory, and he says that if he had it all to do again, he would do it just the same."

This passage, as far as the writer is concerned, has all the distinguishing marks of total sincerity; this is crystal clear even in the sentence where M. le Comte de Las Cases says that Bonaparte would have "vigorously pardoned" a man who was not guilty. But the master's theories are ingenuities devised to reconcile the irreconcilable. By making a distinction between "common law or the established rules of justice" and "natural law or deviations of violence," Napoleon appears satisfied with a sophism that, in fact, he found unsatisfactory. He was not able to subdue his conscience as he had subdued the world. One weakness natural to superior men and little men alike, when they have committed an error, is the wish to pass it off as a work of genius—a monumental scheme beyond the grasp of the vulgar. Pride dictates these things, and folly believes them. No doubt Bonaparte regarded the sentence he reeled off, in all his great man's solemnity, as the mark of a superlative mind: "My dear friend, there you see what passes for distributive justice here below!" What truly philosophical emotion! What impartiality! How it justifies, chalking it all up to destiny, the evil that we do ourselves! People today think everything is excused when they say, "Well, what do you want? It was my nature, it was human frailty." When a man has killed his father, he repeats, "I was made like that!" And the crowd stands gape-mouthed, and they examine the skull of this oddity, and they recognize that he *was* "made like that." But what do I care if you were made like that? Am I expected to submit to your way of being? The world would be a fine mess if everyone who was "made like that" took it into their heads to impose themselves on each other. When people cannot erase their errors, they deify them; they make a dogma of their misdeeds, they change their sacrileges into a religion, and they would consider themselves apostates if they gave up worshipping their vices.

9.

WHAT SHOULD BE CONCLUDED FROM THIS ACCOUNT—ENMITIES PRODUCED BY THE DEATH OF THE DUC D'ENGHIEN

THERE IS a serious lesson to be drawn from Bonaparte's life. Two actions, both bad, initiated and brought about his fall: the death of the Duc d'Enghien and the war with Spain. It did no good for him to ride over them in glory; they remained, and they ruined him. His destruction came from the side where he thought himself strong, profound, invincible, when he violated the laws of morality while neglecting and scorning his true strength, which is to say his superior capacity for order and equity. As long as he concentrated his attacks on anarchy and the foreign enemies of France, he was victorious; he found himself robbed of his vigor only when he entered upon the paths of corruption. The hair cut by Delilah is nothing less than virtue lost. Every crime bears within it a radical incapacity and a germ of tragedy: let us therefore practice goodness in order to be happy, and let us be just in order to be able.

As proof of this truth, note that the prince's death prompted the dissent that, little by little, led to the downfall of the man who authorized the tragedy at Vincennes. The Russian cabinet, responding to the Duc d'Enghien's arrest, made vigorous protests against the violation of the territory of the Empire: Bonaparte felt the blow, and replied, in the *Moniteur*, with a blistering article that dredged up the death of Paul I.[16] In Saint Petersburg, a funeral service was held for the young Condé. The cenotaph read: "For the Duc d'Enghien *quem devoravit bellua corsica*."[17] The two powerful adversaries seemed to reconcile afterward, but the mutual wound politics had made, and insult had deepened, remained in their hearts. Napoleon did not consider himself avenged until he slept in Moscow, and Alexander was not satisfied until he marched into Paris.

The hatred of the Berlin cabinet issued from the same origin: I have spoken of the noble letter from M. de Laforest, in which he tells M. de Talleyrand of the effect the murder of the Duc d'Enghien had on the Potsdam Court. Madame de Staël was in Prussia when the news from Vincennes arrived. "I was staying in Berlin," she said, "on the Spree quai, and my apartment was on the ground floor. One morning at eight I was awakened and told Prince Louis-Ferdinand was on horseback outside my windows, asking whether I would come and speak with him.

"'Are you aware,' he said, 'that the Duc d'Enghien was captured in the territory of Baden, handed over to a military commission, and executed by firing squad twenty-four hours after he arrived in Paris?'

"'What nonsense!' I said to him. 'Can't you see this is nothing but a rumor spread by the enemies of France?'

"Indeed, I admit, my hatred of Bonaparte, strong as it was, did not go so far as to make me credit the possibility of such a heinous crime.

"'Since you doubt what I say,' Prince Louis told me, 'I will send you the *Moniteur*, where you can read the sentence.'

"With these words he left, wearing an expression that promised vengeance or death. A quarter of an hour later, I had the *Moniteur* of March 21 (Pluviôse 30) in my hands. It contained the death sentence passed by the military commission, sitting at Vincennes, against 'the man called Louis d'Enghien'! This is what the French called the grandson of the heroes who were the glory of their country! Even if one were to abjure all the prejudices of high birth which the return of monarchical formalities would necessarily recall, was it possible to blaspheme the memories of the Battle of Lens and Rocroi? This Bonaparte, who has won so many battles, does not even know how to respect them; there is no past and no future for him; his imperious and scornful soul refuses to recognize anything for the public to hold sacred. The only respect he allows is respect for the force in power.

Prince Louis wrote to me, beginning his note with these words: 'The man called Louis of Prussia asks of Madame de Staël...' He felt the insult offered to the royal blood whence he sprang and to the memory of the heroes among which he longed to enlist. How, after such a horrible thing, could a single monarch in Europe ally himself with such a man? Necessity, will you say? There is a sanctuary within the soul where necessity must never hold sway; if this were not so, what would virtue be upon the earth? A liberal pastime, suited only to the peaceful leisure of private men."

The prince's resentment, for which he was to pay with his life, lasted until the Prussian campaign began, in 1806. Frederick William III, in his manifesto of October 9, said, "The Germans have not avenged the death of the Duc d'Enghien, but the memory of this heinous crime will never fade from their minds."

These historical details, which are rarely noted, deserve to be, for they explain enmities whose first cause would be very difficult to locate elsewhere, and at the same time they reveal those steps by which Providence leads the destiny of a man from the crime to the punishment.

10.

AN ARTICLE IN THE *MERCURE*—A CHANGE IN BONAPARTE

I AM GLAD at least to say that my life was not troubled by fear, or touched by infection, or distracted by others' examples. The satisfaction I feel today when I think of what I did then assures me that conscience is no illusion. Happier than all those potentates and nations fallen at the feet of the triumphing soldier, I reread with pardonable pride this page that I have kept as my sole belonging and that I owe to myself alone. In 1807, still dismayed by the murder I have just described, I wrote these lines, which led to the suppression of the *Mercure* and once more jeopardized my freedom:

> When, in the silence of abjection, no sound remains except the rattle of the slave's chain and the informer's voice; when everyone trembles before the tyrant and it is as dangerous to curry his favor as to incur his disapproval, the historian appears, entrusted with the wrath of the nations. Nero prospers in vain, for Tacitus has already been born within the Empire. He is still growing up, unknown, not far from the ashes of Germanicus, but already incorruptible Providence has handed the glory of the master of the world over to an obscure child. If the role of the historian is glorious, it is often full of danger; but it is one of those altars, like that of honor, which, though abandoned, still demands sacrifices. The god has not disappeared because the temple is empty. If there is some chance of fortune for us, there is no heroism in what we do. Magnanimous actions are

those whose anticipated result is misfortune or death. After all, what do reversals matter, if our name, when spoken by posterity, will set generous hearts pounding two thousand years after our life is over?

The death of the Duc d'Enghien introduced a new principle into Bonaparte's conduct and diverted his mind from its proper course. He was compelled to make a shield of maxims whose full force was not at his command, for he was constantly distorting them with his glory and genius. He became suspicious; he inspired fear; people lost confidence in him and in his destiny; he was compelled to see, if not to seek out, men he would never have seen before, and who, because they had been admitted into his company, believed they had become his equals. Their defilement infected him. He did not dare reproach them, for he no longer had the virtuous freedom to criticize. His great qualities remained the same, but his good inclinations degenerated and no longer supported his great qualities. With the corruption of this original sin, his nature began to deteriorate. God ordered his angels to derange the harmonies of this universe, to change its laws, to tilt it on its poles. Says Milton:

> They with labor push'd
> Oblique the centric globe. Some say the sun
> Was bid turn reins from the equinoctial road...
> Boreas, and Caecias, and Argestes loud,
> And Thracias, rend the woods, and seas upturn.[18]

II.

LEAVING CHANTILLY

WILL BONAPARTE'S corpse be exhumed like the Duc d'Enghien's? If it had been up to me, the latter would still be sleeping in the moat of the Château de Vincennes. This "excommunicate" would have been left, like Raymond of Toulouse, in an open coffin;[19] no human hand would have dared to board up the sight of this witness to the incomprehensible judgment and wrath of God. The abandoned skeleton of the Duc d'Enghien and the deserted grave of Napoleon on Saint Helena would mirror one another. There could be nothing more rememorative than these remains at opposite ends of the earth.

At least the Duc d'Enghien did not go to rest on foreign soil, like the man exiled by the nations. The latter took care to restore the former to his homeland, a bit harshly, it is true; but will it be forever? France (as so much dust winnowed by the Revolution's breath attests) is not loyal to the bones of its dead. The old Condé, in his will, declares that he is not sure what country he will be in on the day of his death. Oh, Bossuet, what would you have added to your masterpiece of eloquence if, when you spoke over the coffin of the great Condé, you could foresee the future?[20]

It was here in this very place, Chantilly, that the Duc d'Enghien was born: "Louis-Antoine-Henri de Bourbon, born August 2, 1772, in Chantilly," the death sentence reads. It is on this lawn that he played in his childhood. All trace of his footsteps has been stamped out. And the victor of Freiburg, Nördlingen, Lens, and Seneffe—where has he gone with his "victorious and now-feeble hands"? And his descendants, the Condés of Johannisberg and Berstheim, and his son, and his grandson—where are they? That castle, those gardens, those jets of water "that were never silent, day or night"—what has become of them? Mutilated statues, lions with claws or jaws restored; trophies carved in a crumbling wall; escutcheons of fleurs-de-lis obliterated; the foundations of razed turrets; a few marble steeds atop the empty stables no longer animated by the whinnying of the horse of Rocroi; a high, unfinished gate by a riding arena: that is what remains of the memories of a heroic race. A legacy strangled by a rope has altered the line of inheritance.[21]

The whole forest has repeatedly fallen under the ax. Famous characters from days gone by have ridden over those hunting grounds now silent but once reverberant with noise. How old were they, and what did they feel, when they paused beneath those ancient oaks? What illusions were they pursuing? Oh, my useless *Memoirs*, I cannot now say to you:

> May Condé sometimes read you in Chantilly,
> And may Enghien be moved![22]

Obscure men, what are we compared to these famous men? We will disappear, never to return. You will be reborn, Sweet William, who lie on my table beside this sheet of paper, and whose late little flower I gathered among the heathers; but we, we shall not live again like the sweet-scented solitary who has diverted my thoughts.[23]

BOOK SEVENTEEN

I.

1804—I COME TO LIVE ON THE RUE DE MIROMESNIL—VERNEUIL—ALEXIS DE TOCQUEVILLE—LE MESNIL—MEZY—MÉRÉVILLE

Now removed from active life, and still safe, thanks to Madame Baciocchi, from Bonaparte's wrath, I left my temporary lodgings on the rue de Beaune and went to live on the rue de Miromesnil. The little house I rented has since been occupied by M. de Lally-Tollendal and Madame Denain, his "best beloved," as they used to say in the age of Diane de Poitiers. There, my narrow garden ended in a lumberyard, and my window looked out on a tall poplar that M. de Lally-Tollendal, to dry the air, chopped down with his own broad hands, which seemed gaunt and transparent to him: one illusion among many. In my day, the paved street petered out at my front door. Higher up, the road, or path, wound through a wasteland called Rabbit Hill. There were only a few lonely houses scattered over Rabbit Hill, which on the right led to the Tivoli Gardens, where I had set off with my brother for the Emigration, and on the left led to the Parc de Monceaux. I went strolling fairly often in that abandoned park, where the Revolution had begun among the orgies of the Duc d'Orléans. This hideaway had been embellished with marble nudes and mock ruins—symbols of the frivolous, debauched politics that were to flood France with prostitution and debris.

I did nothing with my time. At most I talked to the rabbits in the park, or chatted about the Duc d'Enghien with three crows on the bank of an artificial stream hidden beneath a carpet of green moss.[1] Deprived of my Alpine legation and my Roman friendships as abruptly as I had been cut off from my attachments in London, I did not know what to do with my imagination or my feelings. Every evening I set them trailing after the sun, but its rays could not carry them beyond the sea. I went indoors and tried to sleep, to the rustling of my poplar.

Yet my resignation had bolstered my reputation. In France, a bit of courage is always becoming. Certain people who had been acquainted with Madame de Beaumont introduced me to new country estates.

M. de Tocqueville, my brother's brother-in-law and guardian of my two orphaned nephews, lived in Madame de Senozan's house: the legacies of the scaffold were everywhere.* There, I saw my nephews growing up with their three de Tocqueville cousins, one of whom was Alexis, the author of *Democracy in America*; he was more spoiled in Verneuil than I had been in Combourg. Is this the last eminence I will have seen unknown in his swaddling clothes? Alexis de Tocqueville has traveled through a civilized America, whose forests I once wandered.

Madame Rosambo lived near Mantes, at Le Mesnil, where my nephew, Louis de Chateaubriand, later married Madame Rosambo's niece, Mademoiselle d'Orglandes. This young woman no longer promenades her beauty around the pond and beneath the willows of the manor; she has passed away. When I went from Verneuil to Le Mesnil, I stopped to see Le Mezy: Madame de Mezy was a novelistic character shut away in her virtue and maternal grief. If only her child, who fell from a window and broke his skull, had been able, like the young quails we hunted, to fly over the house and take refuge on the Île-Belle, the happy isle of the Seine: *Coturnix per stipulas pascens!*[12]

On the other side of the Seine, not far from Le Marais, Madame de Vintimille had introduced me to Méréville. Méréville was an oasis created by the smile of a muse, but by one of those muses the Gallic poets call the "learned Fairies."[3] Here, the adventures of Blanca and Velléda were read before the elegant generations, who, issuing from one another like flowers, now listen to the plaints of my years.

---

*Verneuil has again changed hands and is now owned by Madame de Saint-Fargeau, whose fame she owes to her father and to the Revolution that adopted her as its daughter. (1838)

Gradually my brain, weary of its repose on the rue de Miromesnil, saw faraway phantoms taking shape. *The Genius of Christianity* inspired me with the idea of demonstrating this work by mixing Christian characters with mythological ones. A shade, whom a long time later I came to call Cymodocée, vaguely began taking shape in my mind: all of her features were in flux. Once I had firmed her up, I immured myself alone with her, as I always do with the daughters of my imagination; but before they emerge from the dream state and arrive from the Lethean shores through the gate of ivory, they often change their form. If I create them out of love, I deconstruct them out of love, and the single and cherished object I eventually bring into the light is the product of a thousand infidelities.

I stayed only a year on rue de Miromesnil, for the building was sold. I made arrangements with Madame la Marquise de Coislin, who rented me the attic of her house on the Place Louis XV.

2.

MADAME DE COISLIN

MADAME de Coislin was a very impressive woman. Nearing eighty, her proud and domineering eyes wore a look of wit and irony. She was not well read and proud of it; she had passed through the Voltairean age unaware. If she had conceived any idea of it at all, it was as an age of bourgeois volubility. She did not altogether avoid the subject of her birth, but she was far too high-minded to fall into that sort of inanity. She knew quite well how to talk to the "little people" without stooping; but after all she was the child of the premier marquis of France. If she happened to be descended from Drogon de Nesle, killed in Palestine in 1096; from Raoul de Nesle, the constable knighted by Louis IX; from Jean II de Nesle, regent of France during Saint Louis's last crusade, Madame de Coislin acknowledged this was an error of fate, for which she could not be held responsible. She was naturally of the Court just as others—more happily for them— are of the streets: there are racehorses, and there are hackneys. She could do nothing about these accidents, and she was forced to endure the unhappiness with which it had pleased Heaven to afflict her.

Did Madame de Coislin have liaisons with Louis XV? She never admitted it to me. She did, however, let on that she had been very much beloved, though she claimed to have treated the royal lover with the greatest severity. "I have seen him at my feet," she told me; "he had charming eyes and a silver tongue. One day he offered to give me a porcelain dressing table like Madame de Pompadour had. 'Oh, sire!' said I, 'that would only be for me to hide under!'"

By a singular coincidence, I happened to see this dressing table at Marchioness Conyngham's house in London; she had been given it by George IV, and she showed it off to me with wonderful informality.

Madame de Coislin lived in the room of her house beneath the colonnade corresponding to the colonnade of the Garde-Meuble.[4] Two seascapes by Vernet, which Louis the Well Beloved had given the noble lady, were hung on a greenish old satin tapestry. Madame de Coislin stayed in bed until two o'clock in the afternoon, sitting propped up with pillows on a large mattress surrounded by similarly greenish silk curtains. A sort of nightcap, poorly tied around her head, left her gray hair hanging out, and old-fashioned pendant diamond earrings dangled over the epaulettes of her bed coat, which was stained with snuff, as in the days of the elegant ladies of the Fronde. Around her, on the blanket, lay a scattering of little bits of paper inscribed with addresses detached from their letters, on which Madame de Coislin wrote her thoughts every which way. She never bought paper—for the postman furnished her with all she needed. From time to time, a little dog called Lili would poke her nose out from the sheets, come bark at me for five or six minutes, and then go growling back into her mistress's kennel. This is what time had arranged for the young love of Louis XV.

Madame de Châteroux and her two sisters were cousins of Madame de Coislin. The latter would not, like the repentant Christian Madame de Mailly,[5] have had the right sort of temperament to reply to a man who insulted her, in the Church of Saint-Roch, with a rude name:

"My friend, since you know me so well, pray to God for me."

Madame de Coislin, who was miserly, as so many clever people are, hoarded her money in her wardrobes. She was consequently pursued by a verminous swarm of écus,[6] which clung to her skin: her servants relieved her of them. Whenever I saw her lost in a labyrinth of numbers, she reminded me of the miser Hermocrates, who, dictating his will, named himself his own heir.[7] She did, however, give dinners now and then; but she inveighed against coffee, which she said nobody liked and served no purpose except to drag out the meal.

Madame de Chateaubriand once made a trip to Vichy with Madame de Coislin and the Marquis de Nesle. The Marquis rode on ahead and made arrangements for an excellent dinner. Madame de Coislin came later, and asked for only half a pound of cherries. On leaving, she was presented with an enormous bill and a horrible brouhaha ensued. She would not hear talk of anything but cherries, while the host maintained that, whatever one might have eaten or not eaten, the custom, at an inn, was to pay for your dinner.

Madame de Coislin had worked up an illuminism of her own devising. Credulous and incredulous, her lack of faith led her to mock beliefs that superstition made her fear. She had met Madame de Krüdener; but the secretive Frenchwoman was illuminated only with the benefit of inventory and was not well liked by the fervent Russian, whom she did not like any better. In a fit of passion, Madame de Krüdener said to Madame de Coislin, "Madame, who is your confessor inside?" and Madame de Coislin replied, "I have no idea who my confessor inside is. All I know is my confessor is inside his confessional." After that, the two ladies did not see each other again.

Madame de Coislin was proud to have introduced a novelty at Court, the fashion of loose chignons—despite the strongly pious Queen Marie Leczinska, who objected to this dangerous innovation. She maintained that, in the old days, no respectable person would ever have thought of paying her doctor. Crying out against the abundance of women's linen:

"That smacks of the upstart," she said. "We women of the Court never had more than two shifts; when they wore out, we got fresh ones. We dressed in silk gowns and never looked like shopgirls. Not like these young women nowadays."

Madame Suard, who lived on rue Royale, had a rooster whose song, carrying across the interior courtyards, irritated Madame de Coislin. She wrote to Madame Suard, "Madame, have your rooster's throat cut." Madame Suard sent the messenger back with this note: "Madame, I have the honor of informing you that I will not have my rooster's throat cut." The correspondence stopped there. Madame de Coislin said to Madame de Chateaubriand:

"Ah, my dear, what a time we live in! But it's that Panckoucke girl, that Academy member's wife, you know?"[8]

M. Hénin, a former civil servant at the Ministry of Foreign Affairs, and as boring as bureaucratic protocol, used to scribble fat novels. One day he read some pages aloud to Madame de Coislin: a woman in tears, abandoned by her lover, was lugubriously fishing for salmon. Madame de Coislin, who was impatient and did not care for salmon, interrupted the author and asked him in that serious manner that made her so comic:

"Monsieur Hénin, could you not have this lady catch a different fish?"

The stories Madame de Coislin told do not bear repeating, for there was nothing to them. It was all in the gestures, the emphasis, and the tone of the storyteller: not once did she laugh. There was in particular a dialogue between Monsieur and Madame Jacqueminot she performed to perfection. When in the conversation between the two spouses, Madame de Jacqueminot replied, "But, Monsieur *Jacqueminot*!" this name was pronounced in such a way that you were overcome with giddy laughter. Obliged to let this laughter pass, Madame de Coislin would wait, gravely taking snuff.

Reading of the death of several kings in a newspaper, she removed her glasses and blew her nose:

"There appears to be an epizootic among the crowned beasts."

When she was on the verge of death, someone at her bedside insisted that we only die because we let ourselves go; that if we only paid close enough attention and never lost sight of the enemy, we would never die.

"I believe it," she said, "but I'm afraid I'm becoming distracted."

She breathed her last breath.

I went downstairs the next day to her room. I found Monsieur and Madame d'Avaray, her sister and her brother-in-law, sitting in front of the fireplace with a little table between them counting up the louis from a sack that they had taken from a hollow panel in the wall. The poor dead woman was still lying there in her bed, the curtains half closed. She no longer heard the clink of gold, which should have woken her, now being counted by fraternal hands.

Some of the thoughts scribbled by the deceased in the margins of leaflets and on the addresses ripped from letters were extremely beautiful. Madame de Coislin showed me what remained of the Court of Louis XV, under Bonaparte and after Louis XVI, just as Madame d'Houdetot had allowed me to see what still lingered, in the nineteenth century, of the old philosophical circles.

3.

VOYAGE TO VICHY, AUVERGNE, AND MONT BLANC

IN THE summer of 1805, I went to meet Madame de Chateaubriand in Vichy, where Madame de Coislin had taken her, as I have just mentioned. There I found no trace of Jussac, Termes, or Flamarens, whom Madame de Sévigné had "before and after" her in 1677; they had been asleep for some 128 years. I left behind my sister Lucile in Paris, where she had been living since the autumn of 1804. After a short visit to Vichy, Madame de Chateaubriand suggested we travel and get away from political aggravations for a while.

You may find in my complete works two little travelogues I wrote in Auvergne and Mont Blanc. After an absence of thirty-four years, men, unfamiliar with my person, welcomed me to Clermont with the sort of reception usually reserved for old friends. A man who has long concerned himself with the principles shared by the whole human race has friends, brothers, and sisters in every family, for if man is unappreciative, humanity is grateful. For those who have come to know you through a gracious reputation, and who have never seen you, you are always the same; you are always the age they have ascribed to you. In their fondness, undisturbed by your presence, they always see you young and beautiful, like the sentiments they love in your writings.

When I was a child in my Brittany, and heard stories of Auvergne, I imagined that it was a very, very distant country where you would see strange things, where you could only go at great peril, traveling under the protection of the blessed Virgin. I am always moved to see those little Auvergnats who go to seek their fortune in the great world with a little pine box. They have scarcely anything other than hope in that box when they go clambering down their rocks, and they are lucky if they bring it back intact.

Alas, Madame de Beaumont had rested on the Tiber's shore less than two years when I first set foot on her native soil in 1805. I was only a few leagues from Mont d'Or, where she had gone in search of the life she endured just long enough to make her way to Rome. Last summer, in 1838, I traveled through Auvergne again. Between these dates, 1805 and 1838, I can place the transformations society has undergone around me.

We left Clermont and, on our way to Lyon, passed through Thiers and Roanne. This route, which was then unfrequented, here and there followed the banks of the Lignon. The author of *Astrée*,[9] who is not a great mind, invented lively settings and characters all the same. What creative power fiction has, when it is suited to its era! There is, besides, something ingeniously fantastic in this resurrection of nymphs and naiads rubbing shoulders with shepherds, ladies, and knights: these different worlds go together well, and we are pleased to find mythological tales combined with novelistic fibs. Rousseau tells us how he was bewitched by d'Urfé.[10]

In Lyon, we met M. Ballanche. He went with us to Geneva and Mont Blanc. He would go anywhere he was taken without having the least bit of business there. In Geneva, I was not greeted at the city gate by Clotilde, the betrothed of Clovis: M. de Barante the Elder had become prefect of Léman. I went to see Madame de Staël at Coppet. I found her alone at the back of her house, where her melancholy heart was entombed. I spoke to her of her fortune and her solitude as a precious means of independence and happiness, but in doing so I offended her. Madame de Staël loved society; she regarded herself as the unhappiest of women, in an exile I would have found delightful. How could there be any misery, as I understood it, in living on your own land with all of life's comforts? How could there be any misery in having fame, leisure, peace, and a sumptuous sanctuary with a view of the Alps, when compared with those millions of breadless, nameless, helpless victims banished to every corner of Europe whose every relation had died on the scaffold? It is vexing to be afflicted with a malady that the crowd cannot understand, for the malady grows all the more intense: it is not lessened by being confronted with the pain of others; what afflicts one person gives joy to someone else. Hearts have different secrets, incomprehensible to other hearts. Let us not deny anyone his suffering. Sorrows are like countries: each man has his own.

The next day Madame de Staël called on Madame de Chateaubriand in Geneva and we left for Chamouny. My perspective on the mountainous landscape made people say I was seeking to make myself stand out. You will see, when I speak of Saint-Gotthard, that my perspective remains the same. In *Voyage au Mont-Blanc*, there is a passage I would like to recall because it links together the events of my past with what were then the events of my future, which has become the past in turn:

> There is only one circumstance in which it may be true that the mountains inspire us to forget our earthly sorrows, and that is when we retire far from the world and devote ourselves to religion. An anchorite who is vowed to the service of humanity, a saint who wants to meditate upon God's grandeurs in silence, can find peace and joy on desert rocks; but it is not the tranquility of these spots that passes into the souls of solitary men, it is on the contrary their souls that extend their serenity outward over the stormy regions…
>
> There are mountains I would still be extremely pleased to visit, in Greece and Judea. I would like to travel through the places where my latest studies compel me to spend each day; I would gladly seek out new colors and new harmonies on Tabor and Taiyetos after depicting the nameless hills and unknown valleys of the New World.

This last phrase presaged the voyage I would in fact take the following year, 1806.

On our return to Geneva, unable to go and see Madame de Staël a second time at Coppet, we found the inns all full. If it had not been for the consideration of M. de Forbin, who appeared and procured us a wretched dinner in a lightless antechamber, we would have left Rousseau's hometown without so much as a meal. M. de Forbin was at that time in a state of beatitude; his face beamed with the inner happiness that inundated him; his feet did not touch the ground. Borne up by his talent and his bliss, he descended from the mountain as though from the sky, with his tight-fitting painter's jacket, his palette on his thumb, his brushes in a quiver. He was a good man, despite being excessively cheerful, and he was preparing to imitate me one day—after I made my trip to Syria. He would have liked to go as far as Calcutta. By taking an unusual route, he was hoping to revive his passions, which he had lost along the beaten track.[11] He regarded me with protective pity; I was poor, humble, a little unsure of myself, and I did not have princesses in the palm of my hand. In Rome, I had the good fortune to be able to repay M. de Forbin for his lakeside dinner: I then had the merit of having become an ambassador. But we are always finding, in these days of ours, that the poor devil we left that morning in the street has by evening become a king.

The noble Forbin, a painter on the far side of the Revolution, was the first of that generation of artists who dress themselves up like grotesques or caricatures. Some wear dreadful mustaches, so you might think they were going off to conquer the world; their brushes are halberds and their palette knives, swords. Others have enormous beards, scraggly or puffed-up hair, and smoke cigars volcanically. These "cousins of the rainbow,"[12] as old Régnier said, have their heads filled with floods, seas, rivers, forests, waterfalls, and storms, or else with carnage, torture, and scaffolds. At home they keep human skulls, foils, mandolins, headpieces, and Turkish robes. Braggadocious, enterprising, rude, broad-minded (down to the portrait of the tyrant they are willing to paint), they aspire to form a species somewhere between the monkey and the satyr; they want to make it clear that the secrets of the studio have their dangers and that no model is safe. But how abundantly are these peculiarities redeemed by their exalted lives, their suffering and sensitive natures, their total abnegation of self, an uncalculating devotion to the miseries of others, a delicate, superior, idealized way of feeling, a poverty proudly hailed and nobly supported—and finally, sometimes, by immortal talents, the product of work, passion, genius, and solitude!

Leaving Geneva at night to return to Lyon, we were stopped at the foot of the Fort l'Écluse while we waited for the gates to be opened. During this witches-of-*Macbeth* sojourn on the moor, strange things went on within me. My dead years came back to life and surrounded me like a gang of phantoms. Old seasons of ardor returned to me with all their fire and melancholy. My existence—hollowed out by the death of Madame de Beaumont—had remained empty. Airy forms, houris or dreams, emerging from this abyss, took me by the hand and led me back to the days of my sylph. I was no longer in the places where I was living, I was dreaming of other shores. Some secret influence was pushing me toward the regions of dawn, where I was called to go by thoughts for my new work and by the priestly voice that lifted the vow the villager, my nurse, once made. Because all of my faculties had accumulated, because I had never abused my life, it overflowed with the sap of my intellect, and art, triumphing in my nature, was added to the inspirations of a poet. I had what the Desert Fathers of the Thebaid called "ascensions" of the heart. Raphael (let the blasphemy of the analogy be forgiven), standing before the *Transfiguration* roughed out on the easel, could not have been more electrified by his masterpiece than I was by Eudore and Cymodocée, whose names I still did not know and whose image I glimpsed through a mist of love and glory.

This is the way the native genius that tormented me in the cradle sometimes retraces its steps and returns to me after long abandonment, rekindling the sorrows I have forgotten. I am never healed. If my wounds close instantly, they open again without warning, like those medieval crucifixes that used to bleed on the anniversary of the Passion. I have no resource, to alleviate these crises of mine, other than to give free rein to my feverish thoughts, as a man has his veins lanced when the blood rushes to his heart or mounts to his head. But what am I talking about? Oh, Religion, where are your powers, your reins, your balms? Am I not writing all these things countless years after I brought René into being? I have had a thousand reasons to believe myself dead, and I am alive! It's a great pity. These afflictions of a lonely poet, condemned to suffer the spring despite Saturn,[13] are unknown to the man who never strays from the common laws; for him, the years are always young:

"So do the young goats care for their dear parents in their old age, when sorrowful bonds fetter their limbs. They cull with their mouths and proffer them dewy food and flowery, and for drink they bring them fresh water which they draw with their lips from the nearest stream."[14]

4.

RETURN TO LYON

WHEN I returned to Lyon, I found letters from M. Joubert letting me know it was impossible for him to be in Villeneuve before September. I replied:

> Your departure from Paris is too far off and this upsets me; you know my wife would never agree to arrive in Villeneuve before you do. She has a mind of her own, and since she has been with me I find myself minding two minds both very difficult to govern. We'll stay on in Lyon, where anyway they make us eat so prodigiously I barely have the energy to leave. Abbé de Bonneville is here—back from Rome. He's doing marvelously, cheerful and preachifying, all his troubles behind him. He says hello and is going to write to you. In short, everybody's happy but me; you're the only one grouching. Tell Fontanes I dined with M. Saget.

This M. Saget was a godsend among canons; he lived on the Sainte-Foix hill, in good wine country. The road to his house passed very close by the place where Rousseau had spent the night on the bank of the Saône. "I remember," he writes, "having passed a most delightful night at some distance from the city, on a road by the Saône. Raised and terraced gardens bordered the road on the other side. It had been a very hot day, the evening was delightful, the dew moistened the fading grass, no wind was stirring, the air was fresh without chillness, the setting sun had tinged the clouds with a beautiful crimson, which was again reflected by the water, and the trees that bordered the terrace were filled with nightingales who were continually answering each other's songs. I walked along in a kind of ecstasy, giving up my heart and senses to the enjoyment of so many delights, and sighing only with the regret of enjoying them alone. Absorbed in this pleasing reverie, I lengthened my walk till it grew very late, without perceiving I was tired; at length, however, I discovered it, and threw myself on the step of a kind of niche, or false door, in the terrace wall. The tops of the trees formed a stately canopy for my bed, a nightingale perched directly over me, and with his soft notes lulled me to sleep: how pleasant my slumber was; my awaking more so. It was broad day; on opening my eyes I saw the water, the verdure, an admirable landscape before me."[15]

With Rousseau's charming itinerary in hand, we arrived at M. Saget's. This gaunt ancient man, who had once been married, wore a green cap, a gray camlet coat, nankeen pants, blue stockings, and beaver slippers. He had often lived in Paris and had been an intimate of Mademoiselle Devienne. She wrote him witty letters, rode him hard, and gave him good advice. He did not take it, for he did not take the world seriously, apparently believing, like the Mexicans, that the earth had already burned through four suns and that, with the fourth (the one that lights us today) men had been changed into maggots. He rolled his eyes at the martyrdoms of Saint Pothin and Saint Irenaeus, and at the massacre of Protestants arrayed side by side—by order of Mandelot, governor of Lyon—so they could all have their throats cut more quickly. He recounted the details of the killing fields of Brotteaux as he strolled among his vines, punctuating his narrative with verses by Loyse Labbé. He wouldn't have missed a meal during the latest slayings in Lyon, under the True Charter.[16]

On certain days at Sainte-Foy, they used to serve a calf's head, marinated for five nights, cooked in Madeira wine, and stuffed full of exquisite things; very pretty young peasant girls waited at table, pouring excellent homegrown wine from demijohns the size of three bottles. We descended, the cassocked chapter and I, upon the Saget feast, until the hillside was black with our presence.

Our "dapifer"[17] soon came to the end of his provisions. In the ruin of his final days, he was taken in by two or three old mistresses who ransacked his life—"the sort of women," as Saint Cyprian says, "who live as though they could be truly loved," *quae sic vivis ut possis adamari.*

5.
RIDE TO THE GRANDE CHARTREUSE

WE TORE ourselves away from the delights of Capua to go see the Chartreuse, still in the company of M. Ballanche. We rented a calash whose disjointed wheels made a lamentable noise. Arriving in Voreppe, we stopped at an inn at the top of the town. The next day at dawn, we mounted our horses and set off behind a guide. In the village of Saint-Laurent, below the Grande Chartreuse, we crossed the threshold of the valley and followed the path, between two rocky slopes, up to the monastery. I have told you, when remembering Combourg, what I experienced in this place. The abandoned buildings were crumbling under the gaze of a sort of keeper of the ruins. A lay brother had stayed on there to take care of a sick hermit, who had only recently died. Faith had charged friendship with loyalty and obedience. We saw the narrow grave freshly covered: Napoleon was, at that very moment, about to dig an immense one at Austerlitz. We were shown the convent's outer wall and its cells, each fitted with a garden and a workshop. We cast our gaze over the wooden benches and the lathes; a hand had dropped its chisel. On the walls of one gallery, we studied the portraits of the superiors of the Chartreuse. The ducal palace in Venice displays a series of *ritratti* of the doges; but what different places, what different memories! Higher up, at some distance, we were taken into the chapel of Le Sueur's immortal hermit.[18]

After dining in a vast kitchen, we set off again and crossed paths with a man being carried in a palanquin like a raja. This was M. Chaptal—once an apothecary, then a senator, then the owner of

Chanteloup and inventor of beet sugar, the money-mad heir of the fine Indian reeds of Sicily perfected by the Tahitian sun.[19] Riding down through the forests, I was put in mind of the old cenobites. For centuries they had carried pine saplings and a handful of dirt in the folds of their robes, and now these saplings had grown into trees on the rocks. Oh, blessed are ye who passed noiselessly through this world, not even turning your heads in passing!

We had only just reached the threshold of the valley when a storm erupted. A flood surged, and turbulent mountain streams scrabbled down roaring from every ravine. Madame de Chateaubriand, who had grown bold from fear, galloped through the stones, the waters, and the lightning. She had thrown away her umbrella the better to hear the thunder. The guide shouted to her:

"Recommend your soul to God! In the name of the Father, the Son, and the Holy Ghost!"

We rode into Voreppe to the sound of the alarm bell, the last ragged remnants of the storm hanging before us. Far off in the countryside, we could see a village on fire and the moon ballooning the upper part of its disc above the clouds, like the pale, bald brow of Saint Bruno, the founder of the silent order. M. Ballanche, dripping all over with rain, said, with his unflappable placidity, "I'm like a fish in water."

I have just, in 1838, seen Voreppe again. The storm was long gone, but with me I had two witnesses, Madame de Chateaubriand and M. Ballanche. I mention this only because I have too often, in these *Memoirs*, had to dwell on the dead.

Back in Lyon, we took leave of our companion and traveled on to Villeneuve. I have told you something about this little town—about my walks and my fits of despondency along the banks of the Yonne with M. Joubert. There also lived, not far from this river, three old maiden ladies called the sisters Piat. They reminded me of my grandmother's three friends in Plancoët (excepting the slight difference in social position). The virgins of Villeneuve died one after the other, and I thought of them every time I passed the grassy front steps that led up to their vacant house. What had these village spinsters discussed in their day? They talked about a dog, or a muff their father had bought for them once at the fair in Sens. To me, this was at least as charming as the council held in that same city, where Saint Bernard had Abelard, my countryman, condemned. The maids of the muff were perhaps Héloïses; perhaps they loved, and their letters, rediscovered one day, will enchant posterity. Who knows? They may well have written to their "lord and father and brother and husband," *domino suo, imo patri*, etc.,[20] that they felt honored by the name of "lover," "mistress," or "courtesan," *concubinae vel scorti*.[21] "Amidst all his learning," says a serious scholar,[22] "I find Abelard reveals a streak of admirable folly when he suborned his student Héloïse to love."

6.

DEATH OF MADAME DE CAUD

A GREAT new misery surprised me in Villeneuve. To tell you about it, I must go back a few months, prior to my journey to Switzerland. I was still living in the house on rue Miromesnil then, in the autumn of 1804, when Madame de Caud moved to Paris. Madame de Beaumont's death had destroyed what was left of my sister's sanity. She came close to disbelieving in this death and suspecting some mystery underlay her friend's disappearance, or else to thinking that Heaven itself was among the enemies pulling the strings of her unhappy existence. She had nothing.

I had found an apartment for her on rue Caumartin, playing coy about the cost of the rent and the arrangements I'd made with a nearby restaurateur. Like a flame about to go out, her spirit gave off the liveliest sparks—she was completely dazzling. She would scribble a few lines and then toss them in the fire, or else copy a few passages from a book she found in harmony with the arrangement of her soul. She did not stay long on rue Caumartin; she went to live at the Dames Saint-Michel on rue du Faubourg Saint-Jacques, where the mother superior was a woman called Madame de Navarre. Lucile was given a little cell overlooking the garden, and I noticed she stared, with I know not what gloomy desire, at the nuns strolling in the yard around the vegetable patches. One might suppose she envied the blessed and, going further, aspired to the angelic. I will sanctify these *Memoirs* by depositing, like relics, these notes from Madame de Caud, written before she took flight for her eternal home.

January 17, 1803

I had put all my hope in you and Madame de Beaumont, I fled from my troubles and my pains in the thought of you two—all I wanted was to love you both. Last night, I thought long and hard about your character and your ways. As you and I are always near each other, it takes some time, I think, to understand me, my head is so flooded with ideas, my shyness and my seeming weakness are so at odds with my real inner strength! But that is more than enough about me. My illustrious brother, accept the kindest thanks for all your indulgence and all the tokens of friendship you have never ceased to show me. This is the last letter you will receive from me this morning. Even if I share my thoughts with you, they nevertheless remain entirely within me.

Undated

Do you seriously believe I am safe, my love, from some impertinence on the part of M. Chênedollé? My mind is quite made up not to invite him to continue his visits; I resign myself to thinking that last Tuesday's was the last. I don't want to abuse his politeness. I am closing the book of my fate forever and sealing it with the seal of reason. I shall stop consulting its pages about either the trifles or the important things in life. I renounce all my foolish ideas, and I don't want to involve or vex myself with those of others either. I am going to give myself over body and soul to everything that happens during my passage through the world. What a pity I should pay myself so much attention! God can now afflict me only through you. I thank him for the precious, good, and dear present that he has given me in you, and for having kept my life unstained. These are all the treasures I have in the world. If I were to choose the emblem of my life, I think it would be the moon in a cloud with this motto: "Often obscured, never tarnished." Farewell, my love. You will perhaps be surprised by my language after yesterday morning.

Since I saw you, my heart has again lifted toward God, and I lay it whole at the feet of the cross, its one true home.

Thursday

Hello, my love. What color are your thoughts this morning? As for me, I am remembering that the only person who could comfort me when I feared for Madame de Farcy's life was the woman who told me, "But it is within the realm of possibility that you will die before her." Doesn't that strike just the right note? There is nothing, my love, like the idea of death to relieve us of the future. I am hurrying to relieve you of me this morning, for I feel too wound up to say nice things. Have a good day, my poor brother. Be happy.

Undated

When Madame de Farcy was alive and I was always with her, I did not notice how much a person needs to air one's thoughts to someone else. I had this consolation and was unaware of it. But since we have lost our friend—and with circumstances keeping you and me apart—I have become acquainted with the torture of never being able to relax and renew one's mind in conversation with another. I feel my thoughts do me harm if I cannot rid myself of them—which is surely the fault of my poor constitution. Yet I have been happy enough, since yesterday, with my courage. I pay no attention to my suffering or the sort of weakness I feel within me. I have given myself up. Continue to be kind to me, always: before long it will be a question of humanity. Have a good day, my love. Till very soon, I hope.

Undated

Be easy, my love; my health is visibly improving. I often wonder why I go to such lengths to shore it up. I am like a madman who would build a fortress in the middle of a desert. Farewell, my poor brother.

Undated

Since tonight I have a bad headache, I've quite simply written you a few thoughts taken at random from Fénelon, to keep my promise:

"We are confined within narrow limits when we shut ourselves up in our own existence; on the contrary, we feel at liberty when we leave this prison and enter the immensity of God."

"We shall soon find once more all that we have lost. We are daily approaching it with rapid strides. A little while longer and we shall have no more reason to weep. It is we who die: what we love lives on and never dies."

"You are giving yourself false strength, such as a raging fever gives a sick man. For the last few days, you have been gesturing convulsively, playing at courage and cheer when, deep down, you are in agony."

That is all my head and my poor pen allow me to write you tonight. If you like, I will begin again tomorrow and tell you perhaps a little more. Good night, my love. I will never stop telling you how overcome I am by Fénelon, whose tenderness seems so profound, and whose virtue so exalted. Goodbye, my love.

I am writing you again now that I am up and send you a thousand affections and a hundred blessings. I am feeling well this morning and am worried about whether you will be able to read my scrawl and whether those thoughts of Fénelon's will seem well chosen to you. I am afraid I have let myself become far too concerned with whether you will.

Undated

Would you believe that I have been madly busy since yesterday editing you? The Blossacs have entrusted me, in the greatest secrecy, with a ballad of yours.[23] As I do not think you have made the most of your ideas in this ballad, I am amusing myself trying to give them their full worth. Can one push audacity further than that? Pardon me, great man, and don't forget I'm your sister, which means I'm permitted to exploit your riches a little.

Saint-Michel

I'm no longer going to tell you "Don't come see me again," because, now that you only have a few more days in Paris, I feel your presence is essential to me. Do not come today until four; I expect to be out until then. Oh my friend, my head is full of a thousand contradictory ideas about things which seem both to exist and not to exist, which for me are like objects that can only be seen in a mirror and whose reality therefore cannot be verified, even if I see them distinctly. I don't want to get mixed up with all that anymore. From this moment on, I'm giving myself up. I don't have the energy, as you do, to change shores, but I have enough strength not to attach any importance to the people and things on *my* shore, and to concentrate entirely, irrevocably, on the author of all justice and all truth. There is only one displeasure that I fear will make dying difficult, and that is accidentally hurting, not intending to, some other person's life—not because of the interest they might take in me; I am not crazy enough to think *that*.

Saint-Michel

My love, never did the sound of your voice give me so much pleasure as yesterday when I heard it on my staircase. My thoughts, then, sought to master my courage. I was overcome with pleasure, feeling you so close to me; you appear, and everything inside me is all right again. Sometimes I am repelled at having to drink from the bitter cup. How can this heart, which takes up so little space, contain so much life and so much grief? I am greatly displeased with myself, greatly displeased. My worries and thoughts consume me. I hardly ever give a thought to God anymore and have to limit myself to asking him a hundred times a day: "Hear me speedily, O Lord, my spirit faileth."[24]

Undated

Brother, do not grow weary of my letters or my company. Think that soon you will be forever rid of my importunities. My life is shedding its last rays, like a lamp that has burned out in the darkness of a long night and now sees the breaking dawn in which it shall die. Old friend, my brother, cast a single glance back at the first days of our life. Remember that often we were bounced on the same knee and pressed, both together, to the same bosom. Remember that even then you mixed your tears with mine, that from the earliest days of your life you protected and defended my frail existence, that we played together, and that I shared your first studies. I will not speak to you of our adolescence, of the innocence of our thoughts and pleasures, or of the need we both felt to have each other constantly in sight. If I retrace the past for you now, I candidly confess, dear brother, it is to make you feel my life more keenly in your heart. When you left France for the second time, you put your wife in my hands and you made me promise not to part from her. Loyal to this precious vow, I voluntarily let my hands be shackled and went into those precincts set aside exclusively for victims condemned to death. In those places, all my worries were for you; I never ceased to dwell upon my forebodings about your fate. When I was free again, amid the miseries that came to weigh upon me, the mere thought of seeing you again sustained me. Today, when I am irreversibly losing all hope of running my course by your side, bear with my sorrows. I will resign myself to my destiny, and it is only because I am still struggling with it that I suffer such wrenching anguish; but when I submit to my fate... And what a fate! Where are my friends, my protectors, my riches? Who cares about my life, this life abandoned by everyone, borne up only by itself? My God, I am weak. Are my present woes not enough, without adding fear for the future to their number? Pardon me, my precious friend, I will resign myself; I will fall into a deathlike sleep and meet my destiny. But for the few days I have to spend in this city, let me find my last consolations in you; let me think my presence is sweet to you. Believe me, among the hearts that love you, none approaches the sincerity and tenderness of my helpless affection for you. Fill my memory with pleasant recollections that will prolong my life with you. Yesterday, when you spoke to me of coming to your house, you seemed anxious and serious, though your words were affectionate. What, my brother—could I too be a source of estrangement and boredom for you? You know I am not the one who proposed the welcome distraction of coming to visit you, that I promised you not to take up your time; but if you've changed your mind, couldn't you tell me so straight-out? I don't have the courage to stand up to your politeness. In the old days, you distinguished me a little more from the common crowd and did me more justice. Since you're counting on me to come today, I will go straightaway to see you at eleven o'clock. Let's arrange together what will suit you best for the future. I have written you, certain that I would not have the courage to speak a single word of what this letter contains.

This poignant and quite admirable letter is the last I received from Lucile. The surge of sadness it expresses alarmed me. I rushed to the Dames Saint-Michel: my sister was out walking in the garden with Madame de Navarre. She came in when she was told I had gone up to her cell. She made visible efforts to collect her thoughts and suffered a repeated convulsive movement of the lips. I begged her to return to her senses, to stop writing me such unjust things that tore at my heart, to stop thinking that I could ever be weary of her. She seemed to calm a little at these words, which I drew out to distract and console her. She told me that she thought the convent was doing her harm, that she would feel better living alone, near the Jardin des Plantes, where she could visit doctors and go for walks. I urged her to do exactly as she wished, adding that, to make things easier on Virginie, her maid, I would assign her old Saint-Germain. The prospect of this seemed to give her great pleasure, in memory of Madame de Beaumont, and she assured me she would look into finding herself a new place to live. When she asked me what I was planning to do that summer, I said I was going to Vichy to meet my wife, then to M. Joubert's house in Villeneuve, and from there back to Paris. I suggested she come with us. She told me she wanted to spend the summer alone and was going to send Virginie back to Fougères. She seemed calmer when I left.

Madame de Chateaubriand departed for Vichy and I prepared to follow her. Before leaving Paris, I went to see Lucile again. She was affectionate. She spoke to me of our little compositions, whose lovely fragments you have seen in the third book of these *Memoirs*. I encouraged the great poet to get to work. She embraced me, wished me safe travels, made me promise to come back soon. She led me out onto the landing of the staircase, leaned on the railing, and tranquilly watched as I made my way down. At the bottom of the steps, I paused, and, lifting my head, called up to the sad creature who still stood looking at me:

"Goodbye, dear sister! Until soon! Take good care of yourself. Write to me in Villeneuve. I'll write to you. I hope next winter you'll agree to live with us."

That night I saw the good Saint-Germain and gave him orders and some money so that he could secretly reduce the cost of anything she might need. I implored him to keep me posted about whatever was happening and not fail to tell me to come back to town if I was needed. Three months went by. When I arrived in Villeneuve, I found two rather soothing letters about Madame de Caud's health; but Saint-German forgot to tell me anything about my sister's new address or arrangements. I had started to write her a long letter when, out of the blue, Madame de Chateaubriand fell dangerously ill. I was at her bedside when I was brought another letter from Saint-Germain. I opened it. One devastating line informed me of the sudden death of Lucile.

I have seen to many tombstones in my life, but it was my lot, and my sister's destiny, that these ashes would be scattered to the wind. I was not in Paris when she died and had no relatives there. Kept in Villeneuve by my wife's perilous condition, I could not rush to the sacred remains; orders relayed from afar arrived too late to prevent a common burial. Lucile knew no one and had no friends. The only person acquainted with her was Madame de Beaumont's aged retainer, Saint-Germain; it was as if he had been charged with linking the destinies of the two women. He alone followed the forsaken coffin, and he himself was dead before Madame de Chateaubriand's sufferings allowed me to take her back to Paris.

My sister was buried among the poor. In what cemetery was she lain? By what still wave in what ocean of the dead was she swallowed up? In what house did she pass away, after leaving the Dames Saint-Michel? If by making inquiries, if by consulting the city archives and the parish registers, I found my sister's name, what would that avail me? Would I find the same caretaker in charge? Would I find the man who dug a grave that has remained anonymous and unmarked? Would the rough hands that were the last to touch such pure clay have retained the memory? What nomenclator of shades would point out to me the obliterated site of her burial? Might he not make some mistake about the dust? Since Heaven has willed it, let Lucile be lost forever! I find, in this absence of locality, a distinction from the graves of my other friends. My predecessor in this world and the next is praying for me to the Redeemer; she is praying to him from among the remains of the paupers with which her own are mingled. So, too, does our mother lie, lost, among those whom Jesus Christ loved best. God will have been able to recognize my sister, and she, who did not much cling to the things of this earth, was bound not to leave any trace here. She has left me, that sainted genius. Not a single day goes by I do not mourn her. Lucile loved to hide, and I have set aside a place for her alone in my heart. She will leave it only when I have ceased to live.

These are the true, the only, events of my real life! What did it matter to me, at the moment I lost my sister, the millions of soldiers who were falling on the battlefields, the crumbling of thrones—the changing of the face of the world?

Lucile's death struck at the roots of my soul. When she disappeared, my childhood, my family, and the first vestiges of my life disappeared with her. Our lives are like those fragile buildings held in the air by flying buttresses: they do not come down all at once but crumble piece by piece; the buttresses still support some gallery or other even when they have already let the sanctum or the vault of the building fall. Madame de Chateaubriand, still smarting from Lucile's imperious whims, saw in her death only a happy release for a Christian woman now gone to rest in the Lord. Let us be mild if we wish to be mourned. Only angels weep for lofty genius and superior qualities. As for me, I do not find I am able to share in Madame de Chateaubriand's consolation.[25]

BOOK EIGHTEEN

I.

1805 AND 1806—I RETURN TO PARIS—I LEAVE FOR THE LEVANT

Paris, 1839; Revised in December 1846

WHEN, traveling back to Paris along the Burgundy road, I saw the cupola of Val-de-Grâce and the dome of Sainte-Geneviève, which overtowers the Jardin des Plantes, my heart sank: yet another of my life's companions had been left along the way! We returned to the Hôtel de Coislin, and, though M. de Fontanes, M. Joubert, M. de Clausel, and M. Molé came to while away the evenings with me, I was so overwhelmed by memories and thoughts I was utterly exhausted. Stranded alone behind the precious things gone from me, like a foreign sailor whose engagement is over and discovers he has neither home nor homeland, I paced restlessly on shore. I longed to dive into a new ocean and swim—to refresh myself and cross over to the other side. A nursling of Pindus, a crusader to Jerusalem, I was impatient to go and mix my own ruination with the ruins of Athens, my sorrows with Magdalene's tears.

I went to see my family in Brittany and, after a brief return to Paris, left for Trieste on July 13, 1806. Madame de Chateaubriand accompanied me as far as Venice, where M. Ballanche came to stay with her.

My life having been recorded hour by hour in the *Itinerary*, I would have nothing more to say here if I did not have a handful of hitherto unpublished letters written or received during and after my voyage. Julien, my servant and companion, wrote, for his part, an itinerary parallel with mine, as passengers on a ship keep their private journal on a voyage of discovery. The little manuscript he put at my disposal will serve as a check upon my narrative: I shall be Cook, and he shall be Clerke.[1]

To more fully illuminate the ways in which we are all of us stamped by the social order and the intellectual hierarchy, I am going to interweave my narrative with Julien's. I will let him speak first because he recounts a few days' sailing without me, from Methoni to Smyrna.

JULIEN'S ITINERARY

We went aboard on Thursday, August 1, but the wind was not favorable to leaving the port and we stayed there until daybreak the next morning. Then the harbor pilot came to tell us he could bring us out. As I had never been to sea, I had exaggerated ideas about the dangers, for I experienced none for two days. But on the third day a storm broke out; lightning, thunder, in brief a terrible tempest assailed us and dreadfully stirred up the sea. Our crew consisted of only eight sailors, a captain, an officer, a pilot, and a cook, along with five passengers, including M. de Chateaubriand and me, which made seventeen men in all. Then we all set to helping the sailors furl the sails, despite the rain that soon drenched us to the skin. (We had taken off our coats to be able to move more freely.) This work kept me busy and prevented me from thinking of the danger, which is more terrifying in thought than in reality. For two days straight, there was one storm after another, which seasoned me in my first days of seafaring. I was in no way upset, though M. de Chateaubriand was afraid I might get seasick. When calm was restored, he said to me: "This has put my mind at rest about your health; seeing you have weathered these two stormy days, you have nothing more to worry about, whatever troubles may arise." No more troubles arose during the remainder of our journey to Smyrna. On the tenth, which was a Sunday, Monsieur had them set him ashore near a Turkish town called Methoni, where he disembarked to go to Greece. Among the passengers with us were two men from Milan, who were going to Smyrna to practice their trade of tinsmithing and smelting. Monsieur proposed that one of the two, Joseph, who spoke passably good Turkish, accompany him as a servant-interpreter, as he mentions in his *Itinerary*. He told us before leaving that this trip would only take a few days, that he would rejoin the boat on an island we would pass in four or five days, and that he would wait for us on this island if he arrived there before us. As Monsieur found this man sufficient for this short journey,* he left me aboard to continue on to Smyrna and look after our things. He had given me a letter of recommendation to the French Consul in case he did not rejoin us in time, which was indeed what happened. On the fourth day, we arrived at the appointed island. The captain went ashore and Monsieur was not there. We spent the night and waited until seven o'clock in the morning. The captain went back ashore to leave word that he was forced to go on, having a good wind and being obliged to take his crossing into consideration. Besides, he saw a pirate who was trying to get at us and it was important to put ourselves promptly on the defensive. He had the four cannon loaded and his rifles, pistols, and swords brought on deck, but, as the wind favored us, the pirate gave us up. We arrived on Monday, the 18th, at seven o'clock in the evening, in the port of Smyrna.

After traveling across Greece, stopping off in Zea and Chios, I caught up with Julien in Smyrna. Today, in my memory, I see Greece like one of those luminous rings we sometimes behold when we close our eyes. Outlined in this mysterious phosphorescence is the fine and admirable architecture of the ruins, rendered all the more resplendent by the inexpressible brightness of the Muses. When will I see the thyme of Mount Hymettus or the oleander that grows along the Eurotas again? One of the people I have envied most in my travels on foreign shores was the Turkish customs officer in Piraeus. He lived alone, the guardian of three deserted ports, casting his gaze over

*From Sparta to Athens.

bluish islands, gleaming promontories, and gilded seas. There, I heard nothing but the sound of the waves in the ruined tomb of Themistocles and the murmur of distant memories. Amidst the silence of Sparta's wreckage, glory itself was mute.

I left my poor Milanese dragoman, Joseph, at his tinsmith's shop in the motherland of Homer, and set out for Constantinople. I passed through Pergamos, wanting first to visit Troy out of poetic piety, but a fall from my horse awaited me at the start of my journey—not because Pegasus stumbled, but because I fell asleep. I recalled this accident in my *Itinerary*. Julien recounts it, too, and he makes some remarks, whose accuracy I confirm, concerning the roads and the horses.

JULIEN'S ITINERARY

M. de Chateaubriand, who had fallen asleep on his horse, fell off it without waking up. The horse stopped right away, as did mine, which was following after it. I dismounted immediately to see what had happened, for it was impossible for me to see from six feet away. I saw Monsieur half asleep beside his horse and quite startled to find himself on the ground. He assured me he was uninjured. His horse had not tried to get away, which would have been dangerous, for there were cliffs very close by.

Leaving Soma, after passing through Pergamos, I had a dispute with my guide that is recorded in the *Itinerary*. Here is how Julien tells it:

We left the village very early after refreshing our supplies. A little way from the village, I was very shocked to see Monsieur raging at our guide; I asked him why. Then Monsieur told me he had made a deal with the guide, in Smyrna, that he would take him through the plains of Troy, and that now he was refusing, saying these plains were infested with robbers. Monsieur wouldn't believe a word of it and refused to listen to anyone.

As I saw that he was becoming angrier and angrier, I gestured to the guide to come over near the interpreter and the janissary to explain to me what he had been told about the dangers we would encounter on the plains Monsieur wished to visit. The guide told the interpreter he had been assured that great numbers were needed to ward off attacks. The janissary told me the same thing. Then I went over to Monsieur and repeated to him what all three of them had told me and, furthermore, that we were a day's walk from a little village where there was a sort of consul who could inform us of the truth. Following my report, Monsieur calmed down and we continued on our way toward that village. As soon as we arrived, he went straight to the consul, who told him all the dangers he would be facing if he persisted in going out with so few men upon the plains of Troy. So Monsieur was forced to give up his plan, and we continued on our way to Constantinople.

I arrived in Constantinople.

MY ITINERARY

The almost total absence of women, the lack of wheeled carriages, and the packs of wild dogs were the three things that struck me first in this extraordinary town. Because nearly everyone walks around in slippers, because there are no sounds of carriages or carts, because there are no bell towers and hardly any hammering trades, the silence is unbroken. Around you, you see a mute crowd who seem to wish to pass unseen and always appear to be hiding from the gaze of the master. And you are continually stumbling from a marketplace into a cemetery—as if the Turks were here only to buy, sell, and die. The cemeteries, unwalled and planted in the middle of the streets, form magnificent cypress forests where the doves build their nests and partake of the peace of the dead. Here and there, you come upon monuments that have no connection either with modern men or the new-fashioned monuments that surround them. You might almost think they had been transported by magic into this oriental city. No sign of joy or look of happiness meets your eyes here. What you see is not a people, but a herd led by an imam and slaughtered by a janissary. Amid the prisons and penal colonies stands a seraglio, the capital of servitude; inside, a sacred guardian carefully preserves the germs of pestilence and the primitive laws of tyranny.

Julien, for his part, does not lose himself in the clouds:

JULIEN'S ITINERARY

Constantinople is very unpleasant the way it slopes toward the canal and the port. On all the streets descending in this direction (all very badly paved), people are forced to cram very close together to keep to the strips of land that the water is eroding. There are not many vehicles: the Turks make much more use of saddle horses than other nations. There are, in the French Quarter, some sedan chairs for the ladies. There are also camels and horses for hire for transporting merchandise, as well as Turkish porters who work in pairs with very thick long sticks. They each put five or six of these sticks at each end of the load and can carry an enormous amount of weight at a steady pace. Single men can also carry very heavy loads: they have a sort of hook that goes from their shoulders down to their lower backs, and with a remarkable show of balance, they carry all sorts of parcels without even having to tie them on.

2.

FROM CONSTANTINOPLE TO JERUSALEM—I EMBARK IN CONSTANTINOPLE ON A SHIP CARRYING GREEK PILGRIMS TO SYRIA

MY ITINERARY

There are nearly two hundred passengers—men, women, children, and old people—on this boat, and as many mats laid out in rows on both sides of steerage. In this republic, everyone does as he pleases: women look after their children, men smoke or make their dinner, old folks chat in groups. From every direction, you hear the sound of mandolins, violins, and lyres— singing, dancing, laughing, praying. Everyone is cheerful. Someone said to me, "Jerusalem!" pointing to the south, and I replied, "Jerusalem!" If it weren't for fear, we would be the happiest people in the world, but at the slightest wind the sailors pull in the sails and the pilgrims cry out, "*Christos, Kyrie eleison!*" As soon as the storm has passed, we regain our boldness.

Here Julien has me beat:

JULIEN'S ITINERARY

We had to attend to our departure for Jaffa, which took place Thursday, September 18. We embarked on a Greek vessel where there are at least 150 Greek men, women, and children all going on pilgrimage to Jerusalem and this has caused a great deal of crowding on board.

Like all the other passengers, we had our supply of food and kitchen utensils that I bought in Constantinople. I had, moreover, another rather complete set of provisions that the ambassador gave us, including very fine biscuits, hams, sausages, cervelats; wines of various sorts, rum, sugar, lemons, and even quinine wine to ward off fever. I thus found myself supplied with a very abundant provision, which I meted out and consumed only with great economy, knowing this was not the only crossing we had to make: everything was locked up where the other passengers could not go.

Our crossing, which took only thirteen days, seemed to me very long because of all sorts of unpleasantness and uncleanliness aboard. During the several days of bad weather we had, the women and children were sick, vomiting everywhere, to the point where we had to leave our room and go sleep on deck. We ate there much more comfortably than elsewhere, after we decided to wait until all our Greek friends had finished with their slop.

I passed through the Dardanelles, touched land at Rhodes, and hired a pilot for the Syrian coast. We were stopped by a calm below the Asian continent, more or less across from the ancient cape of Chelidonia. —We remained at sea two days not knowing where we were.

MY ITINERARY

The weather was so fine and the air so mild that all the passengers stayed the night on deck. I had contended for a spot on the quarterdeck with two fat Greek monks, who ceded it to me only under protest. That is where I was sleeping on September 30, at six o'clock in the morning, when I was awoken by a noisy confusion of voices: I opened my eyes and saw the pilgrims looking at the ship's prow. I asked what it was and they

shouted to me: "*Signor, il Carmelo!*" Mount Carmel! The wind
had risen at eight the previous evening and, overnight, we had
arrived in sight of the Syrian coast. Since I had slept in my
clothes, I was soon on my feet, inquiring about the holy mountain. Everyone rushed to point it out to me, but I saw nothing,
for the sun had begun to rise across the water. That moment
had something religious and august about it; all the pilgrims,
rosaries in hand, stood silently in the same attitude, waiting
for the appearance of the Holy Land. The leader of the old
folks prayed out loud, and all you could hear was this prayer
and the sound of the ship, racing before the most favorable
wind, over a shining sea. From time to time a cry went up from
the prow when Mount Carmel reappeared. At last, I saw the
mountain myself, like a roundish blot beneath the rays of the
sun. I got down on my knees then, like the Latins. I did not
feel the agitation I experienced when I first set eyes on the coast
of Greece, but the sight of the cradle of the Israelites and the
homeland of Christians filled me with joy and reverence. I was
going to set foot in the land of wonders, source of the most
astonishing poetry, in places where, even humanly speaking,
the greatest event that has ever changed the face of the world
occurred . . .

The wind failed us at noon; it picked up again at four o'clock;
but, due to the pilot's ignorance, we had passed our destination.
At two o'clock in the afternoon we saw Jaffa again.

A boat pulled away from the shore with three monks aboard.
I got down with them into the longboat and we entered the
port through an opening made between rocks, dangerous even
for a caïque such as ours.

The Arabs on the beach came out in water to their waists
to take us on their shoulders. There followed a quite amusing
scene. My servant was dressed in a long whitish coat, and white
being the color of distinction among the Arabs they thought
Julien was the sheikh. They took hold of him and carried him

off in triumph, despite his protests, while, thanks to my blue coat, I made my humble landing on the back of a ragged beggar.

Now let us hear Julien, the principal actor in the scene:

JULIEN'S ITINERARY

What greatly surprised me was seeing six Arabs come to take me ashore while there were only two for Monsieur, who was greatly entertained to see me being carried like a wooden saint. I am not sure whether perhaps my appearance impressed them more than Monsieur's. He was wearing a brown frock coat with brown buttons, whereas mine was whitish with white metal buttons, which were rather glittery in the sunshine; this, probably, is what caused the mistake.

On Wednesday, October 1, we entered the monastery in Jaffa. The monks are Franciscans and speak Latin and Italian but very little French. They have welcomed us very graciously and done everything possible to procure us whatever we need.

I arrived in Jerusalem. On the advice of the fathers of the monastery, I passed quickly through the Holy City and went to the Jordan. After stopping off at a monastery in Bethlehem, I set out with an escort of Arabs, pausing in Saba. At midnight, I found myself on the shore of the Dead Sea.

MY ITINERARY

When you travel in Judea, you are at first overwhelmed by a great boredom; but when, moving from solitude to solitude, space extends unbounded before you, gradually your boredom dissipates, you experience a secret terror that, far from disgracing the soul, gives you courage and exalts the mind. Extraordinary views reveal a land embroidered with miracles in every direction: the burning sun, the impetuous eagle, the barren fig tree—all the poetry and imagery of scripture are there. Every name contains a mystery; every cave declares the future; every summit resounds with a prophet's voice. God himself has spoken on these shores: waters dried up, rocks split in two, tombs half opened—all attest to wonders. The wilderness itself still seems mute with terror, as though it has not dared to break the silence since it heard the voice of Eternity.

We descended from the rounded top of the mountain to spend the night on the shore of the Dead Sea before going back toward the Jordan.

JULIEN'S ITINERARY

We dismounted our horses to let them rest and eat, as did we, who had a fair enough supply of food, provided for us by the monks of Jerusalem. After we finished our meal, our Arabs went off a little way from us to listen, ears to the ground, for any noise. Having assured us we could rest easy, everyone went to sleep. Although lying on pebbles, I slept very well, until Monsieur came to wake me at five in the morning to get our whole band ready to depart. He had already filled a tinplate bottle with water from the Dead Sea to bring back to Paris.

MY ITINERARY

We pulled up stakes and made our way for an hour and a half with excessive difficulty over a thin white sand. We were proceeding toward a little forest of balsam and tamarind, which, to my great astonishment, I saw rising up in the midst of the barren ground. All of a sudden, the Bethlehemites stopped and pointed out to me, deep in a ravine, something I had not noticed. Without being able to say what it was, I perceived a sort of stream of sand in motion over the stillness of the ground; I approached this unusual phenomenon and saw a yellow river that I had trouble distinguishing from the sand of its two shores. It was deeply embanked, and flowed slowly in a thick stream. This was the Jordan...

The Bethlehemites stripped down and plunged into the Jordan. I did not dare imitate them because of the fever that was constantly tormenting me.

JULIEN'S ITINERARY

We arrived at the Jordan at seven in the morning through sands that came up to our horses' knees and ditches they only barely managed to scramble out of. We followed the river until ten, and for our refreshment bathed very comfortably in the shadows of the bushes that border the river. It would have been very easy to swim to the other side, the spot where we were being very narrow, perhaps two hundred and fifty feet across; but it was not prudent to attempt, for there were some Arabs trying to catch up with us and very soon they would be there in great numbers. Monsieur filled his second tinplate bottle with water from the Jordan.

We returned to Jerusalem. Julien was not much impressed by the sacred sites. Like a true philosopher, he was dry: "Calvary," he said, "is in the same church,[2] on a hill, similar to many other hills we climbed, and from which you can see, in the distance, nothing but wastelands and woods everywhere, bushes and scrub nibbled by animals. The valley of Jehoshaphat lies just beyond the walls of Jerusalem and looks like a moat."

I left Jerusalem, arrived in Jaffa, and embarked for Alexandria. From Alexandria I went to Cairo and left Julien with M. Drovetti, who had the goodness to charter an Austrian ship to Tunis for me. Julien continued his journal in Alexandria: "There are," he wrote, "Jews who practice stockjobbing here, as they do wherever they are. Half a league from the city stands Pompey's Pillar, which is made of a reddish granite and stands on a bed of quarried stone."

MY ITINERARY

On November 23, at noon, the wind having turned favorable, I went aboard the ship. I embraced M. Drovetti on the shore and we made promises of friendship and remembrance: I am now acquitting myself of my debt.

We raised anchor at two o'clock. A pilot took us out of the harbor. The wind was weak and from the south. For three days, we remained in sight of Pompey's Pillar, which hovered on the horizon. At dusk on the third day, we heard the evening gun from the port of Alexandria. This served as the definitive signal of our departure, for the north wind picked up, and we set sail for the west.

On December 1, the winds, blowing westerly, barred our path. Gradually they descended to the southwest and turned into a tempest that did not end until our arrival in Tunis. To pass the time, I copied and organized my notes on the voyage and my descriptions for *The Martyrs*. At night I walked on the deck with the second mate, Captain Dinelli. Nights spent among the waves, on a ship battered by storms, are not barren; the uncertainty of our future lets us see everything for exactly what it's worth: the land, contemplated from a stormy sea, is like life considered by a man about to die.

JULIEN'S ITINERARY

After we left the port of Alexandria, we went along fairly well for the first day, but this did not last, for we have had continual bad weather and bad wind for the rest of the voyage. There was, without fail, always an officer, the pilot, and four sailors on watch on deck. When we saw, at the end of the day, that we were going to have a bad night, we also went up on deck. Around midnight, I made our punch. I always began by giving some to our pilot and the four sailors before serving Monsieur, the officer, and myself; but we did not drink it as calmly as we would in a café. The officer was much more used to it than the captain, and he spoke very good French, which was a very pleasant thing for us during our journey.

We continued our voyage and anchored before the Kerkennah Isles.

MY ITINERARY

A storm rose up from the southeast, to our great joy, and in five days we arrived in the waters of the island of Malta. We sighted it on Christmas Eve, but Christmas Day itself, the wind, shifting to the west-northwest, drove us south of Lampedusa. For eighteen days, we remained off the eastern coast of the kingdom of Tunisia, caught between life and death. I will never, as long as I live, forget the day of the twenty-eighth.

We dropped anchor before the Kerkennah Isles. For eight days we lay at anchor in Syrtis Minor, where I saw the year 1807 begin. Under how many different stars and how many different circumstances had I already seen the renewal of the years—years that pass so quickly or that seem so long! How far away were those days of childhood when, with my heart pounding, I used to receive my father's gifts and blessing! How I used to look forward to New Year's Day! And now, on a foreign ship, in the middle of the sea, in sight of a barbarous land, this first day has flown from me, without witnesses, without pleasures, without the embrace of my family, without those tender well wishes that a mother forms for her son with such sincerity! This day, emerging from the womb of the tempests, has brought me nothing but worries, regrets, and silver hairs.

Julien was exposed to the same fate and catches me in one of those fits of impatience which, fortunately, I have since outgrown.

JULIEN'S ITINERARY

We were very near the island of Malta, and we had reason to fear we might be sighted by some English vessel or other, which would have forced us to enter the harbor; but we encountered none. Our crew was very tired and the wind continued to be unfavorable to us. The captain, seeing on his chart an anchorage called Kerkennah, which was not far off, set sail without alerting Monsieur, who, seeing we were approaching this anchorage, became furious at not having been consulted, telling the captain that he ought to continue on his course, since we had been through worse weather already. But we were too far along to resume our course and, besides, the captain's prudence was borne out by the very strong wind and very bad sea we had that night. When we were obliged to stay another twenty-four hours longer than expected in the anchorage, Monsieur was not shy about showing the captain his displeasure, despite the good reasons the captain had given him.

For nearly a month, we had been at sea, and we were only seven or eight hours from arriving in the port of Tunis when, suddenly, the wind became so violent we had to put out to sea again. It would be three more weeks until we could approach the port once more, and it was at this moment that Monsieur again reproached the captain for having wasted thirty-six hours in the anchorage. He could not be persuaded that something much worse might have happened if the captain had been less cautious. The real trouble, as I saw it, was that our provisions were running low and we had no idea when it would be possible to go ashore and replenish them.

At last I set foot on Carthaginian soil. I found the most generous hospitality with Monsieur and Madame Devoise. Julien describes my host well; he also speaks of the countryside and the Jews. "They pray and weep," he writes.

An American warship gave me passage aboard and I crossed the

Lake of Tunis to La Goulette. "On the way," Julien says, "I asked Monsieur if he had taken the gold he had put in the writing desk of his bedroom; he told me he had forgotten it and I was obliged to return to Tunis." I can never keep my mind on money.

When I arrived in Alexandria, we dropped anchor opposite the ruins of the city of Hannibal. I looked at them from aboard the ship unable to tell what they were: I made out a few Moorish huts, a Muslim hermitage on the end of a jutting cape, some sheep grazing among ruins so hard to see I could scarcely distinguish them from the soil that bore them up. This was Carthage. I visited it before setting sail for Europe.

MY ITINERARY

From the summit of Byrsa, the eye embraces the ruins of Carthage, which are more numerous than is generally believed. They are like the ruins of Sparta in that nothing important has been preserved, yet they occupy a considerable space. I saw them in February; the figs, olives, and carobs were already putting forth their first leaves; tall angelicas and acanthus formed tufts of verdure among the many-colored marble debris. In the distance, I cast my gaze over the isthmus, a twofold sea, faraway islands, charming countryside, bluish lakes, and azure mountains; I scanned the forests, ships, aqueducts, Moorish villages, Mohammedan hermitages, minarets, and white buildings of Tunis. Millions of starlings, assembled in battalions and resembling clouds, flew above my head. Surrounded by the greatest and most moving memories, I thought of Dido, Sophonisba, Hasdrubal's noble wife; I contemplated the vast plains where the legions of Hannibal, Scipio, and Caesar lie buried; my eyes sought out the site of the palace in Utica. Alas, the ruins of Tiberius's palace still exist in Capri, but one searches in vain for the place where Cato's house stood in Utica. The terrible Vandals and the frivolous Moors passed in turn through my memory, which offered me, as a last tableau, Saint Louis dying among the ruins of Carthage.

Like me, Julian takes his last look at Africa in Carthage.

JULIEN'S ITINERARY

On the seventh and eighth we walked in the ruins of Carthage, where a few foundations are still level with the ground, which proves the durability of ancient building methods. There are also hollows for baths now submerged by the sea. Three fine cisterns still exist, and one can also see others, which have filled in. The few inhabitants who live in the area work the land necessary to their survival. They harvest various marbles and stones, as well as medallions, which they sell to travelers as antiquities: Monsieur bought some of these to bring back to France.

3.
FROM TUNIS TO MY RETURN TO FRANCE THROUGH SPAIN

JULIEN briefly recounts our crossing from Tunis to the Bay of Gibraltar. From Algeciras, he quickly moves on to Cádiz and from Cádiz to Granada. Indifferent to Blanca, all he notes is that "the Alhambra and other lofty buildings stand on immensely high rocks." My own *Itinerary* does not offer many more details about Granada. I content myself with saying "the Alhambra seems to me worthy of note, even after the temples of Greece. The valley of Granada is delightful and looks a great deal like Sparta. One understands why the Moors mourn for such a country as this."

I describe the Alhambra in detail in *The Last of the Abencérages*. The Alhambra, the Generalife, and the Sacromonte have engraved themselves in my memory like those imaginary landscapes that, often at the break of day, we believe we glimpse in a fine ray of dawn. I still feel I have a sufficient sense of nature to depict the Vega, but I would not dare attempt it for fear of the "archbishop of Granada."[3] During my sojourn in the city of sultans, a guitarist, driven by an earthquake from a village I had just passed through, became devoted to me. Deaf as a post, he followed me everywhere: when I sat on a ruin in the Moorish palace, he stood singing by my side, accompanying himself on his guitar. The tuneful beggar would perhaps not have composed the symphony of the *Creation*, but his bronzed chest showed through his ragged shirt, and he might well have written, as Beethoven did to Mademoiselle von Breuning:

"My highly esteemed Eleonore, my dearest friend, I am anxious to be so fortunate as again to possess an Angola waistcoat knitted by your own hand."[4]

I crisscrossed the country of Spain, where Heaven reserved a great role for me sixteen years later, helping stifle anarchy among a noble people and saving a Bourbon's life. The honor of our arms was reestablished, and I would have rescued the Legitimacy, if the Legitimacy had been capable of understanding what conditions would allow it to endure.

Julien did not leave my side until he had brought me back to the Place Louis XV, on June 5, 1807, at three o'clock in the afternoon. From Granada, he went with me to Aranjuez, Madrid, and El Escorial, at which point he skips forward to Bayonne:

"We left Bayonne," he writes in his itinerary, "on Tuesday, May 9, for Pau, Tarbes, Barèges, and Bordeaux, where we arrived on the 18th very tired and both feeling feverish. We left again on the 19th and went to Angoulême and Tours, and arrived on the 28th in Blois, where we slept the night. On the 31st, we continued on our way to Orléans and made our last stop, in Angerville."

There I was, five miles from a house whose inhabitants my long voyage had not caused me to forget.[5] But where were the gardens of Armida? Two or three times, returning to the Pyrenees, I have caught sight, from the highway, of the column in Méréville; like Pompey's Pillar, it spoke to me of the desert: like my seafaring fortunes, everything has changed.

I arrived in Paris in advance of the news I had sent there: I had outpaced my life. As insignificant as these notes are, I riffle through them the way one pores over second-rate representations of the places one has visited. These notes posted from Methoni, Athens, Zea, Smyrna, and Constantinople, from Jaffa, Jerusalem, Alexandria, Tunis, Granada, Madrid, and Burgos; these lines scrawled on all sorts of paper with all sorts of ink, carried by every wind, interest me. I even love unrolling my firmans; I touch their vellum with pleasure, I am delighted by the elegant calligraphy, I am amazed by the pomposity of their style. What a great personage I was then! We are rather poor devils, with our three-sou letters and our forty-sou passports, compared with those turbaned lords.

Osman Seïd, pasha of Morea, addresses whomever it may concern in my firman for Athens:

Men of law of the townships of Misitra and Argos, qadis, nabobs, and effendis, may your wisdom ever increase; honor of your peers and our grandees, vaivodes, and you through whose eyes your master sees, who assume his place in each of your jurisdictions, men of position and men of business, whose credit can only increase:

We inform you that among the nobles of France, one particular noble from Paris, the bearer of this order, accompanied by an armed janissary and a servant, has requested permission and explained his intention to pass through some of the places and localities within your jurisdictions in order to travel to Athens, which is an isthmus lying beyond, and separate from, your jurisdictions.

Effendis, vaivodes, and all others named above, when the aforesaid personage arrives in the places under your jurisdiction, you shall take the greatest care that he be treated with all the particular consideration which friendship makes a law, etc., etc.

Year 1221 of the Hegira.

My passport from Constantinople for Jerusalem reads:

To the sublime tribunal of His Excellency the Qadi of Kouds (Jerusalem), most venerable effendi Scherif:

Venerable effendi, may Your Excellency seated on your august tribunal accept our sincere blessings and our affectionate greetings.

We inform you that a noble personage from the Court of France named François-Auguste de Chateaubriand is at present on his way toward you, to make the *holy* pilgrimage (of the Christian).

Would we likewise seek to protect the fate of an unknown traveler with words addressed to the mayors and gendarmes who will inspect his passport along the way? In these firmans, we can also see the revolution of nations at work. How many "passes" did God have to give these empires before a Tartar slave could impose his orders upon a vaivode of Misitra (that is, a magistrate in Sparta), before a Muslim could recommend a Christian to the qadi of Kouds (that is, Jerusalem).

The *Itinerary* has found its place among the elements that make up my life. When I set out in 1806, a pilgrimage to Jerusalem seemed a great undertaking. Now that the crowd has followed in my footsteps and everybody is packed into the diligence, the wonder of the thing has disappeared. Hardly anything remains unique to me except Tunis. People less often go in that direction, and it is agreed that I pointed out the real location of the ports of Carthage. This honorable letter from M. Dureau de La Malle proves it:

Monsieur le Vicomte,

I have just received a relief map complete with contour lines of the ground and ruins of Carthage; it has been made trigonometrically on a basis of 1,500 meters and rests upon barometrical observations made with corresponding barometers. It is a work of ten years of precision and patience, and it confirms your opinions regarding the location of the ports of Byrsa.

I have taken this exact map, gone over all the ancient texts, and, I believe, determined the outer circumference and the other portions of the Cothon, Byrsa, Megara, etc., etc. I wish to do you justice—which is your due upon so many scores.

If you are not afraid to see me swoop down upon your genius with my trigonometry and my heavy erudition, I will be with you at your first sign. If we, my father and I, follow you, in literature, *longissimo intervallo*, at least we shall have tried to imitate you in the noble independence of which you have set France such a fine example.

I have the honor to be, and I am proud of it, your frank admirer,

Dureau de la Malle

So accurate an identification of the sites would, in past centuries, have been enough to give me a name in geography. If I had, thereafter, still been infatuated with making people talk about me, who knows where I would have gone to attract the public's attention? Perhaps I would have taken up my old plan to discover a passage to the North Pole; perhaps I would have traveled up the Ganges. There, I would have seen the long black line of woods that bars the way to the Himalayas and, reaching the pass between the two principal peaks of the Gangotri, beheld the immeasurable amphitheater of the eternal snows; when I asked my guides, like the Anglican bishop of Calcutta, Heber, the name of the other mountains to the east, they would have told me that they border the Chinese Empire. Excellent stuff! But to come back to Paris from the Pyramids now is like coming back from Montlhéry.[6] I recall in this regard one pious antiquarian, who lived near Saint-Denis in France, writing to ask me whether Pontoise did not resemble Jerusalem.

The page that ends the *Itinerary* seems to have been written this very moment, so accurately does it reflect what I feel today. "For twenty years," I said, "I have dedicated myself to study amid all manner of hazard and grief, *diversa exilia et desertas quaerere terras*:[7] a great number of pages in my books have been written in tents, in deserts, on the waves; I have often gripped the pen not knowing how much longer I would live ... If Heaven grants me the peace I have yet to experience, I shall, in perfect silence, seek to raise a monument to my homeland; if Providence refuses me this peace, I must think only of keeping my last days free from the anxieties that poisoned the first. I am no longer young, I have no interest in fame. I know that literature, whose commerce is sweet in secret, invites nothing but trouble from without. In any case, I have written enough if my name is destined to survive and much too much if it is destined to vanish."

It is possible that my *Itinerary* remains a sort of manual for the use of Wandering Jews like me: I have been scrupulous about marking the waypoints and drawing the road map. Many travelers to Jerusalem have written to congratulate me and thank me for my accuracy. I will cite one witness:

> Monsieur, a few weeks ago you did me the honor of receiving me and my friend M. de Saint-Laumer at your home. Bringing you a letter from Abu Ghosh, we came to tell you how meritorious we found your *Itinerary* when it came to particular places and how much we appreciated the entire work even down to the quite humble and modest title that you chose for it, seeing it justified at each step by the scrupulous accuracy of the descriptions, which are still true today, give or take a few ruins, the only change to these regions ...
>
> Jules Folentlot
rue Caumartin, no. 23

My accuracy is due to my good common sense; I am a child of the pedestrian race of Celts and tortoises, not of the race of Tartars and birds who are endowed with horses and wings. Religion, it is true, has often ravished me in its embrace; but when it has set me down on earth again, I have walked, leaning on my stick and resting on boundary walls to lunch on olives and brown bread. If I have "most gladly and gallantly gone into the woods," as Frenchmen will do,[8] I have never loved change for change's sake; the road bores me; I love travel only because of the independence it gives me, just as I am inclined toward the countryside not for the countryside itself, but for the solitude it offers. "All skies are alike to me," says Montaigne; "let us live and laugh among our friends, let us go die and look sour among strangers."[9]

Among the things that remain to me from the Eastern lands are a few letters that reached their destination many months after they were sent. Some priests from the Holy Land, some consuls and families, supposing I had become powerful under the Restoration, wrote me to request the rights of hospitality. From afar, it is easy to be mistaken and believe what seems plausible. M. Gaspari wrote me in 1816, asking for my support on behalf of his son, and addressing this letter to "Monsieur le Vicomte de Chateaubriand, Grand Master of the Royal University in Paris."

M. Caffe,[10] not losing sight of what is happening around him and giving me news of his world, wrote me from Alexandria:

"Since your departure, the country has not improved, though peace reigns. While the leader may have nothing to fear from the Mamluks, who remain in Upper Egypt, it remains necessary to stay on guard. The Abd el Ouad are still causing trouble at Mecca. The Manouf canal has just been closed; Muhammad Ali will be remembered in Egypt for having completed this project," etc.

On August 13, 1816, M. Pangalo the Younger wrote me from Zea on August 3, 1816:

Your Lordship,

Your *Itinerary from Paris to Jerusalem* has reached Zea, and I have read aloud with my family what Your Excellency was kind enough to say of us. Your stay with us was so short that we far from merit Your Excellency's praise for our hospitality and the overly familiar manner with which we received you. We have also recently learned, with the greatest satisfaction, that Your Excellency's titles have been restored and that he occupies a rank he deserves both by merit and by birth. We congratulate him and hope that, in the heights of his grandeur, Monsieur le Comte de Chateaubriand will wish to remember Zea and the aged Pangalo's large family, a family who have served as consuls of France since the reign of Louis the Great, who signed our father's brevet. That long-suffering elder has passed away; I have lost my father; I find myself, with a very mediocre fortune, responsible for my entire family. I have my mother, six sisters to marry off, and several widows in my charge, as well as their children. I have recourse to the goodness of

Your Excellency. I beg him to come to the aid of our family by obtaining the Vice Consulate of Zea, which is very necessary for the frequent harboring of the king's ships...

Your Excellency's very humble and very obedient servant,

M. G. Pangalo

Whenever the slightest smirk plays upon my lips, I am punished as if for a transgression. This letter filled me with regret when I reread a passage (softened, it is true, by expressions of gratitude) about the hospitality of our consuls in the Levant:

"The Pangalo daughters," I say in the *Itinerary*, "sang 'Ah! vous dirai-je, maman?' in Greek. M. Pangalo shouted aloud, the roosters crowed, and thoughts of Iulis, Aristo, and Simonides were completely obliterated."[11]

These requests for my assistance almost always arrive in the midst of my discredits and woes. At the very beginning of the Restoration, on October 11, 1814, I received this other letter sent from Paris:

Monsieur l'Ambassadeur,

Mademoiselle Dupont, from Saint Pierre and Miquelon, who had the honor of meeting you on those islands, requests a brief audience with Your Excellency. As she knows that you live in the country, she implores you to inform her when you are in Paris and can grant her this audience.

Dupont

Memory is so ungrateful, I no longer recalled this young woman I met during my travels on the other side of the ocean. Yet I have retained a perfect recollection of the unknown girl who sat beside me in the sadness of the frozen Cyclades:

"A young fisher-girl appeared on the upper declivities of the crag. Her knees were bare despite the cold, and she walked barefoot in the dew."

Circumstances beyond my control kept me from seeing Mademoiselle Dupont. If, by chance, she was Guillaumy's fiancée, how would a quarter century have changed her? Had she been ravaged by the New World's winters, or did she retain the spring freshness of the beans in flower, sheltered in the moat of the fort on Saint Pierre?

In their preface to an excellent translation of the letters of Saint Jerome, M. Collombet and M. Grégoire sought to find, on the subject of Judea, a resemblance between this saint and myself which, with respect, I do not accept. Saint Jerome, in the depths of his solitude, depicted his inner struggles: I could never have approached the Bethlehemite cave dweller's expressions of genius; at most, I might have sung with Saint Francis, my patron saint in France and my host at the Holy Sepulchre,[12] those two canticles in Italian, from the era that precedes the Italian of Dante:

> *In foco l'amor mi mise,*
> *In foco l'amor mi mise.*[13]

I love receiving letters from overseas. These letters seem to bring me some murmur of the winds, some ray of the suns, some emanation from the different destinies that waters divide and that memories of hospitality bind together. Would I like to see these distant countries again? One or two, perhaps. The sky of Attica produced an enchantment in me that has never been effaced; my imagination is still perfumed with the myrtles near the temple of Aphrodite of the Gardens and the iris along the banks of the Cephissus.

Before Fénelon left for Greece, he wrote Bossuet a letter in which the future author of *Télémaque* reveals the ardor of a missionary and a poet:

> Various trifling occurrences have hitherto delayed my return to Paris, but at last, Your Lordship, I am about to start, and I shall make good speed! But I am contemplating a lengthier journey. The whole of Greece lies open before me—the Sultan

is retreating, Peloponnesus already breathes at ease, and the Church of Corinth will revive and lend its ear once more to the voice of the Apostle. I fancy myself transported to those glorious scenes, among those precious ruins, harvesting the very spirit of antiquity from their venerable rubble. I long to seek out that Areopagus from which Saint Paul proclaimed the Unknown God to heathen sages. Then, following what is sacred, come profaner memories, and I do not disdain to descend to Piraeus, and Socrates planning his Republic. I ascend the twin summits of Parnassus, I gather the Delphic laurels, and revel in the charms of Tempe.

When will Turkish and Persian blood mingle on the plains of Marathon, and leave Greece to religion, philosophy, and art, whose true home she is?

Arva, beata
Petamus arva, divites et insulas.[14]

Neither shall I forget thee, island consecrated by the heavenly visions of the Beloved Disciple! Oh, blessed Patmos, I will hasten to kiss the footprints left on thee by the Apostle, and to imagine Heaven opened to my gaze! To burn with indignation at the false prophet who presumed to interpret the oracles of the true; and to bless the Almighty, who, instead of casting down the Church, like Babylon, has chained the dragon, and led her to victory. Already I see schism healed, East and West reunited, Asia waking to the light after her long sleep; the Holy Land, once trodden by our Savior's Feet and watered with His Blood, delivered from profaners and filled with new glory; the children of Abraham, more numerous than the stars, now scattered over the face of the earth, gathered from all her quarters to confess the Christ they crucified, and to rise again with Him. But enough of all this, Your Lordship. You will be glad to know that this is my last letter, and the end of my enthusiasm, which may perhaps be troublesome. Forgive me on the plea of my need to pour it out to you from afar, until I can do so in person.[15]

This was the true second Homer, the only man worthy of singing Greece and recounting its beauty to the latter-day Chrysostom.

4.

REFLECTIONS ON MY VOYAGE—DEATH OF JULIEN

I RETAIN nothing of the sites of Syria, Egypt, and the Punic lands except what was in harmony with my solitary nature. These places pleased me for reasons that had nothing to do with antiquity, art, or history. The Pyramids impressed me, not because of their immensity but because of the desert against which they were raised. Diocletian's columns held my attention less than the scalloped edges of the sea on the Libyan sands. At the Pelusiac mouth of the Nile, I would not have wanted a monument to remind me of this scene painted by Plutarch:

> Philip the freedman sought up and down about the sands until at last he found some rotten planks of a little fishing boat, not much, but enough to make up a funeral pyre for a naked body, and that not quite entire. As he was busy gathering and putting these old planks together, an old Roman citizen, who in his youth had served in the wars under Pompey, came up to him and demanded who he was that was preparing the funeral of Pompey the Great. And Philip answering that he was his freedman, "Nay, then," said he, "you shall not have this honor alone; let even me, too, I pray you, have my share in such a pious office that I may not altogether repent me of this pilgrimage in a strange land, but in compensation of many misfortunes, may obtain this happiness at last, even with mine own hands to touch the body of Pompey, and do the last duties to the greatest general among the Romans."[16]

Caesar's rival no longer rests in Libyan soil, yet a young Libyan slave was given a tomb by a woman called Pompeia near the same city of Rome from which the great Pompey was banished. Considering these games that fortune plays, it is easy to understand why the Christians went to hide in the Thebaid.[17]

> Born in Libya, buried a virgin in Ausonian earth, I lie on this sandy shore near Rome. Pompeia who reared me wept for me as for a daughter and laid me, a slave, in a freewoman's grave. The flames upon my funeral pyre forestalled the flames of my nuptials. Persephone's torch betrayed our hopes.[18]

The people of Europe, Asia, and Africa I met have been scattered to the winds. One fell from the Acropolis in Athens, another from the rocks on Chios. One threw himself from Mount Zion and others failed to emerge from the waters of the Nile or the cisterns of Carthage. The places, too, have changed: as American cities have been built where once I saw forests, so an empire has formed in the sands of Egypt, where my own gaze met only the "bare horizons round like the bump of a shield," as the Arab poems say, "and wolves so thin that their jaws are like stick splinters."[19] Greece has regained the liberty I wished it would regain as I crossed it in the custody of a janissary. But does she enjoy her national liberty, or has she merely changed yokes?

I am, in a certain sense, the last person to visit the Turkish empire while it still practiced its old way of life. Revolutions, which precede or follow me everywhere I go, have spread across Greece, Syria, and Egypt. Is a new Orient coming into being? What will emerge from it? Will we receive the punishment we deserve for having taught the modern art of warfare to nations whose social state is founded on slavery and polygamy? Have we carried civilization abroad, or have we brought barbarism into Christendom? What will result from the new interests, the new political relations, and the creation of the powers that might emerge in the Levant? No man can tell. I will not let myself be impressed by a few steamboats and railroads, by the sale of manufacturers' products, or by the wealth of a handful of French-men, Englishmen, Germans, and Italians enrolled in the service of a pasha. All that is not civilization. We may perhaps see the return, by means of the disciplined troops of future Ibrahims, of the dangers that menaced Europe in the age of Charles Martel and were averted thanks only to the generosity of Poland. I pity the travelers who will follow me: the harem will no longer hide its secrets from them. They will never see the old sun of the Orient and the turban of Muham-mad. The little Bedouin cried to me, in French, as I was passing through the mountains of Judea: "Forward march!" The order was given, and the Orient marched.

And the shipmate of Ulysses, Julien—what became of him? He had asked, when he gave me his manuscript, to be the concierge in my house on rue d'Enfer; but this position was occupied by an old porter and his family whom I could not send away. Heaven's wrath having made Julien willful and a drunkard, I supported him for a long time. Finally, we were obliged to go our separate ways. I gave him a small sum and arranged for a little pension from my coffer, which is fairly insubstantial, but always copiously filled with excellent notes borrowed against my castles in Spain. At his own request, I had Julien admitted to the Old Men's Hospital, where he finished the last great voyage. I will soon go and fill his empty bed, as I once lay down to sleep, in the camp at Emir Capi, on the mat from which a plague-stricken Muslim had just been carried away. My vocation is plainly for the almshouse, where the old society lies. It pretends to be living and is nevertheless at death's door. When it has passed away, it will rot and be reproduced in new forms; but first it must succumb. The first necessity for peoples, as for men, is to die: "When God bloweth there cometh frost," says Job.[20]

5.

1807, 1808, 1809, 1810—ARTICLE IN THE *MERCURE*, JUNE 1807—I BUY THE VALLÉE-AUX-LOUPS AND RETIRE THERE

Paris, 1839; Revised in June 1847

MADAME de Chateaubriand had been very ill during my voyage, and several times my friends had believed me lost. In a few notes that M. de Clausel wrote for his children and which he was good enough to let me browse, I find this passage:

> M. de Chateaubriand left on his voyage to Jerusalem in July 1806: during his absence, I have been going to see Madame de Chateaubriand every day. Our traveler had the kindness to write me a letter of several pages from Constantinople which you will find in the drawer of our bookcase in Coussergues. During the winter of 1806 to 1807, we knew that M. de Chateaubriand was at sea and returning to Europe. One day I was walking in the Tuileries Garden with M. de Fontanes in a frightful westerly wind; we took shelter on the terrace by the pond. M. de Fontanes said to me: "Perhaps at this very moment, a gust of this dreadful wind is about to wreck his ship." We have since learned this presentiment was very nearly realized. I note this to express the keen friendship; the interest in M. de Chateaubriand's literary glory, which this voyage was bound to increase; the noble, profound, and rare feelings that animated M. de Fontanes, an excellent man from whom I have also received great services and whom I urge you to remember in your prayers to God.

If my name survives and if, through my work, I could make the people who are dear to me survive, with what pleasure I would take all my friends with me!

Filled with hope, I brought back under my roof my fistful of gleanings, but this period of peace was not destined to last long.

Through a series of arrangements, I had become the sole proprietor of the *Mercure*. At the end of June 1807, M. Alexandre de Laborde published a travelogue of Spain. In July, I published the article I quoted when speaking of the death of the Duc d'Enghien. Bonaparte's successes, far from subjugating me, had revolted me. The energy of my feelings and my fire had redoubled; my face had not been darkened by the sun in vain: I was not delivered from heaven's wrath to tremble with blackened brow before one man's rage. If Napoleon had washed his hands of kings, he had not washed his hands of me. My article, appearing amid his successes and marvels, shocked France. Innumerable copies passed from hand to hand; many of the *Mercure*'s subscribers cut the article out and had it separately bound. It was read aloud in salons and peddled from house to house. One would need to have been alive during those years to form an idea of the effect produced by a voice ringing out alone in the universal silence. The noble sentiments driven down into the depths of men's hearts were revived. Napoleon lashed out: we are irritated less by an offense in itself than by the offense to the idea that we have formed of ourselves. What! Would I scorn him even in his glory; would I risk my life a second time at the feet of the man who had brought the world to its knees? "Does Chateaubriand think I am an imbecile—that I don't understand him? I shall have him cut down on the steps of the Tuileries!" He gave the order to suppress the *Mercure* and have me arrested. My property was lost; my person miraculously escaped. Bonaparte had to deal with the world; he forgot about me, but I remained under the onus of his threat.

My position was a deplorable one. When I thought I was bound to act according to the inspirations of my honor, I found myself burdened by both my personal responsibilities and the sufferings of my wife. Her courage was great, but she suffered nonetheless, and these storms, called down one after another on my head, upset her. She had suffered so much for me during the Revolution! It was natural that she desired a bit of rest. All the more so since Madame de Chateaubriand admired Bonaparte without reservation. She had no illusions about the Legitimacy. She never ceased predicting to me what would befall me if the Bourbons really did return.

The first book of these *Memoirs* is dated October 4, 1811, from the Vallée-aux-Loups. There you will find the description of this little retreat I bought to hide myself away during these years. Leaving our apartment in Madame de Coislin's attic, we first went to stay on rue des Saints-Pères in the Hôtel de Lavalette, which took its name from the mistress and master of the house.

M. de Lavalette, squat, dressed in a plum-colored coat, walking with a gold-pommeled cane, became my business representative, if indeed I have ever had any business. He had been a cook for the king, and whatever I did not consume, he drank.

Toward the end of November, seeing that the repairs to my cottage were not progressing, I decided to go oversee them myself. We arrived at night in the Vallée. We took the usual road, entering through the gate at the bottom of the garden. The soil in the alleys, soaked by the rain, bogged down the horses. The carriage overturned. The plaster bust of Homer sitting next to Madame de Chateaubriand jumped out the door and broke its neck. A bad omen for *The Martyrs*, at which I was then at work.

The house, full of laborers laughing, singing, and banging, was warmed by wood shavings and lit by candle-ends. At night, in the woods, it looked like a hermitage illumined by pilgrims. Delighted to find two rooms passably furnished—and in one of which a meal had been prepared—we sat down at the table. The next day, woken by hammering and singing, I watched the sun rise with far fewer worries than the master of the Tuileries.

I was endlessly enchanted. Though no Madame de Sévigné, I went, shod in a pair of wooden clogs, to plant my trees in the mud, to walk the same alleys up and down, to look and look again at every little corner, to crouch down out of sight wherever I found a bit of brush, telling myself that this would be my park in the future, for at that time the future was still abundant. Today, searching my memory, trying to reopen a view that has been closed off, I no longer find quite the same perspective, though I do discover others. I lose myself in my vanished thoughts. The illusions I encounter are perhaps no less lovely than earlier ones; but they are no longer young. What I once saw in the splendor of the south, I now see in the light of the setting sun. —If only I could stop being harassed by dreams! Bayard, called on to surrender, replied: "Wait until I have made a bridge of corpses, so that I might cross over with my garrison." I fear that the only way I will be able to leave this world is by crossing over the corpses of my dreams.

My trees, still saplings, did not catch the sounds of the autumn winds, but in springtime the breezes that inhaled the flowers of the neighboring fields held their breath, and exhaled over my valley.

I made a few additions to the cottage. I embellished its brick wall with a portico supported by two black marble columns and two white marble caryatids: I was remembering my visit to Athens. My plan was to add a tower at one end of the house. In the meantime, I simulated battlements on the wall separating me from the road. Thus I anticipated the medieval mania that stupefies us at present. Of all the things that have escaped me, the Vallée-aux-Loups is the only one I miss. But I cannot keep hold of anything. After losing the Vallée, I built the Infirmerie de Marie-Thérèse, and again, I have just had to leave it. I defy fate to burden me now with even the smallest parcel of earth. My only garden henceforth will be the avenues honored with such fine names around the Invalides, where I stroll with my limping or one-armed colleagues. Not far from these alleys, Madame de Beaumont's cypress rears its head. In these desert spaces, the great and light-footed Duchesse de Châtillon once leaned on my arm. These days I offer my arm only to Time: she is very heavy!

I worked on my *Memoirs* with pleasure and *The Martyrs* progressed; I had already read some books of it to M. de Fontanes. I had housed myself amid my memories as though in an enormous library: I consulted this one or that one, then closed the register with a sigh, for I saw that the light, when it shone there, destroyed the mystery. Shine a light on the days of your life, and they will no longer be what they are.

In July 1808, I fell ill and was obliged to return to Paris. The doctors made the illness perilous. In the days of Hippocrates, there was a deficit of dead men in the underworld, says the epigram: thanks to our modern Hippocrates, there is a surfeit today.

This was perhaps the only time when, at death's door, I desired to go on living. Whenever I felt myself growing faint, which was often, I would say to Madame de Chateaubriand: "Don't you worry; I will come to." I lost consciousness, but with a great inner impatience, for I held on, God knows to what. I was passionate about finishing what I believed and still believe to be my most correct work, but I was also paying the price for the fatigue I had suffered during my travels in the Levant.

Girodet had put the finishing touches to my portrait. He made me look gloomy, as I then was; but he put all his genius into the picture. M. Denon took the masterpiece for the Salon[21] and like a noble courtier hid it prudently from sight. When Bonaparte reviewed the gallery, he said, after scanning the paintings, "Where is the portrait of Chateaubriand?" He knew it must be there, and they were forced to bring the outcast from his hiding place. Bonaparte, whose fit of generosity had ended, said:

"He looks like one of those conspirators who come down the chimney."

One day, coming back to the Vallée alone, I was informed by Benjamin, the gardener, that a strange fat gentleman had asked to see me. Not finding me in, he said he would wait for me, ordered the cook to make him an omelet, went upstairs, and hurled himself on my bed. I went up, entered my bedroom, and saw something enormous sleeping there. Shaking this mass of flesh, I cried out: "Eh! Eh! Who are you?" The mass quivered and sat upright. It wore a furry hat on its head and a speckled wool top and trousers sewn together; its face was stained with tobacco and its tongue was hanging out. It was my cousin Moreau! I had not seen him since Thionville. He had returned from Russia and wished to enter public service. My old cicerone in Paris went off to die in Nantes. Thus one of the first characters to appear in these *Memoirs* vanished. I hope that, stretched out on a bed of asphodels, he still talks up my verse to Madame de Chastenay, if that charming shade has gone down to the Elysian Fields.

6.

THE MARTYRS

IN THE spring of 1809, *The Martyrs* appeared. The work was painstaking: I had consulted knowledgeable critics of taste (Fontanes, Bertin, Boissonnade, Malte-Brun), and I had submitted to their arguments. I wrote, unwrote, and rewrote the same page a hundred times or more. Of all my writings, it is the one whose language is the most correct.

I was not mistaken in the scheme of the book. Today, when my ideas have become commonplace, no one denies that the struggle between two religions, one dying and the other being born, offers one of the richest, most fertile, and most dramatic subjects. For this reason, I thought I might harbor some not too far-fetched hopes, but I was forgetting the success of my previous work. In this country, you can never count on two successes in a row. One success annihilates the next. If you have some talent in prose, think twice about showing it off in verse; if you are respected in literature, lay no claim to politics. Such is the French way of thinking—and its poverty. The selfish insecurities and jealousies awakened by an author's successful debut conspire and lie in ambush for his second publication so as to exact their dazzling revenge:

> Everybody with his fingers in the *inkwell* vows to take vengeance.[22]

I had to pay for the foolish admiration I had underhandedly won with the appearance of *The Genius of Christianity* and return what I had stolen! Alas, they should not have gone to so much trouble to rob me of what I myself didn't think I deserved. If I had liberated Christian Rome, all I would request is a crown of grass, harvested from the Eternal City.

The executor of the justice of the vanities was M. Hoffmann, to whom God grant peace! The *Journal des Débats* was under state control; its owners no longer had power over its contents, and censorship relegated me to condemnation. M. Hoffmann spared the battle of the Franks and a few other pieces of the work; but if Cymodocée appealed to him, he was too good a Catholic not to be indignant about the profane reconciliation of Christian truths and mythological fables. Velléda did not save me. I was charged with the crime of having transformed the German druidess into a Gallic woman— as if I had wanted to borrow anything beyond a sweet-sounding name! And here were the Christians of France, to whom I had rendered such great services by rebuilding their altars, rushing to be stupidly scandalized at the gospel word of M. Hoffmann! The title of *The Martyrs* had misled them; they were expecting to read a martyrology, and the tiger who ripped only a daughter of Homer to pieces seemed a sacrilege to them.

The actual martyrdom of Pope Pius VII, whom Bonaparte had brought as a prisoner to Paris, did not scandalize them, but they were quite roused by my unchristian fictions, as they were called. The Bishop of Chartres[23] himself undertook to do justice to my horrible impieties. Alas! He must now realize his zeal is needed for quite different battles.

The Bishop of Chartres is the brother of my esteemed friend M. de Clausel, a faithful Christian who has never let himself be carried away by a virtuousness so sublime as that of his sibling the critic.

I thought I should respond to my censure, as I had done with *The Genius of Christianity*; I was emboldened by Montesquieu's defense of his *Spirit of the Laws*. But I was wrong. Authors who have been attacked might say the finest things in the world, and they will only excite the laughter of impartial minds and the mockeries of the crowd. They place themselves on poor terrain: the defensive position is disagreeable to the French character. When, to answer objections, I pointed out that, by stigmatizing this or that passage, they were attacking some fine relic of antiquity, finding themselves beaten on the facts, they dodged and said *The Martyrs* was no more than a "pastiche." If I proved the simultaneous presence of the two religions, citing the Church Fathers, they replied that, by the era in which I had set the action of *The Martyrs*, the great minds had given up on paganism.

I thought in good faith that the work had failed. The violence of the attack had shaken my authorial conviction. A few friends consoled me, maintaining that the ban was unjustified and that the public, sooner or later, would issue another ruling. M. de Fontanes especially was firm: I was no Racine, but he might have been Boileau, and he never ceased to say to me, "They will come around to it." His conviction in this regard was so profound that it inspired him to a few charming stanzas—"Tasso, wandering from town to town," etc.— without fear of compromising his taste or the authority of his judgment.

Indeed, *The Martyrs* has risen from the dust. It has had the honor of four consecutive editions and has even enjoyed a particular favor among men of letters. They have expressed their appreciation for a work that testifies to serious study, some pains taken as to style, and a great respect for language and taste.

Criticism of the subject matter was promptly abandoned. To say that I had mixed the profane with the sacred because I had depicted two religions that existed at the same time, each with its own beliefs, altars, priests, and ceremonies, would have been like saying I ought to have renounced history itself. For whom did the martyrs die? For Jesus Christ. To whom were they sacrificed? To the gods of the Empire. There were thus two religions.

The philosophical question regarding whether, under Diocletian, the Romans and Greeks believed in the gods of Homer, and whether public worship had undergone changes, did not concern me as a *poet*; as a *historian*, I might have had a great number of things to say.

None of this matters anymore. *The Martyrs* has endured, contrary to what I first expected, and I have only had to revise the text with care. The fault of the book is the fantastic *directness* that, with what remained of my classical prejudices, I had awkwardly employed. Affrighted by my own innovations, it seemed impossible for me to make do without a "heaven" and "hell." The good and bad angels sufficed, however, to keep the action going, without relying on this worn-out machinery. If the battle of the Franks, Velléda, Jérôme, Augustin, Eudore, Cymodocée, and the descriptions of Naples and Greece do not pardon *The Martyrs*, there is no heaven or hell that will save it. One of the passages that pleased M. de Fontanes most was this one:

> Cymodocée sat by the prison window and, resting her head, adorned with the martyrs' veil, in her hand, sighed these harmonious words:
>
> "Light vessels of Ausonia, rend the calm and brilliant sea; slaves of Neptune, leave the sail to the loving breath of the winds and bend over the nimble oar. Restore me to the protection of my husband and my father, on the fortunate shores of Pamisus.
>
> "Fly, birds of Lybia, whose pliant necks so gracefully curve, fly to the summit of Ithome and say that a daughter of Homer is coming to gaze upon the laurels of Messenia once more!
>
> When shall I return to my ivory bed, to the daylight so dear to mortals, to the meadows scattered with flowers that a pure stream waters and modesty adorns with its breath?

The Genius of Christianity will remain my great work, for it produced or determined a revolution and initiated a new literary era. It is not the same with *The Martyrs*, which came after the revolution and only served as superabundant proof of my doctrines. My style was no longer a novelty, and even, apart from the episode of Velléda and the depiction of the mores of the Francs, my writing is too marked by its influences. The classical overpowers the romantic.

Finally, the circumstances that contributed to the success of *The Genius of Christianity* no longer existed. The government, far from being favorable to me, was against me. *The Martyrs* earned me the renewed attention of persecution. The striking allusions in the portrait of Galérius and the description of the Court of Diocletian could not escape the notice of the imperial police—all the more so since the English translator, who had no reason to be circumspect and who did not care a whit about compromising me, had, in his preface, pointed out these allusions.

The publication of *The Martyrs* coincided with a fatal occurrence. This did not disarm the aristarchs, whose ardor was far too inflamed by the force in power; they felt that literary criticism that tended to diminish the interest attached to my name might be pleasing to Bonaparte, and he—like those millionaire bankers who throw huge banquets and charge you for mailing your letters—did not neglect his lesser profits.

7.

ARMAND DE CHATEAUBRIAND

ARMAND de Chateaubriand, whom you have seen as my boyhood friend and encountered again in the Army of Princes with Libba the deaf and dumb, had stayed behind in England. Married on Jersey, he was entrusted with transporting the correspondence of the Princes. Setting sail on September 25, 1808, he found his bearings on Brittany that same day, at eleven o'clock at night, near Saint-Cast. The crew of his boat consisted of eleven men: only two were French, Roussel and Quintal.

Once ashore, Armand went to the house of M. Delaunay-Boisé-Lucas the Elder, who lived in the village of Saint-Cast, where the English had, long ago, been driven back to their ships.[24] His host advised him to depart at once, but the boat was already on its way back to Jersey. Armand, having made arrangements with M. Boisé-Lucas's son, gave him the packages entrusted to him by M. Henri Larivière, an agent of the Princes.

"I went down to the coast on September 29," he said during one of his interrogations, "where I stayed two nights without seeing my boat. The moon being very bright, I went away and came back on October 14 or 15. I stayed until October 24. I spent every night among the rocks, but to no avail; my boat did not come, and I spent the days with Boisé-Lucas. The same boat and the same crew, including Roussel and Quintal, were supposed to come fetch me. Regarding the precautions taken with M. Boisé-Lucas the Elder, there were none other than those I have already described to you."

The intrepid Armand, landing a stone's throw from his paternal fields as if on the inhospitable coast of Taurida, swept his gaze over the moonlit waves in vain, searching for the boat that might have saved him. Many years earlier, when I had left Combourg and was preparing to travel to the Indies, I cast my melancholy eyes over those waters. Between the rocks of Saint-Cast where Armand hid and the Pointe de la Varde where I sat, a few leagues of sea, traversed by our mirrored stares, have borne witness to the troubles, and separated the destinies, of two men united by name and blood. It was on this same choppy sea that I met Gesril for the last time. Again and again, in my dreams, I see Gesril and Armand washing their wounded brows in the depths, while the water where we used to play in our childhoods turns red and laps at my feet.*

Armand managed to embark on a boat bought in Saint-Malo, but driven back by the northwest wind, he was again forced to lower the sails. Finally, on January 6, aided by a sailor named Jean Brien, he put to sea in a little rowboat that had washed ashore and got hold of another afloat. He gives an account of his journey, which seems to be under the same star as my own adventures, in his interrogation of March 18:

> From nine o'clock at night, when we set out, until two o'clock in the morning, the weather favored us. Judging then that we were not far from the rocks called the Minquiers, we dropped anchor, intending to wait for daylight; but, the wind, having freshened, and afraid it would grow still stronger, we continued on our course. A few minutes later, the sea became very rough and, our compass having been broken by a wave, we were uncertain of which way to go. The first lands we sighted on the seventh (it was perhaps about midday) were the coasts of Normandy and Jersey, which forced us to tack, and once again we dropped anchor, near the rocks called Écrého between the coasts of Normandy and Jersey. Strong and contrary winds

*The documents relating to Armand's trial were sent to me by an anonymous and generous hand.

obliged us to remain in this situation the whole rest of the day and the day of the eighth. On the morning of the ninth, as soon as it was light, I said to Depagne that it seemed to me the wind had died down, given our boat was not rolling or pitching, and that we ought to see which way the wind was blowing. He told me he could no longer make out the rocks where we had dropped anchor. I understood then that we were drifting and had lost our anchor. The violence of the storm left us no other recourse except to launch ourselves toward the coast. Since we could not see the land, I did not know how far we were from it. That was when I threw my papers in the sea, though not before taking the precaution of weighting them with a stone. We then scudded before the wind and made landfall at about nine o'clock in the morning, at Bretteville-sur-Ay, in Normandy.

We were greeted at the coast by the customs agents, who dragged me from my boat at death's door, with my feet and legs frozen. We were both lodged at the house of the lieutenant of the Bretteville brigade. Two days later, Depagne was taken to the Coutances prison and I have not seen him since. A few days after that, I myself was transferred to the jail of that town and the next day taken by the marshal to Saint-Lô, where I stayed for eight hours with this same marshal. I appeared once before the prefect of the *département* and on January 26 went with the captain and the marshal of the gendarmes to be transported to Paris, where I arrived on the twenty-eighth. I was taken to the office of M. Demaret, at police headquarters, and from there to the prison called La Grande Force.

Armand had the winds, the waves, and the imperial police against him; Bonaparte was in connivance with the storms. The gods expended no small amount of wrath in dealing with this one man's ragged existence.

The packet he had thrown into the sea washed up on the beach of Notre-Dame-d'Alloue, near Valognes. The papers contained in this packet—thirty-two in all—were used to convict them. Quintal, who

had come back to the beaches of Brittany with his boat to retrieve
Armand, had also, by the dictates of froward fate, been shipwrecked
in the waters off Normandy a few days prior to my cousin. The crew
of Quintal's boat had talked. The prefect of Saint-Lô had known M.
de Chateaubriand was the leader of these expeditions for the Princes.
When he learned that a boat with only two men had run aground,
he had no doubt Armand was one of the two shipwrecked sailors, for
all the fishermen spoke of him as of the most fearless man they had
ever seen at sea.

On January 20, 1809, the prefect of Manche reported Armand's
arrest to the police. His letter begins as follows:

> My conjectures are completely verified: Chateaubriand has
> been arrested; it is he who landed on the coast of Bretteville
> and who had taken the name of "John Fall."
>
> Worried that, despite the very precise orders I had given,
> John Fall had not arrived in Saint-Lô, I ordered Marshal Mauduit,
> a trustworthy and energetic man, to track down this John Fall
> wherever he may be and bring him to me in whatever state he
> found him. He came upon him in Coutances, just as they were
> arranging to transfer him to the hospital, to treat his legs, which
> were frozen.
>
> Fall appeared before me today. I had had Lièvre put in a
> separate room, from which he could see John Fall arrive with-
> out being observed. When Lièvre saw him coming up a flight
> of stairs near this room, he exclaimed, clapping his hands and
> changing color:
>
> "It's Chateaubriand! How did they catch him?"
>
> Lièvre was in no way forewarned. This exclamation took
> him by surprise. He begged me not to say that he had named
> Chateaubriand, for then he would be lost.
>
> I did not let John Fall know that I knew who he was.

Armand was transported to Paris, lodged at La Force, and underwent a secret interrogation at L'Abbaye, the military prison. Bertrand,

captain of the first demi-brigade of veterans, had been appointed by General Hulin, who had become the military commander of Paris, to serve as the judge-rapporteur of the military commission charged, by a decree of February 25, with inquiring into Armand's case.

The persons compromised were M. de Goyon, sent to Brest by Armand, and M. de Boisé-Lucas the Younger, entrusted with the task of delivering letters from Henri de Larivière to M. Laya and M. Sicard in Paris.

In a letter written March 13, addressed to Fouché, Armand said:

"May the Emperor deign to set at liberty the men who languish in prisons for having shown me too much kindness. In any event, let them all be set free. I recommend my ill-fated family to the generosity of the Emperor."

These misjudgments made by a man with human innards, addressing a hyena, are painful. Bonaparte was, besides, not the lion of Florence; he did not relinquish the child at the sight of the mother's tears.[25] I wrote to request an audience with Fouché. He granted me one and assured me, with frivolous revolutionary aplomb, that he had seen Armand, that I could rest easy, that Armand had said he would die well, and that in fact he "seemed rather intent on it." If I had suggested that Fouché himself should die, would he still have used such a steely tone with such superb insouciance?

I went to speak with Madame de Rémusat and begged her to take a letter to the Empress asking the emperor for justice or mercy. Madame la Duchesse de Saint-Leu told me, in Arenenberg, the fate of my letter: Josephine gave it to the emperor; he seemed to hesitate while reading it, then came upon some words that offended him and tossed it impatiently in the fire. I had forgotten that no one is supposed to admit he is proud of anyone but himself.

M. de Goyon, condemned together with Armand, received the same sentence. However, Madame la Baronne-Duchesse de Montmorency, the daughter of Madame de Matignon, with whom the Goyons were allied, had interceded on his behalf. A Montmorency should have been enough to obtain anything, if prostituting a name were enough to make peace between a new power and an old monarchy.

In any case, Madame de Goyon, who could not save her husband, did save the young Boisé-Lucas. All sorts of people became involved in this tragedy that struck men no one had ever heard of. You might have thought the downfall of a world was at stake: tempests upon the waters, ambushes on shore, Bonaparte, the sea, the murderers of Louis XVI, and perhaps some *passion*, the mysterious lifeblood of sublunary calamities. But no, no one has even taken notice of any of these things; they have struck only me and have survived only in my memory. What did Napoleon care about the insects he crushed against his crown?

The day of the execution, I wanted to accompany my friend to his final battleground. I could not find a cab, I ran on foot to the Plain of Grenelle. I arrived, covered in sweat, a second too late: Armand had been shot against the outer wall of Paris. His face was shattered; a butcher's dog was licking up his blood and brains. I followed the cart that carried the bodies of Armand and his two companions, plebeian and noble, Quintal and Goyon, to the Cimetière de Vaugirard, where I had buried M. La Harpe. I saw my cousin for the last time, and was unable to recognize him: the shot had disfigured him and his face was gone. I could not read the ravages of the years in it, or even see death in that shapeless, bloody orb. He remained young in my memory, as he was in the days of Libba. He was shot on Holy Saturday: the crucifix appears to me at the end of all my adversities. Whenever I walk on the boulevard by the Plain of Grenelle, I stop to look at the mark left by the firing squad, which is still plain to see on the wall. If Bonaparte's bullets had left no other traces, no one would talk about him any longer.

Strange interlocking of destinies! General Hulin, the military commander of Paris, appointed the commission who blew out Armand's brains. He had formerly been named chairman of the commission that shattered the Duc d'Enghien's skull. Shouldn't he have abstained, after his earlier misfortune, from any connection with a council of war? And I, I have spoken of the death of the son of the great Condé without reminding General Hulin of the part he played in the execution of the obscure soldier, my kinsman. I, for my part, must have received my commission to judge the judges of the tribunal at Vincennes from Heaven above.

8.

**1811, 1812, 1813, 1814—PUBLICATION OF THE *ITINERARY*
—LETTER FROM THE CARDINAL DE BEAUSSET—
DEATH OF CHÉNIER—I AM ADMITTED AS A MEMBER
OF THE INSTITUTE—AFFAIR OF MY SPEECH**

Paris, 1839

THE YEAR 1811 was one of the most remarkable in my literary career.

I published the *Itinerary from Paris to Jerusalem*, I took M. de Chénier's seat at the Institute, and I began to write the *Memoirs* that I am now bringing to a close.

The success of the *Itinerary* was as consummate as the success of *The Martyrs* had been disputed. There is no scribbler, however slight, who at the appearance of his farrago does not receive letters of congratulation. Among the new compliments addressed to me, I cannot allow myself to let go of a letter written by a man of virtue and merit who has composed two works whose authority is recognized, and who has left us almost nothing more to say about Bossuet or Fénelon. The Bishop of Alais, Cardinal de Beausset, is the historian of these great prelates. The cardinal went infinitely too far in praising me, which is the custom when writing to an author and means nothing; yet he manages to express the general feeling about the *Itinerary* when it was published. He discerns, relative to Carthage, the objections that might be raised against my sense of the geography, even if this sense has prevailed and I have restored Dido's ports to their proper place. His letter is, besides, a fine example of the diction of a select society, a style rendered grave and sweet by politeness, religion, and manners, with an excellence of tone that is far from us today.[26]

On January 10, 1811. M. de Chénier died. My friends had the fatal idea of urging me to replace him at the Institute.[27] They claimed that, exposed as I was to the enmities of the head of the government, the suspicion and harassment of the police, it was essential for me to become a member of a body then powerful because of its renown and because of the men who composed it. They thought that, sheltered behind this shield, I could work in peace.

I had an unconquerable repugnance for occupying seats, even outside the government; I could never forget what the first one had cost me. Becoming Chénier's successor seemed dangerous to me; I could not say what I thought without laying myself bare. I did not want to pass over regicide in silence, even if Cambacérès was Arch-Chancellor and second-in-command. I was determined to make my claims in favor of liberty heard and to raise my voice against tyranny. I wanted to have my say about the horrors of 1793, to express my regrets for the fallen family of our kings, and to mourn the misfortunes of those who remained loyal to them. My friends replied that I was deluded; that a few words of praise for the head of the government, obligatory in Academic speeches (praise that, in one respect, I thought Bonaparte deserved), would make him swallow all the truths I wished to speak; and that I would at the same time enjoy the honor of having maintained my opinions and the happiness of putting an end to Madame de Chateaubriand's terrors. They laid siege to me, and I surrendered, weary of war, but I insisted they were being taken in; that Bonaparte himself would not be taken in by a string of commonplaces about his son, his wife, and his glory; that he would only feel the sting of my message more keenly; that he would recognize the man who resigned at the death of the Duc d'Enghien and the author of the article that made him suppress the *Mercure*; that, finally, far from assuring me peace and quiet, I would end up reviving the persecutions directed against me. They were soon forced to recognize the accuracy of my predictions. It is true they had not foreseen the temerity of my speech.

I went to pay the customary visits to the members of the Academy. Madame de Vintimille took me to see the Abbé Morellet. We found him sitting in an armchair before his fire; he was asleep, and the *Itinerary*, which he was reading, had fallen from his hands. Waking with a start at the sound of my name announced by his servant, he raised his head and cried: "What monotonous passages there are! So long!" I told him, laughing, that I saw that, and would abridge the new edition. He was a good man and promised me his vote, in spite of *Atala*. When later *The Monarchy According to the Charter* appeared, he could not believe such a political work was written by the bard of "the Floridian girl." Hadn't Grotius written the tragedy *Adam and Eve*[28] and Montesquieu *The Temple of Gnide*? It is true that I was neither Grotius nor Montesquieu.

The election was held, and I was voted in by a fairly large majority. I started writing my speech right away. I wrote and rewrote it twenty times, never to my satisfaction. Sometimes, wanting to make it possible to read aloud, I found it too strongly worded; other times, anger got the better of me and I found it too tepid. I did not know how to measure out the proper dose of Academic praise. If, despite my antipathy for the man, I had wanted to express the admiration I felt for the public part of his life, I would have gone well beyond the peroration. Milton, whom I quote at the beginning of the speech, furnished me with a model; in his *Second Defense of the People of England*, he gave high-flown praise to Cromwell. He says:

> You have not only eclipsed the achievements of all our kings, but even those which have been fabled of our heroes. Often reflect what a dear pledge the beloved land of your nativity has entrusted to your care; and that liberty which she once expected only from the chosen flower of her talents and her virtues, she now expects from you only, and by you only hopes to obtain. Revere the fond expectations which we cherish, the solicitudes of your anxious country; revere the looks and the wounds of your brave companions in arms, who, under your banners, have so strenuously fought for liberty; revere the shades of those who perished in the contest; revere also the opinions and the hopes which foreign states entertain concerning us, who promise to themselves so many advantages from that liberty, which we have so bravely acquired, from the establishment of that new govern-

ment, which has begun to shed its splendor on the world, which, if it be suffered to vanish like a dream, would involve us in the deepest abyss of shame; and lastly, revere yourself; and, after having endured so many sufferings and encountered so many perils for the sake of liberty, do not suffer it, now it is obtained, either to be violated by yourself, or in any one instance impaired by others. You cannot be truly free, unless we are free too; for such is the nature of things, that he who entrenches on the liberty of others is the first to lose his own and become a slave.

Doctor Johnson quoted only the praise given the Protector in order to place the Republican in contradiction with himself; the fine passage I have just quoted counterweighs that praise. Johnson's criticism is forgotten; Milton's defense has remained: everything that holds to partisan politics and passing passions dies like them and with them.[29]

My speech now ready, I was called to read it before the commission appointed to hear it. All but two or three members rejected it. You should have seen the terror of the proud Republicans who listened to me and whom the independence of my opinions turned pale. They shuddered with indignation and fear at the mere mention of liberty. M. Daru took the speech to Saint-Cloud. Bonaparte declared that if it had been read aloud, he would have closed the Institute's doors and had me thrown into a dungeon for the rest of my life.

I received this note from M. Daru:

Saint-Cloud, April 28, 1811
I have the honor of notifying Monsieur de Chateaubriand that, when he has the time or the opportunity to come to Saint-Cloud, I shall be able to return the speech with which he has been so good as to entrust me. I take this opportunity to repeat to him the assurance of the high consideration in which I have the honor to hold him.

Daru

I went to Saint-Cloud. M. Daru gave me the manuscript, ripped here and there, marked *ab irato* with Bonaparte's parentheses and pencil marks: the lion's claw had thrust everywhere, and I took a sort of irritated pleasure in thinking I felt it dig into my side. M. Daru made no bones about Napoleon's anger, but he informed me that, by keeping the peroration, save a dozen or so words, and by changing almost all the rest, I would be received with great applause. The speech had been copied out at the palace, eliminating several passages and interpolating several others. Not long after, this version appeared in print in the provinces.

This speech is one of the clearest proofs of the independence of my opinions and the constancy of my principles. M. Suard, a firm and impartial man, said that if it had been read to the whole Academy, it would have brought down the rafters with thunderous applause. Can you imagine, indeed, warm praises of liberty being read out amid the slavishness of the Empire?

I had kept the marked-up manuscript with religious care. Misfortune willed that, when I left the Infirmerie de Marie-Thérèse, it was burned with a heap of papers.[30] I regret its loss, not for its worth as an Academic speech but for its uniqueness as an artifact. In it, I had set down the names of my colleagues whose works had provided me with a pretext for expressing honorable sentiments.

In the manuscript that was handed back to me, the beginning of the speech, relating to the opinions of Milton, was *struck through* from one end to the other by Bonaparte's hand. A part of my complaint against the isolation of literature from politics was likewise *stigmatized* by the pencil. The praise for Abbé Delille, which called up memories of the Emigration, the poet's loyalty to the misfortunes of the royal family, and the sufferings of his companions in exile, was put between *parentheses*; the praise for M. de Fontanes had been given a *cross*. Almost everything I said about M. de Chénier, about his brother, about my own, about the expiatory altars that were being prepared at Saint-Denis, was *slashed through* with pencil marks. The paragraph beginning with the words "M. de Chénier worshipped liberty" had a *double longitudinal line* through it. I am still baffled that the corrupted text of the speech published by agents of the Empire preserved this paragraph almost entirely intact:

> M. de Chénier worshipped liberty. Can we call this a crime? The knights themselves, were they to emerge from their tombs today, would follow the lights of our age. We would see an illustrious alliance formed between honor and liberty, as, under the reign of the Valois, an architecture borrowed from Greece was crowned, with infinite grace, by Gothic crenellations.
> Is liberty not the greatest good and the first need of mankind? It kindles genius, it elevates the heart, it is as necessary to the friend of the Muses as the air he breathes. The arts may, up to a certain point, thrive in a state of dependence, because they make use of a language apart, which is not understood by the crowd; but literature, which speaks a universal language, languishes and dies in irons. How might we write pages worthy of posterity if we are warned away from every magnanimous feeling, every great and powerful thought? Liberty is so naturally the friend of science and letters that it takes refuge with them when it is banished from the nations. It is you, gentlemen, who are charged with writing her annals, taking revenge on her enemies, transmitting her name and her cult to the end of time.

I invent nothing and change nothing. The same passage can be read in the clandestine edition. The objurgation of tyranny that followed this passage on liberty, and which serves as its counterpart, was suppressed in full by the police. The peroration is preserved: only the praise of our triumphs, which I credited to France, is turned entirely to Napoleon's advantage.

All was not over when they handed my speech back to me. They wanted to force me to write a second one. I said that I stood by the first and would not write another. The committee then told me I would not be admitted to the Academy. Some very gracious people, whom I did not know, took up my cause. Madame Lindsay, who had brought me back from Calais in 1800, spoke to Madame Gay, who went and saw Madame Regnault de Saint-Jean-d'Angély; they managed to reach the Duc de Rovigo and called on him to leave me alone. The women of that era interposed their beauty between power and misfortune.

All this rigmarole was drawn out by the decennial prizes until 1812. Bonaparte, who was persecuting me, asked the Academy, with regard to these prizes, why it had not nominated *The Genius of Christianity*. The Academy explained that several of my colleagues had written unfavorable assessments of my work. I might have said to them what a Greek poet said to a bird:

Attic maid, honey-fed, chatterer, snatchest thou and bearest the chattering cricket for feast to thy unfledged young, thou chatterer the chatterer, thou winged the winged, thou summer guest the summer guest, and wilt not quickly throw it away? for it is not right nor just that singers should perish by singers' mouths.[31]

9.

DECENNIAL PRIZES—*ESSAI HISTORIQUE SUR LES RÉVOLUTIONS*—*THE NATCHEZ*

THE MIXTURE of anger and attraction Bonaparte felt toward me is constant and strange. He wants to lock me up at Vincennes for the rest of my days and then abruptly asks the Institute why it has not considered me for the decennial prizes. He goes further; he tells Fontanes that, since the Institute has not found me worthy to compete for the prizes, he will give me one; that he will appoint me superintendent-general of all the libraries of France, an appointment equivalent to a first-class ambassadorship. Bonaparte's original idea of employing me in the diplomatic service had not gone away: he never admitted, for reasons he well knew, that I had ceased to serve the Ministry of Foreign Affairs. And yet, despite these plans to be munificent, his prefect of police contradictorily invites me to remove myself from Paris, and I go to continue my *Memoirs* in Dieppe.

Bonaparte stoops to the role of teasing schoolboy. He unearths the *Essai historique sur les révolutions* and delights in the attacks he draws down on me by quoting from its pages. A man called M. Damaze de Raymond makes himself my champion: I go to thank him on rue Vivienne. On his mantel, with his knickknacks, he had a human skull; some time later, he was killed in a duel, and his charming face went to join the dreadful visage that seemed to be summoning him. Everyone was at war then: one of the informers charged with arresting Georges was repaid with a bullet in the head.[32]

To cut short my powerful adversary's bad faith attack, I appealed to M. de Pommereul, whom I mentioned to you when recounting my first arrival in Paris: he had become the Director General of the Press and Booksellers. I asked him permission to reprint the *Essai* in full. A reader can find this correspondence and the result of this correspondence in the preface to the *Essai historique sur les révolutions*, edition of 1826, volume two of my *Complete Works*. Of course, the imperial government was quite right to refuse to reprint the book *in full*; the *Essai* was not, when it came to freedoms or legitimate monarchy, a book that should have been published when despotism and usurpation reigned. The police put on airs of impartiality and allowed something to be said in my favor, then laughed and prevented me from doing the one thing that could serve as my defense. When Louis XVIII returned, the *Essai* was exhumed yet again. Just as, in the time of the Empire, they had wanted to use it against me in political matters, so in the time of the Restoration they wanted it to contradict me in religious matters. I made such a complete rectification of my errors in the notes to the new edition of the *Essai* that now there is nothing left to reproach me with. Posterity will come and have its say about the book and its commentary, if such old-fashioned stuff is still of any interest to it. I dare to hope that it will judge the *Essai* as my own gray head has judged it, for as we go on in life, we begin to assume the fair-mindedness of the future we are approaching. The *book* and the *notes* respectively show me to my readers as I was at the beginning of my career and as I am at the end of it.

Moreover, this work that I have treated with pitiless severity is the compendium of my existence as a poet, a moralist, and a future politician. The sap of the work overflows, the audacity of the opinions is pushed as far as it can go. It must be acknowledged that, whatever roads I have taken, I have never been led along by prejudice, I have never been blinded by any cause, I have been guided by no special interests, and the sides I have taken have always been of my own choosing.

In the *Essai*, my independence in matters of religion and politics is complete. I examine everything. I am a republican who serves the monarchy and a philosopher who honors religion. These are not contradictions; they are the inevitable consequences of the uncertainty of theory and the certainty of practice in human life. My mind, made to believe in nothing, not even myself, made to disdain everything, whether splendors or miseries, nations or kings, has nevertheless been dominated by a rational instinct that ordered it to submit to what is acknowledged to be good: religion, justice, humanity, equality, liberty, glory. What people today dream for the future, what the current generation imagines it has discovered, concerning a society still to be born, founded on principles quite different from those of the old society, is plainly foreshadowed in the *Essai*. I was thirty years ahead of those who call themselves heralds of an unknown world. If my actions have been those of the ancient city, my thoughts have been those of the new; the former were in keeping with my duty, and the latter are in line with my nature.

The *Essai* was not an impious book; it was a book of doubt and desolation. But I have already said this.*

Besides, I have had to exaggerate my faults and redeem the many impassioned ideas scattered through my works with orderly ideas. I was afraid, at the beginning of my career, of doing harm to the young; I need to make it up to them, and at the very least I owe them some other lessons. Let them realize that a person can struggle and triumph against a troubled nature. Moral beauty, divine beauty, superior to all earthly dreams—I have seen it. All it takes is a bit of courage to reach out and grasp it.

To conclude what I have to say about my literary career, I must mention the work that began it and that remained in manuscript until the year I inserted it in my *Complete Works*.†

A manuscript from which I drew *Atala, René*, and several descriptions set down in *The Genius of Christianity* is not completely barren. This original manuscript was written without stopping and without sections; all the subjects were mixed together: travelogue, natural history, fiction, etc. But, in addition to this unbroken manuscript,

*Book 11 of these *Memoirs*.
†The preface to *The Natchez* recounts how the work was rediscovered in England thanks to the careful and obliging research of M. de Thuisy.

there was another, divided into books. In this second work, I had not only proceeded to separate the material, I had also changed the genre of the composition, transforming it from a novel into an epic.

A young man who heaps up his ideas, inventions, studies, and readings at random is bound to produce chaos; but in this chaos there is also a certain fecundity that owes something to the potency of his youth.

What has perhaps never happened to another author happened to me, and this was to reread, thirty years later, a manuscript I had utterly forgotten.

There was one thing that worried me. By retouching the picture, I might dull the colors; a surer, though less rapid, hand ran the risk of erasing not only lines that were less than correct but also the liveliest strokes of youth. The composition had to retain its independence, which is to say its fervency. The foam had to be left on the reins of the young courser. If there are things in *The Natchez* I would hazard only with fear and trembling today, there are also things that I would no longer wish to write, notably René's letter in the second volume. It is in my early manner, and reproduces all of *René*. I doubt that the Renés who have followed me can have said anything more nearly approaching madness.[33]

The Natchez opens with an invocation to the wilderness and the star of night, the supreme divinities of my youth:

In the shadow of the American forests, I want to sing songs of solitude such as have never been heard by mortal ears; I want to tell the story of your misfortunes, oh Natchez! oh nation of Louisiana gone but for memories! Should the misfortunes of an obscure inhabitant of the woods have less claim to our tears than those of other men? Are the mausoleums of the kings in our temples more touching than the grave of an Indian buried beneath his native oak?

And thou, beacon of contemplation, star of night, be thou for me the star of Pindar! Go before me across the unknown regions of the New World and with thy light reveal to me the enchanting secrets of these wild lands!

My two natures are intermingled in this bizarre work—particularly in the primitive original. There you find political incidents and novelistic intrigues, but throughout the narrative you hear a voice that sings and that seems to issue from an undiscovered world.

END OF MY LITERARY CAREER

The years 1812 to 1814 saw the end of the Empire, and I spent these same years, as readers have already glimpsed, researching the history of France and composing a few books of these *Memoirs*; but I published nothing more. My life of poetry and study really came to an end with my three major works, *The Genius of Christianity*, *The Martyrs*, and the *Itinerary*. My political writings began under the Restoration. With these writings my active political life likewise began. Here, then, my literary career, properly so called, comes to an end. Dragged away by the stream of days, I had omitted it; not until this year of 1839 did I recall the bygone times of 1800 to 1814.

This literary career, as you have by now been able to see for yourself, was no less troubled than my career as a traveler and a soldier; there were trials, battles, and blood in the arena. It was not all Muses and Castalian Spring. My political career was even more tempestuous.

Perhaps some rubble will mark the site of Akademos's grove. *The Genius of Christianity* begins the religious revolution against the philosophism of the eighteenth century. At the same time, I laid the groundwork for the revolution that threatens our language, for there can be no renovation in thought without an innovation in style. Will there be other art forms, at present unknown, when I am gone? Will the people of the future be able to proceed from our studies, as we proceeded from the studies of the past so as to take a step forward? Are there limits we should not pass beyond because by doing so we will collide with the nature of things? Do these limits not lie in the division of modern languages, in the caducity of these same languages, in human vanities such as the new society has made them? Languages keep pace with the movement of civilization only until they attain perfection; reaching their zenith, they remain stationary for a moment, then decline, and are never able to rise again.

Now the story I am bringing to a close is catching up with the first books that mention my political life, written earlier, at various dates. I feel slightly more confident returning to the finished parts of my edifice. When I first got back to work, I worried the ancient son of Caelus would see the Troy-builder's golden trowel turn into a trowel of lead.[34] Yet it seems that my memory, tasked with meting out my recollections, has not failed me entirely. Have you keenly felt the ice of winter in my narrative? Do you find an enormous difference between the extinguished dust I have just tried to reanimate and the living personages I made you see when recounting my early youth? My years are my secretaries; when one of them dies, she passes the pen to her younger sibling and I continue to dictate. As they are sisters, their handwriting is very nearly the same.

BOOK NINETEEN

I.

ON BONAPARTE

YOUTH is a charming thing. It sets forth from life's harbor crowned with flowers, like the Athenian fleet off to conquer Sicily and the pleasant plains of Enna. The prayer is read by the priest of Neptune; the libations are mixed in cups of gold; the crowd, lined up along the seaside, unites its invocations with those of the pilot; the paean is sung as the sail is unfurled in the beams and breath of the dawn. Alcibiades, arrayed in purple and beautiful as Love, stands out upon the triremes, proud of the seven chariots he has launched upon the Olympian course. But no sooner has Alcinous's island passed behind them than the illusion vanishes. Exiled Alcibiades goes to live out his days far from home and dies transfixed by arrows on Timandra's breast. The men who shared his early hopes, enslaved in Syracuse, have nothing now to lighten the weight of their chains except a few verses of Euripides.[1]

You have seen my youth push off from shore. It was not so fine as Pericles's pupil, brought up in Aspasia's lap;[2] but it had its matitudinal hours, and its desires, and its dreams—God knows! I have painted them for you, these dreams. Now, returning to land after long exile, all I have left to tell you are truths sad as my age. If now and then I still sound the chords of the lyre, these are the last harmonies of a poet endeavoring to heal the wounds of time's arrows, to console himself for the enslavement of the years.

You know how changeable my life was when I was a traveler and a soldier; you have read about my literary existence, from 1800 to 1813, the year you left me at the Vallée-aux-Loups, which still belonged to me, when my "political career" began. We are now approaching this career. Before entering into it, I must retrace the history I passed over when writing about my works and adventures. This history is of Napoleon's making. Let us therefore turn to him; let us speak of the vast edifice that was being raised beyond the realm of my dreams. I shall now become a historian without ceasing to be a writer of memoirs. A subject of public interest will now undergird my private confidences, and my own little stories will be grouped around my narrative here.

When the war of the Revolution broke out, the kings did not understand it at all; they saw a revolt where they should have seen the changing of the nations, the end and the beginning of a world. They flattered themselves that, for them, all it would entail was the addition of a few French provinces to their domains. They put their faith in antiquated military tactics, antiquated diplomatic treaties, and cabinet negotiations—and soon enough conscripts were going to rout Frederick's grenadiers, monarchs were going to go plead for peace in the antechambers of obscure demagogues, and the terrible revolutionary attitude would unravel old Europe's entanglements on the scaffold. Old Europe thought it was only warring with France and did not perceive that a new age was marching on it.

Bonaparte, in the course of his ever-increasing successes, seemed called upon to alter royal dynasties, to make his the oldest of them all. He had made kings of the Electors of Bavaria, Württemberg, and Saxony. He had given the crown of Naples to Murat, that of Spain to Joseph, that of Holland to Louis, and that of Westphalia to Jérôme. His sister, Élisa Baciocchi, was Princess of Lucca. He was, by his own appointment, the Emperor of the French and the King of Italy, a kingdom that included Venice, Tuscany, Parma, and Piacenza (Piedmont had been incorporated into France). He agreed to let one of his captains, Bernadotte, reign in Sweden. According to the treaty that created the Confederation of the Rhine, he exercised the rights of the House of Austria over Germany. He declared himself the mediator of the Helvetic Confederation. He brought down Prussia. Though he didn't possess so much as a rowboat, he declared the British Isles blockaded. England, despite her fleets, at that time could find almost no port in Europe where she was allowed to unload a bale of merchandise or post a letter.

The Papal States formed part of the French Empire and the Tiber was a French *département*. In the streets of Paris, you saw quasi-incarcerated cardinals stick their heads out the doors of their fiacres and ask:

"Is this where the King of —— lives?"

"No," the messenger would reply: "it's farther up."

Austria bought back her independence only by handing over her daughter: the horseman of the South claimed Honoria from Valentinian, along with half the provinces of the empire.[3]

How were these miracles worked? What qualities did the man who produced them possess? I am going to follow the monumental fortune of Bonaparte, who, nevertheless, passed away so swiftly that his days take up only a small portion of the time contained in these *Memoirs*. Fastidious reproductions of genealogies, cold disquisitions on the facts, insipid verifications of dates will now burden and enslave the writer.

2.

BONAPARTE—HIS FAMILY

THE FIRST Buonaparte (Bonaparte) mentioned in modern annals is Jacopo Buonaparte, who—portent of the conquering future—left us a history of the sack of Rome in 1527, to which he was an eyewitness. Napoléon-Louis Bonaparte, Duchesse de Saint-Leu's son, who died following the insurrection in Romagna,[4] translated this curious document. Preceding the translation, there is a genealogy of the Buonapartes. The translator says that he will "limit himself to filling in the gaps in the preface written by the Cologne editor, publishing authentic details about the Bonaparte family—scraps of history," he calls them, "which have been almost entirely forgotten but are interesting, at least for those who love to uncover in the annals of bygone times the origin of a more recent fame."

There follows a genealogy in which we find one Chevalier Nordille Buonaparte, who, on April 2, 1266, stood surety for Prince Conradin of Swabia (the one the Duc d'Anjou had beheaded) for the value of the customs rights of the said prince's effects. Around 1255, the banishment of Trevisan families began.[5] A Bonaparte branch went to settle in Tuscany, where we encounter them in high-ranking government positions. Louis-Marie-Fortuné Buonaparte, from the branch established in Sarzana, emigrated to Corsica in 1612, settled in Ajaccio, and became the head of the Corsican branch of the Bonapartes.[6] The Bonapartes' coat of arms was a field of gules[7] crossed by two bars of gold attended by two stars.

There is another genealogy, which M. Panckoucke has placed at the head of a collection of Bonaparte's writings; it differs on several points from the one given by Napoleon-Louis. Madame d'Abrantès, for her part, thinks Bonaparte may be a Komnenos. Napoleon-Louis feels it necessary to conclude his genealogy with these words: "I have omitted many details, for noble titles are an object of curiosity for very few people, and in any case the Bonaparte family gains no luster from them: *Qui sert bien son pays n'a pas besoin d'aïeux.*"[8]

Notwithstanding this philosophical verse, the genealogy *still exists*. Napoléon-Louis wanted to make concessions to his era by quoting a democratic maxim without submitting to its ramifications.

All of this is bizarre. Jacopo Buonaparte, a historian of the sack of Rome and the detention of Pope Clement VII by the soldiers of Constable de Bourbon, is of the same blood as Napoleon Bonaparte, who destroyed so many cities and changed Rome into a prefecture, the King of Italy, the controller of the Bourbon crown, and the jailor of Pius VII—the pontiff who consecrated him Emperor of the French. The translator of the work of Jacopo Buonaparte is Napoleon-Louis Bonaparte, a nephew of Napoleon and the son of his brother, the King of Holland—and this young man happens to die during the latest insurrection in Romagna, only a short distance from the two towns where the mother and the widow of Napoleon are exiled, at the exact moment when the Bourbons are falling from the throne for the third time.

As it would have been rather difficult to make Napoleon out to be the son of Zeus Ammon, who took the shape of a serpent and made love with Olympias, or to be the grandson of Venus and Anchises,[9] some more freethinking scholars* found another marvel to suit their purposes: they demonstrated to the emperor that he was directly descended from the Man in the Iron Mask. The governor of the Île Sainte-Marguerite was named "Bonapart"; he had a daughter; the Man in the Iron Mask, Louis XIV's twin brother, fell in love with his jailer's daughter and married her in secret, by the Court's own admission. The children born of this union were clandestinely taken

*Las Cases.

to Corsica under their mother's name, and the "Bonaparts" were transformed into Bonapartes due to the difference in tongues. Thus the Man in the Iron Mask became a mysterious, brazen-faced ancestor of the great man, who was thereby linked with the great king.

The branch of the Franchini-Bonapartes bears on its blazon three golden fleurs-de-lis. Napoleon smiled incredulously at this genealogy—but he did smile. It was still a claim on royalty, to his family's advantage. The indifference Napoleon affected was false. It was he himself who sent for his genealogy from Tuscany (Bourrienne). Yet it is the very lack of divinity surrounding Bonaparte's birth that makes this birth wondrous. "I saw Philip," Demosthenes says, "against whom we had fought for the liberty of Greece and the salvation of its republics, with one eye gouged out, one shoulder broken, a crippled hand, a wounded thigh, freely and gladly offering up his body to the blows of fate, so that he might enjoy what remained of his life with glory and renown!"[10]

Now, Philip was Alexander's father. Alexander was thus the son of a king and of a king worthy of being one. By these two facts alone, he commanded obedience. Alexander, born on the throne, did not, like Bonaparte, have a small life to lead before arriving at a great one. Alexander does not present the disparity of two separate trajectories; Aristotle was his private tutor, taming Bucephalus his boyhood pastime. Napoleon was given his lessons by a common schoolteacher and had no coursers available to him. He was the least well off of his fellow students. And this servantless sublieutenant of the artillery goes on, in a few brief years, to force Europe to acknowledge him. This "little corporal" summons the mightiest sovereigns of Europe to his antechambers:

> Ils ne sont pas venus, nos deux rois? Qu'on leur die
> Qu'ils se font trop attendre et qu'Attila s'ennuie.[11]

Napoleon—who so sensibly exclaimed, "Oh! If only I were my grandson!"—did not find power in his family; he created it. How many different capabilities such creation suggests! Would you have

Napoleon be merely the implementer of the social thinking that swirled around him—a way of thinking that unprecedented events and extraordinary dangers had brought into being? If we were to accept this proposition, it would make him no less astonishing. Indeed, how could there be a man capable of harnessing and steering so many strange supremacies?

3.
THE BONAPARTES IN CORSICA

IF NAPOLEON was not born a prince, he was nevertheless born, as the old saying goes, a young man of means. M. de Marbeuf, governor of the island of Corsica, had enrolled Napoleon at a school near Autun. Later, he was admitted to the Brienne military school. Élisa (Madame Baciocchi) received her education at Saint-Cyr:[12] Bonaparte reclaimed his sister when the Revolution broke down the doors of these religious retreats. Thus we see Napoleon's sister was one of the last students at an institution whose first young women had chanted the choruses of Racine for Louis XIV.

The proofs of nobility required for Napoleon's admission to a military school were drawn up. They contain the baptismal certificate of Carlo Bonaparte, Napoleon's father, whose lineage can be traced back ten generations to Francesco; a certificate from the senior nobles of the town of Ajaccio, testifying that the Bonapartes have always been among the most ancient and most noble families; a deed of recognition stating that the Bonapartes of Tuscany are patrician and that their origins are shared with the Bonapartes of Corsica, and so on.

"When Bonaparte entered Treviso," M. Las Cases says, "he was told that his family had been powerful there; in Bologna, that they had been inscribed in the golden book ... At the Conference of Dresden, Emperor Francis told Emperor Napoleon that his family had been sovereigns in Treviso and that he himself had seen the documents: he added that it was invaluable to have been a sovereign and that he must tell Marie Louise, who would be greatly pleased to know this."

Born of a race of gentleman that forged alliances with the Orsinis, the Lomellis, and the Medicis, Napoleon, attacked by the Revolution, was a democrat only momentarily. This is apparent in everything he says and writes. Dominated by his blood, his leanings were aristocratic. Napoleon's godfather was not Pascal Paoli, as he said: it was the obscure Laurent Giubega de Calvi. One learns this peculiarity from the baptismal register kept in Ajaccio by the priest and bursar Diamante.

I am afraid of compromising Napoleon by restoring him to the ranks of the aristocracy. Cromwell, in his speech to parliament on September 12, 1654, declared that he was born a gentleman. Mirabeau, Lafayette, Desaix, and a hundred other partisans of the Revolution were noblemen too. The English claimed the emperor's first name was Nicolas, which they derisively shorted to "Nick." The fine name of Napoleon devolved to the emperor from one of his uncles, who married off his daughter to an Ornano. Saint Napoleon was a Greek martyr. According to Dante's commentators, Count Orso was the son of Napoleon of Cerbaia. It used to be that no one reading history gave a second thought to this name borne by several cardinals, but today it is impossible to ignore. A man's glory does not rise up; it flows down. No one, except for some Ethiopian or other, knows the Nile at its source, but, at its mouth, who is ignorant of it?

4.
BONAPARTE'S BIRTH AND CHILDHOOD

NO ONE contests that Bonaparte's real name was Buonaparte. He himself signed it this way all through his Italian campaign and until he was thirty-three. He then Gallicized it and began to sign himself Bonaparte: I will leave him the name that he gave himself and that is engraved at the foot of his indestructible statue.*

Did Bonaparte make himself a year younger so that he would be French, which is to say so that his birth would not predate the incorporation of Corsica into France? This question is treated in depth, briefly but substantially, in a pamphlet by M. Eckard. His conclusion is that Bonaparte was born February 5, 1768, and not April 15, 1769, despite M. Bourrienne's assertions. That is why the Sénat conservateur, in its proclamation of April 3, 1814, treats Napoleon as a foreigner.

The certificate of the marriage of Bonaparte and Marie-Josèphe-Rose de Tascher, inscribed in the civil registry of the second arrondissement of Paris, on Ventôse 19, year IV (March 9, 1796), states that Napoleon Buonaparte was born in Ajaccio on February 5, 1768, and that his birth certificate, endorsed by the registrar, confirms this date. This same date accords perfectly with what is said in the marriage certificate—that the bridegroom is twenty-eight years old.

Napoleon's birth certificate, presented at the *mairie* of the second

---

*The name Buonaparte was sometimes written with the "u" subtracted: the bursar of Ajaccio who signs for Napoleon's baptism wrote Bonaparte three times without using the Italian *u*.

arrondissement at the time of his marriage to Josephine, was removed by one of the emperor's aides-de-camp in early 1810, when the annulment of Napoleon's marriage to Josephine was already underway. M. Duclos, not daring to resist an imperial command, wrote at this time, regarding one of the documents in the "Bonaparte bundle": "His birth certificate has been handed over to him, since it was not possible, at the time of his request, to make him a copy." The date of Josephine's birth is altered on the marriage certificate, scratched out and written over, though with a magnifying glass the original lines can still be made out. The Empress divested herself of four years. The jokes made on this subject at the Tuileries palace and on Saint Helena are hateful, and in poor taste.

Bonaparte's birth certificate, removed by the aide-de-camp in 1810, has disappeared; all attempts to find it have proved fruitless.

These are irrefutable facts, and I think, in the light of these facts, that Napoleon was born in Ajaccio on February 5, 1768. However, I am not blind to the chronological quandaries that arise if that date is adopted.

Joseph, Bonaparte's older brother, was born on January 5, 1768. His younger brother, Napoleon, could not have been born the same year unless the date of Joseph's birth was likewise altered. This is conjecturable, for all the civil status records relating to Napoleon and Josephine are suspected of being false. Notwithstanding a reasonable suspicion of fraud, the Comte de Beaumont, subprefect of Calvi, in his *Observations on Corsica*, confirms that the civil registry in Ajaccio records Napoleon's birthdate as August 15, 1769. Finally, the papers M. Libri has lent me demonstrate Bonaparte himself believed that he was born on August 15, 1769, at a time when he could have had no reason to wish to make himself younger. But the fact of the *official* date on the documents of his first marriage and the suppression of his birth certificate remains.

Be that as it may, Bonaparte would gain nothing from this biographical transposition. If you set the date of his birth on August 15, 1769, you are forced to postpone his conception to mid-November 1768. Now, Corsica did not surrender to France until the treaty of

May 15, 1768, and the last submissions of the *pieves* (the cantons of Corsica) did not take place until June 14, 1769. According to the most indulgent calculations, Napoleon would still not have been French until he had passed a few nocturnal hours in his mother's womb. Ah, well! If he *was* the citizen of a disputed land, this only sets his nature further apart: his was an existence come down from on high, capable of belonging to any time and any country.

However, Bonaparte inclined toward Italy. He detested the French, until their valiance gave him power. Evidence of this aversion abounds in the writings of his youth. In a note Napoleon wrote about suicide, one finds this passage: "My shackled compatriots grasp the oppressor's hand in trembling... Frenchmen, not satisfied to have taken from us everything we cherish, have moreover corrupted our mores."

A letter written in 1789 to Paoli in England, which has previously been published, begins as follows:

> General,
> I was born when the homeland was dying. Thirty thousand Frenchmen vomited up on our coasts, drowning the throne of liberty in waves of blood—such was the odious spectacle that first struck my sight.

Another letter from Napoleon to M. Gubica, chief clerk of the Estates of Corsica, reads:

> While France is being reborn, what will become of us Corsican wretches? Servile as ever, will we continue to kiss the insolent hand that oppresses us? Will we continue to see all the roles that natural right destined for us occupied by foreigners as contemptible in their mores and conduct as their birth is abject?

Finally, the draft of a third letter handwritten by Bonaparte, concerning the Corsican recognition of the National Assembly of 1789, begins as follows:

Messieurs,

Through bloodshed, the French came to govern us; through bloodshed, they strove to complete their conquest. The soldier, the lawman, the financier banded together to oppress us, despise us, and force us to take long drafts from the cup of ignominy. Long enough have we suffered their vexations—but since we have not had the courage to free ourselves of them, let us forget them forever; let them sink back down into the scorn they deserve, or at least let them go looking in their own country for the trust of the people: certainly, they will never obtain ours.

Napoleon's aversion to his motherland never entirely disappeared. On the throne, he seemed to forget us. He spoke solely of himself, his empire, his soldiers, and almost never of the French. This phrase escaped his lips:

"You people, the French."

The emperor, in the papers he wrote on Saint Helena, recounts that his mother, whose labor pains took her by surprise, had let him fall from her womb on a carpet crawling with foliage and depicting the heroes of *The Iliad*. He would have been no less a man if he had fallen into a pile of straw.

I have just spoken of some rediscovered papers. When I was ambassador to Rome in 1828, Cardinal Fesch, showing me his paintings and books, told me he was in possession of some manuscripts from Napoleon's youth. He attached so little importance to them he offered to show them to me. I left Rome before finding time to consult the documents. After Madame Mère[13] and Cardinal Fesch died, various items of the estate were scattered; the box that contained Napoleon's essay was taken to Lyon with several others and fell into the hands of M. Libri. In the *Revue des Deux Mondes* of March 1, this year of 1842, M. Libri printed a detailed itemization of Cardinal Fesch's papers. He has since been good enough to send me the box. I have taken advantage of this transfer of documents by expanding the original text of my memoirs concerning Napoleon, adding all the reservations that come with a greater stock of information, all the contradictory details and doubts that arise.

5.
BONAPARTE'S CORSICA

BENSON, in his *Sketches of Corsica*, writes of the country house where the Bonaparte family resided:

> I took a very interesting walk along the shore toward the Isle Sanguiniere. At about a mile from Ajaccio, one meets with two square stone pillars, the remains of a doorway leading up to a dilapidated country house, formerly the property of the half brother of Madame Bonaparte, whom Napoleon appointed Cardinal Fesch. The remains of a sort of summer house beneath a rock are still visible, the entrance to it is nearly closed by a very luxuriant fig tree. It was once Napoleon's favorite retreat, in which he followed his studies during the vacation allowed by the College of Brienne.

Napoleon retained a love of his native country all through his ordinary life. In 1788, Bonaparte wrote, concerning M. de Sussy, that "Corsica offered a perpetual spring." Once he had come up in the world, however, he no longer said a word about his island; he even despised it. He felt it was too cramped a cradle. It was only on Saint Helena his homeland returned to haunt his memory. "Corsica held a thousand charms for Napoleon; it explained some of his greatest features and the bold lines of his physical structure. Everything was better there, he said, even down to the smell of the soil itself: he would have been able to identify it blindfolded by that smell alone, which he had never found elsewhere. He saw himself there in his earliest years, with his earliest loves—a young man among the cliffs, traversing the high summits and deep valleys."

Napoleon found romance in his birthplace. That romance started with Vanina, killed by her husband, Sampietro.[14] Baron Neuhoff, or rather King Theodore, had put in an appearance on every shoreline, asking for assistance from England, the pope, the Grand Turk, and the Bey of Tunis, after having been crowned King of the Corsicans, who did not know what they were doing: Voltaire laughed at it all.[15] The two Paolis, Giacinto and especially Pasquale, had made Europe resound with their names. Buttafuoco implored Rousseau to be Corsica's lawmaker, and the Genevese philosopher considered settling down in the country of the man who, bedeviling the Alps, would carry off Geneva under one arm. "In Europe there is still one country where new legislation might be enacted," Rousseau wrote: "this is the island of Corsica. The courage and persistence with which this brave people has managed to recover and defend their liberty richly deserve the advice of some wise man who will teach them how to preserve it. I have a feeling that one day this little island will astonish Europe."[16]

Reared in Corsica, Bonaparte was educated in that primary school of the revolutions. To begin with, he brought us neither the calm nor the passions of the young but a spirit already stamped with political passions. This observation alters the idea that has been formed of Napoleon.

When men become famous, antecedents are found for them. As children, they are, according to their biographers, spirited, rowdy, and untamable; they learn everything, or they learn nothing. More often than not they are also melancholy children who do not take part in their companions' games, who daydream at a distance and are already pursued by the reputation that looms before them. Consider how one enthusiast has dug up Napoleon's extremely ordinary letters to his grandparents (no doubt written in Italian) and forced us to swallow these asinine puerilities. Predictions about our futures are pointless. We are what circumstances make us. Let a child be cheerful or glum, silent or talkative; let him show or not show an aptitude for schoolwork: it augurs nothing. Halt a schoolboy at the age of sixteen, and however intelligent you may imagine him, this child prodigy, frozen at three lustra, will remain an idiot. The child lacks the most wonderful grace of all, a smile. He laughs, but he does not smile.

Napoleon was thus a little boy no more or less distinguished than his disciples. "I was merely," he himself says, "a curious and obstinate child." He liked buttercups, and he ate cherries with Mademoiselle Colombier. When he left his father's house, he knew only Italian. His ignorance of the language of Turenne was almost complete. Like the German Marshal de Saxe, the Italian Bonaparte could not spell a single word; Henri IV, Louis XIV, and Marshal de Richelieu, who had less of an excuse, were not much more precise. It is clearly to conceal the negligence of his education that Napoleon made his handwriting indecipherable. Leaving Corsica at the age of nine, he did not lay eyes on his island again until eight years later. At the college in Brienne, there was nothing out of the ordinary about his studies or comportment. His comrades made fun of his first name and his homeland. He told his friend Bourrienne: "I will do you Frenchman all the harm I can." In a report to the king in 1784, M. de Kéralio attests that "the young Bonaparte would make an excellent sailor," but the sentence is suspicious, because this report was not disinterred until Napoleon was inspecting the fleet in Boulogne.

Leaving Brienne on October 14, 1784, Bonaparte went to the military academy in Paris. The civil list paid for his room and board, and he found this pension painful. That these funds were kept can be seen in some of the Fesch papers passed on to me by M. Libri:

> I, the undersigned, acknowledge having received from M. Bier-court the sum of 200 originating from the scholarship that the king has granted me, as a former cadet of the school in Paris, from the funds of the military academy.

Madame de Comnène (Madame d'Abrantès), who lived with her mother in Montpellier, Toulouse, and Paris, has still not lost sight of her countryman Bonaparte. "Today, when I am walking on the Quai de Conti," she writes, "I cannot help looking up at the fourth-floor mansard on the left side of the building: that is where Napoleon stayed whenever he came to visit my family."

Bonaparte was not well liked at his new school. Morose and rebellious, he irritated his teachers. He criticized everything ruthlessly. He sent the headmaster a note outlining the defects of the education he was receiving there. "Would it not be better to oblige them (the students) to be self-sufficient, viz. take away their little cooking that they won't be doing in the field and make them eat *Kommissbrot* or something like it, get them accustomed to beating the bushes, brushing their clothes, cleaning their boots and shoes?" This is what he later ordered at Fontainebleau and Saint-Germain.

The repudiator relieved the school of his presence and was appointed a sublieutenant in La Fère's artillery regiment.

Napoleon's literary career extends from 1784 to 1793: short in terms of time, but long in terms of the body of work he produced. Wandering with various artillery corps in Auxonne, Dôle, Seurres, and Lyon, Bonaparte was drawn to the sites like a bird lured by a mirror or hastening to a call. Attentive to academic questions, he replied to them; he spoke confidently to powerful people he had not previously met: he made himself the equal of all men before becoming their master. Sometimes he wrote under an assumed name and sometimes signed his own name, which in no way betrayed his anonymity. He wrote to Abbé Raynal and M. Necker; he sent ministers notes on the organization of Corsica; on defense plans for Saint-Florent, Mortella, and the Gulf of Ajaccio; on how to arrange the artillery batteries. He went unheeded, just as Mirabeau went unheeded when, in Berlin, he drafted plans regarding Prussia and Holland. He studied geography. It has been noted that, when speaking of Saint Helena, he summed it up in two words: "Small island." He took an interest in China, the Indies, and Arabia. He labored over the historians, philosophers, economists, Herodotus, Strabo, Diodorus Siculus, Filangieri, Mably, Smith. He refuted the *Discourse on the Origin of Inequality*, saying: "I do not believe it; I do not believe a word of it." Lucien Bonaparte recounts how he, Lucien, had made two copies of a historical work sketched out by Napoleon. A part of the manuscript of this sketch has been found in Cardinal Fesch's box: the research is uninteresting, the style common, the story of Vanina told unmovingly. Sampietro's retort to the great lords of the Court of Henri II after Vanina's murder are worth more than Napoleon's whole narrative:

"What do the quarrels of Sampietro and his wife matter to the King of France?"

Early in life, Bonaparte did not have the smallest inkling of his future; it was only once he began moving up in the world that he took it into his head to rise higher. But if he did not aspire to climb, he did not wish to fall either, and once he'd set foot in a place, he could not be moved. Three handwritten notebooks (Fesch box) are given over to research on the Sorbonne and the Gallican Liberties. There is also correspondence with Paolo, Saliceti, and especially with Father Dupuis, a Franciscan Minim and headmaster of the College of Brienne, a man of good sense and religion who advised his young student and addressed Napoleon as his "dear friend."

Along with these sterile studies, Bonaparte wrote a few imaginative pages. He spoke of women. He wrote *Le Masque Prophète*, *Le Roman Corse*, and a novella set in England, *Le Comte d'Essex*. He has dialogues on love, which he treats with scorn, and yet he drafts a passionate letter to an unknown beloved. He shows little regard for glory, deeming love of country more important—and the country in this case was Corsica.

Anyone who wishes to do so can look up a request he made to a bookseller in Geneva: the romantic sublieutenant was looking for Madame de Warens's *Memoirs*. Napoleon was also a poet, as were Caesar and Frederick. He preferred Ariosto to Tasso, for in Ariosto he found portraits of his future generals and a horse bridled for his voyage to the stars.[17] The following madrigal, addressed to Madame Saint-Huberty playing the role of Dido, has been attributed to Bonaparte, but while the substance may belong to the emperor, the form is the product of a more proficient hand:

> *Romains, qui vous vantez d'une illustre origine,*
> *Voyez d'où dépendait votre empire naissant!*

> *Didon n'a pas d'attrait assez puissant*
> *Pour retarder la fuite où son amant s'obstine.*
> *Mais si l'autre Didon, ornement de ces lieux,*
> > *Eût été reine de Carthage,*
> *Il eût, pour la server, abandonné ses dieux,*
> *Et votre beau pays serait encor sauvage.*[18]

Right around the time he wrote these lines, Bonaparte seems to have been tempted to kill himself. Thousands of youngsters are obsessed with the idea of suicide, which they believe to be proof of their superiority. The following handwritten note is found among the papers passed on by M. Libri:

"Always alone among men, I go home and dream by myself, giving myself over to all the strength and energy of my melancholy. Which way does it turn today? Toward death. If I were sixty, I would respect the prejudices of my contemporaries and patiently wait for nature to take its course, but since I am beginning to feel unhappy, since nothing gives me pleasure, why should I tolerate these days when nothing brings me joy?"

These are reveries of the sort found in every novel. The acme and nadir of such thoughts can be found in Rousseau, whose sentences Bonaparte has altered with a few phrases of his own.

Here is an essay of another kind. I transcribe it letter for letter. Education and blood should not lead princes to be too disdainful of it. Let them remember their eagerness to line up before the orderly of a man who drove them at will from the rooms of kings.

FRASES, CERTIFICATS, AND OTHER ESSENCIAL THINGS RELATIVE TO MY CURRENT STATE.

Procedure for requesting leave.

When one is in the midst of the semester and one wishes to obtain a summer leave due to illness, a physician and a surgin of the town must draw up a certificate saying that before the period stated, your helth does not permit you to rejoin the garrison. You will note that this certificate may be on stamped paper, which must be stamped by the judge and the commandant of the place.

You will then draw up your note to the Minister of War using the following frases:

Ajaccio, April 21, 1787

REQUEST FOR LEAVE

ROYAL ARTILLERY CORPS
Monsieur Napolione de Buonaparte, second lieutenant in the regiment of La Fère, artillery

LA FÈRE ARTILLERY REGIMENT
We emplore Your Excellency the Marshal de Ségur to be so good as to grant him a leave of five months and a half beginning next May 16, which he needs for the restoration of his helth according to the physician and surgeon certificate herewith. Given my meager fortune and the costly cure, I ask the grace that the leave be granted with pay.

Buonaparte

All of this should be sent to the colonel of the regiment at the address of the minister or of the *commissaire ordonnateur*, M. de Lance, i.e., one writes to him at the address of M. Sauquier, the *commissaire ordonnateur des guerres* at the Court.

What a detailed way of teaching yourself how to lie! One can almost see the emperor, laboring to legalize the seizure of kingdoms in an office overcrowded with illicit paperwork.

The style of the young Napoleon is declamatory. It is worth noting if only as the activity of a vigorous pioneer shoveling out the sands. The sight of these early works reminds me of my own juvenile hodge-podges, my *Essais historiques*, and my thousand-folio-page manuscript of *The Natchez* bound with string; but in their margins I did not scribble any little houses, or childish drawings, or schoolboy scrawlings, such as you see in the margins of Bonaparte's drafts. Among my juvenilia, there was no stone ball that might have been a design for a cannonball.

Here ends my prologue to the emperor's life. An obscure Bonaparte preceded the great Napoleon. The idea of Bonaparte was there in the world before becoming present in the man himself: it secretly troubled the earth. In 1789 everyone felt something tremendous in the air about the time Bonaparte appeared—a disturbance no one could name. When the globe is threatened by a catastrophe, we are warned of it by a sort of simmering agitation. We feel afraid. We listen in the night. We stare up at the heavens not knowing why, or what is going to happen.

6.

PAOLI

PAOLI had been recalled from England on a motion of Mirabeau's in 1789. He was presented to Louis XVI by the Marquis de Lafayette and named lieutenant general and military commander of Corsica. Did Bonaparte keep up with the exile whose protégé he had been and with whom he had exchanged several letters? It has been presumed so. He wasted no time turning against Paoli. The crimes of our earliest troubles demoralized the old general, who handed Corsica over to England to escape the Convention. Bonaparte, in Ajaccio, had joined a Jacobin club, but when a rival club was formed Napoleon was forced to flee. Madame Letizia and her daughters took refuge in the Greek settlement of Cargèse, where they set sail for Marseille. Joseph was married in this town on August 1, 1794, to Mademoiselle Clary, the daughter of a rich trader. In 1792, the Minister of War, the unknown Lajard, dismissed Napoleon from duty for a moment, for not having been present at a review.

We find Bonaparte again in Paris with Bourrienne in this same year of 1792. Deprived of any resources, he transformed himself into an entrepreneur: he professed to rent houses under construction on rue Montholon with the aim of subletting them. By this time the Revolution was in full swing and the twentieth of June came to pass. Bonaparte, leaving a restaurant on rue Saint-Honoré near the Palais-Royal with Bourrienne, saw five or six thousand ragged men and women shouting on their way to the Tuileries. He said to Bourrienne, "Let's follow these beggars," and went to take his place on the paving stones by the river. When the king, whose house had been invaded, appeared in one of the windows wearing a red cap, Bonaparte cried out indignantly:

"*Che coglione!* How did that rabble get in? They only had to blow away four or five hundred of them with a cannon and the rest would still be running even now."

You know that on June 20, 1792, I was very near Napoleon. I was walking in Montmorency, where Barère and Maret were seeking solitude for reasons very different from my own. Was it at this time that Bonaparte had to deal in those small assignat banknotes called Corsets? Following the death of a wine seller on rue Sainte-Avoye, Bonaparte's name was found in an inventory made by the lawyer Dumay and the auctioneer Chariot, owing a debt of fifteen francs rent, which he was unable to pay. This poverty adds something to his greatness. On Saint Helena, Napoleon said: "When I heard about the attack on the Tuileries, on August 10, I rushed to the Carrousel, to the house of Fauvelet, Bourrienne's brother, who kept a furniture shop." Bourrienne's brother had a going concern he called the "National Auction" where Bonaparte pawned his watch. A dangerous precedent. How many poor students believe themselves Napoleons because they've pawned their watches!

7.
TWO PAMPHLETS

BONAPARTE returned to the south of France on January 2, year II, and found himself present at the Siege of Toulon. There, he wrote two pamphlets. The first is a letter to Matteo Buttafuoco, whom he treats dishonorably, even as he makes Paoli out to be a criminal for having put power in the people's hands. "It is a strange error," he exclaims, "that places the man who, by dint of his education, high birth, and wealth, is the only man fit to govern, under the thumb of a brute and a mercenary!"

Although a revolutionary, Bonaparte everywhere shows himself to be an enemy of the people. He was nevertheless complimented on his leaflet by Masseria, the president of the patriotic club of Ajaccio.

On July 29, 1793, he had another pamphlet printed, titled *The Supper at Beaucaire*. Bourrienne provides a manuscript of it reviewed by Bonaparte, but this manuscript is abridged and revised to be more in line with the emperor's opinions at the time he reread his work. *The Supper at Beaucaire* is a dialogue involving a man from Marseille, a man from Nîmes, a soldier, and a manufacturer from Montpellier. The dialogue turns on current affairs—the attack of Avignon by Carteaux's army, in which Napoleon had taken part as an artillery officer. He announces to the man from Marseille that his party will be beaten because it has ceased to adhere to the Revolution. The man from Marseille tells the officer, a stand-in for Bonaparte:

"We can never forget that monster who was one of the leaders of the club. He had a citizen hanged from a lamppost, looted his house, and raped his wife, after forcing her to drink a glass of her husband's blood."

"How horrid!" the soldier cries out, "but is it true? I have my doubts. You know no one goes in for rape anymore nowadays."

The previous century's frivolity blossomed in Bonaparte's icy brain. This accusation—of having drunk blood, or having had someone drink it—is often repeated. When the Duc de Montmorency was beheaded in Toulouse, the men-at-arms drank his blood in order to possess themselves of the virtue of a great heart.

8.

BREVET OF CAPTAIN

WE NOW arrive at the Siege of Toulon. Here, Bonaparte's military career begins. Regarding the rank Napoleon then occupied in the artillery, Cardinal Fesch's box contains a strange document. This is a document brevetting Napoleon to artillery captain, dated August 30, 1792, by Louis XVI, twenty days after his dethronement, which occurred on August 10. The king had been locked up in the Temple on August 13, two days after the massacre of the Swiss Guards. In this brevet, it says that the August 30 appointment will retroactively promote the officer to his new position as of the previous February 16.

Ill-starred men are often prophets, but this time the martyr's foresight had nothing to do with Napoleon's future glory. There are still blank brevets in the Ministry of War signed in advance by Louis XVI with their empty spaces waiting to be filled; the aforementioned commission will have been of this kind. Louis XVI, locked up in the Temple with his family on the eve of his trial, had other things on his mind besides seeing to the advancement of a stranger.

The date of the brevet is made clear by the countersignature, which belongs to Servan. Appointed to the Ministry of War on May 8, 1792, Servan was removed from office on June 13 the same year. Dumouriez had the ministry until the 18th, when Lajard, in turn, took over until July 23. Dabancourt succeeded him until August 10—the day that the National Assembly recalled Servan, who submitted his resignation on October 3. Our ministers were as hard to tally in those days as our victories were later.

Napoleon's brevet cannot be from Servan's first ministry, since the document bears the date of August 30, 1792; it must be from his second ministry. However, there is a letter from Lajard, dated July 12, addressed to "artillery captain Bonaparte." Explain this however you like. Did Bonaparte acquire the document in question through bureaucratic corruption, the chaos of the times, or revolutionary *fraternité*? What protector was overseeing the Corsican's affairs? This protector was the immortal Lord. France herself, by divine impetus, delivered the brevet to the First Captain of the earth; this brevet was legalized by the signature of Louis, who left behind his head, on the condition that it would be replaced by Napoleon's—the bargains of Providence, in the face of which we can only raise our hands to the heavens.

9.
TOULON

TOULON had recognized Louis XVII and opened its ports to the English fleets. Carteaux on one side and General Lapoype on the other, requested by representatives Fréron, Barras, Ricord, and Saliceti, made their way to Toulon. Napoleon, who had until recently been serving under Carteaux at Avignon, was summoned to a military council. There he argued for the seizure of Fort Murgrave, built by the English on the heights of the Caire, and for the placement of batteries on the two promontories, L'Éguillette and Balaguier, which, firing down at both the large and the small roadsteads, would force the enemy fleet to abandon them. Everything would happen as Napoleon predicted it—offering up a first glimpse of his destiny.

Madame Bourrienne has inserted a few notes in her husband's *Memoirs*. I will quote a passage that depicts Bonaparte at Toulon:

"I noticed," she says, "that in those days (1795, in Paris) his manner was cold and often somber; his smile was false and frequently quite misplaced; and, on this same subject, I recall that in those same days, not long after our return, he had one of those moments of savage hilarity that disturbed me and made me feel very little disposed to him. He told us, with charming good cheer, that when he was in charge of the artillery in Toulon, one of the officers under him had a visit from his wife, whom he had only recently married and loved dearly. A few days later Bonaparte received orders to make another attack on the city, and this officer was called. His wife came to find General Bonaparte and begged him, with tears in her eyes, to exempt her husband from duty that day. The general was unmoved, as he himself told us with ferocious and charming good cheer. When the time for the attack arrived, this officer who had always been extraordinarily brave, as Bonaparte himself said, had a presentiment of his approaching fate; he turned pale and trembled. He was positioned beside the general, and when the fire from the town turned thunderous, Bonaparte called to him, 'Look out! There's a shell coming at us!' The officer, he said, instead of stepping aside, bent down and was cut in two. Bonaparte laughed out loud talking about the parts that were blown clean off him."

Once Toulon had been recaptured, the scaffolds were raised. Eight hundred victims were gathered on the Champ de Mars and gunned down. The police captains came forward shouting, "Those who aren't dead, stand up; the Republic will show you mercy," and the wounded who stood were all massacred. The scene was so fine that after the siege it was acted out on stage in Lyon:

> Que dis-je? aux premiers coups du foudroyant orage
> Quelque coupable encor peut-être est échappé:
> Annonce le pardon, et, par l'espoir trompé,
> Si quelque malheureux en tremblant se relève,
> Que la foudre redouble et que le fer achève.
> (L'ABBÉ DELILLE)[19]

Did Bonaparte, as chief of artillery, personally oversee the execution? Fellow feeling would not have stayed his hand, though he was not cruel by nature.

We find this letter to the commissioners of the Convention:

"Citizen representatives, it is from the field of glory, marching in the blood of the traitors, that I joyfully announce to you your orders have been executed and France is avenged: no one of any age or either sex was spared. Those who had only been wounded by republican gunfire were dispatched by freedom's blade and equality's bayonet. Farewell, with admiration. BRUTUS BUONAPARTE, citizen sans-culotte."

This letter was printed for the first time, I believe, in *La Semaine*, the gazette published by Malte-Brun. The Vicomtesse de Fors (a pseudonym) included it in her *Mémoires sur la Révolution française*, noting that it was written on the shell of a drum. Fabry reproduced it in the Bonaparte entry in the *Biographie des hommes vivants*. Royou, in the *Histoire de France*, declares that no one knows who issued the murderous order. Fabry, quoted above, says, in *Les Missionnaires de 93*, that some attribute the order to Fréron and others to Bonaparte. The executions on Toulon's Champ de Mars were recounted by Fréron in a letter to Moïse Bayle of the Convention and by Mottedo and Barras to the Committee of Public Safety.

When all is said and done, who issued the first report of the Napoleonic victories? Was it Napoleon or his brother? Lucien, detesting his errors, admits in his *Memoirs* that he was at first an ardent republican. Put in charge of the revolutionary committee at Saint-Maximin in Provence, "we attended closely," he says, "to the speech and panache of the Jacobins of Paris. As the fashion was to take on classical names, my friend the ex-monk took, I believe, the name of Epaminondas, while I assumed the name of Brutus. A pamphlet attributed to Napoleon this borrowed name Brutus, but it was mine alone. Napoleon thought to raise his own name *above* those of ancient history, and even if he had wanted to figure in these masquerades, I doubt he would have chosen *Brutus*."

There is courage in this confession. Bonaparte, in the *Memorial of Saint Helena*, keeps profoundly silent about this part of his life. This silence, according to Madame la Duchesse d'Abrantès, is explained by the thorniness of his position: "Bonaparte had become more prominent than Lucien," she says, "and although he had gone to great lengths to put Lucien in his place, we should make no mistake. Bonaparte must have believed the *Memorial of Saint Helena* would be read by one hundred million people, among whom perhaps a thousand would be aware of the facts he found objectionable. These thousand people would then preserve the memory of these facts in a minimally disturbing manner, through oral tradition, and the *Memorial* would therefore be irrefutable."

Distressing doubts still hover over the note Lucien or Napoleon signed. How would Lucien, who was not a representative of the Convention, have arrogated to himself the right to report on the massacre? Was he deputized by the commune of Saint-Maximin to witness the carnage? And how would he have assumed responsibility for such a report when there were "bigger" men than him at play in the amphitheater—among them witnesses of the execution carried out by his brother? It would cost something to bring the eyes of men so low after raising them so high.

Let us say that the narrator of Napoleon's exploits was Lucien, president of the committee of Saint-Maximin: it would then follow that one of the first shots Bonaparte fired was aimed at Frenchmen. There is no question at least that Napoleon was called upon to spill their blood on the 13th of Vendémiaire, and he reddened his hands with it again with the killing of the Duc d'Enghien. The first time our sacrifice brought Bonaparte to the attention of the world, the second slaughter elevated him to the rank that makes him master of Italy, and the third paved his way to empire.

He grew strong on our flesh; he broke our bones and fed on the marrow of lions. It is a deplorable thing, but it must be recognized if we don't wish to turn away from the mysteries of human nature and the tenor of the times: a *part* of Napoleon's power comes from having been steeped in the Terror. The Revolution is more comfortable serving those who have been tainted by its crimes. An innocent past is an obstacle.

The young Robespierre had taken a liking to Bonaparte and wanted to make him commander of Paris, replacing Hanriot. At that time, Napoleon's family had settled at the Château Sallé, near Antibes. "I had come there from Saint-Maximin," says Lucien, "to spend a few days with my family and my brother. We were all together there, and the general gave us every moment he could spare. One day he appeared more than usually preoccupied and, walking between me and Joseph, announced it was up to him whether he should leave for Paris as early as the following day with the aim of establishing us there to great advantage. I, for my part, was enchanted by this announcement: to arrive in the capital at last struck me as a good that no other consideration could outweigh. 'They have offered me Hanriot's position,' Napoleon told us. 'I must give my answer tonight. Well...what do you make of it?' We hesitated a moment. 'Yes,' the general continued, 'it deserves a good long think: it would not be as easy to keep one's head in Paris as it is in Saint-Maximin.' 'Young Robespierre is an honest man, but his brother is not to be trifled with. You would have to serve him.' 'Me, support that man? Never! I know how useful I would be to him, replacing his idiot commander in Paris, but *that is not what I want to be.* The time isn't right. The only honorable place for me at the moment is in the army. Be patient. *I will take Paris by the horns later on.'* These were Napoleon's words. He then expressed the indignation he felt toward the Reign of Terror, whose demise he predicted, and concluded by repeating several times, at once solemn and smiling, 'Why would I board that ship?'"[20]

After the siege of Toulon, Bonaparte found himself involved in our army's maneuvers in the Alps. He received orders to go to Genoa: secret instructions bid him reconnoiter the condition of the fortress at Savona and gather intelligence about the Genoese government's intentions relative to the coalition. These instructions, delivered to Loano on Messidor 25, year II of the Republic, are signed by Ricord.

Bonaparte fulfilled his mission. Then came the 9th of Thermidor: the terrorist deputies were replaced by Albitte, Salicetti, and Laporte. Suddenly they declared, in the name of the French people, that General Bonaparte, commanding the artillery of the Army of Italy, had completely lost their confidence through his most suspicious conduct and above all through the trip he had recently made to Genoa.

The decree of Barcelonnette on Thermidor 9, year II of the unified, indivisible, and democratic French Republic (August 6, 1794) states that General Bonaparte will be "placed under arrest and brought to the Committee of Public Safety in Paris under careful guard." Salicetti examined Bonaparte's papers; he responded to those who took an interest in the prisoner by saying it was only right to proceed rigorously when investigating accusations of treason from Nice and Corsica. These accusations were the result of the direct instructions given by Ricord: it was easy to insinuate that instead of serving France, Napoleon had served foreign interests. The emperor was not sparing with his own accusations of espionage; he should have remembered the dangers to which similar accusations had exposed him.

Napoleon, struggling to defend himself, said to the representatives:

"Salicetti, you know me . . . Albitte, you don't know me at all, but you nevertheless know how expertly slander can sing. Listen to me; if you restore me in the eyes of my fellow patriots and an hour later the wretches are still calling for my life . . . Well, I don't place much value on it! I have so often scorned it!"

A sentence of acquittal followed. Among the documents that, in these years, served as proof of Bonaparte's good behavior, we note a certificate signed by Pozzo di Borgo. Bonaparte was set at liberty only "provisionally," but in this interval he had time to imprison the world.

Salicetti, the accuser, wasted no time ingratiating himself with the accused; but Bonaparte would never trust his former enemy. He later writes to General Dumas:

"Let him (Salicetti) stay in Naples; he should be happy there. The place is full of *lazzaroni*; I know it well; he's frightened them: he's meaner than they are. Let him know I don't have enough power to protect wretches who voted for the death of Louis XVI from scorn and public indignation."*

Bonaparte, who then hastened to Paris, lodged on rue du Mail—the same street where I landed when I first arrived from Brittany with Madame Rose. Bourrienne joined him, as did Murat, suspected of terrorism and escaped from his garrison in Abbeville. The government tried to transform Napoleon into an infantry brigadier general and wanted to send him off to the Vendée. When he declined the honor, saying he had no wish to change his weaponry, the Committee of Public Safety deleted the decliner from the official list of officers. One of the signatories of the annulation is Cambacérès, who would become second in power under the Empire.

Embittered by these persecutions, Napoleon thought to emigrate,

Souvenirs du lieutenant général comte Dumas, vol. III, p. 317.

but Volney stopped him. Had he carried out his plan, the fugitive Court would have ignored him. There was, besides, on that side, no crown for him to take; I would have found myself with an outsize companion—a giant bowed beside me in exile.

With the idea of emigration behind him, Bonaparte turned his thoughts toward the East, which, in its love of despotism and pomp, was doubly congenial to his nature. He undertook to write a letter offering his sword to the Sultan: inaction and obscurity were like death to him. "I will be useful to my country," he exclaimed, "if I can make the Turkish forces more formidable to Europe." The government, apparently, did not respond to this madman's note.

When all these various plans came to nothing, Bonaparte felt a mounting distress. He was difficult to help; he accepted favors with the same grudgingness he had shown when he was promoted by the king's munificence. He resented anyone more fortunate than he was. Here we see a glimmering—in the soul of the man for whom the treasuries of nations would later be depleted—of the loathing the communists and proletarians of the present time express for the rich. When a man shares in the sufferings of the poor, he gets a feeling for social inequality, and is no more eager to ride in a carriage than he is to sneer at people on foot. Bonaparte especially hated the *muscadins* and *incroyables*, young gallants of the day who wore their hair pulled back with a comb, imitating the heads severed by the blade. He liked to pour cold water on their whoops and roars. He visited Baptiste the Elder and got to know Talma. The Bonaparte family professed a taste for the theater: the idleness of garrison life often prompted Napoleon to go see the show.

Whatever efforts democracy may make to improve its manners by means of the great purpose it sets itself, its habits drag its manners down. It feels a strong resentment toward any sense of restriction. During the Revolution, believing it could put restriction behind it, democracy spilled torrents of blood; but the remedy didn't work, for it couldn't kill everyone, and in the end democracy found itself faced with the insolence of the dead. The necessity of passing through petty circumstances gives life a somewhat common cast; an unusual idea is reduced to being expressed in vulgar language, and genius is imprisoned in slang, just as surely as, in a decrepit aristocracy, abject sentiments are expressed in noble words. If we wish to highlight the inferior side of Napoleon with examples drawn from antiquity, we need look no further than Agrippina's son—and yet the legions worshipped the husband of Octavia, and the Roman Empire shuddered at his memory.[21]

In Paris, Bonaparte visited Mademoiselle de Comnène again. She was soon to marry Junot, whom Napoleon had befriended in the South.

"At that period of his life," the Duchesse d'Abrantès writes, "Napoleon was ugly. Since then he has undergone a complete transformation. I do not refer to the prestigious halo of his glory but the physical change that gradually occurred in the space of seven years. Everything that was bony, sallow, and sickly in his appearance filled out, cleared up, and became attractive. His features, which were nearly all angular and pointy, have grown round. His gaze and his smile remain as admirable as they always were, but otherwise he has undergone a total alteration. His hair, which now looks so remarkable to us in the etchings of the crossing of the Pont d'Arcole, was then quite simple, because those same *muscadins* against whom he ranted and raged wore theirs long; but his color was so yellow at that time, and he took such poor care of himself, that his badly combed, badly powdered hair gave him a disagreeable appearance. His small hands have also undergone a metamorphosis; they were then thin, long, and dark. Everyone knows how vain he has become of them since, and for good reason. Finally, when I think of Napoleon in 1795 coming into the courtyard of the Hôtel de la Tranquillité on the rue des Filles-Saint-Thomas, crossing it with a clumsy and uncertain gait, a round hat pulled down over his eyes, and two badly powdered braids falling over the collar of his iron-gray coat, which has since become a glorious banner no less famous than Henry IV's white plume; wearing no gloves because, he said, they were a pointless expense, and shod in poorly made, poorly polished boots; looking sickly from top to toe owing to his thinness and his jaundiced tint—in short, when I call up my memory of him from those days, compared to the times I saw him again later, I cannot believe that these two images are of the same man."

10.

DAYS OF VENDÉMIAIRE

THE DEATH of Robespierre was not the end. The prisons disgorged their prisoners only gradually. The murders were so well organized, death proceeded with such order and obedience, that the day before the doomed orator was taken to the scaffold eighty victims were sacrificed. The two executioners Sanson were brought to trial; but more fortunate than Roseau, who hanged Tardif on the orders of the Duc de Mayenne, they were acquitted: the blood of Louis XVI had washed them clean.

The released prisoners did not know what to do with their lives any more than the unemployed Jacobins knew how to spend their days; hence the dances and sorrows of the Terror. It was only gradually that justice was torn from the hands of the Convention, whose members did not wish to leave off their crimes for fear of losing power. The Revolutionary Tribunal was abolished.

André Dumont had suggested prosecuting Robespierre's successors. The Convention, urged on against its will following a report by Saladin, reluctantly ordered the arrest of Barère, Billaud de Varennes, and Collot d'Herbois. (The latter two were friends of Robespierre's who had nevertheless played a part in his downfall.) Carrier, Fouquier-Tinville, and Joseph Lebon were tried, and their unbelievable offenses and crimes were revealed—in particular, the "republican marriages" and the drowning of six hundred children in Nantes.[22] The sections,[23] among which the National Guardsmen were divided, accused the Convention of past wrongdoings and feared seeing them repeated.

The Society of Jacobins still fought on, unable to turn up their nose at death. Legendre, who had once been so violent, now returned to humanity and joined the Committee of Public Safety. The night of Robespierre's agony, he had the lair sealed; but eight days later the Jacobins had settled in again under the name the "rejuvenated" Jacobins. The women with their knitting found their way there, too. Fréron resurrected his paper, the *Orateur du peuple*, and while he applauded the fall of Robespierre, he sided with the authority of the Convention. Marat's bust remained on display, and all the various committees—which had changed nothing but their outward form—went on existing.

Bitter cold and famine, combined with political disturbances, complicated the calamities. Armed groups filled with women crying "Bread! Bread!" were formed. Finally, on the 1st of Prairial (May 20, 1795), the door to the Convention was forced, Feraud murdered, and his head plopped down upon the president's desk. Tales are told of how stoically impassive Boissy d'Anglas remained throughout the whole ordeal: woe betide the man who stands in the way of a virtuous act!

This revolutionary vegetation grew vigorously on the bed of manure, watered with human blood, that served as its base. Rossignol, Huchet, Grignon, Moïse Bayle, Amar, Choudieu, Hentz, Granet, Léonard Bourdon—all men who had distinguished themselves by their excesses—were parked between the barriers; and meanwhile our renown increased in foreign lands. When opinion turned against the Convention, our triumphs abroad stifled the public clamor. There were two Frances: a horrible one at home and an admirable one abroad. Our glory was set against our crimes, as Bonaparte set it against our liberties. Our victories have always loomed, like a pitfall, before us.

It is worth noting the anachronism that people commit by attributing our success to our enormities. Our successes were obtained before and after the Reign of Terror, and thus the Terror had nothing to do with our military might. But these successes had one drawback: they formed a halo around the head of the revolutionary ghosts. Without examining the dates, many believed this holy light belonged to them. The capture of Holland and the crossing of the Rhine appeared to be conquests of the ax, not the sword. In this confusion, no one could see how France would manage to throw off the shackles that, despite the catastrophe met by the guiltiest parties, continued to oppress her. Yet the liberator was already in our midst.

Bonaparte had kept most—and certainly the worst—of the friends he had made in the South. Like him, they had taken refuge in the capital. Salicetti, who remained powerful thanks to the Jacobin brotherhood, had grown closer with Napoleon, and Fréron, who had become intimate with Pauline Bonaparte (Princess Borghèse), whom he would later marry, lent his support to his future brother-in-law.

Far from the grousing of the forum and the podium, Bonaparte took his evening stroll in the Jardin des Plantes with Junot. Junot told him about his passion for Paulette, and Napoleon confided in him his feelings for Madame de Beauharnais. Events, incubating, were going to hatch a great man. Madame de Beauharnais was on friendly terms with Barras. It is probable this connection jogged the commissioner's memory when the decisive days arrived.

11.

DAYS OF VENDÉMIAIRE, CONTINUED

FREEDOM of the press, momentarily restored, was a step in the direction of deliverance; but as the democrats had never cared for this freedom, which criticized their errors, they accused it of being royalist. Abbé Morellet and La Harpe launched pamphlets that piled up alongside those of the Spaniard Marchenna, a vile scholar and spiritual runt. The young went around in gray coats with black lapels and collars—the reputed uniform of the Chouans. The meeting of the new legislature served as an excuse for the sections to assemble. The Le Pelletier section, previously called the Filles-Saint-Thomas section, was the liveliest; it appeared several times at the bar of the Convention to complain. Lacretelle the Younger lent his voice to it with the same courage he showed the day Bonaparte gunned down Parisians on the steps of Saint-Roch. Foreseeing the fighting to come, the sections sent to Rouen for General Danican and appointed him their leader. Something of the fear and feelings that the Convention stirred up can be divined from the defenders it found. "To lead these republicans," Réal writes in his *Essay on the Days of Vendémiaire*, "who are called the 'holy battalion of the patriots of '89,' and into their ranks, they summoned those veterans of the Revolution who had seen six campaigns, who had fought beneath the walls of the Bastille, who had laid tyranny low, and who were now preparing to defend the same building they had attacked on August 10. Among them I found the precious remains of the old battalions of Liège and Belgium, led by their old general Fyon."

Réal ends this enumeration with an apostrophe:

"Oh, you who allowed us to conquer Europe with a government without governors and armies without pay, Spirit of Liberty, you watch over us yet!"

These proud champions of liberty survived more than a few "days"; they went to finish their hymns to independence in the offices of a tyrant's police force. Today, this period seems only a broken step over which the Revolution passed: how many men have spoken and acted with conviction, have been passionate about events that we no longer care anything about! Every one of us reaps the fruit of forgotten lives squandered so that we might live.

The Convention was soon to be renewed; the first assemblies were called: the committees, clubs, and sections made a terrible thunder.

The Convention, threatened by widespread aversion, saw it needed to defend itself. Against Danican,[24] it pitted Barras, the new leader of the armed forces of Paris. Having met Bonaparte in Toulon and been reminded of him by Madame de Beauharnais, Barras thought such a man might be useful to him and appointed him second-in-command. The future Director, keeping up the Convention through the days of Vendémiaire, said that Bonaparte's quick and expert thinking had preserved the outer wall, around which he had posted troops with great skill. Napoleon fired on the sections and said, "I have made my mark on France." Attila before him had said, "I am the hammer of the world," *ego malleus orbis*.[25]

After the battle was won, Napoleon feared he had made himself unpopular, and he had to dedicate several years of his life to erasing this page of his history.

There is an account of the days of Vendémiaire written by Napoleon, in which he tries to prove the sections were the first to fire. Facing them, he might have imagined he was back in Toulon: General Carteaux was leading a column on the Pont-Neuf; a company of Marseillais were marching on Saint-Roch; the positions occupied by the National Guards were taken one after the next. Réal, in the narrative I have already mentioned, concludes with a string of inanities that Parisians firmly believe. There is a wounded man crossing the arena of victory who spies a flag he had taken earlier. "Let us go no farther," he says in a fading voice, "I want to die right here." There is General Dufraisse's wife, who cuts up her blouse to make bandages. There are Durocher's two daughters, who administer vinegar and eau-de-vie. Réal attributes everything to Barras—a sycophantic omission which proves that Napoleon, in year IV of the Revolution, was a nobody who won victory for the benefit of another.

In spite of his triumph, Bonaparte did not expect immediate success, for he wrote to Bourrienne:

"Look for a little property in your beautiful Valley of the Yonne; I will buy it as soon as I have the money; but don't forget I have no interest in national property."*

Bonaparte changed his mind during the Empire: he set great store by national property then.

These Vendémiaire riots ended the era of riots: they were not repeated until 1830, to put an end to the monarchy.

Four months after the days of Vendémiaire, on the 19th of Ventôse (March 9), year IV, Bonaparte married Marie-Josèphe-Rose de Tascher. The act makes no mention of the widow of the Comte de Beauharnais. Tallien and Barras stood as witnesses. In June, Bonaparte was called to command the troops cantoned in the maritime Alps—an appointment for whose honor Carnot[26] implored Barras. Generalship of the Army of Italy was nicknamed "Madame Beauharnais's dowry." Napoleon, who spoke of this disdainfully on Saint Helena, knew very well that he was allying himself with an influential lady and showed a want of gratitude.

At this point, Napoleon enters fully into his destiny. He had needed men, and now men are going to need him; events had fashioned him, and now he is going to fashion events. He has passed through those trials that superior natures are doomed to undergo before they are recognized—forced to bow and scrape before the mediocrities whose patronage they require. The seed of the tallest palm must first be sheltered by the Arab beneath a vase of clay.

*Madame de Beaumont and Monsieur Joubert lived in the Yonne Valley then.

12.

ITALIAN CAMPAIGNS

ARRIVING at the Army of Italy's headquarters in Nice, Bonaparte finds the soldiers lacking everything: shoes, bread, discipline. He was twenty-eight years old, and under his orders Masséna was commanding thirty-six thousand men. It was the year 1796. He began his first campaign on March 20—a date that was to be engraved several times in his life. He defeats Beaulieu at Montenotte; two days later, at Millesimo, he separates the Austrian and the Sardinian armies. In Ceva, Mondovi, Fossano, and Cherasco, his successes continue. The spirit of warfare itself has descended. The following proclamation reveals a voice hitherto unheard, as the battles had announced a man hitherto unseen:

"Soldiers! In fifteen days, you have won six victories, taken twenty-one flags, fifty-five pieces of cannon, fifteen thousand prisoners, and killed or wounded more than ten thousand men. You have won battles without cannon, crossed rivers without bridges, made forced marches without boots, bivouacked without brandy and often without bread. The Republican phalanxes and the soldiers of liberty alone were capable of suffering what you have suffered; thanks be to you, soldiers! . . .

"People of Italy, the French army is coming to break your chains; the French people are the friends of all the peoples. All we want to take from you are the tyrants that oppress you."

By March 15, peace is concluded between the French Republic and the King of Sardinia; Savoy, Nice, and Tende are ceded to France. Napoleon is still advancing, and he writes to Carnot:

From headquarters, Plaisance, May 9, 1796

We have finally crossed the Po. The second campaign has begun. Beaulieu is bewildered. He strategizes poorly and constantly falls into the traps laid for him. Perhaps he would prefer to fight in battle, for he is a man of bold fury, not genius. Another victory and we will be masters of Italy. The moment we cease our maneuvers, we will suit the men up again. They are still dreadful enough, but growing quite fat; the soldiers eat nothing but Gonesse bread, good meat and plenty of it, etc. Discipline is reestablished every day, but it is often necessary to have them shot, for there are intractable men who cannot control themselves. What we have taken from the enemy is incalculable. The more men you send me, the more easily I will feed them. I am having twenty paintings by the greatest masters, Correggio and Michelangelo, sent to you. I owe you special thanks for the attentions you have so kindly shown my wife. I recommend her to you: she is a sincere patriot, and I love her to distraction. I hope that things will go well, which will put me in a position to send you twelve million in Paris. That won't be too shabby for the Army of the Rhine. Send me four thousand unseated cavalrymen and I will find them horses here. I make no secret of the fact that, since Stengel died, I don't have a single decent senior cavalry officer. I'd like it if you could send me two or three adjutant generals who have some fire to them, and a firm resolve never to make textbook retreats.

This is one of Napoleon's most remarkable letters. What vivacity! What a wide-ranging mind! Along with the hero's reports, we find a few paintings by Michelangelo haphazardly tossed in to the triumphal profusion, and a very piquant potshot at a rival,[27] who is distinguished from those adjutant generals with "a firm resolve never to make textbook retreats." The same day, Bonaparte wrote to the Directory to advise it of the ceasefire granted to the Duke of Parma and the dispatch of Correggio's *Saint Jerome*. On May 11, he informed Carnot of the crossing of the Lodi Bridge, which puts us in possession of Lombardy. If he did not go to Milan right away, it was only because he wanted to follow Beaulieu and finish things: "If I take Mantua, nothing can stop me from reaching Bavaria; in twenty days I can be in the heart of Germany. If the two Armies of the Rhine launch a campaign, please let me know their positions. It would be a feat worthy of the Republic to go and sign a peace treaty among three armies in the heart of Bavaria with Austria stunned."

The eagle does not walk, he flies, with the banners of victory trailing from his neck and wings.

He complains about Kellermann being sent to serve as his second-in-command:

"I cannot willingly serve with a man who thinks he is the premier general of Europe, and I believe that one bad general is better than two good ones."

On June 1, 1796, the Austrians are entirely expelled from Italy and our outposts light up the hills of Germany. "Our grenadiers and riflemen," Bonaparte writes to the Directory, "laugh and sport with death. Nothing equals their boldness, unless it's the gaiety with which they go on the longest forced marches. You would think that once they'd made camp they would go straight to sleep, but no: they write their own reports or plan their operations for the next day—and often one can pick out the sharpest of them by these things. The other day I was watching a half-brigade file past when a cavalryman approached my horse: 'General,' he said, 'we must do such-and-such.' 'You runt,' I told him, 'you ought to shut your mouth!' He disappeared at once; I had him searched for in vain; it was exactly what I had ordered to be done."

The soldiers promoted their commander: in Lodi they made him a corporal and in Castiglione a sergeant.

On November 17, they arrive at Arcole and the young general crosses the bridge that made him famous; ten thousand men crowd into the square. "It was a song from *The Iliad*!" Bonaparte used to exclaim at the mere memory of this day.

In Germany, Moreau executes the famous retreat that the envious Napoleon called a "sergeant's retreat." Bonaparte, defeating the Archduke Charles, was getting ready to say to his rival:

Je suivrai d'assez près votre illustre retraite
Pour traiter avec lui sans besoin d'interprète.[28]

On January 14, 1797, hostilities break out again with the Battle of Rivoli. Two clashes with Wurmser, at Saint Georges and La Favorite, result in five thousand dead and twenty thousand enemies taken prisoner. Those remaining barricade themselves in Mantua; the blockaded city capitulates. Wurmser, with the twelve thousand men left to him, surrenders.

Soon the March of Ancona is invaded; later the treaty of Tolentino delivers us pearls, diamonds, precious manuscripts, the *Transfiguration*, the Laocoön, the Apollo Belvedere, and ends this series of operations by which, in less than a year, four Austrian armies were destroyed, upper Italy was subjugated, and the Tyrol breached. There is no time to come to grips with any of this—the thunder and lightning arrive all at once.

Archduke Charles, who had rushed in to defend the Austrian front with new troops, is now forced to cross the Tagliamento; Gradisca falls; Trieste is taken; the preliminaries of peace between France and Austria are signed at Leoben.

Venice, formed amid the fall of the Roman Empire, troubled and betrayed, had opened its lagoons and palaces to us; a revolution on May 31, 1797, took place in Genoa, its rival, and the Ligurian Republic was born. Bonaparte would have been quite surprised if, in the midst of his conquests, he had been able to see that he had seized Venice for Austria, the Legations for Rome, Naples for the Bourbons, Genoa for Piedmont, Spain for England, Westphalia for Prussia, and Poland for Russia, like those soldiers who, during the sack of a city, load themselves up with more spoils than they can possibly carry and must throw them away, while at the same time they lose their native land.

On July 9, the Cisalpine Republic proclaimed its existence. In Bonaparte's correspondence, one can see the shuttle racing through the warp of the revolutions attached to ours. As Muhammad went forth with the sword in one hand and the Koran in the other, so we went forth with the sword and the *Rights of Man*.

Throughout all of this, Bonaparte does not let one detail escape him. Now he fears lest the "old men" painted by the great artists of Venice, Bologna, and Milan get wet while crossing Mont Cenis; now he worries a papyrus manuscript from the Biblioteca Ambrosiana may be lost; he implores the Minister of the Interior to tell him when it has arrived at the Bibliothèque Nationale. He gives his opinion of his generals to the Directory:

Berthier: talent, energy, courage, character, everything going for him.

Augereau: a great deal of character, courage, firmness, energy; is loved by the soldiers, lucky in maneuvers.

Masséna: active, tireless, has the boldness, sharp eye, and promptitude needed to make decisions.

Seurier: fights like a soldier, lacks initiative, firm, does not think highly enough of his troops; is ill.

Despinois: flabby, spiritless, no boldness, not made for warfare, not liked by the soldiers, does not lead them into battle; is also high-minded and witty and has sound political principles; good for command at home.

Sauret: good, very good soldier, not intelligent enough to be a general; unlucky.

Abbatucci: not fit to command fifty men.

To the leader of the Maniots, Bonaparte writes: "The French esteem the small, brave people that, alone of ancient Greece, have retained their virtue, the worthy descendants of Sparta who only lack a greater theater to equal their ancestors in renown." He instructs the authorities to take possession of Corfu. "The island of Corcyra," he remarks, "was, according to Homer, the land of Princess Nausicaa." He dispatches the peace treaty concluded with Venice: "Our navy acquired four or five men-o'-war there, three or four frigates, and three or four million lines of rigging—Give me French or Corsican sailors," he writes; "I will take those of Mantua or Guarda. —A million for Toulon, as I told you, goes off tomorrow, plus two million . . .

makes five million that the Army of Italy has supplied in the latest campaign. —I have instructed so-and-so to go to Sion to try to open negotiations with Valais. —I have sent an excellent engineer to find out how much this road (the Simplon) would cost to build . . . I have asked the same engineer to go see what it would take to explode the rock that chokes the Rhône and exploit the forests of the Valais and Savoie." He gives notice that he is going to have a load of wheat and steel shipped from Trieste to Genoa. He presents four cases of rifles to the Pasha of Scutari, as a mark of his friendship. He has several suspicious men removed from Milan and several others arrested. He writes to Citizen Grogniard, the chief naval officer in Toulon: "I am not your judge, but if you were under my command, I would place you under arrest for having complied with a ridiculous requisition." A note delivered to the pope's minister reads: "The pope will perhaps think it worthy of his wisdom, and of the holiest of religions, to issue a bull or mandate ordering priests to obey the government."

All of this is done in between negotiations with new republics, arrangements for festivals dedicated to Virgil and Ariosto, explanatory notes regarding twenty paintings and five hundred manuscripts from Venice; all of this takes place in an Italy deafened by the noise of battle, in an Italy that has become an inferno where our grenadiers lived like salamanders in the fire.

During this whirlwind of events and victories comes the 18th of Fructidor, fostered by Bonaparte's proclamations and discussions among his troops, which are hostile toward the Army of the Meuse. This spelled the end for a man[29] who, perhaps wrongly, had passed for the author of the plans that led to the Republican victories (no doubt Danissy, Lafitte, and d'Arçon, three military masterminds, were all behind these plans): Carnot found himself, through Bonaparte's influence, banished.

On October 17, the latter signed the peace treaty of Campo Formio: the first continental war of the Revolution came to an end thirty leagues from Vienna.

13.

CONGRESS OF RASTATT—NAPOLEON'S RETURN TO FRANCE—NAPOLEON IS APPOINTED LEADER OF THE SO-CALLED ARMY OF ENGLAND—HE DEPARTS ON THE EXPEDITION TO EGYPT

ONCE A congress was put together at Rastatt and the Directory appointed Bonaparte their representative, he took his leave of the Army of Italy. "I shall find no consolation," he said to his men, "except in the hope of seeing myself by your side again soon, fighting new dangers." On November 16, 1797, his agenda announces that he left Milan to preside over the French legation at the congress and that he sent the Army of Italy's flag, embroidered on one side with a list of his conquests,[30] to the Directory.

After a purely military convention, which stipulated that Mainz be handed over to the soldiers of the Republic and Venice to the soldiers of Austria, Bonaparte went away from Rastatt, leaving the remainder of the congress in the hands of Treilhard and Bonnier.

During the last days of the Italian campaign, Bonaparte suffered greatly from the envy of various generals and politicians of the Directory. Twice he offered his resignation, which the members of the government wanted but did not dare accept. Bonaparte's sentiments ran contrary to the spirit of the age; he yielded only reluctantly to the interests born of the Revolution—and this was the cause of his contradictory actions and ideas.

Back in Paris, he arrived at his house on rue Chantereine, which then took the name it still bears today: rue de la Victoire. The Council of Ancients in fact wanted to give Napoleon the Château de Chambord, the work of François I, which now recalls nothing so much as the exile of Saint Louis's last descendant.[31] Bonaparte was presented to the Directory on December 10, 1797, in the courtyard of the Luxembourg Palace. In the middle of this courtyard stood an altar to France surmounted by statues of Liberty, Equality, and Peace. The flags of the conquered formed a canopy above the five directors clothed in classical attire; the shadow of Victory descended from these flags beneath which France would, for a moment, halt. Bonaparte was dressed in the uniform he wore in Arcole and Lodi. M. de Talleyrand received the champion at the altar—recalling how, in another era, he had said Mass upon another. Having fled to the United States and then returned, the old Bishop of Autun had been appointed by Chénier as Minister of Foreign Affairs and stood with a sword at his side, sporting a Henri IV hat. Events forced these travesties to be taken seriously.

The prelate praised the conqueror of Italy, gloomily declaring that he loved "the songs of Ossian, above all because they untether us from earth. Far from fearing what is called his ambition, we shall perhaps need to go and call upon it one day, wresting him from the sweet pleasures of his studious retirement. The whole of France will be free, though he, perhaps, never will be: such is his destiny."

What marvelous clairvoyance!

Saint Louis's brother at Grandella, Charles VIII at Fornoue, Louis XII at Agnadel, François I at Marignano, Lautrec at Ravenna, and Catinat at Turin—none can be compared with the new general. Napoleon's success was peerless.

The Directory, fearing a supreme despotism that would threaten the existence of every other despotism, had worriedly observed the homages paid to Napoleon and were attempting to rid themselves of his presence. They encouraged his passion for an expedition to the Orient. He had said:

"Europe is a molehill; all the great empires and revolutions have been in the East. I have won all the glory I can win here. This little Europe of ours is not enough."

Napoleon, like a child, was elated to have been elected a member of the Institute.[32] He asked for a mere six years to reach the Indies and return.

"I am only twenty-nine," he said; "that is no great age. I will be thirty-five when I get back."

Appointed general of the so-called Army of England, whose corps were scattered from Brest to Antwerp, Bonaparte passed the time with inspections and visits to civil and scientific authorities while the troops who would compose the Army of Egypt were assembled. Then came the skirmish in Vienna over the red cap and the tricolor flag, which our ambassador, General Bernadotte, had hoisted over the door of his palace. The Directory was preparing to retain Napoleon, in order to ward off the possibility of another war, when Count von Cobentzel prevented the rupture, and Bonaparte was ordered to depart. With Italy turned republican and Holland transformed into a republic, peace left France—whose borders now extended as far as the Rhine—many useless soldiers, and in its fearful foresight, the Directory rushed to send the victor abroad. This Egyptian adventure would change Napoleon's fortune as well as his genius—gilding this genius, which was already too bright, with a ray of sun that struck at the pillars of cloud and smoke.[33]

14.

EGYPTIAN EXPEDITION—MALTA—BATTLE OF THE PYRAMIDS—CAIRO—NAPOLEON IN THE GREAT PYRAMID—SUEZ

Toulon, May 19, 1798

PROCLAMATION

SOLDIERS, you are one of the wings of the Army of England.

You have waged war on the mountains and in the plains. You have laid siege to cities. All that remains for you is to wage war at sea.

The Roman legions you have sometimes imitated, but not yet equaled, fought Carthage on this same sea and on the plains of Zama. Victory never abandoned them, for they were forever brave, disciplined, ready to endure fatigue, and united among themselves.

Soldiers, all of Europe is watching you! You have great destinies to fulfill, battles to win, dangers and struggles to overcome. You will do more than you have ever done for the prosperity of the homeland, for the happiness of mankind, and for your own glory.

Following this proclamation of memories, Napoleon embarked, as though he were Homer, or as though he were the hero who closed up the songs of Maeonides in a golden coffer.[34] He is a man who never maunders. No sooner has he set foot in Italy than he appears in Egypt—a fantastical episode that makes his real life larger. Like Charlemagne, he linked an epic with his story. In the library he took with him were Ossian, *Werther*, *The New Héloïse*, and the Old Testament—

an indication of the chaos in Napoleon's brain. He combined positive ideas and novelistic feelings, systems and chimeras, serious studies and flights of the imagination, wisdom and folly. From these incoherent productions of the age, he drew the Empire: an immense dream, which passed as swiftly as the disorderly darkness that brought it into the world.

Entering Toulon on May 9, 1798, Napoleon alighted at the Hôtel de la Marine. Ten days later, he boarded the flagship *L'Orient* and set sail that same day. He pulled away from the shore where he had first spilled blood, French blood: the massacres at Toulon had steeled him for the massacres at Jaffa. With him, he took the firstborn generals of his glory: Berthier, Caffarelli, Kléber, Desaix, Lannes, Murat, Menou. Thirteen ships of the line, fourteen frigates, and four hundred transport ships accompanied him.

Nelson allowed him to slip out of the harbor and did not sight the fleets, although at one point our ships passed within six leagues of the English vessels. From the sea of Sicily, Napoleon spied the summit of the Apennines and said: "I cannot look at Italian earth without emotion. There is the Orient. That is where I am going." At the sight of Ida, an explosion of admiration for Minos and ancient wisdom. During the crossing, Bonaparte amused himself by bringing scholars together and provoking arguments; he usually sided with the most daring or absurd opinion. He asked whether the planets were inhabited or could be destroyed by water or fire—as if he had been charged with inspecting the Heavenly host.

He lands in Malta and unearths the old knights long hidden in the wave-rent rocks; then he descends among the ruins of the city of Alexandria. At dawn he sees Pompey's Pillar, which I had spied from aboard my ship as we sailed away from Libya. At the foot of the monument immortalized by a great and melancholy name, he takes flight; he climbs the walls behind which there used to be a "storehouse of remedies for the soul" and some Cleopatra's Needles, now sunk into the earth and stalked by rawboned dogs. The Gate of Rosetta is forced and our troops rush into the two harbors and the beacon house. What dreadful slaughter ensues! Adjutant General Boyer wrote to his family:

"The Turks, driven back on all sides, are taking refuge in their god and prophet; their mosques are filled; men and women, young and old—everyone is being massacred."

Bonaparte had said to the Bishop of Malta:

"You can assure your diocesans that the Holy Roman and Apostolic Catholic religion will not only be respected but its ministers specially protected."

He said, on arriving in Egypt:

"People of Egypt, I respect God, his Prophet, and the Koran more than the Mamluks. The French are friends to Muslims. Not long ago they marched on Rome and overthrew the throne of the pope, who embittered Christians against those who profess Islam; soon after they set sail for Malta and chased away the infidels who believed God willed them to wage war on Muslims… If Egypt is the Mamluks' farm, let them produce the lease God has given them."

Now Napoleon marches to the Pyramids and shouts to his men:

"Soldiers, from the heights of these monuments, forty centuries fix their eyes upon you!"

He enters Cairo; his fleet is blown to bits at Aboukir; the Army of the Orient is cut off from Europe. Julien de la Drôme—the son of Julien, the member of the National Convention—records it minute by minute:

"It is seven o'clock; night falls and the firing is becoming more frequent. At a few minutes past nine, the ship blows up. At ten, the firing slows and the moon rises to the right of the spot where the ship exploded."

Bonaparte tells the chief justice of Cairo that he will be the restorer of the mosques; he makes his name known throughout Arabia, Ethiopia, and the Indies. Cairo revolts; he bombards it in the middle of a storm; the inspired man says to the believers:

"I could compel every one of you to confess the most secret feelings in your hearts, for I know everything, even what you have never told anyone."

The Grand Sharif of Mecca names him, in a letter, the "protector of the Kaaba"; the pope, in a missive, calls him "my dearest son."

A native weakness often caused Bonaparte to prefer his small side to his great one. What he could win in one fell swoop was boring to him. The hand that shattered the world amused itself with shell games, although when he used his faculties, he surely made up for for his losses. His genius was the repairer of his character. Why did he not present himself from the first as the successor to the knights? His two-faced approach only made him, in the eyes of the Muslim masses, a false Christian *and* a false Muslim. To admire a system's impieties and not to recognize their wretchedness is to be miserably mistaken: we must weep when a giant stoops to such hypocrisy. The infidels offered the crown of Egypt to the imprisoned Saint Louis because he had remained, the Arab historians say, the proudest Christian they had ever seen.

When I passed through Cairo, the city still bore traces of the French: a public garden we had built was planted with palm trees; restaurants had once surrounded it. Unfortunately, like the Ancient Egyptians before them, our soldiers had paraded a coffin around at their feasts.

What a memorable scene, if one could believe in it: Bonaparte sitting inside the Pyramid of Cheops, on the sarcophagus of a pharaoh whose mummy had vanished, chatting with muftis and imams! But let us assume this article in the *Moniteur* is an invention of the Muse. Still, if not a factual story about Napoleon, it is still a story about his intelligence and therefore worthy our attention. Let us listen to a voice that the centuries will hear, speaking from the depths of a tomb:

Le Moniteur, November 27, 1798

Today, 25 Thermidor, year IV of the French Republic, corresponding to the twenty-eighth of the moon of Mucharim, year of Hegira 1213, the commander in chief, accompanied by several officers and members of the National Institute, was transported to the great pyramid called Cheops, in the interior of which several muftis and imams awaited his arrival, charged with the duty of showing him the structure of the interior.

The last room that the commander in chief visited is a flat

vault thirty-two feet long by sixteen wide and nineteen high. There is nothing in it except a granite box about eight feet long and four feet thick, which used to contain the mummy of a pharaoh. He sat down on the granite block, invited the muftis and imams, Suleiman, Ibrahim, and Muhammad, to sit beside him, and, in the presence of his retinue, had the following conversation with them:

Bonaparte: God is great and his works are marvelous. But here is a great work made by the hands of men! What did the man have in mind who had this pyramid constructed?

Suleiman: He was a powerful king of Egypt, whose name is believed to have been Cheops. He wished to prevent sacrileges from disturbing the peace of his remains.

Bonaparte: The great Cyrus had himself buried in the open air, so that his corpse would return to the elements. Don't you think that was better? What do you make of it?

Suleiman (bowing): Glory be to God, to whom all glory is due!

Bonaparte: Glory be to Allah! There is no other God but God; Muhammad is his prophet, and I am one of the friends of Muhammad.

Ibrahim: May the angels of victory sweep the dust from your path and cover you with their wings! The Mamluk deserves death.

Bonaparte: He has been handed over to the black angels Moukir and Quarkir.

Suleiman: He stretched forth his plundering hands to steal the lands, harvests, and horses of Egypt.

Bonaparte: The treasures, industry, and friendship of the Franks will be yours to share until you rise to the seventh heaven and sit beside the black-eyed houri, ever young and ever virgin, and rest in the shade of the Laba, whose branches willingly offer faithful Muslims whatever it is they may desire.

Such charades do not at all alter the solemnity of the Pyramids:

Vingt siècles, descendus dans l'éternelle nuit,
Y sont sans mouvement, sans lumière et sans bruit.[35]

If Bonaparte had taken Cheops's place in the ancient crypt, he
would have added to its grandeur; but he never dragged himself into
that vestibule of death.

"During the rest of our navigation of the Nile," I wrote in the
Itinerary, "I stood on the deck gazing at these tombs ... Great monuments are an essential part of the glory of any human society: they
perpetuate the memory of a people beyond its own existence and
revive it in the minds of the generations who come to settle in its
abandoned lands."

We ought to thank Bonaparte at the Pyramids for vindicating all
of us little statesmen, tainted by poetry and marauding the ruins with
our heads full of piddling lies.

In light of Bonaparte's proclamations, orders of the day, and speeches,
it is clear he saw himself as Heaven's emissary, like Alexander. Cal-
listhenes (whom the Macedonian later treated so unmercifully, no
doubt as a punishment for the philosopher's flattery) was once tasked
with proving that the mortal son of Philip was the son of Jupiter, as
we read in a fragment preserved by Strabo. Pasquier's *The Parley of
Alexander* is a dialogue of the dead between Alexander the great
conqueror and Rabelais the great scoffer:

"Cast your eye," Alexander says to Rabelais, "over all the countries
you see below, and I challenge you to find one man worth his salt
who, to lend weight to his ideas, wouldn't want it bandied about that
he was related to the gods."

Rabelais replies:

"To tell you the truth, Alexander, I never liked any of your little
idiosyncrasies, even the ones involving wine. What good does your
greatness do you now? Are you any different from me? Your regrets
fill you with so much rage, it would be much better if you'd lost your
memory along with your body."

And yet by imitating Alexander, Bonaparte misjudged himself,
and the age, and the state of religion—nowadays no one can pass

himself off as a god. As for Napoleon's exploits in the Levant, they were not yet equal to his European conquests; they had not achieved significant enough results to impress the Islamic masses, even if they did call him the "sultan of fire." Alexander, at the age of thirty-three, writes Montaigne, "passed victoriously over all the habitable earth and attained, in half a lifetime, the utmost achievement of human nature. More kings and princes have written his acts than other historians have written the acts of any other king or prince."[36]

From Cairo, Bonaparte travels to Suez and gazes upon the sea that parted for Moses and folded over Pharaoh. He examines the traces of a canal begun by Sesostris, widened by the Persians, continued by the second Ptolemy, and which the Sudanese had begun again in hopes of opening commerce between the Red Sea and the Mediterranean. He makes plans to conduct a branch of the Nile to the Arab Gulf, on the shores of which his imagination traces the site of a new Ophir, where every year a fair would be held for merchants of perfumes, spices, herbs, silks, and all the precious objects of Muscat, China, Ceylon, Sumatra, the Philippines, and the Indies. The cenobites come down from Sinai and implore him to inscribe his name beside the name of Saladin, in the book of their "sureties."

Back in Cairo, Bonaparte celebrates the anniversary of the founding of the Republic, addressing these words to his men:

"Five years ago, the independence of the French people was threatened, but you took Toulon: this was the portent of your enemies' ruin. One year later, you defeated the Austrians at Dego. The following year you were on the summit of the Alps. You fought against Mantua two years ago and won the famous victory of San Giorgio. Last year, returning from Germany, you were at the sources of the Drava and the Isonzo. Who would have predicted that today you would be standing on the banks of the Nile, at the center of the ancient continent?"

15.
OPINION OF THE ARMY

BUT WAS Bonaparte, amid the pains that preoccupied him and the plans he had conceived, truly committed to his ideas? While it seemed he did wish to stay in Egypt, fantasy did not blind him to reality, and he wrote to his brother Joseph: "I think that within two months I'll be back in France. Make sure I have a country place when I arrive, either near Paris or in Burgundy. I plan on spending the winter there." Bonaparte did not suppose that anything could stand in the way of his return: his will was his destiny and his fortune. When this letter fell into the Admiralty's hands, the English were so bold as to posit that Napoleon's only mission was to destroy his army. One of Bonaparte's letters contained complaints about his wife's flirtations.

The French in Egypt were all the more heroic, seeing they were so miserable. One sergeant writes to a friend, "Tell Ledoux not to be so reckless as to embark for this infernal land."

In the words of a man called Avrieury:

Every person that comes from inland tells us that Alexandria is the finest city in Egypt. Egads! What must the rest be like then? Picture a confused mass of makeshift one-story houses, the best of them with a terrace, a little wooden door with a lock likewise wooden, no windows but a lattice of wood so tightly meshed it is almost impossible to see out, and narrow streets except in the neighborhood of the "Franks" and the quarter of the "grandees." The poor inhabitants, who form the vast majority, go about *au naturel* apart from a blue blouse that reaches halfway down their thighs (and which half the time they hike up for ease of motion), a belt, and a ragged turban. I have had it up to *here* with this charming country. Infernal Egypt! Nothing but sand! What a number of people have been taken in, my dear friend! All these fortune-makers, or rather robbers, are down at the mouth and would jump at the chance to go back where they came from. That much is certain!

Captain Rozis, in a letter to his friend Grivet, writes:

"We are much reduced, and with this there is widespread discontent among the men; despotism has never been at such a height before; we have had several soldiers who killed themselves in the presence of the commander in chief, saying to him: 'This is your work!'"

The name of Tallien will conclude these reports from men who are now almost unknown:

TALLIEN TO MADAME TALLIEN

As for me, my love, I am here, as you know, much against my will—my situation becomes more unpleasant every day, since, separated from my country, from everything that is dear to me, I cannot imagine when I will be able to see them again.

I confess to you in all frankness that I would a thousand times rather be with you and our daughter in some quiet corner of the world, far from all passions and intrigues, and I assure you that if I ever have the happiness of setting foot on my native soil again, nothing shall ever induce me to leave it. *Of the forty thousand Frenchmen here, there are not four who feel otherwise.*

Nothing can be more melancholy than the life we lead here! We are short of everything. It is now five days since I have closed my eyes. I lie down on the tiles; flies, bugs, ants, gnats, mosquitoes, insects of every kind devour us, and twenty times a day I long for our charming cottage. Please, my love, I beg you, do not sell it.

Adieu, my sweet Thérésa, my tears are flooding the page. The sweet memory of your goodness, our love, the hope of seeing you again, ever loving and loyal, and of embracing my dear daughter, are the only things keeping me alive.

Loyalty had nothing to do with any of this.

Such a unanimity of complaints is the natural exaggeration of men who have fallen from the heights of their illusions. For centuries, Frenchmen dreamed of the Orient. The knights traced out the route for them. If they no longer had the faith that led them to liberate the Holy Sepulchre, they still had the boldness of crusaders, and a faith in the realms and the beauties that the troubadours and chroniclers had created around Godfrey. These soldiers who conquered Italy had imagined a rich country there for the taking, with caravans to rob and horses, weapons, and seraglios to seize. Poets had envisioned the Princess of Antioch, and scholars added their dreams to the poets' enthusiasms. Everything, even *Le Voyage d'Anténor*,[37] at first passed for verifiable reality. They believed they would penetrate mysterious Egypt, descend into catacombs, excavate pyramids, unearth undiscovered manuscripts, decipher hieroglyphs, and reawaken Thermosiris.[38] When, instead of all this, the scholars, descending upon the Pyramids, and the soldiers, seeing nothing but naked fellahin and huts made of dried mud, found themselves face-to-face with plague, Bedouins, and Mamluks, their disappointment was enormous. But the injustice of their suffering blinded them to the final result. The French sowed seeds of civilization in Egypt that Muhammad Ali has since cultivated: Bonaparte's glory increased, a ray of light stole into the darkness of Islam, and a breach was made in barbarism.

16.

THE SYRIAN CAMPAIGN

ON FEBRUARY 22, 1799, so as to prevent the hostilities of the pashas of Syria and pursue a few Mamluks, Bonaparte entered the part of the world that the Battle of Aboukir Bay had bequeathed him. But Napoleon was deluded; the only thing he was pursuing was a dream of power. Better favored than Cambyses, he crosses the sands with no sign of the southern wind;[39] he camps among the tombs; he scales El Arish and triumphs in Gaza. On February 6, he writes that they have reached "the pillars placed along the border between Africa and Asia. Last night we slept beneath the Asian sky." This colossal man was marching toward the conquest of the world—a conqueror bound for climes that were not to be conquered.

Jaffa is taken. After the assault, part of the garrison, estimated by Bonaparte at twelve hundred men and taken by others to be two or three thousand, surrendered and was mercifully received; two days later, Bonaparte ordered them put to death.

Walter Scott and Sir Robert Wilson have recounted these massacres. Bonaparte, on Saint Helena, had no trouble confessing them to Lord Ebrington and Doctor O'Meara. But he brushed away their repugnance by citing the position he then found himself in: he "could not feed the prisoners"; he "could not send them back to Egypt under escort." Let them go free on their word? "They would not even have comprehended" this point of honor or these European procedures. "In my place," he said, "Wellington would have done the same."

"Napoleon settled on a terrible measure," says M. Thiers, "that is the only cruel act he committed in his life: he had the remaining prisoners put to the sword; the army obediently, but with a sort of terror, carried out the execution he had commanded."

"The only cruel act he committed in his life" is a great deal to claim after the Toulon massacres, and after so many campaigns during which Napoleon treated men's lives as though they counted for nothing. It is to France's credit that our soldiers should have protested "with a sort of terror" against their general's cruelty.

But did the massacres at Jaffa really save our army? Hadn't Bonaparte seen how easily a few Frenchmen overcame Pasha Damas's forces? At Aboukir, hadn't he destroyed 13,000 Ottomans with a handful of cavalrymen? Didn't Kléber later make the Grand Vizier and his myriad Mohammedans vanish into thin air? If it was a question of rights, by what right had the French invaded Egypt? Why had they slit the throats of men who were only exercising their right to defend themselves? Ultimately, Bonaparte could not invoke the rules of war, since the prisoners from the garrison at Jaffa had "laid down their weapons" and their "surrender was accepted." The deed the conqueror struggled to justify discomfited him: this deed is passed over in silence or indicated vaguely in the official dispatches and accounts of men close to Bonaparte. "I shall dispense with speaking of the train of horrors that follows an assault on a place," says Doctor Larrey: "I was the sad witness to those that occurred at Jaffa." Bourrienne exclaimed that the "atrocious scene still makes me shudder when I think of it, just as I did the day I witnessed it. I would like, if it were possible, to forget it rather than be forced to describe it. Every horrible thing you can imagine occurring on a day of bloodshed would still fall short of the reality." Bonaparte wrote to the Directory that Jaffa was given over to "pillage and every horror of war," which had never seemed so hideous to him. But who was it that had ordered these horrors?

Berthier, Napoleon's companion in Egypt, stationed at headquarters in Enns, in Germany,[40] sent, on May 5, 1809, a dispatch to the major general of the Austrian army roundly condemning a so-called fusillade carried out in the Tyrol, where Chasteller was the commander:

"He (Chasteller) has let seven hundred French prisoners and eighteen to nineteen hundred Bavarians be slaughtered—a crime unheard of in the history of nations, which might have caused a terrible reprisal if His Majesty (Bonaparte) did not regard 'his own prisoners as placed under his protection, on his faith and honor.'"

Here, Bonaparte says all that can be said against the execution of the prisoners of Jaffa. But what did he care about such contradictions? He knew the truth and toyed with it; he used it the same way he would have used a lie. He didn't bother about anything except results; the means were meaningless to him. He found the number of prisoners inconvenient, and so he killed them.

There were always two Bonapartes—one great and the other small. When you think you are safe in Napoleon's life, he renders that life atrocious.

Miot, in the first edition of his *Memoirs* (1804), keeps silent about the massacres; only in the edition of 1814 do we read of them. That edition has almost disappeared; I had a hard time finding a copy. To affirm such a painful truth, I needed nothing less than an eyewitness account. It is one thing to know the outlines of an event and another to comprehend its details: the moral truth of an action can only be discerned in the details of that action. Here they are, according to Miot:

On the 20th of Ventôse (March 10), in the afternoon, the prisoners of Jaffa were ushered into the middle of a vast battalion square formed by General Bon's troops. A muffled rumor of the fate that awaited them led me, like so many others, to mount my horse and follow the silent column of victims, to see whether what I had been told had any basis in truth. The Turks, marching pell-mell, could already foresee their destiny; they did not shed any tears; they did not scream or shout; they were resigned. Some wounded men, unable to walk as quickly as was desired, were killed en route with a few jabs of the bayonet. A few others circulated in the crowd and seemed to be giving advice, which was welcome with danger so imminent. Perhaps

the boldest men thought it was not impossible for them to
defeat the battalion that surrounded them; perhaps they hoped
that by scattering themselves over the fields they were crossing,
some of them would escape death. Every precaution had been
taken in this regard, however, and the Turks made no attempt
to escape.

Arriving at last in the sand dunes southwest of Jaffa, they
were told to halt by a pool of yellowish water. Then the officer
who was commanding the troops had the mass divided into
smaller parts, and these platoons, led to several different points,
were shot. This horrible operation took a long time despite the
number of troops set aside for the gruesome sacrifice—troops
who, I must say, lent themselves only with extreme repugnance
to the abominable administration of the task required of their
victorious arms. Near the pool of water there was a group with
a few elder chiefs, whose expressions were noble and dauntless,
and a young man who had been shaken to the core. At such a
tender age, he must have believed himself innocent, and that
belief brought him to commit an act that appeared to shock
those around him. He rushed at the legs of the horse ridden by
the commander of the French troops; he embraced the knees
of this officer and begged for mercy, shouting "What am I guilty
of? What have I done wrong?" The tears he wept, his touching
cries, were useless; they could not alter the fatal judgment that
had been passed on him. With the exception of this young man,
all the other Turks calmly performed their ablutions in the
stagnant water, then, taking each other by the hand, after having brought these hands to their hearts and mouths, as Muslims
do when they greet one another, they bade each other eternal
farewell. Their courageous souls appeared to defy death, and
one saw, in their tranquility, the confidence that their religion
and their faith in a happy future inspired in them, in those
final moments. They seemed to be saying to themselves: "I am
leaving this world to go enjoy a lasting happiness by Muham-

mad's side." Thus the posthumous serenity that the Koran promises him sustains the Muslim, vanquished but proud in his misfortune.

I saw a respectable old man whose bearing and manners announced a high rank; I saw him . . . coldly ordering a hole dug before him in the shifting sands, a hole deep enough for him to be buried alive in. No doubt he did not want to die except by the hands of his own men. He stretched out on his back in this dreadful, tutelary tomb, and his comrades, addressing their suppliant prayers to God, covered him quickly with sand, and then stamped on the earth that served as his shroud, probably with the idea of hastening the end of his sufferings.

This spectacle, which makes my heart beat faster, and which I have sketched far too faintly, took place during the execution of the groups distributed in the dunes. Finally, no more of these many prisoners remained except those near the pool of water. Our soldiers had exhausted their ammunition and had to stab them with bayonets and knives. I could not bear this horrible sight; I rushed away, pale and about to faint. Several officers reported to me that night that these unfortunate men, yielding to that irresistible natural impulse that urges us to escape from death, even when we no longer have any hope of escaping from it, threw themselves upon each other and received in their limbs the blows directed at their hearts, and which would have ended their sad lives on the spot. They formed, since it must be said, a horrible pyramid of dead and dying men dripping with blood. The bodies of the already dead had to be dragged away to reach the unfortunates who, shielded by this dreadful rampart, had not yet been struck. This description is exact and faithful, though memory makes my hand tremble so fiercely it cannot give a full picture of the horror.

Napoleon's life, juxtaposed with such pages, explains why we feel so remote from him.

Taken by the monks from the Jaffa monastery to the sands south-west of town, I toured the burial site that was once a mound of corpses and is today a pyramid of bones; I went for a walk through the orchards of pomegranate trees laden with vermillion fruits, while nearby the first swallow to arrive from Europe was skimming the funereal ground.

Heaven punishes the violation of human rights. It sent the plague—but the plague did not wreak havoc right away. Bourrienne points out the error committed by historians who place the scene of the *Plague Victims of Jaffa*[41] during the French army's first passage through that city. In fact, the plague did not take place until their return from the Siege of Saint-Jean d'Acre. Several people from our army had already assured me that this scene was pure fable, and Bourrienne confirms these reports:

"The beds of the infected," Napoleon's secretary recounts, "were on the right as we entered the first hall. I was walking beside the general; I maintain that I never saw him touch a victim of the plague. He crossed the halls rapidly, lightly striking the yellow top of his boot with the riding crop he held in his hand. Walking with hasty steps, he kept repeating: 'I must return to Egypt to preserve it from the enemies who will soon be there.'"

In the major general's official report for May 29, there is not a word about the victims of the plague, the visit to the hospital, or the touching of the infected.

What is to become of Gros's painting of Bonaparte's visit? It will remain a masterwork of art.

Saint Louis, though less well favored by painters, was more heroic in deed:

"When the good king, so gallant and gentle-hearted, saw this, he felt a wave of pity and set all other things aside, and had graves dug in the fields, and a cemetery dedicated there by the legate ... With his own hands, King Louis helped bury the dead. Hardly anyone would lend his hand to this effort. After hearing Mass, the king went to the spot every morning, for the five days it took to inter the dead, saying to his men: 'Come, let us bury the martyrs who have suffered for Our

Lord, and let us not be diverted from this task, for they have suffered more than we.' Also present there in their priestly clothes were the Archbishop of Tyre and the Bishop of Damietta and their clergy, who said the service for the dead. But they plugged their noses at the stench. No one ever saw the good king Louis plug his nose. He went about his duty with firm devotion."[42]

Bonaparte lays siege to Saint-Jean d'Acre. Blood is spilled in Cana, where Christ healed the centurion's son;[43] in Nazareth, where the Savior's childhood passed in peace; in Tabor, which witnessed the Transfiguration and where Peter said: "Lord, it is good for us to be here; if thou wilt, let us make here three tabernacles; one for thee, and one for Moses, and one for Elias."[44] It was from Mount Tabor, too, that the order of the day goes forth to all the troops occupying Sour, which is the ancient Tyre; Caesarea; the cataracts of the Nile and its Pelusian mouths; Alexandria; and the banks of the Red Sea that bear the ruins of Kolsum and Arsinoë. Bonaparte was charmed by these names, and delighted in bringing them together.

In this land of miracles, Kléber and Murat renewed the military feats of Tancred and Rinaldo. They scattered the populations of Syria, seized control of the Pasha of Damascus's camp, shot a glance at the Jordan and the Sea of Galilee, and took possession of Scafet, the ancient Bethulia: Bonaparte remarks that the inhabitants showed him the place where Judith killed Holofernes.

The Arab children of the mountains of Judea taught me the most deeply rooted traditions when they shouted at me in French, "Forward march!" "Those deserts"—I wrote in *The Martyrs*—"had already seen the armies of Sesostris, Cambyses, Alexander, and Caesar. Centuries to come, you shall send armies no less numerous and warriors no less renowned to these lands."

Having been guided in Bonaparte's still-recent footsteps in the East, I was led back when there was nothing left to do but retrace his route.

Saint-Jean d'Acre was defended by Jezzar the Butcher. Bonaparte had written him from Jaffa on March 9, 1799:

"Since entering Egypt, I have several times written to inform you I had no intention of making war with you and that my only aim was to drive out the Mamluks...In a few days, I will be marching on Acre. But what reason do I have to take a few years off the life of an old man I do not know? What are a few more leagues compared to the countries I have conquered?"

Jezzar did not let himself be taken in by these flatteries. The old tiger defied his young colleague's claws. He was surrounded by servants mutilated by his own hand:

"They say Jezzar is a cruel Bosnian," he said of himself (according to General Sébastiani), "a contemptible man. But I need no one and other people need me. I was born poor; my father left me nothing but his courage. I have come up in the world through hard work, but I am not proud of this: for everything comes to an end, and today perhaps, or tomorrow, Jezzar will come to an end, not because he is old, as his enemies say, but because God has ordered it so. The King of France, who used to be powerful, has perished; Nebuchadnezzar was killed by a gnat," and so on.

After sixty-one days' entrenchment, Napoleon was forced to lift the siege of Saint-Jean d'Acre. Our soldiers, coming out of their clay huts, ran after the enemy balls that our cannons then sent back. Our troops, having to defend themselves both against the city and the English flotilla in the harbor, launched nine assaults and five times climbed the ramparts. In the time of the Crusaders, Rigord says, there was a tower in Saint-Jean d'Acre called "the accursed one." This tower had perhaps been replaced by the large tower that foiled Bonaparte's attack. Our soldiers jumped into the streets, where they fought hand to hand through the night. General Lannes was wounded in the head, Colbert in the thigh; Boyer, Venoux, and General Bon (the man who oversaw the massacre of the prisoners in Jaffa) were among the dead. Kléber said of this siege: "The Turks are defending themselves like Christians, and the French are attacking like Turks." —The criticism of a soldier who disliked Napoleon. Bonaparte went away proclaiming he had razed Jezzar's palace and bombarded the city until not one stone was left standing, that Jezzar had retreated with his men into one of the coastal forts, that he was grievously wounded, and that, at Napoleon's orders, our frigates had captured thirty Syrian ships loaded with troops.

Sir Sidney Smith and Phélippeaux, an émigré artillery officer, aided Jezzar: the former had been a prisoner at the Temple, the latter a schoolfellow of Napoleon's.[45]

In former times, the flower of chivalry perished at Saint-Jean d'Acre, under Philip Augustus. My countryman Guillaume le Breton sings these losses in twelfth-century Latin verse:

"In all the kingdom, there was hardly a place in which someone did not have a man to mourn, so great was the disaster that sped our heroes to the grave, when death struck them down in the city of Ascaron (Ascalon, near Acre)."

Bonaparte was a great magician, but he did not have the power to transform General Bon, killed at Ptolemais,[46] into Raoul, Sire de Coucy, who, breathing his last below the walls of this city, wrote to the Lady of Fayel: *Mort por loïalement amer son amie.*[47]

Napoleon would not have been in a favorable position to reject the song of the *canteors*; he fed on many other fables at Saint-Jean d'Acre. In the last days of his life, beneath a sky we have never seen, he was glad to divulge what he was contemplating in Syria—that is, assuming he was not inventing these plans after the fact and amusing himself constructing a fictitious future, in which he would have liked us to believe, out of the real materials of the past. "Taking possession of Ptolemais," the revelations of Saint Helena inform us,[48] "Napoleon would have founded an empire in the East and France would have been left to its fate. He would have flown to Damascus, Aleppo, and on to the Euphrates. The Christians of Syria, and even those of Armenia, would have come to reinforce his army. Whole nations would have been shaken to the core. The last remnants of the Mamluks, the Arabs of the Egyptian desert, the Druze of Lebanon, and the *Mutualis* or oppressed Mohammedans of the Sect of Ali, might have joined the army overmastering Syria, and the commotion would have spread over all Arabia. The Arabic-speaking provinces of the Ottoman Empire would have called for a great change and awaited a man favored by fortune. He might have found himself on the Euphrates, in midsummer, with a hundred thousand auxiliaries and a reserve of twenty-five thousand Frenchmen he had sent for from Egypt. He might have reached Constantinople and the Indies and changed the face of the world."

Before retreating from Saint-Jean d'Acre, the French army halted at Tyre. Deserted by Solomon's fleets and the Macedonian's phalanx, Tyre now held nothing but the imperturbable solitude of Isaiah—a solitude in which "the mute dogs refuse to bark."[49]

The Siege of Saint-Jean d'Acre was lifted May 20, 1799. Arriving in Jaffa on May 27, Bonaparte was forced to continue his retreat. There were about thirty to forty plague-stricken men (a number that Napoleon reduced to seven) who could not be transported. Not wanting to leave them behind him, for fear, he said, that they would be exposed to the cruelty of the Turks, he suggested to Doctor Desgenettes that they be administered a strong dose of opium. Desgenettes gave the well-known reply: "My profession is to cure men, not kill them." "No opium at all was administered to them," writes M. Thiers, "and this reported exchange has only served to propagate a disgraceful defamation that has by now been disproved."

Is it defamation? Has it been disproved? That is something I cannot confirm quite as conclusively as the brilliant historian. His reasoning seems to be this—that Bonaparte did not poison the victims of the plague because he *suggested* poisoning them.

Desgenettes, from a poor family of Norman gentlemen, is still venerated among the Arabs of Syria, and Wilson says that his name should not be written except in letters of gold.

Bourrienne writes ten whole pages to support the fact of the poisoning against those who deny it:

"I cannot say I saw the potion administered," he says; "I should state an untruth if I did. But I know for certain the decision was made and must have been made after deliberation, that the order was given, and that the infected are dead. What! Shall something that the whole headquarters discussed, on the day after we left Jaffa, without any question regarding its reality—something that we regarded as a dreadful misfortune—go down as an atrocious invention meant to tarnish the reputation of a hero?"

Napoleon never abandoned any of his errors. Like a tenderhearted father, he preferred the most disgraced of his children. The French army was less indulgent than admiring historians; they believed Napoleon had ordered the poisoning, not only of a handful of sick men, but of several hundred. Robert Wilson, in his *History of the British Expedition to Egypt*, was the first to level the accusation, saying it was supported by the accounts of French officers taken prisoner by the English in Syria. Bonaparte issued a denial to Wilson, who replied that he had only told the truth. Wilson is the same major general who served as Great Britain's liaison to the Russian army during the retreat from Moscow and who later had the good fortune to have a hand in M. de Lavalette's escape. He raised a legion against the Legitimacy during the Spanish War of 1823, defended Bilbao, and sent M. de Villèle back his brother-in-law, M. Desbassayns, who had been forced to ride at harbor. Thus, from various points of view, Robert Wilson's word carries great weight. Most accounts are in agreement regarding the poisoning. M. de Las Cases admits that the rumor of the poisoning was believed in the army. Bonaparte, who became more sincere in his captivity, told M. Warnen and Doctor O'Meara that, had *he* been in the state in which he found the infected, he would have looked to opium to put an end to his pains, and that he would have administered the poison to his own son. Walter Scott reports everything said on the subject, but he rejects the version of events in which a large number of sick men are put to death. He insists that such a multitude of people could not have been successfully poisoned and adds that, in the Jaffa hospital, Sir Sidney saw the *seven* Frenchmen mentioned by Bonaparte. Walter Scott has the greatest impartiality. He defends Napoleon, as he would have defended Alexander, against the reproaches we can heap upon his memory.*

The retreat beneath the Syrian sun was marked by miseries that recall the miseries of our soldiers during the snowbound retreat from Moscow. "There were still some unfortunate men on the shore," says Miot, "waiting to be transported. Among them, a soldier was stricken by

---

*This is practically the first time I have spoken of Walter Scott as a historian of Napoleon, and I will soon refer to him again. Here, I must say that we are prodigiously mistaken when we accuse the illustrious Scotsman of prejudice against a great man. His *Life of Napoleon* occupies no fewer than eleven volumes. The work has not had the success one might have hoped for it because, except in two or three places, the imagination of the author of so many brilliant works has failed him: he is dazzled by the fabulous successes he describes and overwhelmed by the wondrousness of glory. The entire *Life* also lacks panoramic views, which the English rarely take of history, because they do not conceive of history as we do. Still, the *Life* is exact, except for a few errors of chronology. The whole section relating to Bonaparte's internment on Saint Helena is excellent: the English were in a better position than we to understand this part of Napoleon's life. Encountering an existence so filled with marvels, the novelist was conquered by the truth. Reason dominates Walter Scott's work; he is on guard against himself. Indeed, the moderation of his judgments is so great it degenerates into apology. The narrator takes his courteousness to such lengths that he accepts sophisticated excuses made by Napoleon which are simply not acceptable. Those who speak of Walter Scott's work as a self-serving book written under the influence of English national prejudices have plainly never read it—but no one reads anymore in France. Far from exaggerating any accusations against Bonaparte, the author is frightened by public opinion; he makes countless concessions and ceaselessly capitulates. If at first he ventures a firm judgment, later he takes it up again and adds further considerations, which he thinks he owes to impartiality. He does not dare stand up to his hero or look him in the face. Despite this quasi-cowardice in the face of the public's Napoleonic infatuation, Walter Scott has lost all credit for his condescension by having uttered, in his foreword, this simple truth:

"If the general system of Napoleon has rested upon force or fraud, it is neither the greatness of his talents, nor the success of his undertakings, that ought to stifle the voice or dazzle the eyes of him who adventures to be his historian."

The humble audacity that leads one, like Magdalene, to wipe the dirt from God's feet with his hair is nowadays taken for a sacrilege.

the plague and, in the delirium that sometimes accompanies the death agony, he presumably supposed, seeing the army marching to the noise of the drum, that he was about to be abandoned. His imagination led him to see how grave his misfortune would be if he were to fall into the Arabs' hands. It may be further supposed that this fear prompted him to suggest they follow the troops. He picked up and shouldered his rucksack, which he had been using as a pillow, and made an effort to stand up. The venom of the horrible disease coursing through his veins was draining his strength, and after three steps he fell back down on the sand and hit his head. This fall only increased his fear, and after spending a few moments staring at the tail end of the moving columns, he rose a second time and was no more fortunate. On his third attempt, he succumbed and, falling closer to the sea, remained in the place the Fates had chosen for his grave. The sight of this soldier was appalling; the disorder that reigned in his meaningless speech, his face distorted with pain, his wide-open, staring eyes, and his ragged clothes embodied everything most hideous about death. With his eyes fixed on the marching troops, it did not occur to him—as it would have readily occurred to someone with a cooler head—to turn his gaze in the other direction, where he would have seen the Kléber division and the cavalry division leaving Tentoura on the others' heels, and the hope of salvation might have been kept alive in him for a few days more."

When our soldiers, who had by now become quite impassive, saw one of their unfortunate comrades following them like a drunken man, stumbling, falling, getting up, and falling down again, they would say:

"He's been assigned to barracks."

A page of Bourrienne will complete the picture:

"The devouring thirst," the *Memoirs* say, "the total lack of water, the excessive heat, the exhausting march over burning-hot sand dunes—all of this demoralized the men, and the most distressing indifference and cruel self-interest took the place of their generous feelings. I saw officers with limbs missing, whose transport had been ordered and who had even handed out money in compensation for the soldiers' fatigue, thrown off their stretchers. I saw amputees and wounded men, the plague-stricken and those suspected of being plague-stricken, abandoned in the barley. The march was lighted by the same torches used to burn the little towns, villages, hamlets, and the rich harvests that covered the ground. The whole country was aflame. Those who had orders to preside over these disasters seemed to want to avenge their defeats and find relief from their sufferings by spreading desolation everywhere. We were surrounded by the dying, by looters and arsonists. Dying men thrown down by the side of the road said in weak voices: 'I do not have the plague, I am only wounded.' And to persuade the passersby, you would see them reopening their wounds or making new ones. Nobody believed them. They would say: 'His battle days are done.' We passed by, we held our tongues, and all was forgotten. The sun, despite its brightness in those climes, was obscured by the ceaseless smoke of our fires. The sea was to our right. To our left and behind us was the desert we were leaving. Before us were the privations and sufferings to come."

17.

RETURN TO EGYPT—CONQUEST OF UPPER EGYPT

"HE WAS gone and now returns, putting the storms to flight; his coming has sent them back into the desert." This is how the defeated conqueror sang and praised himself when he returned to Cairo. He carried off the world with anthems.

During his absence, Desaix had finished subduing Upper Egypt. Up the Nile, there are ruins whose grandeur Bossuet acknowledged and magnified with his pen. "In the Said," he writes in the *Universal History*, "they have discovered temples and palaces, almost still intact, where the columns and statues are numberless. One palace especially is admired there whose remnants seem to have endured only in order to eclipse the glory of all the grandest works. Four walks that stretch as far as the eye can see, bordered on both sides by sphinxes of a material as rare as their size is remarkable, serve as avenues to four porticos whose height dazzles the eye. What magnificence, and what extent! Even those who have described this prodigious edifice have not had time to go around it, and are not even sure of having seen half of it; but all that they saw was surprising. A hall, which probably stood in the middle of this superb palace, was supported by twenty-six pillars six armfuls thick and proportionately tall, intermixed with obelisks, which so many centuries have not been able to demolish. The very colors, and they are what soonest feel the power of time, are still undefaced amid the ruins of that admirable structure, and still preserve their vividness, so versed was Egypt in the art of imprinting the character of immortality upon all her works. Now that the name of Louis XIV penetrates to the most unknown parts of the world, would it not be an object worthy of his noble curiosity to discover the beauties that the Thebaid contains in its deserts? What beauties would we not find, should we arrive in the royal city, since so far from it we discover such wonders? The Roman power, despairing of equaling the Egyptians, thought it sufficient for its grandeur to borrow the monuments of their kings."[50]

Napoleon sought to take the advice that Bossuet gave Louis XIV. "Thebes," writes M. Denon, who traveled with Desaix's expedition, "this regelated city the imagination makes out only through the mists of time remained such a giant and staggering specter, the army halted of their own accord and clapped their hands. When I made a drawing of the sight, the enthusiastic soldiers were happy to lend me their knees for a table and shade me with their bodies ... Arriving at the cataracts of the Nile, our soldiers, who were still fighting with the beys and suffering incredible fatigue, amused themselves by setting up, in the streets of Syene, tailor shops, jewelers, barbers, and prix-fixe *traiteurs*. Beneath the straight rows of trees in one alley, they planted a milestone with the inscription: *Route de Paris.*"

On their way back down the Nile, the army had frequent clashes with Maghrebis. The Arabs' entrenchments were set on fire, but they had no water; they had to put out the fire with their feet and hands. "Black and naked, they could be seen running through the flames," says M. Denon; "it was the very image of the demons in hell: I could not look at them without a feeling of horror and admiration. There were moments of silence in which a voice could be heard; it was answered by sacred hymns and battle cries."

These Arabs sang and danced like the Spanish soldiers and monks set ablaze in Saragossa; the Russians burned Moscow with their own hands. Whatever sublime madness animated Napoleon, he communicated it to his victims.

18.

THE BATTLE OF ABOUKIR BAY—NAPOLEON'S NOTES AND LETTERS—HE RETURNS TO FRANCE—THE EIGHTEENTH OF BRUMAIRE

BACK IN Cairo, Napoleon wrote to General Dugua:

"Citizen General, you are to have beheaded: Abdall-Aga, the former governor of Jaffa. According to what the Syrians have told me, he is a monster whose country must be emancipated...You are to have shot: Hassan, Joussef, Ibrahim, Saleh, Mahamet, Bekir, Hadj-Saleh, Mustapha, Mahamed, all Mamluks."

Again and again, he issues these orders against Egyptians who have spoken badly of the French. Such was Napoleon's understanding of the law. But should even the rules of war allow so many lives to be sacrificed on the basis of such a simple order: *you are to have shot...* To the Sultan of Darfur, he writes: "I wish you to send me *two thousand male slaves* above the age of sixteen." How he loved slaves.

An Ottoman fleet one hundred ships strong anchored at Aboukir and sent an army ashore. Murat, supported by General Lannes, hurled them back into the sea. Bonaparte informs the Directory of his successes: "The shore where last year the currents bore French and English corpses today is strewn with the corpses of our enemies." Men tire of walking in these victorious heaps just as surely as they tire of walking in the sparkling desert sands.

The following note fills us with sadness:

I have been dissatisfied, Citizen General, with all of your operations during the maneuver that has just taken place. You received an order to come to Cairo and you have done nothing.

All the events that may arise must never prevent a soldier from obeying orders, and skill in warfare consists in *removing* difficulties that can make an operation difficult and never missing your chance. I tell you this for the future.

Ungrateful in advance, Bonaparte's surly order was addressed to Desaix, who, to the soldiers in Upper Egypt, offered countless examples of humanity and courage: marching at the pace of his horse, chatting about ruins, longing for his homeland, saving women and children, he was beloved by the people, who called him the "just Sultan." This was the same Desaix who was later killed at Marengo, in the charge that transformed the First Consul into the master of Europe. The character of the man permeates Napoleon's note: aggression and resentment abound. We sense a person afflicted by every form of fame—the predestinator provided with a language that stays and constrains. But without this spirit of authority, would Bonaparte have been able to bring down everything in his path?

Ready to leave the ancient land where the man of old cried out as he breathed his last, "Oh, powers that dispense life to men, receive me, and grant me a dwelling place among the immortal gods!" Bonaparte thinks only of his earthly future. From the Red Sea, he sends a note to the governors of the Île-de-France and the Île-de-Bourbon; he sends his greetings to the Sultan of Morocco and the Bey of Tripoli. He tells them of his affectionate solicitude for the caravans and pilgrims of Mecca. At the same moment, Napoleon seeks to talk the Grand Vizier out of the invasion that the Ottoman Empire is contemplating, assuring him that he is as ready to do battle and win as he is to enter into any negotiation.

One thing would do our character very little credit if our imagination and love of novelty were not more to blame than our national sense of justice. French people raved about the Egyptian expedition and did not observe that it was a violation of both probity and political rights. Though we are at peace with the oldest ally France has, we attack it, we rob it of its fertile province of the Nile, without a declaration of war, like the Algerians who, during one of their surprise attacks, tried to seize Marseille and Provence. When the Ottomans arm themselves in lawful self-defense, we are so proud of our ambush we ask them what is wrong and why they are angry; we tell them that the only reason we took up arms was to keep order in their house and rid them of those Mamluk brigands who were holding their pasha prisoner. Bonaparte writes to the Grand Vizier: "How could Your Excellency not understand that every Frenchman killed has died for the Porte?[51] I, for my part, will hold the best day of my life to be the day I can help end a war that is both *impolitic and pointless.*" Bonaparte wanted to be on his way; he himself could see the war was pointless and impolitic. But the old monarchy was as guilty as the Republic in this regard: the archives in the Ministry of Foreign Affairs preserve several plans for French colonies to be established in Egypt. Leibniz himself had suggested an Egyptian colony to Louis XIV. The English esteem only practical politics, founded on interests; they consider fidelity to treaties and moral scruples childish.[52]

Finally the hour had come. Halted at the borders of Asia, Bonaparte would first seize the scepter of Europe before heading north to seek the gates of the Himalayas and the splendors of Kashmir by another route. His last letter to Kléber, dated from Alexandria, August 22, 1799, is quite excellent in its combination of logic, experience, and authority. The end of this letter reaches a pitch of serious and penetrating pathos:

You will find enclosed, Citizen General, an order to assume command of the army. The fear that the English squadron may reappear at any moment causes me to hasten my departure by two or three days.

I am taking with me Generals Berthier, Andréossi, Murat, Lannes, and Marmont, and Citizens Monge and Berthollet.

Enclosed are English and Frankfurt newspapers up through June 10. You will see that we have lost Italy and that Mantua, Turin, and Tortona are besieged. I have reason to hope the first will hold out till the end of November. If fortune smiles on me, I hope to reach Europe before the beginning of October.

Specific instructions follow:

You can appreciate as well as anyone, Citizen General, how important the possession of Egypt is for France: this Turkish Empire, which threatens ruin on every side, is now collapsing, and our evacuation of Egypt would be a misfortune, all the more so seeing that we would be sure, in our own lifetimes, to see this fine province pass into other European hands...

What you hear of the successes or reversals of the Republic in Europe must enter strongly into your calculations...

You know my views on the internal politics of Egypt. Whatever you do, the Christians will always be our friends. You must prevent them from becoming too insolent, so that the Turks do not have the same fanaticism against us as against the Christians, which would make them irreconcilable to us...

I have already asked for a troupe of actors several times and will take special care to send you one. This would be very important for the army and for starting to alter the the culture of the country.

The important position that you are about to occupy will finally put you in a position to deploy the talents nature has given you. Interest in what happens here is keen, and the effects on trade, and on civilization itself, will be immense. This will be a time when great revolutions begin.

Accustomed to seeing the reward for life's pains and labors in the opinions of posterity, I am leaving Egypt with the greatest regret. If I were not considering my duty, the interests and glory of the fatherland, and the extraordinary events that have occurred here, I would not now pass through the enemy squadrons and return to Europe. I shall be with you in spirit. Your successes will be as dear to me as if they were my own, and I shall regard as wasted all the days of my life in which I do not do something for the army that I am leaving at your command, in order to consolidate the magnificent establishment whose foundations have just been laid.

All the soldiers of the army I confide to you are like my children; at all times, even amid the greatest hardships, I have had signs of their affection. Nurture these feelings in them; you owe it to the very special regard and friendship I feel for you—and to the very real affection I feel for them.

Bonaparte

Never has a warrior spoken in such tones; it is Napoleon himself who ends this letter. The emperor to come will no doubt be even more astonishing, but how much more detestable! His voice will no longer have a youthful ring; time, despotism, and the intoxication of prosperity will have altered it.

Bonaparte would have been much to be pitied had he been compelled, under ancient Egyptian law, to hold in his arms the *children* he put to death. For the soldiers he left exposed to the blistering sun, he dreamed up the same diversions Captain Parry would use thirty-two years later to keep his sailors busy through the icy polar nights.[53] He bequeathed his Egyptian legacy to his brave successor—who was soon to be murdered—and slipped furtively away, as Caesar once saved himself by jumping into the harbor of Alexandria and swimming to shore. Cleopatra, the queen whom the poet called a "fatal marvel,"[54] was not waiting for Napoleon; he was bound for the secret rendezvous that another faithless potentate, Destiny, had made with him. Having plunged into the Orient, the source of unbelievable fortune and fame, he returned to us without having ever reached Jerusalem, just as he never reached Rome. The Jew who cried "Woe, woe!" wandered around the holy city without ever entering its eternal habitations.[55] A poet, fleeing Alexandria, was the last to board the adventurous frigate. Steeped in the miracles of Judea and the memories of the sepulchral Pyramids, Bonaparte crossed the seas, heedless of their ships and depths. This giant could traverse anything—be it waves or events.

Napoleon sailed the same route I did, coasting along Africa in contrary winds. After twenty-one days, he doubled Cape Bon, reached the coast of Sardinia, was forced to stop off at Ajaccio, looked around at the place of his birth, received some money from Cardinal Fesch, and reembarked. He crossed paths with an English fleet, which did not pursue him. On October 8, he entered the bay of Fréjus, not far from Golfe-Juan, where years later he would appear one terrible and final time. He landed, set off, traveled on to Lyon, and took the Bourbonnais road, entering Paris on October 16. Everyone seemed disposed against him—Barras, Sieyes, Bernadotte, Moreau—and every one of these opponents served him as though by some miracle. A conspiracy was brewing; the government was transferred to Saint-Cloud. Bonaparte went to harangue the Council of Ancients: he was agitated, he stammered the words *brothers in arms*, *volcano*, *victory*, *Caesar*. He was called a Cromwell, a tyrant, a hypocrite. He wanted to accuse them, and they accused him. He claimed to be guided by the god of war and the god of fortune and went away shouting: "Whoever loves me, follow me!" They demanded his indictment, and Lucien, president of the Council of Five Hundred, yielded his chair so as not to have to banish Napoleon. He drew his sword and swore to pierce his brother's breast if he ever tried to infringe upon liberty. They talked of having the deserting soldier, the breaker of sanitary laws, the bearer of the plague, shot, and he was crowned. Murat blew the representatives out the windows: it was the 18th of Brumaire. The consular government was born, and freedom died.

Change now sweeps the world. The man of the last century steps down from the stage and the man of the new century steps up. Washington, who has come to the end of his wonders, gives way to Bonaparte, who begins to work his. On November 9, the President of the United States brings the year 1799 to a close, and the First Consul of the French Republic opens the year 1800:

> *Un grand destin commence, un grand destin s'achève.*
> (CORNEILLE)[56]

I wrote the first part of my *Memoirs* over these immense events, like a modern text profaning ancient manuscripts. I reckoned my lowliness and obscurity in London against the heights and radiance of Napoleon; the sound of his footsteps mingled with the silence of mine on my solitary walks; his name pursued me even into the hovels where I shared the sad poverty of my companions in misfortune, as well as the merry destitution or—as our old tongue would have had it—the "hilarious" penury of Pelletier. Napoleon was my age. We both emerged from the army, but when he had already won one hundred battles, I was still languishing in the shadows among those émigrés who formed the pedestal of his fortune. Having fallen so far behind, could I ever catch up to him again? And yet, though he imposed laws on monarchs; though he subdued them with his armies and trod their blood beneath his boots; though, with flag in hand, he crossed the bridges of Arcole and Lodi; though he triumphed at the Pyramids—for all these victories, would I have given up even one of the unremembered hours I spent in an out-of-the-way little town in England? Oh, magic of youth!

BOOK TWENTY

I.

FRANCE'S POSITION AT THE TIME OF BONAPARTE'S
RETURN FROM THE EGYPTIAN CAMPAIGN

I LEFT England a few months after Napoleon left Egypt, and we returned to France at almost the same time—he from Memphis, I from London. He had captured cities and kingdoms; his hands were full of powerful realities. I still had nothing but dreams.

What had happened in Europe during Napoleon's absence?

War breaks out again in Italy, the kingdom of Naples, and the states of Sardinia; Rome and Naples are momentarily occupied; Pius VI is taken prisoner and led away to die in France; a treaty of alliance is concluded between the cabinets of Petersburg and London.

A second continental coalition is formed against France. On April 8, 1799, the Congress of Rastatt is broken off and the French plenipotentiaries are assassinated. General Suvorov comes from Italy and beats the French at Cassano. The citadel of Milan surrenders to the Russian general. One of our armies, forced to evacuate Naples, struggles to survive, commanded by General Macdonald. Masséna defends Switzerland.

Mantua succumbs after a seventy-two-day blockade and a twenty-day siege. On October 15, 1799, General Joubert is killed at Novi and leaves the field open to Bonaparte, who was destined to play the latter's role. Woe betide those who, like Hoche, Moreau, and Joubert, stand in fatal fortune's way! Twenty thousand Englishmen descend on Den Helder to no purpose; their fleet is partly blocked in by the ice; our cavalry charges the ships and takes them. Eighteen thousand Russians—all that were left of Suvorov's army after so many battles and so long a road—cross the Saint Gotthard massif on September 24 and enter the Valley of the Reuss. Masséna saves France at the battle of Zurich. Suvorov, back in Germany, casts aspersions on the Austrians and pulls back to Poland. Such is the position of France when Bonaparte reappears, overthrows the Directory, and establishes the Consulate.

Before going any further, I should say something you have surely already noticed: I am not attempting to write the entirety of Bonaparte's life. I am giving a synopsis and a summary of his actions. I am evoking his battles, not describing them. After all, one can find descriptions of these battles everywhere—in Pommereul, who published the *Campagnes d'Italie*; in the works of our generals, critics of battles in which they took part; and in the writings of foreign tacticians from England, Russia, Germany, Italy, and Spain. Napoleon's public bulletins and secret dispatches form the rather shaky foundation of these narratives. The works of General Jomini furnish the best source of information: he is especially credible since he has displayed his expertise elsewhere, in the *Traité de la grande tactique* and *Traité des grands opérations militaires*. An admirer of Napoleon until he became unjust, a member of Marshal Ney's staff, he has given us a critical and military history of the Revolutionary campaigns. He saw with his own eyes the wars in Germany, Prussia, Poland, and Russia up to the taking of Smolensk; he was present in Saxony during the battles of 1813, after which he went over to the Allies. He was sentenced to death by Bonaparte's war council and, at the same moment, appointed Emperor Alexander's aide-de-camp. Attacked by General Sarrazin in his *Histoire de la guerre de Russie et d'Allemagne*, Jomini replied. He had at his disposal the materials deposited at the Ministry of War and other archives of the kingdom. He saw, from the other side, our army's rearward march, after having helped guide them forward. His account is lucid and interspersed with many fine and judicious reflections. Whole pages of his have been borrowed without the least acknowledgement; but I have no vocation as a copyist, and no desire for the dubious renown of being an unrecognized Caesar—capable of subjugating the world once more, if only he had a helmet. Had I wanted to come to the rescue of the memory of the veterans by maneuvering over maps, running around battlefields now covered with peaceful crops, quoting document after document, piling up description after identical description, I would have accumulated volume upon volume and earned a reputation for my ability, but at the risk of burying myself, my reader, and my hero beneath my labors. Being but a humble soldier, I bow before the knowledge of Vegetius.[1] It is doubtful that many of my readers are officers on half pay, and the lowliest corporal knows more about these matters than I do.

2.

CONSULATE: SECOND INVASION OF ITALY—THIRTY-DAY CAMPAIGN—VICTORY AT HOHENLINDEN—TREATY OF LUNÉVILLE

TO ENSURE he would keep the seat he had taken, Napoleon needed to outdo himself in miracles.

On April 25 and April 30, 1800, the French crossed the Rhine, with Moreau leading the way. The Austrian army, beaten four times in eight days, retreated on one side as far as Vorarlberg and on the other as far as Ulm. Bonaparte marched through the Great Saint Bernard Pass on May 16, and on the 20th the Little Saint Bernard, the Simplon, the Saint-Gotthard, Mont Cenis, and Montgenèvre were scaled and captured. We entered Italy through three passages reputed to be impregnable—mere caves for bears and rocks for eagles. The army took Milan on June 2 and the Cisalpine Republic was reorganized, but Genoa was forced to surrender after a memorable siege, supported by Masséna.

The occupation of Pavia and the glorious business at Montebello preceded the victory at Marengo, which began with a defeat. The exhausted soldiers led by Lannes and Victor ceased to fight and abandoned the terrain, and the battle started up again with four thousand infantrymen led by Desaix and supported by Kellerman's cavalry brigade. Desaix was killed. Kellerman's charge carried the day, which at last laid Mélas's stupidity bare.

Desaix—a gentleman from Auvergne, a second lieutenant in the Breton regiment, and General Victor de Broglie's aide-de-camp—had commanded, in 1796, a division of Moreau's army and crossed to the Orient with Bonaparte. His character was selfless, naive, and easygoing. After the Convention of El Arish released him, he was kept on by Lord Keith in the lazaretto at Livorno. "When the lamps were out," says Miot, his traveling companion, "our general would tell us stories of robbers and ghosts. He shared in our pleasures and settled our quarrels; he loved women more than words can say and would have liked to win their love only through his love of glory." When at last he landed in Europe, he received a letter from the First Consul calling him to his side. This letter softened Desaix's heart, and he said: "Poor Bonaparte is covered with glory, and he is still not happy." Reading in the papers about the march of the reserve army, he wrote: "He won't leave us anything to do." But he left him time enough to win victory and die.

Desaix was buried high in the Alps at the Hospice of Mont Saint Bernard, like Napoleon on the hills of Saint Helena.

Kléber, assassinated, was killed in Egypt the same day Desaix met his death in Italy. After the departure of the commander in chief, Kléber, with eleven thousand men, had defeated one hundred thousand Turks under the orders of the Grand Vizier, at Heliopolis—a feat to which Napoleon has nothing to compare.

On June 16, the Convention of Alessandria is signed. The Austrians retreat to the left bank of the lower Po. The fate of Italy is decided in this so-called thirty-day campaign.

The triumph at Hochstedt obtained by Moreau consoles the shade of Louis XIV. However, the armistice between Germany and Italy, concluded after the Battle of Marengo, was denounced on October 20, 1800.

December 3 sees Hohenlinden's victory in the thick of a snowstorm—another victory obtained by Moreau, a great general over whom another great genius dominated. Du Guesclin's compatriot then marches on Vienna, and twenty-five leagues from this capital concludes the Steyer armistice with Archduke Charles. After the Battle of Pozzolo, the crossing of the Mincio, the Adige, and the Brenta, there followed, on February 9, 1801, the Treaty of Lunéville.

And not quite nine months earlier Napoleon had been on the banks of the Nile! Nine months had been enough to overthrow the people's revolution in France and to crush the absolute monarchies of Europe.

I am not sure whether it was during this period that an incident, related in certain memoirs, took place—or even whether the incident is worth recalling; but there's no shortage of little anecdotes about Caesar. Life does not all happen on the same plane; at times one ascends, and very frequently one descends. In Milan, so it is said, Napoleon was joined in bed by an Italian girl, sixteen years old and as beautiful as could be; in the middle of the night he sent her away, in the same manner he would have had a bouquet of flowers thrown out the window.

Another time, one of these vernal creatures had slipped into the same palace as Napoleon; she came in at three in the morning, bewitched him, and wound her youth around the head of the lion, who was that night more patient.

These dalliances, which had nothing to do with love, held no real power over a man so devoted to death. He would have burned Persepolis on his own account—not for the pleasure of a courtesan. "François I," Tavannes says, "gets down to work when he doesn't have any more women; Alexander gets down to women when he doesn't have any more work."[2]

Women, in general, hated Bonaparte as mothers. They did not much care for him as women either, for they were not beloved by him. He insulted them without delicacy or sought them out only in passing. He inspired a few imaginative passions only after his fall, for then—and always in the hearts of women—the poetry of wealth is less seductive than the poetry of misfortune. Flowers grow among ruins.

Following the example of the Chevaliers de Saint-Louis, the Légion d'Honneur is created. This institution, with its old monarchical tinge, introduces an obstacle to the new equality. The transfer of Turenne's ashes to the Invalides brings Napoleon esteem, and Captain Baudain's expedition broadcasts his fame around the globe.[3] Everything that might have harmed the First Consul comes to nothing. He eludes the assassination plotted on Vendémiaire 18 and escapes the infernal machine on Nivôse 3. Pitt retires. Paul dies, and Alexander succeeds him. There is still no sign of Wellington. But India sets out to rob us of our conquest of the Nile; Egypt is attacked from the Red Sea, while the Kapudan Pasha comes at it from the Mediterranean. Napoleon agitates empires. Nowhere on earth is free of him.

3.
TREATY OF AMIENS—RUPTURE OF THE TREATY—
BONAPARTE MADE EMPEROR

THE PRELIMINARIES of peace between France and England, interrupted in London on October 1, 1801, are converted into a treaty at Amiens. The Napoleonic world was not yet fixed; its limits changed with the rising and falling tides of our victories.

It is around this time that the First Consul appointed Toussaint L'Ouverture governor for life of Saint-Domingue and incorporated the isle of Elba into France; but Toussaint, traitorously abducted, was to die in a Jura guardhouse, and Bonaparte supplied himself with his own prison at Portoferraio: accommodations for the emperor of the world who no longer had any place in it.[4]

On May 6, 1802, Napoleon is elected consul for ten years and, soon after, consul for life. He feels cramped by the vast dominion that peace with England has given him: without troubling about the Treaty of Amiens, without a thought for the new wars into which his decision is going to plunge him, under the pretext of the refusal to evacuate Malta, he claims the provinces of Piedmont for the French State, and citing political unrest in Switzerland, he occupies it. England breaks with us. This break occurs between March 13 and 20, 1803, and on May 22, the savage decree ordering the arrest of all English people working or traveling in France is issued.

Bonaparte invades the Electorate of Hanover on June 3, the very moment I, in Rome, was closing the eyes of a woman unknown to the world.

On March 21, 1804, the Duc d'Enghien dies, as I have described to you. On the same day the Civil Code, or Napoleonic Code, is decreed to teach us respect for the laws.

Forty days after the death of the Duc d'Enghien, a member of the Tribunat named Curée presents a motion elevating Bonaparte to a position of supreme power, apparently because the Tribunat was sworn to liberty. A more dazzling master has never issued from the proposal of a more obscure slave.

The Sénat conservateur alters the Tribunat's proposal in a decree. Bonaparte does not imitate either Caesar or Cromwell: more confident before the crown, he accepts it. On May 18, he proclaims himself emperor at Saint-Cloud, in halls from which he himself had driven out the people, not far from where Henri III was assassinated, Henrietta of England poisoned, Marie Antoinette greeted with a few fleeting joys that led her to the scaffold, and Charles X left for his final exile.

Speeches of congratulation bubble over.

Mirabeau, in 1790, had said:

"We are providing a new example of that blind and ever-shifting inconsideration that has led us, from one age to the next, into all the crises that have successively afflicted us. It seems the scales shall never fall from our eyes and we have resolved to be children to the end of time—sometimes rebels, and always slaves."

When the plebiscite of December 1, 1804 is presented to Napoleon, the emperor replies:

"My descendants shall keep this throne for a long time."

When we see the illusions with which Providence envelops power, we are consoled by their short duration.

4.
EMPIRE—CONSECRATION—KINGDOM OF ITALY

ON DECEMBER 2, 1804, the consecration and coronation of the emperor took place at Notre-Dame de Paris. The pope read a prayer:

> Almighty and eternal God, who made Hazael ruler of Syria and Jehu king of Israel, manifesting your will to them through the organ of the prophet Elijah; who likewise anointed the heads of Saul and David with the holy oil of kings through the ministry of the prophet Samuel, let the treasure of your grace and blessings pour through my hands upon your servant Napoleon, who, despite our personal unworthiness, we today consecrate emperor in your name.

When Pius VII was still Bishop of Imola, he had said, in 1797:

> Yes, my cherished brethren, *siate buoni cristiani, e sarete ottimi democratici.*[5] Moral virtues make good democrats. The first Christians were animated by the spirit of democracy: God favored the works of Cato of Utica and the illustrious republicans of Rome.

Quo turbine fertur vita hominum?[6]

On March 18, 1805, the emperor declares to the Senate that he accepts the iron crown the electoral colleges of the Cisalpine Republic have offered him: he was both the secret inspirer of the wish and its public object. Little by little, the whole of Italy lies down beneath his laws. He fastens the country to his diadem like a sixteenth-century war chief putting a diamond in place of a button on his cap.

5.

INVASION OF GERMANY—AUSTERLITZ—PEACE
TREATY OF PRESSBURG—THE SANHEDRIN

INJURED Europe was attempting to bandage its wounds: Austria adheres to the Treaty of Petersburg concluded between Great Britain and Russia. Alexander and the King of Prussia meet in Potsdam, providing Napoleon with a subject for ignoble mockery. The Third Coalition is formed. These coalitions were continually being conceived out of mistrust and fear. Napoleon reveled in turmoil. He took advantage of it.

From the coast of Boulogne, where he ordered the construction of a column[7] and threatened Albion with ships, he embarks. An army organized by Davoust is transported like a cloud to the bank of the Rhine. On October 1, 1805, the emperor harangues his 160,000 soldiers: the speed of his movements disconcerts the Austrians. Battle of Lechfeld, Battle of Wertingen, Battle of Günzburg. On October 17, Napoleon appears near Ulm; he orders Mack: *Lay down your arms!* Mack and his thirty thousand men obey. Munich surrenders; the Inn is crossed, Salzburg taken, the Traun forded. On November 13, Napoleon reaches one of those capitals he would visit now and again: he marches through Vienna. Chained to his own triumphs, he is led along by them to the center of Moravia, where he runs into the Russians. On the left, Bohemia rebels; on the right, the Hungarians rise up. Archduke Charles comes rushing in from Italy. Prussia, which has clandestinely entered the coalition and has not yet declared itself, sends Minister Haugwitz bearing an ultimatum.

Then comes December 2, 1805—the day of Austerlitz. The Allies are waiting for a third Russian corps that is no more than eight days distant. Kutuzov maintains that battle must be avoided at all costs, but Napoleon's maneuvers force the Russians to engage: they are defeated. In less than two months the French, starting from the North Sea, have marched beyond the capital of Austria and crushed Catherine's legions. The Prussian minister comes to congratulate Napoleon at his headquarters:

"Here," the conqueror tells him, "is a compliment whose recipient has been changed by the dictates of Fortune."

Francis II in turn presents himself at the lucky soldier's camp:

"Allow me to welcome you," says Napoleon, "to the only palace I've slept in for the past two months."

"You know how to put the place to such good use," replies Francis, "you must enjoy it."

Were such sovereigns worth being slaughtered for?

An armistice is granted. The Russians retreat in three columns, one at a time, in the order determined by Napoleon.

After the Battle of Austerlitz, almost everything Bonaparte does is in error.

The Treaty of Pressburg is signed December 26, 1805. Napoleon manufactures two kings, the Elector of Bavaria and the Elector of Württemburg. The republics Bonaparte had created, he now destroys and transforms into monarchies. Departing from his usual system, on December 27, 1805, at Schönbrunn Palace, he declares that "the dynasty of Naples has ceased to reign"; but this is because he is replacing it with his own. At his command, kings came in or jumped out at the windows. Yet the designs of Providence were fulfilled no less surely than those of Napoleon: we can see both God and man together on the march. After his victory, Bonaparte orders the construction of the Pont d'Austerlitz in Paris, and Heaven orders Alexander to cross it.

The war begun in the Tyrol had continued even as it raged on into Moravia. Amid so many prostrations, when you see a man standing up for himself, you breathe a sigh: Hofer the Tyrolean did not capitulate like his master;[8] yet magnanimity meant nothing to Napoleon.

It struck him as stupidity or madness. The Emperor of Austria abandoned Hofer. When I crossed Lake Garda, immortalized by Catullus and Virgil, I was shown the spot where this huntsman was felled by the firing squad. That is all I personally have experienced of the courage of the subject and the cowardice of the prince.

On January 14, 1806, Prince Eugène marries the daughter of the new king of Bavaria: thrones were pouring down on every side upon the Corsican soldier's family.

On February 20, the emperor decrees the restoration of the Church of Saint-Denis. He dedicates the reconstructed vaults as burial places for the princes of his race, but Napoleon himself will never be buried there. Man digs the grave, and God fills it.

Berg and Cleves are allotted to Murat and the Two Sicilies to Joseph. The memory of Charlemagne crosses Napoleon's mind and the University is established.

On June 5, 1806, the Batavian Republic,[9] forced to love princes, sends a message begging Napoleon to appoint his brother Louis as their king.

The idea of allying Batavia and France through a more or less surreptitious union arose from an acquisitiveness without rhyme or reason: it meant favoring a little cheese-making province over the advantages that would result from a friendly alliance with a great kingdom—all while stoking, to no purpose, the fears and envies of Europe; it meant confirming English possession of India and obliging them, for their own safety, to hold onto the Cape of Good Hope and Ceylon, which they had taken when we first invaded Holland. The scene was set for the granting of the United Provinces to Prince Louis: at the Tuileries Palace, there was a reenactment of Louis XIV showing off his grandson Philip V at Versailles. The next day, a gala luncheon took place in the Salon de Diane. One of Queen Hortense's children entered, and Bonaparte said to him:

"My darling, why don't you recite the fable you have learned?"

Without so much as taking a breath, the child said, "The Frogs Who Asked for a King," and recited:

> Although democratic then,
> The frogs begged a royal yoke,
> Croaking again and again
> Till Jupiter sent a king to calm the constant croak.[10]

Sitting behind the newly made sovereign of Holland, the emperor, in one of his frequent acts of uncouth behavior, pinched her ears: he may have been of high society, but he was not always well mannered.

On July 17, 1806, the Treaty of the Confederation of the Rhine was signed. Fourteen German princes seceded from the Holy Roman Empire and were united with each other and with France: Napoleon takes the title "protector" of the Confederation.

On July 20, after a treaty between France and Russia was signed, Francis II, following the Confederation of the Rhine, renounces the dignity of being elective emperor of Germany and becomes hereditary emperor of Austria: the Holy Roman Empire collapses. This immense event was hardly remarked. After the French Revolution, everything was trifling. After the fall of the throne of Clovis, one scarcely noticed the sound of the fall of the Germanic throne.

At the start of our Revolution, Germany had a multitude of kings and queens. Two principal monarchies tended to draw different powers: Austria created by time, and Prussia by a man. Two religions divided the country and somehow rested upon the foundations of the Treaty of Westphalia. Germany dreamed of political unity, but it lacked the political education needed to attain liberty—just as Italy lacked the military education needed to attain it. Germany, with its ancient traditions, was like those basilicas with multiple bell towers, which sin against the rules of art but nevertheless represent the majesty of religion and the power of the centuries.

The Confederation of the Rhine is a great unfinished work, which required a good deal of time and a special knowledge of the laws and interests of the nations; but it fell quite suddenly to pieces in the mind of the man who had conceived it. All that remained of this profound scheme were a military and a fiscal machine. Once the genius of his

374 · MEMOIRS FROM BEYOND THE GRAVE

early vision passed, Bonaparte thought of nothing but money and soldiers. The tax collector and recruiting officer took the place of the great man. A Michelangelo of politics and war, he left behind cartons full of enormous sketches.

Around this time, stirring up everything, Napoleon dreamed up the Grand Sanhedrin. This assembly did not award him Jerusalem, but, by and by, it did let the finances of the world go to the stalls of the Jews, and thereby produced a fateful subversion in the social economy.[11]

The Marquis de Lauderdale came to Paris to replace Mr. Fox in the pending negotiations between France and England—diplomatic talks that boil down to the English ambassador's remark regarding M. de Talleyrand:

"He's a piece of dung* in a silk stocking."

---

*I have used the polite word.

6.

FOURTH COALITION—PRUSSIA VANISHES—BERLIN DECREE—WAR CONTINUED IN POLAND AGAINST RUSSIA—TILSIT—PLAN TO SHARE OUT THE WORLD BETWEEN NAPOLEON AND ALEXANDER—PEACE

IN THE course of 1806, the Fourth Coalition breaks up. Napoleon leaves Saint-Cloud, arrives in Mainz, takes the enemy's supplies in Saalburg. At Saalfeld, Prince Ferdinand of Prussia is killed. At Auerstadt and Jena, on October 14, Prussia goes up in smoke. When I returned from Jerusalem, I found it gone.

The Prussian Bulletin describes it all in one line: "The king's army has been beaten. The king and his brother are alive." The Duke of Brunswick did not survive his wounds. In 1792, his proclamation had roused France; and he had saluted me on the road when I, a poor soldier, was on my way to join the brothers of Louis XVI.

The Prince of Orange and Möllendorf, along with several officers imprisoned in Halle, were granted permission to retreat due to the city's capitulation.

The octogenarian Möllendorf had known Frederick, who praised him in his *History of My Time*, as Mirabeau did in his *Mémoires secrets*. He had witnessed our disasters at Rosbach and our triumph at Jena, as the Duke of Brunswick had seen Assas killed at Kloster Kamp[12] and, at Auerstadt, Ferdinand of Prussia—a man guilty only of largehearted hatred for the murder of the Duc d'Enghien. These specters of the old wars of Hanover and Silesia had locked eyes with the soldiers of both our empires. But the powerless shades of the past could not halt the forward march of the future. Between the smoke of our old tents and our new camps, they appeared and disappeared.

*

Erfurt capitulates; Leipzig is seized by Davoust; the passages of the Elbe are breached; Spandau surrenders. In Potsdam, Bonaparte takes Frederick's sword prisoner. On October 27, 1806, the great King of Prussia hears, in the dust around his empty palace in Berlin, what can only be the noise of foreign grenadiers: Napoleon has come. While this monument of philosophy was crumbling on the banks of the Spree, I was in Jerusalem, visiting the imperishable monument of religion.

Stettin and Custrin surrender; another victory at Lübeck; the capital of the Wagria is stormed; Blücher, destined to enter Paris twice, remains in our hands. It is the old story of Holland and its forty-six towns taken by Louis XIV during his "voyage" of 1672.[13]

On November 27, the Berlin Decree on the Continental System appears—a sweeping decree that ejects England from the world, which very nearly came to be the case. This decree seemed like madness, but it was merely immense. However, if the continental blockade on one hand helped create the factories of France, Germany, Switzerland, and Italy, on the other it extended English trade to the rest of the globe. Discommoding governments allied with us, it incensed industrial interests, fomented hatred, and contributed to the rupture between the cabinet at the Tuileries and the cabinet of Saint Petersburg. The blockade was, then, an action of dubious merit: Richelieu would not have undertaken it.

Soon, following Frederick's other states, Silesia is crossed. The war between France and Prussia had begun October 9: in seventeen days our soldiers, like a flock of raptors, soared over the gorges of Franconia, above the waters of the Saale and the Elbe. The 6th of December finds them on the far side of the Vistula. Murat has been garrisoned since November 29 at Warsaw, from which the Russians have retreated, coming too late to the aid of the Prussians. The Elector of Saxony, inflated into a Napoleonic king, accedes to the Confederation of the Rhine and commits, in the event of war, to providing a contingent of twenty thousand men.

The winter of 1807 suspends hostilities between the French and Russian empires; but these empires have collided, and already we can see that both their destines have changed. Still, despite his aberrations, Bonaparte's star continues to rise. In 1807, on February 7, he surveys the battlefield at Eylau, and what remains of this place of carnage is one of the most beautiful pictures Gros ever painted, adorned with Napoleon's idealized head. After a fifty-one-day entrenchment, Danzig opens its gates to Marshal Lefebvre, who, during the siege, kept saying to his gunners: "I can't make heads or tails of it, but you make me a hole and I'll be the first to go through." The former sergeant in the French Guards was made "Duc de Dantzick."

On June 14, 1807, the Battle of Friedland costs the Russians seventeen thousand dead and wounded, as many prisoners, and seventy guns. But we paid too dearly for this victory; our enemies had changed, and we could henceforth triumph only by sacrificing seas of French blood. Könisberg is taken, and an armistice is signed in Tilsit.

There, Napoleon and Alexander meet in a pavilion on a raft. Alexander keeps the King of Prussia, whom hardly anyone notices, on a leash. The fate of the world floats on the Niemen, where later it will be fulfilled. In Tilsit, a secret treaty of ten articles was discussed. By this treaty, European Turkey was devolved to Russia, along with whatever conquests the Muscovite armies could make in Asia. Meanwhile, Bonaparte was to become master of Spain and Portugal, reunite Rome and its dependencies with the Kingdom of Italy, cross to Africa, capture Tunis and Algiers, possess Malta, invade Egypt, opening the Mediterranean to the ships of France, Russia, Spain, and Italy alone. Such were the endless cantatas that played in Napoleon's head. A plan to invade India by land had already been arranged between Napoleon and Emperor Paul I in 1800.

The treaty is concluded on July 7. Napoleon, who hated the Queen of Prussia from the start, chose to ignore her intercessions. She lived in a small, forsaken house on the right bank of the Niemen and was done the honor of twice being asked to attend the emperors' banquets. Silesia, which had been unjustly invaded by Frederick, was returned to Prussia: the legality of the old injustice was respected, for whatever came of violence was considered sacred. A portion of Polish territories passed under the sovereignty of Saxony, and Danzig's independence was reestablished. The men killed in its streets and ditches counted for nothing—the ridiculous, pointless murders of war! Alexander recognized the Confederation of the Rhine and Napoleon's three brothers, Joseph, Louis, and Jérôme, as kings of Naples, Holland, and Westphalia.

7.

WAR WITH SPAIN—ERFURT—WELLINGTON APPEARS

THE FATE that Bonaparte used to threaten kings also threatened him. Almost simultaneously he attacks Russia, Spain, and Rome—three enterprises doomed to failure. You can read in the *Congress of Verona*, whose publication has preceded that of these *Memoirs*, the history of the invasion of Spain. The Treaty of Fontainebleau was signed on October 29, 1807. Junot, arriving in Portugal, had declared that according to Bonaparte's decree the House of Braganza "had ceased to reign," although, as you know, it reigns even to this day. They were so well informed in Lisbon of what was happening in the world that Prince John only learned of this decree when he happened on an issue of the *Moniteur* by chance, when the French army was three days' march from the capital of Lusitania. The only thing left for the Court to do was to escape to those seas that had hailed Da Gama's sails and harkened to the songs of Camões.

At the same time that Bonaparte, to his misfortune, had entered Russia in the north, the curtain was being raised in the south. Other regions and other scenes appeared—the sun of Andalusia, the palm trees of the Guadalquivir, which our soldiers saluted with guns in their hands. They saw bullfights in the arena, half-naked guerillas in the mountains, monks at prayer in the cloisters.

With the invasion of Spain, the spirit of the war changed. Napoleon found himself face-to-face with England, his evil genius, which taught him something about battle. England destroyed Napoleon's fleet at Aboukir, stopped him in his tracks at Acre, robbed him of

380 · MEMOIRS FROM BEYOND THE GRAVE

his last ships at Trafalgar, forced him to evacuate Iberia, captured the south of France up to the Garonne, and lay in wait for him at Waterloo. Today, the English guard his tomb on Saint Helena just as they once occupied his birthplace of Corsica.

On May 5, 1808, the Treaty of Bayonne cedes all of Charles IV's monarchical rights to Napoleon; but the seizure of Spain only shows Bonaparte to be an Italian prince in the Machiavellian manner, save the enormity of the theft. The occupation of the Iberian Peninsula diminishes his forces against Russia, with whom he is ostensibly still a friend and ally, but toward whom he harbors a hatred he conceals. In a proclamation, Napoleon had said to the Spanish:

"Your nation is dying: I have seen your ills, and now I will cure them; I want your grandchildren's grandchildren to remember me and say: 'He brought our country back to life.'"

Yes, Napoleon did bring Spain back to life, but he spoke words he did not understand. A catechism from that time, composed by the Spanish, explains the real meaning of the prophecy:

"Tell me, my child, who are you?"
"A Spaniard, by the grace of God."
"Who is the enemy of our happiness?"
"The Emperor of France."
"Who is he?"
"A bad man."
"How many natures does he have?"
"Two, one human and one diabolical."
"How did Napoleon come to be?"
"Through the wages of sin."
"What punishment does the Spaniard who shirks his duty deserve?"
"Death, and the infamy of traitordom."
"What are Frenchmen?"
"Erstwhile Christians who have become heretics."

Once he had fallen from grace, Bonaparte himself unequivocally condemned his Spanish enterprise. "I started out on the wrong foot with that business," he said. "*The immorality must have been too obvious or the injustice too cynical,* and the whole thing seems quite horrible since I've bowed out; for the *assault,* deprived of all the grandeur and the innumerable advantages that drove me to make it, looks simply shameful. Still, posterity would have approved of it had I succeeded, and perhaps rightly so, given its good and great results. That plan was my undoing. It destroyed my moral reputation in Europe and served as a training ground for English soldiers. That wretched Spanish War was a real scourge—the root cause of France's misfortunes."

This confession, to reemploy Napoleon's phrase, is too cynical, but make no mistake: by accusing himself, Bonaparte's objective is to send this attack out into the desert laden with maledictions like a scapegoat, demanding our unreserved admiration for all his other actions.

With the loss of the Battle of Bailén, the cabinets of Europe—astonished by the Spaniards' success—blush at their own faintheartedness. Wellington appears for the first time on the horizon, where the sun is setting; an English army disembarks near Lisbon on July 31, 1808, and on August 30 French troops evacuate Lusitania. Marshall Soult's briefcase then contained proclamations that titled him Nicolas I, King of Portugal. Napoleon recalled the Grand Duke of Berg from Madrid. He was now pleased to perform a transmutation between Joseph, his brother, and Joachim, his brother-in-law: he took the crown of Naples from the head of the former and placed it on the head of the latter; with a brusque gesture, he thrust this headwear on the skulls of the two new kings, and off they scurried, in different directions, like two conscripts who have exchanged shakos.

On September 27, at the Congress of Erfurt, Bonaparte gave one of his last shows of glory. He thought he had got the better of Alexander by intoxicating him with praise. One general wrote:

"We've just made the czar swallow a glass of opium. While he's sleeping, we'll go and see to other business."

A warehouse had been transformed into a theater. In front of the orchestra pit, armchairs were set out for the two potentates, flanked left and right by upholstered seats for the monarchs, with benches for the princes in the rear. Talma, the king of the stage, performed before an audience of kings. At the verse

L'amitié d'un grand homme est un bienfait des dieux,[14]

Alexander took the hand of his great friend, bowed, and said:

"I have never felt it more keenly."

Bonaparte believed Alexander a fool in those days. He made him the butt of his jokes and admired him only when he thought he was being deceitful. "He's a Greek of the Late Empire," he would say; "you have to watch out for him." In Erfurt, Napoleon affected the brazen false bravado of a victorious soldier, while Alexander pretended to be a conquered prince. Cunning did battle with lies. The politics of the West and the politics of the East did not depart from their usual character.

London eluded the overtures of peace that were made to it, and the cabinet of Vienna slyly decided on war. Once again left to his imagination, Bonaparte, on October 26, said to the Corps Législatif:

"The Emperor of Russia and I met in Erfurt; we are in agreement and invariably united in peace and in war."

He added:

"When I loom up on the other side of the Pyrenees, the terrified Leopard will flee to the ocean to save himself from shame, defeat, or death." And then the Leopard loomed up *on this side* of the Pyrenees.

Napoleon, who always believed whatever he liked, thought he would return to Russia after subduing Spain in four months' time, as has since happened to the Legitimacy. Consequently, he withdraws eighty thousand old soldiers from Saxony, Poland, and Prussia, and he himself makes his way to Spain. To the deputation of the city of Madrid, he says:

"Nothing can stand in the way of my plans for long. The Bourbons must no longer rule in Europe—no power under the influence of England can exist on the continent."

It was thirty-two years ago this prophecy was delivered, and the capture of Saragossa, on February 21, 1809, heralded the deliverance of the world.

All the bravery of the French was to no avail. The forests armed themselves, the bushes became enemies. The reprisals stopped nothing, for in that country reprisals are natural phenomena. The Battle of Bailén, the defense of Girona and Ciudad Rodrigo, signaled the resurrection of a people. La Romana, from the faraway Baltic, led his regiments back to Spain, as once the Franks, escaping the Black Sea, landed triumphantly at the mouths of the Rhine. Conquerors of the finest soldiers of Europe, we shed the blood of monks with that impious rage that France displayed in both Voltaire's buffooneries and the atheistic insanity of the Terror. Yet it was these militias of the cloister that put an end to our old soldiers' successes: they hardly expected to encounter these frocked friars riding horses like fire-breathing dragons over the burning timbers of the buildings of Saragossa, loading their rifles amid the flames, to the music of mandolins, and boleros, and the requiem mass for the dead. The ruins of Saguntum applauded.

But still the secret places of the palaces of the Moors, transformed into Christian basilicas, were violated. The churches were stripped of masterpieces by Velázquez and Murillo. Some of Rodrigo's bones were stolen from Burgos. French soldiers were so covered with glory they didn't think twice about rousing El Cid's ghost against them: no more than the executioners of the Duc d'Enghien had feared provoking the ire of Condé's shade.

When, emerging from the ruins of Carthage, I traveled through Hesperia before the French invasion, I saw Spaniards still protected by their ancient customs. The Escorial showed me, in one site and one monument, all the severity of Castile. A cenobite barracks built by Philip II in the shape of a martyr's grill, in memory of one of our disasters, the Escorial was built on hard ground among dark hills. It contained royal tombs, filled or ready to be filled; a library on which the spiders had set their seal; and masterpieces by Raphael growing mold in an empty sacristy. Its 1,140 windows, three-quarters broken, opened on mute reaches of Heaven and earth. The Court and the Hieronymites who once gathered there represented the times and disgust for the times brought together.

Next to that redoubtable edifice, the embodiment of the Inquisition driven out into the desert, were a park streaked with broom and a village whose smoke-blackened hearths revealed the ancient passage of man. This Versailles of the steppes had no inhabitants except during the intermittent sojourns of kings. I saw the redwing, the lark of the heath, perched on the roof in the sunlight. Nothing could be more imposing than these dark sacred architectures, with their invincible faith, their nobility, their taciturn look of experience. An irresistible force drew my eye to the sacred dosserets—stone hermits who were bearing religion on their heads.

Farewell, monasteries, at whom I have cast a glance in the valleys of the Sierra Nevada and on the shingle beach near Murcia! There, at the tolling of a bell that will soon cease to chime, beneath crumbling archways, among lavras abandoned by anchorites, voiceless tombs, and dead men deserted by the Manes; there, in empty refectories and forsaken courtyards where Bruno left his silence, Francis his sandals, Dominic his torch, Charles his crown, Ignatius his sword, and Rancé his hairshirt; there, at the altar of a dying faith, the faithful were used to despising life and time: if we still dreamed of passions, your solitude lent them something well suited to the vanity of dreams.

Through these funereal constructions, the shadow a dark man could still be seen wandering: this was the shadow of Philip II, their creator.

8.

PIUS VII—FRANCE'S ANNEXATION OF THE ROMAN STATES

BONAPARTE had entered the orbit of what the astrologers used to call an "evil planet." The same politics that launched him into vassal Spain now troubled him in acquiescent Italy. What did he gain from these quarrels with the clergy? Were the sovereign pontiff, the bishops, the priests, and even the very catechism not overflowing with praise for his power? Did they not sufficiently preach submission? Did the weaker Roman States, diminished by half, stand in his way? Could he not do with them as he pleased? Had Rome itself not been despoiled of its masterpieces and treasures? Only its ruins remained.

Perhaps it was the moral and religious power of the Holy See that Napoleon feared. But, by persecuting the Papacy, did he not increase that power? Wouldn't Saint Peter's successor, submissive as he was, have been more useful to him walking side by side with his master—instead of being forced to defend himself against his oppressor? What *drove* Bonaparte? The evil side of his genius, his inability to remain at rest. An eternal gambler, when he wasn't laying bets on new empires, he was chancing fantasies.

Probably, at the root of this restless irritableness, there was some deep need for domination—some historical memories gone awry in his mind with no real relevance to his era. All authority (even the authority of time and faith) not attached to him personally struck the emperor as usurpation. Russia and England whetted his appetite for preponderance—the one with its autocracy, the other with its spiritual supremacy. He recalled the days when the popes used to stay in Avignon, when France contained within its borders the source of religious dominion. A pope on his payroll would have charmed him. He did not see that by persecuting Pius VII, and thus making himself guilty of pointless ingratitude, he lost the advantage of passing, among Catholic populations, for the restorer of religion. With his greed, he won the last vestments of the obsolete priest who had crowned him and the honor of playing jailer to a dying old man. But finally Napoleon had to have a *département* of the Tiber. Apparently no conquest is complete if the eternal city is not taken: Rome is always the world's greatest prize.

Pius VII had consecrated Napoleon. On the brink of returning to Rome, the pope was told that he might be detained in Paris. "It has all been taken care of," the pontiff replied; "before leaving Italy, I signed a formal abdication. It is in the hands of Cardinal Pignatelli in Palermo, out of the reach of French power. Instead of a pope, you will now only be detaining a monk named Barnaba Chiaramonti."

The first pretext for the quarrel-seeker's quarrel was the permission the pope granted to the English (with whom he as the sovereign pontiff was at peace) to come to Rome like all other foreigners. Then there was the matter of Jérôme Bonaparte having married Miss Patterson in the United States—an alliance Napoleon disapproved of. Mrs. Jérôme Bonaparte, who was about to give birth, could not land in France and was obliged to go ashore in England. When Bonaparte demanded the marriage be annulled by Rome, Pius VII refused, finding no cause to nullify the contract, even if it was made between a Catholic and a Protestant. Who defended the rights of justice, liberty, and religion—the pope or the emperor? The latter exclaimed: "In my era, I find priests more powerful than I; they reign over spirits, whereas I reign only over matter: the priests keep the soul and throw me the body." Remove Napoleon's bad faith from the correspondence between these two men—the one standing on new ruins and the other sitting upon old ones—and there still remains an extraordinary fund of grandeur.

A letter sent from Benavente in Spain, from the theater of destruction, mixes the comic with the tragic; you might think you were witnessing a Shakespearean scene: the master of the world orders his foreign minister to write to Rome and tell the pope that he, Napoleon, will not accept the Candlemas candles that the King of Spain, Joseph, doesn't want either. The kings of Naples and Holland, Joachim and Louis, must also refuse the aforesaid candles.

The French consul was ordered to tell Pius VII "it was neither the purple nor power that gives value to these things (the purple and power of an elderly prisoner!), that there may well be popes and priests in hell, and that a candle blessed by a priest can be just as holy as a candle blessed by a pope." Miserable outrages of sophomoric philosophy!

Then Bonaparte, having taken a giant leap from Madrid to Vienna, resumed his old role of exterminator and issued a decree dated May 17, 1809, annexing the Papal States to the French Empire, declaring Rome a free imperial city, and appointing a *consulte* to take possession of it.

The dispossessed pope was still living in the Quirinal and still commanded a few devoted authorities and Swiss Guards. This was too much. Bonaparte needed an excuse for one last act of violence and found it in a ridiculous incident, which, nevertheless, serves as naive evidence of the people's affection. Some fishermen on the Tiber had caught a sturgeon and wanted to take it to their new Saint Peter in Chains. Immediately, the French agents call "Riot!" and what remains of the papal government is sent packing. The sound of the cannon from Castel Sant'Angelo announces the fall of the pontiff's temporal sovereignty. The lowered pontifical flag gives way to the tricolor that, in every corner of the world, presaged glory and ruins. But Rome had seen many other storms pass and vanish. They merely raised the dust from her ancient brow.

9.

PROTEST OF THE SOVEREIGN PONTIFF—HE IS TAKEN FROM ROME

CARDINAL Pacca—one of the the successors of Consalvi, who had retired—races to the Holy Father's side. Both of them exclaim: *Consummatum est!*[15] The cardinal's nephew, Tiberio Pacca, brings a printed copy of Napoleon's decree. The cardinal takes the decree, goes to a window whose closed shutters do not let in enough light to read by, and tries to decipher the page. He only barely manages to do so, with his star-crossed sovereign a few steps away from him and the sound of triumphant imperial cannon fire in the distance. Two old men in the darkness of a Roman palace were battling, alone, against a power that was crushing the world. They drew strength from their age. When a man is ready to die, he is invincible.

The pope first signed a solemn protest; but before signing the bull of excommunication prepared long ago, he asked Cardinal Pacca:

"What would you do?"

"Raise your eyes to Heaven," his servant replied, "then give your orders: what you say shall be the will of Heaven."

The pope raised his eyes, signed his name, and said:

"Let the bull go out."

Megacci hung the first posters of the bull on the gates of the three basilicas: San Pietro, Santa Maria Maggiore, and San Giovanni in Laterano. The posters were torn down. General Miollis sent one to the emperor.

If anything could give excommunication something of its former strength, it was the virtue of Pius VII. Among the ancients, the lightning that crackled across a serene sky was the most menacing thing imaginable. But the bull still retained a certain weakness: Napoleon, grouped among the "spoliators" of the Church, was not *expressly* named. Fear was in the air, and the timid took refuge, in good conscience, in the absence of any explicit excommunication. What was needed was to battle against the thunder—to fight lightning with lightning, since no one had decided to defend themselves; what was needed was to put an end to worship, lock the doors of the temples, ban churchgoing, order the priests not to administer the sacraments. Whether or not the time was right for this lofty venture, it would have been useful to give it a try: Gregory VII would not have failed to do so. If on one hand there was not enough faith to support an excommunication, on the other there was not enough left for Bonaparte, playing at being Henry VIII, to become leader of a separate church. Through complete excommunication, the emperor would have found himself in inextricable difficulties. Violence can close churches, but it cannot open them. People cannot be forced to pray, nor priests compelled to offer the holy sacrifice. No one ever made the move against Napoleon that might have been made.

A seventy-one-year-old priest, without a single soldier, held the empire in check. Murat sent seven hundred Neapolitans to Miollis, who inaugurated the feast of Virgil in Mantua.[16] Radet, general of the gendarmerie in Rome, was tasked with kidnapping the pope and Cardinal Pacca. Military precautions were taken. Orders were given in the greatest secrecy, and it was just as it had been on Saint Bartholomew's Night: when the hour after midnight struck on the Quirinal's clock, the troops, who had assembled in silence, boldly scaled the heights of the prison where the frail priests lay captive.

At the agreed-upon hour, General Radet entered the courtyard of the Quirinal by the large gate; Colonel Siry, who had slipped into the palace, opened the doors for him from inside. The general ascended to the upper rooms: arriving in the Hall of Sanctifications, he found the Swiss Guard forty men strong, but they offered no resistance, having received orders to restrain themselves. The pope wanted nothing before him but God.

The windows of the palace overlooking the street to Porta Pia had been smashed with axes. Startled out of bed, the pope rose in his rochet and mozzetta and went into the Audience Hall with Cardinal Pacca, Cardinal Despuig, and a few prelates and members of his secretarial staff. He was sitting at a table between the two cardinals. Radet entered, and all were silent. Pale and disconcerted, Radet finally spoke: he declared to Pius VII that he must renounce temporal sovereignty over Rome and that if His Holiness refused to obey, he had orders to take him to General Miollis.

The pope replied that if vows of loyalty obliged Radet to obey Bonaparte's injunctions, all the more reason why he, Pius VII, had to hold to the oaths he had made when he received the papal tiara. He could not cede or abandon the domain of the Church, for the Church did not belong to him; he was only its administrator.

When the pope asked if he had to go alone, the general replied: "His Holiness may take his minister with him."

Pacca hastened to don his cardinal's robes in a neighboring chamber.

On Christmas Night 1075, Gregory VII, while celebrating Mass at Santa Maria Maggiore, was torn from the altar, hit on the head, robbed of his ornaments, and led into a tower by order of the prefect Cencius. The people took up arms. Cencius took fright and fell at the feet of his captive. Gregory appeased the people, was brought back to Santa Maria Maggiore, and finished Mass.

On September 8, 1303, Nogaret and Colonna went into Anagni at night, forced their way into the house of Boniface VIII, who was waiting for them with the pontifical cape over his shoulders, his head circled by the tiara, his hands armed with the keys and the cross. Colonna hit him in the face, and Boniface died of it, from rage and pain.

Humble, dignified Pius VII did not show such human audacity or such worldly pride. The example he followed was much closer to him: his trials most resembled those of Pius VI. These two popes, who shared the same name and served successively, were both victims of our revolutions: both were dragged to France along the *via dolorosa*! The one, at the age of eighty-two, went to die in Valence; the other, a septuagenarian, was imprisoned in Fontainebleau. Pius VII seemed to be the ghost of Pius VI, traveling the same road once again.

When Pacca returned in his cardinal's robe, he found his august master already in the hands of the henchmen and gendarmes who forced him down the stairs, stumbling over the debris of the broken-down door. Pius VI, abducted from the Vatican on February 20, 1798, three hours before sunrise, abandoned the world of masterpieces, which seemed to mourn him, and left Rome by the Porta Angelica, to the murmur of the fountains in Saint Peter's Square. Pius VII, taken from the Quirinal on July 6 at daybreak, left by the Porta Pia and followed the walls around to the Porta del Popolo. This Porta Pia, which I have seen so often on my solitary walks, was the gate through which Alaric entered Rome. Following the wall-walk where Pius VII passed, I saw nothing on the Villa Borghese side but Raphael's retreat and, on the side of the Pincian Hill, the refuges of Claude Lorrain and Poussin—wonderful reminders of the beauty of women and the light of Rome; reminders of the spirit of the arts protected by pontifical power, which could follow and console a captive and despoiled prince.

When Pius VII left Rome, he carried in his pocket a twenty-sous *papetto*, like a soldier carrying five sous for the road: later, he would recover the Vatican. Bonaparte, at the time of General Radet's exploits, had his hands full of kingdoms: and what remains of them? Radet published the account of his exploits; he had a painting made of them, which he left to his family. Notions of justice and honor are so muddled in men's minds, it is incredible.

In the courtyard of the Quirinal the pope had encountered the Neapolitans, his oppressors; he blessed them as well as their city: this apostolic blessing that encompasses everyone, rich and poor, gives a special quality to the events of the lives of these pontiff-kings who are nothing like the kings of earth.

Post horses were waiting outside the Porta del Popolo. The louvers of the carriage into which Pius VII climbed had been nailed shut on the side where he sat. Once the pope was in, the doors were double-locked, and Radet put the keys into his pocket. The leader of the

392 · MEMOIRS FROM BEYOND THE GRAVE

gendarmes was to accompany the pope as far as the Charterhouse of Florence.

In Monterossi, women wept on their doorsteps. The general implored His Holiness to lower the curtains of the car and hide. The heat was oppressive. Toward evening, Pius VII asked for a drink; Cardigny, the quartermaster, filled a bottle with water from a stream that ran alongside the road and Pius VII drank with great pleasure. In the hills of Radicofani, the pope stayed at a poor inn; his clothes were drenched with sweat, and he had no others. Pacca helped the maid to make His Holiness's bed. The next day the pope crossed paths with some peasants, saying to them: "Have courage and pray!" They passed through Siena and entered Florence, where one of the wheels of the carriage broke. The people, filled with emotion, cried out: *Santo Padre! Santo Padre!* The pope was dragged out of the carriage through the door. Some prostrated themselves, while others touched His Holiness's vestments, as the people of Jerusalem had touched the robe of Christ.

Finally, the pope was able to set out again for the Charterhouse. In this lonely place, he inherited the bed that Pius VI had occupied ten years earlier, when two grooms had hoisted him into the carriage as he groaned in pain. This Charterhouse belonged to Vallombrosa Abbey. Through a series of pine forests, they then reached the Camaldolese Monastery, and from there, proceeding from rock to rock, that Apennine summit overlooking the two seas. A sudden order forced Pius VII to take off again for Alessandria; he barely had time to ask the prior for a breviary. Pacca was at this point separated from the pontiff.

From the Charterhouse to Alessandria, the crowd poured in from every side. They threw flowers to the prisoner, gave him water and fruit. Country people offered to liberate him, saying: *Vuole? Dica.* A pious thief robbed him of a pin—a relic that was to open the gates of heaven to the brigand.

Three miles from Genoa, the pope was put on a litter and taken to the seashore. A felucca transported him to the other side of the city to Sampierdarena. Through Alessandria and Mondovi, Pius VII

BOOK TWENTY · 393

made his way to the first French village, where he was welcomed with effusions of religious feeling. He said:

"Could God order us to appear unmoved by such marks of affection?"

The Spaniards taken prisoner in Saragossa were detained in Grenoble. Like those garrisons of Europeans forgotten on the mountains of India, they sang through the night and made the foreign air ring with their song. Suddenly the pope appeared. He seemed to have heard these Christian voices. The captives fly to meet this new unfortunate. They fall to their knees. Pius VII pushes almost his whole body through the door; he extends his thin and trembling hands to these warriors who had defended Italy's liberty with the sword as he had defended Spain's liberty with the faith. Twin swords cross over their heroic heads.

From Grenoble, Pius VII reached Valence. There, Pius VI had died; there, he had shouted when he was shown to the people, "*Ecce homo!*" There, too, Pius VI parted ways with Pius VII. The dead man, encountering his tomb, returned to it, and put an end to the ghostly duplication; for until then they were like two popes moving together, as a shadow accompanies a body. Pius VII wore the ring that Pius VI had on his finger when he died—a sign that he had accepted the miseries and destiny of his predecessor.

Two leagues from Comana, Saint Chrysostom lodged at the church of the martyr Saint Basilisk, who appeared to him during the night and said to him: "Be of good courage, John! Tomorrow we shall be together." John replied: "God be praised!" He lay down on the ground and died.

In Valencia, Bonaparte started on the path that would send him hurtling toward Rome. There was no time for Pius VII to visit the ashes of Pius VI. He was hurriedly pushed on to Avignon. There, in that little Rome, he could see the ice cellar beneath the palace of another line of pontiffs, and hear the voice of the coronated poet of old, recalling Saint Peter's successors on the Capitol.[17]

Driven on at random, he returned to the Maritime Alps. At the Pont du Var, he said he wished to cross it on foot. He saw the population divided into guilds, the clergy dressed in their vestments, and ten thousand people kneeling in silence. The Queen of Etruria with her two children, all of them kneeling, waited for the Holy Father at the far end of the bridge. In Nice, the city streets were strewn with flowers. The captain who was transporting the pope to Savona took an unfrequented road through the woods at night and, to his great surprise, wandered into a wilderness of light—a lantern had been hung from every tree. Along the seafront, the corniche was similarly illuminated; from afar, the ships could see these beacons kindled by piety, tenderness, and respect for the shipwreck of a captive monk. Was this the way Napoleon came back from Moscow? Was he preceded by the news of his goodness and the blessings of the people he passed?

During this long journey, the Battle of Wagram had been won and the marriage of Napoleon with Marie Louise delayed. Thirteen of the cardinals sent to Paris were exiled, and the Roman *consulte* formed by France had again announced the union of the Holy See and the Empire.

The pope, detained in Savona, tired and besieged by Napoleon's homunculi, issued a writ chiefly authored by Cardinal Roverella which allowed bulls of confirmation to be sent to several different bishops. The emperor had not counted on so much complacency; he rejected the writ because it would have given him no choice but to set the pontiff free. In an outburst of anger, he had ordered the cardinals who opposed him to give up their vestments. A few of them were locked up at Vincennes.

The prefect of Nice wrote to Pius VII that he was forbidden to communicate with any church in the Empire lest he be considered disloyal; that he, Pius VII, had ceased to be the organ of the Church because he preached rebellion and his soul was all bile; that, since nothing could bring him to his senses, he would soon learn that His Majesty "is powerful enough to depose a pope."

Was it really the victor of Marengo who dictated such a letter?

Finally, after three years of captivity in Savona, on June 9, 1812, the pope was summoned to France. He was ordered to change his clothes. Headed for Turin, he arrived at the hospice of Mont Cenis in the middle of the night. There, at death's door, he received extreme unction. He was allowed to stop only as long as it took to administer the last rites; they did not want him staying so close to heaven. But he did not complain. He followed the clement example set by the woman martyred in Vercellae. At the foot of the mountain, just as she was about to be beheaded, she saw the clasp of the headsman's chlamys fall to the ground and said to him:

"Here, look, a golden clasp has fallen from your shoulder. Pick it up, lest you lose what you have earned through such hard toil."[18]

During his passage through France, Pius VII was not allowed to get out of his carriage. If he ate a meal, it was in this same carriage, which was locked up in the storerooms of the post offices. On the morning of June 20, he arrived in Fontainebleau; three days later, Bonaparte crossed the Niemen to begin his expiation. The concierge refused to receive the captive because no order had yet reached him. Once the order from Paris came, the pope entered the palace. He brought celestial justice with him. On the same table where Pius VII rested his faltering hand, Napoleon signed his abdication.

If the iniquitous invasion of Spain turned the political world against Bonaparte, the disagreeable occupation of Rome repulsed the moral world. For no reason at all, as though it gave him pleasure, he alienated himself from both the nations and the churches, from both man and God. Between the two precipices he had carved out at the edges of his life, he went along a narrow road, seeking his destruction at the bottom of Europe, as if on the bridge that Death, abetted by Sin, had built over Chaos.[19]

Pius VII is no stranger to these *Memoirs*. He is the first sovereign to whom I fulfilled a mission in the political career that began and abruptly came to an end under the Consulate. I can still see him receiving me at the Vatican with *The Genius of Christianity* open on his table, in the same office where I was admitted at the feet of Leo XII and Pius VIII. I love to remember what he suffered. May my remembrance of his torments pay the debt of gratitude I owe him for the torments he blessed in Rome, in 1803.[20]

10.

**FIFTH COALITION—THE TAKING OF VIENNA—
BATTLE OF ESSLING—BATTLE OF WAGRAM—PEACE
TREATY SIGNED IN THE AUSTRIAN EMPEROR'S
PALACE—DIVORCE—NAPOLEON WEDS MARIE
LOUISE—BIRTH OF THE KING OF ROME**

ON APRIL 9, 1809, between England, Austria, and Spain, the Fifth
Coalition was declared and tacitly supported by the discontent of
other sovereigns. The Austrians, complaining of the violation of treaties, abruptly crossed the Inn at Braunau: they had been reproached
for their slowness and wanted to proceed in Napoleonic fashion, but
such a pace didn't suit them. Glad to leave Spain, Bonaparte made
for Bavaria and named himself commander of the Bavarians without
waiting for the French; all soldiers were the same to him. He defeats
Archduke Louis at Abensberg, Archduke Charles at Eckmühl, saws
the Austrian army in half, and crosses the Salza.

He enters Vienna. On May 21 and 22, the terrible Battle of Essling
takes place. Archduke Charles's account tells us that on the first day
288 Austrian guns fired 51,000 balls and that on the second day more
than 400 guns were fired on both sides. Marshal Lannes was mortally
wounded. Bonaparte spoke a few words to him and then forgot him;
the attachments between men cool as quickly as the bullets that strike
them.

The Battle of Wagram (July 6, 1809) encapsulates the various
battles fought in Germany. There, Bonaparte deploys all his genius.
Colonel César de Laville, charged with going to warn him of disaster
on the left flank, finds him on the right flank directing Marshal
Davout's assault. Napoleon returns immediately to the left and wins
back the ground lost by Masséna. It was then, at the moment when
the battle seemed lost, that Napoleon alone, incongruously interpet-

ing the enemy's maneuvers, exclaimed, "The fight is won!" He sets
his sights on vacillating Victory and hauls her back to the field of
carnage like Caesar hauling his astonished soldiers back to battle by
the beard. Nine hundred brazen mouths roar. The fields and the crops
go up in flames. Whole villages vanish. In all, the fighting lasts twelve
hours. During one charge, Lauriston marches at a trot toward the
enemy at the head of a hundred cannon. Four days later, soldiers
would be harvested from among the grain—men who had died beneath the rays of the sun, on trampled stalks of wheat. The worms
were already working themselves into the wounds of the corpses in
the most advanced state of decay.

In my youth, we carefully read the commentaries of Folard, Gui-
schardt, Tempelhoff, and Lloyd. We studied "deep order" and "thin
order." I used to map out maneuvers on my little sublieutenant's table
with little squares of wood. But military science was changed, like
everything else, by the Revolution. Bonaparte invented large-scale
war—inspired by the conquests of the Republic, which had requisitioned the masses. He despised strongholds, which he was satisfied
to protect with troops, ventured into the invaded country, and won
battles one after the next. He was uninterested in retreats. He went
straight ahead, like those Roman roads that cross mountains and
precipices, never bending. He brought all his strength to bear on a
single point, then gathered the isolated corps whose lines he had
broken. This maneuver, which was peculiar to him, was well suited
to French fury, but would never have worked with less agile and
impetuous soldiers. Toward the end of his career, he also ordered
artillery charges and captured redoubts with cavalry. And what was
the result? When France went to war, Europe learned to march. Then
it was simply a question of multiplying the means. The masses have
counterbalanced the masses. Instead of one hundred thousand men,
six hundred thousand have been taken; instead of one hundred cannon, five hundred were dragged out. Military science has not increased
one whit; only the scale has been enlarged. Turenne knew as much
as Bonaparte, but he was not absolute master and did not have forty
million men at his disposal. Sooner or later, we must return to the

civilized warfare still known by Moreau—warfare that leaves populations alone while a small number of soldiers do their duty. We must return to the art of retreat, to the defense of a country by means of strongholds, to patient maneuvers that cost nothing but time and spare men's lives. The enormous battles of Napoleon go beyond glory; the eye cannot comprehend those fields of carnage, which ultimately bring about no results commensurate with their calamities. Europe, barring unforeseen events, will be fed up with fighting for a long time to come. Napoleon killed war by blowing it out of proportion. Our war in Africa is only an experimental school open to our soldiers.[21]

Among the dead, on the battlefield at Wagram, Napoleon displayed his characteristic impassivity, which he affected in order to appear above other men. He said coldly, or rather he repeated what he usually said under such circumstances:

"What an enormous outcome!"

When injured officers were mentioned to him, he would say:

"They are absent."

If military experience teaches some virtues, it weakens many others: the too-human soldier could not carry out his work; the sight of blood and tears, suffering, the cries of pain, stopping him at every step, would destroy whatever it is in him that makes the Caesars—a race that, in the final analysis, we would gladly do without.

After the Battle of Wagram, an armistice is signed at Znaim. The Austrians, whatever our bulletins may say, had retreated in good order and not left a single mounted gun behind. Bonaparte, in possession of Schönbrunn, was working for peace there.

"On October 13," says the Duc de Cadore,

I had come from Vienna to work with the emperor. After a few moments' discussion, he said to me:

"I'm going to the review. Stay in my office. You can draw up that note, and I'll give it a look after the review."

I remained in his office with M. de Meneval, his private secretary, and a moment later he returned.

"The Prince of Lichtenstein," Napoleon said to me: "didn't he tell you he often had offers to assassinate me?'

"Yes, sire. He told me of the horror with which he rejected these proposals."

"Well! Someone just tried. Follow me."

I walked with him into the drawing room. There were a few people who looked very agitated standing around a young man of eighteen or twenty, with a pleasant, very gentle-looking face that suggested a sort of candor; he alone seemed to have retained his calm. This was the assassin. He was questioned quite gently by Napoleon himself, with General Rapp acting as the interpreter. I will only relate a few of his answers, which struck me most forcefully:

"Why did you want to murder me?"

"Because there will never be peace for Germany as long as you're alive."

"What inspired this plan?"

"Love of my country.

"Have you not conspired with anyone else?"

"I undertook it alone."

"Were you aware of the dangers you would face?"

"I was, but I would be happy to die for my country."

"You have religious principles; do you believe that God authorizes murder?"

"I hope God will forgive me in light of my motives."

"Have you been taught this doctrine in the schools?"

"Many of my fellow students share my sentiments and would be willing to sacrifice their lives to protect their country."

"What would you do if I released you?"

"I would kill you."

The terrible naiveté of these answers, the cold and unshakable resolution they proclaimed, and this fanaticism so far distant from all human fear, made an impression on Napoleon—an impression I thought deepened the more composure he showed. He sent everyone out of the room, until I alone remained with him. After making a few remarks about blind and willful fanaticism, he said to me: "We must make peace."

This account, written by the Duc de Cadore, deserves to be quoted in full.

The nations had begun to rise up. They would prove to be more powerful enemies of Bonaparte than any king. The resolution of a single commoner saved Austria. Yet Napoleon had not been entirely abandoned by Fortune. On August 14, 1809, in the palace of the emperor of Austria, he made peace. This time, the daughter of Caesars was the proffered palm. But Josephine had been consecrated, and Marie Louise was not. With the departure of his first wife, the virtue of divine anointment seemed to draw away from the victor. I could have seen the same ceremony I saw at the Cathedral of Reims at Notre-Dame de Paris. With the exception of Napoleon, the same people were there.

One of the secret actors who played the largest part in this affair was my friend Alexandre de Laborde, who was wounded among the émigré ranks and honored with the Croix de Marie-Thérèse for his wounds.

On March 11, the Prince de Neuchâtel[22] married in Vienna, by proxy, the Archduchess Marie Louise. She left for France, accompanied by Princesse Murat, and on the way was decorated with the emblems of the sovereign. She arrived in Strasbourg on March 22, and on the 28th, at Compiègne Castle, where Bonaparte was waiting for her. The civil marriage ceremony took place at Saint-Cloud on April 1. The next day Cardinal Fesch bestowed the nuptial blessing on the newlyweds in the Louvre. Bonaparte taught this second wife to be unfaithful to him, just as the first had been, by cheating in his own bed, enjoying intimacy with Marie Louise before the celebration of the religious marriage, showing a contempt for the majesty of royal manners and holy law that did not bode well.

Everything seems finished; Bonaparte has obtained the only thing he lacked. Like Philip Augustus allying himself with Isabella of

Hainaut, he mixes the most recent race with the "race of great kings." The past is united with the future. He is now, in every sense, master of the ages—if only he had wished to settle at the summit. Yet, while he has the power to stop the world, he does not have the power to stop himself. He will go on until he has conquered the last crown, which gives meaning to all the others, the crown of misfortune.

On March 20, 1811, the Archduchess Marie Louise gives birth to a son—supposed sanction of earlier felicities. From this child hatched like a polar bird, under the midnight sun, there will remain only a sad waltz composed by himself at Schönbrunn and played on organs in the streets of Paris, around his father's palace.

11.

PLANS AND PREPARATIONS FOR THE WAR IN RUSSIA
—EMBARRASSMENT OF NAPOLEON

BONAPARTE had no more enemies. Not knowing where he could capture an empire, and for lack of anything better, he had the kingdom of Holland taken from his brother. Yet in the depths of his heart, Napoleon had retained a secret enmity for Alexander, dating back to the time of the death of the Duc d'Enghien. He was animated by rivalry for power; he knew what Russia could do and at what cost he had won the victories at Friedland and Eylau. The conferences at Tilsit and Erfurt, the cease-fires, a peace that Bonaparte's character could not endure, declarations of friendship, handshakes, embraces, fantastic plans for mutual conquest—all this was nothing but an extended postponement of hostility. There remained one country on the continent where Napoleon had not set foot, an empire standing face-to-face with the French Empire. The two colossi were bound to take each other's measure. By expanding the boundaries of France, Bonaparte had collided with the Russians, as Trajan, crossing the Danube, had collided with the Goths.

A natural calm, sustained by sincere piety since his return to religion, inclined Alexander toward peace. He would never have broken it if no one had come looking for him. The whole year of 1811 was spent in preparations. Russia invited tame Austria and panting Prussia to ally themselves with her in the event of an attack; England arrived with her purse. The example of the Spaniards had elicited the sympathy of the nations. The League of Virtue (Tugendbund) had already been formed and was beginning to take root in young Germany.

Bonaparte negotiated and made promises. He let the King of Prussia think he could possess the German-populated Russian provinces. The kings of Saxony and Austria were flattered into thinking they might enlarge their domains with what still remained of Poland. The princes of the Confederation of the Rhine dreamed of altering the map as they saw fit. Even France, Napoleon thought, might be expanded, although it had already overrun Europe. He nominally added Spain to its territory. General Sebastiani said to him: "And what about your brother?" Napoleon replied: "Who cares about my brother? Why should we give him a kingdom like Spain?" With a word, the master disposed of a kingdom that had cost Louis XIV so many sacrifices and miseries—but he did not hold onto it very long. As for the nations, no man has ever shown them less attention or more scorn than Bonaparte. He threw scraps to the pack of kings he led to the hunt with whip in hand. "Attila," writes Jordanes, "took with him a crowd of tributary princes who waited in fear and trembling for a sign from the master of monarchs to do whatever they were ordered to do."[23]

Before marching into Russia with his allies Austria and Prussia, with the Confederation of the Rhine made up of kings and princes, Napoleon had wanted to secure his two flanks, which touched the two edges of Europe, and he negotiated two treaties: one in the south with Constantinople, the other in the north with Stockholm. These treaties failed.

Napoleon, during the Consulate, had renewed contact with Constantinople: Selim and Bonaparte had exchanged portraits and kept up a secret correspondence. Napoleon wrote to his accomplice from Osterode, on April 3, 1807:

"You have shown yourself the worthy descendant of Selims and Suleimans. Tell me what you need: I am powerful enough and interested enough in your success, both as a man and a leader, not to deny you anything."

A charming outpouring of tenderness between two sultans chatting beak to beak, as Saint-Simon would have said.[24]

With Selim overthrown, Napoleon returns to his Russian plan

and thinks of sharing Turkey with Alexander; then, overwhelmed again by yet another cataclysm of ideas, he makes up his mind to invade the Muscovite empire. But it is not until March 21, 1812, that he asks Mahmud to be his ally, abruptly demanding from him a hundred thousand Turks on the banks of the Danube. In exchange for this army, he offers the Wallachia Gate and Moldavia to the Porte. The Russians had beat him to it, however: their treaty was about to be concluded, and was signed on May 28, 1812.

In the north, events were also turning against Bonaparte. The Swedes were in a position to invade Finland, and the Turks threatened Crimea; by this combination Russia, with two wars on her hands, would have been unable to unite her forces against France. Politics today would be conducted on a grand scale if the contemporary world had not been shrunk, both morally and physically, by the communication of ideas and railroads. Stockholm, confining itself to a national politics, came to an agreement with Petersburg.

After losing Pomerania to the French invasion of 1807 and Finland to the Russian invasion of 1808, Gustav IV had been deposed. Loyal and mad, he went to swell the ranks of kings wandering upon the earth—and I, I gave him a letter of recommendation for the Fathers of the Holy Land: at the tomb of Jesus Christ, all of us must be consoled. Gustav's uncle replaced his dethroned nephew. Bernadotte, the former leader of the French army in Pomerania, had won the esteem of the Swedes, who now looked to him. Bernadotte was chosen to fill the void left by the newly elected and recently deceased Prince of Holstein-Augustenburg, Crown Prince of Sweden.[25] Napoleon looked on the election of his old friend with displeasure.

The enmity between Bonaparte and Bernadotte went back a long way. Bernadotte had opposed the 18th of Brumaire and contributed— through his lively conversation and influence over public opinion— to those squabbles that brought Moreau before a court of law. Bonaparte took revenge in his own fashion: by seeking to debase his character. After Moreau's sentencing, Napoleon presented Bernadotte with a house in rue d'Anjou which had been seized from the condemned general. Out of a weakness all too common in those days, Joseph

Bonaparte's brother-in-law didn't dare refuse this dishonorable munificence. Grosbois was granted to Berthier.[26] Fortune having placed the scepter of Charles XII in the hands of a compatriot of Henri IV, Charles John[27] refused Napoleon's overtures; he thought it safer to ally himself with Alexander, his neighbor, than with Napoleon, a distant enemy. He declared himself neutral, advised peace, and offered to mediate between Russia and France.

Bonaparte is furious. He yells:

"He, that wretch, he gives *me* advice! He wants to lay down the law to me! A man who owes everything to my benevolence! What ingratitude! I know how to make him bend to my sovereign will!"

Following this outburst, Bernadotte signed the Treaty of Saint Petersburg on March 24, 1812.

Do not ask what right Bonaparte had to call Bernadotte a wretch, forgetting he had sprung from the exact same origin and source: war and the Revolution. His insulting language bespoke neither hereditary rank nor greatness of soul. Bernadotte was not ungrateful; he owed nothing to Bonaparte's benevolence.

The emperor had transformed himself into the monarch of an old race who attributes everything to himself, who speaks only of himself, who thinks he can reward or punish by saying he is satisfied or dissatisfied. Many centuries passed beneath the crown, a long succession of tombs at Saint-Denis: not even these would excuse such arrogance.

Fortune brought two French generals back to Europe—one from the United States and the other from the north—to the same battleground, to wage war with a man they had first united against, before he had separated them. Soldier or king, no one then thought it would be a crime to want to overthrow the oppressor of liberties. Bernadotte triumphed, Moreau succumbed. Men who go young are vigorous voyagers; they are quick to take a route that feebler men are still trudging slowly toward.

12.

THE EMPEROR BEGINS THE RUSSIAN EXPEDITION— OBJECTIONS—NAPOLEON'S MISTAKE

IT WAS not for lack of warnings that Bonaparte persisted in waging war on Russia. The Duc de Frioul, the Comte de Ségur, and the Duc de Vicence were all consulted, and all opposed this enterprise with a horde of objections. "It was not right," says the Duc de Vicence courageously (*Histoire de la grande armée*), "while seizing the continent and even the States of his ally's family, to accuse this ally of defecting from the continental system. When the French armies swarmed over Europe, how could they reproach the Russians for their army? Was it therefore necessary to launch ourselves beyond the nation of Germany, whose wounds, which we had made, were not yet healed? The French no longer recognized each other in the vastness of a country delimited by no natural border. Who shall defend the real France now abandoned? 'My reputation,' was the emperor's reply." Medea had provided him with this answer: Napoleon brought down tragedy upon himself.[28]

He announced the plan to organize the empire into cohorts of *ban* and *arrière-ban*: his brain was a jumble of history and memory. To the objection of the various parties still extant in the empire, he replied:

"The royalists fear my loss more than they desire it. The most useful and difficult thing I have done was to put a stop to the revolutionary torrent, which would have engulfed everything. You fear I'll lose my life in battle? It is impossible for me to be killed. Have I fulfilled the will of Fate? I feel driven toward an object I do not understand. When I reach it, an atom will be enough to bring me down."

This, too, was duplication: the Vandals in Africa, Alaric in Italy, said that they yielded only to a supernatural impulse, *divino jussu perurgeri*.[29]

Seeing the absurd and shameful dispute with the pope increased the dangers that Bonaparte confronted, Cardinal Fesch begged him not to attract the enmity of both heaven and earth. Napoleon took his uncle by the hand, led him to a window (it was night), and said:

"Do you see that star?"

"No, Sire."

"Look carefully."

"Sire, I do not see it."

"Well, I do."

"You, too," said Bonaparte to M. de Caulaincourt, "have become a Russian."

"Often," says M. de Ségur, "we have seen him (Napoleon) half collapsed on a sofa, sunk in deep meditation; then suddenly he comes out of it with a start, convulsing and shouting; he thinks he hears someone saying his name and shouts: 'Who's calling me?' Then he gets up and walks around in great agitation."

When Le Balafré was approaching his violent end, he climbed to the terrace of the Château de Blois called the Bretons' Perch. Under an autumn sky, with the deserted countryside stretching out in every direction, he could be seen strolling, making furious gestures.

Bonaparte, in salutary hesitation, said:

"Nothing around me is well enough settled for me to go and make war so far away; it must be delayed for three years."

He proposed declaring to the czar that he would neither directly nor indirectly contribute to the reestablishment of the Kingdom of Poland: the old and new France alike have abandoned this faithful and unfortunate country.

Of all the political errors Bonaparte committed, this abandonment was among the most serious. He would say, after the mistake was made, that he did not help reestablish this kingdom because he was afraid of displeasing his father-in-law. Bonaparte was a fine one to be restrained by family considerations! The excuse is so feeble all it managed to do was curdle his marriage with Marie Louise. Hardly sharing his enthusiasm for this marriage, the Emperor of Russia exclaimed:

"Then the next task will be to drive me back to my forests!"[30]

Bonaparte was simply blinded by his hatred for the liberty of the nations.

Prince Poniatowski, during the French army's first invasion, had organized Polish troops. Political bodies had been assembled. France maintained two successive ambassadors in Warsaw: the Archbishop of Malines and M. Bignon. The Poles, those Frenchmen of the north—brave and lighthearted like us—spoke our language; they loved us like brothers; they laid down their lives for us out of loyalty enflamed by their aversion to Russia. France had long ago caused their ruin, and it was up to France to restore them to life. Did we owe nothing to this nation that had saved the people of Christendom? In Verona, I said to Alexander: "If Your Majesty does not restore Poland, Poland will be forced to exterminate you." To claim that this kingdom was condemned to occupation by its geographical position is to grant too much to hills and rivers: a score of nations, protected only by their courage, have maintained their independence, while Italy, walled in by the Alps, has fallen under the yoke of whoever has taken a notion to cross them. It would be more correct to acknowledge another inevitability: that warlike people who inhabit the plains are condemned to be conquered. All the various invaders of Europe have swooped down on the plains.

Far from favoring Poland, the French wanted her soldiers to take the national cockade; poor as it was, they made her responsible for feeding a French army of eighty thousand men; they promised the Grand Duchy of Warsaw to the King of Saxony. If Poland had been reformed into a kingdom, the Slavic race from the Baltic to the Black Sea would have regained its independence. Notwithstanding the lurch in which Napoleon had left the Poles—exploiting them all the while—they asked to serve as the vanguard; they boasted that they alone could enter Moscow without us: an inopportune proposition! The armed poet Bonaparte had reappeared; he wanted to ascend the Kremlin to sing and sign a decree on the theaters.[31]

Whatever may be published today in praise of Bonaparte the great democrat, his hatred of constitutional governments was invincible. It did not abandon him even when he had ventured into the menacing wilderness of Russia. Senator Wibicki brought to him, in Vilna, the resolutions of the Warsaw Diet:

"It is up to you," he said with sacrilegious exaggeration; "it is up to you who dictate the history of the age, and in whom the strength of Providence lies; it is up to you to support efforts that you must approve."

Wibicki came to ask Napoleon the Great to say the words:

"'Let the kingdom of Poland exist,' and the kingdom of Poland will exist. The Poles will be more than glad to obey the orders of a leader before whom the centuries are but a moment and space but a point."

Napoleon replied:

"Gentlemen, deputies of the Polish Confederation, I have listened to what you have just said to me with great interest. If I were Polish, I *would think and act* as you do; I would have voted, as you have, in the Warsaw assembly. Love of country is the first duty of a civilized man.

"*In my situation, I have many interests to reconcile* and many duties to fulfill. If I had reigned during the first, second, or third division of Poland, I would have armed my people to defend it.

"I love your nation! For sixteen years, I have seen your soldiers fighting beside me in the fields of Italy and Spain. I applaud what you have done; I authorize the efforts you wish to make: I will do everything in my power to second your resolutions.

"I have been saying these things to you since I first entered Poland. I must add that *I have promised the Emperor of Austria that his domains will remain intact and that I cannot therefore sanction any maneuver, or any action, which would disturb the peaceful possession of what remains of the provinces of Poland.*

"I will reward your country's devotion, which makes you so distinguished and entitles you to my great esteem and protection, with *all that I am able to do under the circumstances.*"

Thus Poland was abandoned. We let her be crucified for the

redemption of the nations. We indolently insulted her Passion. We presented her with a sponge dipped in vinegar when, on the cross of liberty, she said *sitio*, "I am thirsty."[32] "When Liberty," Mickiewicz cries, "sits on the throne of the world, she will judge the nations; she will say to France, 'I called for you and you did not listen: go, therefore, into slavery.'"[33]

"Must so many sacrifices and so much effort," asks the Abbé de Lamennais, "produce nothing? Have the holy martyrs sown only eternal slavery in the fields of their country? What do you hear in those forests? The sad murmur of the winds. What do you see on those plains? The migrating bird, searching for a place to rest."[34]

13.

MEETING IN DRESDEN—BONAPARTE REVIEWS HIS
TROOPS AND ARRIVES AT THE BANK OF THE NIEMEN

ON MAY 9, 1812, Napoleon left for the army and went to Dresden. It was in Dresden that he gathered the scattered resources of the Rhine Confederation and that, for the first and last time, he set the machine he had made in motion.

Among the exiled masterpieces that mourn for the Italian sun is a picture of the meeting between the Emperor Napoleon and the Empress Marie Louise, the Emperor and Empress of Austria, and a mob of sovereigns, great and small. These sovereigns and their various courts aspire to form circles subordinate to the primary court. They are fighting over vassalage. One wants to be the Brienne sublieutenant's cupbearer and another his pantler. The history of Charlemagne is called upon by the erudite of the German chancelleries. The higher born one is, the more one must grovel:

"A Dame de Montmorency," Bonaparte says in Las Cases, "would have gladly stooped down to tie the Empress's shoes."

When Bonaparte crossed the Palace of Dresden on his way to a gala, he led the pack, with his hat on his head; Francis II followed with his hat pulled down over his eyes, next to his daughter, the Empress Marie Louise. The gang of princes brought up the rear, in respectful silence. The Empress of Austria was missing from the procession. She said she was ill and only emerged from her rooms in a porter's chair, to avoid giving her arm to Napoleon, whom she detested. What noble sentiments remained had withdrawn into the hearts of women.

Only one king, the King of Prussia, was at first kept out. "What does that prince want from me?" Bonaparte shouted impatiently. "Isn't there enough *beseeching* in his letters? Why does he want to persecute me again in person? I don't need him."

The great crime of Frederick William in the eyes of the "republican" Bonaparte was to have abandoned the cause of kings. The Berlin Court's negotiations with the Directory revealed, according to Bonaparte, a "timid, self-interested, ignoble politician concealed in this prince who sacrifices his dignity and the royal cause to petty territorial expansions." When he looked at a map of New Prussia, he exclaimed: "How can it be I let this man have so many countries!" Of the three commissioners of the Allies who escorted him to Fréjus, the Prussian was the only one Bonaparte treated badly and wanted nothing to do with. The secret reason for the emperor's aversion to Frederick William has been sought and sometimes laid at the door of some little trifle or another. In speaking of the death of Duc d'Enghien, I think I have come closer to the truth.

Bonaparte waited in Dresden for the columns of his armies to advance. Marlborough, in that same city, on his way to meet Charles XII, saw a route marked on a map leading to Moscow; he guessed the monarch would take this route and not meddle in the war in the west. By not confessing his plan of invasion aloud, however, Bonaparte could not conceal it. For the diplomats, he put forth three complaints: the ukase of December 31, 1810, prohibiting certain imports into Russia, which destroyed the "continental system"; Alexander's protest against the annexation of the Duchy of Oldenburg; and Russia's armament. If one were not accustomed to the abuse of words, one would be astonished to see the customs regulations of an independent state and the violation of a system this state had not accepted cited as legitimate causes for the declaration of war. As for the annexation of the Duchy of Oldenburg and Russian armament, you have just seen the Duc de Vicence's valiant attempt to make Napoleon see the insolence of these reproaches. Justice is so sacred, it seems so necessary to the success of everything, that even people who trample it underfoot claim to be acting only according to its principles.

Meanwhile, General Lauriston was sent to Saint Petersburg and the Comte de Narbonne to Alexander's headquarters—messengers of suspicious words of peace and goodwill. The Abbé de Pradt had been dispatched to the Polish Diet and came back with a new nickname for his master: Jupiter Scapin.[35] The Comte de Narbonne reported that Alexander was neither boastful nor despondent and preferred war to accepting a shameful peace. The czar still professed a naive enthusiasm for Napoleon, but he said that the cause of the Russians was just and that his ambitious friend was in the wrong. This truth, expressed in the Moscow bulletins, became the opinion of the nation: Bonaparte was transformed into the Antichrist.

Napoleon leaves Dresden on May 29, 1812, and travels to Posen and Thorn, where he sees the Poles plundered by his other allies. He descends the Vistula and stops at Danzig, Königsberg, and Gumbinnen.

Along the way, he reviews his various troops. To the old soldiers, he speaks of the Pyramids, Marengo, Austerlitz, Jena, Friedland. With the young men, he expresses his concern for their needs, their equipment, their pay, their captains. He is playing, for the moment, at being kind.

BOOK TWENTY-ONE

I.

INVASION OF RUSSIA—VILNA: THE POLISH SENATOR WIBICKI; THE RUSSIAN PARLIAMENTARIAN BALASHOV—SMOLENSK—MURAT—PLATOFF'S SON

WHEN BONAPARTE crossed the Niemen, 85,500,000 souls recognized his dominion or that of his family; half the population of Christendom obeyed him; his orders were carried out in a space that spanned nineteen degrees of latitude and thirty degrees of longitude. Never had so gigantic an expedition been seen, nor will it be seen again.

On June 22, at his headquarters in Wilkowiski, Napoleon declares war:

"Soldiers, the Second Polish War has begun; the first ended at Tilsit; Russia is being dragged along by fate; its destiny must be fulfilled."

Moscow replies to this youthful voice again with the mouth of its metropolitan, aged 110:

"The city of Moscow receives Alexander, its Christ, like a mother in the arms of her zealous sons, singing Hosanna! Blessed be he who cometh!"

Bonaparte addressed himself to Destiny, Alexander to Providence.

On the night of June 23, 1812, Bonaparte reconnoitered the Niemen and ordered three bridges thrown over it. At dusk of the following day, some sappers cross the river in a boat and find no one on the other side. A Cossack officer, commanding a patrol, comes to them and asks who they are.

"Frenchmen."

"Why have you come to Russia?"

"To wage war with you."

The Cossack disappears into the forest; three sappers shoot into the trees; there is no answering fire. Universal silence.

Bonaparte had spent a whole day tired but restless. He felt something retreating from him. The columns of our army advanced through the forest of Pilwisky, keeping to the darkness like the Huns led by a doe through Palus Maeotis.[1] The Niemen was invisible. To know where it ran, they had to touch its edges.

In plain day, instead of Muscovite battalions or Lithuanian populations advancing before their liberators, they saw nothing but bare sands and deserted forests:

"Three hundred paces from the river, on the highest height, the emperor's tent was visible. Around it all the hills, their slopes, and the valleys were covered with men and horses." (Ségur.)

All the forces under Napoleon's command amounted to 680,300 infantry and 176,850 horses. In the War of the Succession, Louis XIV had 600,000 men—all French. The active infantry, under the immediate orders of Bonaparte, was divided into ten corps. These corps consisted of 20,000 Italians, 80,000 men from the Confederation of the Rhine, 30,000 Poles, 30,000 Austrians, 20,000 Prussia, and 270,000 Frenchmen.

The army crosses the Niemen. Bonaparte himself rides over the fateful bridge and sets foot on Russian soil. He stops and watches his soldiers parade past, then flies from view and goes galloping haphazardly through a forest as though called to a council of spirits on the heath. He returns; he listens. The army listens, too. They think they hear the rumble of far-off cannon fire and become excited. But it is only a storm. The fighting faded into the distant. Bonaparte took shelter in an abandoned convent—an asylum of peace twice over.

It has been said that Napoleon's horse fell and people murmured, "This is a bad omen; a Roman would retreat." The same story is told of Scipio, William the Bastard, Edward III, and Malesherbes setting out for the Revolutionary Tribunal.

It took three days for the troops to cross the river, then they fell into line and advanced. Napoleon hurried onward. Time shouted at him, "go! go!" as Bossuet once preached.[2]

In Vilna, Bonaparte receives senator Wibicki of the Warsaw Diet. A Russian parliamentarian, Balashov, now introduces himself, saying it is still possible to negotiate, that Alexander is not the aggressor, that the French are in Russia without any declaration of war. Napoleon replies that Alexander is just a general on parade, that he has only three real generals: Kutuzov, for whom he, Bonaparte, does not care because he is Russian; Bennigsen, who was already too old six years earlier and is now in his second childhood; and Barclay, whose sole expertise was retreats. The Duc de Vicence, believing himself insulted by Bonaparte's words, interrupts him angrily and says:

"I am a good Frenchman; I have proven it, and I will prove it again by repeating that this war is impolitic, dangerous, and spells the downfall of the army, France, and the emperor."

Bonaparte had told the Russian envoy:

"Do you think I'm worried about your Polish Jacobins?"

Madame de Staël, whose friends in high places kept her well informed, reports this remark. She also affirms there was a letter written to M. de Romanzoff[3] by one of Bonaparte's ministers which proposed striking the words "Poland" and "Polish" from European acts—superabundant proof of Napoleon's aversion to his brave supplicant.

Bonaparte asks Balashov how many churches were in Moscow and, hearing the answer, exclaims:

"Why so many churches when no one is Christian anymore?"

"I beg your pardon, Sire," the Muscovite replied, "but the Russians and the Spanish still are."

Balashov is dismissed with unacceptable proposals and the last glimmer of peace fades. The bulletins say:

"Here, then, is the empire called Russia—so formidable from afar! Up close it's a desert. It took more time for Alexander to muster his recruits than it will for Napoleon to get to Moscow."

Bonaparte, reaching Vitebsk, thought for a moment he might stop there. Returning to his headquarters after seeing Barclay retreating again, he threw down his sword on his maps and cried:

"I'm calling a halt to things here! My 1812 campaign is over. My 1813 campaign will finish the job."

He would have been better off if he had kept to this resolution, as all his generals advised him! He had fooled himself into thinking he would receive new proposals for peace. Seeing none coming, he grew bored; he was only twenty days' march from Moscow. "Moscow, the holy city!" he kept repeating. His eyes began to sparkle and his expression turned fierce: the order to depart was given.

Men advised him, and he disdained their advice; Daru, when questioned, told him he could see neither "the aim nor the necessity of such a war."

"Do you take me for a fool?" the emperor replied. "Do you think I'm making war on a whim?" Hadn't everyone heard him, the emperor, say that "the war with Spain and Russia were two cankers eating away at France"? But to make peace, two were required, and he had not received a single letter from Alexander.

And who was the cause of those "cankers"? Such inconsistencies pass unnoticed and are even altered, if necessary, to serve as proof of Napoleon's ingenuous sincerity.

Bonaparte would consider himself humiliated were he to acknowledge his mistake and stop. His soldiers complain he no longer sees them except during battle—that he is always sending them to their deaths and never offering them support. To these complaints, Bonaparte turns a deaf ear. The news of peace between the Russians and the Turks reaches him and does not change his mind. He hurries on to Smolensk.

The Russians' proclamations say:

"Napoleon is coming with betrayal in his heart and loyalty on his lips, he is coming to bind us with his legions of slaves. Let us carry the cross in our hearts and the iron in our hands; let us rip out this lion's teeth; let us overthrow the tyrant who is overthrowing the earth."

On the heights of Smolensk, Napoleon finds the Russian army

120,000 strong. "I have them!" he cries. On the seventeenth, at day-break, Belliard pursues a band of Cossacks and drives them into the Dnieper. The curtain is drawn back, and the enemy army can be seen on the road to Moscow, retreating. Bonaparte's dream still eludes him. Murat, who had contributed too much to this pointless pursuit, despairs and wants to die. He refuses to leave one of our batteries leveled by fire from the citadel of Smolensk, which has not yet been evacuated. "All of you, retreat! Leave me alone here!" he cries. A ter-rible attack was taking place against this citadel and, ranged on the heights that rose like an amphitheater, our army stood contemplating the fighting below. When they saw the assailants launch themselves through the fire and shrapnel, they clapped their hands, as they had done at the sight of the ruins of Thebes.

During the night, a fire attracts attention. One of Davoust's of-ficers scales the walls and enters the citadel in a cloud of smoke. The sound of distant voices reaches his ear. With his pistol in his hand, he moves in their direction and, to his great astonishment, comes upon a friendly patrol. The Russians had abandoned the city, and Poniatowski's Poles had occupied it.

Murat, due to his extraordinary costume and his valor, which so resembled theirs, excited the enthusiasm of the Cossacks. One day, when he was leading a furious charge against their bands, he loses his temper with them, upbraids them, and commands them. The Cos-sacks do not understand, but they surmise his meaning, turn their horses around, and obey the orders of the enemy general.

When we saw the hetman Platov in Paris, we did not know of his fatherly afflictions. In 1812, he had a son as splendid as the Orient who rode a fine white Ukrainian horse. This seventeen-year-old war-rior fought with all the fearlessness of the age of hope and bloom. A Polish uhlan killed him. After he was laid out on a bearskin, the Cossacks came and respectfully kissed his hands. They said funeral prayers, buried him on a hillock covered with pines, then, pulling at their hair, paraded around the tomb with their lances reversed and pointing toward the ground. A man might have thought he was witnessing the funerals described by the historian of the Goths[4] or the Praetorian Guard reversing their fasces before the ashes of Germanicus, *versi fasces*.[5] "The wind blows the snowflakes from the northern spring's hair." (*Edda of Saemund.*)

2.

THE RUSSIANS RETREAT—THE BORYSTHENES— BONAPARTE'S OBSESSION—KUTUZOV SUCCEEDS BARCLAY AS COMMANDER OF THE RUSSIAN ARMY— BATTLE OF MOSKVA OR BORODINO—BULLETIN— THE BATTLEFIELD

BONAPARTE wrote to France from Smolensk that he was now master of the Russian saltworks and that his treasury minister could count on eighty million more.

Russia was fleeing toward the pole. Lords, deserting their wooden houses, left with their families, serfs, and herds. The Dnieper, the ancient Borysthenes, whose waters had once been declared sacred by Vladimir, was crossed. This river had sent civilized people barbarian invasions; now it was being subjected to invasion by the civilized. A savage, disguised with a Greek name, it no longer recalled even the first migrations of the Slavs; it continued on its course, unknown, bearing shawls and perfumes to the women of Saint Petersburg and Warsaw instead of the children of Odin. It had no place in world history except east of the mountains where Alexander's altars stand.[6]

From Smolensk, an army could be led equally well to Saint Petersburg or Moscow. Smolensk should have cautioned the victor to stop. For a moment, he wished to do so. "The Emperor was discouraged," M. Fain says, "and spoke of halting at Smolensk." Medical supplies were already beginning to run low: General Gourgaud recounts how General Lariboisière had to sacrifice the tow from his cannon to bandage the wounded. But Bonaparte could not restrain himself; he took too much delight in contemplating the dawns, at either end of Europe, which would break upon his armies over sunburnt plains and icy plateaus.

Orlando, in his narrow chivalric circle, chased after Angelica.[7]

The conquerors of the first race pursued a higher sovereign. There was no rest for them until they had clasped in their arms that divinity crowned with towers, the bride of Time, the daughter of Heaven, the mother of the gods.[8] Consumed by his own existence, Bonaparte saw everything in relation to himself; Napoleon had taken possession of Napoleon; there was no longer anything in him but him. Previously he had explored only places well known to history. Now he was wandering a nameless road along which Peter had scarcely begun to sketch out the future cities of an empire that was not yet a century old. Had he heeded the past, Bonaparte might have been disquieted by the memory of Charles XII, who passed through Smolensk on the way to Moscow. At Kolodrina, there was a murderous clash: the French corpses were buried in haste, so that Napoleon could not measure the enormity of his losses. At Dorogobuzh, there was an encounter with a Russian whose magnificent white beard came down over his chest: too old to flee with his family, left alone at his hearth, he had seen the marvels of the end of the reign of Peter the Great and was there to witness, in silent indignation, his country's devastation.

A series of battles offered and refused led the French to the field by the Moskva. Whenever they made camp, the emperor would go to talk with the generals and listen to their contentions while he sat on the branches of a fir tree or toyed with a Russian shell he pushed around with his foot.

Barclay, the Livonian pastor turned general, was responsible for the system of retreat that made it possible to catch up with him in the autumn: an intrigue at Court lost him his position. Old Kutuzov, beaten at Austerlitz because no one had listened to what he said—which was to refuse to fight until the arrival of Prince Charles—replaced Barclay. The Russians saw Kutuzov as their proper leader, the disciple of Suvorov, who had conquered the Grand Vizier in 1811 and made peace with the Ottomans, which was then quite necessary for Russia.

At this juncture, a Muscovite officer presented himself at Davoust's outposts; he came bearing only vague proposals; his real mission seemed to be to look and see: he was shown everything. The French, with their careless, fearless curiosity, asked him what they would find between Vyazma and Moscow:

"Poltava," he replied.[9]

Arriving at the heights of Borodino, Bonaparte finally laid eyes on the Russian army, halted and formidably entrenched. It consisted of 120,000 men and 600 guns, which were equally matched on the French side. Scrutinizing the Russian left, Marshal Davoust proposed turning the enemy's flank.

"That would lose me too much time," the emperor answered.

Davoust insisted, saying he could complete his maneuver before six in the morning.

Napoleon interrupted him brusquely:

"Ach, all you ever want to do is turn the enemy's flank."

There was a great commotion in the Muscovite camp. Troops were under arms; Kutuzov, surrounded by Orthodox priests and archimandrites, preceded by religious emblems and a holy icon salvaged from the ruins of Smolensk, spoke to his soldiers of Heaven and homeland. Napoleon he called the "universal despot."

Amid war songs and triumphant choruses mixed with sorrowful cries, a Christian voice also made itself heard in the French camp. It separated itself from all the rest; it was the sacred hymn that rose, alone, beneath the temple vaults. This soldier, whose calm voice full of feeling rang out, was the aide-de-camp of the marshal in charge of the cavalry. He had taken part in all the battles of the Russian campaign; he spoke of Napoleon with the greatest admiration; but he recognized his failings; he redressed the lies that had been told, and declared that every error committed arose from the leader's pride and the captains' forgetfulness of God.

"In the Russian camp," writes Lieutenant-Colonel de Baudus, "they hallowed the night that was sure to be the last for so many soldiers...The spectacle offered to my eyes by the enemy's piety, as well as the pleasantries it inspired among far too many of our officers, reminded me that the greatest of our kings, Charlemagne, also prepared for the most perilous of his undertakings with religious ceremonies...Ah! The good faith of many among those misguided Christians must have sanctified their prayers; for if the Russians were beaten at the Moskva, our utter annihilation, whose glory they cannot claim, since it was the manifest work of Providence, went to prove, some months later, that they had received what they had asked for."

But where was the czar? He had only recently told the fugitive Madame de Staël, in all modesty, that he regretted "not being a great general."[10] Around this time, M. de Bausset, an officer of the palace, appeared in our camps. Leaving the tranquil woods of Saint Cloud and following the horrible traces of our army, he arrived the day before the funeral at the Moskva, bearing the portrait of the King of Rome that Marie Louise was sending to the emperor. M. Fain and M. de Ségur describe the feelings that seized Bonaparte at the sight of it. According to General Gourgaud, Bonaparte exclaimed after looking at the portrait:

"Take it away; he shouldn't see a field of battle so soon."

The day preceding the storm was extremely calm. "All the knowledge used to prepare such cruel follies," writes M. de Baudus, "suggests something shameful about human reason when I consider it today, at my age; for in my youth I found it rather beautiful."

Toward evening on the sixth, Bonaparte dictated this proclamation, unknown to most of the soldiers until after the victory:

"Soldiers, this is the battle you have longed for. From now on, victory depends upon you. We need it. It will grant us abundance and a speedy return to the homeland. Conduct yourselves as you did at Austerlitz, at Friedland, at Vitebsk and Smolensk, and let remotest posterity cite your conduct on this day. Let it be said of you: 'He was at the great battle beneath the walls of Moscow.'"

Bonaparte passed an anxious night. At times he thought the enemies were retreating, at times he worried over the deprivation of his soldiers and the weariness of his officers. He knew people around him were saying:

"Why have we been made to travel eight hundred leagues for nothing but marshy water, famine, and bivouacs on ashes? Every year the war gets worse; new conquests demand we seek new enemies. Soon Europe will no longer be enough for him, and he will go after Asia."

In fact, Bonaparte had not been unmoved on seeing the tributaries that flow into the Volga. Born for Babylon, he had already tried to reach it by another route. Stopped at Jaffa, at the western gates of Asia, he would die in the seas bordering that part of the world, from which man and the sun both arise.

In the middle of the night, Napoleon sent for one of his aides-de-camp, who found him with his head in his hands. "What is war?" he said. "An occupation for barbarians! The whole art of it consists in being the strongest at any given point." He lamented the inconstancy of fortune and asked for a report on the enemy's position. When he was told the fires were burning with the same brightness and in equal numbers, he calmed down. At five in the morning, Ney sent an envoy requesting permission to attack. Bonaparte roused himself and exclaimed:

"Let us go and open the gates of Moscow!"

Dawn broke, and Napoleon, pointing to the Orient just beginning to blush, shouted:

"Here is the sun of Austerlitz!"

3.

EXCERPT FROM THE EIGHTEENTH BULLETIN OF THE GRAND ARMY

Mozhaysk, September 12, 1812

ON THE sixth, at two o'clock in the morning, the emperor surveyed the enemy's outposts; the day was spent in reconnoitering. The enemy was in a very strong position.

This position appeared good and well defended. *It would have been easy to maneuver and force the enemy to abandon it; but this would have delayed the fighting.*

On the seventh, at six o'clock in the morning, General Comte Sorbier, who had armed the right battery with the Imperial Guard artillery, commenced firing.

At half past six o'clock, General Compans was wounded. At seven o'clock, Prince d'Eckmühl's horse was killed.

At seven o'clock, Marshal Duc d'Elchingen (Ney) charges again and, protected by sixty pieces of cannon that General Foucher had aimed at the enemy's center the previous night, advanced toward the center. A thousand pieces of cannon vomit death on both sides.

At eight o'clock, the enemy's positions were taken, their redoubts captured, and our artillery crowned their hillocks.

The enemy retained its redoubts on the far bank. General Comte Morand marched there and took them, but at nine o'clock in the morning, attacked on every side, he could no longer remain there. The enemy, emboldened by this success, advanced their reserve and the last of their troops to try their luck once more. The Russian Imperial Guard took part in this maneuver. It attacked our center, on which our right had pivoted. For a moment it was feared they would take the burned village, and Friant's division went there. Eighty pieces of French cannon first stopped and then crushed the enemy columns, which were held tight for two hours under fire, not daring to advance, unwilling to retreat, and renouncing any hope of victory. The King of Naples (Murat) decided things for them; he had the Fourth Cavalry Corps charge into the breaches that the grapeshot of our cannon had made in the serried ranks of the Russians and their cuirassier squadrons. They scattered in every direction.

At two o'clock in the afternoon, all hope abandoned the enemy: the battle was done, the cannonade continued; they fought to retreat and save themselves, but not for victory.

Our total losses can be estimated at ten thousand men; those of the enemy at forty or fifty thousand. No one has even seen such a battlefield. Of every six corpses, one was French and five were Russian. Forty Russian generals were killed, wounded, or captured: General Bagration was wounded.

We have lost the division general Comte Montbrun, killed by a cannon shot; General Comte Caulaincourt, who had been sent to replace him, killed by the same cause an hour later.

The brigadier generals Compère, Plauzonne, Marion, and Huart were killed; seven or eight generals were wounded, for the most part lightly. Prince d'Eckmühl was uninjured. The French troops covered themselves with glory and demonstrated their great superiority over the Russian troops.

Such is, in a few words, the outline of the Battle of the Moskva, which occurred two leagues back of Mozhaysk and twenty-five leagues from Moscow.

The Emperor was never in any danger. The Imperial Guard, on foot and on horseback, lost not a single man. Victory was never uncertain. If the enemy, forced into their positions, had not wished to retake them, our losses would have been greater than theirs; but they destroyed their army by keeping it under the fire of our batteries from

eight o'clock to two o'clock and attempting to recover what they had
lost. This was the cause of their immense losses.

This cold bulletin, filled with things unspoken, gives no idea of the
Battle of the Moskva, least of all the dreadful massacres that took
place at the great redoubt. Eighty thousand men were put out of action; thirty thousand were French. Auguste de La Rochejaquelein
had his face split by a saber and was taken prisoner by the Muscovites:
he recalled other battles and another flag. Bonaparte, reviewing the
nearly annihilated Sixty-First Regiment, said to his colonel:

"Colonel, what have you done with one of your battalions?"

"Sire," he replied, "they are at the redoubt."

The Russians have always maintained and still do maintain that
they won the battle: they have even raised a triumphal funeral column
on the heights of Borodino.

M. de Ségur's account supplies what is missing from Bonaparte's
bulletin:

"The Emperor surveyed," he writes, "the field of battle. Never had
there been another so horrible. Everything converged on it: a gloomy
sky, a cold rain, a violent wind, houses burnt to ashes, a devastated
plain covered with ruins and debris; the sad, dark trees of the north
on the horizon; soldiers everywhere, wandering among the corpses,
looking for food even in the sacks of their dead companions; horrible
wounds, for the Russian balls are larger than ours; noiseless bivouacs;
no more songs or tales—only mournful silence.

"Around the great generals were what remained of the officers and
sub-officers, and a handful of soldiers—hardly enough to guard the
flag. Their clothes were torn by tenacious combat, blackened by powder, soiled by blood; and yet, despite their rags, their misery, their
disaster, they had a proud look about them, and even, at the sight of
the emperor, let out a few cries of triumph, but these were strange
and excited: for in this army capable of both analysis and enthusiasm,
each man judged the position of all…

"The emperor could only reckon his victory by the dead. The

ground was so littered with Frenchmen fallen at the redoubts, they seemed to belong there more than did the men still standing. There appeared to be more dead victors than living ones.

"In this crowd of corpses, which one had to walk over to follow Napoleon, a horse's hoof touched a wounded man, eliciting from him a last sign of life or pain. The emperor, who until then, overburdened by the sight of so many victims, had been as silent as his victory, roared; he relieved himself with cries of indignation and by insisting a multitude of cares be lavished on this unfortunate. Then he sent the officers riding with him to go help the men who could be heard screaming on every side.

"They were mostly found at the bottom of the ravines where the greatest number of our soldiers had been hurled, and where many others had dragged themselves to shelter from the enemy and the storm. Some, groaning, spoke the name of their native country or their mother: these were the youngest. The oldest waited for death with an impassive or sardonic look, not deigning either to implore or complain; others asked to be killed on the spot; but everyone passed quickly by these unfortunate men, having neither the useless pity to help them, nor the cruel pity to finish them off."

Such is M. de Ségur's account. Cursed be victories not won in defense of the homeland, which merely serve a conqueror's vanity!

The Imperial Guard, composed of 25,000 elite men, did not take part in the Battle of the Moskva. Citing various excuses, Bonaparte refused to engage them. Contrary to custom, he kept away from the action and could not have followed the maneuvers with his own eyes. He sat or walked near one of the city's redoubts, which had been captured the day before the battle. When someone came to tell him of the death of one of his generals, he made a gesture of resignation. His impassivity was looked upon with astonishment. Ney exclaimed:

"What is he doing *behind* the army? There, all he hears about are reversals, not successes. Since he no longer wages war himself, since he is no longer a general, since he wants to act the emperor everywhere, let him go back to the Tuileries and leave the generaling to us."

Murat admitted that, on that important day, he no longer saw any signs of Napoleon's genius.

Uncritical admirers have attributed Napoleon's torpor to the worsening of the ailments that, so they tell us, were then afflicting him. They claim he was continually forced to dismount from his horse and often remained motionless, resting his forehead against the barrel of a cannon. This may be. A passing illness might have contributed to the curbing of his energy. But if we remark how this energy returned to him during the Saxon campaign and his famous French campaign, we are forced to seek another cause for his inaction at Borodino. What! You admit in your bulletin "it would have been easy to maneuver and force the enemy to abandon it; but this would have delayed the fighting"; and you, who have enough *mental vigor* to condemn millions of our soldiers to death, do not have sufficient *bodily strength* to order your Guard at least to go to their aid? We can find no explanation for this other than in the very nature of the man. Adversity arrived, and its first touch froze him. Napoleon's greatness was not of the kind that makes friends with calamity. Prosperity alone left him with his faculties intact. He was not fashioned for misfortune.

4.

FORWARD MARCH OF THE FRENCH—ROSTOPCHIN—
BONAPARTE AT SALVATION HILL—VIEW OF MOSCOW
—NAPOLEON ENTERS THE KREMLIN—MOSCOW
FIRE—BONAPARTE REACHES PETROVSKY WITH
DIFFICULTY—ROSTOPCHIN'S SIGN—SOJOURN ON
THE RUINS OF MOSCOW—BONAPARTE'S OCCUPATION

BETWEEN the Moskva and Moscow, Murat engaged in battle out-side Mozhaysk. The French entered the city to find ten thousand dead and dying. The dead were thrown out the windows to make room for the living. The Russians were withdrawing in good order to Moscow.

On the evening of September 13, Kutuzov had called a war coun-cil. All the generals said "Moscow is not the motherland." Buturlin (*Histoire de la campagne de Russie*), the same officer that Alexander sent to the Duc d'Angoulême's barracks in Spain, and Barclay, in his *Mémoire justificatif*, give the reasons for the council's point of view. Kutuzov proposed a ceasefire to the King of Naples, while Russian troops passed through the old capital of the czars. The ceasefire was accepted because the French wanted to keep the city. Only Murat was close up on the enemy rear guard, and our grenadiers followed on the heels of the retreating Russian grenadiers. But Napoleon was a long way from achieving the success he believed within reach: Kutuzov was concealing Rostopchin.

Count Rostopchin was governor of Moscow. He had made plans for vengeance to rain from the sky. A monstrous balloon, built at great cost, was to soar over the French army, pick out the emperor among thousands, and rain iron and fire on his head. On a trial run, the wings of the airship broke, and the idea of a bombshell falling from the clouds had to be abandoned—but Rostopchin kept the flares. While news of the disaster at Borodino had reached Moscow, the rest of the empire was still reading one of Kutuzov's bulletins and celebrating victory. Rostopchin composed various proclamations in rhyming prose, saying:

"Let us go, my Muscovite friends, let us march into battle! We shall muster a hundred thousand men, take the image of the Blessed Virgin, 150 pieces of cannon, and put an end to it all!"

He advised the inhabitants simply to arm themselves with pitchforks, since a Frenchman weighed no more than a bundle of wheat.

We know Rostopchin later denied he had a hand in the Moscow fire, and we know Alexander never made any statement on the subject. Did Rostopchin want to avoid the reproaches of the nobles and merchants whose fortunes went up in flames? Did Alexander fear being called a barbarian by the Institute? It was such a miserable era, and Bonaparte so monopolized its greatness, that when something praiseworthy occurred, everyone defended themselves and disclaimed responsibility for it.*

The burning of Moscow will go down in history as a heroic decision that saved one nation's independence and contributed to the liberation of several others. Numantia has not lost its rights to the admiration of mankind.[11] What does it matter if Moscow burned? Hadn't it happened seven times already? Is it not now bright and rejuvenated, despite Napoleon's prediction that the burning of this capital would set Russia back one hundred years? "The tragedy of Moscow," Madame de Staël writes with admirable good sense, "regenerated the empire: this religious city has perished like a martyr whose spilled blood reinvigorates the brethren who survive him." (*Ten Years' Exile.*)

Where would the nations be if Bonaparte, ensconced in the Kremlin, had wrapped the world in his despotism like a mortuary sheet? The rights of humanity come first. Speaking for myself, if the earth

---

*Count Rostopchin, a witty and educated man, has been seen around Paris. In his writings, thought lies hidden beneath a certain buffoonery. A sort of polite barbarian; an ironic, even depraved, poet, he is capable of generous feelings, although he despises both peoples and kings. The Gothic churches, in their grandeur, admit grotesque decorations.

were an explosive globe, I wouldn't hesitate to set it on fire were it a question of delivering my country from an oppressor. However, nothing less than the supreme interests of human liberty are needed to induce a Frenchman—his head covered in mourning and his eyes full of tears—to speak of a decision that would prove fatal to so many of his countrymen.

The evacuation of Moscow had already begun. The roads to Kazan were filled with fugitives on foot and in carriages, alone or with servants. An omen had momentarily raised people's spirits. A vulture had got caught in the chains supporting the cross of the principal church. Rome, like Moscow, would have seen Napoleon's captivity in this omen.

When the long convoys of wounded Russians arrived at the gates, all hope vanished. Kutuzov had promised Rostopchin to defend the city with the 91,000 men who remained to him. But you have just seen how the war council forced him to withdraw. Rostopchin was left to his own devices.

Night fell. Emissaries secretly went to knock on doors, saying all must leave, for Nineveh was doomed.[12] Flammable materials were placed in public buildings and bazaars, private houses and shops; water pumps were removed. Then Rostopchin ordered them to open the prisons. A Russian and a Frenchman were frog-marched out of this filthy troupe. The Russian, belonging to a sect of German Illuminati, was accused of having tried to hand his country over to the enemy and of having translated the proclamation of the French. His father ran up. The governor granted him a moment to bless his son. "Me, bless a traitor!" cried the old Muscovite, and cursed him. The prisoner was handed over to the crowd and killed.

"As for you," Rostopchin said to the Frenchman, "you were bound to want your countrymen to come. You are free. Go tell your people that Russia had only one traitor, and he has been punished."

The other criminals were given, along with their freedom, instructions for setting fire to the city when the time was right. Rostopchin was the last to leave Moscow, as a captain is the last to leave a sinking ship.

Napoleon, on horseback, had meanwhile rejoined his vanguard. One hill remained to be crossed. It butts up against Moscow as Montmartre butts up against Paris, and it is called Salvation Hill, for the Russians used to pray there, in sight of the holy city, like pilgrims before Jerusalem. Moscow, "with its gilded cupolas," as the Slavic poets say, shone in the daylight with its 295 churches, its 1,500 palaces, its ornate wooden houses painted yellow, green, and pink: nothing was missing but the cypresses and the Bosphorus. The Kremlin was part of this mass covered with polished or painted iron. The Moskva, in the midst of elegant villas built of brick and marble, ran between parks planted with forests of pine—the palms of this latitude. Venice in its glory days was no less resplendent amid the Adriatic's waves.

It was on September 14, at two o'clock in the afternoon, that Bonaparte, under a sun adorned with polar diamonds, set eyes on his newest conquest. Moscow, like a European princess at the farthest reaches of his empire, bedecked with all the riches of Asia, seemed to have been brought there specially to marry Napoleon.

A cheer went up. "Moscow! Moscow!" our soldiers cried. They clapped their hands yet again. In the old days of French glory, they used to cry, in victory or defeat, "Long live the king!" "It was a wonderful moment," says Lieutenant-Colonel de Baudus, "when the magnificent panorama presented by the whole huge city was suddenly revealed. I will never forget the emotion displayed among the ranks of the Polish division, made all the more striking by the religious feeling that imbued their gesture. On seeing Moscow, entire regiments fell on their knees and thanked the Lord of hosts for having led them victoriously into the capital of their bitterest enemy."

The cheers faded. Mutely, they descended toward the capital. No deputation came forth from the gates to offer up the keys in a silver bowl. The motion of life had ceased in the great city. Moscow staggered silently before the strangers; three days later, she had perished;

the Circassian of the North, the beautiful bride, had laid down on her funeral pyre.

While the city was still standing, Napoleon, walking toward it, cried out, "So here is the famous town!" And he gazed at it. Moscow, abandoned, looked like the city mourned in the Book of Lamentations.[13] Already Eugène and Poniatowski had overrun the walls. A few of our officers entered, then came back and told Napoleon:

"Moscow is deserted!"

"Moscow deserted? That's unlikely! Bring me the boyars."

But there were no boyars, only poor people in hiding. Empty streets, shuttered windows: no smoke rising from the houses that would soon explode with clouds of it. No noise at all. Bonaparte shrugged.

Murat, who had advanced as far as the Kremlin, was greeted by the howling of prisoners released in order to liberate their country: the gates had to be blown apart with cannon fire.

Napoleon had come to the Dorogomilovo Gate. He stopped at one of the first houses in the outskirts, went riding along the Moskva, and saw no one. He returned to his quarters, appointed Marshal Mortier governor of Moscow, General Durosnel commander, and M. de Lesseps civil administrator in the capacity of quartermaster-general. The Imperial Guard and troops were dressed in full regalia to appear before an absent populace.

Bonaparte soon learned for certain that the city was threatened with some imminent event. At two in the morning, he was told a fire had broken out. The conqueror left the suburb of Dorogomilovo and took shelter in the Kremlin. It was the morning of the fifteenth. He experienced a moment of joy, entering the palace of Peter the Great. In his satisfied pride, he wrote a few words to Alexander, by the light of the bazaar just beginning to burn, as the defeated Alexander had once written him a note from the battlefield at Austerlitz.

In the bazaar, the long rows of stalls were all shut. At first the fire was contained, but on the second night it breaks out in every quarter. Fireballs, thrown up, burst in the air and fall in luminous sheaves on palaces and churches. A violent north wind scatters the sparks and hurls flaming brands at the Kremlin. Inside was a powder magazine; an artillery park had been left under Bonaparte's very windows. From district to district, our soldiers are pursued by volcanic effluvia. Gorgons and Medusas, torches in hand, roam the livid intersections of this inferno, while others fan the flames with tarred wooden spears. Bonaparte, in the halls of the new Pergamum, rushes to the windows, shouting:

"What extraordinary determination! What men! They are Scythians!"

A rumor is spreading that the Kremlin has been mined. Servants swoon, soldiers steel themselves. Outside, the mouths of the infernos gape, move closer, combine. The tower of the Arsenal, like a tall candle, burns above a sanctuary in flames. Soon the Kremlin is nothing more than a black island washed by the waves of an undulating sea of fire. The sky, reflecting the glow, looks as if it were crisscrossed by the shifting lights of an aurora borealis.

Then the third night began to fall. Men could scarcely breathe in the suffocating air. Fuses were twice fastened to the building that Napoleon occupied. How to escape? A solid block of flame barred the doors of the citadel. After a long search in every direction, a postern gate leading to the Moskva was found. The victor, with his Guard, slipped out through this safety hatch. All around him in the city, arches groaned and burst; bell towers streaming with torrents of liquefied metal tilted, tottered, and fell. Beams, rafters, roofs cracked, crackled, crumbled, were ruined in a Phlegethon[14] whose burning waves they sent surging, sparkling with millions of golden spangles. Bonaparte was only able to escape over the cooled coals of a neighborhood that had already been reduced to ash. He reached Petrovsky, the palace of the czar.

General Gourgaud, criticizing M. de Ségur's description of events, accuses the emperor's executive officer of having made a mistake. In fact, the account written by M. de Baudus, who served as aide-decamp to Marshal Bessières and acted as Napoleon's guide, proves that the emperor did not escape through a postern at all, but by going out through the main gate of the Kremlin. From the shores of Saint Helena, Napoleon still saw the city of the Scythians ablaze:

"Never," he said, "for all their poetry, can any of the fictions of the burning of Troy ever equal the reality of the burning of Moscow."

Remembering this catastrophe earlier, Bonaparte had written:

"My evil genius came to me then and proclaimed my destiny, which I have met on the isle of Elba."

Kutuzov had at first gone east. Then he fell back to the south. His night march was cast in a half light by the distant conflagration of Moscow, from whose precincts there issued a lugubrious hum. One might almost have thought the bell never mounted because of its enormous weight had been magically suspended at the top of a burning steeple to sound a death knell for the expiring city.[15] Kutuzov reached Voronovo, Count Rostopchin's estate. No sooner had he glimpsed this exquisite demesne than it vanished into the maw of the fire. On an iron church gate, they read the sign, *la scritta morta*,[16] written in the proprietor's own hand:

> I embellished this estate for eight years and lived here happily with my family; the inhabitants of these grounds, numbering 1,720, have fled at your approach, and I have set my house ablaze so that it will not be defiled by your presence. Frenchmen, I left you my two houses in Moscow with furniture worth half a million rubles. *Here*, you will find nothing but ashes.
>
> > Rostopchin

Initially, Bonaparte had admired the fires and the Scythians as a spectacle kindred to his imagination; but the misfortune this catastrophe caused him soon cooled his enthusiasm and prompted him to resume his injurious diatribes. Sending Rostopchin's letter to France, he adds: "It would appear that Rostopchin has gone mad; the Russians regard him as a sort of Marat." He who fails to understand greatness in another will not understand what it would mean for himself, when the time for sacrifices comes.

Alexander betrayed no despondency when he learned of his adversities. "Why should we draw back," he wrote in his circular instructions, "when Europe encourages us with her eyes? Let us rather set her an example! Let us bless the hand that has chosen us to be the first among nations in the cause of virtue and liberty." This is followed by an invocation to the Almighty.

A style that incorporates the words *God, virtue, freedom*, is powerful; it pleases the people, reassures and consoles them. How superior it is to those affected phrases, sadly scrounged from pagan locutions and defined by fatalism: *it was to be, they had to be, destiny drags them on!*—empty phraseology, which is always barren, even when it refers to the most significant acts.

After leaving Moscow on the night of September 15, Napoleon returned the eighteenth. Coming back, he had spied campfires ablaze on the miry soil fed with mahogany furniture and gilded paneling. Around these open-air hearths, soldiers, blackened with smoke and covered with mud, their uniforms in tatters, lounged on silk couches or sat in velvet armchairs. Kashmir shawls, Siberian furs, golden Persian fabrics served as rugs over the sludge at their feet. Their dinners—of black paste or bloody grilled horseflesh—they ate off silver dishes.

No sooner had irregular looting begun than it became regulated. Each regiment scrambled for spoils in their turn. Peasants driven from their huts, Cossacks, and enemy deserters prowled around the Frenchmen—feeding on what our troops had already gnawed to the bone. Our men took everything they could carry with them. Soon, weighed down with their spoils, they threw them away, as though suddenly remembering they were two thousand miles from home.

Expeditions for provisions produced many pitiful scenes. One French foraging party was bringing back a cow when they were approached by a woman, accompanied by a man who carried a child only a few months old in his arms. They pointed to the cow that had just been taken from them. The mother tore the wretched clothes that covered her breasts to show that she had no more milk; the father made a gesture as though he would dash his child's head against a stone. The officer in charge ordered the cow returned. He adds:

"The effect this scene had on my soldiers was such that for a long time not one word was spoken in the ranks."

Bonaparte's dreams had changed. He now said he wanted to march on Saint Petersburg; he was already starting to trace out the route on his maps. He explained that his new plan was excellent and that they were sure to enter the second capital of the Russian empire. "What was left for him to do, among ruins? Was it not glorious enough for him to have ascended to the Kremlin?" But such were the new chimeras that filled Napoleon's head. The man was on the brink of madness, yet his dreams were still those of a great mind.

"We are only fifteen days' march from Saint Petersburg," says M. Fain: "Napoleon is thinking of setting out for this capital." Instead of a march of *fifteen days*, considering the time and the circumstances, we must read *two months*. General Gourgaud adds that all the news from Saint Petersburg revealed the fear the Russians had of Napoleon's maneuvers. There is no doubt that, if he had gone to Saint Petersburg, the emperor would have been successful; but they were even then preparing to leave him another smoldering shell of a city, and the retreat to Archangel had already been mapped out. It is not possible to subjugate a nation whose last stronghold is the North Pole. Besides, the English fleets, sailing into the Baltic in the spring, would have reduced the taking of Saint Petersburg to mere destruction.

But while Bonaparte's unbridled imagination toyed with the idea of a journey to Saint Peterburg, he seriously considered the opposite idea. His belief in his prospects was not firm enough to rob him of good sense altogether. His principal plan was to bring a peace treaty signed in Moscow back to Paris. By doing so, he would have avoided the dangers of retreat, carried off a breathtaking conquest, and returned to the Tuileries with an olive branch in hand. After the first note he had written to Alexander on arriving at the Kremlin, he did not miss a single opportunity to renew his advances. During a benign meeting with a Russian officer called Toutelmine, the deputy director of the Moscow Foundling Hospital that had been miraculously spared from the flames, he had let slip some words favorable to compromise. Through Mr. Jacowlef, brother of the former Russian minister in Stuttgart, he wrote directly to Alexander: Mr. Jacowlef undertook to deliver this letter to the czar without an intermediary. At last, General Lauriston was sent to Kutuzov. The latter pledged his good offices in any negotiation leading to peace, but he refused General Lauriston a safe-conduct for Saint Petersburg.

Napoleon was still convinced he exercised the same sway over Alexander which he had exercised at Tilsit and Erfurt, and yet Alexander wrote to Prince Michael Larcanowitz on October 21:

"I have learned, to my extreme displeasure, that General Benningsen has met with the King of Naples ... All the decisions stated in the orders I have addressed to you must persuade you that my resolve is unshakable, that at this time no proposal from the enemy could induce me to end the war and thereby impede the sacred duty to avenge the homeland."

The Russian generals exploited the self-regard and simplicity of Murat, the commander of our vanguard. Still charmed by the eager attentions of the Cossacks, he borrowed jewels from his officers to give his sycophants as gifts. But the Russian generals not only had no interest in peace, they dreaded it. Despite Alexander's resolve, they knew their Emperor's weakness and feared our Emperor's charm. As for revenge, it was only a matter of gaining a month, of waiting for the first frost: the prayers of Muscovite Christendom implored Heaven to hasten its storms.

General Wilson, in his capacity as British liaison officer to the Russian army, had arrived. He had already crossed paths with Bonaparte in Egypt. Fabvier, for his part, had returned from our southern to our northern army. The Englishman urged Kutuzov to attack, and everyone knew the news Fabvier brought was not good. From the two extremities of Europe, the only two nations still fighting for their freedom joined hands over the head of the victor at Moscow. Alexander's reply did not come; France's couriers tarried; Napoleon's anxiety increased. The peasants began warning our soldiers, "You don't know our climate; in a month the cold will make your nails fall out." Milton, whose great name lends greatness to everything, expresses himself just as naively in his *Moscovia*: "Here it is so cold in winter, that the very sap of their woodfuel burning on the fire, freezes at the brand's end, where it drops."[17]

Bonaparte, feeling that a backward step would damage his prestige and invalidate the terror of his name, could not bring himself to move. Despite many warnings of the dangers to come, he remained, waiting from one moment to the next for a reply from Saint Petersburg. He, who had hurled so many insults, was now pining for a few merciful words from the vanquished. At the Kremlin, he kept busy with regulations for the Comédie Française, devoting three evenings to completing this august work; he discussed the merit of some new Parisian poetry with his aides-de-camp. Those around him admired the great man's sangfroid while there were men wounded in his latest battles still dying in excruciating pain—and while, by delaying these few days, he was sentencing the 100,000 men left to him to death. The servile stupidity of the age attempted to make this pathetic affectation pass for the workings of a fathomless mind.

Bonaparte visited the buildings of the Kremlin. He went up and down the steps where Peter the Great had ordered the Streltsy slaughtered; he passed through the banquet hall where Peter had the prisoners assembled, cutting off a head after each glassful and urging his guests—princes and ambassadors—to amuse themselves in the same fashion. The remaining men were then beaten upon the breaking wheel, and the women buried alive. All in all, two thousand Streltsy were hanged and their bodies displayed for days around the city walls.[18]

Rather than composing an ordinance on the theaters, Bonaparte would have done better to write the Sénat conservateur the letter that Peter sent from the banks of the Prut to the Senate at Moscow:

"I inform you that, through no fault of my own, deceived by fallacious counsel, I am trapped here in my camp, surrounded by an army four times stronger than mine. If I am captured, you should no longer consider me your czar and ruler, or take account of anything I tell you, even if you are sure I have written it with my own hand. If

I die, you should choose amongst yourselves the one most worthy of being my successor."

A note from Napoleon, addressed to Cambacérès, contained some unintelligible orders. The recipients deliberated, and though the note was signed with an elongated classical name, because the writing was recognizably Bonaparte's, it was decided the unintelligible orders should be executed.

The Kremlin contained a double throne for two brothers: Napoleon did not share his. In one of the rooms you could still see the stretcher, splintered by a cannonball, on which the wounded Charles XII was carried during the Battle of Poltava. Always inferior to others in matters of magnanimous feeling, did Bonaparte visiting the tombs of the czars recall that on feast days they used to be covered with magnificent mortuary sheets; that when a subject had a favor to solicit, he would lay his petition on one of these tombs; and that only the czar had the right to remove it?

These appeals from the unfortunate, presented to the powerful by the dead, were not to Napoleon's taste. He was occupied with other things. Partly out of a desire to deceive, partly because it was his nature, he professed, as he had done on leaving Egypt, to be bringing actors from Paris to Moscow, and he promised an Italian singer would soon arrive. He pillaged the churches of the Kremlin and piled his coaches with sacred ornaments and icons, to be mingled with the crescents and horse tails he had taken from the Mohammadans. He ordered the huge cross on the tower of Ivan the Great removed, planning to stick it on the dome of the Invalides: it would have been in perfect keeping with the Vatican masterpieces he had hung in the Louvre. While they were taking down the cross, cawing crows flew around and around it.

"What do those birds want with me?" said Bonaparte.

The fatal moment was at hand. Daru raised objections to the various projects that Bonaparte laid out.

"What should we do then?" the emperor shouted.

"Stay here, turn Moscow into a huge fortified camp, spend the winter, salt the horses that can't be fed, wait for spring. Then our reinforcements and the Lithuanians will rescue us and complete the conquest."

"That is brave advice," Napoleon replied, "but what would Paris say? France isn't used to my absence."

"What," Alexander used to wonder, "are they saying about me in Athens?"[19]

He plunges again into a sea of uncertainties. Will he leave or stay? He cannot make up his mind. He deliberates, then deliberates further. Finally, a skirmish at Vinkovo on October 18 abruptly prods him to leave the wreckage of Moscow with his army. That very day, without any preparations or rigmarole or looking back, wishing to avoid the direct route to Smolensk, he takes one of the two roads to Kaluga.

For thirty-five days, like those brooding African dragons that fall asleep once they've eaten their fill, he had forgotten himself. Apparently this was all the time it took to alter forever the fate of such a man. In this interval, his star sank in the heavens. Finally he awoke, caught between the winter and an ashen capital. He crept out of the rubble, but it was too late. A hundred thousand men were doomed. As they began their retreat, Marshal Mortier, the rear-guard commander, ordered his soldiers to blow up the Kremlin.*

* The official records regarding this campaign, found in Alexander's office after his death, have just been printed in Saint Petersburg. These five or six volumes' worth of documents will no doubt shed new light on the curious events of this part of our history. We ought to read the enemy's version of events cautiously, but with less suspicion than we bring to Bonaparte's official documents. It is impossible to imagine how thoroughly he altered reality—to such a degree it became difficult to ascertain. Still, within his phantasmagorical accounts, there remained a grain of truth; namely, that Napoleon, for one reason or another, was the master of the world. (Paris, 1841)

5.
RETREAT

ON OCTOBER 18, Bonaparte—fooling himself or wishing to fool others—wrote the Duc de Bassano a letter copied out by M. Fain. "By the first weeks of November," he said, "I shall have led my troops back into the country between Smolensk, Mohyliv, Minsk, and Vitebsk. I have decided on this maneuver because Moscow is no longer a practical military position; I will look for a more favorable one at the start of my next campaign. Operations will then have to be directed toward Petersburg and Kiev." Such conceitedness would be pitiful if it were merely meant to palm off a lie; but with Bonaparte, the idea of conquest, no matter how improbable, may always be supposed sincere.

The French army marched on Maloyaroslavets. What with all they carried and the poorly coupled caissons, on the third day of the march they were still no more than ten leagues from Moscow. Their intention was to overtake Kutuzov, and indeed Prince Eugène's vanguard did reach Fominskoye before him. There were still 100,000 infantrymen when the retreat began. The cavalry was almost annihilated, except for 3,500 horsemen of the Imperial Guard. Our troops, having reached the new Kaluga road on the twenty-first, entered Borovsk on the twenty-second, and on the twenty-third Delzons's division occupied Maloyaroslavets. Napoleon was elated. He believed he had escaped.

On the 23rd of October, at half past one in the morning, the earth shook: 183,000 pounds of powder, laid beneath the Kremlin's vaults,

446

destroyed the palace of the czars. Mortier, who brought down the Kremlin, was himself destined to be brought down by Fieschi's *machine infernale*.[20] How many worlds passed between these two explosions, whose men and moment were so different!

In the wake of this muffled roar, a booming cannonade cut through the silence from the direction of Maloyaroslavets. Napoleon, in retreat, dreaded this sound at least as much as he had longed for it during his invasion. One of the viceroy's aides-de-camp announced the Russians were on the attack. During the night, Generals Compans and Gérard came to the aid of Prince Eugène. Many men perished on both sides. The enemy, who had managed to bar the road to Kaluga, closed off the entrance to the undisturbed path that we had hoped to follow. Our last resort was to fall back onto the road to Mozhaysk and return to Smolensk by the old paths which had been the scenes of our disaster. The birds of the sky had not yet finished eating what we had sown when we passed that way again.

Napoleon stayed that night at Ghorodnia in a poor house so small the officers attached to the various generals found no room to shelter there. They gathered beneath Bonaparte's window, which had no shutters or curtains. A light shone from it, while the officers outside were plunged in darkness. Napoleon, sitting in his wretched room, lowered his head into his hands; Murat, Berthier, and Bessières stood at his side, silent and still. He gave no orders, and, on the morning of the twenty-fifth, mounted on horseback to go examine the position of the Russian army.

He had hardly left the house when a landslide of Cossacks tumbled at his feet. This living avalanche had crossed the Luja and hid along the edge of the woods. Every man drew his sword, including the emperor. If the marauders had only been a little more daring, Bonaparte would have been taken prisoner.

In the burnt ruins of Maloyaroslavets, the streets were filled with bodies half roasted, dismembered, gouged, and mutilated by the wheels of the cannon that had run them over. To keep on toward Kaluga, they would have needed to fight a second battle, but the emperor did not think it a good idea. There is, in this regard, a disagreement between the supporters of Bonaparte and the friends of the marshals. Who suggested they return by the route they had already traveled? Evidently, Napoleon. Pronouncing a death sentence as enormous as this one hardly troubled him at all. He was used to it.

Returning to Borovsk near Wercia the next day, the twenty-sixth, General Wintzingerode and his aide-de-camp, Count Nariskin, were presented to our commander in chief: they had allowed themselves to be captured by entering Moscow too soon. Bonaparte flew into a passion. "Let that general be shot," he shouted, beside himself: "he is a deserter from the kingdom of Württemburg, which belongs to the Confederation of the Rhine." He went wild with invectives against the Russian nobility, said "I shall go to Saint Petersburg and knock it into the Neva," and then abruptly ordered his men to burn down a mansion visible on a hill nearby. The wounded lion pounced on anything within reach.

Still, in the midst of his frantic anger, when he gave Mortier the order to destroy the Kremlin, he conformed to his double nature. At the same moment, he was writing sentimental notes to the Duc de Trévise. Thinking these missives would be read, he implored him, with quite paternal concern, to spare the hospitals. "For that," he added, "is how I conducted myself in Saint-Jean d'Acre." In Palestine, he had ordered the Turkish prisoners shot and—had it not been for the opposition of Desgenettes—would have poisoned the sick! Berthier and Murat saved the life of General Wintzingerode.

Meanwhile, Kutuzov was indolently pursuing us. Wilson urged the Russian general to act with more energy, and the general replied: "Just wait until the snow comes." On October 29, our army reached the fatal hills of the Moskva. A cry of grief and shock went up among the men. A vast scene of butchery lay before them, with forty thousand corpses in various stages of decay. The carcasses lined up, row upon row, continued to observe military discipline. Detachments of skeletons toward the front, on beheaded hillocks, indicated commanders, who were still presiding over the melee of the dead. Everywhere broken weapons, staved-in drums, fragments of armor and uniforms, and tattered flags lay scattered between the trunks of trees, shattered a few feet above the ground by cannonballs. Here was the great redoubt of Borodino.

At the center of this motionless destruction something could be seen moving: a French soldier missing both legs cut a path through these cemeteries that seemed to have vomited up their innards. The body of a horse gutted by a shell had been this soldier's sentry box; he had lived there by gnawing on the flesh of his lodging. The rotten meat of the dead within his reach served as both the charpie to dress his wounds and the substance to sheathe his bones. This fearful remorse of glory was dragging itself toward Napoleon. Napoleon did not wait for it.[21]

The silence of the soldiers, hurried along by cold, hunger, and the enemy, was profound. They wondered whether they, too, would soon be like the companions whose remains they had seen. In this reliquary, nothing was heard but the agitated breath and involuntary shudders of the retreating batallions.

Farther on, they found the Kotloskoi abbey transformed into a hospital. There were no more supplies; but the men were still alive enough to be conscious of death. Bonaparte, arriving on the premises, warmed himself with the wood of his dismantled wagons. When the army resumed its march, the dying men rose, went to the threshold of their final refuge, let themselves be set down upon the road, and held out their shaking hands to the comrades who were leaving them: they seemed at once to implore and to summon them.

Time and again, the air resounded with the detonation of caissons we were forced to abandon. The sutlers threw the sick into ditches. The Russian prisoners, escorted by foreigners in the service of France, were dispatched by their guards—killed in a uniform manner, their brains left leaking from their heads. Bonaparte had taken Europe with him. Every language was spoken in his army; every cockade and every flag could be seen there. The Italian, forced into battle, fought no differently from the Frenchman; the Spaniard had borne out his reputation for valor: Naples and Andalusia were no more than vague traces of a sweet dream to them. They say Bonaparte could only be defeated by the whole of Europe, and that is true; but they forget that

Bonaparte could conquer only with the help of Europe, allied to him willingly or by force.

Russia alone resisted the Europe herded by Napoleon. France, left alone and defended by Napoleon, fell to another Europe, which had turned against it; but it must be said that Russia was defended by its climate, and that Europe marched only regretfully under its master's orders. France, on the contrary, was defended neither by its climate nor its decimated population—only by courage and the remembrance of its glory.

Indifferent to the miseries of his soldiers, Bonaparte cared for nothing but his own interests. When he was encamped, his conversation revolved around the ministers who had sold themselves, he said, to the English—these ministers being the fomenters of the war. He would not admit that he alone was responsible for it. The Duc de Vicence, who persevered in trying to redeem our misfortunes with his noble conduct, burst forth in the midst of this nonsense at the camp:

"What horrible cruelties! Is this the *civilization* we're bringing to Russia?"

In response to Bonaparte's incredible words, he made a gesture of anger and incredulity, and left. The man who was enraged by the smallest sign of dissension put up with Caulaincourt's asperities as punishment for the letter that, years earlier, he had charged him with carrying to Ettenheim.[22] When you have committed a reproachable act, Heaven imposes on you the sanction of witnesses. The ancient tyrants killed them in vain, for, going down into the underworld, these witnesses entered the bodies of the Furies and returned.

Napoleon, passing through Gzhatsk, pushed on to Vyazma, which he passed without encountering the enemy he feared he would find there. On November 3, he arrived in Slawskowo and learned a battle had taken place behind him, at Vyazma. This clash with Miloradovich's troops was lethal to us. Our soldiers, our wounded officers, their arms in slings, their heads wrapped in bandages, threw themselves with miraculous valor upon the enemy's cannon.

This series of engagements in the same places, these layers of dead mounting atop layers of dead, these battles twinned by battles, would have doubly immortalized the fatal fields if forgetfulness did not so swiftly settle on our dust. Who thinks of those peasants left behind in Russia? Are those rustics glad to have been at "the great battle beneath the walls of Moscow"? Perhaps I am the only one who, on autumn evenings, watching the birds of the north wheel high in the sky, remembers that they have seen our countrymen's graves. Industrial companies have moved into the wilderness with their furnaces and boilers; the bones have been converted into animal black. Whether it comes from dogs or men, the pigment is worth the same price; its source, in glory or obscurity, makes no difference to its brilliancy. This is what we are doing with the dead nowadays! These are the sacred rites of the new religion! *Diis Manibus*.[23] Oh, happy companions of Charles XII, you were never visited by such sacrilegious hyenas! During the winter the ermine frequents the virginal snows, and during the summer the flowering mosses of Poltava.

On November 6, 1812, the thermometer plummeted to eighteen degrees below zero. The whole world vanishes into whiteness. The shoeless soldiers feel their feet going numb; their stiff, purplish fingers let go of the musket, now hot to the touch; their hair bristles with frost, their beards with their frozen breath; their tattered clothes turn to cloaks of ice. They fall, and the snow covers them; on the ground, they form row upon row of tombs. They can no longer tell which way the rivers are flowing and must break the ice so that they know where to direct their steps. Lost and bewildered in the whiteness, the various battalions build fires to recall and recognize one another, as ships in peril will fire a signal cannon. The firs, turned into motionless crystals, rise here and there—the candelabras of these funereal solemnities. Crows and packs of white dogs without masters follow the retreating corpses at a distance.

It was hard, after the day's march, at a wilderness camp, to have to take the precautions proper to a healthy, well-supplied army; to station sentinels, assign patrols, set up outposts. During the sixteen-hour nights, blasted by the cruel northern winds, no one knew where to sit or lie. The trees brought down with all their alabaster refused to catch fire. The men hardly managed to melt a little snow in which to boil up a spoonful of rye flour. They hadn't been resting on the bare ground a moment before the Cossacks came, filling the forest with their cries. The horse artillery of the enemy rumbled in the distance. Our soldiers' fast was saluted like the feast of kings whenever they sat down to eat; the shells rolled like iron loaves among the famished diners. At first light, which came long before sunrise, they heard the beating of a drum sheeted with frost and the hoarse blare of a trumpet. Nothing could be sadder than this dismal reveille, which called to arms warriors who would never wake again. The growing daylight soon illuminated whole circles of soldiers, lying stiff and dead around the smoking watch fires.

The few survivors set off. They were advancing toward unknown horizons that, forever receding, vanished with every step into the fog. Beneath a sky panting as though tired after the previous day's turmoil, our thinning ranks crossed heath after heath, forest after forest where the ocean seemed to have left its foam on the tousled branches of the birches. In those woods, they did not even see that sad little winter bird who sings, as I do, among the leafless bushes. If in making this comparison, I suddenly find myself in the presence of my memories, oh my comrades (all soldiers are brothers), your sufferings return me to my younger years, when, retreating before you, I crossed the heath of the Ardennes, poor and forsaken.

The great Russian armies were following ours, which was now separated into several divisions and subdivided into columns. Prince Eugène commanded the vanguard, Napoleon the middle, and Marshal Ney the rear. Delayed by various obstacles and skirmishes, these corps did not always keep their distance. Sometimes one went ahead and sometimes they marched in parallel, very often without seeing each other or communicating, for want of cavalry. Night and day, the Tauridians, on their little horses whose hair swept the earth, harried our soldiers, worn down by these hibernal horseflies. The landscape had changed: where previously there had been a rivulet, there was now a torrent suspended by chains of ice on the steep banks of its ravine. "In a single night," says Bonaparte (*Papiers de Sainte-*

Hélène), "thirty thousand horses were lost; we were forced to abandon almost all the artillery, then five hundred guns strong. Neither ammunition nor provisions could be taken. We were unable, for want of horses, to go on reconnaissance or send a cavalry vanguard to scout the road ahead. The soldiers lost heart, lost their minds, fell into confusion. The most trivial circumstance alarmed them. Four or five men were enough to spread fear through a whole battalion. Instead of staying together, they wandered away separately seeking fire. Men sent out as scouts left their posts and went looking for ways to warm themselves in nearby houses. They fanned out in every direction, drifted away from their corps, and easily fell prey to the enemy. Others would lie down on the ground and fall asleep: a bit of blood leaked from their nostrils and they died dreaming. Thousands of soldiers perished. The Poles held onto some of their horses and some of their artillery; but the French and the soldiers of other nations were no longer the same men. The cavalry suffered enormously. Out of forty thousand men, I don't think more than three thousand escaped with their lives."

And you, who recounted this under the warm sun of another hemisphere—were you merely the *witness* to so many sorrows?

The same day (November 6) the temperature fell so low, the first courier anyone had seen from France in a very long time arrived like a bird of ill omen gone astray. He brought the bad news of Malet's conspiracy.[24] This conspiracy had something of the prodigiousness of Napoleon's star. According to General Gourgaud's report, what most struck the emperor was the unignorable proof it afforded that "monarchical principles, in their application to his monarchy, had taken such shallow root that high officials, hearing news of the emperor's death, forgot the deceased sovereign had a successor."

On Saint Helena, Bonaparte (according to Las Cases) claimed to have said to his Court in the Tuileries, on the subject of Malet's conspiracy:

"Well, gentlemen, you claimed you were done with your revolution. You thought I was dead—but the King of Rome, your oaths, your principles, your doctrines? You make me shudder for the future!"

Bonaparte's thoughts were logical. It was a question of his lineage. Would he have been so logical if it were a question of the line of Saint Louis?

Bonaparte learned of the trouble in Paris in the middle of a wilderness, among the wreckage of an almost annihilated army whose blood was being drunk by the snow. The rights that Napoleon had founded on force were being destroyed, along with his forces, by Russia, while in the capital all it took was one man to cast them into doubt. Outside of religion, justice, and freedom, there are no rights at all.

Almost at the same time that Bonaparte heard what had happened in Paris, he received a letter from Marshal Ney. This letter informed him that "the best soldiers have been asking themselves why it was up to them alone to fight so that others might escape; why the eagle no longer protected but killed them; why it was necessary to sacrifice whole battalions when there was nothing left to do but flee?"

When Ney's aide-de-camp began to mention the woeful particulars, Bonaparte interrupted him:

"Colonel, I did not ask you for these details."

The Russian expedition was a true extravagance, which all the civil and military authorities of the Empire had condemned. The victories and losses the soldiers recalled as they retreated along that road embittered and discouraged the soldiers. Along this same road, taken both ways, Napoleon might also have found an illustration of the two parts of his life.

6.

SMOLENSK—THE RETREAT, CONTINUED

ON NOVEMBER 9, the French army finally arrived in Smolensk. An order from Bonaparte had forbidden anyone from entering until the posts had been handed over to the Imperial Guard. The soldiers outside congregated below the walls; the soldiers inside hunkered down where they were. The air resounded with the imprecations of the desperate men who had been shut out. They wore filthy Cossack jackets, patched greatcoats, tattered cloaks and uniforms, bedclothes and horse blankets, caps or kerchiefs, staved-in shakos, bent or broken helmets—all covered with blood or snow, pocked by bullets or slashed by sabers. With haunted, sunken faces, their eyes dark and gleaming, they gazed up at the ramparts grinding their teeth, like those mutilated prisoners who, under Louis le Gros, carried their severed left hand in their right. They might have been taken for a party of frantic masqueraders or for maniacs escaped from the hospital. The Young and Old Guard arrived. They entered the square incinerated on our first visit. Cries are raised against the privileged troop: "Will the army never get anything but *their* scraps?" And the starving cohorts run tumultuously toward the magazines like an insurrection of ghosts. They are driven back. Fighting ensues. Meanwhile, the dead lay in the streets, the women, the children, the dying on the carts. The air was rank with the rotten smell of corpses. Many have been stricken with stupidity or insanity. Some, whose twisted hair stood on end, blaspheming or laughing like cretins, fell down dead in the street. Bonaparte vents his fury on a poor helpless supplier, whose orders had not been executed.

The army of 100,000 men, reduced to 30,000, was now surrounded by a band of 50,000 stragglers. Only 1,800 horsemen remained. Napoleon turned over command of them to M. de Latour-Maubourg. This officer, who led the cuirassiers in the attack on Borodino's great redoubt, had his head slashed by a saber; later, he would lose a leg at Dresden. Seeing his servant weeping, he said to him: "What are you sorry for? Now you'll only have one boot to wax." This general, who remained loyal to misfortune, became tutor to Henri V during the young prince's first years in exile.[25] I take off my hat as I pass before him, as though in the presence of Honor itself.

They were forced to stay in Smolensk until November 14. Then Napoleon ordered Marshal Ney to team with Davoust and destroy the place with mines. As for him, he proceeded on to Krasnoi, which he reached on the fifteenth, after this station had been looted by the Russians. The Muscovites were tightening their noose. The great Moldavian army was in the vicinity. They were preparing to surround us completely and drive us into the Berezina.

The rest of our batallions were dwindling day by day. Kutuzov, informed of our miseries, scarcely stirred:

"Just leave your headquarters for a moment," Wilson exclaimed, "go up onto the heights, and you'll see that Napoleon has run out of luck. Russia can claim this victim. All you need to do is strike. One charge will suffice. In two hours' time, the face of Europe will be changed."

This was true; but only Bonaparte would have been particularly struck, and God wished to lay his hand on France.

Kutuzov replied:

"I allow my soldiers to rest every three days. I would be embarrassed, I would stop at once, if there weren't enough bread, even for a moment. I am escorting the French army as my prisoner, and I will punish her whenever she attempts to stop or to leave the main road. Napoleon's destiny has already been written. In the marshes of the Berezina, the meteor will be extinguished in sight of all the Russian armies. I shall have delivered them a Napoleon enfeebled, disarmed, and dying. That is glory enough for me."

Bonaparte had spoken of "old" Kutuzov in that tone of disparaging disdain with which he was so prodigal.[26] Old Kutuzov, for his part, was disdainful of disdain.

Kutuzov's army was more impatient than their leader. The Cossacks themselves exclaimed:

"Are we going to let these skeletons come out of their graves?"

Meanwhile, the fourth corps, which was supposed to leave Smolensk on the fifteenth and rejoin Napoleon on the sixteenth at Krasnoi, was nowhere to be seen. Communications had been severed. Prince Eugène, who was commanding the corps, vainly sought to reestablish them: all he managed to do was to turn the Russians' flank and link up with the guard at Krasnoi. But Marshal Davout and Marshal Ney still did not appear.

Then Napoleon suddenly recovered his genius. He left Krasnoi on the seventeenth with the baton in his hand, leading his Guard, now reduced to thirteen thousand men. They would do battle with innumerable enemies, clear the road to Smolensk, and cut a path for the two marshals. Bonaparte spoiled this maneuver only by conjuring a phrase out of proportion with his mask:

"I have played Emperor enough; now it's time for me to play the general."

Henri IV, leaving for the Siege of Amiens, had said:

"I have played long enough at being King of France; now it's time for me to play the King of Navarre."

The surrounding heights, beneath which Napoleon marched, were loaded with artillery and could at any moment strike him down. He glanced at them and said, "Let a squadron of my cavalrymen take them!" The Russians could have simply let the guns roll down the slope; the weight alone would have crushed them; but, at the sight of this great man and the remnants of the Guard marching in good order in a square battalion, they stood stock-still, as though hypnotized. His glance alone halted 100,000 men upon the heights.

For this engagement at Krasnoi, Kutuzov was honored in Petersburg with the title of Smolensky—apparently for not having, with Bonaparte in command, despaired of being saluted by the Republic.

7.

CROSSING THE BEREZINA

AFTER this pointless effort, Napoleon crossed the Dnieper again on the nineteenth and made camp at Orsha. He burned the papers he had brought for the purpose of writing his memoirs during the long, dull winter, if Moscow, still intact and unscorched, had allowed him to stay there. As he saw it, he was forced to throw the huge cross of Saint John into Semlewo Lake. It was fished out again by some Cossacks and set back upon the tower of Ivan the Great.

At Orsha, everyone was on edge. In spite of Napoleon's attempts to rescue Marshal Ney, he was still missing. Finally, news of him reached Baranni. Eugène had succeeded in finding him. General Gourgaud recounts the pleasure that Napoleon experienced on hearing this news (although the bulletins and accounts written by the friends of the emperor continue to speak with cautious discretion of any fact not directly related to him). The joy of the army was, however, quickly stifled; they proceeded from one danger to the next. Bonaparte was on his way from Kokhanow to Talachyn when an aide-de-camp informed him of the loss of the bridgehead at Borisov, taken by the Moldavian army under General Dabrowski. The Moldavian army, surprised in turn by the Duc de Reggio in Borisov, retreated behind the Berezina after destroying the bridge. Tchitchagov thus found himself facing us, on the other side of the river.

General Corbineau, commanding a brigade of our light cavalry, guided by a peasant, had discovered the ford of Veselovo downriver from Borisov. Hearing this news, Napoleon, on the night of the twenty-fourth, sent Eblé and Chasseloup out with pontooners and sappers. At Studienka, on the Berezina, they found the ford as indicated.

Two bridges were constructed. An army of forty thousand Russians camped on the opposing shore. How surprised the French were when, at daybreak, they saw the riverbank deserted and the rear guard of Tchaplitz's division in full retreat! They couldn't believe their eyes. A single ball, or the fire from a Cossack's pipe, would have been enough to break or burn Eblé's frail pontoons. They run to tell Bonaparte, who rises in a hurry, goes out, looks, and exclaims, "I have fooled the admiral!" The exclamation was natural. The Russians miscarried at the start, making a mistake that was to prolong the war for three more years. But their leader had not been fooled. Admiral Tchitchagov had seen what was happening; he had simply yielded to his character. Though he was an intelligent and fiery man, he also loved his comforts; he was afraid of the cold, stayed by the stove, and thought he would always have time to wipe the French out later, after he had warmed up. He surrendered to his own disposition. Today, retired in London, having abandoned his fortune and renounced Russia, Tchitchagov has furnished the *Quarterly Review* with some curious articles on the campaign of 1812: he tries to excuse himself, and his countrymen fire back at him. It's a quarrel among Russians.

Alas! If Bonaparte, by building his two bridges and the incomprehensible retreat of the Tchaplitz division, was saved, the French were not. Two other Russian armies were gathering on the riverbank that Napoleon was preparing to leave. Here, he who has not seen with his own eyes must be silent and let the witnesses speak:

"The devotion of Eblé's pontooners," writes Chambray,[27] "will live in men's minds as long as the memory of the crossing of the Berezina endures. Although weakened by the miseries they had so long suffered, although deprived of liquors and substantial nourishment, they could still be seen braving the cold, which had by then become very severe, and sometimes standing in water up to their chests. This meant almost certain death, but the eyes of the army were upon them, and they sacrificed themselves for its salvation."

"Disorder reigned among the French," Ségur writes in his turn, "and materials were lacking for the two bridges. Twice, on the nights of the twenty-sixth and twenty-seventh, the bridge constructed for vehicles broke, and the crossing was delayed by seven hours. It broke a third time on the twenty-seventh, about four o'clock in the evening. On the other hand, the stragglers scattered in the surrounding woods and villages had not taken advantage of the bridges the first night, and on the twenty-seventh, when day dawned again, everyone came at the same time to make the crossing.

"Things became especially dire when they saw the Imperial Guard, whom they were watching like hawks, begin to move. Its departure was like a signal: they ran in from every side and piled up on the shore. Instantly we saw a confused mass of men, horses, and wagons besieging the narrow entrance to the bridges, which overflowed with them. The first men onto the bridge, pushed forward on one side by those who followed them and held back on the other by the Guards and pontooners, or stopped by the river, were crushed, trampled underfoot, or launched into the ice floes borne by the Berezina. From this huge and horrifying crowd there rose sometimes a low hum, sometimes a deafening clamor, mingled with groans and dreadful imprecations... The disorder was so great that, around two o'clock, when the emperor appeared, it was necessary to use force to make a path for him. A corps of grenadiers of the Guard, as well as Latour-Maubourg, gave up, out of pity, trying to shoulder their way through this crush of wretches...

"The immense multitude who thronged the shore with their horses and carriages formed a terrible encumbrance. It was about noon when the first enemy balls fell in the midst of this chaos. This was the signal for universal despair...

"Many of those who had first hurled themselves into this desperate crowd, having missed the bridge, tried to climb its sides; but most were driven back into the river. It was there that one saw women among the ice floes, with their children in their arms, lifting them up as they sank; already submerged, their stiffened arms still held them above them.

"In the midst of this horrible disorder, the artillery bridge gave way and broke. The column entangled on this narrow passage tried in vain to retreat. The deluge of men coming on behind, unaware of the catastrophe that had occurred and not hearing the cries of those before them, pushed blindly onward and sent them flying into the abyss, where they in turn were soon thrown.

"Everything then went over to the other bridge. A multitude of large caissons, heavy wagons, and artillery poured in from every direction. Led by their conductors, and carried swiftly down a steep, uneven slope, cutting through this mass of men, they crushed the poor wretches caught between them, then collided, turned over violently, and knocked down still others as they fell. Whole ranks of desperate men pushed against these obstacles that blocked them in, lost their balance, and were crushed beneath the weight of other miserable wretches, who succeed one another without interruption.

"These waves of unfortunates rolled like a dreadful human tide. All you could hear were cries of pain and rage. In this dreadful melee, those being trampled and suffocated struggled under the feet of their companions, to whom they clung tooth and nail; those still standing beat them back without mercy, like enemies. Amid the horrible din of cannon fire, whistling bullets, and bursting bombs, of shouts and moans and fearful imprecations, the disordered crowd did not even hear the laments of the victims they were swallowing up."

The other testimonies agree with M. de Ségur's account. For the purpose of collation and proof, I will quote this one passage from the *Mémoires de Vaudoncourt*:

"The rather large plain near Veselovo presents, this evening, a spectacle whose horror is difficult to describe. It is covered with wagons and coaches—most of them overturned and broken. It is littered with corpses of nonmilitary individuals, among whom one sees far too many women and children who had trailed behind the army to Moscow, or who were fleeing this city to follow their compatriots, and whom death has struck in various ways. The fate of these unfortunates, in the melee of the two armies, was to be crushed under wagon wheels or horse hooves; hit by bullets or balls from either side; drowned in attempting to cross the bridges with the troops, or stripped by enemy soldiers and thrown naked in the snow, where the cold soon put an end to their suffering."

What mourning wail does Bonaparte have for this catastrophe; for this woeful event—one of the worst recorded by history; for these disasters surpassing those of Cambyses's army? What cry is wrung from his inmost soul? These thirteen words in his bulletin: "During the days of the twenty-sixth and twenty-seventh the army crossed the river." You have just seen how! Napoleon's heart was not even touched by the sight of those women lifting their infants up above the surface of the water. The other great man who, through France, came to rule the world, Charlemagne, to all appearances a coarse barbarian, sang and mourned (poet that he was) the child engulfed by the Ebro while playing on the ice:

Trux puer adstricto glacie dum ludit in Hebro.[28]

The Duc de Bellune was charged with protecting the ford. He had left behind General Partouneaux, who was forced to capitulate. The Duc de Reggio, wounded again, was replaced by Marshal Ney. We crossed the marshes of the Gaina. The slightest forethought on the part of the Russians would have made the roads impassable. At Maladzyechna, on December 3, all the couriers who had been holed up there for three weeks were found. It was then that Napoleon considered abandoning the flag.

"Can I remain," he said, "at the head of a rout?"

At Smorgoni, the King of Naples and Prince Eugène urged him to return to France. The Duc d'Istrie, acting as spokesman, had only begun to speak when Napoleon flew into a rage, shouting:

"Only my mortal enemy could suggest I leave the army in its current situation."

He made as if to lunge at the marshal, sword in hand. In the evening, he sent for the Duc d'Istrie and said to him:

"Since it's what you all want, I have no choice but to go."

The scene had been arranged beforehand; the plan for his departure had been decided before it was carried out. M. Fain assures us that, in fact, the emperor had already made up his mind to leave the army "on the fourth, during the march that took him from Maladzyechna to Biclitza." Such was the comedy with which the great actor brought his tragic drama to a close.

At Smorgoni, the emperor wrote his twenty-ninth bulletin. On December 5, he climbed into a sleigh with M. de Caulaincourt. It was ten o'clock at night. He crossed Germany concealed under his companion's name. With his disappearance, everything fell to pieces: when, during a windstorm, a granite colossus is buried beneath the sands of the Thebaid, not a shadow remains in the desert. A few soldiers who were dead up to their heads ended up cannibalizing each other under shelters made of pine branches. Conditions that seemed incapable of worsening came to a head. Winter, which until now had only been the autumn of those climes, descended. The Russians no longer had the heart to fire, in those icy wastes, at the frozen shades Bonaparte had left to wander after him.

At last the French army reached the Niemen. Of the three bridges over which our troops had marched, not one still existed. A single bridge, the work of the enemy, hung over the frozen waters. Of the five hundred thousand men and countless pieces of artillery that, in June, had crossed the river eastward, only a thousand infantrymen, a scant few guns, and thirty thousand wounded wretches were still to be seen passing through Kaunas. No more music, no more songs of victory. The blue-faced band, whose eyes were kept open only by their frozen lashes, walked in silence over the bridge, or clambered from floe to floe until they reached the Polish shore. When they finally entered houses heated by stoves, the unfortunate ones died, their lives melting like the snow that shrouded them. General Gourgaud claims that 127,000 men crossed the Niemen the second time. Even by this count, 313,000 men would have been lost, in a campaign that lasted four months.

Murat, in Gumbinnen, assembled his officers and said to them:

"It is no longer possible to serve a madman. We are no longer safe with him. Not a prince in Europe believes his words or his treaties."

From Gumbinnen, he went to Posen and disappeared. Twenty-three days later, the Prince of Schwarzenberg left the army, which then passed under the command of Prince Eugène. General Yorck, who was at first ostensibly castigated by Frederick William but soon reconciled with him, withdrew and took the Prussians with him. European defection had begun.

8.

JUDGMENT OF THE RUSSIAN CAMPAIGN—LAST BULLETIN OF THE GRAND ARMY—BONAPARTE'S RETURN TO PARIS—EXHORTATION OF THE SENATE

THROUGH the whole length of this campaign, Bonaparte was inferior to his generals, and particularly to Marshal Ney. The excuses that have been made for Bonaparte's flight are inadmissible: the proof is plain to see, since his departure, which was supposed to save everything, saved nothing. His abandonment of the army, far from repairing their misfortunes, created further misfortunes and hastened the dissolution of the Confederation of the Rhine.

The twenty-ninth and final bulletin of the Grand Army, sent from Maladzyechna on December 3, 1812, arrived in Paris on the 18th, preceding Napoleon by only two days. It struck France dumb, even if it did not express itself with the frankness for which it has since been praised. There are some conspicuous contradictions that nevertheless fail to veil the truth legible between every line. On Saint Helena (as we have already heard), Bonaparte spoke more honestly. Then his revelations could no longer compromise the diadem that had fallen from his head. We must, however, listen for a moment to the ravager:

"This army," he writes in the bulletin of December 3, 1812, "so fine on the sixth, was very different by the fourteenth. With almost no cavalry, artillery, or transports, we could not reconnoiter so much as a quarter of a league before us...

"Those whom nature had not sufficiently steeled to be superior to fate and fortune seemed shaken, lost their gaiety and good humor, and thought of nothing except calamities and catastrophes; those whom she created superior to everything preserved their spirits and ordinary manners, and saw new glories in the different difficulties to be overcome...

"Throughout all these movements, the emperor has always marched in the midst of his Guards; the cavalry under the Duc d'Istrie (Marshal Bessieres; and the infantry under the Duc de Dantzick (Marshal Lefebvre). His Majesty has been well pleased with the fine spirit shown by his Guards. They have always been ready to go wherever circumstances required; but the circumstances have always been such that their mere presence has sufficed, and we were never in a position that required them to charge.

"The Prince de Neuchâtel (Marshal Berthier), the Grand Marshal (Duroc), the Grand Equerry (Caulaincourt), and all the aides-de-camp and military officers of the emperor's household always accompanied His Majesty.

"Our cavalry was dismounted so thoroughly that it was necessary to summon the officers who still had horses in order to form four companies of 150 men each. The generals acted as captains and the colonels as sublieutenants. This sacred squadron, commanded by General Grouchy and under the orders of the King of Naples, never lost sight of the emperor through all his movements. The health of His Majesty has never been better."

What a summing up of so many victories! Bonaparte had said to the Directors:

"What have you done with one hundred thousand Frenchmen—all my companions in glory? They are dead!"

France could now say to Bonaparte:

"What have you done with five hundred thousand soldiers along the Niemen—all my children and allies? They are dead!"

After the loss of Napoleon's hundred thousand Republican soldiers, at least the homeland was saved: the final results of the Russian campaign led to the invasion of France and the loss of all that our glory and sacrifices had accumulated over twenty years.

Bonaparte was constantly watched over by a "sacred squadron" that "never lost sight of him through all his movements." What a compensation for the three hundred thousand lives sacrificed! But why hadn't nature "sufficiently steeled" them? Then they might have retained their "ordinary manners." Could this lowly cannon fodder deserve to have their "movements" as carefully monitored as those of His Majesty?

The bulletin concludes, like so many others, with the words "His Majesty's health has never been better."

Families, dry your tears: Napoleon is feeling fine.

Following this report, we read this official comment in the papers:

"It is a historical document of the first rank. Xenophon and Caesar wrote thus: the former in his *Retreat of the Ten Thousand*, the latter in his *Commentaries*."

What a demented academic comparison! But, leaving aside the unpaid literary publicity, consider that one is expected to be *glad* that the terrible tragedies Napoleon himself caused have now given him an opportunity to show off his talents as a writer! Nero has set fire to Rome, and he sings about the burning of Troy. We had reached a form of flattery so savagely stupid it dug up the buried memories of Xenophon and Caesar in order to insult the eternal mourning of France.

The Sénat conservateur doesn't waste a moment. "The Senate," says Lacépède, "hastens to the foot of the throne of Your Imperial and Royal Majesty to offer homage and congratulations on *the blessed arrival* of Your Majesty among his people. The Senate, the emperor's first council, *whose authority does not exist unless* the monarch calls for it and sets it in motion, is established for the preservation of this monarchy and the hereditary transmission of your throne, *in our fourth dynasty*. France and posterity shall find it in all circumstances faithful to this sacred duty, and all its members shall always be ready to lay down their lives for the defense of this *palladium* of national security and prosperity." The members of the Senate later proved this marvelously by proclaiming Napoleon's demise!

The emperor replies:

"Senators, I am very gratified by your address. I am committed to THE GLORY AND THE POWER of France, but our first thoughts are FOR ALL that can be done to perpetuate peace at home ... AS FOR THIS THRONE, which is now linked FOREVER to the destinies of the fatherland ... I have asked Providence for a *certain number of years* ... I have reflected on what has been achieved in different epochs, and I shall continue to reflect on it."

The reptilian historian,[29] daring to congratulate Napoleon on public prosperity, is nevertheless frightened by his own courage. He is afraid of *existing*. He is extremely careful to say that the authority of the Senate "does not exist" unless the monarch summons and sets it in motion. The independence of this Senate was truly fearful!

Bonaparte, making excuses for himself on Saint Helena, said:

"Was it the Russians who destroyed me? No, it was false reports, silly intrigues, betrayals, stupidity, and many other things we shall perhaps know about someday and which may mitigate or justify the two fundamental errors, in diplomacy and war, that should rightly be ascribed to me."

Errors that lead only to the loss of a battle or a province permit of excuses couched in enigmatic words, but errors that convulse society and subjugate a whole nation's independence cannot be effaced by eating humble pie.

After so many calamities and such heroic feats, it is very bleak, in the end, to read the Senate's words and feel nothing except horror or contempt.

BOOK TWENTY-TWO

I.

FRANCE'S MISFORTUNES—COMPULSORY CELEBRATIONS—SOJOURNS IN MY VALLEY—ROUSING OF THE LEGITIMACY

Revised February 22, 1845

WHEN BONAPARTE, preceded by his bulletin, arrived in Paris, consternation was general. "All that was left in the Empire," Ségur says, "were men aged by time or war, and children. There were hardly any men in the prime of life. Where were they? The tears of wives, the cries of mothers, told the tale. Bending laboriously over the earth that, were it not for them, would have gone uncultivated, they cursed the war he represented."

Yet even after Bonaparte's return from the Berezina, some were still willing to dance by order, as we read in Queen Hortense's *Souvenirs pour servir à l'histoire*.[1] People were forced to go to balls with their hearts filled with sorrow, inwardly praying for his relatives or friends. Such was the dishonor to which despotism had condemned France. One saw in the salons what we sometimes see in the streets: creatures distracting themselves from their lives by singing of their woes to divert the passersby.

For three years, I had hidden away in Aulnay. From my pine-covered slope, I had watched the comet that, in 1811, soared over the forested horizon; it was beautiful and sad and queen-like, trailing as it did a long train behind it. Who had this lost stranger come seeking in our universe? To whom was she speaking in the desert of the sky?[2]

On October 23, 1812, I paid a brief visit to Paris and stayed at the Hôtel Lavalette on the rue des Saints-Pères. My hostess, Madame

Lavalette, who was deaf, came to wake me, armed with her long hearing-trumpet:

"Monsieur! Monsieur! Bonaparte is dead! General Malet has killed Hulin. All the authorities have changed. The revolution is done."

Bonaparte was so beloved that for a few moments Paris was in ecstasies (except for the authorities, who were burlesquely arrested.) A breath of wind had almost toppled the Empire. At midnight a soldier broke out of prison and by daybreak he was master of the world. A dream came close to blowing away a formidable reality.

The more moderate said:

"If Napoleon is not dead, he will come back chastened by his errors and misfortunes. He will make peace with Europe, and the rest of our children will be safe."

Two hours after his wife had roused me, M. Lavalette came into my room to tell me that Malet had been arrested. He "would not conceal from me (a phrase he harped on) that it was all over." No one could tell if it was day or night. I have already recounted how Bonaparte received this news in a snowfield near Smolensk.

The *sénatus-consulte*[3] of January 12, 1813, put 250,000 men at Napoleon's disposal: inexhaustible France watched as blood poured from its wounds in the form of new soldiers. Then a long-forgotten voice made itself heard. A few old French ears thought they recognized its timbre. It was the voice of Louis XVIII. The brother of Louis XVI announced principles that would later be set down in a constitutional charter—the first hopes of liberty, which came to us from our ancient kings.[4]

Alexander, entering Warsaw, addressed a proclamation to Europe:

If the North imitates the sublime example offered by the Castilians, the world's mourning shall soon be at an end. Europe, on the brink of becoming prey to a monster, would recover both peace and independence. May there soon be nothing left of the *bloodthirsty colossus who has threatened the continent with his endless criminality* but a long-abiding memory of horror and pity!

This monster, this bloodthirsty colossus who threatened the continent with his endless criminality, had learned so little from misfortune that he had scarcely escaped the Cossacks before he hurled himself at an old man whom he was holding prisoner.

2.

THE POPE AT FONTAINEBLEAU

WE HAVE seen the abduction of the pope from Rome, his sojourn in Savona, and his detention at Fontainebleau. Discord had arisen in the Sacred College. One group of cardinals wanted the Holy Father to stand up for the faith and received an order to wear only black stockings; a few of them were sent into exile in the provinces or imprisoned at Vincennes. Another group of cardinals were in favor of the pope's total submission and held onto their red stockings. It was the case of the Candlemas candles all over again.

When, at Fontainebleau, the pope succeeded in breaking away from the pesky red-stockinged cardinals, he would walk alone in the galleries of François I. There, he could see some trace of the arts which carried him back to the holy city. From his windows, he could look out on the pines that Louis XVI had planted opposite the somber chambers where Monaldeschi was murdered. From this desert, like Jesus, he could take pity on the kingdoms of the earth. The dying septuagenarian, whom Bonaparte came to torment in person, mechanically signed the Concordat of 1813, which he later denounced, after Cardinal Pacca and Cardinal Consalvi had arrived.

When Pacca came to see the prisoner he had accompanied out of Rome, he thought he would find a large crowd around the royal jail, but in the courtyards he only met a few servants and a single sentinel stationed atop the horseshoe staircase. The windows and doors of the palace were shut. In the first antechamber of the apartments he saw Cardinal Doria, in the other rooms a few French bishops. Pacca was announced to His Holiness, who stood motionless, pale, stooped, gaunt, his eyes sunk deep in his skull.

The cardinal told him he had come there in great haste so that he might throw himself at the pontiff's feet, to which the pope replied:

"Those cardinals dragged us to the table and made us sign."

Pacca withdrew to the apartment that had been prepared for him, still confused by the desolate rooms, the silent stares, the dejected faces, and the deep sorrow impressed upon the pope's brow. When Pacca returned to His Holiness, he himself writes, "I found him in a state worthy of compassion which made me fear for his life. He was overwhelmed by inconsolable sorrow when he spoke of what had happened. The thought of it so tormented him he could not sleep and could hardly eat. 'This thing,' he said, 'is going to drive me mad. I am going to die insane, like Clement XIV.'"

In the privacy of these vacant galleries where the voices of Saint Louis, François I, Henri IV, and Louis XIV had long fallen silent, the Holy Father spent several days writing the original and the copy of the letter that was to be delivered to the emperor. Cardinal Pacca kept the dangerous paper concealed in his robe while the pope went on adding new lines. When it was finished, on March 24, 1813, the pope delivered it to Colonel Lagorsse and asked him to take it to the emperor. At the same time, he gave an address to the cardinals around him. He regarded the writ he had issued in Savona and the concordat of January 25 as null and void. "Blessed be the Lord," he said in his address, "who has continued to bless us in His mercy! He has graciously humbled us with salutary confusion. We have therefore been shamed and humiliated for the good of our soul. For of Him and through Him and to Him are all things, to whom be glory forever. (From the Palais de Fontainebleau, March 24, 1813.)" No finer writ has ever issued from that palace. Once the conscience of the pope was eased, the martyr's face became serene. His smile and his sleep returned to him.

At first Napoleon threatened to hack off the heads of a few of the priests at Fontainebleau. He considered declaring himself the official head of the state religion. Then, falling back into his usual way of doing things, he pretended he was not even aware of the pope's letter.

But his luck was on the wane. The pope, who had emerged from an order of poor monks, and returned, through his misfortunes, into the bosom of the crowd, now seemed to have resumed his great role as the tribune of the nations, giving the signal to depose the oppressor of public liberties.

3.
DEFECTIONS—DEATH OF LAGRANGE AND DELILLE

ILL FORTUNE encourages treason but does not justify it. On February 28, 1813, Prussia allies itself with Russia at Kalisch. On March 3, Sweden signs a treaty with the cabinet at Saint James's Palace and obliges itself to provide thirty thousand men. Hamburg is evacuated by the French, Berlin occupied by the Cossacks, and Dresden taken by the Russians and Prussians.

The defection of the Confederation of the Rhine is brewing. Austria allies itself with Russia and Prussia. War begins again in Italy, where Prince Eugène has conveyed himself.

In Spain, the English army defeats Joseph at Vitoria, and the paintings stolen from churches and palaces fall into the Ebro. I had seen them in Madrid and at the Escorial, and I saw them again when they were being restored in Paris; the tide and Napoleon had passed over these Murillos and Raphaels, *velut umbra.*[5]

Wellington, still advancing, defeats Marshal Soult at Roncevaux. The sites of our oldest memories formed the background for the scenes of our new destinies.

On February 14, at the opening of the Corps Législatif, Bonaparte declared that he had always wanted peace and that the world was in need of it. But this world no longer had any wish to serve him. Besides, from the mouth of the man who called us "his subjects," there came no words of sympathy for France's sorrows: Bonaparte imposed sufferings on us as if they were a tribute that we owed him.

On April 3, the Sénat conservateur added 180,000 combatants to those it had already allocated. This was an extraordinary number of men, especially considering the number already taken. On April 10, Lagrange breathed his last; Abbé Delille died a few days later. If, in heaven, nobility of feeling is held in higher regard than loftiness of thought, the bard of *La Pitié* must be seated nearer the throne of God than the author of the *Théorie des fonctions analytiques*.[6] Bonaparte left Paris on April 15.

4.

THE BATTLES OF LÜTZEN, BAUTZEN, AND DRESDEN—
REVERSALS IN SPAIN

Paris, April 14, 1846;
Revised July 28, 1846

THE LEVIES of 1812, coming one after the other, had stopped in Saxony. Napoleon arrives. The honor of the old army is transferred to two hundred thousand conscripts who fight like the grenadiers at Marengo. On May 2, the Battle of Lützen is won: Bonaparte, in these new clashes, employs almost nothing but artillery. Marching into Dresden, he says to the populace: "I am aware of the transports of joy with which you welcomed Emperor Alexander and the King of Prussia within your walls. One can still see the wet mess from the flowers your young girls scattered in the monarchs' footsteps." Was Napoleon remembering the "girls of Verdun"?[7] That had been in the days of his youth.

At Bautzen, another triumph; but both Kirgener, the General of the Engineers, and Duroc, Grand Marshal of the Palace, are killed. "There is another life," the emperor says to Duroc; "we shall see each other again." But would Duroc have *liked* to see him again?

On August 26 and 27, the French army reaches the banks of the Elbe, in fields already famous. Back from America, having visited with Bernadotte in Stockholm and Alexander in Prague, Moreau loses his legs to a cannonball in Dresden while talking with the Emperor of Russia—by then a traditional Napoleonic fate. News of the death of the victor at Hohenlinden was brought into the French camp by a lost dog on whose collar the new Turenne's name was written; the animal, now masterless, scampered at random among the dead: *Te, janitor Orci!*[8]

The Prince of Sweden, who had become generalissimo of the North German Army, had, on August 15, sent a proclamation to his soldiers:

"Soldiers, the same feeling which guided the French of 1792, and which led them to unite and combat the armies on their territory, must now direct your valor against the man who, having invaded your native soil, still keeps your brothers, your wives, and your children in chains."

Bonaparte, incurring unanimous reprobation, lunged against liberty, which attacked him from every side, in every form. A *sénatus-consulte* issued on August 28 annulled the decision of a jury in Antwerp. This was, no doubt, a rather minor infraction against the rights of citizens, compared with the arbitrary enormities the emperor had previously committed. But there is, in the law, a sacred independence whose cries are heard. The oppression of this single jury made more of a stir than all the various oppressions to which France had already fallen victim.

Finally, in the South, the enemy had entered our territory. The English—Bonaparte's obsession, and the cause of almost all his errors—crossed the Bidasoa on October 7. Wellington, the fatal man, was the first to set foot on French soil.

Insisting on remaining in Saxony, despite the capture of Vandamme in Bohemia and Bernadotte's defeat of Ney near Berlin, Napoleon returned to Dresden. Then the Landsturm rose up. A national war—much like the one that had liberated Spain—was set in motion.

5.

THE SAXON CAMPAIGN, OR CAMPAIGN OF THE POETS

THE BATTLES of 1813 have been called the Saxon Campaign, but they are more accurately called the Young Germany Campaign or the Campaign of the Poets. Bonaparte had reduced us to a low state of despair indeed, since, even when we were seeing French blood being shed, we could not help feeling some sympathy for those generous young men taking up the sword in the name of independence. Each of these battles was a protest for the rights of the nations.

In one of his proclamations, written in Kalisch on March 25, 1813, Alexander called the people of Germany to arms, promising them, in the name of his royal brethren, free institutions. This was the signal for the Burschenschaft, which had already secretly formed.[9] The universities of Germany were opened; the students and professors set aside their pain and directed all their energy toward mending the wound. "Let tears and lamentations be dismissed, but let grief and sorrow long linger," said the Germans of old; "it is becoming for a woman to weep and for a man to remember": *Lamenta ac lacrymas cito, dolorem et tristitiam tarde ponunt. Feminis lugere honestum est, viris meminisse.* It was at this point Young Germany made to liberate their homeland—at this point they showed themselves to be those "allies of the Empire" whom ancient Rome had used, as though they were weapons or javelins, *velut tela atque arma.*[10]

In 1813, Professor Fichte delivered a lecture on duty in Berlin. He spoke of Germany's afflictions and concluded with these words:

"This course of lectures will be suspended until the end of the

482 · MEMOIRS FROM BEYOND THE GRAVE

campaign. We shall resume it if our country becomes free, or else we shall have laid down our lives in the cause of liberty."

The young people in the audience rose to their feet and cheered: Fichte stepped down from his lectern, hurried through the crowd, and went to enlist in a militia that would soon be on its way to the army.

Everything Bonaparte had despised and insulted now becomes dangerous to him. Intelligence descends into the arena to do battle with brute force. Moscow is the torch by which Germany girded up its loins. "To arms!" the Muse exclaimed: "The Phoenix of Russia has risen from its ashes!" The Queen of Prussia, so frail and so lovely, on whom Napoleon had heaped so many ungenerous abuses, was transformed into an implored and imploring shade:

"Thou sleep'st so sweetly!" sang the Bards: "Oh, fair lady, sleep on! until thy sons, their rusty swords unsheathing, temper their steel in the blood of our foe! —Then, awake! Be thou a guardian angel to the holy cause of liberty and vengeance!"

Körner feared nothing, except dying prosaically: "Poetry! Poetry!" he cried, "give me death at daybreak!"

At his last bivouac, he composed *Lyre and Sword*:

THE KNIGHT
Thou Sword upon my thigh,
Those beaming glances why?—
    Thou look'st so pleas'd on me,
    I've all my joy in thee—
                    Hurrah!

THE SWORD
In the belt of a gallant knight
My glance is ever bright;
    A freeman is my lord,
    And this makes glad the Sword—
                    Hurrah!

THE KNIGHT
Yes, trusty Sword, I'm free—
And fondly cherish thee;
    Dear as a Bride thou art,
    The treasure of my heart!—
                    Hurrah!

THE SWORD
Ah! would thy vows were mine,
As my iron-life is thine!
    If our nuptial-knot were tied,
    When dost thou fetch thy Bride?—
                    Hurrah![11]

Wouldn't you swear you were hearing the words of one of those warriors of the North, one of those men of war and wastes about whom Saxo Grammaticus says, "He fell, he laughed, and he died."[12]

Körner's was not the cold passion of a skald well out of harm's way.[13] He carried a sword at his side. Young, fair, and handsome, an equestrian Apollo, he sang by night like an Arab in his saddle; his *mawwal*, as he charged the enemy, was accompanied by the sound of his galloping steed.[14] Wounded at Lützen, he dragged himself through the woods, where some peasants found him. He reappeared on the fields of Leipzig and died, scarcely twenty-five years old. He had torn himself away from the arms of the woman he loved and died in the midst of all of life's pleasures. "Women like to behold a lovely young man," said Tyrtaeus, "and find him no less lovely when he falls in the vanguard."[15]

These nineteenth-century Arminiuses, brought up on the Greeks, had a war song all their own. When these students abandoned the peaceful sanctuary of knowledge for the fields of battle, the silent joys of study for the noisy perils of war, Homer and the Nibelungen for the sword—what did they pit against our bloody, Revolutionary, hymn? Stanzas full of religious feeling and sincere human nature that sang of God, loyalty, and Germany.[16]

These schoolmates who had become companions in arms did not join clubs where Septembriseurs[17] vowed to murder men with daggers. Faithful to the poetry of their dreams, the traditions of history, the cult of the past, they made an old castle or an ancient forest the conservative asylums of the Burschenschaft. The Queen of Prussia became their patroness, taking the place of the Queen of Night.

At the top of a hill, among the ruins, the schoolboy-soldiers with their teacher-captains spied the summit of their cherished university halls. Moved by the memory of their ancient scholarly past, touched by the sight of the sanctuary of study and their childhood games, they swore to liberate their country, as Melchthal, Fürst, and Stauf-facher once pronounced their triple oath in the high air of the Alps, which immortalized them.[18] The German spirit has something inex-plicable about it; Schiller's Thekla is still a Teutonic girl endowed with foresight and graced with the divine. Today, the Germans wor-ship freedom in an indefinable wave, just as they once called God "the secret of the woods": *Deorum nominibus appellant secretum illud*.[19] The man whose life was a dithyramb in action fell only when the poets of Young Germany had sung and taken up the sword against their rival, Napoleon, the poet of arms.

Alexander was worthy of being the herald sent to the young Ger-mans. He shared their lofty sentiments, and he was in a position powerful enough to make their plans a reality; but he let himself be scared by the fearful monarchs around him. These monarchs did not keep their promises; they did not provide their people with liberal institutions. The children of the Muse (the flame with which the inert mass of soldiers had been animated) were thrown into dungeons as a reward for their devotion and noble credulity. Alas! The genera-tion that gave the Teutons back their independence has gone; all Germany has left are weary old ministers. They call Napoleon a "great man" as loudly as they can, as though their admiration in the present could make up for their servility in the past. In this foolish enthusi-asm for a man who continued humiliating governments even after he had flogged them, one is hardly reminded of Körner. "Arminius, the liberator of Germania," writes Tacitus, "is unknown to the Greeks, who are interested only in their own affairs; nor is he very much celebrated among us Romans, whom he defeated; but the barbarous nations still sing about him," *caniturque barbaras apud gentes.*[20]

6.

BATTLE OF LEIPZIG—BONAPARTE RETURNS TO
PARIS—TREATY OF VALENÇAY

ON THE fields of Leipzig, from October 18 and 19, the battle that the Germans called the Battle of the Nations took place. At the end of the second day, the Saxons and Württembergians, deserting Napoleon's camp under Bernadotte's flags, decided the outcome of the action. Victory was besmirched by betrayal. The Prince of Sweden, the Emperor of Russia, and the King of Prussia entered Leipzig through three different gates. Napoleon, having suffered enormous losses, retreated. As he knew nothing about "sergeant's retreats," as he once said, he blew up the bridges behind him. Wounded twice, Prince Poniatowski drowned in the Elster: Poland went down with its last defender.

Napoleon did not stop until he reached Erfurt. The bulletin he composed there declared that his army, which was always victorious, "arrived *like* an army defeated." Erfurt, not long before, had seen Napoleon at the height of his glory.

The Bavarians are the last to follow suit and desert a falling fortune. At Hanau, they try to exterminate what remains of our soldiers. Wrede is defeated by the Guards of Honor alone. A few conscripts, already veterans, force him to fall back. They save Bonaparte and take up their position behind the Rhine. Arriving like a fugitive in Mainz, Napoleon reaches Saint-Cloud on November 9. The indefatigable Lacépède returns to tell him, "Your Majesty has overmastered all." M. de Lacépède may have written quite correctly about the oviparous, but he did not know how to stand on his own two feet.

Holland regains its independence and recalls the Prince of Orange. On December 1, the Allied powers declare that they are "not waging war with France, but only with the emperor, or rather with that ascendancy which he has too long exerted beyond the limits of his empire, to the misfortune of Europe and France."

When we saw the time approaching when we would be confined to our former territory, we wondered what the use of massacring so many millions of men had been. Time engulfs us and calmly continues on its course.

By the Treaty of Valençay on December 11, poor Ferdinand VII was sent back to Madrid. Thus the Spanish affair, the first cause of Napoleon's downfall, came abruptly to an end. Anyone can turn to evil, anyone can kill a people or a king; but to come back from it is difficult. Jacques Clément kneeled, mending his sandals for the journey to Saint-Cloud; his fellow monks, laughing, asked him how long he thought his handiwork would last. "Long enough to take me where I'm going," he answered: "I only have to get there, not back."[21]

7.

THE CORPS LÉGISLATIF IS CONVOKED, THEN ADJOURNED—THE ALLIES CROSS THE RHINE— BONAPARTE'S ANGER—JANUARY 1, 1814

THE CORPS Législatif was convoked on December 19, 1813. Astonishing on the battlefield, remarkable in his Council of State, Bonaparte was not nearly so impressive in the public forum: he was not fluent in the language of liberty. He sought to express congenial affections and paternal sentiments, but his emotions were all wrong; he tried to plaster over his insensitivity with words:

"My heart has need of the presence and affection of my subjects. I have never been seduced by prosperity. Adversity will find me beyond its reach. I have conceived and executed great designs for the happiness of the world. As a monarch and a father, I feel that peace is conducive to the security of thrones and families alike."

An official article printed in the *Moniteur* had said, in July 1804:

"Under the Empire, France would never go beyond the Rhine and its armies would never cross it again."

The Allies crossed this river on December 21, 1813, from Basel to Schaffhausen, with more than one hundred thousand men. On December 31, the Army of Silesia, commanded by Blücher, crossed it from Mannheim to Koblenz.

By the emperor's order, the Senate and the Corps Législatif had appointed two commissions tasked with reviewing documents relative to the negotiations with the Allied powers—the foresight of a ruler who, refusing the now inevitable consequences, wished to relinquish responsibility to another authority.

The Corps Législatif's commission, presided over by M. Lainé, dared to say that "the means of peace would have assured effects, if the French were convinced their blood would henceforth be shed only to defend their native land and its laws; that His Majesty must be entreated to maintain the full and constant execution of the laws that guarantee individuals the rights of liberty and property, and the nation the free exercise of its political rights."

The Minister of Police, the Duc de Rovigo, orders the proofs of the report confiscated. A decree of December 31 adjourns the Corps Législatif; the doors to the hall are locked. Bonaparte called the members of the commission "paid English agents." "The man named Lainé," he said, "is a traitor who has been corresponding with the prince regent, using Desèze as an intermediary; Raynouard, Maine de Biran, and Flauguergues are likewise dissenters."

The soldier was shocked not to find any more of those Poles whom he had abandoned, and who, while drowning themselves in obedience to his orders, continued to cry out, "Long live the Emperor!" He called the commission's report "a motion issued by a club of Jacobins."

Not one speech by Bonaparte failed to reveal his aversion to the Republic that spawned him; but he hated its crimes less than he did its liberties. Regarding this same report, he also said:

"Do you wish to restore the sovereignty of the people? Very well, in that case, I declare myself the people, for I claim to be where sovereignty resides, now and forever."

Never has a despot so emphatically explained his nature. It is the famous phrase of Louis XIV refigured:

"The State, *c'est moi*."

At the reception on the first day of the year 1814, some sort of scene was anticipated: I knew one man attached to this Court who was prepared to take his sword in hand. Napoleon did not, however, go beyond verbal violence, although he did let himself run on so unrestrainedly it sometimes caused confusion even among his halberdiers:

"Why," he exclaimed, "should we talk about these domestic debates in the presence of Europe? One should always wash one's dirty linen at home, among family. What is a throne? A piece of wood covered with a piece of cloth. It all depends on who's sitting there. France needs me more than I need France. I am one of those men who are killed but not dishonored. Three months from now we shall have peace, or the enemy shall be driven out of our territory, or I shall be dead."

Bonaparte was used to washing Frenchmen's linen in blood. Three months later, we had no peace, the enemy had not been expelled from our territory, and Bonaparte had not lost his life; death was not his preferred maneuver. Stricken by so many tragedies—and by the ingrate obstinacy of the tyrant she had created—France watched herself being invaded with the inert stupor brought on by despair.

An imperial decree had mobilized 121 National Guard battalions. Another decree had formed a Regency Council chaired by Cambacérès, composed of ministers and led by the Empress. Joseph, the monarch on call, returned from Spain with his loot and was declared Commander General of Paris. On January 25, 1814, Bonaparte left his palace for the army, off to burn brightly once more, before fizzling out.

8.

POPE SET FREE

TWO DAYS earlier, the pope had been set free; the hand that would soon be wearing chains was at that moment forced to break them. Providence had changed the fortunes of the world, and the wind, blowing in Napoleon's face, was pushing the Allies toward Paris.

When he was informed of his deliverance, Pius VII hastened to say a short prayer in the chapel of François I. He climbed into a carriage and crossed the forest where, according to popular tradition, one can see the great huntsman Death appear whenever a king is going to descend into the vaults of Saint-Denis.

The pope was traveling under the supervision of an officer of the gendarmerie, who followed him in a second carriage. At Orléans, he learned the name of the city he was entering.

He followed the road south, to the cheers of the crowd, in those provinces through which Napoleon was soon to pass, in danger of being killed, even while guarded by foreign commissaries. His Holiness was slowed in his progress by the fall of his oppressor. The authorities had ceased to fulfill their duties. No one was obeyed. An order written by Bonaparte—an order that twenty-four hours earlier would have brought down the loftiest head and overthrown a kingdom—was now a worthless piece of paper. If Napoleon had power for a few minutes more, he might have been able to protect the captive he had persecuted. A provisional mandate from the Bourbons was needed to liberate a pontiff who had set their crown on a foreign head. What a confusion of destinies!

Pius VII made his way amid hymns and tears, to the sound of bells and cries of "Long live the pope! Long live the head of the Church!" They brought him not keys to cities or blood-soaked capitulations obtained by murder, but the sick to heal, and newlyweds to bless beside his carriage. To the former he said, "May God console you!" To the latter he reached out his peaceful hands. He kissed little children in their mothers' arms. Only those unable to walk remained in the cities. Pilgrims slept the night in fields, waiting for the arrival of the old priest now emancipated. Peasants, in their simplicity, said the Holy Father resembled Our Lord. Protestants, full of emotion, said, "Here is the greatest man of his age." Such is the greatness of true Christian society, where God ceaselessly mingles with men. Such is the superiority of the power of the weak, sustained by religion and adversity, over the power of the sword and the scepter.

Pius VII passed through Carcassonne, Béziers, Montpellier, and Nîmes before reentering Italy. On the banks of the Rhône, one might almost have thought the numberless crusaders of Raymond of Toulouse were still passing in review at Saint-Remy. Once more, the pope saw Nice, Savona, Imola—witnesses to his recent afflictions and the first mortifications of his life. We love to weep where we have wept before; under ordinary conditions, we tend to remember the happy places and times. But Pius VII lived both his blessings and sufferings over again, as a man, in his memory, relives his long-ago passions.

In Bologna, the pope was left in the hands of the Austrian authorities. Murat, Joachim-Napoleon, King of Naples, wrote to him on April 4, 1814:

> Most Holy Father, the fortune of war having rendered me the ruler of the states you possessed when you were compelled to quit Rome, I do not hesitate to restore them to your authority, renouncing in your favor all my rights to these countries gained by conquest.

What was left to the dying Joachim and the dying Napoleon? The pope had not yet reached Rome when he granted asylum to

Bonaparte's mother, but his legates had already regained possession of the eternal city. On May 23, in the fullness of spring, Pius VII set eyes on Saint Peter's dome. He has said that he wept when he saw the sacred basilica. Then, on the verge of entering through the Porta del Popolo, he was stopped: twenty-two orphans dressed in white robes and forty-five girls holding huge golden palm leaves came forward singing hymns. The crowd shouted "Hosanna!"

Pignatelli, who led the troops to the Quirinal when Radet stormed Pius VII's Gethsemane, now led the march of the palms. At the same moment Pignatelli was changing roles, noble perjurers in Paris were gathering behind the armchair of Louis XVIII and becoming great servants again. Prosperity is transmitted to us along with its slaves, as a seigniorial domain used to be sold with its serfs.

9.

NOTES FOR WHAT WILL BECOME THE PAMPHLET
DE BONAPARTE ET DES BOURBONS—I TAKE AN
APARTMENT ON RUE DE RIVOLI—THE ADMIRABLE
CAMPAIGN IN FRANCE, 1814

IN THE second book of these *Memoirs*, you have read (I had just come back from my first exile in Dieppe):

"I have been permitted to return to my Valley. The earth trembles under the footsteps of foreign soldiers. I write this, like the last Romans, amid the tumult of Barbarian invasion. By day, I scribble pages as agitated as the events of the moment; by night, when the rumble of distant gunfire fades from my woods, I return in silence to those years that sleep in the grave, to the peace of my earliest memories."

These agitated pages I was scribbling by day were notes regarding the events of the moment, which, scrambled together, would become my pamphlet *De Bonaparte et des Bourbons*. I had such a high opinion of Napoleon's genius and of his soldiers' valor that foreign invasion, happy though its eventual result might be, had never before entered my head; but I thought now that this invasion, by making France aware of the danger to which Napoleon's ambition exposed him, would bring about a movement within the country, and that the liberation of the French would be accomplished by their own hands. This was what I had in mind and why I wrote my notes, so that, if our political assemblies halted the march of the Allies and decided to break with a great man who had by then become a scourge, they would know whom to turn to. Our refuge seemed to me to be in the authority, modified to suit the times, under which our ancestors had lived for eight centuries. When you are caught in a storm and all you can find is an old building, however ruined it may be, that is where you go.

494

In the winter of 1813 and 1814, I took an apartment on rue de Rivoli, opposite the first gate of the Tuileries Garden, near where I had heard the news of the Duc d'Enghien's death. All one saw in that street were a few arcades constructed by the government and some houses, rising here and there, with their jagged, lateral toothing stones.

If France had not been so stricken with grief, it never could have maintained the aversion that Napoleon inspired while still warding off the admiration he elicited the moment he went into action. He had the greatest genius for action that has ever existed. His first campaign in Italy and his last campaign in France (I do not speak of Waterloo) are his two finest campaigns. He was Condé in the first, Turenne in the second; a great warrior in the former, a great man in the latter—but the consequences were different. By one he gained the Empire, and by the other he lost it. His last days in power, rootless and untethered though they were, could not be drawn from him, like a lion's tooth, except by the effort of all Europe's arms. The name *Napoleon* was still so imposing that enemy armies crossed the Rhine in terror; they kept looking behind them to make sure they could still retreat. Even when they had conquered Paris, they continued to tremble. Alexander, casting his eyes back to Russia while invading France, congratulated anyone who was able to get away, and wrote to his mother of his worries and regrets.

Napoleon beat the Russians at Saint-Dizier and the Prussians and Russians at Brienne, as though to do honor to the fields in which he had been raised. He trounced the Army of Silesia at Montmirail and Champaubert, and a part of the Grand Army at Montereau. He made headway everywhere; marched and then retraced his steps; beat back the columns that surrounded him. When the Allies proposed an armistice, Bonaparte tore up the preliminaries of peace, shouting:

"I am closer to Vienna than the Emperor of Austria is to Paris!"

Russia, Austria, Prussia, and England, for their mutual consolation, concluded a new treaty of alliance, but, in secret, alarmed by Bonaparte's resistance, they were thinking of retreat. In Lyons an army was formed on the Austrian flank, while in the South Marshal Soult was stopping the English in their tracks. The Congress of

Chatillon, which was not dissolved until March 18, was still in progress. Bonaparte chased Blücher from the heights of Craonne. The main Allied army had triumphed on February 27 at Bar-sur-Aube only because they had so many more men. Bonaparte, multiplying his, had recovered Troyes, which the Allies then occupied again. From Craonne he went to Reims. "Tonight," he said, "I shall go take my father-in-law at Troyes."[22]

On March 20, a battle took place near Arcis-sur-Aube. Among constant artillery fire, a shell comes down at the fore of a square of Guards; the square appears to make a slight movement: Bonaparte rushes to the projectile with its smoking wick and makes his horse sniff at it. The shell explodes, but the emperor emerges safe and sound from a cloud of smoke.

The battle was to begin again the next day, but Bonaparte, yielding to the inspiration of genius—an inspiration that was, however, fatal to him—retreated in order to come up behind the Allied troops, separate them from their magazines, and swell his ranks with the garrisons along the frontier. The foreigners were getting ready to retreat toward the Rhône when Alexander, operating under one of those heavenly decrees that change a whole world, decided to march toward Paris, seeing nothing in his way. Napoleon thought he was leading the best part of the enemy army behind him, but he was followed only by ten thousand cavalrymen, whom he believed to be the vanguard of the main army, and who masked the real movements of the Prussians and the Muscovites. When he dispersed his ten thousand horses at Saint-Dizier and Vitry, he at last saw that the main Allied army was not behind him. This army had nothing but Marshals Marmont and Mortier and about twelve thousand conscripts between it and the capital.

Napoleon hurriedly set off for Fontainebleau. The sainted victim recently gone from there had left behind the remunerator and the avenger. The two things always go hand in hand in history. When a man clears a path to injustice, at the same time he clears a path to perdition. Somewhere along the way, at a marked distance, the first path merges with the second.

10.

I BEGIN PRINTING MY PAMPHLET—A NOTE OF
MADAME DE CHATEAUBRIAND'S

MINDS were greatly agitated. The hope of seeing, whatever it may cost, an end to a cruel war that for twenty years had overburdened France—which had now had more than enough of tragedy and glory—took precedence over nationhood for most of the populace. Everyone was thinking of the side he would have to take in the approaching catastrophe. Evening after evening, my friends came to talk with Madame de Chateaubriand, recounting and commenting on the events of the day. Fontanes, Clausel, and Joubert were running with that crowd of transient friends whom events provide and take away. The beautiful, peaceable, devoted Duchesse de Lévis, whom we shall meet again in Ghent, was keeping Madame de Chateaubriand company. The Duchesse de Duras was also in Paris then, and I often went to see Madame la Marquise de Montcalm, the Duc de Richelieu's sister.

I continued to be persuaded, despite the fields of battle drawing ever nearer, that the Allies would not enter Paris and that a national insurrection would put an end to our fears. My fixation on this idea kept me from feeling the presence of the foreign armies as keenly as I might have—but I could not keep from thinking of the sufferings we had inflicted on Europe, even as I saw Europe inflicting them on us.

Noon and night, I went on working on my pamphlet; I was preparing it like an antidote for the moment when anarchy struck. This is not the way we write today, quite cozily, with nothing to fear but the wars in periodicals. At night I locked myself up in my room. I

498 · MEMOIRS FROM BEYOND THE GRAVE

kept my papers under my pillow, two loaded pistols on my table, and, between these two muses, lay down to sleep. My text was twofold; I had composed it as a pamphlet, which form it retained, and as a speech, which differed in certain respects from the pamphlet. I supposed that, when France revolted, everyone would assemble at the Hôtel de Ville, and I had prepared myself to speak on two subjects.

Madame de Chateaubriand has written a few notes at various periods of our life together, and among these notes I find the following paragraph:

> M. de Chateaubriand was writing his pamphlet *De Bonaparte et des Bourbons*. If this pamphlet had been seized, there was no doubt about the sentence: he would have gone to the scaffold. Yet the author was incredibly careless about hiding it. Often, when he went out, he forgot it on his table; his prudence never went beyond putting it under his pillow, which he did in front of his valet de chambre, a very honest fellow, but not above temptation. For my part, I was in mortal terror. As soon as M. de Chateaubriand went out, I would take the manuscript and conceal it on my person. One day, crossing the Tuileries, I realized I no longer had it with me and, being quite sure I had felt it on leaving the house, was in no doubt I had lost it along the way. I could already see the fatal letter in the handwriting of the police and M. de Chateaubriand arrested. I fainted in the middle of the garden. Some kind people assisted me and took me back to the house, a short distance away. What a torture it was when, climbing the stairs, I wavered between my fear, which was very nearly certainty, and the slight hope I had forgotten to take the pamphlet with me! Approaching my husband's room, I felt myself growing faint again. Finally, I went in: nothing on the table. I went over to the bed, pushed at the pillow, and at first felt nothing. I lifted it, and saw the roll of papers! My heart pounds every time I think about it. I have never experienced such a joyous moment in my life. Certainly, I can say in all honesty I would not have been so glad if I had

been saved at the foot of the scaffold, for in fact it was someone much dearer to me than myself whom I saw saved from that fate.

How unhappy I would be if I might have caused Madame de Chateaubriand a moment of pain!

I did, however, have to let a printer in on my secret. He agreed to take the risk. According to the news of the hour, he would fetch or return my half-finished proofs, as the noise of gunfire drew nearer or farther from Paris. For two weeks, I played with my life as though it were a game of heads or tails.

I I.

THE WAR COMES TO THE GATES OF PARIS—
VIEW OF PARIS—SKIRMISHES AT BELLEVILLE—
FLIGHT OF MARIE LOUISE AND THE REGENCY—
M. DE TALLEYRAND REMAINS IN PARIS

THE NOOSE was tightening around the capital. Moment by moment, we followed the news of the enemy's progress. Russian prisoners and wounded French soldiers in carts flowed in haphazardly through the gates; some, half dead, fell beneath the wheels, which they stained with their blood. Conscripts called up from the interior crossed the capital in a long line on their way to the armies. At night, we heard artillery trains on the outer boulevards and could not tell whether the far-off detonations signaled decisive victory or conclusive defeat.

The war came and installed itself outside the gates of Paris. From the towers of Notre-Dame, we saw the leading edge of the Russians columns, the first waves of the oceanic tide breaking on the shore. I felt what a Roman must have felt when, from the apex of the Capitol, he saw the soldiers of Alaric and the old city of the Latins far below him, as I saw the Russian soldiers and, far below me, the old city of the Gauls. Farewell, then, paternal Lares, hearths that preserved the country's traditions, roofs beneath which Verginia was sacrificed to liberty and chastity by her father, and Héloïse was vowed to literature and religion by love.[23]

It had been centuries since Paris had seen the smoke of enemy camps. Bonaparte, after so many triumphs, had led the Thebans within sight of the women of Sparta. Paris was the place he had left to go and roam the earth; now he returned there, leaving behind him the immense inferno of his pointless conquests.

Everyone rushed to the Jardin des Plantes, which in former times might have offered them the protection of the fortified Abbaye Saint-Victor. The little world of swans and banana trees, which our power had promised eternal peace, was disturbed. From the heights of the labyrinth, above the towering cedar, over the public granaries Bonaparte had not had time to finish, beyond the site of the Bastille and the keep of Vincennes (places that told our story, chapter by chapter), the crowd watched the infantry fire in the fighting at Belleville. Montmartre was taken. The cannonballs fell as far as the Boulevards du Temple. A few companies of National Guardsmen made a sortie and lost three hundred men in the fields around the tomb of the martyrs.[24] Never had French soldiers shone more brightly in the midst of their reversals. The last heroes were the one hundred and fifty young men of the École Polytechnique, transformed into gunners in the redoubts on the road to Vincennes. Surrounded by enemies, they refused to surrender and had to be torn from their guns. The Russian grenadier captured them, blackened with powder and covered with wounds. While they struggled in the enemy's arms, the grenadier lifted these young French palm leaves up into the air with shouts of victory and admiration, before restoring them, bleeding, to their mothers.

Meanwhile, Cambacérès was fleeing with Marie Louise, the King of Rome, and the regency. We read this proclamation plastered on the walls:

KING JOSEPH,
LIEUTENANT GENERAL OF THE EMPEROR,
COMMANDER IN CHIEF OF THE NATIONAL GUARD

Citizens of Paris,

The Regency Council has provided for the safety of the Empress and the King of Rome: I remain with you. Let us arm ourselves to defend this city, its monuments, its riches, our women and children, all that is dear to us. Let this vast city become a camp for a little while, and let the enemy come to shame beneath its walls, which he hopes to clear in triumph.

Rostopchin had not pretended to defend Moscow; he burned it down. Joseph declared he would never abandon the Parisians and then decamped on the sly, leaving us signs of his courage placarded at street corners.

M. de Talleyrand was one of the members of the regency appointed by Napoleon. Since the day the Bishop of Autun had ceased to be, under the Empire, Minister of Foreign Affairs, he had dreamed of only one thing: Bonaparte's disappearance, followed by the regency of Marie Louise—a regency of which he, the Prince de Bénévent, would have been the head. Bonaparte, by appointing him a member of the provisional regency in 1814, seemed to have favored his secret desires. But the Napoleonic death had not occurred. All M. de Talleyrand could do was hobble at the feet of the colossus he could not bring down and await the moment when he could advance his own interests. The genius of that man of bargains and compromise lay in knowing how to act. His position was difficult: to remain in the capital was the obvious course, but if Bonaparte returned, the prince, separated from the fugitive regency, the laggard prince, ran the risk of being shot. On the other hand, how could he slip out of Paris the moment the Allies slipped in? Wouldn't that be as good as giving up the spoils of success and betraying the endless train of events for which M. de Talleyrand was made? Far from inclining toward the Bourbons, he feared them, due to his various apostasies. However, since there was some sort of chance for them, M. de Vitrolles, with the assent of the married prelate, had gone in secret to the Congress of Châtillon as an undeclared whisperer for the Legitimacy. This precaution taken, the prince, in order to extricate himself from his predicament in Paris, had recourse to one of those tricks at which he was a past master.

M. Laborie, who would soon become, under M. Dupont de Nemours, private secretary to the provisional government, went to M. de Laborde, who was attached to the National Guard. He informed him of M. de Talleyrand's departure, saying:

"He is preparing to follow the regency. It will perhaps seem necessary to you to stop him, in order to be in a position to negotiate with the Allies if need be."

The comedy was played to perfection.

The prince's carriages were loudly loaded up, and by midday March 30 he was on his way out. At the Barrière d'Enfer, he was inexorably sent back home despite his protests. In case of a miraculous return, there was now proof the former minister had tried to join Marie Louise and that the armed forces had turned him back.

12.

PRINCE SCHWARTZENBERG'S PROCLAMATION— ALEXANDER'S SPEECH—CAPITULATION OF PARIS

IN THE meantime, the moment the Allies appeared, Comte Alexandre de Laborde and M. Tourton, two high-ranking officers of the National Guard, had been sent to the Generalissimo, Prince von Schwartzenberg, who had been one of Bonaparte's generals during the Russian campaign. The Generalissimo's proclamation was published in Paris on the evening of March 30. It read:

> For twenty years Europe has been flooded with blood and tears: attempts to put an end to these misfortunes have come to nothing because, at the very heart of the government that oppresses you, there is an insurmountable obstacle to peace. Parisians, you know the situation of your country: the preservation and peace of your city will be the object of the Allies' attention. It is with these sentiments that Europe, in arms before your walls, addresses you.

What a magnificent admission of the grandeur of France: "Europe, in arms before your walls, addresses you!"

We who respected nothing were respected by those whose towns we had ravaged and who, in their turn, had become stronger than we. We appeared to them to be a sacred nation; our lands seemed to them to be an Elis[25] that, the gods decreed, no battalion could trample. If, notwithstanding, Paris had believed it ought to resist, as it quite easily could have, for twenty-four hours, the results would have been different. But no one, except for soldiers intoxicated with fire and honor, wanted any more to do with Bonaparte, and, lest he should stay, the people hastened to open the gates.

Paris capitulated on March 31. The military capitulation was signed by Marshals Mortier and Marmont and Colonels Denys and Fabvier, the civil capitulation by the mayors of Paris. The Municipal and Departmental Council sent a deputation to the Russian headquarters to sort out the various articles. My companion in exile, Christian de Lamoignon, was one of the delegates. Alexander said to them:

"Your Emperor, who called himself my ally, marched into the very heart of my dominions and inflicted evils whose traces will last a long time. It is far from my wish to visit upon France the injuries I have received from her. I am a just man, and I know that the French people are not to blame. The French are my friends, and I want to prove to them that I come to return good for evil. Napoleon is my only enemy. I promise my special protection to the city of Paris. I will respect all its public institutions. I will quarter only select troops within its walls. I will preserve your National Guard, which is composed of the elite of your citizens. It is for you to ensure your future welfare; you must secure for yourself a government that will give peace to France and Europe both. It is for you to manifest your wishes. You will always find me ready to second your efforts."

These words were punctually fulfilled. The joy of victory prevailed over every other interest in the eyes of the Allies. What did Alexander feel when he saw the domes of the buildings of this city no foreigner had ever entered except to admire us, except to revel in the marvels of our civilization and intelligence; of that inviolable city, defended for twelve centuries by its great men; of that capital of glory Louis XIV still seemed to safeguard with his shade, and Bonaparte with his return!

13.
THE ALLIES ENTER PARIS

GOD HAD spoken one of those words that, from time to time, interrupts the silence of eternity. Then the hammer rose, in the midst of the present generation, to strike the hour Paris had only heard tolled once before: on December 25, 496, when Reims announced the baptism of Clovis and the gates of Lutetia opened to the Franks. On March 30, 1814, after the blood baptism of Louis XVI, the old, long-motionless hammer again awakened in the belfry of the ancient monarchy and reverberated a second time. The Tartars invaded Paris. In the intervening 1,318 years, foreigner soldiers had hurled abuse at the walls of the capital, but they had never entered it except when summoned there by our own divisions. The Normans besieged the city of the Parisii, and the Parisii cast off the sparrow hawks they carried on their fist. Eudes, the child of Paris and future king, *rex futurus*, says the monk Abbo, beat back the pirates of the north.[26] In 1814, the Parisians let their eagles go, and the Allies entered the Louvre.

Bonaparte had waged an unjust war against Alexander, his admirer, who had begged on his knees for peace; Bonaparte had ordered the carnage at the Moskva; he had forced the Russians to burn Moscow with their own hands. Bonaparte had pillaged Berlin, humiliated its king, hurled insults at its queen. What reprisals were we, then, to expect? You shall see.

I had wandered in the Floridas around nameless monuments long ago devastated by conquerors of whom no trace remained, and I was kept alive to see the Caucasian hordes camped in the courtyard of the Louvre. When it comes to these historical events that, according to Montaigne, "are meager evidence of our worth and capacity,"[27] my tongue cleaveth to my jaws. *Adhaeret lingua mea faucibus meis.*[28]

The Allied army entered Paris on March 31, 1814, at noon, within ten days of the anniversary of the Duc d'Enghien's death. Was it worth it for Bonaparte to commit an action so long remembered for such a short reign? The Emperor of Russia and the King of Prussia led the troops. I saw them file past on the boulevards. Dumbstruck and destroyed, as if my French name had been taken from me and replaced with the number by which I would thenceforth be known in the mines of Siberia, I felt myself at the same time growing more and more exasperated with the man whose glory had reduced us to this disgrace.

Yet this first invasion by the Allies has remained unparalleled in the annals of the world. Order, peace, and moderation reigned throughout. Shops were reopened; six-foot-tall Russian soldiers were piloted through the streets by tiny French scamps, who laughed at them as they would have laughed at puppets and masks at Carnival. The defeated might have been mistaken for the victors; the latter, trembling at their successes, looked apologetic. The National Guard alone were quartered in the interior of Paris, with the exception of the houses where the foreign kings and princes were lodged. On March 31, 1814, countless armies were occupying France. Within a few months, following the restoration of the Bourbons, all these troops recrossed our frontiers without a single musket being fired or a drop of blood being spilled. The boundaries of old France were extended on some of her frontiers, and she received a share of the ships and magazines of Antwerp. Three hundred thousand French prisoners, scattered about in the countries where victory or defeat had left them, were sent home. After twenty-five years of warfare, the din of battle died out from one end of Europe to the other. Alexander departed, leaving us our masterworks and our liberty, set down in the charter—a liberty we owed to his intelligence as well as to his influence. Chief of two supreme authorities, an autocrat of the sword and the church, Alexander alone, of all the sovereigns of Europe, understood that France had reached an age of civilization at which she could only be governed under a free constitution.

In our very natural enmity toward foreigners, we have confused the invasion of 1814 with the invasion of 1815, which was in no way similar.

Alexander considered himself merely an instrument of Providence and claimed nothing for himself. To Madame de Staël, complimenting him on the good fortune that his subjects, denied a constitution, had to be governed by him, he made his well-known reply:

"I am only a happy accident."

A young man, in the streets of Paris, expressed his admiration for the affability he showed even to the humblest citizens, and Alexander said:

"What else is a sovereign for?"

He did not want to take up residence in the Tuileries Palace, recalling the delight that Bonaparte had taken in the palaces of Vienna, Berlin, and Moscow. Looking up at the statue of Napoleon atop the column in the Place Vendôme, he said:

"If I were up so high, I'd be afraid of getting dizzy."

As he was walking around the Tuileries Palace, he was shown the Salon de la Paix:

"What good was this room to Bonaparte?" he asked, laughing.

The day Louis XVIII entered Paris, Alexander hid behind a window, without any mark of distinction, to watch the procession go by.

He sometimes had elegantly affectionate manners. Visiting a madhouse, he asked one woman if there were very many ladies who had gone "mad from love."

"Not at present," she replied, "but it is to be feared that their numbers may increase now that Your Majesty has arrived in Paris."

One of Napoleon's grand dignitaries said to the czar:

"Your arrival here, Sire, has long been waited and wished for."

"I would have come sooner," he replied, "had French valor not delayed me."

There is no doubt that, when crossing the Rhine, he was sorry not to be able to retire in peace and go live with his family.

At the Hôtel des Invalides, he saw the mutilated soldiers who had beaten him at Austerlitz. They were somber and silent; there was nothing to be heard in their empty courtyards and bare chapels but the sound of their wooden legs. Alexander's sympathy was stirred. He ordered twelve Russian cannon presented to these warriors.

Someone proposed changing the name of the Pont d'Austerlitz:

"No," he said, "that I have passed over the bridge with my army is enough."

There was something gentle and melancholy about Alexander. He used to go around Paris on horseback or on foot with no attendants or pomp. He appeared to be astonished by his triumph; his almost tender gaze wandered over a population he seemed to consider superior to himself. It was as if he felt he was a barbarian in our midst, as a Roman might have felt ashamed in Athens. Perhaps, too, he thought that these soldiers had been in his incinerated capital—that his soldiers in turn were now masters of Paris, where he might have found some of those now-extinguished torches by which Moscow had been liberated and consumed. This destiny, this changing fortune, this misery common to subjects and kings, could not fail to make a deep impression on a mind as religious as his.

14.

BONAPARTE AT FONTAINEBLEAU—THE REGENCY AT BLOIS

BUT WHAT was the victor of Borodino doing? As soon as he heard of Alexander's decision, he had sent orders to Maillard de Lescourt, major of artillery, to blow up the Grenelle powder magazine: Rostopchin had set Moscow alight, but only after he had sent away the inhabitants. From Fontainebleau, where he had retreated, Napoleon advanced toward Villejuif, where he cast a glance at Paris. Foreign soldiers guarded the gates, reminding the conqueror of the days when his grenadiers stood sentry on the ramparts of Berlin, Moscow, and Vienna.

Events obliterate events. How paltry it seems to us today, the anguish of Henri IV at Villejuif, hearing of Gabrielle's death and returning to Fontainebleau! Bonaparte, too, returned to that solitude, where nothing awaited him but the memory of his august prisoner. The peaceful captive had only recently vacated the palace, making way for the captive of war—so promptly does misfortune fill its places.[29]

The regency had withdrawn to Blois. Bonaparte had ordered the Empress and the King of Rome to leave Paris, saying he would rather see them at the bottom of the Seine than brought back to Vienna in triumph; but at the same time he had urged Joseph to stay in the capital. His brother's retreat made him furious, and he accused the ex–king of Spain of having cost him everything. Ministers; members of the regency; Napoleon's brothers, wife, and son all came in a mad rush to Blois, carried away by the debacle. Wagons, bags, carriages—

everything was there. Even the king's coaches arrived and were dragged through the mud from Beauce to Chambord, the only piece of France left to Louis XIV's heir. A few ministers did not stop there and went to hide as far away as Brittany, while Cambacérès lounged in a sedan chair on the steep streets of Blois. Various rumors circulated. There was talk of two camps and a general requisition. For several weeks, no one knew what was happening in Paris, and the uncertainty did not cease until a wagoner arrived whose pass was countersigned *Sacken*.[30] Not long after, the Russian general Shuvalov alighted at the Auberge de la Galère, where he was suddenly besieged by grandees, in a hurry to obtain a visa that would save their necks. Before leaving Blois, however, not one of them failed to draw his traveling expenses and outstanding salary from the regency's funds. In one hand they held their passports and in the other their money, making sure, in the meantime, that their support for the provisional government was clear, for they did not lose their heads. Madame Mère[31] and her brother Cardinal Fesch departed for Rome. Prince Esterhazy went looking for Marie Louise and her son on Francis II's behalf. Joseph and Jérôme withdrew to Switzerland after trying, in vain, to force the Empress to share their fate: Marie Louise was eager to be reunited with her father. Indifferently attached to Bonaparte, she found an opportunity to improve her situation and rejoiced at being freed from the double tyranny of a husband and a master. When, the following year, Bonaparte sent the Bourbons scattering in confusion, the latter, who had only recently been rescued from their long tribulations, had not had fourteen years of unprecedented prosperity to grow accustomed to the comforts of the throne.

15.

PUBLICATION OF MY PAMPHLET, *DE BONAPARTE ET DES BOURBONS*

HOWEVER, Napoleon had not yet been dethroned. More than forty thousand of the best soldiers on earth surrounded him. He could have retreated behind the Loire. The French armies, returning from Spain, were growling in the South. The military population, then seething, might have spewed forth its lava. Even among the military leaders, there was still talk of whether Napoleon or his son ought to rule over France. For two days, Alexander hesitated. M. de Talleyrand was secretly inclined, as I have said, toward the policy that would crown the King of Rome, for he dreaded the Bourbons. If he was not entirely enthusiastic about plans to make Marie Louise regent, this was because Napoleon was still alive and he, the Prince de Bénévent, was afraid he would be unable to maintain control with a minority jeopardized by the existence of a man still restless, unpredictable, enterprising, and in the vigor of his years.*

It was during these critical days that I published my pamphlet *De Bonaparte et des Bourbons* in an effort to tip the scales. Its effect is well known. I flung myself headlong into the fray, serving as renascent liberty's shield against the tyranny that was then still standing and whose power had been tripled by despair. I spoke in the name of the Legitimacy to lend my words the authority of practical politics. I taught France what the old royal family was; I told them how many

*Further on, you will find my account of the Hundred Days in Ghent and my portrait of M. de Talleyrand, toward the end of these *Memoirs*. (Paris, 1839)

members of this family still existed, what their names were, and their character. It was as if I had enumerated the children of the Emperor of China, the Republic and Empire had so completely invaded the present and relegated the Bourbons to the past. Louis XVIII said, as I have already mentioned many times, that my pamphlet was more advantageous than an army of a hundred thousand men. He might also have said that, for him, it was a certificate of existence. I helped to give him the crown a second time through the happy outcome of the war with Spain.

From the beginning of my political career, I became popular with the crowd, but I also failed, from the beginning, to win favor with the powerful. All those who had been slaves under Bonaparte abhorred me. On the other hand, I was suspicious to anyone who wished to enslave France. There was not one sovereign on my side at first except for Bonaparte himself. He browsed through my pamphlet at Fontainebleau; Maret had brought it to him. He discussed it impartially, saying: "This is fair; that is not fair. I have no reason to reproach Chateaubriand; he resisted me when I was still in power. But these scoundrels..." And he named them.

My admiration for Bonaparte has always been great and sincere, even when I was attacking him with all my might.

Posterity is not as fair in its judgments as people tend to think. Distance creates passions, infatuations, and errors just as surely as proximity does. When people admire someone unreservedly in retrospect, they are scandalized to learn that the man's contemporaries did not have the same idea of him that they do. This, however, is easy to explain. The things in the person that caused offense have disappeared; his frailties have died along with him. All that remains is his imperishable life. But the evil he did is no less real—evil in itself and in its essence, and especially for those who endured it.

The tendency today is to magnify Bonaparte's victories. Those who suffered are gone. We no longer hear the curses or the sorrowful and painful cries of the victims. We no longer see France depleted, with only women to till her soil. We no longer see parents arrested as pledges for their sons, or the inhabitants of villages made collectively

514 · MEMOIRS FROM BEYOND THE GRAVE

responsible for the penalties applicable to a single deserter. We no longer see the conscription posters pasted up at street corners, and passersby crowded around those enormous lists of the dead, searching them, in dismay, for the names of their children, brothers, friends, neighbors. We forget that everyone deplored the victories. We forget that even the slightest veiled criticism of Bonaparte at the theater, slipping through the censors' net, sent us into transports. We forget that the people, the Court, the generals, the ministers, even the intimates of Napoleon grew tired of his tyranny and his conquests, weary of that game which was always won yet went on being played, of that existence called into question each morning by the impossibility of remaining at rest.

The reality of our sufferings is demonstrated by the catastrophe itself. If France had been fanatical about Bonaparte, would she have abandoned him twice, abruptly and completely, without making a last effort to keep him? If France owed everything to Bonaparte (glory, liberty, order, prosperity, industry, commerce, manufactories, monuments, literature, the fine arts); if, before him, the nation had done nothing; if the Republic, devoid of genius and courage, had neither defended nor expanded its territory; then France would have been very ungrateful, not to mention cowardly, to let Napoleon fall into the hands of his enemies, or at least not to protest the imprisonment of such a benefactor.

This reproach, which might fairly be made against us, never is—and why not? Because it is plain that, at the time of his fall, France did not want to defend Napoleon. In our bitter disgust, we saw him merely as the author and scorner of our miseries. The Allies did not conquer us; it was we ourselves who, making a choice between two scourges, gave up shedding our blood, which no longer flowed for the sake of our liberties.

The Republic had been cruel, there is no doubt, but every man, woman, and child hoped it would pass, that sooner or later we would recover our rights, retaining the conquests the Revolutionaries had given us on the Alps and the Rhine. All the Republic's victories were won in our name; they were always for France. It was France that triumphed, France that conquered; it was French soldiers who had done it all and for whom triumphal or funeral celebrations were organized. The generals (and there were some very great ones) obtained an honorable but modest place in the people's memories: such were Marceau, Moreau, Hoche, and Joubert—the latter two destined to take the place of Bonaparte, who, in the dawn of his glory, suddenly crossed General Hoche and, in his jealousy, brought fame to that peace-loving warrior who died so abruptly after his victories at Altenkirchen, Neuwied, and Kleinnister.

Under the Empire, we disappeared. We no longer mattered. Everything belonged to Bonaparte: *I* have ordered, *I* have won, *I* have spoken; *my* eagles, *my* crown, *my* blood, *my* family, *my* subjects.

Yet what happened under these two regimes, at once so similar and dissimilar? We did not abandon the Republic in its reversals. It killed us, but it honored us; we did not have the shame of being the property of a man. Thanks to our efforts, the country was not invaded. The Russians, defeated beyond the mountains, met their end in Zurich.[32]

As for Bonaparte, he, despite his enormous acquisitions, succumbed not because he was defeated, but because France no longer wanted him. An important lesson! Let it never be forgotten that there is a germ of death in everything that offends human dignity.

Independent minds of every shade and opinion shared a language at the time my pamphlet was published. Lafayette, Camille Jordan, Ducis, Lemercier, Lanjuinais, Madame de Staël, Chénier, Benjamin Constant, Le Brun thought and wrote as I did.

Lanjuinais said, "We went looking for a master among men whom the Romans didn't want as slaves." Chénier did not treat Bonaparte any more favorably.[33] Nor did Madame de Staël spare Bonaparte her rigorous judgment:

> Would it not be a great lesson for the human race if these directors (the five members of the Directory), very unwarlike men, got up, dusted themselves off, and held Napoleon accountable for the barrier of the Rhine and the Alps, conquered by the Republic; for the foreigners who have twice entered Paris; for

the three million Frenchmen who perished from Cádiz to Moscow; above all, for the sympathy the nations used to feel for the cause of liberty in France, which has now changed into inveterate aversion?

(*Considérations sur la Révolution française*)

Let us listen also to Benjamin Constant:

He who, for twelve years, said he was destined to conquer the world, has eaten crow... Even before his territory was invaded, he was overcome by an apprehension he could not conceal. As soon as the enemy reached his borders, he threw all his conquests away. He demanded the abdication of one of his brothers and sanctioned the expulsion of another. Without being asked, he declared he would give up everything.

If kings, even when vanquished, do not abjure their dignity, why should the conqueror of the earth yield at the first setback? His family's cries, he tells us, rend his heart. Were the people who died in Russia in the triple agony of injury, cold, and famine not of the same family? But while they breathed their last, deserted by their leader, this leader thought himself safe. Now that he is in danger, too, he is suddenly sensitive.

Fear is a bad counselor, especially for those without a conscience. In adversity, as in good fortune, there is measure only in morality. Where morality does not rule, good fortune descends into folly, adversity into degradation...

What effect must this blind fear, this sudden faintheartedness, still unexampled amidst all our storms, have on a brave nation? The nation in its pride found (wrongly) a certain reward in being oppressed only by an invincible leader. Today what is left? No more prestige, no more triumphs, a mutilated empire, the world's execration, a throne whose pomp is tarnished, whose trophies have been cast down, and whose only entourage consists of the wandering shades of the Duc d'Enghien, Pichegru, and so many others slaughtered to establish it.[34]

Did I go so far as this in *De Bonaparte and des Bourbons*? Don't the proclamations of the authorities in 1814—which I will soon reproduce—repeat, ratify, and confirm these various opinions? That the authorities who express them may have been sheepish and degraded by their early adulation does take something away from the writers of these words, but it does not weaken the strength of their arguments.

I could multiply quotations, but I shall only recall two, because of the opinions of the two men. If you wonder whether Béranger, that constant and admirable admirer of Bonaparte, thought he should excuse his behavior, witness these words:

"My enthusiastic and unfailing admiration for the emperor's genius, my idolatry, never blinded me to the despotism ever growing in the Empire."

Paul-Louis Courier, speaking of Napoleon's accession to the throne, said:

"Tell me, what does it mean, for a man like him, Bonaparte, a soldier, the leader of an army, the premier general in the world, to want to be called His Majesty! To be Bonaparte and to be called *Sire*! He aspires to descend: but no, he believes he is ascending by making himself the equal of kings. He prefers a title to a name. Poor man, his ideas don't rise to the level of his destiny. Caesar understood much better and was another kind of man altogether: he would not take any antiquated titles but made his own name a title superior to that of 'king.'"[35]

Living talents have taken the same independent route: M. de Lamartine on the tribune, M. de Latouche in retirement, and, in two or three of his finest odes, M. Victor Hugo, who has prolonged these noble accents:

> *Dans la nuit des forfaits, dans l'éclat des victoires,*
> *Cet homme ignorant Dieu, qui l'avait envoyé.*[36]

Abroad, the judgment of Europe was just as severe. I shall mention only the feelings of Englishmen of the opposition, who accommodated themselves to everything in our Revolution and justified it in all regards: read Mackintosh in his defense of Peltier.[37] Sheridan,[38] on the occasion of the Treaty of Amiens, said to Parliament:

"Every man feels when he returns from France that he is coming from a dungeon to enjoy the light and life of British independence."

Lord Byron, in his "Ode to Napoleon," treats him in the most appropriate manner:

> 'Tis done—but yesterday a King!
>   And arm'd with Kings to strive—
> And now thou art a nameless thing:
>   So abject—yet alive!

The whole ode is made of the same stuff; each stanza goes one better than the last. Not that this prevented Lord Byron celebrating the tomb on Saint Helena. Poets are birds: every noise makes them sing.

When the best and most diverse minds agree in their judgment, no admiration, however false or sincere, no arrangement of facts, no system imagined post hoc, can possibly nullify the sentence passed. A man could, like Napoleon, replace the law with his will, persecute all independent life, take joy in disgracing people, upsetting their lives, doing violence to private mores as well as public freedoms—and all unselfish protests against these enormities would be declared slanderous and blasphemous! Who would want to defend the cause of the weak against the strong, if courage, exposed to the vengeance of the vilities of the present, still had to await the blame of the cowardice of the future?

This illustrious minority, formed in part of the children of the Muses, gradually becomes the national majority. By the end of the Empire, everyone detested imperial despotism. One very serious reproach will be attached to Bonaparte's memory: he rendered his yoke so heavy that our hostile feelings toward the foreigner weakened, and an invasion, though deplorable today in memory, seemed, at the moment it occurred, something of a deliverance. This was in fact the opinion of the Republicans, enunciated by my ill-fated and brave friend Carrel. "The return of the Bourbons," Carnot had said in his turn, "produced universal enthusiasm in France. They were received with inexpressible transports of joy, and former Republicans shared sincerely in the general jubilation. Napoleon had oppressed them all so much, every class of society had suffered so much, there was really no one who didn't feel exultant."

The only thing these sanctions lack is an authority to confirm them: Bonaparte undertook to certify their truth. When taking leave of his soldiers in the courtyard of Fontainebleau, he admitted France wanted nothing more to do with him. "France herself," he said, "has chosen other destinies." A memorable and unexpected confession, whose weight and value should not be diminished.

God, in His patient eternity, sooner or later brings justice to bear. In those moments when Heaven appears to sleep, it is a fine thing that honest men look on with disapproval, for this disapproval remains as a rein on absolute power. May France never repudiate the noble souls who cried out against her servitude when all were prostrate, when there were so many advantages to remaining prostrate, so many graces to receive in exchange for flattery, so many persecutions to reap for sincerities sown. Honor, then, to Lafayette, de Staël, Benjamin Constant, Camille Jordan, Ducis, Lemercier, Lanjuinais, and Chénier, who, standing up in the midst of a creeping crowd of subjects and kings, dared to despise victory and protest tyranny!

16.

THE SENATE RENDERS THE DECREE OF HIS DEMISE

Revised February 22, 1845

ON APRIL 2, the senators, to whom we owe only one article of the Charter of 1814 (the ignoble article that allowed them to retain their pensions), decreed Bonaparte's demise. If this decree, which liberated France and dishonored those who rendered it, was an affront to the human race, it also teaches posterity the price that majesty and fortune must pay if they do not deign to sit on the foundations of morality, justice, and liberty.

DECREE OF THE SÉNAT CONSERVATEUR

The Sénat conservateur, considering that, in a constitutional monarchy, the monarch exists only in virtue of the constitution, or the social contract, finds:

That Napoleon Bonaparte after governing for some time with prudence and wisdom had violated the constitution by raising taxes in an arbitrary and lawless manner contrary to his oath.

That he had needlessly adjourned the Corps Législatif and suppressed a report of that assembly as well as disowning its right to represent the people.

That he had published several unconstitutional decrees, particularly those of March 5, 1813, by which he endeavored to render national a war in the interest of his inordinate ambition.

That he had violated the constitution by his decrees respecting state prisons.

That he had abolished the responsibility of judicial authorities.

That the freedom of the press, constituting one of the rights of the nation, had been constantly subjected to the arbitrary censorship of his police, while he himself had simultaneously made use of the same engine to fill the public ear with fabricated facts and false maxims, doctrines favorable to despotism, and insults heaped upon foreign governments.

That he had caused acts and reports, adopted by the Senate, to be altered by his own authority prior to publication.

That instead of reigning, according to his oath, for the honor, happiness, and glory of the French nation, he had put the finishing stroke to the distresses of the country, by a refusal to treat on honorable conditions; by his abuse of the means entrusted to him in men and money; by his abandonment of the wounded, without dressing or sustenance; and by his pursuance of measures whose consequences have been the ruin of towns, the depopulation of the country, famine, and pestilence.

From all these inductive causes, the Senate, considering that the imperial government, established by the decree of Floréal 28, in the year XII, has ceased to exist, and that the manifest desire of all Frenchmen is to obtain a political order whose first result should be peace and concord among the great members of the European family; therefore, the Senate declares and decrees the following: *Napoleon Bonaparte has forfeited the throne and the right of inheritance established in his family; the people and army of France are disengaged and freed from the oath of fidelity that they took to Napolon and his constitution.*

The Roman Senate was less severe when it declared Nero a public enemy: history is merely a repetition of the same facts applied to different men at different times.

How are we to imagine the emperor reading the official document at Fontainebleau? What must he have thought of his actions and of the men who had called him to account for oppressing our freedoms?

522 · MEMOIRS FROM BEYOND THE GRAVE

Could I, when I published my pamphlet, have guessed I would see it developed and converted into a decree issued by the Senate? What prevented these legislators, in times of prosperity, from seeing the evils they attributed to Bonaparte or from perceiving that the Constitution had been violated? How was it these mutes suddenly became so zealous about freedom of the press? How was it those who had heaped praise on Napoleon whenever he came back from one of his wars now found he had undertaken these campaigns "in the interest of his inordinate ambition"? How was it those who had let so many conscripts be devoured by him were suddenly moved by the wounded soldiers abandoned "without dressing or sustenance"? There are times when contempt must be frugally dispensed, considering the large number of people in need of it: I take pity on them for the moment, because they will be in need of it again during and after the Hundred Days.

When I asked what Napoleon at Fontainebleau thought of the Senate's acts, his answer was given: an order of the day for April 5, 1814, not officially published, but collected in several newspapers outside the capital, thanked the army for its loyalty, adding:

"The Senate has taken it upon itself to dispose of the French government. It has forgotten it is indebted to the emperor for the power it now abuses; that the emperor has rescued some of its members from the storms of the revolution and drawn others out of obscurity or protected them from the odium of the nation. The Senate relies on the articles of the Constitution to overthrow it. It does not blush when it reproaches the emperor, without considering that, as the highest political body of the state, it has had a hand in every event it describes. Nor does it blush when it speaks of libels published against foreign governments, apparently forgetting that they were written in its midst. So long as fortune remained faithful to their sovereign, these men remained faithful, and no complaints were heard about the abuse of power. If the emperor had felt the contempt for men he has been accused of feeling, the world would now have to acknowledge that he has had reasons for this contempt."

It is a homage paid by Bonaparte himself to the freedom of the press: he must have believed it had something good about it, since it offered him one last refuge and resort.

And I, who am struggling against time; I, who am striving to hold it accountable for what it has witnessed; I, who am writing this so far removed from these bygone events, under the reign of Philippe, the counterfeit heir to a mighty legacy—what am I in the hands of Time, that great devourer of ages I thought unchangeable, of that Time which makes me pirouette with it through space?

17.

HÔTEL DE SAINT-FLORENTIN—M. DE TALLEYRAND

ALEXANDER had settled at M. de Talleyrand's house. I was not present at the confabulations. One can read about them in the accounts of Abbé de Pradt and the various sharkers who held, in their foul little hands, the fate of one of the greatest men in the history and destiny of the world. I counted for nothing in politics, except among the people; there was no menial schemer less empowered or favored than I. A future man of the possible Restoration, I waited beneath the windows, in the street.

Through the machinations at the Hôtel de Saint-Florentin, the Sénat conservateur appointed a provisional government composed of General Bournonville, Senator Jaucourt, the Duc de Dalberg, Abbé de Montesquiou, and Dupont de Nemours. The Prince de Bénévent took possession of the presidency.

Encountering this name for the first time, I had planned to speak of this character who played such a remarkable part in the affairs of the day; but I shall save his portrait for the end of my *Memoirs*.

The intrigue that detained M. de Talleyrand in Paris, at the time of the Allies' invasion, was the reason he was so well favored at the start of the Restoration. The Emperor of Russia was familiar with him because he had seen him at Tilsit, and in the absence of French authorities, Alexander settled at the Hôtel de l'Infantando,[39] which the master of the house was quick to offer him.

From that moment forward, M. de Talleyrand seemed to be the arbiter of the world; his parlors became centers of negotiation. Putting together the provisional government as he pleased, he found places for his partners at whist: the Abbé de Montesquiou only figured there as a claim to legitimacy.

The first acts of the Restoration were entrusted to the barren Bishop of Autun. He infected this Restoration with sterility and passed on to it a germ of dishonor and death.

18.

ADDRESSES OF THE PROVISIONAL GOVERNMENT—CONSTITUTION PROPOSED BY THE SENATE

THE FIRST acts of the provisional government, placed under the dictatorship of its president, were proclamations addressed to the soldiers and to the people.

"Soldiers," they said, "France has just broken the yoke beneath which she has been groaning with you for so many years. Think of all you have suffered from tyranny. Soldiers, it is time to put an end to your country's ills. You are her noblest children; you cannot belong to the man who has ravaged her, who has tried to make your name odious to all the nations, who has perhaps compromised your glory if a man who IS NOT EVEN FRENCH could ever diminish the honor of our arms and the magnanimity of our soldiers."

Thus, in the eyes of the most servile slaves, the man who won so many victories is no longer "even French"! When, in the days of the League, Du Bourg ceded the Bastille to Henri IV, he refused to remove the black sash[40] and take the money offered him for the place's surrender. Asked to recognize the king, he replied that the man was doubtless a very good prince, but as for him, he had pledged his loyalty to M. de Mayenne. Besides, he added, Brissac was a traitor. To second what he said, he swore he would fight him to the death between four pikes, in the presence of the king, and eat his heart out of his chest.[41] What a difference there is between times and men!

On April 4, a new address from the provisional government to the French people was published:

Emerging from your civil discords, you chose as your leader a man who appeared on the world's stage with all the characteristics of greatness. But on anarchy's ruins, all he established was despotism. He should at least, *out of gratitude, have become French* with you: *he never was.* He has ceaselessly, pointlessly, and unreasonably waged unjust wars like a swaggerer seeking fame. He went on dreaming of extravagant plans even when unprecedented reversals so spectacularly punished the pride and abuse of victory. He did not know how to reign either in the nation's interest nor, for that matter, in the interest of his own despotism. He destroyed everything he wished to create and recreated everything he wished to destroy. All he believed in was force, and now force overwhelms him—a just return for such insane ambition.

These are incontestable truths and merited maledictions; but who was responsible for these maledictions? What had become of my poor little pamphlet, tucked out of sight between these virulent addresses? Had it disappeared completely? The same day, April 4, the provisional government outlawed the signs and emblems of the imperial government. If the Arc de Triomphe had existed, they would have torn it down. Mailhes, who cast the first vote for the death of Louis XVI, and Cambacérès, who was the first to call Napoleon by the name Emperor, eagerly recognized the acts of the provisional government.

On the 6th, the Senate drafted a hasty constitution, built on very nearly the same foundations as the Charter to come. The Senate was preserved as an upper house, the honor of being a senator was declared irremovable and hereditary, and majorats[42] were attached to the endowment of the senatorship. The constitution rendered these titles and majorats transmissible to the descendants of the possessor. Fortunately, these ignoble legacies called down the Parcae, as the ancients would say.[43]

The sordid effrontery of these senators who, in the midst of an invasion, did not lose sight of themselves for a moment is striking even considering the immensity of public events.

Wouldn't it have been more convenient for the Bourbons to adopt the established government, a mute Corps Législatif, and a secret, servile Senate? On reflection, we find the thing impossible. Natural liberties, righting themselves in the absence of the arm that bent them low, would have resumed their verticality under such meager pressure. If the legitimate princes had dismissed Bonaparte's army, as they should have done (this was Napoleon's own opinion on the isle of Elba), and if, at the same time, they had retained the imperial government, it would have been too much for them to break the instrument of glory and preserve only the instrument of tyranny. The Charter was Louis XVIII's ransom.

19.

THE COMTE D'ARTOIS ARRIVES—BONAPARTE'S ABDICATION AT FONTAINEBLEAU

ON APRIL 12, the Comte d'Artois arrived as lieutenant general of the kingdom. Three or four hundred men on horseback went to meet him. I was among their number. He was charming, with his elegant manners—so different from those of the Empire. In his person the French were pleased to recognize their bygone customs, courtesy, and language. The crowd surrounded and pressed at him: a consoling apparition from the past, and a double shield against the victorious foreign forces and Bonaparte, who remained a threat. Alas! This prince had barely set foot back on French soil before he had to witness the murder of his son and go die in the land of exile he had left. There are some men who have had life thrown around their necks like a chain.

I was presented to the king's brother. Someone must have urged him to read my pamphlet, for otherwise he would not have known my name. He would not recall seeing me either in the Court of Louis XVI or in the camp at Thionville, and probably he had never heard a word about *The Genius of Christianity*. It is quite simple really. When a person has suffered much and long, he no longer remembers anything except himself. Personal misfortune is a rather chilly companion, but she is demanding; she obsesses you; she leaves you no time for any other feeling, never leaves you, takes possession of your lap and your bed.

The day before the Comte d'Artois arrived, Napoleon, after pointlessly negotiating with Alexander through M. de Caulaincourt, had published the deed of his abdication:

The Allied powers having proclaimed that the emperor Napoleon was the sole obstacle to the restoration of peace in Europe, the emperor Napoleon, loyal to his pledge, declares that he renounces for himself and his heirs the throne of France and Italy, for there is no personal sacrifice, even that of his life, that he is not prepared to make in the interest of the French.

To these dazzling words, the emperor does not hesitate to give, by dint of his return, a no less dazzling refutation. All he needed was the time to go to Elba. He remained in Fontainebleau until April 20.

When April 20 came, Napoleon descended the horseshoe staircase that led to the peristyle of the empty palace of the Capet monarchy. A few grenadiers—what remained of the conquering soldiers of Europe—formed a line in the big courtyard, as though standing on their final battlefield. They were surrounded on every side by old trees, the mutilated companions of François I and Henri IV. Bonaparte addressed these words to the last witnesses of his battles:

Generals, officers, sub-officers, and soldiers of my Old Guard, I bid you farewell. For twenty years I have been well content with you; I have found you always on the road to glory.

The Allied powers have armed all of Europe against me. A portion of the army has betrayed its duties, and *France herself has chosen other destinies.*

With you and the brave men who have remained loyal to me, I might have kept up a civil war for three years; but France would have been unhappy, which is contrary to the purpose I set for myself.

Be faithful to the new king France has selected. Do not abandon our dear country, which has been unhappy too long! Love her always, love her well, this dear country.

Do not pity me for my lot; I shall be happy if I know that you are happy.

I might have died; nothing would have been easier for me;

but I shall never cease to follow the path of honor. I still have to write what we have done.

Since I cannot embrace you all, I will embrace your general ... Come, General ...

(He clasps General Petit in his arms.)

Bring me the eagle!

(He kisses it).

Dear eagle! May these kisses resound forever in the hearts of all my warriors! Farewell, my children! My prayers will always be with you. Do not forget me.

Having said this, Napoleon struck his tent, which covered the world.

20.

NAPOLEON'S JOURNEY TO ELBA

BONAPARTE had asked the Allies for commissioners to guard him as he made his way to the island that the sovereigns had granted him in fee simple as an advance on his inheritance. Count Shuvalov was appointed for Russia, General Kohler for Austria, Colonel Campbell for England, and Count Waldburg-Truchsess for Prussia. The latter wrote *Napoleon's Journey from Fontainebleau to the Isle of Elba*. This pamphlet and that of Abbé de Pradt on the Polish Embassy are the two accounts that most distressed Napoleon. He then mourned, no doubt, for the days of his liberal censorship, when he had poor Palm, a German bookseller, shot for distributing von Gentz's pamphlet in Nuremberg: *Germany in Its Deep Debasement*. Nuremberg, when this piece of writing was published, was still a free city and did not belong to France. But shouldn't Palm have guessed this conquest was coming?

Count Waldburg first gives an account of several conversations that preceded the departure from Fontainebleau. He reports that Bonaparte praised Wellington to the skies and inquired about his character and habits; he apologized for not having made peace in Prague, Dresden, and Frankfurt; he agreed he was in the wrong, but he also had other views. "I was no usurper," he said. "I did not accept the crown except in compliance with the unanimous wish of the whole nation, while Louis XVIII *has* usurped it, since he has been called to the throne only by a lowly Senate, more than ten members of which voted for the death of Louis XVI."

Count Waldburg continues his narrative as follows:

The emperor set out with his four other carriages on the twenty-first, about noon, following a long conversation with General Kohler, which may be summarized thus: "Well! Yesterday you heard my speech to the Old Guard; you liked it, and you saw the effect it produced. This is the way a man must speak and act with them, and if Louis XVIII does not follow this example, he will never be able to do anything with French soldiers."...

As soon as the French troops were gone, the cries of "Long live the Emperor!" ceased. Already in Moulins we saw the first white cockades, and the inhabitants greeted us with "Long live the Allies!" In Lyons, which we passed through at about eleven o'clock at night, a few people gathered to receive the emperor with "Long live the Emperor!" As Napoleon had expressed a wish to be escorted by an English frigate to the isle of Elba, Colonel Campbell left us at Lyons for the purpose of procuring one, either from Toulon or Marseille. About midday on the twenty-fourth, near Valence, Napoleon met Marshal Augereau. Both stepped down from their carriages. The emperor took off his hat and reached out his hand to the marshal, who took the hand, but did not salute him. The emperor, as he asked him, "Where are you going? To Court?" took the marshal's arm. Augereau replied that for the moment he was only going as far as Lyon. They walked together for a quarter of a league on the road toward Valence, and the emperor reproached the marshal for his conduct toward him, saying: "Your proclamation is very silly; why insult me? You should simply have said that since the nation had declared itself in favor of a new sovereign, the army's sworn duty was to comply. Long live the king! Long live Louis XVIII!" Augereau, speaking as informally as the emperor had spoken to him, bitterly reproached him for his insatiable ambition, to which he had sacrificed everything, even the happiness of France. Suddenly tired of this conversation, Napoleon turned toward the marshal, embraced him, doffed his hat to him a second time, and climbed into his carriage.

Augereau, who stood with his hands clasped behind his back, did not remove his cap from his head, and as the emperor was already in the carriage, only lifted one hand to give him a contemptuous wave farewell . . .

On the twenty-fifth, we arrived at Orange and were received with cries of "Long live the king! Long live Louis XVIII!"

The same morning, close to Avignon, where we were scheduled to change horses, the emperor met with a throng of people shouting "Long live the king! Long live the Allies! Down with the tyrant, the imp, the lowly beggar!" and still coarser abuse.

We did everything in our power to put a stop to this scandal and to divide the crowd attacking his carriage, but we could not stop these fanatics from venting their indignation against the man who, they said, had made them so unhappy, and who only wished to make them more miserable still . . .

In all the places we passed through, he was received in the same manner. In Orgon, a small village where we next changed horses, the behavior of the populace was most outrageous. Just in front of the inn where the horses were taken out, a gallows had been erected, on which a figure in French uniform covered with blood was suspended. On its breast was pinned a paper with this inscription: *Such will be the fate of the tyrant, sooner or later.*

The people clung to Napoleon's carriage on both sides, trying to catch sight of him and hurl their strongest abuses at his face. The Emperor hid in a corner, behind General Bertrand; he looked pale and haggard and did not say a word. Only by addressing the people were we were able to get him out of this mess.

Standing by Bonaparte's carriage, Count Shuvalov harangued the populace in these terms: "Aren't you ashamed to be insulting a poor defenseless soul? He is humiliated enough by the miserable situation in which he finds himself—this man who imagined himself dictating laws to the universe and who is now at the mercy of your generosity! Leave him alone; look at him: you see that contempt is the only weapon you need to use against this man. He is no longer dangerous. It would be below the dignity of the nation of France to take revenge on him any further!" The people applauded this speech, and Bonaparte, seeing the effect it produced, made gestures of approval to Shuvalov, thanking him afterward for the service he had rendered him.

A quarter of a league below Orgon, Napoleon thought it essential to take the precaution of disguising himself. He put on an old blue greatcoat, a round hat with a white cockade, and mounted a post-horse to gallop before his carriage, wanting to pass himself off as a courier. As we could not accompany him, we arrived in Saint-Cannat a long time after him. Not knowing the precautions he had taken to elude the populace, we thought him in the greatest danger, for we saw his carriage surrounded by furious people attempting to open the doors. These were fortunately locked, which saved General Bertrand's life. The tenacity of the women astonished us most; they begged us to hand him over to them, saying: "But he deserves it, considering all the wrongs he's done by us, all we are asking is for you to do the right thing."

Half a league from Saint-Cannat, we caught up with the emperor's carriage, which, soon after, pulled into a miserable roadside tavern called La Calade. We followed him in there, and only at this juncture were we made aware of the emperor's self-made disguise. He had entered the tavern thanks to this bizarre outfit, accompanied by a single courrier. His entourage, from the general to the kitchen boy, were bedecked with white cockades, which they seemed to have procured in advance. His valet de chambre, who met us at the door, implored us to call the emperor "Colonel Campbell," since that is how he had introduced himself to the hostess. We promised to conform to this desire, and I went first into a small sort of room where I was amazed to find the former ruler of the world plunged in deep reflections, with his head in his hands. I didn't recognize him at first and walked over to him. He stood up with a start at the sound of my footsteps, and I could see his face was wet with tears. He motioned for me not to say anything, had me sit down beside him, and while the hostess was in the room spoke to me only of inconsequential matters. But the moment she went out, he resumed his earlier posture. I thought it best to leave him alone; however, he made us promise to go into the room from time to time so as not to raise suspicions about his being there.

We let him know that everyone was aware that Colonel Campbell had passed through this place the day before, on his way to Toulon. He immediately resolved to take the name of Lord Burghers.

We sat down to dine; but as the dinner had not been prepared by his cooks, he could not bring himself to eat it for fear of being poisoned. Yet, seeing us eat with good appetite, he was ashamed to let us know how terrified he was and so took everything offered to him. He pretended to taste it, but returned it without so much as touching it. Sometimes he dropped the food he had taken under the table to make it appear he had eaten it. In the end, all he had for dinner was a little bit of bread and a small bottle of wine he had retrieved from his carriage and went so far as to share with us.

He talked incessantly and was remarkably friendly. When we were alone and the hostess who served us was gone, he told us he believed his life was in danger. He was convinced the French government had taken measures to have him abducted or assassinated in this place.

He had thought of a thousand plans for how to save himself. He had also imagined ways of fooling the people of Aix, for we had already been warned that a very large crowd was waiting at the post office. He told us that, in his view, the best thing to do would be to go all the way back to Lyon and take another route; he could then board a ship in Italy. We could not, in any event, consent to this plan and tried to persuade him to go directly to Toulon, or via Digne to Fréjus. We endeavored to convince him it was impossible the French government could have such perfidious intentions without our knowledge and that the populace, despite the great impropriety they allowed themselves, would not commit a criminal act of the kind he described.

In an effort to make us see his point of view—and to demonstrate how well his fears were founded—he told us what had transpired between him and the hostess, who had not recognized him.

"Well!" she had said to him, "have you seen Bonaparte?"

"No," he had replied.

"I am curious," she continued, "to see if he can make it out alive. I still think the people are going to kill him. Of course, you must admit that devil deserves it! Tell me, though, are they really going to put him on a boat and send him out to his own island?"

"Indeed."

"Oh, won't they drown him then?"

"I surely hope so!" said Napoleon.

"So you see," he told us at table, "the dangers I am facing."

Then he began to weary us with his worries and indecision all over again. He even entreated us to look around and see if we could find a secret door through which he could escape, or if the window, whose shutters he had closed the moment he set foot inside the tavern, was too tall for him to jump out and flee.

The window, however, was covered with a metal grate, and I felt very awkward communicating this discovery to him. He would start and change color at the drop of a pin.

After dinner was over, we left him to his thoughts, and whenever, according to his wishes, we went into his room, we always found him in tears...

General Shuvalov's aide-de-camp came to say that most of the people in the street had dispersed. The emperor decided to leave at midnight.

Being outrageously cautious, he assumed yet another disguise.

He forced General Shuvalov's aide-de-camp to put on the blue greatcoat and round hat he had been wearing when he entered the tavern.

Bonaparte, who now wished to pass himself off as an Austrian general, dressed in General Kohler's uniform, pinned himself with the Order of Saint Theresa which the general wore, put my traveling cap on his head, and threw General Shuvalov's cloak over his shoulders.

After the Allies had thus equipped him, the carriages drove up; but before going out, we rehearsed, in our room, the order in which we were supposed to walk. The procession was headed by General Drouot, followed by the impostor Emperor, General Shuvalov's aide-de-camp, General Kohler, the emperor, General Shuvalov, and me: I

538 · MEMOIRS FROM BEYOND THE GRAVE

had the honor of forming the rear guard, which would be immediately followed by the rest of the imperial entourage.

So it was we passed through the astonished crowd, who vainly tried to identify *their tyrant* among us.

Shuvalov's aide-de-camp (Major Olevieff) took Napoleon's seat in his carriage and Napoleon set off with General Kohler in his calash . . .

Yet the emperor was still not reassured. He remained in the Austrian general's calash and ordered the driver to smoke, thinking this familiarity might conceal his presence. He even asked General Kohler to sing, and when the general told him he did not know how to sing, Bonaparte told him to whistle.

Thus he went on his way, hidden in the depths of a calash, pretending to be asleep, lulled by the general's pleasant whistling and shrouded in the driver's smoke.

In Saint-Maximin, he lunched with us. Having learned that the sub-prefect of Aix was there, he sent for him and gave him a speech: "You ought to be embarrassed to see me in an Austrian uniform. I have had to put it on to protect myself from the abuses of the Provençals. I came into your midst in good faith when I might have brought six thousand Guardsmen, and I've found nothing here but a pack of madmen threatening my life. The Provençals are a wicked race: they committed all sorts of horrors and crimes during the Revolution and are quite ready to start up again anytime. But when it comes to fighting with valor, they are cowards. I've never been satisfied with a single regiment from Provence—not in any of my armies. Probably they'll be as dead set against Louis XVIII tomorrow as they appear to be against me today," and so on.

Then, turning to us, he said that Louis XVIII would never be able to do anything with the nation of France if he treated us with too much restraint. "He is going to have to raise considerable taxes," he said, "and those measures will make his subjects hate him immediately."

He told us that it had been eighteen years since he had been sent to this part of the country, with several thousand men, to liberate two royalists sentenced to be hanged for wearing the white cockade. "It was no easy thing prying them out of the hands of those madmen. And today," he continued, "these same men would inflict the same abuses on anyone who *refused* to wear the white cockade! Such is the inconstancy of the French people!"

We learned there were two squadrons of Austrian hussars in Le Luc and, at Napoleon's request, sent orders to the commandant to await our arrival there so that they might escort the emperor to Fréjus.

———

Here Count von Waldburg's account comes to an end. These stories are painful to read. What! Could the commissioners not offer better protection to the man they had the honor to serve? Who were they to affect such superior airs with such a person? Bonaparte rightly says that, if he had wished to do so, he could have traveled with a part of his Guard. It is obvious that the men around him were indifferent to his fate. They enjoyed his degradation, and they were all too pleased to consent to the marks of contempt necessary to keep him safe. It is so *sweet* to trample beneath one's feet the destiny of a man who marched over the loftiest heads—to avenge pride with insults! This is why the commissioners don't say a word (not even a word of abstract compassion) about such a reversal of fortune to admonish mankind of his nothingness and the greatness of God's judgments! In the Allied ranks, Napoleon had found no shortage of grovelers. When one has gone on his knees before brute force, he has no right to hold himself above misfortune. I grant you that Prussia had need of an effort of virtue to forget what she had suffered—she, her king, and her queen. But this effort should have been made. Alas, Bonaparte had taken pity on no one, and now everyone's heart was hardened against him. The moment he showed himself cruelest was in Jaffa—but he was smallest on the way to Elba. In the first case, military necessity served as his excuse; in the second, the callousness of the foreign commissioners changes the feelings of the reader and diminishes his disgrace.

The provisional government of France itself does not seem to me entirely beyond reproach. I reject Maubreuil's slanderous claims.[44] Nevertheless, in the terror Napoleon still inspired in his former servants, a fortuitous catastrophe might have appeared to them merely an unfortunate incident.

One would like to doubt the truth of the facts reported by Count von Waldburg-Truchsess, but General Kohler has confirmed, in a sequel to the Waldburg itinerary, much of his colleague's narrative. General Shuvalov, for his part, also lends credence to the accuracy of these facts: his restrained language said much more than Waldburg's effusions. Finally, Fabry's *Itinerary* is based on authentic French documents, provided by eyewitnesses.

Now that we have done justice to the commissioners and the Allies, we must ask: Is this really the conqueror of the world we see in Waldburg's *Journey*? The hero reduced to disguises and tears, weeping in a courier's jacket in the back room of a tavern? Was it thus that Marius stood upon the ruins of Carthage, or that Hannibal died in Bithynia or Caesar in the Senate? What disguises did Pompey wear? Did he cover his head with his toga? He who had donned the purple took cover beneath the white cockade, shouting "Long live the king!"— the same king whose heir he had shot! The master of the earth encouraged the humiliations that the commissioners lavished on him to keep his identity hidden: he bid General Kohler to whistle and the coachman to blow smoke in his face; he forced Shuvalov's aide-de-camp to play the part of the emperor while he himself shouldered the clothes of an Austrial colonel and draped himself in a Russian cloak! The love of life is cruel indeed. Such immortals cannot consent to die.

Moreau said of Bonaparte, "His defining characteristics are a love of lying and a love of life: I will beat him and see him begging for mercy at my feet." This is what Moreau believed, because he could not comprehend Bonaparte's nature. In this regard, he fell into the same error as Lord Byron. At least on Saint Helena, Napoleon—made large by the Muses, though not very noble in his quarrels with the English governor—had to bear only the weight of his immensity. In France, the harm he had done appeared to him personified in widows and orphans, and compelled him to tremble at the thought of what a few women might do to him.

All this is true. But Bonaparte cannot be judged according to the rules we apply to the great geniuses, for he lacked magnanimity. There are men who are very good at ascending and very bad at descending. Napoleon was very good at both things. Like the rebel angel, he could shrink his immeasurable mass down and fit himself into a measurable space; his ductility permitted him both salvation and rebirth. With him, when everything seemed finished, it was not finished. Changing his manners and costume at will, flawless in comedy and tragedy alike, he was an actor who could look natural under the tunic of a slave or the mantle of a king, in the role of Attila or Caesar. In another moment or two, you shall see the dwarf, coming up from the depths of degradation, rear his Briarean head; Asmodeus shall emerge in a storm of smoke from the bottle into which he had squeezed himself.[45] Napoleon judged life according to how much it brought him. He had an instinct for what still remained to be painted. He did not want to run out of canvas before he had finished his pictures.

As for Napoleon's fear, Walter Scott, who is fairer to him than the commissioners, candidly remarks that the people's fury made an enormous impression on Bonaparte, that he shed tears and showed more frailty than seemed consistent with his approved courage; but, he adds, "the danger was of a new and peculiarly horrible description, and calculated to appal many to whom the terrors of a field of battle were familiar. The bravest soldier might shudder at a death like that of the de Witts."[46]

Napoleon was subjected to these Revolutionary distresses in the same places where he began his career with the Terror.

The Prussian general, interrupting his narrative, thought himself obliged to reveal a weakness that the emperor did not hide: Count Waldburg may have confused what he saw with the sufferings Ségur witnessed during the Russian campaign, when Bonaparte, forced to dismount, went and rested his head against the cannon. Among the weaknesses of famous warriors, true history only counts the dagger that pierced the heart of Henri IV or the gunshot that killed Turenne.

After recounting Bonaparte's arrival in Fréjus, Walter Scott, finished with the great scenes, happily relapses into his particular brilliance. He chatters away "like a magpie," as Madame de Sévigné says. He jaws on about Napoleon's voyage to Elba and the charm he exercised over the English sailors, except for one Hinton, "who could never hear the emperor's praises without muttering the vulgar but expressive phrase *Humbug.*" When Napoleon disembarked, Hinton wished "His Honor" good health and best wishes once more. Napoleon was, in one person, all things great and miserable in man.

21.

LOUIS XVIII AT COMPIÈGNE—HIS ENTRY INTO PARIS—THE OLD GUARD—IRREPARABLE ERROR—DECLARATION OF SAINT-OUEN—TREATY OF PARIS—THE CHARTER—DEPARTURE OF THE ALLIES

WHILE Bonaparte, whom the whole world knew, escaped from France under a rain of curses, Louis XVIII, whom all had forgotten, left London under a vault of white flags and crowns. Napoleon, disembarking on the isle of Elba, recovered his strength. Louis XVIII, disembarking at Calais, might have seen Louvel.[47] It is certain he met General Maison, who, sixteen years later, would be charged with putting Charles X aboard a boat at Cherbourg. Apparently to render him worthy of his future mission, Charles X gave M. Maison the baton of the Marshal of France, like a knight, before a duel, conferring knighthood on the man of lower rank with whom he has deigned to measure swords.

I feared what would happen when Louis XVIII appeared. I hastened to precede him at that residence where Joan of Arc fell into English hands and where I was shown a volume pierced by one of the bullets fired at Bonaparte. What were people going to think at the sight of the crippled royal replacing the horseman who could have said, like Attila: "The grass never grows again where my horse has gone"? With no mission or taste for it, I undertook (a spell had been cast on me) a difficult task—that of describing the arrival of the son of Saint Louis in Compiègne, idealizing him as best I could with the help of the Muses. I expressed myself thus:

The carriage of the king was preceded by the generals and marshals of France, who had gone to meet His Majesty. There were no longer cries of "Long live the king!" but a confused uproar, in which all one could hear were the accents of tenderness and joy. The king wore a blue coat, distinguished only by a badge and epaulets; his legs were wrapped in broad red velvet gaiters edged with a bit of gold cord. When he sat in his armchair with his old-fashioned gaiters, holding his cane between his knees, you might have thought you were seeing Louis XIV at fifty...

Marshals Macdonald, Ney, Moncey, Serrurier, Brune, Prince de Neuchâtel, all the generals, all the people present, obtained the most affectionate words from the king. In France, such is the power of the legitimate sovereign—that magic attached to the very name of the king. A man returns alone from exile dispossessed, with no entourage or guards or riches; he has nothing to give, almost nothing to promise. He steps out of his carriage, leaning on the arm of a young woman; he presents himself to captains who have never seen him, to grenadiers who hardly know his name. Who is this man? He is the king! Everyone falls at his feet.

What I said of the military, to accomplish the purpose I set myself at that time, was true of the generals; but I was lying about the soldiers. I can see, in my mind's eye, as though I were seeing it still, the spectacle I witnessed when Louis XVIII, riding into Paris on the 3rd of May, went down to Notre-Dame. Everyone had wanted to spare the king the sight of the foreign troops, and it was a regiment of the Old Guard that lined the Quai des Orfèvres from the Pont Neuf to Notre-Dame. I cannot believe human faces and bodies have ever worn such menacing and terrible expressions. These grenadiers covered with wounds, the conquerors of Europe who had seen so many thousands of balls pass over their heads, who smelled of fire and powder; these same men, stripped of their captain, were forced to salute an old king—enfeebled by time, not battle—while being guarded by an army of Russians, Austrians, and Prussians in Napoleon's invaded capital. Some of them, by knitting their brows repeatedly, caused their bearskins to fall down over their eyes, so as not to have to look; others lowered the corners of their mouth in furious contempt; still others, like tigers, bared their teeth through their mustaches. When they presented arms, it was with a gesture of rage, and the noise of these weapons made one tremble. Never, it must be said, have men been put to such a test or suffered such torment. If at that moment they had been called to vengeance, they would have had to be exterminated to the last man, or else they would have devoured the earth.

At the end of the line was a young hussar on horseback. He was holding his sword unsheathed, making it leap and dance with convulsive gestures of rage. His flesh was pale; his eyes swiveled in their sockets; he opened his mouth and closed it over and over, snapping his teeth and choking back shouts only the first strangled sound of which could be heard. He caught sight of a Russian officer: the look he gave him cannot be described. When the king's carriage passed him, he made his horse rear up, and there is no question he was tempted to rush upon the king.

The Restoration, at its start, committed an irreparable error. It should have dismissed the army, retaining the marshals, generals, military governors, and officers with their pensions, honors, and ranks. The soldiers would then have come back little by little to an army reconstituted, as it later happened with the Royal Guard. The Legitimacy would then not have begun with all those soldiers of the Empire against them—organized, recruited, and denominated exactly as they were in the days of their victories, incessantly talking with each other about the past, harboring regrets and feelings hostile to their new leader.

The miserable resurrection of the Maison Rouge, that motley collection of soldiers of the old monarchy and soldiers of the recent empire, made things worse. To think that veterans who had distinguished themselves on a thousand battlefields would not be shocked to see young men no doubt very brave but for the most part new to the soldiering profession—to see them bearing, without having earned, the marks of high military rank—was to take no heed of human nature.

546 · MEMOIRS FROM BEYOND THE GRAVE

During Louis XVIII's stay in Compiègne, Alexander had come to visit him: Louis XVIII offended him with his haughtiness. Out of this meeting came the declaration of Saint-Ouen, issued on May 2, in which the king declared that he had resolved on the following guarantees as a foundation for the constitution he intended for his people: representative government divided into two bodies, taxes freely consented to, public and individual liberty, freedom of the press, freedom of religion, inviolable and sacred rights of property, the previous sale of national lands held irrevocable, ministers made responsible, judges irremovable, and judiciary power independent, all Frenchmen admissible to every form of employment, etc., etc.

This declaration, although in keeping with Louis XVIII's cast of mind, did not belong either to him or his advisers. It belonged, quite simply, to the era when he had gone into exile. His wings had been tied, his flight suspended, since 1792. Now he was climbing into the air again, wanting to continue on his way. The Terror's excesses and Bonaparte's despotism had driven ideas in a backward direction; but as soon as the obstacles that had encumbered them were destroyed, they poured into the bed they had to follow and dig at the same time. Things were taken up again exactly at the point where they had been dropped, and what had taken place was as good as null and void. The human race, brought to a halt at the beginning of the Revolution, had only lost forty years of its life. But what are forty years in the life of society? The gap disappeared as soon as the two torn sections of time were stitched together.

On May 30, 1814, the Treaty of Paris was concluded between the Allies and France. It was agreed that, within two months, all the powers that had been involved in the war would send plenipotentiaries to Vienna in order to settle the final arrangements at a general congress.

On June 4, Louis XVIII held a *lit de justice* with the entire Corps Législatif and a fraction of the Senate present. He read a noble speech—old-fashioned, dull, obsolete, these tedious details only serve as a historical thread.

The Charter, for the greater part of the nation, had the drawback of being "vouchsafed."[48] This entirely useless word was bound to rake up the smoldering question of royal, as opposed to popular, sovereignty. Louis XVIII also dated his gift to the people from the year of his reign, as if Bonaparte had never existed—just as Charles II leapfrogged over Cromwell. It was a sort of insult to the sovereigns who had all recognized Napoleon and who, at that very moment, happened to be in Paris. This outmoded language and these pretensions taken from old monarchies contributed nothing to legal legitimacy and were merely childish anachronisms. Still, the Charter, by replacing despotism and bringing us legal liberty, was sufficient to satisfy men of conscience. The royalists, however, who reaped so many advantages, who, emerging from their villages or wretched homes, from the obscure places where they had lived under the Empire, were called to a high and public existence, and accepted the gift grumbling all the while. Whereas the liberals, who had become quite content under Bonaparte's tyranny, regarded the Charter as a veritable slave code. We had gone back to the time of Babel, but we were no longer working on a building in common, however confused; now everyone was building his own tower at his own height, according to his particular strength and size. In the end, if the Charter seemed defective, it was because the Revolution wasn't over; the principles of equality and democracy had rooted themselves in men's minds and worked against the monarchical order.

The Allied princes wasted no time leaving Paris. Alexander, before going away, had a religious sacrifice celebrated in the Place de la Concorde. An altar was raised where Louis XVI's scaffold once stood. Seven Muscovite priests celebrated the office, and the foreign troops marched before the altar. The Te Deum was sung to one of those beautiful ancient Greek melodies. The soldiers and sovereigns kneeled to receive benediction. The French people present then thought back to 1793 and 1794, when the oxen refused to walk over the cobblestones, which they found repulsive, they smelled so foully of blood. What hand had led these men from every land, these sons of the ancient barbarian invasions, these Tartars, some of whom lived in sheepskin tents at the foot of the Great Wall of China, to the feast of atonement? Spectacles such as this will never be seen again by the feeble generations that come after my time has run out.

22.

FIRST YEAR OF THE RESTORATION

DURING the first year of the Restoration, I was witness to a third social transformation. I had seen the old monarchy pass into a constitutional monarchy and the latter into a republic; I had seen the Republic convert itself into a military autocracy, and now I was seeing military autocracy revert to a free monarchy, new ways of thought and new generations coming to terms with old principles and old men. The marshals of the Empire became marshals of France. The uniforms of the Royal Bodyguard and the Maison Rouge, tailored using the same old patterns, were mingled with the uniforms of Napoleon's Imperial Guard. The ancient Duc d'Havré, with his powdered wig and black cane, marched with shaking head as captain of the Bodyguard, next to Marshal Victor, lame like Bonaparte. The Duc de Mouchy, who had never heard a shot fired, paraded at Mass next to Marshal Oudinot, who was riddled with wounds. The Tuileries Palace, so tidy and military under Napoleon, was filled with, instead of the smell of gunpowder, the stench of luncheons wafting in every direction: under the gentlemen of the bedchamber, the gentlemen officers of the royal kitchen and wardrobe, everything resumed an air of domesticity.[49] In the streets, one saw old-fashioned émigrés who perfectly preserved the airs and clothes of the past—no doubt the most respectable of men, but strangers in a crowd of moderns, as the Republican captains were strangers among Napoleon's soldiers. The ladies of the imperial Court brought in the dowagers of the Faubourg Saint-Germain[50] and instructed them in the "ins and outs" of the palace.[51] Brassarded deputations arrived from Bordeaux, and from the Vendée came captains of parishes topped with hats à la Rochejaquelein. These various personages held fast to the expression of the feelings, thoughts, habits, and customs familiar to them. Liberty, which lay at the bottom of this period, made what seemed, at first glance, not to have any chance of coexisting, coexist; but it was difficult to perceive this liberty, for it wore the colors of the old monarchy and of imperial despotism. Also, no one spoke the constitution's language very well. The royalists made boorish mistakes when speaking of the charter; the imperialists were still less fluent in it; and the former members of the National Convention, who had in their turn become Napoleon's counts, barons, and senators, as well as Louis XVIII's peers, sometimes fell into the Republican dialect they had nearly forgotten, and sometimes into the idiom of absolutism they had so thoroughly learned. Lieutenants general were promoted to the rank of gamekeeper and put in charge of the hares. Aides-de-camp to the recently departed military tyrant could be heard discussing the inviolable freedom of the nations, while regicides lent their support to the sacred dogma of legitimacy.

Such metamorphoses would be repugnant were they not partly attributable to the flexibility of the French spirit. The people of Athens governed themselves; orators appealed to their passions in the public square; the sovereign crowd was made up of sculptors, painters, workers, "spectators of words and hearers of actions," says Thucydides.[52] But when, good or bad, the decree was issued, who emerged from this incoherent, inexpert mass to carry it out? Socrates, Phocion, Pericles, Alcibiades.

23.

SHOULD ROYALISTS BE BLAMED FOR THE RESTORATION?

SHOULD royalists "take the blame" for the Restoration, as most argue today? Not in the slightest. Does it now seem that thirty million men were dismayed, while a handful of Legitimists, against everyone's wishes, brought about a hated restoration by waving a few handkerchiefs and pinning their wives' ribbons to their hats? The vast majority of Frenchmen were, in truth, overjoyed; but this majority was not Legitimist in the strict sense of the word, which is applicable only to rigid partisans of the old monarchy. This majority was a mob who held all manner of opinions: they were glad to be liberated and angry at the man they blamed for all their troubles. Hence the success of my pamphlet. How many avowed aristocrats were among those proclaiming the king's name? Mathieu and Adrien de Montmorency, the Messieurs de Polignac who had escaped from their jail, M. Alexis de Noailles, M. Sosthène de La Rochefoucauld. Did these seven or eight men, whom the people neither knew nor followed, lay down the laws to a whole nation?

Madame de Montcalm had sent me a sack of 1,200 francs to distribute to the pure Legitimist race: I sent it back to her, not knowing where to invest a single coin. A shameful rope was fastened around the neck of the statue atop the column in the Place Vendôme, but there were so few royalists to heave away that it was up to the Bonapartists to bring down the effigy of their master, with the aid of a gibbet. The colossus bowed his head and fell at the feet of those sovereigns of Europe, who had so often bowed low before him. It was the men of the Republic and the Empire who most enthusiastically welcomed the Restoration. The conduct and ingratitude of personages raised by the Revolution toward the man they claim to mourn and admire today were abominable.

Imperialists and liberals, it is you into whose hands the power fell, you who knelt down before the sons of Henri IV! It was quite natural that the royals should be happy to recover their princes and see the reign of the man they regarded as a usurper come to an end; it was not at all natural that you, creatures of this usurper, should have grossly exaggerated the feelings of royalists. Ministers and dignitaries pledged an oath to the Legitimacy. All the civil and judicial authorities stood in line to swear to their hatred for the new dynasty now outlawed and their love for the ancient race they had condemned a hundred times over. Who composed those proclamations and addresses accusing and insulting Napoleon which were then inundating France? Royalists? No. Ministers, generals, and officials chosen and maintained by Bonaparte. Where was the Restoration rigged? In the homes of royalists? No, at M. de Talleyrand's, with M. de Pradt, chaplain of the god Mars and mitered mountebank. With whom and in whose rooms did the lieutenant general of the kingdom dine? Among royalists in royalist houses? No, at the Bishop of Autun's, with M. de Caulaincourt. Where were the banquets thrown for the infamous foreign princes? In royalist mansions? No, at Malmaison, at the Empress Josephine's. What did Napoleon's dearest friends (Berthier, for example) most ardently support? Legitimacy. Who was spending all their time at the house of the autocrat Alexander, that brutal Tartar? The ranks of the Institute, the scholars, the men of letters, the philanthropic philosophers, the theophilanthropists, and many others; they came back charmed, sated with praise and snuff-boxes. As for we Legitimists, poor devils, we were not admitted anywhere and counted for nothing. In the street sometimes we used to be told to go on home to bed; at other times, we were advised not to shout "Long live the king!" quite so loudly, seeing that others had taken charge of this cause. Far from forcing anyone to be Legitimist, the powerful declared no one would be required to change their role or their language, that the Bishop of Autun would be under no more obligation to say Mass in the kingdom than he had been during the Empire. I saw no chatelaine, no Joan of Arc, proclaiming the sovereignty of right with a falcon on her fist or a lance in her hand; but Madame de Talleyrand, whom Bonaparte had fastened to her husband like a sign,[53] did roam the streets in a carriage singing hymns about the pious Bourbon family. A few sheets hanging from the windows of the families of the imperial Court led the good Cossacks to believe there were as many fleurs-de-lis in the hearts of the converted Bonapartists as there were white rags at their windows. Contagion, in France, is a wonder. A Frenchman would shout "Off with my head!" if he heard his neighbor shouting it. The imperialists went so far as to enter our homes and make us other Bourbonists put out, for spotless flags, whatever scraps of white our linen closets contained. This happened at my house; but Madame de Chateaubriand would have none of it, and valiantly defended her muslins.[54]

24.

FIRST MINISTRY—I PUBLISH *POLITICAL REFLECTIONS* —MADAME LA DUCHESSE DE DURAS—I AM NAMED AMBASSADOR TO SWEDEN

THE CORPS Législatif, transformed into the Chamber of Deputies and the Chamber of Peers, composed of 154 members appointed for life, among whom there were more than sixty senators, formed the first two legislative chambers. M. de Talleyrand, installed in the Ministry of Foreign Affairs, left for the Congress of Vienna, which was set to open November 3, according to Article 32 of the treaty of May 30. M. de Jaucourt took over the ministry during the interim, which lasted until the Battle of Waterloo. The Abbé de Montesquiou became Minister of the Interior with M. Guizot as secretary general. M. Malouet entered the Navy and when he died was replaced by M. Beugnot. General Dupont took charge of the Ministry of War before his place was taken by Marshal Soult, who distinguished himself by raising a monument to the memory of those who had fallen at Quiberon. Duc de Blacas was Minister of the Maison du Roi, M. Angles prefect of police, the councillor Dambray Minister of Justice, and Abbé Louis Minister of Finances.

On October 21, Abbé de Montesquiou presented the first law on the subject of the press, which submitted all writings under twenty printed pages to censorship, and M. Guizot drew up this first law of liberty.

Carnot addressed a letter to the king, admitting that the Bourbons "had been received joyously," but, taking no account either of how little time had passed or of all that the Charter had granted, he gave high-toned lessons and impertinent advice. None of this is seemly when you have had to accept the rank of "minister" and the title of "count" of the Empire. There is no reason to be arrogant when dealing with a weak and liberal prince when you have submitted to a violent and despotic one—when you, a worn-out machine of the Terror, have not been up to the task of calculating the proportions of the Napoleonic Wars. In reply, I published my *Political Reflections*, which contains the substance of *Monarchy According to the Charter*; M. Lainé, president of the Chamber of Deputies, spoke glowingly of this work to the king, who always seemed charmed by the services I had the good fortune to render him. The heavens appeared to have thrown the mantle of the Herald of Legitimacy over my shoulders; but the more successful the work was, the less the author pleased His Majesty. My *Political Reflections* disclosed my constitutional doctrines: the Court received from them an impression which my fidelity to the Bourbons has not been able to erase. To his familiars, Louis XVIII used to say:

"Be careful never to allow a poet into your affairs; he will be a dead loss. Those people are good for nothing."[55]

A strong and lively friendship was then filling my heart. The Duchesse de Duras[56] had imaginative powers—and even certain facial expressions—reminiscent of Madame de Staël. One can judge her authorial talent by reading *Ourika*. After returning from the Emigration and being locked up for several years in the Château d'Ussé on the banks of the Loire, it was in the lovely gardens of Méréville that I first heard about her for the first time, although I must have passed by her in the London streets without ever meeting her. She moved to Paris for the education of her charming daughters, Félicie and Clara. Affinities of family, province, and literary and political opinion introduced her into my life. Her warmth of soul, nobility of character, loftiness of mind, and generous feelings made her a superior woman. At the start of the Restoration, she took me under her wing, for, despite what I had done for the legitimate monarchy and the services that Louis XVIII had admitted receiving from me, I had been so thoroughly marginalized I thought of disappearing to Switzerland. Perhaps that would have been best. In those solitudes Napoleon had intended for me as his ambassador to the mountains, I may well have been happier than in the Tuileries. When I entered its halls during the first days of the Legitimacy, I felt almost as distressed by them as I had been on the day I saw Bonaparte there, prepared to kill the Duc d'Enghien. Madame de Duras mentioned me to M. de Blacas. He told her I was free to go where I wished. Madame de Duras was so tempestuous, was so courageous on behalf of her friends, that a vacant embassy, the Swedish embassy, was disinterred. Louis XVIII—who had already grown tired of my noise—was happy to present me to his good brother King Bernadotte. Did the latter perhaps imagine I was being sent to Stockholm to dethrone him? Oh, good Lord, princes of the earth, I am not interested in dethroning anyone! Hold onto your crowns, if you can manage it, and above all don't give them to me. I've had enough of them.[57]

Madame de Duras, an excellent woman who used to let me call her "my sister"—and whom I had the happiness to see in Paris over the course of many years—went to die in Nice: another wound reopened. The Duchesse de Duras knew Madame de Staël very well. I cannot understand how I did not come across Madame Récamier, who had by then returned to France from Italy. I would have greeted the solace she would have brought into my life. Even then, I had ceased to belong to those morning hours that console themselves and was fast approaching those hours that can only be consoled by others.

25.

EXHUMATION OF THE REMAINS OF LOUIS XVI—FIRST JANUARY 21 AT SAINT-DENIS

ON DECEMBER 30, 1814, the legislative chambers were adjourned until May 1, 1815, as if summoned to assemble for Napoleon's Champ de Mai. On January 18, the remains of Marie Antoinette and Louis XVI were exhumed. I was present at this exhumation in the cemetery where Fontaine and Percier have since raised, at the pious behest of Madame la Dauphine—and in imitation of a sepulchral church at Rimini—what is perhaps the most remarkable monument in Paris.[58] This chapel, formed of a series of tombs, captures the imagination and fills it with sadness. In Book Four of these *Memoirs*, I spoke of the exhumations of 1815. Among the bones, I recognized the queen's head by the smile this head had given me at Versailles.

On January 21, the first stone was laid for the base of the statue that was to be raised in the Place Louis XV, though this would never come to pass. I wrote a funeral oration for January 21, saying:

> The successors of those monks who came bearing the oriflamme before the Reliquary of Saint Louis will never receive the holy king's descendant. *In these subterranean dwellings where the dead kings and princes used to sleep, Louis XVI will find himself alone* ... How did so many dead men rise and go? Why is Saint-Denis deserted? Let us ask instead why its roof has been restored and why its altar still stands! What hand has rebuilt these vaults and prepared these empty tombs? The hand of the same man who once sat on the Bourbon throne. Oh, Providence! He

believed he was preparing sepulchres for his race, and he was only building the tomb of Louis XVI.[59]

For a long time, I wanted the statue of Louis XVI to be set upon the very spot where the martyr shed his blood. I would no longer be of this opinion. The Bourbons must be praised for having thought of Louis XVI from the moment they returned. They had to smear their forehead with his ashes before they put his crown on their heads. Nowadays, I think they shouldn't have gone any further. In Paris it was not, as in London, a commission that judged the monarch; it was the entire National Convention—hence the annual reproach the repetition of the funeral ceremony seemed to make to the nation, which had ostensibly been represented by a complete assembly. All nations have set anniversaries for the celebration of their victories, insurgencies, and tragedies, because they have all collectively wanted to retain the memory of these things. The French have had solemnities for the barricades, songs for the Saint Bartholomew's Day Massacres, celebrations of the death of Capet—yet isn't it remarkable that the law is powerless to establish days of remembrance, whereas religion has caused even the obscurest saint to survive, century after century? If the fasts and prayers instituted for the sacrifice of Charles I still endure, this is because in England the state has both religious and political supremacy, and under this supremacy January 30 has become established as a national holiday. In France, this is not the case. Only Rome has the right to give orders in matters of religion; thus, what good is an ordinance issued by a prince or a decree issued by a political assembly if another prince or assembly has the right to annul them? That is why I now think the symbolic significance of a holiday that can be abolished, the testimony to a tragic calamity not consecrated by worship, does not belong in the path of the crowd going heedlessly about its pleasures. Besides, at the present time it is to be feared that a monument raised with a view to remembering the terror of populist excesses may well instill a desire to imitate them. Evil is more tempting than good. In our efforts to perpetuate our pain, we often merely perpetuate examples of how to inflict it. Future generations do not adopt the legacies of mourning; they have more than enough present reasons to weep without taking on the burden of shedding hereditary tears.

On leaving Desclozeaux's graveyard,[60] I gazed at the catafalque laden with the remains of the queen and king, and felt quite overcome; I followed its progress with my eyes, filled with foreboding. Finally Louis XVI went to rest at Saint-Denis; Louis XVIII, for his part, would go to slumber in the Louvre. Together, the two brothers inaugurated another era of legitimate kings and scepters—a vain restoration of the throne and the tomb whose double dust time has already swept away.

Since I have been speaking of these funeral ceremonies, which were so often repeated, I shall tell you about the nightmare that oppressed me when, after the ceremony was over, I went for an evening stroll in the half-becalmed basilica. That I considered the vanity of human grandeur among those devastated tombs goes without saying: such a moral would occur to anyone. But my mind did not stop there. I bore down to the nature of man. Is everything emptiness and absence in the region of the grave? Is there nothing in this nothing? Is there no life at all in the void, no thoughts at all to be had by dust? Who knows the passions, the pleasures, the embraces of the dead? The things they dreamed, believed, expected: are these, like they themselves, idealities which are swallowed up with them? Dreams, plans, joys, pains, freedoms and enslavements, strengths and infirmities, honors and infamies, riches and poverty, talent, genius, intelligence, glory, illusions, loves: are you but momentary perceptions, perceptions that pass away with the nullified skull that engendered them, the defunct breast where once beat a heart? In your eternal silence, oh, tombs, if tombs you be, does a man hear nothing but mocking laughter forever and ever? Is this laughter God, the only derisory reality, which will survive the imposture of the universe? Let us close our eyes; let us fill the desperate abyss of life with the great and mysterious words of the martyr: "I am a Christian."

26.

THE ISLE OF ELBA

BONAPARTE had refused to embark on a French ship, setting store solely by the English navy, because it was victorious. He had forgotten his hatred, the calumnies and insults he had heaped upon perfidious Albion. He now saw no one more worthy of his admiration than the victors, and it was the *Undaunted* that carried him to the port of his first exile. He was not unworried about how he would be received. Would the French garrison hand the territory it was guarding over to him? Of the Italians who lived on the island, some wanted to call in the English, while others wanted to remain free of any master. The tricolor and the white flag fluttered on some headlands side by side. Everything, however, was arranged. When it became known that Bonaparte was arriving with millions, the people generously decided to welcome the "august victim." The civil and religious authorities were brought around to the same conviction. Joseph-Philippe Arrighi, the vicar general, published a pastoral letter, which piously declared that divine Providence had decreed "in the future we should be the subjects of Napoleon the Great. The isle of Elba, raised to so sublime an honor, receives the Lord's Anointed in its bosom. We order a solemn Te Deum to be sung in thanksgiving," and so on.

The emperor had written to General Dalesme, the commander of the French garrison, that he wished to inform the people of Elba that he "had chosen" their island for his dwelling place because of the mildness of their manners and climate. He touched land at Portoferraio to a double salute from the English frigate that had carried him and some of the batteries on shore. From there he was led under the parish canopy to the church, where the Te Deum was sung; the beadle, who acted as master of ceremonies, was a short man so fat he could not clasp his hands around his paunch. Napoleon was then taken to the town hall, where an apartment had been prepared for him. The new imperial flag was unfurled—a white background, crossed by a red band sown with three gold bees. Three violins and two basses followed him with gleeful scraping. The throne, set up hastily in the public dance hall, was decorated with gilt paper and scarlet rags. The theatrical side of the prisoner's nature was not indifferent to such pageantry: Napoleon performed in the chapel, as he used to amuse his Court with trifling old games in the Tuileries Palace, before going off to kill men for sport. He organized his household, which would consist of four chamberlains, three orderly officers, and two palace stewards. He declared he would receive ladies twice a week, at eight in the evening. He gave a ball. He expropriated, for his personal residence, a pavilion intended for military engineers. Wherever he went, Bonaparte always rediscovered the two sources from which his extraordinary life had sprung: democracy and royal power. His power came from the masses, his rank from his genius. Thus you see him passing effortlessly from the public square to the throne, kings and queens thronging around him in Erfurt, bakers and oil merchants dancing in his barn at Portoferraio. He had something of the people among the princes and something of the princes among the people. At five o'clock in the morning, in silk stockings and buckled shoes, he would preside over his masons on the isle of Elba.

Installed in his empire, which had been an inexhaustible source of steel since the days of Virgil,

Insula inexhaustis Chalybum generosa metallis,[61]

Bonaparte did not forget the outrages he had suffered. He had not given up the idea of tearing off his shroud; but it suited him to seem to be buried, to make no more than a few phantasmal appearances around his tomb. That is why, as if he had nothing else on his mind, he hastened to descend into his quarries of magnet and crystallized iron; he might have been mistaken for the former inspector of mines of his ci-devant states. He regretted having once appropriated the revenue from Ilva's forges to feed the Légion d'Honneur. Five hundred thousand francs now seemed more valuable to him than a blood-bathed cross on the chests of his grenadiers.

"What was I thinking?" he said. "But I have issued several stupid decrees of that sort."

He made a commercial treaty with Livorno and proposed to make another with Genoa. Somehow or other, he built thirty or so feet of highway and traced out the sites of four great cities, as Dido limned the bounds of Carthage. A philosopher fed up with human greatness, he said that henceforth he wished to live like a justice of the peace in an English county. And yet, as he climbed a hillock overlooking Portoferraio, at the sight of the sea advancing on him from every direction at the foot of the cliffs, these words escaped his lips:

"Damn! It must be admitted, my island is very small."

Within a few hours he had toured his whole domain and wanted to add a rock called Pianosa to it.

"Europe will accuse me," he laughed, "of having already made a conquest."

The Allied powers delighted in the derision of leaving him a mere four hundred soldiers; but that was all he needed to call them all back beneath his flag.

Napoleon's presence on the shores of Italy, which had seen his glory dawn, and which retains his memory, agitated everyone. Murat was his neighbor. His friends, as well as strangers, secretly or openly landed on his sanctuary. His mother and his sister, Princess Pauline, visited him. It was expected that Marie Louise and her son would soon be seen. In fact, a woman and child did appear: she was received with great secrecy and went to stay in a secluded villa in the remotest corner of the island. On the shore of Ogygia, Calypso spoke of her love to Odysseus, who, instead of listening to her, thought of how to defend himself against the suitors.[62] After two days' repose, the northern swan put out to sea again, to land among the myrtles of Baiae, taking her little one away in her white yawl.[63]

If we had been less trusting, it would have been easy for us to see a catastrophe approaching. Bonaparte was too close to his cradle and his conquests. His funeral island ought to have been farther away and hemmed in by far more waves. It is hard to understand what possessed the Allies to think of relegating Napoleon to the rocks where he was to serve his apprenticeship in exile. How could they believe that in gazing at the Apennines, smelling the powder of the battlefields of Montenotte, Arcola, and Marengo, spying on Venice, Rome, and Naples, his three beautiful slaves, the most irresistible temptations would not take hold of his heart? Had they forgotten that he had shaken the earth, and that his admirers and debtors—all of them his accomplices—were everywhere? His ambition had been disappointed, not extinguished; misfortune and vengeance were rekindling its flames. When the Prince of Darkness looked from the edge of the created universe at the world and man, he determined to ruin them.[64]

Before breaking out, the terrible prisoner restrained himself for a few weeks. In the immense public game of Pharoah[65] he was playing, he brilliantly negotiated for a fortune or a kingdom. Fouchés and Guzmán de Alfaraches swarmed.[66] The great actor had long allocated melodrama to his police force and reserved the best roles for himself; now he amused himself with vulgar victims who vanished through the trapdoors of his theater.

Bonapartists, during the first year of the Restoration, moved from simple desire to outright action, as it became progressively clearer to them how weak the Bourbons' character was. While others wove intrigue without, they wove it within, until the conspiracy became flagrant. Under the able administration of M. Ferrand, M. de Lavalette initiated the correspondence: the postmen of the monarchy carried the dispatches of the Empire. Nothing was hidden anymore. Cartoons represented the wished-for return: eagles could be seen flying in through the windows of the Tuileries Palace, while a flock of turkeys doddered out through the gates. *The Green Dwarf* and *The Yellow*

Dwarf spoke of "plumes de cane."⁶⁷ Warnings poured in from every side, and no one was willing to believe them. The Swiss government had pointlessly hastened to warn the king's government of the movements of Joseph Bonaparte, who had retired to the district of Vaud. A woman back from Elba gave the most particular details of what was going on in Portoferraio, and the police had her thrown into prison. Everyone was sure that Napoleon wouldn't dare try anything until the Congress had ended, and that in any case his sights would be set on Italy. Others, even more wisely, hoped the little corporal, the ogre, the prisoner, would land on the coast of France—that would be too good! It would all be over in a flash! Pozzo di Borgo, in Vienna, declared the delinquent would be hung from a tree branch. If one could get his hands on certain papers, he would find proof in them that, as early as 1814, a military conspiracy had been hatched and had progressed in conjunction with the political conspiracy that the Prince de Talleyrand was conducting in Vienna, at Fouché's instigation. Napoleon's friends wrote to tell him that if he didn't hurry up and come back he would find his place at the Tuileries taken by the Duc d'Orléans. Some imagine this revelation accelerated the emperor's return. As for me, I am convinced of the existence of these intrigues, but I also believe that what finally made up Bonaparte's mind was simply the nature of his genius.

The Drouet d'Erlon and Lefebvre Desnouettes conspiracy had only recently erupted.⁶⁸ A few days before these generals rose up in arms, I dined at the home of Marshal Soult, who had been appointed Minister of War on December 3, 1814. A simpleton was describing Louis XVIII's exile at Hartwell House, and the marshal listened intently. With every new detail, he would say, "That's historic."

"His Majesty was brought his slippers."

"That's historic!"

"On lean days, the king would swallow three fresh eggs before eating his dinner."

"That's historic!"

This reply struck me. When a government is not firmly established, every man whose conscience is worth nothing becomes—depending on how much energy he has—a quarter, a half, or three quarters a conspirator. He awaits the dictates of fate. More traitors are made by events than by opinions.

BOOK TWENTY-THREE

I.

COMMENCEMENT OF THE HUNDRED DAYS—RETURN FROM THE ISLE OF ELBA

Revised in December 1846

SUDDENLY the telegraph announced to the brave and the incredulous alike that the man had landed. *Monsieur*[1] rushed to Lyon with the Duc d'Orléans and Marshal Macdonald, then returned at once. Marshal Soult, denounced in the Chamber of Deputies, was succeeded on March 11 by the Duc de Feltre. Bonaparte had already crossed paths with this general, Louis XVIII's Minister of War in 1815, who had been his own last Minister of War in 1814.

The boldness of the enterprise was unprecedented. From a political point of view, one might regard this enterprise as Napoleon's irremissible crime and capital error. He was aware that the princes were still at the Congress and that Europe, which remained under arms, would not suffer his restoration. His judgment should have warned him that, even if he was successful, it could last but a day. To his passion for strutting on the stage once more, he sacrificed the tranquility of a people who had given him their blood and wealth; he lay the country he credited for all that he had been in the past and all that he would be in the future open to dismemberment. In his outlandish thinking, there was a ferocious egotism and an appalling lack of gratitude or generosity to France.

All this is true according to practical reason, for a man of heart rather than a man of brain; but for creatures of Napoleon's species, another kind of reason exists. These creatures of high renown keep a pace all their own. Comets describe curves that elude calculation; they are unrelated to anything, appear good for nothing; if there is an object in their path they obliterate it and proceed through the abysses of the sky. Their laws are understood by God alone. Extraordinary individuals are the monuments of human intelligence; they are not the rule.

Bonaparte was therefore less swayed to this undertaking by the false reports of his friends than by the inmost need of his genius. He embarked on the crusade by virtue of the faith he had in himself. It is not enough, for a great man, to be born; he must die. Was the isle of Elba any place for Napoleon to meet his end? Could he accept sovereignty over a vegetable patch, like Diocletian in Salona?[2] If he had held out longer, would he have had a better chance of success—when the memory of him would have stirred up fewer emotions, his old soldiers had left the army, and new social positions had been adopted?

Ah, well: he went up against the world on the spur of the moment. At first, he had good reason to think he had not been mistaken about the prestige of his power.

One night, between the 25th and 26th of February, at the end of a ball at which Princess Borghèse was doing the honors, he escapes in triumph, his longtime accomplice and companion. He crosses a sea covered with our fleets, encounters two frigates, a seventy-four, and the brig the *Zephyr*, which comes up alongside and interrogates him. He personally answers the captain's questions. The sea and the waves salute him, and he continues on his course. The deck of his little ship the *Inconstant* serves him as promenade and office; he dictates amid the winds and has three proclamations, to the army and to France, drawn up on this turbulent table. A few feluccas, loaded up with his companions in adventure, hoist, around his admiral's bark, a white flag spangled with stars. On March 1, at three in the morning, he lands on the coast of France between Cannes and Antibes, in Golfe-Juan. He disembarks, strolls along the seashore, picks some violets, and bivouacs in an olive grove. The dumbstruck locals keep out of the way. He avoids Antibes and hastens into the mountains of Grasse, passing through Sernon, Barrème, Digne, and Gap. At Sisteron, twenty men might have stopped him, but he encounters no one. He advances unhindered among those men and women who, a few months previous, had wanted to murder him. If a few soldiers stumble into the void that forms around his gigantic shadow, they are irresistibly drawn along by the attraction of his eagles. His mesmerized enemies seek but do not find him; he hides in his glory as the lion of the Sahara hides in plain day, evading the sunstruck eyes of the hunters. Enveloped in a burning whirlwind, the bloody phantoms of Arcole, Marengo, Austerlitz, Jena, Friedland, Eylau, Borodino, Lützen, and Bautzen parade for him together with a million dead. From within that column of fire and smoke, at the entrance to the towns, come a few trumpet blasts mingled with the signals of the tricolor labarum—and the gates of the towns fall. When Napoleon crossed the Niemen at the head of four hundred thousand foot soldiers and a hundred thousand horses to blow up the palace of the czars in Moscow, it was less astonishing than when, breaking his ban, throwing his chains in the faces of the kings, he came alone from Cannes to Paris, to sleep peacefully at the Tuileries.

2.

TORPOR OF THE LEGITIMACY—BENJAMIN CONSTANT'S ARTICLE—MARSHAL SOULT'S ORDER OF THE DAY—ROYAL SESSION—THE LAW SCHOOL'S PETITION

ALONGSIDE the wonder of a one-man invasion, we must point out another, which was the result of the first: the Legitimacy swooned and collapsed. The state's pusillanimousness spread to its limbs and paralyzed France. For twenty days, Bonaparte marched on, step by step; his eagles flew from steeple to steeple, and on a road two hundred leagues long the government, master of all, equipped with money and weapons, found neither the time nor the means to bring down a lone bridge or fell a single tree, delaying the man whom the populace did not oppose (but did not follow either) at least by an hour.

This governmental torpor seemed all the more deplorable considering that public opinion in Paris was extremely animated and would have lent itself to anything, notwithstanding Marshal Ney's defection. Benjamin Constant wrote in the gazettes:

> After visiting every plague possible upon our country, he left French soil. Who did not imagine he had left it for good? Suddenly he returns and again promises Frenchmen freedom, victory, peace. Responsible for the most tyrannical constitution that ever ruled France, today he speaks of freedom? Yet it was he who, for fourteen years, undermined and annihilated freedom. He had no memories to excuse him, no long habituation to power; he was not born in the purple. It was his fellow citizens he enslaved, his equals he enchained. He did not inherit power; he desired and plotted tyranny. What freedom can he

promise? Are we not a thousand times freer now than under his empire? He promised victory and three times abandoned his troops, in Egypt, Spain, and Russia, handing his comrades-in-arms over to the triple agony of cold, misery, and despair. He drew down upon France the humiliation of foreign invasion and lost the conquests we had made before him. He promises peace, but his very name is a war cry. The nation unhappy enough to serve him would again become the object of European hatred. His triumph would be the beginning of a fight to the death with the civilized world . . . He therefore has nothing to claim and nothing to offer. Whom could he convince or seduce? War at home, war abroad—these are the gifts he brings us.

Marshal Soult's Order of the Day for March 8, 1815, very nearly repeats Benjamin Constant's ideas with an effusion of loyalty:

Soldiers,

The man who not so long ago abdicated, before the eyes of Europe, a usurped power, which he put to such fatal use, has landed on the soil of France, which he was never supposed to see again.

What does he want? Civil war. What is he looking for? Traitors. Where will he find them? Among the soldiery he has tricked and sacrificed so many times by misleading their bravery? In families where the very mention of his name inspires horror?

Bonaparte despises us enough to believe we can abandon a legitimate and beloved sovereign to share the fate of a man who is no better than an adventurer. This is what he believes, the fool! His latest act of lunacy shows his true colors.

Soldiers, the French army is the bravest in Europe, and it shall also be the most loyal.

Let us rally around the banner of the lilies, to the voice of that father of the people, of that worthy heir to the virtues of Henri the Good. He himself has traced out the duties you have to fulfill. In charge of you, he places that prince, the model of French knighthood, whose happy return to our country has already chased out the usurper, and who today is going, with his presence, to destroy his last and only hope.

Louis XVIII appeared before the Chamber of Deputies on March 16. The future of France and the world were at stake. When His Majesty entered, the deputies and the spectators in the galleries took off their hats and rose to their feet. Applause shook the walls of the room. Louis XVIII climbed slowly to his throne; the princes, marshals, and captains of the Guards ranged themselves on either side of the king. The shouts ceased. Everything was silent, and in this interval of silence one seemed to hear the far-off footsteps of Napoleon. His Majesty, seated, regarded the assembly a moment before reading out his speech in a firm voice:

Gentlemen,
    In this moment of crisis, when a public enemy has penetrated into a part of my kingdom and threatens the liberty of the rest of it, I come among you to tighten the bonds that, uniting you with me, form the strength of the state; I come to address you to express my feelings and my wishes to the whole of France.
    I have laid eyes on my native land again. I have reconciled it with foreign powers, which—have no doubt—will remain faithful to the treaties that have brought us peace. I have worked for the happiness of my people. I have received, every day I receive, the most touching tokens of their love for me. At sixty years of age, in what better way could I end my career than by dying in defense of my country?
    Thus I do not fear for myself, I fear for France. He who comes to light the fire of civil war also brings with him the scourge of foreign war. He is coming to place our country under his iron yoke once again. He is coming, finally, to destroy that constitutional Charter I have given you; that Charter, my finest title in the eyes of posterity; that Charter which every

Frenchmen cherishes and which I swear, here and now, to uphold. Let us rally, then, around it.

The king was still speaking when a cloud cast the room in darkness. All eyes turned toward the ceiling, seeking the cause of this sudden night. When the law-giving monarch stopped speaking, the cries of "Long live the king!" began again amid tears. "Everyone," the *Moniteur* truthfully reported, "was electrified by the king's sublime speech and stood with their hands outstretched toward the throne. All that could be heard were the words, 'Long live the king! We shall die for the king! The king in life and in death!' repeated with an enthusiasm that every French heart will share."

Indeed, the spectacle was full of pathos: an old, crippled king, who, in return for the murder of his family and twenty-three years of exile, had brought France peace and freedom, putting every outrage and misfortune behind him; this patriarch among sovereigns comes to declare to the representatives of the nation that, at his age, having laid eyes on his native land again, there could be no better end to his career than to die in defense of his people! The princes swore fidelity to the Charter; these tardy oaths came to an end with that of the Prince de Condé and the adhesion of the Duc d'Enghien's father. This heroic dynasty on the verge of extinction—this dynasty of the patrician sword seeking, in the name of liberty, a shield against a plebeian sword that was younger, longer, and crueler—had, with all the many memories it evoked, something extremely melancholy about it.

Louis XVIII's speech, repeated outside the chamber, excited inexpressible transports. Paris was quite royalist and remained so during the Hundred Days. Women in particular were Bourbonistes.

The young today worship the memory of Bonaparte because they are humiliated by the role the current government is forcing France to play in Europe. In 1814, the young hailed the Restoration because it brought down despotism and restored liberty. M. Odilon Barrot, a large number of students from the medical school, and the entirety of the law school joined the ranks of the royal volunteers. The law students petitioned the Chamber of Deputies on March 13:

Gentlemen,

We offer our services to the king and the country; the entire School of Law asks to march. We will not abandon our sovereign or our constitution. Loyal to French honor, we ask you for arms. The feeling of love we bear toward Louis XVIII is responsible for constancy of our devotion. We want no more shackles—we want freedom. At the moment we have it, but they are coming to take it from us. We will defend it to the death. Long live the king! Long live the constitution!

In this energetic, natural, and sincere language, we discern the generosity of youth and a love of liberty. Those who nowadays tell us that the French received the Restoration with revulsion and sorrow are ambitious men playing a part, or striplings who never experienced Bonaparte's oppression, or old imperialized revolutionary liars, who, having applauded like everybody else when the Bourbons returned, now insult, according to their custom, what has fallen, and return to their instinct for murder, policing, and servitude.

3.
PLAN TO DEFEND PARIS

THE KING'S speech had filled me with hope. Conferences took place at the home of the president of the Chamber of Deputies, M. Lainé. This was where I met M. de Lafayette. Until then, I had never seen him except from afar, in another era, under the Constituent Assembly. The proposals were many and various, and most were weak, as they tend to be in times of danger. Some wanted the king to leave Paris and take refuge in Le Havre; others spoke of transporting him to the Vendée. On one side men muttered ambiguous phrases, while on the other they said we had to wait and see what was coming. What was coming, however, was very plain to see. I expressed a different opinion (how unusual!), and M. de Lafayette warmly supported me.* M. Lainé and Marshal Marmont were also of my opinion. I said:

"Let the king keep his word and stay in his capital. The National Guard is on our side. Let us secure Vincennes. We have weapons, and we have money: because we have money, there will be weakness and greed. If the king leaves Paris, Paris will let Bonaparte in, and Bonaparte, once he becomes ruler of Paris, is ruler of France. The army has not gone over entirely to the enemy. Several regiments, many generals and officers, have not yet betrayed their oath. If we remain firm, they

*M. de Lafayette confirms, in his posthumously published memoirs, precious for their store of facts, the rare agreement of his opinion and mine at the time of Bonaparte's return. M. de Lafayette was a man who sincerely loved honor and liberty. (Paris, 1840)

will remain loyal. Let us scatter the royal family and keep only the king here. Let the king's brother go to Le Havre, the Duc de Berry to Lille, the Duc de Bourbon to the Vendée, the Duc d'Orléans to Metz. Madame la Duchesse and Monsieur le Duc d'Angoulême are already in the South. Our multiple points of resistance will prevent Bonaparte from concentrating his force. Let us barricade ourselves in Paris. The National Guards of the nearest *départements* are already coming to our aid. Even as we are making these maneuvers, our old monarch, under the protection of the will of Louis XVI, with the Charter in hand, shall remain calmly seated on his throne at the Tuileries. The diplomatic corps will range themselves around him. The two Chambers will gather in the two pavillions of the palace. The Maison du Roi will camp on the Carrousel and in the Tuileries Garden. We will line the quais and the riverside with guns. Let Bonaparte attack us in this position; let him take our barricades one by one. Let him bombard Paris, if that is what he wishes to do, and if he has enough mortars. Let him make himself odious to the whole population, and we shall see what comes of his undertaking! If we can hold out for three days at most, then victory is ours. The king defending his palace will elicit universal enthusiasm. And if it is destined he should die, let him die worthy of his rank. Let Napoleon's last exploit be to slit an old man's throat. Louis XVIII, sacrificing his life, shall win the only battle he has ever fought, and he shall win it for the benefit of the liberty of humanity."

That is what I said. One is never entitled to say all is lost if he has attempted nothing. What could have been finer than an old son of Saint Louis, supported by the French, overthrowing, in a matter of moments, a man whom all the Allied kings of Europe had taken so many years to lay low?

This resolution, desperate though it sounded, was at bottom quite reasonable and presented no danger at all. I will remain permanently persuaded that Bonaparte, finding Paris against him and the king at home, would not have used force against them. Without artillery, food, or money, all he had was a ragtag collection of troops, still not quite certain what was going on, surprised by their sudden change of cockade, their oaths sworn en route and on the fly: they would have quickly become divided. A few hours' delay would be Napoleon's undoing. All that was needed was a bit of courage. We could already count on a portion of the army; the two Swiss regiments were holding fast to their oaths; and is it not true that, in the event, Marshal Gouvion Saint-Cur ordered the Orléans garrison to resume the white cockade two days after Bonaparte's entry into Paris? Everyone, from Marseille to Bordeaux, recognized the authority of the king for the whole month of March. In Bordeaux, the troops hesitated; they would have remained with the Duchesse d'Angoulême had they heard the king was in the Tuileries and Paris was defending itself. The provincial towns would have imitated the capital. The Tenth Regiment of the Line fought very well under the Duc d'Angoulême; Masséna was sly and uncertain. In Lille, the garrison responded to the stirring proclamation of Marshal Mortier. If all these proofs of possible fidelity occurred *despite* the king's flight, what wouldn't men have done in the case of resistance?

Had my plan been adopted, foreigners would not have ravaged France a second time; our princes would not have returned with the hostile armies; the Legitimacy would have been saved by its own hands. There would have been only one thing to fear in the wake of such success: that the royalty would be too confident of its strength and, consequently, encroach on the rights of the nation.

Why was I born into an era where I was so badly placed? Why was I a royalist against my instincts, at a time when a miserable race of courtiers could neither hear nor understand me? Why was I hurled into this horde of mediocrities, who took me for a fool when I spoke of courage and a revolutionary when I spoke of freedom?

It was a question of defense! The king had no fear, and my plan pleased him well enough with its rather Louis XIV grandeur; but other faces had lengthened. The crown diamonds (long ago acquired with the private funds of the sovereigns) were packed up, leaving thirty-three million écus in the treasury and forty-two million in securities. Those seventy-five million were the fruit of taxation: Why was it not returned to the people, instead of being left behind for a tyrant?

A two-headed procession stumbled up and down the staircases of the Pavillon de Flore. Everyone was inquiring of everyone else what needed to be done, but no one had an answer. You asked the captain of the Guards; you asked the chaplains, the cantors, the almoners—but still, nothing. Pointless chitchat, pointless blathering about the news. I saw young people weeping with rage, asking for orders and weapons in vain; I saw women growing faint with anger and scorn. To reach the king? Impossible. Etiquette closed the door.

The great measure decreed against Bonaparte was an order to "run him down." Limp-legged Louis XVIII was to *run down* the conqueror who bestrode the world? This old legal formula, revived for the occasion, tells you all you need to know about the narrow-mindedness of the statesman of that era. *Run down* in 1815! And *run down* what? A wolf? A bandit chief? A perfidious lord? No—Napoleon, who had run down kings, had seized them and branded their shoulders forever with his indelible *N*!

This ordinance, considered more closely, disclosed a political truth that no one saw. The Bourbons, made strangers to the nation for twenty-three years, had remained stuck in the day and place to which the torrents of the Revolution had borne them, while the nation had continued on both in time and space. Thus the impossibility of understanding or supporting each other. Religion, ideas, interests, language, earth, and heaven—everything was different for the people and the king, for they were separated by a quarter century equivalent to centuries.

But if the order to *run down* seemed strange in its insistence on the old legal idiom, did Bonaparte ever intend to do better while using a new language? The papers of M. d'Hauterive, inventoried by M. Artaud, prove it was very difficult to prevent Napoleon from having the Duc d'Angoulême shot, despite the official piece in the *Moniteur*, the showpiece that remains to us. He thought it wrong for this prince to defend himself. And yet the fugitive from Elba, on leaving Fontainebleau, had urged his soldiers to be loyal to the monarch that France had chosen. Bonaparte's family had been respected: Queen Hortense had accepted the title of Duchesse de Saint-Leu from Louis XVIII; Murat, who still reigned in Naples, did not see his kingdom sold until M. de Talleyrand took care of it during the Congress of Vienna.

This era, when no one spoke frankly, weighed heavy on the heart. Everyone hurled forth professions of faith like bridges to scurry across the difficulty of the day; even if you had to change direction, at least you had traversed the difficulty. Only the young, still fresh from their cradle, were sincere.

Bonaparte solemnly says he is giving up the crown, leaves, and returns nine months later. Benjamin Constant publishes his vigorous protest against the tyrant and changes his mind within twenty-four hours—we shall see later, in another book of these *Memoirs*, who inspired him to this noble gesture, which his changeable nature did not allow him to uphold. Marshal Soult rouses the troops against their former leader; a few days later, he laughs aloud at his proclamation in Napoleon's office at the Tuileries and becomes major general of the army at Waterloo. Marshal Ney kisses the king's hands, swears to bring him Bonaparte locked in an iron cage, then delivers every soldier he commands to the latter. And the King of France? He says that at sixty he cannot imagine a better end to his career than dying in defense of his people . . . and he flees to Ghent! Faced with such an absolute absence of truth in human sentiments, such discrepancy between words and deeds, one feels overcome with disgust for mankind.

Louis XVIII, on March 20, said he wished to die in France. If he had kept his word, the Legitimacy might have lasted another century. Nature herself seemed to have deprived the old king of his capacity for retreat by saddling him with advantageous infirmities; but the future destinies of the human race would have been hampered had the author of the Charter done as he said he would. Bonaparte hastened to the future's aid. This Christ of unholy power took the new man sick of the palsy by the hand and said to him: "Arise, and take up thy bed." *Surge, tolle lectum tuum.*[3]

4.

THE KING'S ESCAPE—I DEPART WITH MADAME DE CHATEAUBRIAND— TROUBLES ALONG THE WAY— THE DUC D'ORLÉANS AND THE PRINCE DE CONDÉ— TOURNAY, BRUSSELS—MEMORIES—THE DUC DE RICHELIEU—THE KING IN GHENT SUMMONS ME

IT WAS obvious an escape was being planned. For fear of being detained, they did not even warn those who, like me, would have been shot an hour after Napoleon waltzed into Paris. I saw the Duc de Richelieu on the Champs-Élysées.

"We're being deceived," he told me. "I'm going to stand guard here: I have no intention of waiting for the emperor at the Tuileries by myself."

Madame de Chateaubriand had sent a servant to the Carrousel on the evening of the nineteenth with orders to return only when he was certain that the king had fled. At midnight, when the servant had still not returned, I retired for the evening. I had just climbed into bed when M. Clausel de Coussergues came in. He told us that His Majesty had left and was on his way to Lille. He brought me this news from the chancellor, who, knowing I was in danger, betrayed the secret and sent me 12,000 francs to cover my salary as minister to Sweden. I insisted on staying, not wanting to leave Paris until I was physically sure the royals had removed themselves. The servant sent to ascertain this returned: he had seen the carriages of the Court pass by. Madame de Chateaubriand pushed me into her carriage at four o'clock in the morning, March 20. I was in such a rage that I didn't know where I was going or what I was doing.

We left the city by the Barrière Saint-Martin. At dawn, I saw crows peacefully descending from the roadside elms where they had passed the night, going to have their first meal in the fields, not bothering their heads about Louis XVIII or Napoleon at all. They were under no obligation to leave their country and, thanks to their wings, could scoff at the bad road on which I was being jerked and jolted. Old friends of Combourg! We were much more alike when, at the break of day, we used to eat blackberries together from the brambles in the Breton woods.

The road was bumpy, the weather rainy, Madame de Chateaubriand suffering: she kept constantly looking through the rear window of the carriage to see if we were being followed. We slept in Amiens, where Du Cange was born; then in Arras, which Robespierre called home. There I was recognized. When we sent for horses on the morning of the twenty-second, the postmaster said they had been reserved for a general who was bringing news of "the triumphal entry of the emperor-king to Paris." Madame de Chateaubriand was dying of fear, not for herself but for me. I ran to the post office and, with money, removed the obstacle.

Under the ramparts of Lille at two in the morning on the twenty-third, we found the gates locked—orders had been given not to open them to anyone. Not a soul could or would tell us whether the king had entered the city. For a few louis, I hired the postilion to guide us, outside the glacis, to the other side of the place and then on to Tournay: in 1792, I had walked, overnight, this same road with my brother. Arriving in Tournay, I learned that Louis XVIII had indeed entered Lille with Marshal Mortier, and that he intended to defend himself there. I sent a courier to M. de Blacas, imploring him to send me a permit to be received in the place. My courier returned with a permit from the commandant but no word from M. de Blacas. Leaving Madame de Chateaubriand in Tournay, I had climbed back into a carriage and was on my way to Lille when we ran into the Prince de Condé. From him we learned that the king had departed and Marshal Mortier had gone with him to the border. If this was the case, Louis XVIII was no longer in Lille by the time my letter arrived there.

The Duc d'Orléans kept a close eye on the Prince de Condé. A sullen-looking man, he was, at bottom, happy to find himself above the fray. The ambiguity of his declarations and behavior bore the stamp of his character. As for the old Prince de Condé, emigration was his Lar.[4] He was not afraid of Monsieur de Bonaparte; he would fight if called to, flee if called to—things were a bit confused in his brain. He was not too sure whether he would stop at Rocroi for battle or go to dinner at the Grand-Cerf. He pulled up stakes a few hours before us, telling me to recommend the coffee at the inn to the members of his household he had left behind. He did not know I had resigned when his grandson died. He was not sure he had had a grandson. He felt in the sound of his name only a certain swelling of glory, which might well be due to some Condé he no longer recalled.

Do you remember the first time I passed through Tournay, with my brother, during my first emigration? Do you remember, then, the man turned into an ass, the girl with wheat stalks growing out of her ears, the rain of crows that set everything on fire?* In 1815, we ourselves were rather a rain of crows; but we did not set fire to anything. Alas! My fortuneless brother was no longer with me. Between 1792 and 1815, the Republic and the Empire had passed away—and how many revolutions had likewise rolled through my own life! Time had ravaged me like the rest. And you, youthful generations of the moment, let twenty-three years go by, and when I am dead and buried, you, too, shall be asking yourselves what happened to the loves and illusions you cherish today.

In Tournay, I found both Bertin brothers: M. Bertin de Vaux soon went back to Paris, while the other Bertin, the elder Bertin, my friend, remained. You know from Book Fifteen of these *Memoirs* what bound me to him.[5]

From Tournay we traveled on to Brussels. There, I found neither Baron de Breteuil, nor Rivarol, nor any of those young aides-de-camp now dead or grown old, which amounts to the same thing, nor any sign of the barber who had given me shelter. In any case, I was no

*Book 9, Chapter 7.

longer wielding a musket but a pen; the soldier had become a quill-driver. I was in search of Louis XVIII, who, unbeknownst to me, was already in Ghent, where M. Blacas and M. Duras had taken him. Their intention had at first been to put the king on a boat bound for England. If the king had agreed to this, he would never have regained the throne.

Entering an inn to take a look at a room, I spotted the Duc de Richelieu smoking, half reclined on a sofa at the back of a dark room. He spoke to me about the princes most brutally, saying he was headed for Russia and no longer wanted to hear about "those men." The Duchesse de Duras, arriving in Brussels, had the sorrow to lose her niece there.

The capital of Brabant is an abomination to me. I have never found it anything but a passageway to exile, and it has always brought bad luck to me and my friends.

An order from the king at last summoned me to Ghent. The royal volunteers and the Duc de Berry's little army had been dismissed at Béthune amid the mud and accidents of a military debacle: they had movingly bidden each other farewell. Two hundred men of the Maison du Roi stayed behind and were billeted in Aalst—my two nephews, Louis and Christian de Chateaubriand, among them.

5.

THE HUNDRED DAYS IN GHENT: THE KING AND HIS
COUNCIL—I BECOME ACTING MINISTER OF THE
INTERIOR—M. DE LALLY-TOLLENDAL—MADAME
LA DUCHESSE DE DURAS—MARSHAL VICTOR—
ABBÉ LOUIS AND COMTE BEUGNOT—ABBÉ DE
MONTESQUIOU—WHITE-FISH DINNERS AND DINERS

I HAD BEEN offered a billet I did not make use of. A baroness,
whose name I have forgotten, came to find Madame de Chateaubri-
and at the inn and offered us an apartment in her house. She implored
us with such good grace! "Pay no attention," she told us, "to what my
husband tells you: he's a bit . . . in the head, you know? My daughter
is so unusual; she has terrible moments, poor child! But she's gentle
as a lamb. Alas! She's not the one that causes me the most grief; that
would be my son Louis, my youngest. If God doesn't get ahold of him
soon, he'll be worse than his father." Madame de Chateaubriand
politely declined to go and live with such reasonable people.[6]

The king, well housed, with his servants and guards, now formed
his council. This great monarch's empire comprised a single house in
the United Kingdom of the Netherlands—a house located in a town
that, in addition to being the birthplace of Charles V, had been the
seat of one of Bonaparte's prefectures. All these names together
conjure quite a number of eras and events.

With the Abbé de Montesquiou away in London, Louis XVIII
appointed me acting Minister of the Interior.[7] My correspondence
with the *départements* did not give me much trouble. It was easy to
keep in touch with the prefects, sub-prefects, mayors, and deputy
mayors of our good cities within our borders. I did not repair very
many roads and, it's true, I allowed some steeples to collapse. My
budget, however, did not make me rich; I had no secret funds—only,
in a flagrant abuse of power, I was holding two positions at once: I

remained Minister Plenipotentiary of His Majesty to the King of
Sweden, who, like his countryman Henri IV, ruled by right of conquest,
if not by right of birth.[8] We ministers held our talks around a table
covered with green baize in the king's study. M. de Lally-Tollendal,
who was, I believe, Minister of Public Education, delivered speeches
even ampler and plumper than his person: he quoted his illustrious
ancestors, the kings of Ireland, and confused the trial of his father
with the trials of Charles I and Louis XVI.[9] In the evenings, he took
a rest from the tears, sweat, and words he poured out at the council
with a lady who had rushed there from Paris, infatuated with his
genius. He virtuously tried to cure her of her infatuation, but his
eloquence eclipsed his virtue and drove the stinger further in.[10]

Madame la Duchesse de Duras had come to join her husband
among the exiled. I would not wish to speak ill of misfortune, since
it allowed me to spend three months in the company of this excellent
woman, talking about everything that honest minds and hearts can
find in a perfect harmony of tastes, ideas, beliefs, and feelings. Madame
de Duras was ambitious for me. At first, she alone knew what I might
be worth in political life. She was always saddened by the envy and
blindness that kept me away from the king; but she was far more
distressed by the ways in which my character hampered my fortune.
She scolded me, she wanted to educate me out my indifference, my
frankness, my naiveté, and make me adopt airs and graces that she
herself could not bear. Perhaps nothing makes us more affectionate
or grateful than when we feel we are under the auspices of a superior
friendship which, by virtue of its ascendancy over society, makes your
defects pass for qualities, your imperfections for charms. A man
protects you with what he is worth, a woman with what you are worth:
that is why, of these two empires, the former is so odious and the
latter so sweet.

Since I have lost this large-hearted person, whose soul was so
noble, whose mind united something of the forcefulness of Madame
de Staël's thinking with the graceful talent of Madame de La Fayette,
I have never ceased, while mourning her, to reproach myself for the
inequities I have sometimes inflicted on hearts devoted to me. Let us

keep a close watch on our character! Let us recall that, with a deep attachment, we can nevertheless poison the days we buy back at the cost of all our blood. When our friends have gone down to the grave, what means do we have to right our wrongs? Are our useless regrets and our vain repentance remedies for the sorrows we have caused them? They would have preferred a single smile from us while they were alive to all the tears we shed after they have gone.

The charming Clara* was in Ghent with her mother. We both, the two of us, composed bad couplets to the tune of "La Tyrolienne." I dandled many pretty little girls on my knee who are now young grandmothers. If you leave a woman you have seen wedded at sixteen and return sixteen years later, you will find her exactly the same as before: "Ah! Madame, you have not aged a day!" Indeed—but you are speaking to the daughter, the girl you will again lead to the altar. But you, the melancholy witness of the two nuptials, box up the sixteen years you have received at each union: they are a wedding present that will hasten your own marriage with a pale, rather scrawny lady.

Marshal Victor had come to Ghent and displayed admirable simplicity. He asked for nothing and never pestered the king with eager attentions. He was scarcely seen. I do not know whether he ever once had the honor of being invited to one of His Majesty's dinners. Years later, I met him again; I was his colleague in office, and he always seemed to me to display the same excellent nature. In Paris, in 1823, the Dauphin was quite severe with this honest soldier. It was very kind to repay the Duc de Bellune's humble devotion with such easy ingratitude![11] Candor entrances and moves me, even when it is naive in the extreme. Thus the marshal told me about the death of his wife in the language of a soldier, and he moved me to tears: he spoke coarse words so quickly, and with such decorum, one could almost have written them down.

M. de Vaublanc and M. Capelle also joined us. The former said he had a bit of everything in his portfolio. Did you want some Mon-

*Madame la Duchesse de Rauzun.

tesquieu? Here it is. Some Bossuet? Here you go. As the game seemed to be taking a different turn, more and more travelers arrived.

The Abbé Louis and the Comte Beugnot alighted at the inn where I was staying. Madame de Chateaubriand was having terrible difficulty breathing, and I was sitting up with her. The two newcomers were put in a room separated from my wife's only by a thin partition. It was impossible not to hear, at least without stopping up your ears. Between eleven o'clock and midnight, the transplants raised their voices; Abbé Louis, who talked like a stuttering wolf, said to M. Beugnot:

"You, a minister? You'll never be one again! All you've done is make one blunder after another!"

I did not hear Comte Beugnot's answer clearly, but he said something about thirty-three million left in the royal treasury. The abbé, apparently in a rage, knocked over a chair, which clattered to the floor. Beneath this clangor, I picked out a few words:

"The Duc d'Angoulême? He'll have to buy his national property at the gates of Paris. I will sell off what is left of the state forests. I will cut everything down—the elms along the high road, the Bois de Boulogne, the Champs-Elysées. What is it good for, eh?"

Brutality was Louis's chief merit. His talent lay in a stupid love of material interests. If the Minister of Finance drew the forests after him, he must have had a very different sort of secret from Orpheus, who "made the woods go after him with his fair fiddling."[12] In the slang of the time, M. Louis was called a "special" person. His specialty, when it came to financial matters, had been piling up taxpayers' money in the treasury for Bonaparte to steal. However, Napoleon wanted nothing to do with this man, who was at best suited to the Directory, and who, though special, was by no means unique.

Abbé Louis had come all the way to Ghent to claim his office. He was very well liked by M. de Talleyrand, beside whom he had officiated at the first Federation Day on the Champ de Mars. The bishop played the priest, Abbé Louis the deacon, and Abbé d'Ernaud the subdeacon. M. de Talleyrand, remembering this admirable profanation, said to Baron Louis, "Abbé, you were very good as the deacon on the Champ de Mars!" We tolerated this shame under the great tyranny of Bonaparte. But should we have tolerated it later on?

The "most Christian" king screened himself from all accusations of hypocrisy. In his cabinet, he had a married priest, M. de Talleyrand; a concubinal priest, M. Louis; and a non-practicing priest, M. de Montesquiou.

The latter, a man as feverish as a consumptive, who had a certain facility with words, was in possession of a petty and deprecatory mind, a hateful heart, and a sour character. One day when I made a speech calling for freedom of the press in the Luxembourg, the descendant of Clovis, passing before me (a man related merely to the Breton Mormoran),[13] gave me a great blow in the thigh with his knee, which was not in good taste; I returned the blow, which was not polite: we were playing at being the Duc de La Rochefoucauld and the Coadjutor.[14] The Abbé de Montesquiou humorously called M. de Lally-Tollendal "an English-style beast."

In the rivers of Ghent, they catch a very delicate white fish. We would go, *tutti quanti*, to dine on this good fish in an open-air café, waiting for battles and the end of empires. M. Laborie was never missing at these rendezvous: I had met him for the first time in Savigny, when, fleeing from Bonaparte, he had gone in by one window of Madame de Beaumont's house and out by another. A tireless worker, always piling up new pursuits and bills, as fond of rendering services as others are of receiving them, he has been slandered. Slander is not an indictment of the slandered, it is the excuse of the slanderer. I have seen people grow weary of the promises in which M. Laborie was so rich. But why? Illusions are like torture: they are always good for passing an hour or two.[15] I have often, with a golden bridle in my hand, led old nags of memories unable to stand upright, which I took for frisky young hopes.

At these same white-fish dinners, I met M. Mounier, a man of reason and probity. M. Guizot deigned to honor us with his presence.

6.

THE HUNDRED DAYS IN GHENT, CONTINUED: MY REPORT TO THE KING: EFFECT OF THIS REPORT IN PARIS—FALSIFICATION

A *MONITEUR* had been established in Ghent. My report to the king of May 12, inserted in this paper, demonstrates that my feelings on the freedom of the press and on foreign domination have always and in every country been the same. I can quote these passages today. They are not at all at odds with my life.

> Sire, you were on the brink of crowning the institutions whose foundations you had laid. You had determined a period for the commencement of hereditary peerage. The ministry would have acquired greater unity; the ministers would have become members of both Chambers, according to the spirit of the Charter. A law would have been proposed to allow a person to be elected a member of the Chamber of Deputies before the age of forty, so that citizens might be able to have a real political career. A penal code dealing with crimes of the press was to be adopted, after which the press would have been entirely free, for this freedom is inseparable from any representative government...
>
> Sire, this is the occasion to make a solemn protest: all of your ministers, all of the members of your council, are inviolably dedicated to the principles of a wise liberty; from you, they draw that love of law, order, and justice without which there is no happiness for a nation. Sire, may we be allowed to tell you that we are prepared to shed the last drop of our blood on your behalf, to follow you to the end of the earth, to share

with you whatever tribulations it pleases the Almighty to send you, for we believe before God that you will uphold the constitution you have bestowed upon your people, that the sincerest wish of your royal soul is the freedom of the French. If it had been otherwise, Sire, we would still have been willing to die at your feet in defense of your sacred person; but we would have been nothing but your soldiers, we would have ceased to be your advisers and ministers.

Sire, at this moment, we share your royal sadness; there is not one of your advisers or ministers who would not give his life to prevent the invasion of France. Sire, you are French, we are French! Alive to the honor of our country, proud of the glory of our arms, pleased by the courage of our soldiers, we would be willing, enrolled in their battalions, to shed the last drop of our blood in the effort to recall them to their duty, or to share lawful victories with them. We can only look with deepest sorrow upon the misfortunes about to be visited upon our country.

Thus, in Ghent, I proposed to give the Charter what it still lacked, and I expressed my sorrow at the new invasion threatening France. I was, however, merely an exile whose wishes were in contradiction with the facts that could open the doors to my country to me again. These pages were written in the lands of the Allied sovereigns, among kings and émigrés who hated the freedom of the press, among armies marching to conquest who held us, as it were, prisoners. These circumstances perhaps add some force to the feelings I dared to express.

My report, reaching Paris, made a great stir. It was reprinted by M. Le Normant, who was gambling with his life, and for whom I had all the difficulty in the world obtaining a meaningless printer's license from the king. Bonaparte acted, or allowed himself to act, in a manner unworthy of him: when my report appeared, they did what the Directory had done to the publication of Cléry's memoirs; they falsified it to shreds. I was made to seem I had proposed all sorts of stupidities to Louis XVIII concerning the restoration of feudal rights, as if the appearance of the original piece in the Ghent *Moniteur*, on a date fixed and known, did not confound this imposture. But they needed a lie to buy them an hour. The false Chateaubriand charged with writing this disingenuous pamphlet was a soldier of rather high rank. After the Hundred Days, he was dismissed, on the basis of his conduct toward me. He sent his friends to my house, and they begged me to intervene, so that a man of merit would not lose his only means of subsistence. I wrote to the Minister of War and obtained a retirement pension for this officer. He is now dead, but his wife has remained attached to Madame de Chateaubriand out of a gratitude to which I am far from having any rights. Certain kinds of behavior are overly esteemed; the vulgarest people are susceptible to these acts of generosity. It costs very little to give oneself a reputation for virtue: the loftiest soul is not the one who forgives; it is the one who has no need of forgiveness.

I do not know how Bonaparte, on Saint Helena, found out that I had "rendered essential services in Ghent." If he overestimated the part I played, at least there was, behind this estimation, an appreciation of my political worth.

7.

THE HUNDRED DAYS IN GHENT, CONTINUED:
THE BEGUINAGE—HOW I WAS RECEIVED—GRAND
DINNER—MADAME DE CHATEAUBRIAND'S TRIP TO
OSTENDE—ANVERS—A STAMMERER—DEATH OF A
YOUNG ENGLISHWOMAN

IN GHENT I shrunk away, as often as I could, from intrigues disagreeable to my nature and distressing to my eyes; for, deep down, in our piddling catastrophe, I perceived the catastrophe of society. My refuge from idlers and boors was between the walls of the Beguinage. I strolled around this tiny universe of veiled or guimped women devoting themselves to various Christian works—a region of calm set, like the African Syrtes,[16] at the edge of the storms. As I strolled there, no disparities clashed with my thoughts, for religious feeling is so lofty it is never alien to the most serious revolutions. The solitaries of the Thebaid and the barbarians who destroyed the Roman world are in no sense discordant facts or mutually exclusive existences.

I was graciously received, as the author of *The Genius of Christianity*, within the cloister walls. Wherever I go among Christians, priests come to me and mothers bring their children, who recite my chapter on First Communion to me. Then come the unhappy people who tell me the good I have had the happiness to do them. My visit to a Catholic city is announced like that of a missionary and doctor. I am moved by this double reputation. It is the only thing I like about myself. The rest of my person and fame brings me no pleasure at all.

I was many times invited to banquets given by the family of Monsieur and Madame Ops, a venerable father and mother surrounded by thirty children, grandchildren, and great-grandchildren. At M. Coppens's house, a gala, which I had no choice but to attend, went from one in the afternoon until eight in the evening. I counted nine servings: we began with jams and finished with chops. Only the French know how to dine methodically, just as only they know how to compose a book.[17]

My "ministry" kept me in Ghent. Madame de Chateaubriand, who was not so busy, went to see Ostende, where I had embarked for Jersey in 1792. I, exiled and dying, had traveled down the same canals along which I, exiled again, but in perfect health, now walked: my life is full of fables! The miseries and joys of my first emigration came back to me. I revisited England in my mind, saw my companions in fortune, and Charlotte, whom I was to see again. No one is as skilled as I am at creating real companionship for himself by conjuring shadows; it has reached the point where the life of my memories absorbs my sense of my actual life. People I never thought about, when they die, invade my memory. It seems no one can become my companion unless he has gone to the other side of the grave. This leads me to believe that I am a dead man. Where others find eternal separation, I find eternal reunion. If one of my friends takes wing from the earth, it is as if he has come to live at my house; he never leaves me again. The further the present world retreats from me, the more the past world returns to me. If the current generations disdain the old generations, their scorn is wasted where I'm concerned: I don't even notice their existence.

My Golden Fleece was still not in Bruges; Madame de Chateaubriand brought it to me. In Bruges, in 1426, "there was a man called John" who invented or perfected oil painting. Let us give thanks to John of Bruges. Without the propagation of his method, the master-works of Raphael would be obliterated today. Where did the Flemish painters steal the light with which they illuminate their pictures? What Greek ray strayed to the shores of Batavia?[18]

Following her journey to Ostende, Madame de Chateaubriand made a trip to Antwerp. There she saw, in a cemetery, plaster souls in purgatory smeared top to toe with smoke and fire. In Louvain, she recruited me a stammering, very learned professor who came to Ghent expressly to gaze upon a man as strange as my wife's husband. He said to me: "Illus...ttt...rr..." His words failed his admiration, and I asked him to dinner. Once the Hellenist had drunk some curaçao, his tongue was loosed.[19] We launched into discussing the merits of Thucydides, whom the wine made as clear to us as water. In the effort of keeping pace with my host, I ended up, I believe, speaking Dutch, or at least I ceased to understand what I was saying.

Madame de Chateaubriand had a sad night's stay at an inn in Antwerp. A young English girl who had just given birth lay dying. For two hours she wept and wailed; then her voice weakened, and her last moan, which only scarcely reached a stranger's ear, was lost in eternal silence. The cries of that traveler, forsaken and alone, seemed to prelude the thousand agonized voices soon to be heard at Waterloo.

8.

THE HUNDRED DAYS IN GHENT, CONTINUED: UNUSUAL MOVEMENT IN GHENT—THE DUKE OF WELLINGTON—*MONSIEUR*—LOUIS XVIII

THE CUSTOMARY solitude of Ghent was made even more impressive by the foreign mob that then animated it and would soon continue on its way. Belgian and English recruits drilled in the squares and beneath the trees along the promenades. Gunners, suppliers, and dragoons brought down artillery trains, herds of oxen, horses that struggled in the air as they were lowered, hanging in leather straps. Lady sutlers landed with sacks, children, and their husbands' guns in tow. All of them were going, with no idea why, and no interest, to the great rendezvous of destruction that Bonaparte had set for them. One saw politicians gesticulating wildly on the canal side next to a motionless fisherman, émigrés trotting from the king's house to *Monsieur*'s house, from *Monsieur*'s house to the king's. The chancellor of France, M. Dambray, in a green coat and round hat, with an old novel under his arm, rushed off to the Council to amend the Charter. The Duc de Lévis went to pay his court in tramped-down shoes that showed his feet, for—a very brave and new-fashioned Achilles—he had been wounded in the heel. He was extremely witty, as can be seen in the collection of his thoughts.[20]

Louis XVIII rode out every night after dinner in a six-horse carriage with his valet de chambre and his guards to make the rounds of Ghent, exactly as he would have done in Paris. If he happened to cross paths with the Duke of Wellington, he would give him, in passing, a subtle nod of acknowledgement.

Louis XVIII never forgot for a moment the preeminence of his birth. He was a king everywhere, as God is God everywhere, in a manger or a temple, on an altar of gold or clay. Adversity never elicited even the smallest concession from him; the lower he sank, the loftier he became. His name was his diadem. He seemed to say, "You may kill me, but you shall not kill the centuries inscribed on my brow." If they had scraped all his heraldry off the Louvre, why should he care? Was it not engraved upon the globe? Had delegates been shipped to scrape it off in every corner of the earth? Had it been erased in the Indies, Pondicherry, America, Lima, and Mexico; in the East, Antioch, Jerusalem, Acre, Cairo, Constantinople, Rhodes, Morea; in the West, on the walls of Rome, the ceilings of Caserta and El Escorial, the vaults of Regensburg and Westminster, in the coats of arms of every king? Had it been torn from the compass, where it seemed to announce the reign of the lilies to all the various regions of the earth?

His obsession with grandeur, antiquity, dignity, and the majesty of his family gave Louis XVIII true dominion. Everyone felt its power. Even Bonaparte's generals admitted it. They were more intimidated by this helpless old man than by the terrible master who had commanded them in a hundred battles. In Paris, when Louis XVIII granted the triumphant monarchs the honor of dining at his table, he passed unceremoniously by those princes whose soldiers were camped in the courtyard of the Louvre. He treated them like vassals, who had merely done their duty by bringing men-at-arms to their overlord. There is but one monarchy in Europe, and that is the French monarchy. The destiny of the others is linked to the fate of this one. All the royal races are, traced back far enough, of the race of Hugh Capet,[21] and almost all are his daughters. Our ancient royal dynasty has been the ancient royal dynasty of the world. The era of the expulsion of kings will be dated from the banishment of the Capets.

The more impolitic the haughtiness this descendant of Saint Louis became (it was disastrous for his heirs), the more it pleased the nation's pride: the French enjoyed the sight of a sovereign, who, defeated, had borne the chains of a man bearing, victorious, the yoke of a dynasty.

Louis XVIII's unshakable faith in his blood is the real power that put the scepter in his hand. It is this same faith that, on two occasions, caused a crown to fall upon his head—a crown that Europe did not believe in and for which it did not pretend to deplete her populations or her treasuries. The soldierless exile was there to be found at the end of all the battles in which he had not fought. Louis XVIII was the Legitimacy incarnate. It ceased to be visible when he disappeared.

9.

THE HUNDRED DAYS IN GHENT, CONTINUED: MEMORIES OF THE HISTORY OF GHENT—MADAME LA DUCHESSE D'ANGOULÊME ARRIVES IN GHENT—MADAME DE SÈZE—MADAME LA DUCHESSE DE LÉVIS

I WANDERED around Ghent as I wander around everywhere, alone. The boats gliding over the narrow canals, obliged to cross ten or twelve leagues of meadows before arriving at the sea, looked as if they were sailing over the grass. They reminded me of the savage canoes in the wild-oat marshes of Missouri. Pausing by the waterside, where men were soaking lengths of raw canvas, my eyes ranged over the spires of the town, and history appeared to me in the clouds. I saw the citizens of Ghent rising up against Henri de Châtillon, governor for France; Edward III's wife giving birth to John of Gaunt, scion of the House of Lancaster; the populist reign of van Artevelde, who said, "Good people, what has provoked you? Why are you so displeased with me? What have I done to anger you?" And the people shouted at him, "You must die!"—as time shouts at us all. I saw, later, the dukes of Burgundy and the coming of the Spanish. Then the pacification, the sieges, the seizures of Ghent.

When I had mooned among the centuries for a while, the sound of a little bugle or a Scottish musette awakened me. I could see living soldiers coming up to join the battalions of Batavia long dead. Always destruction, power laid low, and, in the end, a few faint shadows and some half-forgotten names.

The coastal regions of Flanders were among the first garrisons of Chlodio and Clovis's companions. Ghent, Bruges, and the countryside around them provided nearly a tenth of the grenadiers of the Old Guard. This terrible militia was taken, in part, from the cradle of our fathers, and it would be exterminated not far from this cradle. Did the Lys give her flower to the sign of our kings?[22]

The Spanish have left their mark on the landscape. The buildings of Ghent set me thinking of those of Granada, minus the sky of La Vega. A large city almost uninhabited, with deserted streets and canals quite as deserted as these streets...twenty-six islands formed by these canals, which were not those of Venice, an enormous medieval cannon: this is what, in Ghent, took the place of the city of the Zegris, the Darro, and the Genil, the Generalife and the Alhambra.[23] Oh, my old dreams—will I ever see you again?

The Duchesse d'Angoulême, sailing from Gironde, arrived via England with General Donnadieu and M. de Sèze, who had crossed the sea with his blue ribbon pinned to his jacket. The Duc and Duchesse de Lévis followed the princess; they had darted into their diligence and escaped from Paris by the Bordeaux road. Some travelers, their companions, talked politics:

"That scoundrel Chateaubriand," said one of them, "is not so stupid! For three days, his carriage sat there packed in his courtyard—the bird flew the coop. They would have made short work of him if Napoleon had got him!"

The Duchesse de Lévis was a very beautiful person, very good, and as calm as the Duchesse de Duras was turbulent. She never left Madame de Chateaubriand's side and was our constant companion in Ghent. No one in my life has ever been the cause of such quietude—a thing I am very much in need of. The least troubled moments of my existence are those I spent at Noisiel, with this woman whose words and feelings never entered your soul without bringing you peace. I recall them regretfully, those moments passed under the tall chestnuts of Noisiel! My spirit calmed, my heart mending, I gazed at the ruins of Chelles Abbey and the little lights on the boats that paused among the willows of the Marne.

My memory of Madame de Lévis is like that of a quiet autumn evening. In no time at all, she was gone; she went to merge with death, the source of all repose: I watched her descend into her grave at the Père-Lachaise cemetery without a sound. She lies a way above Monsieur de Fontanes, who rests next to his son Saint-Marcellin, killed in a duel. Thus, when I bowed my head before Madame de Lévis's grave, I was confronted with two other tombs. Man cannot awaken one pain without reawakening another: those flowers that never open except in shadow flourish during the night.

In addition to Madame de Lévis's affectionate kindness, I also enjoyed the friendship of her father: I may now reckon only by generations. M. de Lévis was a fine writer. He had a varied and fertile imagination that bespoke his noble blood, which he had shed years before on the beaches at Quiberon.

Nor did it all end there. For this friendship would be passed down to the second generation. The Duc de Lévis, who is today one of the Comte de Chambord's councillors, has become dear to me. My hereditary affection will not fail him any more than my loyalty shall fail his august master.[24] The new and charming Duchesse de Lévis, his wife, adds to the great name of d'Aubusson the most brilliant qualities of heart and mind. There is something to live for when the Graces lend history such tireless wings!

IO.

THE HUNDRED DAYS IN GHENT, CONTINUED: PAVILLON DE MARSAN IN GHENT—M. GAILLARD, COUNCILLOR TO THE ROYAL COURT—SECRET VISIT OF MADAME LA BARONNE DE VITROLLES—NOTES WRITTEN IN *MONSIEUR'S* HAND—FOUCHÉ

IN GHENT, as in Paris, there was a Pavillon de Marsan.[25] Every day brought *Monsieur* news from France that had been manufactured by self-interest or imagination.

M. Gaillard, a former Oratorian, a councillor to the royal Court, and a close friend of Fouché's, appeared in our midst; he made himself known and was put in touch with M. Capelle.

When I went to *Monsieur's* house, which was rarely, his entourage talked to me, in veiled words and with many sighs, about a "man who (it must be admitted) is conducting himself marvelously; he is obstructing all the emperor's operations; he is defending the Faubourg Saint-Germain"; and so on. The faithful Marshal Soult was also the object of *Monsieur's* predilections and, after Fouché, the most loyal man in France.[26]

One day, a carriage stopped at the door of my inn and I saw the Baronne de Vitrolles step down from it. She arrived endowed with the authority of the Duc d'Otrante and obtained a note, written in *Monsieur's* hand, in which the prince declared he would be eternally grateful to the man who saved M. de Vitrolles. Fouché was satisfied. Armed with this note, he was sure of his future in the case of another restoration. From that moment forward, there was no discussion in Ghent that did not revolve around the immense obligations everyone had to the excellent M. Fouché de Nantes, unless it revolved around the sheer impossibility of returning to France except at this righteous

604 · MEMOIRS FROM BEYOND THE GRAVE

man's pleasure. The difficulty was how to make the king appreciate this new redeemer of the monarchy.

After the Hundred Days, Madame de Custine forced me to have dinner with Fouché at her house. I had seen him once, five years earlier, in connection with the condemnation of my poor cousin Armand. The ex-minister knew I had opposed his nomination at Roye, at Gonesse, at Arnouville, and, since he thought I was power-ful, wished to make peace with me. The best thing about him was the killing of Louis XVI: regicide was the peak of his innocence. Garrulous, like all revolutionaries, beating the air with empty phrases,[27] he reeled off a string of commonplaces full of words like "fate," "ne-cessity," "the law of things," mixing this philosophical nonsense with nonsense about the progress and march of society, and shameless maxims favoring the strong over the weak; nor did he skimp on cocky assertions about the justice of success, the insignificance of a severed head, the rightness of what prospers, the wrongness of what suffers, all the while affecting to speak of the most horrible disasters with frivolity and indifference, as though he were a genius above such inanities. Not one choice idea, one remarkable insight, escaped him, on any subject whatsoever. I went away shaking my head at crime.

M. Fouché never forgave me my dryness or the minimal effect he had on me. He had thought he would fascinate me by making the blade of the fatal instrument rise and fall before my eyes, like a glory from Sinai;[28] he had imagined I would mistake the fanatic for a co-lossus—a man who, speaking of the soil of Lyon, had said:

"We shall devastate this ground, and on the ruins of this arrogant and rebellious city we shall build cottages here and there, which the friends of equality shall hasten to come live in ... We shall have the energy and courage to walk through the vast graveyard of the con-spirators ... Their bloodstained corpses, floated down the Rhône, shall make everyone, on both banks and at its mouth, see the horror and the omnipotence of the people ... We shall celebrate the victory of Toulon; this evening, we shall dispatch 250 rebels beneath a hail of bullets."

These horrible goffered frills did not impress me in the least. Because M. "de Nantes"[29] had diluted Republican infamies with imperial muck; because the sansculotte, transformed into a duke, had braided the lantern cord into the cord of the Légion d'Honneur, he seemed to me no cleverer and no greater. The Jacobins detest men who ignore their atrocities and deride their murders; their pride is provoked, like that of writers whose talent one contests.

11.

CONGRESS OF VIENNA: NEGOTIATIONS OF M. DE
SAINT-LÉON, SENT BY FOUCHÉ—PROPOSAL RELATIVE
TO M. LE DUC D'ORLÉANS—M. DE TALLEYRAND—
ALEXANDER'S DISPLEASURE WITH LOUIS XVIII—
VARIOUS PRETENDERS—LA BESNARDIÈRE'S REPORT
—ALEXANDER'S UNEXPECTED PROPOSAL TO THE
CONGRESS: LORD CLANCARTHY DEFEATS IT—M. DE
TALLEYRAND RETURNS: HIS DISPATCH TO LOUIS XVIII
—DECLARATION OF THE ALLIANCE, ABBREVIATED
IN THE OFFICIAL NEWSPAPER OF FRANKFURT—
M. DE TALLEYRAND WISHES THE KING TO RETURN
TO FRANCE THROUGH THE SOUTHEASTERN
PROVINCES—PRINCE DE BÉNÉVENT'S DEALS IN
VIENNA—HE WRITES TO ME IN GHENT: HIS LETTER

AT THE same time that Fouché was sending M. Gaillard to Ghent
to negotiate with Louis XVI's brother, his agents in Basel were in
talks with the agents of Prince Metternich on the subject of Napoleon
II, and M. de Saint-Léon, who had also been sent by Fouché, arrived
in Venice to discuss a "possible" crown for the Duc d'Orléans. Friends
of the Duc d'Otrante could not count on him any more than his
enemies could: when the legitimate princes returned, he kept his
former colleague M. Thibaudeau on the list of the exiled, while M.
de Talleyrand, for his part, subtracted or added relegates to this
catalog as he saw fit. Didn't the Faubourg Saint-Germain have good
reason to put their faith in M. Fouché?

M. de Saint-Léon delivered three notes to Vienna, one of which
was addressed to M. de Talleyrand. The Duc d'Otrante suggested that
Louis XVIII's ambassador propel the son of *Égalité*, if he could see a
way to do it, onto the throne.[30] What probity there was in these negotiations! How lucky we were to be dealing with honest people! Yet

we have admired, acclaimed, blessed these Cartouches;[31] we have paid court to them; we have called them "my lord"! This explains the world as it is now. M. de Montrond came in addition, after M. de Saint-Léon.

The Duc d'Orléans did not conspire in deed but tacitly; he let the revolutionary affinities scheme: such a sweet society! In this dark wood, the plenipotentiary of the King of France lent an ear to Fouché's overtures.

As for M. de Talleyrand's arrest at the Barrière d'Enfer, I have already described what must be called M. de Talleyrand's persistent obsession with Marie Louise's regency. He was obliged by this arrest to settle up with the eventuality of the Bourbons, but he was still uneasy; it seemed to him that, under the heirs of Saint Louis, a married bishop would never be sure of his place. The idea of substituting the younger branch for the elder one thus pleased him, all the more so because he was well acquainted with the Palais-Royal.[32]

Taking sides, yet not exposing himself entirely, he ventured to say a few words about Fouché's plan to Alexander. The czar had ceased to be interested in Louis XVIII. He had wounded him in Paris by affecting superiority, and he had wounded him again by rejecting the marriage between the Duc de Berry and the emperor's sister. The princess was refused for three reasons: she was a schismatic, she was not of old enough stock, and she was from a family of madmen—reasons that were not presented straight-out but slantwise, and that, once he saw them, offended Alexander three times over. As a final grievance against the exiled old sovereign, the czar pointed to the planned alliance of England, France, and Austria. Besides, it seemed that the succession was open; everyone was claiming to be the heir of the sons of Louis XIV. Benjamin Constant, on behalf of Madame Murat, pleaded the rights Napoleon's sister believed she had to the Kingdom of Naples; Bernadotte cast a distant glance at Versailles, apparently because the King of Sweden was from Pau.

La Besnardière, a division head in the department of external relations, went over to M. de Caulaincourt and put together a report on "France's grievances and arguments" against legitimacy.[33] Once this kick had been let fly, M. de Talleyrand found a way to pass the report on to Alexander. Displeased and persuadable, the autocrat was struck by La Besnardière's pamphlet. Out of the blue, in the middle of the congress, to the stupefaction of all, the czar asked if it would not be worth examining by what means the Duc d'Orléans could be made a king befitting France and Europe. This is perhaps one of the most surprising things that happened in those extraordinary times, and perhaps it is more extraordinary still that it has since been so little discussed.* Lord Clancarthy thwarted the Russian's proposal. His Lordship declared that he was in no position to handle such a serious question. "As for me," he said, "as a private individual, I think that to put the Duc d'Orléans on the French throne would be to replace military usurpation with familial usurpation, which is more dangerous to monarchs than any other form of usurpation." When the members of the congress went off to dine, they marked the sheet where they had left off in their protocols with the Scepter of Saint Louis, as though it were a wisp of straw.

Regarding the obstacles confronting the czar, M. de Talleyrand did a complete about-face. He foresaw the shot that was going to ring out and reported to Louis XVIII (in a dispatch I saw, No. 25 or 27) on the special session of the congress.† He thought himself obliged to inform His Majesty of such an exorbitant step because this news, he said, would soon reach the king's ears—an unusual instance of naiveté on the part of M. le Prince de Talleyrand.

The special session had turned on a declaration of the Alliance designed to warn the world that all they wanted was Napoleon, and that they did not wish to impose on France either an obligatory form of government or a sovereign not of its choosing. This last part of the declaration was suppressed, but it was plainly announced in the of-

---

*A recent pamphlet, entitled *Letter from Abroad*, which seems to have been written by a clever and knowledgeable diplomat, addresses these secret Russian talks in Vienna. (Paris, 1840)

†It has been claimed that, in 1830, M. de Talleyrand had his correspondence with Louis XVIII removed from the private archives of the crown, just as he had had everything he had written relative to Spain and the death of Duc d'Enghien removed from the archives of the Empire.

ficial paper in Frankfurt. England, in its negotiations with cabinets, always uses this liberal language, which is only a precaution against the parliamentary gallery.

One sees that, in the Second Restoration, as in the first, the Allies did not care about the restoration of the Legitimacy: the event was everything. What did it matter to such shortsighted sovereigns that the mother of the monarchies of Europe had been slain? Would that prevent them from throwing banquets and having guards? Today, monarchs are so firmly seated—the globe in one hand, the sword in the other!

M. de Talleyrand, whose interests were then in Vienna, feared that the English, who no longer held a favorable opinion of him, would engage their military before all the armies were in line and that the Court of Saint James's would then gain the upper hand. That is why he tried to induce the king to go back to France by way of the southeastern provinces—so that he would be protected by the troops of the Empire and the Austrian cabinet. The Duke of Wellington at that time had firm orders not to commence hostilities. It was Napoleon who wanted the Battle of Waterloo. No one can stop the destinies of such a nature as his.

These historical facts—the most curious in the world—have been generally ignored. It is much the same with the treaties of Vienna, whose bearing on France has been the subject of confusion. These treaties have been thought to be the exclusive work of a few victorious sovereigns bent on our ruin, but unfortunately, if they are lethal, they have been envenomed by a French hand. When M. de Talleyrand is not conspiring, he is striking bargains.

Prussia longed to possess Saxony, which will sooner or later be its prey. France ought to have paid attention to this longing, since if Saxony had obtained an indemnification in the Circle of the Rhine, we would have retained Landau along with our surrounding territories; Koblenz and other fortresses would have been passed on to a small, friendly state that, placed between France and Prussia, would have prevented any points of contact. The keys to France would not have been handed over to Frederick's ghost. For the three million

Saxony paid him, M. de Talleyrand opposed the schemes of the Berlin cabinet; but in order to persuade Alexander to assent to the existence of the old Saxony, our ambassador was forced to abandon Poland to the czar, though the other powers wanted a Poland of some shape or form to restrict the Muscovites' movements in the north. The Bourbons of Naples put themselves back in power, like the sovereign of Dresden, with money. M. de Talleyrand claimed he had the right to a subvention in exchange for his duchy of Benevento: he was selling his livery on leaving his master. When France was giving up so much, couldn't M. de Talleyrand have given up something as well? At any rate, Benevento did not belong to the Grand Chamberlain. By virtue of the revival of the old treaties, this principality belonged to the State of the Church.

Such were the diplomatic transactions transpiring in Vienna while we were in Ghent. I received, in this latter residence, the following letter from M. de Talleyrand:

Vienna, April 4

I was very pleased to learn, sir, that you were in Ghent, for the circumstances demand the king be surrounded by strong and independent men.

You will surely have thought it useful to refute, in strongly reasoned publications, the whole of the new doctrine that they are trying to establish in the official documents now appearing in France.

It would be useful if something could appear whose object would be to establish that the declaration of March 31 made in Paris by the Allies, that the forfeiture, that the abdication, that the treaty of April 11 which resulted from them, are so many preliminary, indispensable, and absolute conditions of the treaty of May 30: that is to say that without these conditions the treaty would not have been made. On this basis, whoever violates the aforementioned conditions, or seconds their violation, breaks the peace that the treaty established. It is therefore he and his accomplices who are declaring war on Europe.

A discussion along these lines would do good abroad as well as at home; only it needs to be done right, so make it your business.

Please accept, monsieur, the assurance of my sincere attachment and high regard.

Talleyrand

I hope to have the honor of seeing you at the end of the month.

Our minister in Vienna was loyal to his loathing for the great chimera escaped from among the shades. He feared being thwacked by his wing. This letter shows, besides, what M. de Talleyrand was capable of when he wrote alone: he had the goodness to instruct me in the "gist" of the thing, leaving the flourishes to me. Of course, all it was going to take to stop Napoleon were a few diplomatic phrases about the forfeiture, the abdication, the treaties of April 11 and May 30. I was very gratified by the instructions, seeing I had been brevetted a "strong man," but I did not follow them. An ambassador *in petto*, I kept my nose out of foreign affairs. I was too busy as "acting Minister of the Interior."

But what *was* going on in Paris?

12.

THE HUNDRED DAYS IN PARIS: EFFECT OF THE PASSING OF THE LEGITIMACY IN FRANCE— BONAPARTE'S SURPRISE—HE IS OBLIGED TO CAPITULATE TO IDEAS HE HAD BELIEVED DEAD— HIS NEW SYSTEM—THREE ENORMOUS GAMBLERS REMAIN—LIBERAL CHIMERAS—CLUBS AND FEDER- ATES—THE REPUBLIC'S SLEIGHT OF HAND: THE ADDITIONAL ACT—CHAMBER OF REPRESENTATIVES CONVOKED—POINTLESS CHAMP DE MAI

I AM SHOWING you the reverse side of events, which history does not reveal. History only sets the scene. These *Memoirs* have the advantage of presenting both sides of the fabric. In this regard, they better depict humanity in its entirety by laying out, like Shakespeare's tragedies, scenes low and high. Wherever you go in this world, you will find a cottage beside a palace, a man who is weeping beside a man who is laughing, a ragman toting his sack beside a king who is losing his throne. What did the slave at the Battle of Arbela make of Darius's fall?

Ghent was merely a dressing room behind the scenes of the show being put on in Paris. Some famous characters still remained in Europe. I had begun my career in 1800 with Alexander and Napoleon; why hadn't I followed these actors, my contemporaries, onto the great stage? Why was I alone in Ghent? Because Heaven casts a man where it will. From the "little" Hundred Days in Ghent, let us turn to the "great" Hundred Days in Paris.

I have told you the reasons that ought to have given Bonaparte pause on the isle of Elba, and the overriding reasons, or rather the necessity stemming from the strong trunk of his nature, which forced him to emerge from his exile. But the march from Cannes to Paris used up what remained of the old man. In Paris, the spell was broken.

The few moments in which the laws had reappeared were enough to make the reestablishment of arbitrary rule unimaginable. Despotism muzzles the masses and lets individuals run loose within certain limits; anarchy unleashes the masses and subjugates individual independence. Hence despotism seems like freedom when it takes the place of anarchy, but it remains what it truly is when it takes the place of liberty. A liberator following the constitution of the Directory, Bonaparte was an oppressor coming after the Charter. He sensed this so acutely that he thought himself obliged to go further than Louis XVIII and return to the sources of national sovereignty. He, who trampled the people when he was their ruler, was reduced to being a tribune of the people, to courting the favor of the faubourgs, to parodying the early days of the Revolution, to sputtering out a superannuated language of liberty that made him grimace, and whose every syllable enraged his sword.

His destiny, as a man of power, had been so thoroughly fulfilled that no one saw any further signs of Napoleon's genius during the Hundred Days. His genius was for victory and order, not defeat and liberty; he could do nothing with victory, which had turned its back on him, and nothing for order, since it existed without him. In his surprise, he said:

"Look at how the Bourbons have fixed up France for me in just a few months! It is going to take me years to remake it."

It was not the work of the Legitimacy the conqueror was considering but the work of the Charter. He had left France speechless and prone and found it upright and talking. In the naive confines of his absolutist mind, he mistook liberty for disorder.

And yet Bonaparte must capitulate to ideas he cannot put down all at once. In the absence of real popularity, workers, paid forty sous a head, go around at the end of the day, braying in the Carrousel, "Long live the emperor!" This was called "going on the cry." At first, his proclamations announce marvels of forgetting and forgiving; individuals, the nation, and the press are declared free; the sole ambitions of the ruler are peace, independence, and happiness for the people; the whole imperial system is changed; the golden age is going to be reborn. In order to bring practice in line with theory, France is divided into seven huge police divisions, and the seven lieutenants are invested with the same powers that directors-general had under the Consulate and the Empire. Everyone knows what these protectors of individual liberty were in Lyon, Bordeaux, Milan, Florence, Lisbon, Hamburg, and Amsterdam. Above these lieutenants, in a hierarchy more and more "favorable to liberty," Bonaparte installs "extraordinary commissioners," in the style of the representatives of the people under the Convention.

The police, led by Fouché, told the world, with solemn proclamations, that they would only maintain order and would act strictly according to the principles of virtue.

Bonaparte issued a decree reestablishing the National Guard of the Kingdom, whose name alone had once made his head swim. He was forced to annul the divorce between despotism and demagoguery pronounced under the Empire, and to favor their renewed alliance. Out of this conjugal union there would arise, in the Champ de Mai, a figure of Liberty with a Phrygian cap and a turban on its head, a Mamluk's saber at its belt, and a revolutionary hatchet in its hand— a Liberty surrounded by the shades of thousands of victims sacrificed on the scaffolds or in the scorching Spanish countryside and the icy Russian wastes. Prior to victory, the Mamluks had been Jacobins; in the wake of victory, the Jacobins became Mamluks: Sparta was for the moment of danger, Constantinople for the moment of triumph.[34]

Bonaparte would have very much liked to regain absolute authority for himself, but this was no longer possible. He found men ready to fight him for it: firstly the earnest republicans, freed from the chains of despotism and the laws of the monarchy, who wished to retain an independence that may perhaps be only a noble error, and secondly the madmen of the old Montagnard faction.[35] The latter, humiliated at having been no more than the police spies of a despot, seemed determined to recoup, on their own account, the freedom to do anything and everything which they had ceded to a ruler for fifteen years.

But neither the republicans, nor the revolutionaries, nor Bonaparte's satellites were individually strong enough to win autonomous power or to bring the other parties to their knees. Threatened from without by invasion and from within by public opinion, they understood that if they were divided, they were lost. To avoid this risk, they adjourned their quarrels. Some brought their systems and delusions, others their terror and perversity, to the common defense. But no one was in earnest in this alliance. Every one of them pledged, once the crisis was over, to turn it to his own advantage. All sought, in advance, to secure the spoils of victory. In this dreadful round of thirty-one, three enormous players kept the bank by turns: Liberty, Anarchy, and Despotism, all three of them cheating and conniving to win a game that everyone lost.

Preoccupied by their plans, they did not crack down on the few stray children who were pressing for revolutionary measures: federates emerged in the outskirts and federations were organized under rigorous oaths in Brittany, Anjou, Lyon, and Burgundy. They sang the Marseillaise and the Carmagnole. A club, established in Paris, corresponded with other clubs in the provinces. The resurrection of the *Journal des Patriotes* was announced. But what confidence could the undead of 1793 inspire? Wasn't everyone aware of how they construed liberty, equality, and the rights of man? Were they more moral, more sensible, more sincere after their enormities than they had been before them? Had they become capable of virtues by defiling themselves with every vice under the sun? A man does not abdicate crime quite as easily as a crown; the brow encircled by the dreadful band retains indelible marks.

The idea of making an ambitious man of genius stoop from the rank of emperor to the condition of generalissimo or president of the Republic was delusional. The Phrygian cap they placed on the heads of his busts during the Hundred Days would only have made Bonaparte dream of resuming the diadem—were it given to these athletes who race through the world to run the same course twice.

All the same, a few choice liberals promised victory. Misguided men, like Benjamin Constant, fools, like M. Simonde-Sismondi, spoke of making the Prince de Canino Minister of the Interior, Lieutenant General Carnot Minister of War, and Comte Merlin Minister of Justice. Although he seemed dejected, Bonaparte was not opposed to democratic movements that, in the final analysis, supplied conscripts for his army. He allowed himself to be attacked in pamphlets. Caricatures repeated "the isle of Elba" to him, as the parrots cried "Péronne" to Louis XI.[36] They preached liberty and equality to the jailbird in the most familiar manner possible. He listened to their remonstrances and looked contrite. Then, suddenly breaking the chains with which they played at binding him, he proclaimed, by his own authority, not a plebeian constitution, but an aristocratic constitution, an "additional act" to the constitutions of the Empire.

The dreamed-of republic was changed by this adroit sleight of hand into the old imperial government rejuvenated by feudality. The "additional act" lost Bonaparte the Republican party and caused discontent in almost all the other parties. License reigned in Paris, anarchy in the provinces; the civil and military authorities clashed. Here, people threatened to burn mansions and to slit priests' throats; there, they hoisted the white flag and cried "Long live the king!" Attacked, Bonaparte recoiled. He removed the nomination of the mayors of communes from the list of "extraordinary commissioners" and turned their nomination over to the people. Frightened by the number of votes against the additional act, he abandoned his de facto dictatorship and convoked the Chamber of Representatives by virtue of this act, which had not yet been passed. Drifting from reef to reef, he has hardly been delivered from one danger before he runs into another. Sovereign for a day, how was he to institute a hereditary peerage that the spirit of equality rejects? How was he to govern the two Chambers? Would they show passive obedience? What would their reaction be to the proposed assembly of the Champ de Mai, which no longer had any real purpose, since the additional act had been implemented before the votes were counted? Wouldn't this assembly, composed of thirty thousand electors, think of itself as representing the nation?

This Champ de Mai, so pompously declared and celebrated on June 1, resolved into a simple parade of troops and a parceling out of flags before an execrated altar. Napoleon, surrounded by his brothers, the state dignitaries, the marshals, the civil and judiciary bodies, proclaimed the sovereignty of the people, in which he did not believe. The citizens had imagined they themselves would frame a constitution on that solemn day; the peace-loving bourgeois expected Napoleon would abdicate in favor of his son (an abdication plotted in Basel by the agents of Fouché and Prince Metternich); but it was nothing more than a risible political ruse. The additional act was, besides, a tribute to the Legitimacy. With a few differences—above all the missing "abolition of the confiscation of property"—it was the Charter.

13.

THE HUNDRED DAYS IN PARIS, CONTINUED:
BONAPARTE'S WORRIES AND RESENTMENTS

THESE sudden changes, this confusion of everything, heralded the death throes of despotism. Still, the emperor could not receive the mortal blow from within, for the power combating him was as exhausted as he was. The revolutionary titan that Napoleon had once laid low had not recovered its inborn energy. The two giants now aimed useless punches at one another. It was only a battle between ghosts.

In addition to these general impossibilities, Bonaparte was also dealing with domestic tribulations and palace worries. He had told France the empress and the King of Rome were returning, but neither came. Speaking of the Queen of Holland, whom Louis XVIII had made Duchesse de Saint-Leu, he said:

"When one has accepted a family in its prosperity, one must also embrace its adversity."

Joseph, who had rushed in from Switzerland, only asked him for money. Lucien worried him because of his liberal connections. Murat, after first conspiring against his brother-in-law, was in too great a hurry, on coming back to him, to attack the Austrians: stripped of the kingdom of Naples, a fugitive of ill omen, he waited under arrest near Marseille for the catastrophe that I will tell you about later.

And could the emperor, then, trust any of his former supporters or so-called friends? Hadn't they shamefully abandoned him the moment he fell? Hadn't the Senate that once groveled at his feet, now nestled in the peerage, decreed the demise of its benefactor? Could he believe those men when they came and said to him:

"The interests of France are inseparable from your own. If Fortune betrays your efforts, Sire, reversals would not weaken our perseverance and would only redouble our attachment to you."

Your perseverance! Your attachment redoubled by misfortune! This is what you said on June 11, 1815. What had you said on April 2, 1814? What would you say a few weeks later, on July 19, 1815?

The Minister of the Imperial Police, as you have seen, was in contact with Ghent, Vienna, and Basel. The marshals to whom Bonaparte was compelled to entrust command of his soldiers had recently taken an oath of allegiance to Louis XVIII. They had issued the most violent proclamations against Bonaparte. Since then, it is true, they had reespoused their sultan; but if he had been arrested in Grenoble, what would they have done? Can a violated oath be retaken in full force by breaking another oath? Do two perjuries add up to loyalty?

A few days later, the men who had sworn obedience to Bonaparte at the Champ de Mai would transfer their devotion back to Louis XVIII at the Tuileries; they would approach the sacred table of the God of peace hoping to be appointed ministers at the banquets of war. Heralds and bearers of the royal insignia at Bonaparte's coronation, they would fulfill the same functions at the coronation of Charles X; then, as the agents of another power, they would take that king as a prisoner to Cherbourg, hardly able to find a free corner in their consciences where they could hang up the plaque of their latest oath. It is hard to be born in times of improbity, in days when two men chatting together must be on guard against using certain words for fear of causing offense or making the other man blush.

Those who had not been able to bind themselves to Napoleon through his glory, who had not been able to adhere out of gratitude to the benefactor from whom they had received their wealth, their honors, and their very names—were they now going to sacrifice themselves for his scanty hopes? Were they going to chain themselves to a precarious, reincipient fortune—these ingrates untempted by a fortune consolidated by unprecedented successes and by the spoils of sixteen years of victory? So many chrysalides that, between one spring and the next, had shed and resumed, sloughed off and put on the skin of the Legitimist and the revolutionary, the Napoleonist and the Bourbonist; so many words given and broken; so many crosses moved from the knight's breast to the horse's tail and from the horse's tail to the knight's breast; so many gallant men changing their banners and strewing the lists with their violated oaths of fealty; so many noble ladies waiting on Marie Louise and Marie Caroline by turns, were bound to leave, in the depths of Napoleon's heart, nothing but distrust, horror, and contempt. That great man grown old stood alone among all those traitors, men and fate, on a reeling earth,[37] beneath a hostile sky, face-to-face with his destiny and the judgment of God.

14.
RESOLUTION IN VIENNA—MOVEMENT IN PARIS

NAPOLEON had found no faithful friends except the phantoms of his former glory. These escorted him, as I have told you, from the place where he landed to the capital of France. But the eagles who had "flown from steeple to steeple," from Cannes to Paris, settled wearily on the chimney tops of the Tuileries, unable to go any farther.

Napoleon did not swoop down upon Belgium, at the head of an enthusiastic populace, before an Anglo-Prussian army could assemble there. He paused; he tried to negotiate with Europe and humbly maintain the treaties of the Legitimacy. The Congress of Vienna drew the Duc de Vicence's attention to the abdication of April 11, 1814: by that abdication, Bonaparte "recognized that he was the sole obstacle to the restoration of peace in Europe" and consequently "renounced, for himself and his heirs, the thrones of France and Italy." Now, since he had returned to reestablish his power, he was manifestly violating the Treaty of Paris and placing himself in the same political situation that had existed prior to March 31, 1814. Thus it was he, Bonaparte, who was declaring war on Europe and not Europe on Bonaparte. These logical quibbles made by diplomatic attorneys, as I said regarding M. de Talleyrand's letter, were worth as much as they could be before the fighting began.

The news of Bonaparte's arrival in Cannes had reached Vienna on March 6, in the middle of a feast where men and women were dressed up to represent the divine councils of Olympus and Parnassus. Alexander had just received the proposal for an alliance between

France, Austria, and England. He hesitated a moment between the two new pieces of news, then said:

"It is not a question of myself, but of the safety of the world."

And a courier was sent to Saint Petersburg with orders to dispatch the Guards. The retreating armies halted; their long line reversed direction, and eight hundred thousand enemies turned their faces toward France. Bonaparte prepared for war. He was expected on new Catalaunian Plains.[38] God had summoned him to the battle that was to put an end to the reign of battles.

The warmth of the wings of the fame of Marengo and Austerlitz had been enough to hatch armies in France, which is nothing if not a great nest of soldiers. Bonaparte had restored the epithets "invincible," "terrible," and "incomparable" to his legions. Seven armies resumed the titles of the Armies of the Pyrenees, the Alps, the Jura, the Moselle, and the Rhine: impressive memories meant to serve as a frame for notional troops and hoped-for triumphs. A real army was mustered in Paris and in Laon: 150 cavalry batteries, 10,000 elite soldiers who had enrolled in the Guards, 18,000 sailors who had distinguished themselves at Lützen and Bautzen; 30,000 veterans, officers, and noncommissioned officers garrisoned in the fortified towns; 7 northern and eastern *départements* ready to rise up en masse; 180,000 men of the National Guard mobilized; volunteer units in Lorraine, Alsace, and Franche-Comté; federates offering their pikes and their strength; Paris manufacturing 3,000 rifles a day—such were the emperor's resources. Perhaps he would have overwhelmed the world once more, if he could have brought himself, while liberating his country, to call for foreign nations to assert their independence. It was a propitious moment. The kings, after promising their subjects constitutional governments, had shamefully gone back on their word. But liberty had become revolting to Napoleon as soon as he'd drunk from the cup of power. He preferred being defeated with his soldiers to being victorious with entire nations. The corps he steered toward the Netherlands, one after another, amounted to 70,000 men.

15.

WHAT WE WERE DOING IN GHENT—M. DE BLACAS

WE ÉMIGRÉS, away in the city of Charles V, were like the women of that city. Sitting behind their windows, they watched the soldiers, in a little cheval glass, going by in the street. Louis XVIII was there in a corner, completely forgotten. From time to time, he received a note from the Prince de Talleyrand back from Vienna or a few lines from the members of the diplomatic corps residing with the Duke of Wellington and serving as delegates: M. Pozzo di Borgo, the Baron de Vincent, and the rest. They had plenty to think about besides us! A man unacquainted with politics would never have imagined an ailing man hidden on the banks of the Lys could be flung back on the throne by the collision of thousands of soldiers prepared to slit each other's throats—soldiers of whom he was neither king nor general, who were not thinking of him, who were indifferent to his name and his existence. Never had two points so close together, Ghent and Waterloo, been so different: the former was so dim, the latter so dazzling. The Legitimacy had been stowed in the depot, like a broken old wagon.

We knew Bonaparte's troops were approaching. To defend us, we had only two little companies under the orders of the Duc de Berry, a prince whose blood could not serve us, for it was already demanded elsewhere. A thousand horses, detached from the French army, could have finished us off in a matter of hours. The fortifications of Ghent had been demolished; the boundary wall that remained could have easily been taken, especially when you consider that the Belgian people were not favorably disposed to us. The scene I had witnessed at the Tuileries was repeated: His Majesty's carriages were secretly readied and horses were ordered. We faithful ministers would have had to slog along behind him, by the grace of God. *Monsieur*—assigned to keep a close eye on the army's movements—left for Brussels.

M. de Blacas had become anxious and melancholy. I, poor man, consoled him. In Vienna, no one much cared for him: M. de Talleyrand made fun of him; the royalists accused him of having brought about Napoleon's return. Thus, whatever happened, there would be no more exile in England for him, no more high-ranking positions in France. I was his only supporter. I used to see him fairly often in the horse market, where he trotted about alone; riding beside him, I would "consent to his sad thoughts."[39] This man—whom I defended in Ghent and in England, whom I would defend in France after the Hundred Days, not to mention in the preface to *The Monarchy According to the Charter*—has always been inimical to me. This would not matter if he had not also done harm to the monarchy. I do not repent of my past foolishness; but I am bound, in these *Memoirs*, to redress certain incursions made on my judgment and my good heart.[40]

16.

BATTLE OF WATERLOO

ON JUNE 18, 1815, around noon, I left Ghent by the Brussels gate. I was going to finish my solitary walk on the highway. I had brought Caesar's *Commentaries* with me and was strolling along slowly, immersed in my reading, already more than a league from town, when I thought I heard a dull rumbling: I stopped, looked up at the sky, which was full of clouds, wondering whether I ought to continue on the way I was going or start back toward Ghent for fear of a thunderstorm. I stood and listened. I heard only the cry of a coot in the rushes and the chiming of a village clock: I went on. I had not gone thirty paces when the rumbling began again, now short and now long, at irregular intervals. Sometimes it was perceptible only through a trembling of the air, which was transmitted to the ground over those immense plains, it was so far off. These detonations less vast, less undulant, less rhythmic than thunder made me think of a battle. At that moment, I happened to be standing across from a poplar planted at the corner of a field of hops. I crossed the lane and leaned against the trunk of this tree, turning my face toward Brussels. A southerly wind picked up and brought me the unmistakable sound of artillery. That great battle, nameless as yet, to whose echoes I listened at the foot of a poplar, and whose humble obsequies a village clock had just tolled, was the Battle of Waterloo.[41]

A silent and solitary hearer of the formidable judgment of the Fates, I would have been less moved had I found myself in the fray. The danger, the fire, the deadly mayhem would not have given me time to think; but alone beneath a tree, in the countryside near Ghent, like the shepherd whose flock stood grazing around me, the weight of my reflections was overwhelming. What was this battle? Was it going to be decisive? Was Napoleon there in the flesh? Were lots being cast upon the world, as upon Christ's vesture?[42] Come victory or defeat, what would be the consequence for the nations: liberty or bondage? But how much blood must be flowing! Wasn't every noise that reached my ear the last breath of a Frenchman? Was this a new Crécy, a new Poitiers, a new Azincourt, which would benefit France's most implacable enemies? If they triumphed, wouldn't our glory be lost? If Napoleon won, what would become of our liberty? Although a victory for Napoleon meant eternal exile for me, my homeland, at that moment, prevailed in my heart; my prayers were for France's oppressor, if he should, while saving our honor, wrest us from foreign domination.

And if Wellington triumphed? Then the Legitimacy would return to Paris behind those red uniforms freshly dyed in Frenchmen's blood. Then the kings would have ambulance carts for carriages at the coronation, all filled with mutilated grenadiers. What sort of restoration would it be, under such auspices? —These were only a few of the thoughts tormenting me. Every gunshot gave me a shock and made my heart beat double-quick. A few leagues away from an immense catastrophe, I could not see it; I could not touch the vast funerary monument growing minute by minute in Waterloo, as from the Bulaq shoreline, on the eastern banks of the Nile, I had vainly stretched out my hands toward the Pyramids.

No wayfarer appeared. A few women in the fields, peacefully weeding rows of vegetables, seemed not to hear the noise that had held me spellbound. But here came a courier! I left the foot of my tree and stood in the middle of the road; I flagged down the courier and questioned him. He was employed by the Duc de Berry and was riding from Aalst. He told me that Bonaparte had marched into Brussels yesterday (June 17) after a bloody fight. The battle must have started up again today (June 18). Everyone believed the Allies were going to suffer a definitive defeat and the order to retreat had been given. He continued on his way.

I followed him, walking as quickly as I could, and was passed by the carriage of a merchant who was fleeing with his family. He confirmed the courier's story.

17.

CONFUSION IN GHENT—THE BATTLE OF WATERLOO CONSIDERED

EVERYTHING was in confusion when I got back to Ghent. The gates of the city were being closed; only the wickets remained half open. A few poorly armed civilians and some soldiers from the regimental depot were standing guard. I made my way to the king's house.

Monsieur had just arrived by a circuitous route: he had left Brussels on hearing the false reports that Bonaparte was about to enter the city and that after losing a first battle there was no hope of winning a second. It was rumored that, because the Prussians had not formed their lines, the English had been crushed.

In the aftermath of these reports, it was "every man for himself." Everyone with any resources left. As for me, I am used to having nothing and was, as always, ready and eager to go. I wanted to get Madame de Chateaubriand out of town before me, since, although she was a great Bonapartist, she hated gunfire; but she refused to leave me.

That evening, a council was held at His Majesty's. We listened to *Monsieur*'s reports again, and to all the rumors overheard at the commandant's or at Baron d'Eckstein's. A wagon was loaded with the crown diamonds. I had no need of a wagon to transport my treasure. I put the black silk handkerchief I wrap around my head at night in my limp ministerial portfolio, and I put myself at the prince's disposal, along with that important document on the affairs of the Legitimacy. I was richer on my first emigration, when my rucksack did duty as my pillow and served as a swaddling band for *Atala*; but in 1815 Atala was a tall, gangling little girl of thirteen or fourteen, who ran around the world all alone and, to her father's honor, got herself too much talked about.

On June 19, at one in the morning, a letter from M. Pozzo brought to the king by a courier established the facts. Bonaparte had not entered Brussels, and he had decisively lost the Battle of Waterloo. Leaving Paris on June 12, he had joined his army on the 14th. On the 15th, he broke the enemy's lines on the Sambre. On the 16th, he beat the Prussians on those fields of Fleurus where victory seems forever faithful to the French. The villages of Ligny and and Saint-Amand were taken. At Quatre Bras, another success: the Duke of Brunswick was left among the dead. Blücher, in full retreat, fell back upon a reserve of thirty thousand men under the command of General von Bülow. The Duke of Wellington, with the English and the Dutch, stood with his back to Brussels.

On the morning of the 18th, before the first shot was fired, the Duke of Wellington declared that he could hold out until three o'clock, but that at that time, if the Prussians had not appeared, he would certainly be crushed. Forced back on Plancenoit and Brussels, he was cut off from any possibility of retreat. He had been surprised by Napoleon, and his strategic position was deplorable. He had accepted it, not chosen it.

The French first, on the enemy's left flank, took the heights overlooking the Château d'Hougoumont as far as the farms of La Haye-Sainte and Papelotte. On the right flank, they attacked the village of Mont-Saint-Jean. In the center, La Haye-Sainte Farm was taken by Prince Jérôme. But the Prussian reserves came into sight near Saint-Lambert at six in the evening. A new and furious onslaught was made on the village of La Haye-Sainte. Blücher arrived with fresh troops and isolated the rest of ours, who were already cut off from the squares of the Imperial Guard. Around that immortal phalanx, the torrent of fugitives swept everything away in waves of dust, scorching smoke, and grapeshot, in a blackness crisscrossed by rockets, amid the roar of three hundred cannon and the breakneck galloping of fifty-five thousand horses. It was, as it were, a synthesis of all the battles of the Empire. Twice the French cried *Victory!* and twice their cries were stifled beneath the pressure of the enemy's columns. The fire from our lines died out; the cartridges were exhausted. A few wounded grenadiers, in the midst of thirty thousand dead and a hundred thousand blood-smeared cannonballs that lay cold and conglobated at their feet, remained upright, leaning on their rifles, their broken bayonets, their emptied cannon. Not far from them the man of warfare listened, with a fixed stare, to the last cannon fire he would ever hear in his life. On those fields of carnage, his brother Jérôme was still fighting with his dying battalions outnumbered, but his courage was not enough to bring victory home.

The number of dead on the Allied side has been estimated at eighteen thousand, on the French side at twenty-five thousand. Twelve hundred English officers perished. Almost all of the Duke of Wellington's aides-de-camp were killed or wounded. There was not a family in England who did not mourn. The Prince of Orange had been shot in the shoulder. Baron von Vincent, the Austrian, had been shot through the hand. The English were indebted for their victory to the Irish and the Scottish Highlanders brigades, which the charges of our cavalry could not break. General Grouchy's corps, not having advanced, did not take part in the action. The two armies crossed iron and fire with a bravery and ferocity animated by ten centuries of national enmity. Lord Castlereagh, reporting on the battle to the House of Lords, said: "The battle over, the French and English soldiers washed their bloody hands in the same stream and, from opposite banks, congratulated each other on their bravery." Wellington had always been baleful to Bonaparte, or, rather, English genius, which has long rivaled French genius, barred the road to victory. Nowadays the Prussians dispute with the English and claim the honor of having won this decisive battle; but in war it is not what happens on the field, it is the name, that makes the victor. It was not Bonaparte who won the real Battle of Jena.[43]

The blunders of the French were considerable. They made mistakes regarding friendly or hostile battalions; they occupied the position of Quatre Bras too late; Marshal Grouchy, who was in charge of containing the Prussians with his thirty-six thousand men, allowed them to pass without seeing them. Hence the reproaches addressed to our generals. Bonaparte made a frontal attack as usual, instead of turning the English flank, and, with masterly presumption, set about blocking the retreat of an enemy who had not been defeated.

All kinds of lies and some rather curious truths have been churned out on the subject of this catastrophe. The phrase "The Guard dies but does not surrender" is an invention no one dares defend any longer. It seems certain that, at the beginning of the battle, Soult made some strategic observations to the emperor:

"Just because Wellington has defeated you," Napoleon answered him dryly, "you persist in thinking of him as a great general."

When the fighting was over, M. de Turenne urged Bonaparte to retreat to avoid falling into the enemy's hands. Bonaparte, emerging from his thoughts as if from a dream, at first flew into a passion; then, all of a sudden, in the midst of his rage, he threw himself upon his horse and fled.[44]

18.

THE EMPEROR'S RETURN—REAPPEARANCE OF LAFAYETTE—BONAPARTE'S SECOND ABDICATION— TEMPESTUOUS SESSIONS IN THE CHAMBER OF PEERS —BALEFUL OMENS FOR THE SECOND RESTORATION

ON THE 19th of June, a hundred-gun salute at the Invalides had announced the victories at Ligny, Charleroi, and Quatre Bras: the day before, at Waterloo, men had also been celebrating these triumphs.

The first courier to bring Paris news of the defeat—one of the most significant defeats in history, judged by its consequences—was Napoleon himself. He came back through the gates on the night of the 21st. It was as if his Manes[45] were returning to tell his friends that he was dead. He stayed at the Bourbon Élysée Palace; when he had come back from Elba, he had stayed at the Tuileries. These two asylums, instinctively chosen, revealed how his destiny had changed.

Fallen in a noble fight abroad, Napoleon in Paris had to endure attacks from lawyers who wanted to exploit his misfortunes. He regretted not having dissolved the Chamber before leaving for the army; he also frequently lamented not having Fouché and Talleyrand shot. But there is no question, after Waterloo, that Bonaparte refrains from every form of violence, whether because he was obeying the customary calm of his temperament or because he had been tamed by destiny. He no longer says, as he did before his first abdication, "They shall see what the death of a great man is." This verve is gone. Hostile to liberty, he considered breaking up the Chamber of Representatives presided over by Lanjuinais, who had gone from being a citizen to a senator, a senator to a peer, before again becoming a citizen, who was, once more, about to become a peer. General Lafayette, one of the representatives, read out a motion from the tribune declaring "the

Chamber in permanent session, any attempt to dissolve it a crime of high treason, whosoever should be guilty of it a traitor to the country and to be tried as such" (June 21, 1815).

The general's speech opened with these words:

> Gentleman, when for the first in many years I raise a voice the old friends of liberty will recognize, I feel called upon to speak to you of the dangers facing our country... Now is the moment to rally around the tricolor flag, the flag of '89, the flag of liberty, equality, and public order.

The anachronism of this speech caused a momentary illusion; people thought they saw the Revolution, personified by Lafayette, emerging from its grave and standing pale and wrinkled on the rostrum. But these motions of order, modeled after Mirabeau's, were nothing but obsolete weaponry taken from an old arsenal. Though Lafayette nobly united the end and the beginning of his life, it was not in his power to weld together the two ends of the broken chain of time. Benjamin Constant went to the emperor at the Élysée and found him in his garden. The crowd filled the Avenue de Marigny, crying "Long live the Emperor!"—a touching cry coming from the soul of the people. It was addressed to the vanquished!

Bonaparte said to Benjamin Constant:

"What do these people owe me? I found them poor and have left them poor."

This may be the only phrase that ever emanated from Napoleon's heart, assuming Constant's emotion did not in this case deceive his ear. Bonaparte, who foresaw the event, anticipated the summons they were preparing to serve on him. He abdicated so as not to be forced to abdicate.

"My political life is over," he said; "I declare my son emperor of the French, under the name Napoleon II."

A useless provision, like that of Charles X in favor of Henri V. A man cannot give crowns unless he possesses them, and men break the testament of adversity. Besides, the emperor was no more sincere in descending from the throne a second time than he had been at the time of his earlier withdrawal. When the French delegates went to tell the Duke of Wellington that Napoleon had abdicated, he replied:

"I heard that a year ago."

The Chamber of Representatives, after some debates in which Manuel[46] took the floor, accepted its sovereign's second abdication, but vaguely and without appointing a regency.

An executive commission was created. The Duc d'Otrante chaired it. Three ministers, a counselor of state, and one of the emperor's generals comprised it, and once more they divested their master: these men were Fouché, Caulaincourt, Carnot, Quinette, and Grenier.

During these transactions, Bonaparte was turning over his thoughts. "I no longer have an army," he said to himself. "All I have are some deserters. The majority in the Chamber of Deputies is in my favor. Only Lafayette, Lanjuinais, and a handful of others are against me. If the nation rises up, the enemy will be crushed; if, instead of rising, they quarrel, all will be lost. The nation has not sent the deputies to overthrow me but to support me. I am not afraid of them, whatever they do; I will always be the idol of the people and the army. If I were to say the word, they would be beaten to death. But if we quarrel with each other instead of coming to an understanding, we will suffer the fate of the Western Roman Empire."

When a deputation from the House of Representatives came to congratulate him on his recent abdication, he replied:

"I thank you. I would like to think my abdication shall bring France happiness, but I am not hopeful."

He repented soon after, when he heard the Chamber of Representatives had appointed a governmental commission composed of five members. He said to the ministers:

"I have not abdicated in favor of a new Directory; I have abdicated in favor of my son. If this is not proclaimed, then my abdication is null and void. The Chambers will not force the Allies to recognize the nation's independence by going before the Allies with hangdog looks and on bended knee."

He complained that Lafayette, Sebastiani, Pontécoulant, and

Benjamin Constant had conspired against him and that, moreover, the Chambers did not have sufficient power. He said that he alone could fix things but that the leaders would never agree, that they would rather sink into the abyss than side with him, Napoleon, and seal it.

On June 27, at Malmaison, he wrote this sublime letter:

"By abdicating power, I renounced the most honorable right of a citizen, the right to defend my country. Under these grave circumstances, I offer my services as a general, still regarding myself as the premier soldier of the motherland."

The Duc de Bassano having told him the Chambers would not be in his favor, Napoleon replied:

"Then I see it plain as day, there's no choice but to give in. That villain Fouché is feeding you lies. Only Caulaincourt and Carnot are worth a damn. But what can they do with a traitor, Fouché, and two fools, Quinette and Grenier, and two Chambers that don't know what they want? You all believe, like a bunch of idiots, in the foreigners' fine promises. You think they'll plop a chicken in your pot[47] and give you a prince of their making, don't you? You're wrong."*

Diplomats were sent to the Allies. On June 29, Napoleon requested two frigates, stationed at Rochefort, to transport him out of France. Meanwhile, he had retreated to Malmaison.

The discussions in the Chamber of Peers were lively. Bonaparte's longtime enemy Carnot, who signed the order for the massacres at Avignon without taking the time to read it, had found time, during the Hundred Days, to sacrifice his republicanism to the title of Comte. On June 22, in the Luxembourg, he had read a letter from the minister of war containing an exaggerated report on the military resources of France. The newly arrived Ney could not hear this report without anger. Napoleon, in his bulletins, had spoken of the marshal with ill-disguised displeasure, and Gourgaud had accused Ney of being the chief cause of the loss of the Battle of Waterloo.

Ney stood up and said:

*See the last pages of volume 1 of the *Oeuvres de Napoléon*.

"This report is false, false in every respect. Grouchy can only have twenty or twenty-five thousand men under his command at most. There is not a single soldier of the Guard left to be rallied. I commanded them. I saw them all slaughtered on the field of battle. The enemy is in Nivelles with eighty thousand men; he can be in Paris in six days. You have no means of saving the country except by opening negotiations."

The aide-de-camp Flahaut tried to corroborate the Minister of War's report, but Ney shot back with still greater vehemence:

"I repeat to you, you have no means of salvation except negotiation. You must recall the Bourbons. As for me, I will be retiring to the United States."

At these words, Lavalette and Carnot showered the marshal with reproaches, which Ney answered disdainfully:

"I am not one of those men who care about nothing except their own interests. What would I gain by Louis XVIII's return? I would be shot for the crime of desertion. But I owe my country the truth."

In the session of the Chamber of Peers on the twenty-third, General Drouot, recalling this scene, said:

"I was chagrined to hear what was said yesterday in the interest of diminishing the glory of our military, exaggerating our disasters, and disparaging our resources. My astonishment was all the greater as these speeches were delivered by a distinguished general (Ney) who, through his great valor and military knowledge, has shown himself, time and again, to be deserving of the nation's gratitude."

In the session on the twenty-second, a second storm, swirling around Bonaparte's abdication, had broken out shortly after the first. Lucien insisted that his nephew be recognized as emperor when M. de Pontecoulant interrupted the speaker and asked by what right Lucien, a foreigner and a Roman prince, should be allowed to assign France a sovereign.

"How," he added, "are we to recognize a child who resides in a foreign country?"

At this question, La Bédoyère sprung up from his seat:

"I have heard your voices clamoring around the throne of the fortunate sovereign; today, now that he is in trouble, these same voices are drawing away from it. There are people who do not wish to recognize Napoleon II because they would rather receive the law from foreigners, whom they call 'allies.'

"Napoleon's abdication is indivisible. If you refuse to recognize his son, he must take up the sword, surrounded by Frenchmen who have shed their blood for him and still have the wounds to prove it.

"He will be abandoned only by the vile generals who have already betrayed him. But if we declare that every Frenchman who deserts his flag will be covered with infamy, his house razed to the ground, his family banished, then there will be no more traitors, no more intrigues such as have occasioned the latest catastrophes, some of whose authors are perhaps sitting among us."

The Chamber rose to its feet in an uproar:

"Order! Order! Order!" they thundered, feeling the thrust.

"Young man, you forget yourself!" shouted Masséna.

"Do you think you're still in the guardhouse?" said Lameth.

All the omens of the Second Restoration were baleful. Bonaparte had returned leading four hundred Frenchmen, while Louis XVIII was returning behind four hundred thousand foreigners. He passed by the pool of blood at Waterloo to go to Saint-Denis as though on his way to his funeral.

It was while the Legitimacy was thus advancing that the interpellations of the Chamber of Peers rang out. There was something indescribable about the terrible revolutionary scenes in the great days of our troubles, when the dagger was passed around on the bench from victim to victim. A few soldiers whose ill-fated fascination had brought about the ruin of France by causing the second foreign invasion now fought with one another at the threshold of the palace. Their prophetic despair, their gestures, their words from the grave, seemed to herald a threefold death: death for themselves, death for the man they had blessed, death for the family they had proscribed.

19.

DEPARTURE FROM GHENT—ARRIVAL IN MONS—I MISS MY FIRST CHANCE IN MY POLITICAL CAREER—M. DE TALLEYRAND IN MONS—SCENE WITH THE KING—I FOOLISHLY TAKE AN INTEREST IN M. DE TALLEYRAND

WHILE Bonaparte was retreating to Malmaison with the Empire at an end, we were leaving Ghent with the monarchy beginning anew. Pozzo, who knew how little the Legitimacy was being discussed in high places, hastened to write Louis XVIII a note, telling him to leave and come quickly, before the seat was taken, if he wanted to reign. To this note, Louis XVIII owed his 1815 coronation.

In Mons, I missed the first chance of my political career. I was my own stumbling block and always in my own way. This time, my "good qualities" did me the bad turn my faults might have done me.

M. de Talleyrand, who was feeling very good about the negotiations that had made him rich, claimed to have rendered the greatest services to the Legitimacy and to be returning as its master. Shocked to find they hadn't followed the route back to Paris he had mapped out for them, he was even more displeased to find M. de Blacas in the company of the king. He regarded M. de Blacas as the scourge of the monarchy; but that was not the real reason for his aversion. He considered M. de Blacas the favorite, and therefore his rival; he was also afraid of *Monsieur* and had lost his temper when, a couple of weeks earlier, *Monsieur* had offered him his house on the Lys. To ask for M. de Blacas's removal was as natural as could be; to demand it was too reminiscent of Bonaparte.

M. de Talleyrand rode into Mons at about six o'clock in the evening, accompanied by Abbé Louis. M. de Ricé, M. de Jaucourt, and a few other of his dining companions flew to him. In the grip of a mood no one had seen him in before—the mood of a king who believes his authority has not been recognized—he refused to go and see Louis XVIII right away, ostentatiously replying to those who urged him to do so:

"I am not one to hurry; there will be time enough tomorrow."

I went to see him. He lavished on me the same flatteries he had used to seduce all sorts of ambitious underlings and important fools. He took me by the arm and leaned on me as he spoke—familiarities of high favor, calculated to turn my head, which were completely wasted on me. I did not understand. I invited him to come with me to the king's house, where I was about to go.

Louis XVIII was in deep distress. It was a matter of being separated from M. de Blacas, who could not return to France; opinion had turned against him. Although I had had reason to complain of the favorite in Paris, I had not displayed any resentment toward him in Ghent. The king had been grateful to me for my behavior. In his anguish, he treated me wonderfully. He had already been informed of what M. de Talleyrand was saying.

"He is boasting," he told me, "about having put the crown back on my head a second time, and he is threatening me by saying he will return to Germany. What do you make of it, M. de Chateaubriand?"

"Your Majesty must have been misinformed," I replied. "M. de Talleyrand is merely tired. If it please the king, I shall go back and talk to the minister at home."

The king seemed very happy with this. He hated annoyances more than anything; he longed for repose, even when it cost him his friends.

M. de Talleyrand surrounded by his sycophants was more arrogant than ever. I tried to make him see that, at such a critical moment, he could not think of leaving. Pozzo told him the same thing. Although he was not at all fond of him, Pozzo did like seeing him in the ministry, at that moment, as an old acquaintance; besides, he thought he was in favor with the czar. I could not change M. de Talleyrand's mind; the prince's hangers-on were against me. Even M. Mounier thought he should depart. Abbé Louis, who snapped at everyone, told me, gnashing his teeth three times:

"If *I* were the prince, *I* would not stay in Mons for a quarter of an *hour*."

"Monsieur l'Abbé," I replied, "you and I can go where we please. No one would notice. It's not the same for M. de Talleyrand."

I insisted again, saying to the prince:

"Are you aware that the king is continuing on his journey?"

M. de Talleyrand looked surprised, then said to me, majestically, the way Le Balafré spoke to the men who tried to warn him of Henri III's schemes:[48]

"He would not dare!"

I returned to the king's house, where I found M. de Blacas. I asked His Majesty to excuse his minister, he was sick, but he would very certainly have the honor of paying his court to the king the next day.

"As he pleases," Louis XVIII replied. "I leave at three o'clock."

And then he added, affectionately:

"I am going to part ways with M. de Blacas. The position will be vacant, Monsieur de Chateaubriand."

The Royal Household was being laid at my feet. Not giving M. de Talleyrand another thought, a shrewd politician would have had his horses hitched to his carriage, ready to follow or precede the king. I remained stupidly at my inn.

M. de Talleyrand, who could not be persuaded the king was going on his way that same night, had gone to bed. At three o'clock, they woke him to tell him that the king was leaving. He could not believe his ears.

"Tricked! Betrayed!" he cried.

They got him out of bed, and there he was, for the first time in his life, in the street at three o'clock in the morning, leaning on M. de Ricé's arm. He arrived in front of the king's house; the first two horses of the team were already halfway through the carriage door. Some men gestured for the postilion to stop. The King asked what the matter was, and they cried to him:

"Sire, it is M. de Talleyrand!"

"He is asleep," said Louis XVIII.

"He is here, Sire."

"Come on!" said the king.

The horses moved backward with the carriage; the door was opened; the king got down and hobbled back to his apartment, followed by the limping minister. There, M. de Talleyrand began an angry explanation. His Majesty listened to him and replied:

"Prince de Bénévent, are you leaving us? The waters will do you good. You must be sure to give us your news."

The king left the prince dumbfounded, was led back to his carriage, and departed.

M. de Talleyrand foamed with anger. Louis XVIII's poise had disconcerted him. He, Talleyrand, who prided himself on being so poised, beaten on his own ground and left standing there, on a square in Mons, like the most insignificant of men—he could not believe it! He said nothing, watched the carriage pull away, then seized the Duc de Lévis by one of the buttons on his jacket:

"Go, Monsieur le Duc, go and tell them how I am treated! I have put the crown back on the king's head"—he always came back around to that crown—"and now I'm going to Germany to begin the new Emigration."

M. de Lévis, listening distractedly, raising himself up on his tiptoes, said:

"Prince, I am leaving; there must be at least one true gentleman with the king."

M. de Lévis flung himself into a hired coach that was conveying the Chancellor of France: the two noblemen of the Capetian Monarchy were setting off side by side, sharing expenses, trying to catch up with it in a Merovingian *benna*.[49]

I implored M. de Duras to work toward reconciliation and to keep me informed of his progress.

"What?" M. de Duras asked me, "you are staying here after what the king said to you?"

M. de Blacas, for his part, before leaving Mons, thanked me for the sympathy I had shown him.

I found M. de Talleyrand embarrassed. He regretted not having followed my advice, refusing to go, like a bad-tempered second lieutenant, to the king's house the previous night. He was afraid that arrangements would be made without him and, cut off from political power, he would find himself unable to profit from the chicaneries then in progress. I told him that, although I did not share his opinions, I was nevertheless attached to him, as an ambassador to his minister; that, furthermore, I had friends with the king and soon hoped to hear something good. M. de Talleyrand became the very image of tenderness. He leaned on my shoulder. Certainly, at that moment, he thought me a very great man.

I did not have to wait long for a note from M. de Duras. He wrote me from Cambray that the affair was settled and that M. de Talleyrand was going to receive orders to come along. This time, the prince did not fail to obey.

What devil possessed me? I had not gone with the king, who had, so to speak, offered or rather given me the ministry of his household and who was wounded by my obstinate insistence on staying in Mons. I was breaking my neck for M. de Talleyrand, whom I hardly knew, whom I did not respect, and whom I did not admire—for M. de Talleyrand, who was going to devote himself to aims quite different from my own, and who lived in an atmosphere of corruption in which I could not breathe.

It was also from Mons that, in the midst of his difficulties, the Prince de Bénévent sent M. Duperey to Naples to collect the millions from one of his deals he had made in Vienna. At that time, M. de Blacas was likewise traveling with the Naples embassy in his pocket, and millions more that the generous exile of Ghent had given him in Mons. I had a good rapport with M. de Blacas precisely because everybody hated him; I had incurred the friendship of M. de Talleyrand for my fidelity to one of his volatile whims. Louis XVIII had positively called me to him, and I chose the turpitude of a faithless man over the favor of the king. It was only right I should receive the reward for my stupidity, that I should be abandoned by all for having tried to serve all. I returned to France without the money to pay my way, while wealth poured down on the disgraced. I deserved this correction. It is all very well to fight like a poor knight when everyone else is armored in gold; but one still must not make enormous mistakes. Had I remained with the king, the combination of the Talleyrand and Fouché ministry would have become almost impossible; had the Restoration begun with a moral and honorable ministry, the future might have been different. My lack of concern for myself led me to underestimate the importance of what was happening. Most men err in rating themselves too highly; I err by not rating myself highly enough. I wrapped myself in my habitual disdain for what would become of me, but I ought to have seen that what would become of France was, at that moment, bound up with my own trifling lot. History is full of tangles like this one.

20.

**FROM MONS TO GONESSE—WITH M. LE COMTE
BEUGNOT I OPPOSE FOUCHÉ'S NOMINATION AS
MINISTER: MY REASONS—THE DUKE OF WELLINGTON
WINS THE DAY—ARNOUVILLE—SAINT-DENIS—LAST
CONVERSATION WITH THE KING**

AT LAST I left Mons and arrived in Cateau-Cambrésis. M. de Talleyrand joined me there. It was as though we had come to renegotiate the peace treaty of 1559 between Henri II of France and Philip II of Spain.

At Cambray, it so happened that the Marquis de La Suze, a *maréchal des logis* from the days of Fénelon, had arranged billets for Madame de Lévis, Madame de Chateaubriand, and me: we remained in the street amid the bonfires, the crowd circulating around us shouting "Long live the king!" A student, hearing I was there, took us to his mother's house.

Friends of the different monarchies of France were beginning to appear. They did not come to Cambray for the league against Venice[50] but to join forces against the new constitutions. They hastened to lay their successive loyalties and hatred for the Charter at the king's feet—a passport they thought necessary to reach *Monsieur*. I and two or three other reasonable Pierrots already reeked of Jacobinism.

On June 28, the Declaration of Cambray appeared. In it, the king said:

"I wish to dismiss only those men whose reputation is a subject of grief for France and of terror for Europe."

Yet the name of Fouché was pronounced with gratitude by the Pavillon de Marsan! The king laughed at his brother's new passion and said:

"He has not received it by divine inspiration."

I have already told you how, when passing through Cambray after the Hundred Days, I looked in vain for the building I had called home in the days of the Navarre regiment and the café I had frequented with La Martinière. All of it had vanished, along with my youth.

From Cambray we went to spend the night in Roye. The hostess of the inn there mistook Madame de Chateaubriand for Madame la Dauphine. She was carried in triumph to a huge room with a table set for thirty. This room lit by candles, a chandelier, and a large fire was stifling. The hostess did not want to receive any payment, saying:

"I feel ashamed for not being able to have myself guillotined for our kings."

A last spark from a fire that had animated the French for so many centuries.

General Lamothe, M. Laborie's brother-in-law, came, sent by the authorities of the capital, to let us know it would be impossible for us to appear in Paris without the tricolor cockade. M. de Lafayette and some other commissioners, who were, moreover, poorly received by the Allies, were crawling from one staff office to another, imploring foreigners to appoint someone to rule France: any king, chosen at the Cossacks' discretion, would be excellent, provided he was not descended from Saint Louis and Louis XIV.

In Roye, we held a council. M. de Talleyrand had two nags hitched to his carriage and went to His Majesty's house. His equipage occupied the width of the square, from the minister's inn to the king's door. He stepped down from his chariot carrying a memorandum he read to us: he was considering the course we would have to follow on arrival; he hazarded a few words on the necessity of admitting everyone, indiscriminately, into the sharing out of positions; he let it be known that we might extend our generosity even to the judges of Louis XVI. His Majesty colored and, striking the arms of his chair with both hands, cried:

"Never!"

"Never," for twenty-four hours.

In Senlis, we stopped at a house belonging to a canon. His maid-servant received us like dogs. As for the canon, who was not Saint Rieul, the patron of that town, he would not so much as look at us. His maid had orders to do nothing for us apart from buying us something to eat with our money: *The Genius of Christianity* bought me nothing. Yet Senlis should have been a good omen, since it was in this town that Henri IV broke free from the hands of his jailers in 1576. "I have only mourned two things I left in Paris," said the king and fellow countryman of Montaigne, as he made his escape: "the Mass and my wife."

From Senlis, we went to the birthplace of Philip Augustus, otherwise known as Gonesse. On our approach to the village, we saw two people coming toward us: these were Marshal Macdonald and my loyal friend Hyde de Neuville. They stopped our carriage and asked where M. de Talleyrand was; they made no bones about telling me they wanted to warn him that His Majesty should not think of going through the gates before taking on Fouché as a minister. I was overcome with worry, for despite what Louis XVIII had said in Roye, I was not at all sure of how things would go.

"Are you sure," I asked the marshal, "we cannot return to Paris except under such stringent conditions?"

"Truth to tell, Monsieur le Vicomte," the marshal replied, "I am not quite convinced of it myself."

The king stopped in Gonesse for two hours. I left Madame de Chateaubriand in her carriage in the middle of the high road and went to the council at the town hall. There, a measure was submitted for consideration which would decide the future of the monarchy. When the discussion began, I, alone with M. Beugnot, maintained that under no circumstances should Louis XVIII admit M. Fouché into his councils. The king listened. I saw that he would have liked to keep the word he had given in Roye; but he was absorbed by *Monsieur* and pressed by the Duke of Wellington.

In one of the chapters of *The Monarchy According to the Charter*, I summarized the reasons I set forth in Gonesse. I was excited; the spoken word has a power that is weakened in print:

Wherever there is an open forum, no one who is vulnerable to reproaches of a certain nature ought to be placed at the head of the government. There are certain speeches, certain words, which should oblige such a minister to resign on leaving the Chamber. This check, which is so essential to a free representative government, was forgotten when a combination of delusions conspired to bring a notorious man into the ministry, despite the crown's all-too-well-founded repugnance for him. This man's advancement was to mean one of two things: the abolition of the Charter, or the fall of the whole administration on the first day of the session. Can you imagine the minister I am talking about listening to the discussion in the Chamber of Deputies on January 21—liable to be addressed at any moment by some deputy from Lyon, perpetually threatened by a terrible *Tu es ille vir*?[51] Men of this sort are fit to be openly employed only with the mutes of Bajazet's seraglio, or the mutes of Bonaparte's Corps Législatif. What will become of the minister if a deputy, standing on the rostrum with a *Moniteur* in hand, reads the report of the Convention of August 9, 1795— and if he demands Fouché be expelled as unworthy of holding office by virtue of this report which "expelled" him, Fouché, (I quote verbatim) "for being a thief and a terrorist whose atrocious and criminal behavior would bring dishonor and opprobrium to any assembly that would have him as a member"?

These are the things that have been forgotten!

After all, if they were wretched enough to think a man of his sort could be useful to them, they should have kept him behind the scenes, consulting his miserable experience; but to do violence to the crown and public opinion, to admit such a minister into political life without shame, a man that Bonaparte, at that very moment, called "infamous"—was this not as good as saying they were renouncing liberty and virtue? Is a crown worth such a sacrifice? It left them powerless to turn anyone away. If they accepted Fouché, who could be excluded?

The various parties acted without giving any thought to the form of government they had adopted. Everyone spoke of the constitution, liberty, equality, the rights of the nations, and no one wanted these things; they were merely fashionable verbiage. They asked, unthinkingly, for news of the Charter, hoping all the while it would soon turn up its toes. Liberals and royalists inclined toward absolute government, ameliorated by morality: such is the French temperament and tendency. Material interests dominated. No one wanted to give up what had been, so they said, done during the Revolution. Every man was responsible for his own life and claimed the right to make his neighbor bear the brunt of it. Evil, they asserted, had become a public element, which was henceforth to be incorporated into government and enter, as a vital principle, into society.

My fanciful idea for a Charter set in motion by religious and moral action was the cause of the ill will certain parties bore me. From the royalists' perspective, I loved liberty too much; from the revolutionaries', I was too contemptuous of their crimes. Had I not been there, to my great detriment, making myself a professor of constitutionality, the Ultras and the Jacobins would have tucked the Charter in the pockets of their fleurs-de-lis frocks or their Cassius-style carmagnoles.[52]

M. de Talleyrand did not like M. Fouché. M. Fouché detested and, what was stranger, looked down his nose at M. de Talleyrand: it was difficult to win that privilege. M. de Talleyrand, who at first would have been glad not to be coupled to M. Fouché, sensing the latter was inevitable, agreed to the proposal. He did not see that, under the Charter, especially when he was united with the Butcher of Lyon, he was scarcely more acceptable than Fouché.

What I had predicted quickly came to pass. No one profited from the admission of the Duc d'Otrante; they only suffered reproach. The approaching shadow of the Chambers was enough to scare away ministers who would be too vulnerable in an open forum.

My opposition was useless. As it always is with weak characters, the king closed the session without deciding anything. The ordinance was not to be issued until we came to the Château d'Arnouville.

The council we held at this château was not lawful. Only the intimates and those privy to the secret were summoned. M. de Talleyrand, having got there ahead of us, conferred with his friends. The Duke of Wellington arrived: I saw him drive past in a calash, the feathers on his hat floating in the air. He had come to bestow France on M. Fouché and M. de Talleyrand as a twofold gift for the victory at Waterloo. When it was explained to him that the Duc d'Otrante's regicide was perhaps a drawback, he replied "But that's frivolous!" An Irish Protestant, an English general, unfamiliar with our manners and history, a mind seeing nothing in the French year of 1793 but the antecedent English year of 1649, was charged with sorting out our future! Bonaparte's ambition had reduced us to this misery.

I prowled by myself in the gardens the Comptroller General Machault left, at the age of ninety-three, to go and die in the Madelonnettes; for death, in his great review, does not forget anyone.[53] I was no longer sent for. The familiarities brought about by a common misfortune had ceased between sovereign and subject. The king was preparing to return to his palace, I to my retreat. The vacuum re-forms itself around monarchs as soon as they regain their power. I have seldom crossed, without losing myself in serious reflections, the silent, disused salons of the Tuileries, which used to lead me to the king's office: for me, deserts of another kind—infinite solitudes where the very worlds vanished before God, who is the only real being.

There was a shortage of bread in Arnouville. Had it not been for an officer named Dubourg,* who was, like us, winging away from Ghent, we would have had to fast. M. Dubourg went plundering and brought back half a lamb to the house where we were staying. It belonged to the mayor, who had fled. If the mayor's servant, a heroine of Beauvais in the house by herself, had possessed any weapons, she would have received us like Jean Hachette.[54]

We traveled on to Saint-Denis. The bivouacs of the Prussians and the English stretched out on both sides of the road. In the distance, the eyes met the spires of the abbey. Into its foundations Dagobert had thrown his jewels, in its catacombs the races had buried their kings and great men. Four months earlier, we had laid the bones of

---

*We shall encounter my friend General Dubourg again during the days of July.

Louis XVI there to take the place of other dust. When I returned from my first exile in 1800, I had crossed the same plain of Saint-Denis. At that time, Napoleon's soldiers were camped there; it was still Frenchmen who were superseding the old bands of the Constable de Montmorency.[55]

A baker took us in. Toward evening, around nine o'clock, I went to pay my court to the king. His Majesty was ensconced in the buildings of the abbey: they had all the trouble in the world keeping the little girls of the Légion d'Honneur from shouting "Long live Napoleon!"[56] First, I went into the church; a section of the wall adjoining the cloister had fallen. The ancient abbey was lighted by a single lamp. I prayed at the threshold of the vault into which I had seen Louis XVI lowered. Full of fear for the future, I do not know whether my heart had ever been flooded with a sadness more profound or devout. I then went to His Majesty's dwelling quarters. Introduced into one of the rooms preceding the king's, I found no one, sat in a corner, and waited. Suddenly a door opened, and without a sound Vice, leaning on the arm of Crime, came in: M. de Talleyrand was walking, supported by M. Fouché. The infernal vision passes slowly before me, enters the king's office, and disappears. Fouché had come to swear fidelity and pay homage to his lord. The loyal regicide, on his knees, put the hands that ordered the beheading of Louis XVI into the hands of the martyred king's brother, and the apostate bishop stood surety for this oath.

The following day the Faubourg Saint-Germain arrived. Everyone said his piece about Fouché's already-obtained appointment: the religious and the impious, the virtuous and the vicious, the royalist and the revolutionary, the foreigner and the Frenchmen, shouted from every side, "Without Fouché, no safety for the king; without Fouché, no salvation for France—he alone has already saved the country; he alone can complete his work." The elderly Duchesse de Duras[57] was one of the noblewomen who sang this hymn most passionately. The Bailli de Crussol, a Malta survivor, chanted droningly, saying that if his head was still on his shoulders, it was thanks to M.

Fouché. The fainthearted had been so frightened of Bonaparte they had turned the Butcher of Lyon into a Titus. For more than three months, the salons of the Faubourg Saint-Germain regarded me as an infidel because I disapproved of the appointment of their ministers. But these poor people had prostrated themselves at the feet of parvenus. They never stopped jawing about their nobility, their hatred of revolutionaries, their staunch fidelity, the inflexibility of their principles, and yet they adored Fouché.

Fouché had sensed that his ministerial existence was incompatible with the game of representative monarchy. As he could not amalgamate himself with the elements of a legal government, he had attempted to make the political elements consistent with his own nature. He had created a false terror. Concocting imaginary dangers, he tried to force the crown to recognize Bonaparte's two Chambers and accept a declaration of rights that had been finalized rashly. There were even some murmurs about the necessity of exiling *Monsieur* and his sons. To isolate the king would have been his masterpiece.

Everyone continued to be duped. The National Guard climbed over the walls of Paris and came to protest its devotion in vain; it was said that the Guard was ill disposed to the crown. The faction had the gates closed to prevent the population, which had remained royalist all through the Hundred Days, from rushing in to pay their respects, and it was said that this populace was threatening to butcher Louis XVIII if he so much as rode by. The blindness was miraculous, for at that moment the French army was retreating to the Loire, 150,000 Allies occupied the outposts of the capital, and it continued to be claimed that the king was not strong enough to enter a city where not one soldier remained and there were only civilians, who were more than capable of containing a handful of federates if these federates decided to make trouble. Unfortunately the king, through a series of fateful coincidences, seemed to be the leader of the English and the Prussians. He thought he was surrounded by liberators, and he was encircled by enemies. He appeared to be accompanied by an escort of honor, and this escort was, in reality, merely the gendarmes who were leading him out of his kingdom. He was crossing Paris in the company of foreigners whose memory would one day serve as a pretext for the banishment of his House.

The provisional government formed after Bonaparte's abdication was dissolved by means of a kind of indictment against the crown: a toothing-stone upon which they eventually hoped to construct a new revolution.

At the First Restoration, I was of the opinion that we should keep the tricolor cockade. It shone in all its glory, while the white cockade was forgotten. By retaining colors made legitimate by so many triumphs, we would avoid creating a rallying point for a revolution to come. Not to adopt the white cockade in the first place would have been wise; but to abandon it after it had been worn by Bonaparte's own grenadiers was an act of cowardice. One cannot pass under the Caudine Forks with impunity.[58] What is dishonorable is fatal. A slap in the face does you no harm physically, yet it kills you.

Before leaving Saint-Denis, I was received by the king and had the following conversation with him:

"Well!" said Louis XVIII, opening the dialogue with this exclamation.

"Well, Sire, you are taking on the Duc d'Otrante?"

"It had to be done. Everyone from my brother to the Bailli de Crussol (and the latter is not suspect) said that we could not do otherwise. What do you think?"

"Sire, the thing is done. I ask Your Majesty for permission to say nothing."

"No, no, speak. You know I have held out against this since Ghent."

"Sire, I am only obeying your orders; pardon me for my loyalty: but I believe the monarchy is finished."

The king kept silent. I was beginning to tremble at my boldness, when His Majesty spoke again:

"Well, Monsieur de Chateaubriand, I believe you are right."

This conversation concludes my account of the Hundred Days.

BOOK TWENTY-FOUR

I.

BONAPARTE AT MALMAISON—GENERAL ABANDONMENT

Revised in December 1846

IF A MAN were suddenly transported from the most clamorous scenes of life to the silent shore of the Arctic Ocean, he would experience what I am experiencing at Napoleon's grave, for that, abruptly, is where we find ourselves: beside this grave.

Having left Paris on June 25, Napoleon went to Malmaison, to await the moment of his departure from France. Now I am returning to him. Going back over days past, anticipating future times, I shall not leave him again until after he is dead.

Malmaison, where the emperor settled down for a while, was empty. Josephine had died; Bonaparte found himself alone in that retreat. There, he had begun his triumphant career; there, he had been happy; there, he had become intoxicated by the incense of the world; there, from the heart of his tomb, he had issued orders that caused the earth to tremble. In those gardens where the feet of the crowd once raked the sandy paths, grass and brambles grew green; I saw this for myself when I walked there. Already, for want of attention, the foreign trees were withering. The black swans of Oceania no longer navigated the canals. The tropical birds were gone from their cages: they had flown off to wait for their host in their native land.

Bonaparte might, however, have found consolation by turning back to his early days. Fallen kings grieve above all because they can see nothing, upstream of their fall, except inherited glory and the splendors of their cradle; but what could Napoleon see prior to his prosperity? The manger where he was born in a Corsican village. If he had been a greater soul, he would have proudly put on the goatherd's sayon after casting off the purple mantle; but men do not return to their origins when these were humble. It seems an unjust Heaven deprives them of their patrimony when, in Fate's lottery, they merely lose what they have won, and yet Napoleon's greatness comes from what he made of himself. No one of his blood had gone before him and paved the way for his power.

At the sight of those abandoned gardens, those uninhabited rooms, those galleries discolored by carousing crowds, those halls where the songs and the orchestras had fallen silent, Napoleon could think over all he had done. He could wonder whether, with a little more moderation, he might have held onto his happiness. Foreigners and enemies were not the cause of his banishment now; he was not going away nearly victorious, leaving the nations in awe of him, following the prodigious campaign of 1814. He was retreating in defeat. Frenchmen and friends were demanding his immediate abdication, pressing for his departure, refusing even to have him as a general, sending him one courier after another to force him to leave the soil where he had spread both glory and affliction.

With this harsh lesson came other warnings. The Prussians were prowling around Malmaison. Blücher, drunk, stumblingly ordered them to "string up" the conqueror who had "held his foot against the throats of kings." The rapidly changing fortunes, the vulgar manners, the swift rise and fall of modern personages will, I fear, rob our time of some of the nobility of history: Rome and Greece never talked about "stringing up" Alexander or Caesar.

Scenes that had taken place in 1814 were played out again in 1815, but there was something more offensive about them, for the ingrates were goaded on by fear. They had to get rid of Napoleon quickly. The Allies were coming. Alexander was not there at the beginning to temper the triumph and curb the insolence of victory. Paris was no longer adorned with its lustral inviolability; a first invasion had profaned the sanctuary. What was descending on us was no longer the wrath of God, it was the contempt of the heavens. The lightning had ceased.

All the cowards had acquired a new degree of malignity during the Hundred Days. Pretending to elevate themselves, for love of country, above personal attachments, they cried out that Bonaparte was beyond criminal for having violated the treaties of 1814. But weren't the real culprits the men who had furthered his plans? What if, in 1815, instead of raising new armies for him, after deserting him once only to desert him again, they had told him, when he came to sleep at the Tuileries: "Your genius has deceived you; public opinion is no longer with you; take pity on France. Enjoy this last visit to the country and leave; go and live in the land of Washington. Who knows if the Bourbons will not make mistakes? Who knows if one day France will turn its eyes toward you, once you have learned, in the school of liberty, to respect the laws? You will then return, not as a raptor swooping down on its prey, but as a great citizen bringing peace to his country."

They did not use this language with him; they pandered to the passions of their leader; they contributed to his blindness, sure as they were of benefiting by either his victory or his defeat. Only soldiers died for Napoleon, with admirable sincerity; the rest were nothing but a grazing herd, fattening themselves left and right. Still, if the viziers of the despoiled caliph had been satisfied with turning their backs on him, that would have been one thing! But no; they took advantage of his final moments; they overwhelmed him with their sordid demands. They all wanted to make money from his poverty.

Never was there a more complete desertion. Bonaparte was to blame for it. Insensitive to the sufferings of others, the world repaid his indifference with indifference. Like most despots, he was on good terms with his servants, but deep down he cared for no one. A solitary man, all he needed was himself. Misfortune did nothing but restore him to the desert that was his life.

When I collect my memories, when I recall seeing Washington in his little house in Philadelphia and Bonaparte in his palaces, it seems to me that Washington, retired to his Virginian fields, cannot have undergone the syndereses Bonaparte experienced while awaiting exile in his gardens at Malmaison.[1] In Washington's life, nothing had changed; he fell back on his modest habits; he had not raised himself above the happiness of the farm laborers he had freed. In Bonaparte's life, everything had been turned on its head.

2.

DEPARTURE FROM MALMAISON—RAMBOUILLET— ROCHEFORT

NAPOLEON left Malmaison accompanied by Generals Bertrand, Rovigo, and Becker, the latter acting in the capacity of warder. Along the way, he was seized with a desire to stop at Rambouillet. He left that palace to embark in Rochefort, as Charles X did before embarking in Cherbourg—Rambouillet, an inglorious retreat, where what is greatest in men and dynasties was eclipsed; the fatal place where François I died; where Henri III, escaping the barricades, slept booted and spurred; where Louis XVI left his shadow! How happy Louis, Napoleon, and Charles might have been if they were only the anonymous guardians of the flocks of Rambouillet![2]

When he arrived in Rochefort, Napoleon hesitated. The Executive Commission sent off imperative orders:

"The garrisons of Rochefort and La Rochelle," said the dispatches, "must use main force to make Napoleon take ship...Use force... make him go...his services cannot be accepted!"

Napoleon's services could not be accepted! But hadn't you accepted his gifts and his chains? Napoleon did not go away; he was driven out; and by whom?

Bonaparte had believed in nothing but good fortune. He accorded misfortune neither fire nor water; he had declared ingrates innocent in advance.[3] The rule of like for like justly led him to be judged by his own system. When success ceased to animate him and became embodied by another individual, the disciples abandoned the teacher for the school. I, who believe in the legitimacy of good deeds and the sovereignty of misery, had I served Bonaparte, would not have left him. With my fidelity, I would have shown him the falsity of his political principles. Sharing his disgrace, I would have stayed by his side, like a living contradiction of his barren doctrines and the limited value of the rule of prosperity.

Since the 1st of July, frigates had been riding at anchor, waiting for him, in the harbor of Rochefort. The hopes that never die, the memories inseparable from a final farewell, detained him. How he must have missed the days of his childhood, when his calm eyes had not yet seen the first rainfall! He gave the English fleet time to approach. He could still embark on two luggers that were to join a Danish ship at sea (this was the course taken by his brother Joseph); but as he gazed at the French shoreline, his resolution failed him. He was averse to republics. The equality and liberty of the United States revolted him. He was inclined to ask the English for asylum.

"What disadvantage do you see in this course of action?" he asked those he consulted.

"The disadvantage of dishonoring yourself," replied one naval officer. "You must not fall, even dead, into the hands of the English. They will have you stuffed and show you at a shilling a head."

3.

BONAPARTE TAKES REFUGE WITH THE ENGLISH
FLEET—HE WRITES TO THE PRINCE REGENT

IN SPITE of these observations, the emperor decided to hand himself over to his conquerors. On July 13, when Louis XVIII had already been in Paris five days, Napoleon sent the captain of the English ship *Bellerophon* this letter for the prince regent:

> Your Royal Highness,
> Exposed to the factions dividing my country and to the enmity of the mightiest powers of Europe, I have put an end to my political career and come, like Themistocles, to throw myself upon the hospitality of the British people. I put myself under the protection of their laws, which I ask of Your Royal Highness as of the most powerful, the most constant, and the most generous of my enemies.
> *Rochefort, July 13, 1815*

If Bonaparte had not been insulting the English people, its government, and its king for twenty years, he might have been able to find some suitable tone for this letter; but how did this Royal Highness, so thoroughly despised and insulted by Napoleon, suddenly become "the most powerful, the most constant, and the most generous" enemy by the mere fact of being victorious? It was impossible Napoleon believed what he was saying, and what is not true is not eloquent. The sentence expressing the fact of his fallen grandeur is fine, but the banal allusion to Themistocles is too much.

There is something worse than a lack of sincerity in the step Bonaparte was taking, however; there is a disdain for France. The emperor cared about nothing except his personal catastrophe. As soon as the fall came, we no longer counted for anything in his eyes. Without considering that, by choosing England over America, he was insulting his country's grief, he asked for asylum from the government that, for twenty years, had bribed Europe to fight against us; the government whose commissioner with the Russian army, General Wilson, urged Kutuzov, during the retreat from Moscow, to exterminate us completely. The English, the victors of the final battle, were encamped in the Bois de Boulogne. Go then, O Themistocles, and sit quietly by a British hearth, while the earth has not yet finished lapping up the French blood shed for you at Waterloo! What role could the deserter (who would perhaps be celebrated) have played on the banks of the Thames, with France invaded and Wellington dictator at the Louvre? Napoleon's exalted fortune served him better: the English, letting themselves be carried away by a spiteful, small-minded politics, missed their opportunity for one final triumph. Instead of humiliating their supplicant by letting him in to their fortresses or banquets, they made the crown they believed they had taken from him all the more lustrous. In his captivity he grew larger, fed by the enormous fear of the people in power. The ocean imprisoned him in vain. Europe in arms camped on the shore, her eyes fixed upon the sea.

4.

**BONAPARTE ON THE *BELLEROPHON*—TORBAY—
DECREE CONFINING BONAPARTE TO SAINT HELENA
—HE CROSSES ON TO THE *NORTHUMBERLAND* AND
SETS SAIL**

ON JULY 15, the *Épervier* transported Bonaparte to the *Bellerophon*.
The French ship was so small that, from the deck of the English ship,
they could not see the giant riding on the waves. The emperor, approaching Captain Maitland, said to him:

"I have come to place myself under the protection of the laws of
England."

For once at least, the scorner of the laws admitted their authority.

The fleet set sail for Torbay. A multitude of ships cruised around
the *Bellephron*; the same excitement was evident at Plymouth. On
July 30, Lord Keith issued the petitioner the act that confined him
to Saint Helena.

"It's worse than Tamburlaine cage," said Napoleon.[4]

This violation of the rights of man and hospitality was revolting.
If you greet the day on *any* ship, provided it is *under sail*, you are
English by birth. According to the age-old traditions of London, the
waves are reputed to be the "soil of Albion." Yet an English ship was
not an inviolable altar for a supplicant, nor did it place the great man
who embraced the stern of the *Bellerophon* under the protection of
the British trident! Bonaparte protested. He argued legality, spoke
of treachery and perfidy, and appealed to the future. But was this in
keeping with his character? Hadn't he laughed in justice's face? Hadn't
he, in his days of power, trampled underfoot the sacred things whose
assurance he invoked? Hadn't he abducted Toussaint-Louverture and
the King of Spain?[5] Hadn't he arrested English travelers who happened

to be in France when the Peace of Amiens was broken and kept them as prisoners for years? It was thus allowable for mercantile England to imitate what he himself had done, and to carry out ignoble reprisals; but they could have acted differently.

The greatness of Napoleon's heart did not match the greatness of his head. The quarrels he had with the English are deplorable; they revolt Lord Byron. How could he have deigned to say so much as a word to his jailers? It is painful to see him stooping to verbal skirmishes with Lord Keith in Torbay, with Sir Hudson Lowe on Saint Helena, issuing statements because they break faith with him, quibbling over a title, over a little more, or a little less, gold or honor. Bonaparte, reduced to himself, was reduced to his glory, and that should have been sufficient for him. There was no reason for him to ask others for anything. In the end, he did not treat adversity despotically enough; one could have forgiven him for making misfortune the last of his slaves. I find nothing remarkable about his protest against the contravention of hospitality except the way he signed it: "Aboard the *Bellerophon*, at sea, Napoleon." There are harmonies among these immensities.

From the *Bellerophon*, Bonaparte crossed on to the *Northumberland*. Two frigates laden with the future garrison of Saint Helena escorted him. Some of the officers of this garrison had fought at Waterloo. The explorer of the globe was allowed to keep M. and Madame Bertrand, M. Montholon, M. Gourgaud, and M. de Las Cases by his side—voluntary and generous passengers on the submerged plank. According to one clause in the captain's instructions, "Bonaparte was to be disarmed": Napoleon, by himself, held prisoner on a ship in the middle of the ocean, disarmed! What outlandish fear of his power! But what a lesson from Heaven to men who abuse the sword! The stupid admiralty treated the great convict of the human race like a felon being shipped off to Botany Bay. Did the Black Prince "disarm" King John?[6]

The squadron weighed anchor. Since the boat that carried Caesar, no ship had been laden with such a destiny. Bonaparte was approaching that sea of miracles over which the Arab of Sinai had seen him pass. The last French land Napoleon saw was La Hogue—another trophy of the English.[7]

The emperor had been mistaken, where posterity is concerned, when he expressed his wish to remain in Europe. There, he would have soon been no more than a common, withered prisoner; his old role was finished. But beyond this role, a new situation rejuvenated him with a new renown. No man so universally famous had lived out his days as Napoleon did. He was not proclaimed, as he was at his first fall, the autocrat of some iron and marble quarries: the former to provide him with a sword, the latter a statue. Recognized as an eagle, he was given a rock where he could remain in the sunlight until the end of his days, in plain view of the entire earth.

5.

APPRAISAL OF BONAPARTE

NOW THAT Bonaparte is leaving Europe, giving up his life in order to go and seek his death beneath the fated sky, it is time to inquire into this man who led two lives, to describe the false Napoleon and the true Napoleon. Merged together, they form a heterogeneous whole, composed partly of reality and partly of lies.

From all that has already been said,* it is obvious that Bonaparte was a poet in action; an immense genius in war; an indefatigable, able, and intelligent mind in administration; and an industrious and rational legislator. That is why he continues to have such a hold on the imagination of so many people and such authority over the judgement of practical men. But as a politician he will always seem deficient in the eyes of statesmen. This observation, which has escaped most of his panegyrists, will become, I am convinced, the definitive opinion of him in years to come; it will explain the contrast between his prodigious actions and their miserable results. On Saint Helena, he harshly condemned his own political conduct on two points: the war in Spain and the war in Russia. He might have extended this admission to other failings. His enthusiasts will perhaps maintain that, when he criticized himself, he was mistaken. Let us recapitulate:

---

*I ask you to recall what I have told you about the man when I spoke of the death of the Duc d'Enghien; when I painted him in action in Europe before, during, and after the Russian campaign; when I summarized my pamphlet *De Bonaparte et des Bourbons*. The comparison with Washington that I made in Book 6 of these *Memoirs* also throws some light on Napoleon's character.

Bonaparte acted contrary to all prudence, not to speak again of the loathsomeness of the deed, when he killed the Duc d'Enghien: he attached a weight to his life. Despite all that his puerile apologists may say, this death, as we have seen, was the secret leaven of the discords that later arose between Alexander and Napoleon as well as between Prussia and France.

The war in Spain constituted a clear abuse. The peninsula belonged to the emperor. He could have turned it to good account. Instead, he turned it into a training ground for English soldiers and the seed, sown by the nation's revolt, of his own destruction.

The imprisonment of the pope and France's annexation of the Papal States were nothing but than a tyrannical caprice, which lost him the advantage of passing himself off as the restorer of religion.

Bonaparte did not stop, as he should have done, when he married the daughter of the Caesars—when Russia and England were crying mercy to him.

He did not revive Poland, when the safety of Europe depended on the restoration of that kingdom.

He hurried off to Russia despite the recommendations of his generals and advisers.

Madness having set in, he marched on beyond Smolensk although everything told him he should not go farther, that his first northern campaign was finished, and that his second (as he himself sensed) would make him master of the Empire of the Czars.

He did not know how to assess the distances or foresee the effect of the climate, which everyone in Moscow assessed and foresaw. Consider, too, what I have said of the Continental Blockade and the Confederation of the Rhine: the former was a monumental idea but a dubious act; the latter a considerable achievement, but spoiled in the execution by an instinct born of the barracks and a love of money. Napoleon inherited the old French monarchy as the centuries and an unbroken succession of great men had made it, as the majesty of Louis XIV and the alliances of Louis XV had left it, and as the Republic had enlarged it. He plopped himself down on that magnificent throne, stretched out his arms, grabbed hold of the nations, and gathered them around him; but he lost Europe as swiftly as he had seized it, and he twice brought the Allies to Paris, despite the marvels of his military intelligence. He had the world at his feet, and all he got out of it was a prison for himself, exile for his family, and the loss of all his conquests as well as a piece of old French territory.

This is history proved by facts that no one can deny. But where did the faults I have just indicated originate, faults followed by such a prompt and unfavorable conclusion? They originate in Bonaparte's shortcomings as a politician.

In his alliances, he enchained governments only with concessions of territory, whose boundaries he soon altered, constantly showing a tendency to take back what he had given, and never letting anyone forget the oppressor for a moment. In his invasions, he renovated nothing, Italy aside. Instead of pausing after each step to rebuild, behind him, what he had toppled, he never ceased his forward march through the ruins, moving so fast he scarcely had time to catch his breath as he went. If, by a sort of Treaty of Westphalia, he had settled and assured the existence of the states of Germany, Prussia, and Poland, then on his first rearward march he could have fallen back on contented populations and found shelter among them. But his poetic edifice of victories, lacking a foundation and kept in the air only by his genius, fell the moment that his genius deserted him. The Macedonian founded empires as he went: Bonaparte, as he went, managed merely to destroy them. His one objective was to be ruler of the globe, yet he never troubled his head about how to preserve what he ruled.

People have tried to make Bonaparte into a perfect being, a man of feeling, delicacy, moral virtue, and justice, a writer like Caesar and Thucydides, an orator and historian like Demosthenes and Tacitus. Napoleon's public speeches, his recorded remarks in tent and council, are all the less inspired by the prophetic breath because the catastrophes they foretold have not come to pass, while the Isaiah of the sword has himself disappeared: Ninevehian speeches[8] that go after states, but do not take or destroy them, are childish, not sublime. Bonaparte was Destiny incarnate for sixteen years, but Destiny is mute, as

Bonaparte should have been. Bonaparte was not Caesar; his education was neither scholarly nor elite; a quasi foreigner, he was ignorant of the most basic rules of our language. But what, after all, does it matter if his speech was faulty? He gave the watchword to the universe. His bulletins have the eloquence of victory. Sometimes, in the intoxication of success, his soldiers made a show of tacking them on a drum; the most mournful accents gave rise to fatal roars of laughter. I have carefully read all that Bonaparte has written: the first manuscripts of his childhood, his novels, his letters to Buttafuoco, *The Supper at Beaucaire*, his private letters to Josephine, the five volumes of his speeches, orders, and bulletins, and his unpublished dispatches, spoiled by redaction in the offices of M. de Talleyrand. I know something of these matters, and I have found hardly any thoughts resembling the great islander's nature except for a sorrowful handwritten note left behind on Elba:

My heart refuses both common joys and ordinary pain.

Not having given myself life, I shall not rob myself of it either, as long as it will have me.

My evil genius appeared to me and foretold my end, which I found at Leipzig.

I have conjured up the terrible spirit of novelty that has been flooding the world.

This is most certainly the real Bonaparte.

If Bonaparte's bulletins, speeches, allocutions, and proclamations are distinguished by their energy, this energy did not belong to him in his own right: it was of his time, it came from the revolutionary inspiration that grew weaker in Bonaparte, for he walked in the opposite direction of that inspiration. Danton said, "The metal is bubbling over. Keep an eye on the furnace, or you will all get burned." Saint-Just said, "*Dare!*" The whole policy of our Revolution is contained in that word; a half-hearted revolutionary is simply digging his own grave.

Do Bonaparte's bulletins raise themselves above this prideful speech?

As for the numerous volumes published under the titles *Memoirs of Saint Helena*, *Napoleon in Exile*, etc., etc., etc., these documents—taken from Bonaparte's table talk, or dictated by him to various persons—contain some beautiful passages on military life, some remarkable appreciations of certain men; but in the end Napoleon is only interested in absolving himself, justifying his past, varnishing events with ideas about things he never paused to consider while these events were taking place. In these compilations, where pros and cons parade one after the other, where every opinion finds a favorable authority and a peremptory refutation, it is difficult to untangle what belongs to Napoleon from what belongs to his secretaries. Very likely he gave each of them a different version, so that readers might choose according to their taste and, in the future, create for themselves Napoleons to their liking. He dictated his story the way he wished it to be told, like an author writing reviews of his own work. Nothing therefore could be more absurd than going into ecstasies over these analects composed by multiple hands, which are not, like Caesar's *Commentaries*, a short work conceived by a great mind and written by a superior writer (and yet those brief comments, in the opinion of Asinius Pollio, were neither accurate nor faithful).[9] *The Memorial of Saint Helena* is a fine work, if one makes allowances for its innocent and uncomplicated admiration.

One of the things that most contributed to rendering Napoleon so repellent in his lifetime was his penchant for debasing everything. In a city on fire, he coupled decrees reestablishing theater companies with decrees deposing monarchs—a parody of the omnipotence of God, who decides the fate of the world and of an ant. While empires collapsed, he hurled insults at women. He enjoyed humiliating those he had brought low; he especially slandered and affronted anyone bold enough to resist him. His arrogance was indistinguishable from his happiness; he thought he grew in stature by diminishing others.

Jealous of his generals, he blamed them for his own failings, because, as far as he was concerned, he could never have failed. Contemptuous of all their merits, he rebuked them for their errors. After the disaster at Ramillies, he would never have said, like Louis XIV to Marshal Villeroi, "At our age, Marshal, no one is lucky."[10] Such tender magnanimity was alien to Napoleon. The age of Louis XIV was made by Louis the Great: Bonaparte made his age.

The story of the emperor, altered by false traditions, will be further falsified by the state of society during the imperial period. Any revolution chronicled with freedom of the press allows the eye to go down to the bottom of things, for everyone reports the facts as he has seen them: we know about Cromwell's reign because people told the Protector what they thought of his actions and his person. In France, even under the Republic, despite the inexorable censorship of the executioner, the truth broke through; the victorious faction was not always the same; it swiftly succumbed, and the faction to follow taught you what its predecessor had concealed from you. Between one scaffold and the next, between one severed head and the next, there was freedom. But when Bonaparte seized power, thought was gagged. All that could be heard was a despotic voice that spoke only in praise of itself and did not allow anyone to speak of anything else. Truth disappeared.

The so-called authentic documents from this time are corrupted. Nothing was published, books or newspapers, except at the behest of the master. Bonaparte scrutinized the articles in the *Moniteur*; his prefects in the *départements* sent back recitations, congratulations, and felicitations exactly as they had been dictated and transmitted by the Parisian authorities, exactly expressing a preauthorized public opinion entirely different from the real public opinion. How can anyone write history using such documents? To provide evidence of your impartial studies, cite the authentic documents you have consulted, and you will only be citing a lie in support of a lie.

If it were possible to call this universal imposture into question, if men who have not lived through the days of the Empire persisted in believing everything they come across in its published documents—

or even everything they might dig up in certain ministry files—it would be enough to appeal to an unimpeachable witness, the Sénat "conservateur."[11] There, in the decree I quoted above, you read its own words: "The freedom of the press had been constantly subjected to the arbitrary censorship of his police, while he himself had simultaneously made use of the same engine to fill the public ear with fabricated facts and false maxims"; "acts and reports, adopted by the Senate," had been "altered by his own authority prior to publication"; and so on. Is there anything that can be said in response to this declaration?

The life of Bonaparte was an incontestable truth, which imposture had taken upon itself to write.

6.

BONAPARTE'S CHARACTER

MONSTROUS pride and incessant affectation spoil Napoleon's character. During the days of his dominion, why did he need to exaggerate his stature, when the Lord of hosts had furnished him with the chariot whose "wheels were living creatures"?[12]

He took after his Italian ancestors; his nature was complex. The great men, who form a very small family on the earth, unfortunately find no one to imitate but one another. At once a model and a copy, a real person and an actor playing that person, Napoleon was his own mime; he would not have thought of himself as a hero if he had not put on a hero's costume. This strange weakness lends something false and equivocal to his astonishing reality. One must be careful not to mistake the king of kings for Roscius, or Roscius for the king of kings.[13]

Napoleon's qualities are so distorted in the gazettes, pamphlets, poems, and even in the songs invaded by imperialism, that these qualities are completely unrecognizable. All the touching things these anas attribute to Bonaparte on the subject of "prisoners," "the dead," and "soldiers" are hogwash, which the actions of his life belie.

My illustrious friend Béranger's "Grandmother" is no more than a fine little ditty: Bonaparte had nothing good-natured about him.[14] Domination incarnate, he was dry as a bone. This frigidity counterweighed his fiery imagination. He found, within himself, no words, only actions—and actions ready to become hostile at the slightest sign of independence. A gnat that flew without orders from him was, to his mind, a rebellious insect.

It was not enough to lie to people's ears; it was also necessary to lie to their eyes. Here, in an engraving, we see Bonaparte taking off his hat before the Austrian wounded; there, a little soldier boy prevents the emperor from passing; further on, Napoleon touches the plague victims of Jaffa, when in fact he never touched them; or he crosses the Saint Bernard Pass on a high-spirited horse in driving snow, when in fact the weather could not have been better.

Aren't people now trying to transform the emperor into a Roman of the early days of the Aventine, into a missionary of liberty, into a citizen who instituted slavery only out of love for the opposite virtue? Draw your own conclusions about the great founder of equality by considering these two characteristic acts: he ordered his brother Jérôme's marriage to Miss Patterson annulled because Napoleon's brother could only be joined with the blood of princes; and later, on his return from the isle of Elba, he adorned the new "democratic" constitution with a peerage and crowned it with the "additional act."

That Bonaparte, furthering the Republic's successes, disseminated the principles of independence everywhere; that his victories helped to loosen the bonds between nations and kings, wresting these nations from the power of old customs and ideas; that, in this sense, he contributed to social enfranchisement, I do not pretend to contest; but that, of his own free will, he consciously worked for the political and civil emancipation of the nations; that he established the narrowest despotism with the idea of giving Europe, and France in particular, the broadest constitution; that he was a tribune merely disguised as a tyrant—these are suppositions I cannot accept.

Bonaparte, like the race of princes, wanted nothing and sought nothing but power, which he attained through liberty merely because he stepped onto the world's stage in 1793. It did not take long until the Revolution, Napoleon's wet nurse, began to look like one of his enemies, and he never stopped beating her. The emperor, besides, could recognize evil very well, when the evil did not come directly from the emperor, for he was not devoid of moral sense. The sophism put forward regarding Bonaparte's "love of liberty" proves only one thing: how easily reason can be abused. Nowadays, this abuse of reason lends itself to everything. Hasn't it been demonstrated that the Terror was a time of great humanity? Indeed, weren't the leaders asking for the abolition of the death penalty while they were killing half the world? Haven't the great civilizers, as they are *called*, sacrificed men, and doesn't this mean, as has been *proved*, that Robespierre was carrying on the work of Jesus Christ?[15]

The emperor involved himself in everything. His mind never rested. He suffered from a sort of perpetual agitation of ideas. Naturally reckless, he never moved at a steady, continuous pace; he proceeded by leaps and bounds; he pounced on the universe and throttled it; he wanted nothing from that universe if it required him to wait: an incomprehensible creature, who discovered the secret of debasing his loftiest actions by disdaining them and of raising his lowliest actions up to his own level. Patient by nature but impatient to control, incomplete and, in a certain sense, unfinished, Napoleon had gaps in his genius. His understanding of things was like the sky of that other hemisphere, in which he would die—like that sky whose stars are separated by empty spaces.

One may wonder what magic spell allowed Bonaparte, who was so aristocratic and so hostile to the people, to attain the popularity he enjoys today, for this forger of yokes has most certainly remained popular with a nation whose pretension has been to raise altars to independence and equality. Here is the answer to the riddle:

Daily experience makes it clear that the French instinctively seek out authority. They do not love freedom. Equality alone is their idol. Now, equality and tyranny have secret links. On both counts Napoleon pleased the French, who are militarily inclined toward power and democratically in love with a dead level. Once he ascended the throne, he seated common people beside him. A proletarian king, he humiliated kings and nobles in his antechambers. He leveled the ranks, not by lowering but by raising them. Leveling down would have been more appealing to plebeian envy, but leveling up was more flattering to its pride. French vanity was inflated, too, by the superiority Bonaparte gave us over the rest of Europe. And the affliction of his final days has only added to Napoleon's popularity. After his death, as we learned more about what he suffered on Saint Helena, we began to feel sorry for him; we forgot his tyranny and remembered that, after conquering our enemies, then drawing them to France, he had defended us against them. We imagine he would save us from the shameful situation we are in today. His fame has been heightened by his misfortune, and his glory has profited from his adversities.

Finally, his military miracles have bewitched the young and taught us all to worship brute force. His unprecedented good fortune has given every self-seeking striver the hope of scaling the heights he climbed.

And yet this man, who became so popular by flattening out France with a roller, was the mortal enemy of equality and the most active organizer of aristocracy within democracy.

I cannot acquiesce to the false praise with which some people insult Bonaparte, attempting to justify all of his behavior; I cannot renounce my reason and rhapsodize about what fills me with horror or pity.

If I have managed to convey what I have felt, I will still have made a portrait of one of the leading figures in history; but I have not adopted anything of that fantastic creature composed of lies—lies I witnessed being born and which, although at first taken for what they were, have over time assumed the appearance of truth, due to the infatuation and idiotic credulity of humankind. I have no wish to play the fool and fall into a fit of admiration. I am trying to describe characters conscientiously, without taking away what they possess or giving them what they lack. If success were deemed innocence; if, depraving even posterity, it clapped everything in its irons; if, a future slave, begotten of a slavish past, this suborned posterity became the accomplice of whoever happened to triumph, where would be the right, where would be the reward of sacrifices? Good and evil being merely relative, all morality would be canceled out of human actions.

Such is the difficulty, for the impartial writer, when dealing with a man of dazzling renown. He ignores it as best he can and tries to lay the truth bare, but the glory returns, like a radiant haze, and instantly covers his picture.

7.

WHETHER BONAPARTE HAS BEQUEATHED US IN FAME WHAT HE HAS TAKEN FROM US IN STRENGTH

TO AVOID admitting the loss of territory and power we owe to Bonaparte, the current generation consoles itself by imagining that what he took from us in strength, he paid us back in glory. "Aren't we now renowned," they say, "the world over? Isn't it true that a Frenchman is feared, noticed, sought out, and recognized on every shore?"

But are we limited to these two conditions: either immortality without power, or power without immortality? Alexander made the name of the Greeks known around the globe and left them no fewer than four empires in Asia. The language and civilization of the Hellenes extended from the Nile to Babylon and from Babylon to the Indus. At his death, his patrimonial kingdom of Macedonia, far from being diminished, had become one hundred times stronger. Bonaparte made us known on every shore. Under his leadership, the French brought Europe so thoroughly to its knees that France's name still prevails and the Arc de l'Étoile can tower high and wide without seeming a puerile trophy; but before our reversals, this monument would have stood witness instead of being merely a chronicle. Yet is it not true that Dumouriez with his conscripts had given the foreigner his first lessons, that Jourdan had won the Battle of Fleurus, Pichegru had conquered Belgium and Holland, Hoche had crossed the Rhine, Masséna had triumphed at Zürich and Moreau at Hohenlinden—feats most difficult to accomplish, and which paved the way for others? Bonaparte brought together these scattered successes in one person;

he continued these victories and made them shine. But without those earlier wonders, could he have worked his own later ones? He rose above all things only when the man of reason carried out inspirations worthy of a poet.

Our overlord's fame cost us no more than two or three hundred thousand men a year; we paid for it with no more than three million of our soldiers; our citizens bought it at the low cost of fifteen years of suffering and loss of their liberties. Do such trifles matter? Aren't subsequent generations flourishing? What a pity for those who have perished! The calamities under the Republic were for the salvation of all. Our misfortunes under the Empire have accomplished much more: they have deified Bonaparte! And that is enough for us.

That is not enough for me, I will not stoop so low as to hide my nation behind Bonaparte. He did not make France, France made him. No talent, no eminence will ever induce me to consent to an authority that can, with one word, deprive me of my independence, my home, my friends. If I do not speak of my fortune or honor, this is because fortune does not seem to me worth the trouble of defending. As for honor, it eludes tyranny: it is the soul of martyrdom. Bonds enclose but do not enchain it; it breaks through the prison walls and takes the whole man with it.

The wrong that true wisdom will never forgive Bonaparte is his having habituated society to passive obedience, driven mankind back to times of moral degradation, and perhaps bastardized human character to such a degree that it is impossible to say when hearts will begin to throb with generous feelings again. The weakness that now engulfs us, amongst ourselves and with regard to Europe, our present abasement, is the consequence of Napoleonic slavery: it has left us nothing but the ability to bear the yoke. Bonaparte has deranged the future. I would not be at all surprised to see us, in the unease of our powerlessness, diminishing ourselves still further: barricading ourselves against Europe instead of going out to meet it; giving up our liberties at home to keep ourselves safe from imaginary dangers abroad; losing ourselves in ignoble precautions, contrary to our genius and the fourteen centuries that have gone into the making of our way of life. The despotism that Bonaparte left hanging in the air will come down and enclose us like a fortress.

The fashion nowadays is to greet liberty with a sardonic laugh, to regard it as an antiquated notion fallen into disuse, like honor. I am not at all fashionable. I think that, without liberty, the world is nothing. It makes life worthwhile. Even if I should find myself the last man defending it, I will never cease proclaiming its rights. To attack Napoleon in the name of things past and gone, to assail him with dead ideas, is to let him triumph yet again. He can only be combated with something greater than himself, and that is liberty. He has committed crimes against liberty and, therefore, against the human race.

8.

USELESSNESS OF THE TRUTHS LAID OUT IN THE PREVIOUS CHAPTERS

VAIN WORDS! I sense their uselessness better than anyone. Nowadays any criticism, however moderate it may be, is considered profanation. It takes courage to brave the shouts of the vulgar and not to fear being called narrow-minded, incapable of understanding or appreciating Napoleon's genius simply because, despite the keen and candid admiration you profess for him, you still cannot bring yourself to praise all his imperfections. The world belongs to Bonaparte. What the ravager was unable to conquer, his fame usurps. While alive, he may have failed to win the world, but dead, he possesses it. You can insist all you like, but the generations pass by without heeding you. Antiquity has the shade of the son of Priam say, "Do not judge Hector by his tomb or measure by his barrow the adversary of all Hellas. *The Iliad*, Homer himself, Greece, the Achaeans in flight—these are my tomb—by these all was my barrow built."[16]

Bonaparte is no longer the Bonaparte who lived; he is a legendary figure made up of poets' whims, soldiers' estimations, and the people's stories. He is the Charlemagne and Alexander of the medieval epics we see today. This fantastical hero will replace the real person: divergent portraits will disappear. Bonaparte was so at one with absolute power that, after suffering the despotism of the man himself, we must now submit to the despotism of his memory. The latter despotism is more domineering than the former, for, although a few people resisted Napoleon while he was on the throne, today there is universal agreement we should accept the shackles he throws on us from beyond the grave. He is an obstacle to future events. After him, how can a power issuing from the camps establish itself? Has he not killed all military glory by surpassing it? How can a free government come into being, when he has corrupted the principle of liberty in the hearts of humanity? No legitimate power could now drive the usurping specter from the mind of man. The soldier and the citizen, the republican and the monarchist, the rich person and the poor person, all place busts and portraits of Napoleon in their houses, palaces, cottages—and the erstwhile defeated are of the same opinion as the erstwhile victors. One cannot set foot in Italy without seeing him; one cannot cross the German border without encountering him, for in Germany the young generation that beat him back is gone. Usually the centuries sit down before the portrait of a great man and complete it with their slow and gradual work. In this case, humanity did not want to wait; perhaps it was in too much of a rush to stump a pastel.[17] It is time to place the finished part of the idol side by side with the defective part.

Bonaparte is not great by virtue of his words, his speeches, his writings, or the love of liberty he never possessed and never attempted to establish. He is great for having created a sturdy and powerful government, a code of laws adopted in diverse countries, courts of law, schools, and a strong, active, intelligent administration on which we are still living. He is great for having resurrected, enlightened, and governed Italy extraordinarily well. He is great for having, in France, revived order in the midst of chaos, for having righted its altars, for having reduced the raving demagogues, the vainglorious scholars, the anarchic writers, the Voltairean atheists, the open-air orators, the cutthroats from the prisons and streets, the wormlings of the tribunes, the clubs, and the scaffolds—for having reduced them to serving under him. He is great for having chained up an anarchic mob. He is great for having put an end to the familiarities of a common fortune, for having forced soldiers, his equals, and captains, his superiors or rivals, to bend before his will. He is especially great for having, by himself, created himself; for having been able, with no authority except for his own genius, to compel the obedience of thirty-six million subjects in an age with no illusions about thrones.

He is great for having brought down every king who opposed him, for having defeated every army, no matter much they differed in discipline and valor; for having taught his name to both the savage and the civilized; for having surpassed all the conquerors who preceded him; for having filled ten years with marvels so staggering that it is difficult to comprehend them today.

The famous offender in triumphal matters is gone from the earth. The few men who still understand noble sentiments can pay homage to his glory without fearing it, but they also need not apologize for having declaimed what was baleful about this glory; they need not acknowledge the destroyer of independence as the father of emancipation. Napoleon does not need merits ascribed to him; he was sufficiently endowed at birth.

Now that, untethered from his time, his story is ended and his epic is beginning, let us go see him die. Let us leave Europe. Let us follow him beneath the sky where he apotheosized! The rumbling of the seas, where his ships struck sail, will lead us to the place where he vanished. "At the far end of our hemisphere," says Tacitus, "one can hear the sound the sun makes as it sinks into the sea," *sonum insuper immergentis audiri*.[18]

9.

ISLE OF SAINT HELENA—BONAPARTE CROSSES THE ATLANTIC

JOÃO DA Nova, the Portuguese explorer, had lost his bearings in the waters separating Africa from America. In 1502, on August 18, the feast day of Saint Helen, mother of the first Christian emperor, he spied an island at 16° latitude and 11° longitude; he touched land there and named it for the day of its discovery.

After frequenting this island for a few years, the Portuguese deserted it. The Dutch settled there, then abandoned it for the Cape of Good Hope. The East India Company of England seized it before the Dutch took possession of it again in 1672. Finally, the English occupied it once more and built settlements there.

When João da Nova first appeared on Saint Helena, the interior of the uninhabited island was thick with woods. Fernão Lopes, a Portuguese renegade deported to this oasis, populated it with cows, goats, chickens, guinea fowl, and other birds from every corner of the earth. They gave rise, as on board the ark, to all the animals of creation.

Five hundred whites, fifteen hundred blacks, together with some mulattoes, Javanese, and Chinese, make up the population of the island. Jamestown is the city and the port. Before the English took control of the Cape of Good Hope, the fleets of the East India Company, on their way back from the Indies, rested in Jamestown. The sailors laid out their rubbish in the shade of the palms, and a silent, solitary forest was transformed, once a year, into a noisy, crowded market.

The climate of the island is salutary, but rainy. This innermost keep of Neptune, which is only seven or eight leagues around, attracts the ocean's mists. At midday, the equatorial sun persecutes everything that breathes, forces even the midges to be silent and rest, compels people and animals to hide. At night, the waves are illuminated by what is called "sealight," produced by myriad insects whose amorous pursuits, electrified by the tempests, enkindle the surface of the deep with the festive fires of their ubiquitous nuptials; then the shadow of the island, dark and still, lies in the midst of a shifting plain of diamonds. The sight of the sky is equally magnificent, according to my learned and famous friend M. von Humboldt.* "A strange, completely unknown feeling is awoken in us when nearing the equator and crossing from one hemisphere to another," he writes; "the stars we have known since infancy begin to vanish. Even those with no inkling of astronomy know they are no longer in Europe when they see the enormous constellation of the Ship or the brilliant Clouds of Magellan rise in the night sky."

"On the night of the 4th of July," he continues, "at about the 16th degree of latitude, we saw the Southern Cross clearly for the first time, and I recalled the sublime passage from Dante that the most celebrated commentators have identified with this constellation:

Io mi volsi a man destra ... [19]

"Portuguese and Spaniards are particularly susceptible to this feeling; religious sentiments attach them to a constellation whose shape recalls the sign of the faith planted by their ancestors in the deserts of the New World."[20]

The poets of France and Lusitania have set elegiac scenes on the shores of Melinde and the neighboring islands. It is a far cry from these fictional sorrows to the real torments Napoleon suffered under those stars foretold by the bard of Beatrice, amid those seas of Éléonore and Virginie.[21] Did the great men of Rome, relegated to Grecian islands, care about the charms of those shores, or the divinities of Crete and Naxos? What enchanted Vasco da Gama could not touch Bonaparte.

Personal Narrative of a Journey to the Equinoctial Regions of the New Continent.

Lying on the stern of the ship, he took no note, above his head, of the glister of unknown constellations that his eyes had never seen before. What good, where he was concerned, were those stars he had not beheld from his bivouacs, those stars that had not shone on his empire? And yet no star failed to attend his destiny: one half of the firmament lit up his cradle; the other half was reserved for the pomp of his tomb.

The sea Napoleon was crossing was not the friendly sea that carried him from the harbors of Corsica and the sands of Aboukir, from the rocks of Elba to the shores of Provence; it was a hostile ocean that, after imprisoning him in Germany, France, Portugal, and Spain, opened out before him now only to close again behind him. It is probable that, as he watched the waves urging on his ship, the trade winds driving it farther and farther with their unremitting breath, he did not think about his catastrophe as I am thinking about it. Every man feels his life his own way, and he who gives the world a great spectacle is not so moved or so instructed as the spectator. Dwelling on the past, as if he could live it over again, still hoping and rooting in his memories, Bonaparte scarcely noticed that he was crossing the line, and never asked what hand traced those circles in which the planets are compelled to imprison their eternal passage.

On August 15, the wandering colony celebrated Saint Napoleon's Day on board the vessel that was taking Napoleon to his final halt. On October 15, the *Northumberland* drew abreast of Saint Helena. The passenger went up on deck; he had trouble seeing the imperceptible black spot in the bluish immensity; he took a spyglass and surveyed that speck of earth as he might once have surveyed a fortress in the middle of a lake. He saw the village of Saint James encased in craggy rocks. There was not a wrinkle of that barren crag not fitted with a gun. They seemed to want to receive the captive in a manner suited to his genius.

On October 16, 1815, Bonaparte landed on the rock, his mausoleum, as on October 12, 1492, Christopher Columbus landed in the New World, his monument. There, says Walter Scott, at the entrance to the Indian Ocean, Bonaparte "was debarred from the power of making a second avatar," or incarnation, on the earth.

10.

NAPOLEON LANDS ON SAINT HELENA—HIS SETTLEMENT AT LONGWOOD—PRECAUTIONS—LIFE AT LONGWOOD—VISITS

BEFORE being transported to Longwood House, Bonaparte lived in a hut called The Briars, near Balcomb's Cottage. On December 9, Longwood, hurriedly enlarged by the carpenters of the English fleet, received its guest. The house, situated on a mountain plateau, consisted of a parlor, a dining room, a library, a study, and a bedroom. It was not much. Those who resided in the tower of the Temple and the keep of Vincennes were given even worse accommodation, although, it's true, their hosts were considerate enough to cut their stay short. General Gourgaud, the Montholons and their children, M. de Las Cases and his son, all temporarily camped out in tents. The Bertrands settled at Hutt's Gate, a cottage bordering the grounds of Longwood.

Bonaparte had a stretch of sand twelve miles long to walk on. Sentinels surrounded this space, and lookouts were posted on the highest peaks. The lion could extend his journeys beyond this stretch, but he then had to consent to being watched by an English *bestiarius*.[22] Two camps defended the excommunicate's enclosure. In the evening, the circle of sentries tightened around Longwood. After nine o'clock, Napoleon was not allowed out. The patrols made their rounds; riders on the move, infantrymen stationed here and there, kept watch in the creeks and ravines that ran down to the beach. Two armed brigs cruised, one to leeward, the other to windward of the island. What precautions to keep one man in the middle of the ocean! Once the sun had set, no rowboat could put out to sea; the fishing boats were counted, and at night they remained in port under the watch of a naval lieutenant. The sovereign generalissimo who had summoned the world to his stirrup was called on to appear twice a day before an infantry officer. Bonaparte refused to answer this call; when, by chance, he could not elude the gaze of the officer on duty, this officer would not have dared to say where and how he had seen the man whose absence from the universe was much more difficult to certify than his presence.

Sir George Cockburn, who was responsible for these severe regulations, was replaced by Sir Hudson Lowe. There then began the quibbles that all the memoirs relate to us. If these memoirs are to be believed, the new governor must have belonged to the family of enormous spiders that live on Saint Helena—or he was the reptile of those woods where snakes are unknown. England showed a lack of generosity, Napoleon a lack of dignity. To put an end to the requirements of etiquette, Bonaparte sometimes seemed determined to hide behind a pseudonym, like a monarch in a foreign country. He had the touching idea of taking the name of one of his aides-de-camp, killed at the Battle of Arcole. France, Austria, and Russia appointed commissaries to the Saint Helena residence. The captive was used to receiving the ambassadors of the latter two powers. The Legitimacy, which had not recognized Napoleon as emperor, would have acted more nobly by not recognizing Napoleon as a prisoner either.

A large wooden house, built in London, was shipped to Saint Helena; but Napoleon no longer felt well enough to inhabit it. His life at Longwood was thus arranged: he rose at irregular hours, and M. Marchand, his valet de chambre, read to him in bed. When he got up early, he would dictate to Generals Montholon and Gourgaud, and to M. de Las Cases's son. He breakfasted at ten, wandered around on horseback or in a carriage until about three, returned at six, and went to bed at eleven. He affected the costume in which he is depicted in Isabey's portrait: in the morning he would wrap himself in a caftan and tie an Indian kerchief around his head.

Saint Helena lies between the two poles. Sailors who cross from one place to another welcome the sight of this first way station, where land gives rest to eyes wearied by the sight of the ocean and offers fresh fruits and water to mouths chafed by the salt. Bonaparte's presence had changed this promised land into a plague-ridden rock. Foreign vessels no longer landed there; as soon as they were sighted twenty leagues away, a cruiser went to inspect them and bade them sail off. No one was admitted to this place of respite, save in stormy weather, except ships of the British navy.

Some of the English travelers who had come back from admiring or were about to go see the wonders of the Ganges would, on their journey, visit another wonder: India, accustomed to conquerors, had one in chains at her gate.

Napoleon bore these visits with difficulty. He agreed to see Lord Amherst on his way back from his embassy to China. Admiral Sir Pulteney Malcolm he liked.

"Does your government intend to keep me penned on this rock until I die?" he asked him one day.

The admiral replied he feared that was so.

"Then my death will come soon."

"I hope not, sir. You must live long enough to write about your great deeds. There are so many of them, the task will ensure you a long life."

Napoleon did not take offense at being called simply "sir." At that moment, he revealed his true greatness.

Fortunately for him, he did not write his life. He would have diminished it. Men of his type must let their memories be recounted by that nameless voice that belongs to no one and that emerges from the peoples and the centuries. Only common men like us are permitted to talk about ourselves, for nobody else would ever talk about us.

Captain Basil Hall put in an appearance at Longwood; Bonaparte remembered seeing the captain's father at Brienne:

"Your father," he said, "was the first Englishman I ever met. I have remembered him all my life on that account."

He talked with the captain about the recent discovery of the island of Loo-Choo.

"The inhabitants have no weapons," said the captain.

"No weapons!" Bonaparte exclaimed.

"No cannon, no rifles."

"At least they have spears, bows and arrows?"

"Nothing of the sort."

"No daggers?"

"No daggers."

"But how do they fight?"

"They do not know what goes on in the world. They have no idea that France or England exist. They have never heard of Your Majesty."

Bonaparte smiled in a way that struck the captain. The more serious the countenance, the more beautiful the smile.

All these various travelers noticed that Bonaparte's face had lost all trace of color. His head looked like a marble bust whose whiteness had been rather yellowed by time. There were no wrinkles on his brow, no hollows in his cheeks; his soul seemed serene. His apparent calm led some to believe that the flame of his genius had gone out in him. He spoke slowly, his expression affectionate and almost tender. Sometimes he would shoot a dazzling glance, but the dazzle quickly faded; his eyes would cloud over and grow melancholy.

Ah! But other travelers known to Napoleon had once appeared on those shores.

After the explosion of the infernal machine, a *sénatus-consulte* of January 4, 1801, decreed without trial, by a simple police order, that 130 republicans should be exiled overseas. Put to ship on the frigate *Chiffonne* and the corvette *Flèche*, they were taken to the Seychelles islands and shortly thereafter dispersed along the archipelago of the Comoros, between Africa and Madagascar, where they almost died. Two of the deportees, Lefranc and Saunois, managed to escape on an American vessel and touched land at Saint Helena in 1803. It was there, twelve years later, that Providence had imprisoned their great oppressor.

The notorious General Rossignol, their companion in misfortune, a quarter of an hour before he breathed his last, exclaimed:

"I am dying in the most horrible pain; but I would die happy if I could hear that my country's tyrant was enduring the same agonies!"

Thus, even in the other hemisphere, freedom's imprecations awaited the man who betrayed her.

11.

**MANZONI—BONAPARTE'S ILLNESS—OSSIAN—
NAPOLEON'S REVERIES AT THE SIGHT OF THE SEA—
RESCUE PLANS—BONAPARTE'S LAST PURSUIT—
HE TAKES TO BED AND DOES NOT RISE AGAIN—
HE DICTATES HIS WILL—NAPOLEON'S RELIGIOUS
FEELINGS—CHAPLAIN VIGNALI—NAPOLEON
APOSTROPHIZES TO ANTOMARCHI, HIS DOCTOR—
HE RECEIVES EXTREME UNCTION—HE DIES**

ITALY, torn from her long sleep by Napoleon, turned her eyes to the illustrious child who wished to restore her to her glory and under whose yoke she had fallen. The sons of the Muses, the noblest and most grateful of men, when they are not the basest and most ungrateful, cast their gaze on Saint Helena. The last poet of Virgil's homeland sang of the last warrior of Caesar's homeland:

> *Tutto ei provò, la gloria*
> *Maggior dopo il periglio,*
> *La fuga e la vittoria*
> *La reggia e il tristo esiglio:*
> *Due volte nella polvere,*
> *Due volte sull'altar.*
>
> *Ei si nomò: due secoli,*
> *L'un contro l'altro armato,*
> *Sommessi a lui si volsero,*
> *Come aspettando il fato;*
> *Ei fe' silenzio, ed arbitro*
> *S'assise in mezzo a lor.*[23]

Bonaparte was nearing his end. Preyed upon by an internal wound envenomed by sorrow, he had borne that wound all through his days of prosperity. It was the sole inheritance he had received from his father. The rest came from the munificence of God.

Already he had lived six years in exile. It had taken him less time to conquer Europe. He remained indoors nearly all the time, and read Ossian in the Italian translation by Cesarotti. Everything saddened him under that sky where life seemed shorter—the sun shining three days fewer in that hemisphere than in ours. When Bonaparte went out, he walked on crumbling paths bordered by aloes and fragrant broom; he passed between gum trees with strange flowers that the prevailing winds tipped all to one side, or he hid in the thick clouds that rolled along the ground. He sat at the feet of Diana's Peak, the Flag Staff, and Ladder Hill, contemplating the sea through the gaps in the mountains. Before him stretched the ocean which on one side laves the African coasts, on the other the American shores, and which runs like a bankless river and loses itself in the southern seas. No civilized land lies nearer to the Cape of Storms. Who can tell the thoughts of that Prometheus disemboweled alive by death, when he cast his eyes over the waves? Christ was transported to the summit of a mountain from which he saw the kingdoms of the world; but, in Christ's case, it was written to the tempter of man: "Thou shalt not tempt the Lord thy God."[24]

Bonaparte, forgetting what he had written on the isle of Elba ("not having given myself life, I shall not rob myself of it either"), spoke of killing himself. He had also forgotten his order of the day, regarding the suicide of one of his soldiers. He was so confident of the attachment of his companions in captivity he thought they would agree to suffocate with him in the smoke of a fire. His delusion was tremendous. Such are the intoxications of a long dominion. But we must remember, when considering Napoleon's impatience, the degree of suffering he had reached. M. de Las Cases, having written to Lucien on a piece of white silk, in violation of the rules, was ordered to leave Saint Helena. His absence magnified the void that surrounded the outcast.

On May 18, 1817, Lord Holland, in the House of Peers, made a motion concerning the complaints transmitted to England by General Montholon. "Posterity will not ask," he said, "whether Napoleon was justly punished for his crimes, but whether England showed the generosity befitting a great nation." Lord Bathurst opposed the motion.

Cardinal Fesch sent two priests from Italy to his nephew. Princess Borghese begged the favor of being able to join her brother. "No," said Napoleon, "I do not want her to witness my humiliation or the insults I am exposed to here." This beloved sister, *germana Jovis*,[25] never crossed the seas. She died in the place where Napoleon had left his fame behind.

Plans to rescue him were made. One Colonel Latapie, leading a band of American adventurers, plotted a landing on Saint Helena. Johnston—an enterprising smuggler—said he would steal Bonaparte away by means of an underwater boat. Some young lords became involved in these plots and conspired to break the oppressor's chains; humanity's liberator they would have left to die in chains without a second thought. Bonaparte hoped to be set free by political movements in Europe. Had he lived until 1830, perhaps he would have returned to us—but, among us, what would he have done? He would have seemed obsolete and backward amid the new ideas. In the past, his tyranny appeared as liberty to us in our slavishness; in the 1830s, his greatness would appear as despotism to us in our pettiness. In the present era, everything becomes decrepit in a day; he who lives too long dies alive. As we go on through life, we leave behind three or four images of ourselves, all different from one another; we look at them, later, through the mist of the past, like portraits of our different ages.

As Bonaparte's health grew weaker, he kept busy like a child. He amused himself digging a little pond in his garden and put in some fish. A mixture of copperas in the mastic used in cementing the basin had affected the water, and the fish died. Bonaparte said:

"Everything I love—everything that belongs to me—is doomed."

Toward the end of February 1821, Napoleon was obliged to take to bed and did not rise again.

"How low I have fallen," he murmured. "I have stirred up the whole world, and now I cannot lift my eyelids."

He did not believe in medicine and objected to a consultation between Antomarchi and the Jamestown doctors. He did, however, allow Dr. Arnold to be present at his deathbed. From the 13th to the 27th of April, he dictated his will. On the 28th, he ordered his heart be sent to Marie Louise and forbade any English surgeon from laying a hand on him after his death. Convinced he was succumbing to the illness that had afflicted his father, he recommended that the autopsy report be passed on to the Duke of Reichstadt. This paternal precaution would turn out to be useless. Napoleon II has joined Napoleon I.[26]

At this final hour, the religious feeling that had always suffused Bonaparte was awoken. Thibaudeau, in his *Mémoires sur le Consulat*, tells us, in connection with the restoration of worship, that the First Consul had told him:

"'Last Sunday, in the silence of Nature, I was walking in these gardens (of Malmaison); suddenly, the sound of the Rueil church bell struck my ear and brought back to me all the impressions of my youth; I was moved, so strong is the force of early associations, and I said to myself: If this can happen to me, what effect must similar memories not produce on simple, credulous men? Let your philosophers find an answer to that!' ... and, lifting his hands to the heavens, 'who is it who has made all this?'"

In 1797, by his Proclamation of Macerata, Bonaparte authorized French priests who had taken refuge in the Papal States to remain there, forbade them to be disturbed, ordered the monastic orders to feed them, and allotted them a monetary stipend.

His fluctuations in Egypt, his anger with the Church he had restored, show that a spiritual instinct predominated even in his divagations, for his lapses and irritations are not of a philosophical nature and bear the imprint of the religious temperament.

When providing Vignale with the details of the *chapelle ardente*[27] he wanted to surround his remains, he thought he could see Antomarchi wincing at his instructions. He explained himself to the doctor:

"You are above these weaknesses, but what do you want from me? I am neither a philosopher nor a doctor; I believe in God; I am of my father's religion. We cannot all be atheists ... Can you not believe in God? For in the end everything proclaims His existence, and the greatest geniuses have believed in him ... But you are a doctor ... Such people deal only with matter; they never believe in anything."

Oh, you modern rationalists, leave off your admiration of Napoleon; you have nothing in common with that poor man. Did he not imagine that a comet had come to fetch him, just as it had once carried off Caesar? Besides, he "believed in God"; he was "of his father's religion"; he was no "philosopher" or "atheist"; he did not, as you do, fight battles with the Lord, even if he did conquer a number of kings. He thought that everything proclaimed the existence of the Supreme Being; he said that the greatest geniuses had believed in this Being, and he wished to believe as his fathers had. And lastly, monstrous to relate, this first man of modern times, this man of all the ages, was a Christian in the nineteenth century! His will begins with this article:

I DIE IN THE APOSTOLIC AND ROMAN RELIGION, IN THE BOSOM OF WHICH I WAS BORN MORE THAN FIFTY YEARS AGO.

In the third paragraph of Louis XVI's will, we read:

I DIE IN THE UNION OF OUR HOLY MOTHER THE CATHOLIC, APOSTOLIC, AND ROMAN CHURCH.

The Revolution taught us many lessons; but is there any lesson comparable to this one? Napoleon and Louis XVI making the same profession of faith! Do you want to know the value of the cross? Then search the world over for what best befits virtue in misfortune or the man of genius on his deathbed.

On May 3, Napoleon was administered extreme unction and received viaticum. The silence of the bedroom was broken only by the irregular breathing of the dying man and the regular beating of a pendulum clock: the shadow, before coming to a halt on the dial, made a few more rounds; the star that traced its outline was finding it hard to go out. On the fourth, storms worthy of Cromwell's agony arose and nearly all the trees at Longwood were uprooted.[28] Finally, on the fifth, at eleven past six o'clock in the evening, in the midst of the wind and the rain and the rumble of the waves, Bonaparte rendered up to God the mightiest breath of life that ever animated human clay. The last words heard upon the conqueror's lips were "Head . . . army," or "head of the army." His thoughts were wandering over the fields of battle once more. When he closed his eyes forever, his sword, which died with him, was laid on his left side, and a crucifix rested on his chest. The symbol of peace, applied to Napoleon's heart, calmed its throbbing, as a ray from the heavens makes the waves subside.

12.

OBSEQUIES

BONAPARTE first wished to be buried in the Ajaccio Cathedral,
then, by a codicil dated April 16, 1831, he bequeathed his bones to
France. Heaven served him better. His real mausoleum is the rock
where he died—turn again to my account of the Duc d'Enghien's
death. Finally, Napoleon, foreseeing that the British government
would oppose his last wishes, chose a burial site on Saint Helena.

In a narrow valley called the Slane or Geranium Valley, and now
the Valley of the Tomb, there is a burbling spring. Napoleon's Chinese
servants, as faithful as Camões's Javanese, used to fill their amphorae
there. Weeping willows overhang the water, and green grass, dotted
with champas, grows all around. "The champa, despite its brilliancy
and scent, is not a sought-after plant, for it blooms on graves," say the
Sanskrit poets.[29] In the declivities of deforested rocks, bitter lemons,
coconut palms, larches, and gum wood grow poorly, and the people
harvest the gum that clings to the beards of the goats.

Napoleon liked the willows on the spring. He asked for peace
from Slane Valley as the banished Dante had asked for peace at the
cloister of Corvo. In recognition of the fleeting repose he experienced
in the last days of his life, he said, speaking of the spring: "If God
were to grant me good health again, I would raise a monument at the
place where it begins." This monument was his tomb. In the time of
Plutarch, in a place consecrated to the nymphs on the banks of the
Strymon, one could still see a stone seat where Alexander used to
take his ease.

Napoleon, booted and spurred, dressed in the uniform of a colonel of the Guard and decorated with the Légion d'Honneur, was laid in state on his iron bunk. Upon that face, which had never shown surprise, the soul, as it departed, had left a sublime stupor. Planishers and joiners soldered and nailed Bonaparte into a fourfold coffin of mahogany, lead, mahogany again, and tin: it was as if they feared he would never be sufficiently imprisoned. The cloak worn by the old victor at the vast funeral of Marengo was used as a mortuary sheet.

The funeral was held on May 28. The weather was beautiful. Four horses, led by grooms on foot, drew the hearse; twenty-four English grenadiers, unarmed, surrounded him, followed by Napoleon's horse. The garrison of the island lined the cliffs along the road. Three squadrons of dragoons preceded the procession; the Twentieth Infantry Regiment, the marines, the Saint Helena Volunteers; and the Royal Artillery with fifteen guns brought up the rear. Groups of musicians, positioned at intervals on the rocks, traded mournful airs. At a narrow pass, the hearse rolled to a stop. The twenty-four unarmed grenadiers removed the body and had the honor of carrying it on their shoulders to the burial site. Three artillery salvos saluted Napoleon's remains as he went down into the earth: all the noise he had made on this earth did not penetrate six feet below.

A stone, which was to be used in the construction of a new house for the exile, was lowered onto his coffin, like the trapdoor on his final dungeon.

The verses from Psalm 87 were recited: "I am poor, and have labored since my youth; I have been exalted, and I have been humbled and afflicted . . . thy terrors have thrown me into confusion."[30] Minute by minute, the flagship was firing its guns. This warlike music, lost in the immensity of the oceans, answered the *requiescat in pace*. The emperor, buried by those who had defeated him at Waterloo, had heard the last gunfire of this battle; he did not hear the last detonation with which England troubled and honored his sleep at Saint Helena. Finally, everyone withdrew, holding a willow branch in hand, as if returning from the Feast of Palms.

Lord Byron believed that the dictator of kings had abdicated his

698 · MEMOIRS FROM BEYOND THE GRAVE

fame along with his sword and that he would die forgotten. The poet should have known Napoleon's Destiny was a Muse, like all lofty Destinies. This Muse was able to change an abortive conclusion into a tragedy that gave her hero new life. The solitude of Napoleon's exile and tomb has added another layer of prestige to his brilliant memory. Alexander did not die under the eyes of the Greeks; he vanished into the faraway beauties of Babylon. Bonaparte did not die under the eyes of the French; he disappeared into the sumptuous horizons of the torrid zones. He sleeps like a hermit or a pariah in a valley, at the end of a deserted trail. The grandeur of the silence that presses in upon him is equal to the immensity of the noise that once surrounded him. The nations are absent, their crowds gone. The tropicbird, "harnessed," as Buffon says, "to the chariot of the sun," dashes down from the star of light—and where, today, does he take his rest? He takes his rest on ashes whose weight once tilted the globe.[31]

13.

DESTRUCTION OF THE NAPOLEONIC WORLD

Imposuerunt omnes sibi diademata, post mortem ejus,
et multiplicata sunt mala in terra
(MACHABAEORUM)[32]

THESE last words on Alexander from the Books of the Maccabees
seem made for Napoleon. "After his death, they all crowned *themselves*,
and evils were multiplied upon the earth." Scarcely twenty years have
gone by since Bonaparte's death, and already the French and Spanish
monarchies are no more.[33] The map of the world has changed; we
have had to learn a new geography. Separated from their legitimate
sovereigns, nations have been thrown to rulers picked at random.
Famous actors have stepped down from the stage onto which nameless actors have climbed. The eagles have flown from the pine trees
fallen into the sea, while frail mollusks have attached themselves to
the sides of the still-protective trunk.

Since, ultimately, everything marches on toward its conclusion,
"the terrible spirit of novelty that has been flooding the world," as
the emperor called it—that spirit which he dammed with his genius—has resumed its course. The conqueror's institutions have foun-
dered. His will be the last of the great individual lives. From now on,
nothing will dominate in our minor and equalized societies. Napoleon's
shade will stand alone at the far end of the devastated old world, like
the phantom of the deluge at the edge of its abyss. In the distant

future, people will pick out that shade above the chasm into which unknown centuries fall, until the appointed day of the social renaissance.

14.

MY LAST RELATIONS WITH BONAPARTE

SINCE it is my own life I am writing, even as I digress into those of others, large or small, I have no choice but to include certain things and men when, by chance, this life of mine recalls them. Have I gone through, in one breath, without stopping, the memory of the deportee who, in his oceanic prison, awaited the execution of God's decree? No.

The peace Napoleon did not conclude with his jailers the kings, he made with me: I was, like him, a son of the sea; my birthplace, like his, was a rock. I flatter myself that I knew Napoleon better than those who saw him more often and knew him more intimately.

Napoleon on Saint Helena, no longer having any reason to be angry with me, had renounced his enmities, and I, becoming more just in my turn, wrote this paragraph in the *Conservateur*:

> The nations have called Bonaparte a scourge, but God's scourges retain something of the eternity and grandeur of the divine wrath from which they emanate: *Osse arida ... dabo vobis spiritum et viveris.* "O ye dry bones ... I will cause breath to enter into you, and ye shall live."[34] Born on an island to go and die on an island beyond the bourne of three continents; flung amidst the seas where Camões seemed to prophesy him by making the place home to the spirit of storms, Bonaparte cannot so much as stir on his rock but we are apprised of it by a jolt; a single step taken by this new Adamastor[35] at the other

702 · MEMOIRS FROM BEYOND THE GRAVE

pole is felt at this one. If Napoleon, escaping from the hands of his jailers, retired to the United States, his eyes, fixed on the ocean, would be enough to disturb the people of the Old World. His mere presence on the American side of the Atlantic would force Europe to set up camp on the opposing shore.

This article reached Bonaparte on Saint Helena. A hand he believed to be hostile poured the last balm on his wounds. He said to M. de Montholon:

"If, in 1814 and '15, the royal trust had not been placed in men whose souls had been adulterated with circumstances too strong for them, or who, renegades to their country, saw safety and glory for their master's throne only under the yoke of the Holy Alliance; had the Duc de Richelieu, whose ambition was to rescue his country from the presence of foreign bayonets, or Chateaubriand, who had just rendered eminent services at Ghent, been put in charge of affairs, France would have emerged from those two national crises mighty and feared. Nature has accorded Chateaubriand a sacred fire: his works attest to it. His style is not that of Racine, it is that of the prophet. If he ever finds himself at the helm of affairs, it is possible that Chateaubriand would go astray. So many others have come to grief before him! But there is no question that all that is great and national must befit his genius, and that he would have indignantly rejected the shameful acts of the administration of those days."[36]

Such were my last relations with Bonaparte. Why shouldn't I confess that his opinion "pandered to my foible—regal pride"?[37] Many little men to whom I have rendered eminent services have not judged me so favorably as the giant whose power I had dared to attack.

15.
SAINT HELENA SINCE NAPOLEON'S DEATH

WHILE the Napoleonic world began to fade away, I was making inquiries about the places where Napoleon himself had vanished. The tomb at Saint Helena has already outlasted one of the willows that are its contemporaries: every day the decrepit, fallen tree is mutilated by pilgrims. The burial site is surrounded by a cast-iron fence; three slabs have been laid transversely over the grave; a few irises grow at its feet and head. The valley spring still flows in the spot where a prodigious life ran dry. Travelers, carried there by tempests, believe themselves compelled to record their obscurity on the radiant sepulchre. An old woman has set up house nearby and lives in the shadow of a memory. A pensioner stands guard in a sentry box.

The old Longwood House, two hundred paces from the new one, is abandoned. Through an enclosure filled with manure, one arrives at a stable, which used to be Bonaparte's bedroom. A black man shows you a sort of hallway half blocked by a hand mill and tells you, "Here he dead."[38] The room where Napoleon greeted the day was probably no larger or more luxurious.

At the new Longwood, Plantation House, where the governor lives, one sees a portrait of the Duke of Wellington and paintings of his battles. A glass cabinet contains a piece of the tree beside which the English general stood at Waterloo. This relic is displayed between an olive branch picked from the Mount of Olives and some ornaments worn by savages of the South Seas: a bizarre conglomeration on the part of the abusers of the waves. Here, the victor uselessly tries to substitute himself for the vanquished with the aid of a branch taken from the Holy Land and the memory of Cook. It is enough that, on Saint Helena, one finds solitude, the ocean, and Napoleon.

If a man were to research the history of how shores have been changed by the presence of illustrious tombs, birthplaces, and palaces, he must surely discover all manner of things and destinies, seeing that such strange metamorphoses occur even in the obscure dwellings where we lead our own trifling lives! In what hut was Clovis born? In what chariot did Attila greet the day? What mountain stream runs over Alaric's grave? What jackal stands upon the site of Alexander's gold or crystal coffin? How many times have these ashes shifted from place to place? And all those mausoleums of Egypt and India—to whom do they belong? Only God knows the reason for these changes linked with the mysteries of the future. For men, there are truths hidden in the depths of time that only the passage of centuries can reveal, as there are stars so far from the earth that their light has not yet reached us.

16.

EXHUMATION OF BONAPARTE

But while I have been writing this, time has been marching on. It has produced an event that would have a certain grandeur, if events nowadays did not tend immediately to fall into the mud. Again, they petitioned London for Bonaparte's corpse, and this time the request was granted. What does England care about some old bones? She will give us as many presents of that sort as we like. Napoleon's remains have been returned to us at the moment of our humiliation;[39] they might have been subject to search, but the foreigner was lenient: he gave the ashes a pass.

The translation of Napoleon's remains is an offense against fame. No sepulchre in Paris will ever be as good as the Slane Valley. Who would want to see Pompey elsewhere than in the furrow of sand heaped up by a poor freedman, with the help of an old legionnaire?[40] What will we do with these magnificent relics in the midst of our miseries? Would the hardest granite on earth represent the longevity of Bonaparte's achievements, even if we had a Michelangelo to carve the memorial statue? What kind of monument will he be given? To little men mausoleums, to great men a stone and a name. Why not at least hang the coffin from the top of the Arc de Triomphe, so that the nations could see their master from afar, borne on the shoulders of his victories? Wasn't Trajan's urn set atop his column in Rome? Napoleon, among us, will be lost in the swarm of vagrants who steal away in silence. God grant that he will not be exposed to the vicissitudes of our political changes, protected though he may be by Louis

XIV, Vauban, and Turenne! Beware of those violations of tombs so common in our country! Let a certain side of the Revolution triumph, and the dust of the conqueror may join the dust that our passions have previously scattered; people will forget the vanquisher of nations and remember only the oppressor of liberties. Napoleon's bones will not reproduce his genius, they will teach his despotism to mediocre soldiers.

Be that as it may, one of Louis Philippe's sons was given a frigate whose name, dear to our old naval victories, protected it in its passage over the waters.[41] Sailing from Toulon, where Bonaparte had embarked, at the height of his power, to go conquer Egypt, the new *Argo* went to Saint Helena to lay claim to nothingness. The burial site, in its silence, still stood motionless in the Slane Valley. Of the two weeping willows, one had fallen; Lady Dallas, wife of a governor of the island, had eighteen young willows and thirty-four cypresses planted to take the place of the fallen tree. The spring, which remained, flowed as it had when Napoleon drank its water. For the length of one night, under the direction of an English captain named Alexander, men worked to bore open the monument. The four caskets, nested one inside another—the mahogany coffin, the lead coffin, the second mahogany coffin, and the tin coffin—were found intact. These mummy molds were then inspected beneath a tent in the midst of a circle of officers, some of whom had known Bonaparte.

When the last casket was opened, every eye plunged inside. "We saw," says Abbé Coquereau, "a whitish mass which covered the whole length of the body. Dr. Gaillard, touching it, realized that a white satin cushion that had covered the inside of the upper wall of the coffin had detached and enveloped the remains like a shroud ... The whole body seemed to be covered with a light foam; it was as if we were beholding it through a diaphanous cloud. It was indeed his head. A pillow raised it slightly, and we could see his broad brow, his eyes whose sockets were outlined beneath the eyelids, still fringed with a few lashes; his cheeks were bloated; but only his nose had suffered. His half-open mouth revealed three remarkably white teeth. On his chin, the traces of his beard were perfectly clear. His two hands, especially, seemed to belong to someone still breathing, their tone and color was so alive. One of them, the left hand, was raised a little higher than the right; his nails had grown after death; they were long and white. One of his boots had burst its seams and four of the toes on his dull white feet were exposed."

What struck these necrobiae?[42] The inanity of earthly things? The vanity of mankind? No, the beauty of the dead man; only his nails had grown longer, to tear, I presume, at what liberty was left in the world. His feet, restored to humility, no longer rested on royal cushions; they lay bare in their dust. Condé's son, too, was fully dressed in the moat at Vincennes; yet Napoleon, however well preserved he may have been, had now been reduced precisely to the state of those "three teeth" the bullets had left in the Duc d'Enghien's jaw.

The star eclipsed on Saint Helena reappeared, to the great joy of the nations. The world saw Napoleon again, though Napoleon never again saw the world. The wandering remains of the conqueror were watched over by the same stars that guided him into his exile: Bonaparte passed through the tomb, as he passed through everything, without stopping. Landing at Le Havre, the corpse arrived at the Arc de Triomphe—a canopy beneath which the sun shows its brow on certain days of the year.[43] All the way from that arch to the Invalides, one could see nothing but columns of planks, plaster busts, a statue of the great Condé (a hideous, weeping porridge), and pine-board obelisks commemorating the victor's indestructible life. Bitterly cold weather made the generals drop around the hearse as during the retreat from Moscow. Nothing was beautiful, except the funeral barge that had silently carried Napoleon and a crucifix down the Seine.

Robbed of his catafalque of rocks, Napoleon came to be buried amid the rubbish of Paris. Instead of ships saluting the new Hercules, burned upon Mount Oeta, the washerwomen of Vaugirard will roam around him, crossing paths with pensioners unknown to the Grand Army. As a prelude to this inadequacy, little men could think up nothing better than an open-air waxworks show. After a few rainy days, all that was left of these decorations were a few muddy globs. No matter what has been done, men will always see the triumphant one's true sepulchre in the midst of the seas: the body is with us, the life immortal on Saint Helena.

Napoleon brought the era of the past to a close. He made war in such a way, on such a scale, that it no longer interests mankind. He slammed the doors to the Temple of Janus impetuously behind him; and behind those doors he piled up stacks of corpses, so that they could never be opened again.

17.
MY VISIT TO CANNES

IN EUROPE, I have gone to visit the places where Bonaparte landed after breaking his ban and returning from Elba. I alighted at the inn in Cannes at the very moment when the guns were firing in commemoration of the 29th of July: one of the consequences of the emperor's incursion, which he no doubt foresaw.[44] Night had fallen by the time I reached Golfe-Juan. I dismounted at an isolated house along the high road. Jacquemin, a potter and innkeeper, the owner of this house, led me down to the sea. We followed sunken paths between the olive trees under which Bonaparte had bivouacked. Jacquemin himself had housed the exile, and now he was guiding me. To the left of the side road was a sort of shed in which Napoleon, invading France alone, had stored the effects he had brought with him.

When I got to the beach, I saw a calm sea unruffled by the slightest breath of wind. The ripples, thin as gauze, unfurled on the sand without sound or foam. A wondrous sky, all resplendent with constellations, crowned my head—the crescent moon soon dropping and hiding herself behind a mountain. There was only one ship at anchor in the bay, and a pair of boats. To the left you could see the lighthouse at Antibes and to the right the Lérins Islands. Straight ahead of me, the open sea stretched out to the south, toward the city of Rome, where Bonaparte had first sent me.

The Lérins Islands, today called the Sainte-Marguerite Islands, once sheltered a few Christians who had fled the barbarians. Saint Honorat, coming from Hungary, landed on one of these reefs: he climbed a palm tree, made the sign of the cross, and all the serpents died, which is to say: paganism vanished and the new civilization was born in the West.

Fourteen hundred years later, Bonaparte came to finish that civilization in the very place where the saint had started it. The last solitary to live in that monastery was the Man in the Iron Mask—if the Man in the Iron Mask ever in fact existed. From the silence of the Golfe-Juan, from the peace of the islands of the ancient anchorites, came the noise of Waterloo, which crossed the Atlantic, and went to die on Saint Helena.

Standing between the memories of two societies, between a world long gone and a world soon to vanish, in the middle of the night, at the deserted edge of those salt waters, you may imagine what I felt. I left the beach in a kind of religious consternation, leaving the waves to pass to and fro over, yet never to erase, the prints Napoleon's pen-ultimate footsteps had made.

At the end of every great epoch, you hear some doleful voice or other mourning the past and ringing the curfew bell. So those who saw the disappearance of Charlemagne, Saint Louis, François I, Henri IV, and Louis XIV wept and moaned. What couldn't I tell you in my turn, eyewitness that I am to two or three worlds gone by? When, like me, one has met Washington and Bonaparte, what else is there to see beyond the plow of the American Cincinnatus and the tomb at Saint Helena? Why have I outlived the age and the men I belonged to by birth? Why haven't I fallen with my contemporaries, the last of an exhausted race? Why have I remained here alone, seeking their bones in the darkness and dust of a crowded catacomb? I don't relish the thought of lasting much longer. Ah, if only I was as carefree as one of those old waterfront Arabs I saw in Africa! Sitting cross-legged on a little rope mat, their heads wrapped in their burnooses, they while away their final hours watching the beautiful flamingos fly through the azure over the ruins of Carthage. Lulled by the murmur of the waves, they forget their existence and, in a hushed voice, sing a song of the sea: they are going to die.

AFTERWORD

THERE IS, in the oft-mocked parallel between Chateaubriand and Napoleon—a parallel we see running almost like a watermark through the *Memoirs*—at least one respect in which the resemblance is in no way forced: their isolation—at once dazzling and immediate—in superiority. From the moment Chateaubriand appears, he stands alone on his terrain. With *The Genius of Christianity*, which at one fell swoop creates a desert around him, he comes into possession of a voluminous, monumental, administered portion of fame, underwritten by an omnipresent, considerable party. For after 1800, Europe is France, and the French Catholicism of "God perceived by the heart," to whatever degree it grows green again on the scorched earth, is, more or less, Chateaubriand. When he travels, there is not one country priest (we catch a glimpse of this in the *Memoirs*) who doesn't race to the top of his village in order to be the first to present him with bread and salt.[1] And, what's more, he possesses a noble, secret portion: the whole—parsimonious—sum of poetry imparted to his generation. For twenty-five years it is he who dispenses it. Alone and in full. Everything, in his career, is acquired from the first and for good. There is no need to keep the public waiting with bated breath, no pressure to be a "purveyor." After *The Martyrs*, he draws the curtain closed and moves on to other exercises. His glorious sun may have been a dark one, but he never stood in anybody's shadow. When later—much later, and by then he was a minister of state—he senses the young fame of Lamartine or Hugo encroaching, one suspects his vanity was already well protected by that carapace of so-called desert varnish seen on stones long roasted beneath the Saharan sun; he didn't feel the sting. His brood... For his is a singular case—and this is more consequential than one might think—of a "lone wolf" almost unexampled in modern literature: he is a writer, a poet, without peers. (Let us not forget that Madame de Staël—the heiress of a power fallen to the distaff, the power of the philosophical salons—was scarcely in France during Napoleon's rule; she was rather the antenna, pointed toward France, of the liberal intelligentsia of Central Europe: her Coppet is a sort of East Berlin.) The superiorities with which Chateaubriand is confronted are by necessity all of a different order, and in their respective orders they are even less contestable than his own. There is Beauty, and there is Power—Madame Récamier, and Napoleon. The *Memoirs* linger on his long-held grudges against the Bourbons and Talleyrand, Villèle and Polignac. But literary rivalries? There are none to speak of. All we find in the *Memoirs* is a brief fraternal fit of temper against Byron: a lord abounding in women, a poet provisioned with a fame no less voluminous than his own, a man poaching on his turf. But even then he attacks him on moral grounds—a subject on which René occasionally means business. We find, throughout the pages of Chateaubriand—this writer come back to camp all alone in the vastness of imperial France as in a dispossessed palace (though he was, it must be said, well fashioned for the handgonnes of the literary maquis, for collegial formalities)—an illustrious yawn, which we imagine sometimes standing in for something like François Mauriac's *Bloc-Notes*. He had no experience of the Republic of Letters; he lived through the barren, boring Empire. The mind boggles at this singular adventure, this situation almost unthinkable in France: a writer who senses the emptiness around him.

And not only in the ranks of literature. Of the two great bloodlettings France has undergone (1792–1815 and 1914–1918), it so happened that the second—a victory, which left the social foundations to all appearances intact—was made literarily invisible by an unforeseeable, unseasonable burgeoning of new writers. There was no symptom, in literature, of that pernicious anemia: on the plane of art, it corresponds rather with a super-plenitude of being; the history of literature, as we know, has these cavalier ways of *making do*. But at the turn of the nineteenth century everything conspired to not, in any sense, blunt our keen awareness of the hemorrhage: the brutal falling back after enormous effort, society like a field battered by hail, the wrenching separations of exile. There could finally be nothing less triumphant, whatever some may say, than the counterrevolution of 1814: the entire Restoration, aware of its precariously suspended sentence, is dressed in half mourning; the only monument it raises is an ossuary. The interval dividing 1814 from the Hundred Days in the *Memoirs* is something like a long funeral service; the whole literature of the Restoration—a literature of noblemen, terminal survivors, which is called French romanticism—has felt, and cannot forget, the breath of the abyss on its brow. That is why it cannot rid itself of a certain dolorism, a certain "gnawing regret" which makes all of its themes, so different from German romanticism, themes of "losing hold": death, isolation, the crumbling of empires, the fleetingness of time, the decline of love. After the Russian Revolution, literature will find this muted voice again—this voice suffering from heavy losses of blood, this pallor on the brow, these dead-leaf quaverings, this accent of chill, erratic, autumnal religiosity—but not until *Doctor Zhivago*. The France of the Revolution and the Empire found a voice for this "spleen" (as it is so wonderfully called), for these damaged viscera where the red blood cells struggle to be re-formed, right away, and this voice belonged to René. Chateaubriand is not a sacristan tidying up the Gothic cathedral; he is not the exoticism of the savannas, the great world of nature closed and now reopening, the indeterminate treetops of forests. He is the unforgettable poet of the wobbly churching of women and the blood lost by a world brought to bed. This voice that, all through the two thousand pages of the *Memoirs*, proclaims the Great Pan dead, but whose unique timbre—the ample echo of the empty palace and the disfurnished planet—remained unknown to the late Roman Empire, is the voice of History's great entombments.

In the years that Chateaubriand was composing his *Memoirs*, Balzac was writing the Human Comedy. The same world was before their eyes. It so happens that I've just closed one of Balzac's novels and, trying to write this text, reopened the *Memoirs*. What a sudden, extraordinary, *decompression of being*! On the one hand, you have a compact world and an almost insane release of energy; on the other, a strange lacunary universe slowly drifting toward night, riddled with those long intercalary rifts one sees in the clouds at sunset, and broken up by the enormous founderings of memory. The movement of Chateaubriand's imagination is always steered by the same inclination: over every landscape and emotional focal point it presents, it slides successively, like so many "negatives," one, two, three, even four plates, superimposed on the colors of memory—and, as when a disk painted with all the colors of the spectrum is spun rapidly round, it obtains, by this swift superimposition of tones, a sort of negation that is unexpectedly vibrant, a "blank" fringed by a subtle marginal iridescence, which is the color of time peculiar to the *Memoirs* and makes them and the *Life of Rancé* the most shimmering hymns to impermanence in French literature.

When I got to the beach, I saw a calm sea unruffled by the slightest breath of wind. The ripples, thin as gauze, unfurled on the sand without sound or foam. A wondrous sky, all resplendent with constellations, crowned my head—the crescent moon soon dropping and hiding herself behind a mountain. There was only one ship at anchor in the bay, and a pair of boats. To the left you could see the lighthouse at Antibes, and to the right the Lérins Islands. Straight ahead of me, the open sea stretched out to the south, toward the city of Rome, where Bonaparte had first sent me.

The Lérins Islands, today called the Sainte-Marguerite Islands, once sheltered a few Christians who had fled the barbarians. Saint Honorat, coming from Hungary, landed on one of these reefs: he climbed a palm tree, made the sign of the cross, and all the serpents died, which is to say: paganism vanished and the new civilization was born in the West.

Fourteen hundred years later, Bonaparte came to finish that civilization in the very place where the saint had started it. The last solitary to live in that monastery was the Man in the Iron

Mask—if the Man in the Iron Mask ever in fact existed. From the silence of the Golfe-Juan, from the peace of the islands of the ancient anchorites, came the noise of Waterloo, which crossed the Atlantic, and went to die on Saint Helena.

Standing between the memories of two societies, between a world long gone and a world soon to vanish, in the middle of the night, at the deserted edge of those salt waters, you may imagine what I felt. I left the beach in a kind of religious consternation, leaving the waves to pass to and fro over, yet never to erase, the prints Napoleon's penultimate footsteps had made.

At the end of every great epoch, you hear some doleful voice or other mourning the past and ringing the curfew bell. So those who saw the disappearance of Charlemagne, Saint Louis, François I, Henri IV, and Louis XIV wept and moaned. What couldn't I tell you in my turn, eyewitness that I am to two or three worlds gone by? When, like me, one has met Washington and Bonaparte, what else is there to see beyond the plow of the American Cincinnatus and the tomb at Saint Helena? Why have I outlived the age and the men I belonged to by birth? Why haven't I fallen with my contemporaries, the last of an exhausted race? Why have I remained here alone, seeking their bones in the darkness and dust of a crowded catacomb? I don't relish the thought of lasting much longer. Ah, if only I was as carefree as one of those old waterfront Arabs I saw in Africa! Sitting cross-legged on a little rope mat, their heads wrapped in their burnooses, they while away their final hours watching the beautiful flamingos fly through the azure over the ruins of Carthage. Lulled by the murmur of the waves, they forget their existence and, in a hushed voice, sing a song of the sea: they are going to die.[2]

The whole movement of the *Memoirs* is here *in nuce*. But what's striking in this perfect romantic sunset is not so much the unprecedented irruption of history as a sick, incurable dimension of sensibility, by dint of which the *Memoirs* truly inaugurate modern times in literature; it is Chateaubriand's peculiar way of using history as a privileged means of morose delectation; it is the world reduced beneath his gaze to a pure, dreamy transparency, pressed between what has been and what is going to be in a formidable clamp of nothingness.

When you arrive in Combourg on the road from Dol, you still see, as in the *Memoirs*, "a valley, at the bottom of which, not far from a pond, there rises the single spire of a village church. At the western edge of this village, the towers of a feudal castle loom above a copse of trees."[3] All around this characterless, unbeautiful site, which is repeated a hundred times in Brittany, extends the quintessential rural entrenchment, the secret carceral countryside, bushy and hushed, the morose "stilted hedges" of France—the Bocage—which is to a countryside what the cloister is to a house, and which only souls born in its shadow can love. When I passed through Combourg for the first time, it was a gray, misty day at the end of September: the ponderous shade trees that float over the immense lawn were already losing their leaves; there wasn't a soul around. The most dreadful portent of the winter months oozed from the bare, claustral façade hemmed in between its towers, and from the enormous deserted staircase where the dead leaves cascaded down. The causeway by the leaden pond belonged to Roderick Usher, and the whole castle was itself one of Poe's phrases, which, when I was a boy of twelve, opened up the gates to me: "Nevertheless, in this mansion of gloom . . ." This year, under the July sun, the walkers come flocking; from the heights of the crenellations the brown-patched lawn is a garden party of bright summer clothes. Visited, the castle disappoints: one finds it ungainly and strangely inconsistent, like a suit of stage armor on a dwarf. The escutcheon and the enormous staircase, the towers devouring the curtain wall, the pointed roofs, and the machicolations eat cruelly into the habitable space. The external signs of its earliest constructions, rather than forming the building's soul, seem larger than life and even ostentatious: the whole thing somehow smacks of the Gothic parvenu. Inside, the rooms, which were cheaply redone in the last century, are an over-the-top feudal mess of paint, roughly in the style Wilhelm II deployed on the walls of Haut Koenigsbourg, consisting of escutcheons and astragals, pinecones and fleurs-de-lis—almost exactly as in the first chapter of the *Memoirs*, where we read Chateaubriand "a little obliquely," as Louis XVIII did. Chateaubriand hardly ever came back to Combourg, and advisedly so. He went away from here, "leaving family figures behind," and says what Cagliostro said to his judges: "I am a nobleman—and a traveler." The savage odor of the country squire's nest, the long soak in the feudal wallow—all this evaporates between the fingers that flip through the first pages of the *Memoirs*. But this building, this well-preserved piece of Carcassonne, remains, glacial and intact, and the admirable foliage grows green once more. "Everything has changed in Brittany, except for the waves, which are always changing."[4]

Where can we go looking for him today? If the essential thing for a man, as Malraux more or less says, consists in reducing his share of comedy to a minimum, there's no question Chateaubriand falls far short of the mark. Half a dozen motley "turns," which virtually leap out from his usual repertoire with a whimsical intensity hard to describe, give more than one passage in the soliloquy of the *Memoirs* the feel of a transformation act, whose vivacity and nonchalance, not to mention their inimitable wink at the spectator, are almost those of Italian comedy.

There is, yes, the unctuousness of vanity, insufferable vanity, answerable at every turn to Sainte-Beuve's calling him the "lascivious cat, now purring to be stroked the other way."

Ah! Why didn't I follow my sister's advice? Why did I keep writing? Subtract my writings from my century, and would there have been any difference in the events or the spirit of that century?

There is the cockiness of competence, triple underlining his accomplished performance of the traditional "And that's how it's done."

First of all, you will notice that I have an eye for everything; that I occupy myself with Reshid Pasha as well as M. de Blacas; that I defend my privileges and rights as ambassador to Rome against all comers; that I am cunning, false (eminent quality!), and shrewd to the point that, when M. de Funchal, in an equivocal position, writes to me, I do not answer him but go to see him out of wily courtesy so that he cannot show one line that I have written him and will still be satisfied. There is not a single rash word to repeat in my conversations with Cardinals Bernetti and Albani, the two secretaries of state. Nothing escapes me. I stoop to the smallest details ... From there, climbing higher and higher and reaching a greater diplomacy, I take it upon myself to exclude a cardinal ... If a *carbonaro* stirs, I know it, and I judge more or less how much truth there is to the conspiracy; if an abbot is conniving, I know it, and I foil the plans concocted to keep the cardinals from the French ambassador. Finally, I discover that an important secret has been deposited by Cardinal de Latil in the bosom of the Grand Penitentiary. Are you satisfied? Is this not a man who knows his trade? Well, you see, I dispatched all this diplomatic business like any other ambassador without it costing me so much as a thought, the way a simple-minded peasant in Lower Normandy knits his socks even as he keeps his sheep. In my case, my sheep were my dreams.[5]

There is the crazed devotee of the defeated, the liegeman of kings who prefers them fallen (Charles X knew something about this), to such a degree that he even soaped the balance board for the sole purpose of showing them what a wealth of loyalty and probity he preserved for them, *afterward*. There is (a type updated in our own era in more ways than one) the "charming reactionary" who, having plastered the gaudy cockade of the Lost Cause to his hat once and for all, discharges himself from the duty of upholding it and has a gay old time eliciting tributes and smiles, making a mock of his loyalties, from the "progressive" youth on the other side of the aisle.

Suddenly I felt myself surrounded by the crowd, and a cry rang out:

"Long live the defender of the freedom of the press!"

My hair had made me recognizable...One of the young men pushing me from behind suddenly thrust his head between my legs and lifted me onto his shoulders. Fresh cheers rose up, and they shouted to the onlookers in the street and at the windows:

"Hats off! Long live the Charter!"

And I replied:

"Yes, gentleman, long live the Charter! But long live the king!"

This cry was not repeated, but it provoked no anger. And that is how the game was lost! Everything might still be all right, but only popular men could now be presented to the people: in revolutions, a name does more than an army.

I begged my young friends at such length that at last they set me down on the ground...I arrived, in the midst of my triumph, in the main courtyard of the Luxembourg...I was touched by the sentiments of those noble young people. I had cried "Long live the king!" in their company as safely as I might have done locked away in my home...and yet this was the 20th of July, and we had just passed the ditch where they were burying citizens killed by the bullets of the soldiers of Charles X![6]

The hostage struggles, but with one leg only. The soldiers killed for the defense of Charles X do not obtain the noble viscount's commemoration. Cheered one day, he was dismissed the next. However, the times had changed; their spirit inclined toward the pharmacist Cadet Gassicourt. But one suspects the old defector-in-spirit retained a certain nostalgia for that auspicious era when, on his way back from chatting up some noble duke at the lovely Juliette's, he was cheered by the democratic rabble.

This is not a hanging offense, and Chateaubriand himself was willing to laugh at his twofold triumph: he is no fool, even if he can't stop himself harping on his success. There are more serious things. "The destiny of a great man is a Muse," he wrote—magnificently. But the Muses were footloose frolickers, whereas that of his own destiny hobbled along after the fact in a dreadful orthopedic device whose screws the *Memoirs* tighten, moment by moment, with a perceptible cracking. *Ornamentation*, and ornamentation of the most conventional kind, plays—in the after-the-fact arrangement of his life, rather than in this life itself—a significant role. It is regrettable that Chateaubriand, at the end of his days, could sincerely represent his career, in the trompe l'oeil edifice of his *Memoirs*, in a way that, yes, covered almost the whole sweep of human activity, but in which three out of the four windows are false. "My career as a soldier—my career as a traveler— my literary career—my political career": these four little phrases, by accrediting, through a great example, the idea that poetry flows into the "great affairs" of the country, and subsequently the world—more or less as the Mississippi flows into the Gulf of Mexico—weigh heavily on the will to power of the great nervous romantics of the next generation. Four phrases without which the careers of Lamartine or Hugo or Barrès cannot be fully comprehended, and to which Malraux, perhaps—and this to our loss—owes his having passed so quickly from the principality of youth to the category Son et Lumière. There were not so many winning cards in that fine hand fascinated by the imperial "slam": There was only one. There is only one. The halo of the traveler flaked away rather quickly, and we can hardly muster any interest in that abrupt, interrupted, cantankerous, and inconsequential political career, during which, for fifteen years, he squashes may bugs against the boarded-up panes of the Restoration. History has not found a place for the *Conservateur*, a bizarre attempt to impose a Chouan government on the prince in the name of parliamentary sovereignty, and "my Spanish war"—as Chateaubriand paternally calls it—hardly combated anything but the balancing of the budget. As for his pro-Russian Balkan policy of 1823, which Villèle will stop in time, it in several ways anticipates Polignac's Great Plan, which will make Europe smile six years later.[7] Between the life of Stendhal and the career of the noble viscount, in the interest they still hold for us, we do not differentiate—or rather, sad to say, we do! I'm afraid we do. If the enormous "blanks" in the *Memoirs*, beginning with Chateaubriand's return from London, correspond more or less exactly to what would be given full expression in contemporary memoirs—if the feeling of what is seemly for him, or rather for his statue, sometimes disfigures the memorialist's work—it is because he allowed his freedom, fine though it was, to freeze into the drapery of office, which was not a block of marble, as he imagined, but a block of ice. No one can arbitrate his fame, as lesser men knew better than he during his lifetime. "You are going to see one of the powers of the earth; you are going to see M. de Chateaubriand," says Charles X to the young Comte de Chambord, announcing the visit of the old, fallen, ruined minister to Prague.[8] The phrase does honor to the elderly king, a perfect stranger to the viscount's poetry and politics alike: he sovereignly restores this career its proper proportions.

Yes, of course, all of that is true. But so is this: exactly where he shows us how profligate he can be, he saves himself every time—setting a bad example and scoffing at success. Where limp Lamartine, who lacks that drop of bitterness that is essential to aging well, plunges, with the rather bland grace of Young Tarentine, straight into the tempest of '48; where Barrès takes Boulanger for Napoleon and Burdeau for Robespierre, for him everything is a gift and an enrichment. Disburdened of three-quarters of his written work (since hardly anyone anymore reads the *Essay* or *Genius* or *The Martyrs* or *The Natchez*), he gives the impression of being all the better off for it. His name, his somewhat trumped-up travels, his political career (which is real but hardly matters), his amorous career that *The Genius of Christianity* forced him to put between parentheses—probably none of this really enriches him, but all of it endorses a prestigious bill of exchange, permitting him that unaffected equal footing with everyone, which no other French writer has perhaps ever known—that fine human tone, at once major and familiar, not possessed by Saint-Simon, who too frequently speaks the jargon of a fetishist coterie, or Rousseau, who consorts too freely with ancillary loves, or Stendhal, who sniffs out the chocolate of the Jesuits and sometimes writes in the mode of *"quand on conspire, quand sans frayeur."*[9] He saw almost everything. For seventy years—between Cagliostro and Marx!—from the tricorn to the Phrygian cap, from the Phrygian cap to the bicorn, from the bicorn to the gibus, from the gibus to the Desfoux—the bottom becoming the top, the top the bottom—the Jacobin general, the general consul, the emperor consul, Emperor Buonaparte, Buonaparte le Père la Violette, le Père la Violette Badinguet[10]—the whole world dancing to the scarifying jig of Fatimah's sun, which never stops rising and falling—and those faces in the *Memoirs* that grimace vulnerably for a moment between one set of castoffs and the next, unable to stand the transformation scene any longer—no, he is not boasting: in this universe bivouacked between two twilights—women, ministers, garrets, palaces, tween decks, wigwams, and embassies passed through like inns—he has seen humanity and a unique era mingling with his story as with the very stuff of his dreams: *sicut nubes—quasi naves—velut umbra*: this is the *Memoirs'* beautiful epigraph. The life of Napoleon is enshrined in the middle of his great book not, as people spitefully say, to suggest a parallel but rather, I think, as his talisman. God knows he was aware of his own powers, but he was also aware of his luck; he knew how much uniqueness the time in which he lived had added to his genius: he looked at mankind and the world from Bonaparte's shoulders, where the view was the same as it would have been from nowhere. Hence that unquestionable but hard-to-grasp prestige, that indescribable *something* that isolates him from all the romantics, a sort of intimate contact—a prestige in which his social and political career hardly signify but in which literature isn't everything either. Whereas Benjamin Constant, who had much more to do with Bonaparte, derived from that contact no increased prestige, Chateaubriand, on almost every page, catches a glint of the imperial sun. It is as though it were a light belonging to him alone, a furtive phosphorescence revealed through the *Memoirs* just as surely as in the golden backgrounds of Byzantine mosaics. His genius sufficed to set him apart from his own generation, but thinking that perhaps he'd be submerged in those to follow, he knew he would be seen more clearly, and for a longer time, hoisted around Napoleon's neck.

One part of his work, the pseudo-classical part, is dead: he didn't live with one foot on either side of that geological rift of the Revolution and Empire, surrounded and besieged as he was by Morellets, Delilles, Laharpes, and Fontanes, without relinquishing something of himself to the continent sinking beneath the ashes in an orgy of faux-Pompeian style. But anyway, where he ages, he ages well: his prose has that multilayered bouquet that favors only the noblest vintages. Reread the famous description of the Mississippi that opens *Atala*: it no longer discovers America, but it has taken on the inexhaustible charm of an Henri Rousseau. He had the writer's ultimate luck: the gift of masterpieces in old age, where everything is potion or spell—halcyon days, concentration of juices, limpidity, the transparency of the October sun, and that unerring hand which, before the first tremors, separates light from shadow as never before. The *Memoirs* have never been younger: a prodigious and solitary conjunction of a great era, a great style, and a large format. The language of the *Life of Rancé* presses more mysteriously into the future: its jerky, out-of-phase, Morse code messages, which cut into the narrative out of the blue as though they were signals being picked up from another planet, already stammer some news from the country where Rimbaud is going to awaken. Far from all the avenues of the romantic park, at the edge of the reflecting pool, we find this beautiful bird, showing off his plumage. "The peacock's cry in no way deepens the loneliness of the deserted garden" (Claudel). To him, we owe almost everything.

—Julien Gracq (1960)
translated from the French by Alex Andriesse

NOTES

These notes are indebted to many sources. Of special importance were Patrice Gueniffey's biography of Napoleon, John Eldred Howard's *Letters and Documents of Napoleon* (1961), Anka Muhlstein's *Napoléon à Moscou* (2007), the work of Marc Fumaroli and Jean-Paul Clément, and the abridged translations of the *Memoirs* done by Robert Baldick and Alexander Teixeira de Mattos.

As in *Memoirs from Beyond the Grave, 1768–1800*, almost all biblical language, in both the notes and the text, is taken from the King James Version of the Bible. Although this may seem a strange choice for a work so clearly Catholic, Chateaubriand himself, in his *Sketches of English Literature*, calls the King James translation "a masterpiece. The authors of that immense undertaking did for the English language what Luther did for the German, and the writers of Louis XIII's time for French. They established the language."

—A. A.

BOOK THIRTEEN

1. An allusion to the Bourbon princess Anne-Geneviève, aka Madame de Longueville (1619–1679), sister of the Prince de Condé, who helped incite the first and second Fronde (1648–1649, 1650–1653)—civil wars in which the princes, the parliaments, and the people rose up against Louis XIV. In January 1650, Madame de Longueville, having briefly taken refuge at the Château de Dieppe, fled from the advancing royal army and made her way to Stenay, where she found an ally in General Turenne (1611–1675), who was in love with her. Turenne's failure to win the Battle of Rethel in December 1650 may have been what "sullied his laurels."

2. La Rochefoucauld.

3. From Béranger's "Le Vieux Caporal": "Who is that weeping and sobbing below? / Ah, 'tis the drummer's widow."

4. Marie-Caroline de Bourbon-Siciles, Duchesse de Berry (1798–1870), often visited Dieppe in summertime. "The blithe and voluptuous idol of

seduced, insurgent Paris" is Madame de Longueville (see Book 13, note 1).

5   Virgil's *Aeneid*, Book 6, lines 190–211.

6   "Some, coming from the homeland's lares." This is a scrambled quotation from the satirically Latinate "Épître du Limousin," which, although apocryphal, is included in many editions of Rabelais's *Pantagruel*. Lares are ancient Roman deities believed to watch over particular places.

7   The "young kinswoman" was Georgina Howard, Madame d'Aguesseau's illegitimate daughter. Chateaubriand served as her legal guardian until she married.

8   "Liberty, Equality, Fraternity or Death."

9   The phrase "itinerary avenues" is modeled on "itinerary columns," which in ancient Rome were "erected in the cross ways in large roads, having several faces, which by the inscriptions serve to shew the different routes" (Nathan Bailey's *An Universal Etymological English Dictionary*, 3rd ed., London: Thomas Cox, 1735).

10 In 1800, Les Thernes was an only partly developed area with a bad reputation, just beyond the city walls at the Barrière de l'Étoile—a fortified gateway near where the Arc de Triomphe stands today.

11 The "Chemin de la Révolte" was a nickname for a road built by Louis XV, who wanted the royal carriages to be able to bypass Paris, where riots had broken out after a rumor spread that the king was having young children kidnapped, killed, and drained of their blood so that he and his courtiers could bathe in it after their long bouts of debauchery (Jacques Hillairet, *Dictionnaire historique des rues de Paris*, vol. 1, Paris: Éditions Minuit, 1997, p. 433). The road thus ran outside the walls of Paris—not far from where the Boulevard Périphérique runs today.

12 Today, the Place de la Concorde.

13 The younger brother of Joseph Joubert, who would become one of Chateaubriand's closest friends.

14 Auguste-Jacques Lemierre d'Argy (1762–1815), playwright and translator of Thomas Gray, had written Chateaubriand a letter from Paris in July 1797—shortly after Chateaubriand's youthfully ambitious universal history of revolutions was published—telling him he had made "a great splash."

15 Before the revolution of 1789, when Chateaubriand was a young man just arrived in Paris from rural Brittany, he had met both of these older

poets. (See *Memoirs from Beyond the Grave, 1768–1800*, Book 4, Chapters 11 and 12.)

16 The Circus, an underground structure hosting shops, billiard halls, galleries, and an arena for balls, concerts, and equestrian spectacles, was opened in 1789 and destroyed by fire in 1798.

17 The painter Jacques-Louis David (1748–1825) was one of the principal organizers of the Festival of Reason, where young women in white, Roman-style stoles and mantles draped with tricolor sashes paid tribute to the goddess Liberty. In Greek mythology, Corybants are the drumming, dancing worshippers of the earth goddess Cybele.

18 "His virtues and charms make him their worthy father."

19 The Charterhouse of Paris, founded by Saint Louis in 1257, was located south of the Luxembourg Palace, on a plot of land that is now part of the Luxembourg Gardens. The Charterhouse was gradually demolished between 1796 and 1800.

20 The French magician, artist, balloonist, and physicist "Robertson," born Étienne-Gaspard Robert (1763–1837), developed magic-lantern horror shows, complete with sound effects, which he called "phantasmagoria." Robertson had adopted this term—and indeed the whole concept of the magic-lantern horror show—from the magician Paul Philidor, but he had invented a special lantern on wheels, the Fantoscope, which allowed him to change the size of projected images and take horror to new heights.

21 The people responsible for the September Massacres of 1792, when more than one thousand political prisoners were murdered by armed militiamen, sansculottes, National Guardsmen, and police.

22 The assassination of Julius Caesar, by Brutus among others, led to the downfall of the Roman Republic, which was still in its infancy during the late sixth century BCE, when the very likely fictitious assassin Scaevola is said to have lived.

23 Madame Brinvilliers (1630–1676) was accused of poisoning her father and two of her brothers in order to inherit their estates.

24 The Théâtre de Variétés, today called the Théâtre du Palais-Royal.

25 The Place de Grève, where the Hôtel de Ville now stands, was a site of public executions.

26 The phrase "charming pity" is taken from Nicolas Boileau's "Art poétique," Song 3.

27 The "Grand Master of the University" is Fontanes, who in 1808 would be appointed the Grand-Maître de l'Université impériale.

28 An example of Chateaubriand's tact. He alludes here to Étienne-Denis Pasquier and Mathieu Molé, both of whom wrote scathingly about Chateaubriand in their own memoirs.

29 Aubiac, the lover of Marguerite of Valois (Henri IV's first wife), was executed, but not before kissing his true love's sleeve (or muff, as most sources have it), a story that Chateaubriand would have encountered in Pierre Bayle's *Historical and Critical Dictionary*.

30 2 Samuel 12:23.

31 There is no evidence that Céleste de Chateaubriand, who was then living in Fougères, came to visit her husband at this time. Chateaubriand probably did not see Céleste again until after he returned from the South of France. See Book 14, Chapter 3.

32 Among the many roles François-Joseph Talma (1763–1826) played to great acclaim was that of Vendôme in Voltaire's medieval drama *Adélaïde du Guesclin* (1734).

33 Boileau's Epistle VII, lines 4–7: "Iphigenia herself, immolated at Aulis, did not elicit as many tears from the assembled Greeks as the blessed spectacle played out before our eyes, in her name, by Champmeslé." Marie Champmeslé (1642–1698) was the actress who played Iphigenia in the first production of Racine's *Iphigénie* in 1674.

34 Lucien Bonaparte (1775–1840), Napoleon's brother, was an early enthusiast of Chateaubriand's work.

35 Reference to Ponce Denis Écouchard Lebrun's epigram regarding Jean François La Harpe, who dared to criticize Corneille. It was laughable, Lebrun wrote, "To see this dwarf sizing up an Atlas / And, redoubling his Pygmy efforts, / Ludicrously flexing his little arms / As though to topple such a towering fame."

36 Allusion to the Albigensian Crusade of the thirteenth century and perhaps also to the violent repression of the Waldensians from the thirteenth through the sixteenth centuries.

37 Psalm 23:7.

BOOK FOURTEEN

1 The Mathieu Molé depicted was not the owner of Champlâtreux but his ancestor Mathieu Molé (1584–1656), a magistrate and president of the Parliament of Paris, who, according to certain historians, won over a

crowd of rioters with an eloquent, truly magisterial speech (hence the "square cap") in the early days of the uprising that would become the Fronde.

2 The life span of a poplar is much shorter than that of a linden.

3 Henri IV of France.

4 Apparently this is an allusion to one of Franz Joseph Gall's phrenological categories. (Gall had developed his system for categorizing the human cranium by studying ducks, pigeons, chickens, and frogs.) "When I dined with Dr. Gall in London in 1823," the Comte de Marcellus writes in *Chateaubriand et son temps*, "he vehemently defended himself against the gaffe he had made with M. de Chateaubriand ... He took 'the frog affair' quite seriously."

5 Jean-François de Saint-Lambert's *Saisons*, Song III.

6 Laura, the subject of Petrarch's *Canzoniere*, whom the poet had first encountered in Avignon on April 6, 1327.

7 "Here, contained in small space, you may see that which contains great renown.... O sweet soul, being held so dear, who can praise thee but by staying silent? For speech is always repressed when the subject surpasses the speaker." From Domenico Laffi's *A Journey to the West: The Diary of a Seventeenth Century Pilgrim from Bologna to Santiago de Compostela* (trans. James Hall). Although attributed to François I, these verses were very likely composed by the sixteenth-century poet Maurice Scève.

8 Petrarch's *Canzoniere* 323. In Edmund Spenser's translation:
> Within this wood out of a rock did rise
>> A spring of water, mildly rumbling downe,
> Whereto approached not in anie wise
>> The homely shepherd, nor the ruder clowne,
> But manie Muses, and the Nymphs withal,
>> That sweetly in accord did tune their voice
> To the soft sounding of the waters fall.

9 Petrarch's *Canzoniere* 128. In Peter Hainsworth's translation:
> My Italy...
> O deluge that amassed
> from unknown alien wastes
> To inundate the sweet fields that are ours!
> ... Is this ground not the ground that I first touched?
> And this not my first home,
> where I was nurtured with such tenderness?

> This too the fatherland in which I trust,
> kind, pious motherland,
> which covers now my father and my mother?

10 A loose paraphrase of Cicero's *For Flaccus*, Chapter 26.

11 Virgil's *Aeneid*, Book 1, lines 454-493. The Trojan is Aeneas.

12 Act 2, Scene 2, of *Hamlet*, in which the melancholy Dane recites "Aeneas' tale to Dido" to one of the players come to the castle.

13 Lucan's *Pharsalia*, or *De Bello Civili*, Book 3.

14 Pytheas (350–285 BCE) was a Greek geographer, born in Marseille.

15 From the memoirs of the Italian playwright Vittorio Alfieri (1749–1803), which were published in French in 1804.

16 *Volente vel nolente* means "willing or unwilling"; *sed alio modo puniatur*, "but that he be punished in some other way."

17 Joseph Juste Scaliger (1540–1609) was a French historian, classicist, and outspoken convert to Protestantism whose final home was not the university town of Montpellier but the university town of Leiden, in the Netherlands.

18 "The Mount of the Virgins."

19 In 1622, Louis XIII (and his prime minister, Richelieu) laid siege to the Protestant stronghold of Montpellier—an event that Chateaubriand mentions in order to criticize the absolute monarchy inaugurated during Louis XIII's reign.

20 From Corneille's "Sur le canal du Languedoc pour la jonction des Deux-Mers": "The Garonne and the Tarn [Corneille calls it the Atax, the ancient Roman name for the river Aude], in their deep caves, long ago sighed and married their waves, and thereby set to flowing, by a happy bent, the treasures of dawn on the banks of the sunset. But against such sweet wishes, to such beautiful flames, nature, bound to its eternal laws, proudly raised, as invicible obstacles, hills and rocks in a dreadful chain. Oh, France, your great king speaks, and these rocks are rent. The earth opens its breast, the highest mountains descend. Everything yields...."

21 Chateaubriand adopts this testimony to Henri II de Montmorency's conduct in his last battle—shortly before he was captured and beheaded by order of Louis XIII—from Michaud's *Biographie universelle* (1821).

22 From the *Histoire de la Croisade contre les hérétiques albigeois, écrite en vers provençaux par un poète contemporain et traduite par M. Fauriel* (1837).

23 From Montaigne's "Of Vanity" (trans. Donald M. Frame).

24 Allusion to two singers, Honorine Gasc (dates unknown) and Maria Malibran (1808–1836), a soprano renowned in Naples, New York, and Paris, particularly for her performances of Rossini.

25 Clémence Isaure was a semilegendary figure of medieval Toulouse, credited with founding or restoring the Academy of the Floral Games, which preserved the traditions of Occitan poetry and gave awards for the best of it in the form of flowers. Its members have included Ronsard, Voltaire, and Chateaubriand.

26 From Bachaumont and Chapelle's *Voyage* (1656): "Alas, how happy a man would be in that beautiful, enviable place if, forever loved by Sylvie, and forever in love, he could spend his life with her!"

27 An allusion to a Latin proverb in Aulus Gellius's *Attic Nights*, Volume 3, Book 9, line 7: *habet aurum tolosanum*, "He has gold from Toulouse." According to Erasmus's *Adagia*, the proverb was used to refer to anyone who "suffers great and inescapable disasters and dies a strange and pitiable death," especially because of ill-gotten wealth—a meaning that can be traced back to the story of the Roman proconsul Quintus Servilius Caepio, who sacked Toulouse and stole the Gauls' gold, not long after which he was stripped of his citizenship and exiled or, according to some accounts, died in prison. Hence Chateaubriand's pithier explanation: "it brings misfortune."

28 These are the last words of Chateaubriand's *Mémoire sur la captivité de Madame la Duchesse de Berry* (1832).

29 At the age of fifty-nine, La Harpe married Mademoiselle de Hatte-Longuerue, the twenty-three-year-old daughter of an impoverished widow. After three weeks, the young woman declared that she could not overcome her repugnance for the older man and asked for a divorce.

30 The last words of Voltaire's letter to the Encyclopedists were: "*Écrasons l'infâme.*" The infamous, or loathsome, thing to be crushed here is Christianity.

31 An imaginative paraphrase of Eliphaz's vision in Job 4:13–17.

32 "Who is this huge man untouched by the fire?" Dante, *Inferno* 14, lines 46–47. The huge man is the Greek warrior Capaneus, a giant found among the blasphemers in the seventh circle.

33 It is doubtful that Madame de Chateaubriand was getting ready to join her husband. "The fear of being reunited with my wife," Chateaubriand wrote Fontanes in August 1803, "has for a second time driven me to leave my native land."

34 Pope Pius VII was a Chiaramonti, the Italian equivalent of Clermont.

35 The Chevalier de Bayard (1476–1524), known as "the fearless knight be-
    yond reproach," served Charles VIII and Louis XII in many battles.
    Jean-Jacques Rousseau briefly lived in Chambéry, at the house called
    Les Charmettes, with his mistress Madame de Warens, as he chronicles
    in books 5 and 6 of his *Confessions*.

36 Chateaubriand, contemplating Hannibal's tower, tautens thoughts he
    gave freer rein in his *Voyage en Italie* (1826): "Looking over this wilder-
    ness, I could not help but feel a dreadful awe in the face of one man's
    hatred, more powerful than any obstacle—the hatred of a man who,
    starting out from the Gulf of Cadiz, had blazed a trail over the Pyrenees
    and the Alps, in pursuit of the Romans," a "free people."

37 Pascal's *Pensées*, Section 1, 17.

38 From the poem "The Alps, or Italy" (1822), in which Chateaubriand
    again echoes a favorite phrase from *Paradise Lost* ("The world was all
    before them"): "Alps, you have not suffered my fate! Time can do noth-
    ing to you; your brows wear lightly the years that weigh on mine. For the
    first time, when, with my heart full of hope, I overstepped your ram-
    parts—and the horizon—an immense future lay before my eyes. Italy at
    my feet, and all the world before me!"

39 A reference to the giant Adamastor, the genius loci of the Cape of Good
    Hope made legendary by Camões's *The Lusiads*.

40 From an early ninth-century marriage charter.

41 Exodus 2:16–17 "Now the priest of Midian had seven daughters: and
    they came and drew water, and filled the troughs to water their father's
    flock. And the shepherds came and drove them away: but Moses stood
    up and helped them, and watered their flock."

42 Ancient Greek name for lower Italy, here applied to Italy as a whole.

43 Chateaubriand arrived in Jerusalem on October 4, 1806, and was wel-
    comed by Franciscans celebrating the feast of Saint Francis of Assisi.

44 Clermont-Tonnerre.

BOOK FIFTEEN

1 Racine's *Phèdre*, Act 1, Scene 3: "I perish last and most wretched of all."
2 Capistron's *Andronic*, Act 4, Scene 4: "My days aren't worth a sigh to me."
3 Madame de Sévigné's house, the Château des Rochers-Sévigné, near Vi-
   tré, in Brittany.

4 Barbara von Krüdener (1764–1824), known as Madame de Krüdener in France, was a Baltic German writer and Christian mystic. She exerted a tremendous influence over Alexander I of Russia, as well as the Réveil, a Protestant revival moment in western Switzerland that began in 1814.

5 *The Greek Anthology* 346 (trans. W. R. Paton): "In Corinth. This little stone, good Sabinus, is a memorial of our great friendship. I shall ever miss thee; and if so it may be, when with the dead thou drinkest of Lethe, drink not thou forgetfulness of me."

6 The inclusion of letters of condolence is common in nineteenth-century memoirs. In the words of Sainte-Beuve: "Each [letter] speaks in its own manner, and this blending of voices gives something like the effect of a conversation in a mourning carriage, trailing after the hearse."

7 Mathieu de Montmorency (1767–1826). The month before she wrote this letter, Madame de Staël had been sentenced to lifelong exile from Paris, partly for the publication of *Delphine*, a novel that Napoleon declared immoral and anti-Catholic.

8 Wilhelm von Humboldt (1767–1835), the elder brother of the naturalist Alexander von Humboldt and founder of the University of Berlin.

9 John 11:44.

10 Chateaubriand's letter to Fontanes, first published in the *Mercure de France* in 1804, was later printed in the fourth edition of *The Genius of Christianity* and as a separate volume titled *Lettre sur la campagne romaine* (*Letter on the Roman Countryside*). The tomb of the ancient Roman noblewoman Caecilia Metella is on the Appian Way.

11 Allusions to episodes recounted by Jean-Jacques Rousseau in his *Confessions*, although it should be noted that Rousseau did not personally drop off his bastard children at the Foundling Hospital; he delegated that task to their mother, his mistress, Thérèse Le Vasseur.

12 A Russian general in Rome had, on behalf of Emperor Alexander I, offered Chateaubriand a job as tutor to an eight-year-old grand duke. He would have had to serve in this post for eight years, after which he would have been given a "fortune large enough to last me the rest of my days," he wrote Fontanes on November 16, 1803. "But the prospect of another eight years of exile makes me tremble ... and according to a law of the Republic, no French person can receive a foreign pension."

13 Louis XVI was executed on January 21, 1793.

BOOK SIXTEEN

1 One of Madame de Beaumont's final requests had been that Chateaubriand live with his wife again, which he had not done since the three months he had spent with her immediately following their marriage in 1792. Chateaubriand made no move to invite her to Paris, but Madame de Chateaubriand, in the words of Jean-Paul Clément, "took the initiative and joined her husband at the Hôtel de France on or about March 15, 1804."

2 Moreau, Cadoudal, and Pichegru were plotting to depose the First Consul and reestablish the Bourbon Legitimacy by placing the Duc d'Enghien on the throne. They were arrested one by one in February and March 1804. Pichegru was found strangled in his prison cell in April. Cadoudal was executed in June. Moreau was spared and exiled to the United States, where he settled near Trenton, New Jersey, before returning to Europe and dying in the Battle of Dresden in 1813.

3 Étienne-Denis Pasquier (1767–1862) was a relatively liberal Bourbonist lawyer who stayed out of public life from the early 1790s until he was appointed master of requests in 1806.

4 Allusion to Proverbs 6:17, in which three of the seven things that are an "abomination unto the Lord" are listed, including "a proud look [*oculos sublimes*], a lying tongue, and hands that shed innocent blood."

5 John 8:43 "Why do ye not understand my speech? even because ye cannot hear my word."

6 This conversation between Chateaubriand and Charles X at Hradschin Castle took place in 1833, twenty-nine years after the Duc d'Enghien's death.

7 For reasons that are not entirely clear, Nero planned to kill his mother, Agrippina, by having her board a boat that had been designed to sink. The boat sank, but Agrippina didn't die: she swam ashore. Hearing she'd survived, Nero sent an assassin or group of assassins to stab her to death. The deed now done, Nero charged his tutor, Seneca, with the task of composing a letter explaining Agrippina's demise. Seneca, writing in the voice of Nero, claimed that Agrippina had been planning a coup d'état and that, when her treachery was discovered, she had killed herself. Probably no one believed this explanation, but there were, according to Tacitus (*Annals* 14.12), great displays of rejoicing in the Senate and many festivities celebrating the salvation of the empire.

8 The Duc d'Enghien.

9 A *capitaine rapporteur* interrogated the person on trial, as well as the witnesses, and—according to the *Report from His Majesty's Commissioners for Inquiring into the System of Military Punishments in the Army* (London, 1836)—"takes all the steps that may be necessary to enlighten the council to the performance of their sacred duty." He does not, however, have "a deliberative voice in the council."

10 The daughter of the last Holy Roman Emperor, Marie Louise (1791–1847) was Napoleon's second wife and the Empress of the French from 1810 to 1814. Their son, Napoleon II (1811–1832), was declared the King of Rome.

11 In a footnote, Chateaubriand writes: "Allusion to an abominable reply said to have been made to M. le Duc d'Enghien." When the duke asked the firing squad to "shoot straight," one of the gunmen retorted, "You will find you have no friends here."

12 Freiburg im Breisgau was the place where, in 1644, the Duc d'Enghien's ancestor, "the great Condé" (1646–1686), defeated the Bavarians and the troops of the Holy Roman Empire. (See also Book 9, Chapter 12 of the *Memoirs*.) Marengo was the place where, in 1800, Napoleon defeated the Austrians.

13 A condensed quotation from Joinville's *Life of Saint Louis*, adapted here from Caroline Smith's translation.

14 The Comte de Las Cases (1766–1842), who volunteered to go into exile with Napoleon, kept a journal that includes many recorded conversations with the deposed emperor on Saint Helena. It was published as the *Memorial of Saint Helena*.

15 A reference to an emblem of Hercules (called Hercules Gallicus) the second-century Roman writer Lucian claimed to have seen in Marseille. In this emblem, according to George Puttenham's *The Arte of English Poesie* (1589), "they had figured a lustie old man with a long chayne tyed by one end at his tong, by the other end at the peoples eares, who stood a farre of and seemed to be drawen to him by the force of that chayne fastned to his tong, as who would say, by force of his perswasions."

16 Paul I, Emperor of Russia (1754–1801), was strangled by a group of military officers at his palace in Saint Petersburg on March 23, 1801.

17 "For the Duc d'Enghien, whom the Corsican monster devoured."

18 Milton's *Paradise Lost*, Book 10, lines 670–672, 699–700.

19 Raymond of Toulouse (1156–1222) was excommunicated by the Roman Catholic Church multiple times, for, among other things, assassinating

a cardinal and marrying his first cousin. At his death, he remained excommunicate. His body was laid in a coffin and taken to a church but no one dared to bury it. And so the corpse remained, putrescing in an open coffin, reportedly for more than three hundred years.

20 A reference to Bossuet's once-famous oration on the death of Condé. Chateaubriand alludes to this oration again in the next paragraph ("victorious and now feeble hands," etc.) as well as earlier in the *Memoirs* (Book 7, Chapter 10).

21 On a trip to England, the sixty-some-year-old Louis Henri, Duc de Bourbon and Prince de Condé (1756–1830), had, at a house of ill repute, met a young woman called Sophie Dawes. The duke brought Sophie back to France with him and in 1818 contrived to have her marry a penniless young officer named Feuchères, whom he talked Louis XVIII into elevating to the rank of baron. In 1824, Feuchères discovered the role he was playing, separated from Sophie, and caused a scandal. Louis XVIII banned Sophie from Court. Sophie then approached Louis Philippe, Duc d'Orléans (the future King Louis Philippe I), and conspired with him to make her former lover sign over the majority of his fortune to Henri, the son she had had with Louis Philippe. This was in August 1829.

In 1830, when the July Monarchy came to power, it appears that the Duc de Bourbon was thinking of secretly leaving France. On August 27, he was found hanging by the neck from the espagnolette of his window, but with his feet touching the ground. Louis Philippe and Sophie Dawes were both accused of being involved in the death. "In reality," writes Guy Antonetti in *Louis-Philippe* (1994), the new king "knew very well that there had been no suicide but was neither able, nor did he wish, to admit the truth," which was that the duke enjoyed erotic asphyxiation. Very likely the reason that Sophie Dawes had him under her thumb, Antonetti suggests, was her willingness to participate in his pleasure. At any rate, whether the duke's death was suicide, accident, or murder, with him the Condé line came to an end.

22 Boileau's "Epistle VIII, To Monsieur Racine."

23 Proust, in his essay on Chateaubriand (trans. Sylvia Townsend Warner), writes of reading this passage: "We are sure that this person is a poet, a *rara avis*, since what he says is always identical, and does not borrow any grandeur, any authenticity, from any of the things he relates, which do not alter it, whereas quite suddenly, whether it is a matter of the great Condé or of a little flower gathered at Chantilly, one feels that beneath

his sentence there lies another reality, which shows through from beneath it and whose physiognomy is made apparent, beneath the several
clauses of the sentence, by their lineaments which correspond to it."

BOOK SEVENTEEN

1 "This conversation with three crows," writes the Comte de Marcellus,
   "was repeated in London in 1822 with the crows of Regent's Park, and in
   the same number. The author, to distract himself from his thoughts, or
   rather to let them run their course inside him, used to go and watch their
   games, and often told me about their feats of prowess. I can still hear the
   words he would always say to me when he got back from his solitary
   rambles: 'Well, would you believe I saw my three crows again today?'"

2 Literally, "quails feeding on the stalks." An altered quotation of Man-
   tuan's *Villa Refrigerii* (1447–1516), which reads: "*Sedula per stipulas ten-
   era cum prole coturnix / Pascitur*" ("Carefully do the quail with their
   young feed on the tender stalks").

3 Natalie de Noailles (1774–1835), whom Chateaubriand first met in the
   spring of 1805. He spent the summer in Méréville with her in 1807 and
   again in 1808.

4 The Garde-Meuble (the organization responsible for providing and
   keeping up the wardrobe and furnishings of the royal household during
   the Ancien Régime) used to be housed on the north side of what is today
   the Place de la Concorde (formerly the Place Louis XV) in the building
   now known as the Hôtel de la Marine, whose colonnaded façade was
   designed by Anges-Jacques Gabriel. It is directly across rue Royale from
   the Hôtel de Coislin.

5 Louise Julie de Mailly-Nesle (1710–1751) was another of Louis XV's
   mistresses.

6 French coins of the Ancien Régime (although silver five-franc coins
   were still routinely called écus well into the nineteenth century).

7 Reference to an epigram by Lucillius found in *The Greek Anthology*:
   "Hermocrates the miser when he was dying wrote himself his own heir
   in his will, and he lay there reckoning what fee he must pay the doctors
   if he leaves his bed and how much his illness costs him. But when he
   found it cost one drachma more if he were saved, 'It pays,' he said, 'to
   die,' and stiffened himself out" (trans. W. R. Paton).

8 Amélie Panckoucke (1743–1830), wife of the Academy member Jean-
   Baptiste-Antoine Suard (1733–1817), held a famous salon a half-dozen

doors down from the Hôtel de Coislin, at 13 rue Royale. (The room itself has been reassembled and is on permanent display at the Philadelphia Museum of Art.)

9 Honoré d'Urfé (1568–1625).

10 "I recall only that upon drawing near Lyon," Rousseau writes in his *Confessions* (trans. Christopher Kelly), "I was tempted to prolong my route to go to see the banks of the Lignon; for among the novels I had read with my father *Astrée* had not been forgotten, and it was this one that most frequently came back to my heart."

11 Chateaubriand is here referring to the painter Forbin (1779–1841), who in 1817 and 1818 traveled to Greece, Constantinople, Syria, and Egypt to purchase Greek and Roman artworks for the Louvre and the Musée du Luxembourg.

12 Phrase referring to painters, coined by the satirist Mathurin Régnier (1573–1613), and playing on the phrase "knights of the rainbow," which used to be applied to servants dressed in colorful livery.

13 Saturn is the planet associated with melancholy.

14 Oppian's *Cynegetica*, Book 2 (trans. A.W. Mair).

15 Rousseau's *Confessions*, Part 1, Book 4.

16 A series of Lyon-related references, spanning the centuries. Loyse Labé is, in modern orthography, the Lyonnaise poet Louise Labé (1524–1566). "The killing fields of Brotteaux" refer to the open ground where nearly three hundred political prisoners were killed using primitive machine-gun-like methods (three cannons, loaded with grapeshot) in 1793. The "latest slayings"—in another draft, Chateaubriand wrote the "latest disturbances"—are the first Canut revolts (1831), when many Lyonnais silk workers (*canuts*) protested for higher wages and clashed with Guardsmen, resulting in more than one hundred deaths. The "True Charter" is an ironic allusion to the July Monarchy of Louis Philippe, who declared that the Charter, instated by Louis XVIII, would during his reign "be true."

17 A dapifer was, in medieval times, the servant who brought the meat to the table.

18 Saint Bruno of Cologne (c. 1030–1101), founder of the Carthusian order, was depicted in a painting by Eustache Le Sueur (1616–1655).

19 A byzantine sequence of allusions to sugar. Nearchus, an officer in the army of Alexander the Great, referred to sugarcane as "Indian reeds from which honey is made, though without bees." The Arabs brought

sugarcane from Persia to Sicily in the ninth or tenth century, and in the late eighteenth century French colonists began cultivating it in Tahiti. Chaptal (1756–1832) was an active promoter of beet sugar, which he pointed out would be cheaper to produce and might make France less dependent on international trade.

20 This is how Héloïse addressed one of her letters to Abelard.

21 The Latin Chateaubriand quotes (*"concubinae vel scorti"*) is less decorous than his French; Héloïse writes, in William Levitan's translation, "The name of wife may have the advantages of sanctity and safety, but to me the sweeter name will always be *lover* or, if your dignity can bear it, *concubine* or *whore*."

22 François Armand Gervaise (1660–1761), a disciple of Rancé (founder of the Trappist order) and the author of a biography of Abelard.

23 This was probably "Le Montagnard émigré" ("The Exiled Mountain Dweller"), a ballad Chateaubriand later incorporated into *Les Aventures du dernier Abencérage* (and a ballad Nabokov alludes to in both *Ada, or Ardor* and *Lolita*).

24 Psalm 143:7.

25 Chateaubriand was informed of Lucile's death on November 13, 1804, by his sister Marie Anne (Madame de Marigny), who was then living in Paris. The original death certificate was lost when the Hôtel de Ville burned during the Bloody Week in 1871, but based on the documents that survive it appears that on November 9 Lucile left the convent in Montparnasse for a room facing the Jardin des Plantes and that, on November 10, perhaps during her first night in the new apartment, she died. Marie Anne was able to see to her shrouding and her burial, which, according to Maurice Levaillant, probably occurred in the Cimetière Sainte-Catherine (built over in the 1820s), where she was placed in the common grave, as was then not unusual.

"It is more than likely," says Jean-Paul Clément, "that Lucile caused her own death." Certainly Chênedollé thought something of the sort had happened. "A terrible thought occurs to me," he wrote in his journal after hearing the news: "I fear that she may have taken her own life." André Maurois, in his not always plausible biography of Chateaubriand, plausibly suggests that suicide may account for why Lucile left the convent less than twenty-four hours before she died, why Chateaubriand did not go to Paris for the funeral, and why, in the *Memoirs*, he dissembles about the details surrounding her death.

BOOK EIGHTEEN

1   Charles Clerke (1741–1779) was a naval officer who served Captain
    Cook on three of his expeditions.

2   The Church of the Holy Sepulchre.

3   Allusion to Lesage's novel *Gil Blas*.

4   From a letter sent from Vienna on November 2, 1793. The English is
    taken from *Beethoven's Letters, 1790–1826* (trans. Lady Wallace).

5   The Château de Malesherbes, not far from which, in the Jardins de
    Méréville, there is a Trajan column.

6   Sixteen or so miles from Paris.

7   Virgil's *Aeneid*, Book 3, line 4, "seeking various exiles in desert lands."

8   Lines paraphrased from a thirteenth-century historical poem called the
    Chronique rimée, by Philippe Mouskes. See also Book 2, Chapter 3 of
    the *Memoirs*.

9   Montaigne's "Of Vanity" (trans. Donald M. Frame).

10 Caffe (like Gaspari, a former French consul in Athens, and Pangalo, the
    French vice consul in Zea) is mentioned in Chateaubriand's *Itinerary,
    from Paris to Jerusalem*; he was a French merchant living in Rosetta and
    traveled with Chateaubriand in Egypt.

11 "Ah! vous dirai-je, Maman?" is a children's song, sung to the same tune
    as "Twinkle, Twinkle, Little Star."

12 Chateaubriand stayed with Franciscan monks when he visited the Holy
    Sepulchre in Jerusalem.

13 From a canticle attributed to Saint Francis, though probably apocry-
    phal: "Love sets me on fire."

14 Horace's Epode 16, "Let us seek the blessed fields, the fields and blessed
    isles."

15 On October 9, 1675, Fénelon wrote this letter not to Bossuet ("the latter-
    day Chrysostom") but to the Duc de Beauvilliers (1648–1714). In fact,
    Fénelon never went to Greece; the letter was composed when he was
    hoping to be sent there as a missionary. My translation of Fénelon here
    is adapted from Henrietta Louisa Lear's *Fénelon* (1877).

16 Plutarch's "Life of Pompey" (trans. John Dryden).

17 Region of Egypt where the Christian hermits known as the Desert Fa-
    thers lived in the third century CE.

18 Epigraph by Antipater of Thessalonica (first century BCE), collected in
    The Greek Anthology.

19 Allusion to the *Lamiyyat 'al-Arab* by the Arabic poet Al-Shanfara Al-Azdi

(died circa 540 CE). As translated by Robert Irwin in *The Penguin Anthology of Classical Arabic Literature*: "I breakfast poorly, like a lean gray wolf, [one of those who] look as if their jaws / Were all stick-splinters."

20 Says Elihu, in Job 37:10.

21 Girodet's portrait of Chateaubriand was shown at the Salon of 1810 under the title *A Man Meditating on the Ruins of Rome*.

22 A play on a line in Aeschylus's *Seven Against Thebes*, quoted by Longinus in "On the Sublime." In the translation of that essay by Boileau, which Chateaubriand here had in mind, the line runs, "Everybody with his fingers in the blood vows to take vengeance."

23 The Bishop of Chartres was then Claude-Hippolyte Clausel de Montals (1769–1857).

24 The Battle of Saint-Cast, during which the French army repelled the invading English forces, took place on September 11, 1758.

25 Allusion to a story told by the thirteenth-century Florentine chronicler Ricordano Malispini. A lion, escaped from a menagerie and wandering the streets of Florence, snatched up a boy named Orlanduccio in his jaws. When the tearful mother "rushed at the lion and pulled the boy from his mouth, the lion did no harm to the boy or the woman." "The question arose," Malispini adds, "whether this was due to the lion's noble nature or because Fate had kept the boy alive to revenge his father's death, as he later did" (*Storia fiorentina di Ricordano Malisipini: Dall'edificazione di Firenze fino al 1282*, vol. 2).

26 Chateaubriand goes on to quote this letter, which is dated "March 25, 1811, Villemoisson, near Lonjumeau (Seine-et-Oise)," in full. Here, to give some idea of its old-fashioned style, is the first paragraph: "You are right, sir, to have received, as indeed you have received, the just tribute of the public's gratitude and satisfaction; but I can assure you that not one of your readers has enjoyed your interesting work with more genuine feeling than I. You are the first and only traveler who has no need of the aid of engraving or drawing to place before the eyes of his readers the places and monuments which recall fine memories and great images. Your soul has felt all, your imagination depicted all, and the reader feels with your soul and sees with your eyes."

27 In 1811, the Académie française (abolished in 1793) was, like the other academies, not considered its own independent body but the "second class" of the Institut de France. This is why Chateaubriand uses the words "Academy" and "Institute" interchangeably.

28 Hugo Grotius's *The Exile of Adam* (1601).

29 Allusion to Samuel Johnson's "Life of Milton," in which Johnson says that, in the *Defensio Secunda*, "[Milton] shows that his eloquence is not merely satirical; the rudeness of his invective is equaled by the grossness of his flattery."

30 As late as February 1848, Chateaubriand still did not have a copy of the speech. Sometime in the spring (Chateaubriand died on July 4, 1848) he received a copy from Philarète Chasles, but this version is riddled with errors. Probably Chateaubriand, who was by then extremely ill, did not have the energy to review it. In any case, although various versions of the speech have been included in editions of the *Memoirs*, I have decided to omit it, following instead Chateaubriand's manuscript of 1847.

31 Epigram by Evenus (trans. John William Mackail).

32 The Breton royalist Georges Cadoudal (1771–1804). According to the memoirs of Madame de Rémusat, "Cadoudal was arrested in the Place de l'Odéon. He was in a cabriolet, and, perceiving he was being followed, spurred his horse on. A gendarme bravely caught the animal by the head and was shot dead by Cadoudal."

33 René's letter in *The Natchez* interestingly presages many passages in the *Memoirs*: "I am bored of life; boredom has always gnawed away at me: what interests other men doesn't touch me at all. If I were a shepherd or king, what would I do with my scepter or my crook? I would tire of glory and genius, work and leisure, prosperity and misfortune alike. In Europe, in America, I find society and nature both wearisome. I am virtuous without pleasure. If I were a criminal, I would be criminal without remorse. I would prefer never to have born, or to be forgotten forever."

34 Caelus is a Roman sky god sometimes conflated with Uranus. His "ancient son" here may be Saturn, the Greco-Roman god associated with time, or Janus, the Roman god of time, beginnings, endings, and transitions of all sorts. The "Troy-builder" is probably Apollo, who, according to a Homeric tradition, built the city of Troy together with Poseidon.

BOOK NINETEEN

1 Extended allusion to Plutarch's biography of the ancient Greek general Alcibiades in *Parallel Lives*.

2 Pericles was Alcibiades's guardian and tutor; Aspasia was Pericles's lover and, later, wife.

3 "The horseman of the South" conjures Attila, who was traditionally

called "the horseman of the North." Chateaubriand's inversion here is meant to invoke Napoleon's Italian and Corsican origins. Honoria, the eldest sister of the Roman emperor Valentinian (321–375 CE), sent Attila a friendly message he interpreted as a proposal of marriage. As dowry, he demanded half the provinces of the Western Roman Empire.

4 Napoleon-Louis Bonaparte (1804–1831), the son of Napoleon's brother Louis and Napoleon's stepdaughter, Hortense de Beauharnais.

5 Chateaubriand here draws from *Sac de Rome* by Jacopo Buonaparte (though the authorship of this volume is disputed), who records that between 1255 and 1257 Trevisan families were driven out or exiled by the persecutions of the Guelph leader Ezzelino da Romano (1194–1259), a tyrant Dante consigns to the seventh circle of hell.

6 Federico Galantini has indeed definitively established that Napoleon's ancestors came from Sarzana, in Liguria, and emigrated to Corsica in 1529, after Sarzana was annexed by the Republic of Genoa.

7 Red, as one of the heraldic colors.

8 From Voltaire's play *Mérope*, "He who serves his country has no need of ancestors."

9 Alexander the Great, according to Plutarch, is the son of Zeus Ammon and Olympias; Ascanius, according to Virgil, is the grandson of Venus and Anchises (and the son of Aeneas).

10 Demosthenes's oration "On the Crown."

11 Corneille, *Attila*, Act 1, Scene 1, "Our two kings haven't come yet? Let them know that he has been kept waiting too long; now Attila is bored."

12 At the Maison Royale de Saint-Louis, founded by Madame de Maintenon.

13 Napoleon's mother.

14 Sampiero de Bastelica (c. 1501–1567) married the noblewoman Vanina d'Ornano. He was imprisoned by the governor of Corsica for plotting against the government but set free by order of King Henri II, whom he helped invade Corsica in 1553. Vanina, on the run and trying to save her property and her life, denounced Sampietro before the Genoese Senate—a betrayal for which Sampietro later ordered his men to strangle her to death. When she said she accepted his judgment, but that if she had to die, she would rather he killed her himself, he did so—an "act of barbarism that made the name Sampietro odious throughout Europe," in the words of Michaud's *Biographie universelle*.

15 King Theodore appears in *Candide*, Chapter 26.

16   *The Social Contract*, Book 2, Chapter 10.

17   The hippogriff.

18   "Romans, who boast of your illustrious origins, consider the wellsprings of your nascent empire! Dido is not fetching enough to curb her lover's flight, but if the new Dido [Saint-Huberty], who adorns these lands of ours, had been Queen of Carthage, he would have forsaken his gods to serve her, and your fine country would still be uncivilized."

19   From Abbé Delille's *Le Malheur et la Pitié*: "What now? Some of the guilty may have escaped the storm's first bolts. Declare they are pardoned, and if by some deluded hope one of these wretches staggers to his feet, let the thunder roll and the lead cut him dead."

20   A French proverb that seems to have sprung from a line in Cyrano de Bergerac's play *Le Pédant joué* (1646).

21   Nero.

22   In addition to six hundred children, approximately four thousand other people were drowned in the Loire at Carrier's command.

23   The "sections" of Paris, instituted in 1790 and abolished in 1795, were urban subdivisions replacing the twenty-one *quartiers* of the Ancien Régime. Each section had a civil committee (in charge of administrative tasks), a revolutionary committee (in charge of finding suspects to send to the Revolutionary Tribunal), and a police committee (the National Guard).

24   General Danican (Louis Michel Auguste Thévenet, 1764–1848) commanded the royalist group on the 13 Vendémiaire.

25   This phrase, "I am the hammer of the world," is typically attributed to Frederick II, Holy Roman emperor (1194–1250), the "forerunner of the Antichrist" who is supposed to have said to the pope, "The fates warn, the stars teach, and so do the flights of birds / That I will soon be the hammer of the world" (trans. Stephen D. O'Leary).

26   Lazare Carnot (1753–1823) was a French mathematician whose numerical approach to military tactics and mass conscription led him to be elected a member of the Committee of Public Safety in 1793.

27   General Jean Victor Marie Moreau (1716–1813), famous for his well-executed retreats.

28   Corneille's *Sertorius*, Act 3, Scene 1. Sertorius, the Roman general who has revolted against Sulla in Hispania, sparking what is now known as the Sertorian War (80–72 BCE), says to Pompey, "I will follow your il-

lustrious retreat so closely, / I will deal with him [Sulla] without any need of an interpreter."

29 Lazare Carnot.

30 Chateaubriand proceeds to list these conquests, which include the number of prisoners, horses, and weapons taken; the treaties signed; the territories captured; and the artworks stolen and sent to Paris.

31 Henri, Comte de Chambord (1820–1883), the Duc de Berry's son.

32 In May 1798, Bonaparte was elected to the Academy of Sciences.

33 Exodus 3:21 "And the Lord went before them by day in a pillar of a cloud, to lead them the way; and by night in a pillar of fire, to give them light; to go by day and night."

34 In Plutarch's *Life of Alexander*, Alexander places the *Iliad* in a coffer taken from Darius, King of Persia.

35 From Pierre Le Moyne's *Saint Louis* (1653): "For twenty centuries bedded in eternal night, / They have known no movement, no noise, no light."

36 Montaigne, "Of the Most Outstanding Men."

37 A fantastical travelogue and account of the crusades "translated," in the Borgesian sense, from a "Greek manuscript found at Herculaneum" by Étienne-François de Lantier (1734–1826).

38 An allusion to a character in Fénelon's *Aventures de Télémaque*, a book very popular with young French readers in the eighteenth and nineteenth centuries (including Jean-Jacques Rousseau and Chateaubriand). Thermosiris is a "priest of Apollo, who served in a marble temple that the Kings of Egypt had consecrated to the god."

39 Herodotus's *Histories*, Book 3 (trans. Robin Waterfield): "They say that after [Cambyses's army] had left Oäsis and was making its way across the desert … an extraordinarily strong south wind, carrying along with it heaps of sand, fell on them while they were taking their midday meal and buried them."

40 Enns is located in Austria, south of the Danube and west of Vienna.

41 A painting by Antoine-Jean Gros, *Bonaparte Visiting the Plague Victims of Jaffa* (1804), in which Napoleon is shown laying his hand on the bare chest of one of the afflicted.

42 Jean de Joinville's *Memoirs*.

43 Chateaubriand here confuses the episode in John 4, where Jesus heals the nobleman's son in Cana, with the episode in Matthew 8, where Jesus heals the centurion's son in Capernaum.

44 Matthew 17:4.

45 Sidney Smith (1764–1840) was a British naval officer held at the Temple prison in Paris from 1796 to 1798; Antoine de Phélippeaux (1767–1799) was at the École Militaire with Napoleon before he emigrated to England in 1791 and took up arms against the Republic of France.

46 Ptolemais was the Ancient Greek name for Acre.

47 A line adapted from the thirteenth-century romance the *Histoire du châtelain de Coucy et de la dame de Fayel*. Seigneur de Coucy was a knight and poet who went with Richard the Lionheart to Palestine and died at the Siege of Acre in 1191. Legend has it that, when he was mortally wounded, he ordered his squire to bring his heart home to his mistress, Gabrielle de Vergy, whose husband, Sieur de Fayel, intercepted this present and made his wife eat it.

48 Chateaubriand culls this passage from various entries in Las Cases's *Memorial of Saint Helena*.

49 Isaiah 56:10.

50 From Bossuet's *An Universal History, from the Beginning of the World to the Empire of Charlemagne*, here adapted from Ephilstone's translation of 1821.

51 "The Porte" is a metonym for the government of the Ottoman Empire.

52 This non sequitur regarding the English was, as Jean-Paul Clément puts it, a "leitmotif" in Chateaubriand's political thought.

53 In 1822, when Captain Parry's ships were frozen close beside each other in the Arctic ice for ten months, he contrived to keep the men busy performing plays, giving each other lessons, and producing a newspaper.

54 Cleopatra is called *fatale monstrum* (a deadly monster) in Horace's *Odes*, Book 1, Poem 37.

55 Flavius Josephus, in the *History of the Jewish War* (c. 75 CE), writes of "one Jesus, the son of Ananus, a plebeian and husbandman," who during Titus's siege of Jerusalem would not stop shouting "Woe, woe to Jerusalem!" and would never explain what moved him to shout these words.

56 Corneille's *Attila*, Act 1, Scene 2. "A great destiny begins, a great destiny comes to an end."

BOOK TWENTY

1 The Roman Vegetius, who lived in the late fourth century BCE, was author of *De re militari* (Of Military Matters).

2 From the *Memoirs* of Gaspard de Saulx, Seigneur de Tavannes (1509–

1573), a Catholic military leader involved in instigating the Saint Bartholomew's Day Massacres.

3 Captain Nicolas Baudain (1754–1803) led exploratory and cartographical voyages to Australia, Tasmania, the Canary Islands, and the Île de France (Mauritius), among other far-flung locations.

4 Contrary to what Chateaubriand says, it was after Toussaint-Louverture (1743–1803) proclaimed *himself* Saint-Domingue's governor-general for life that Napoleon had him arrested, deported, and imprisoned in a fortress at the eastern edge of France, where he died. Portoferraio is the largest city on the island of Elba.

5 "Be good Christians, and you shall be excellent democrats."

6 "What whirlwinds carry man's life away?" This line comes from the *Supplementum*, Maphaeus Vegius's fifteenth-century conclusion to Virgil's unfinished *Aeneid*.

7 The triumphal Column of the Grande Armée near present-day Boulogne-sur-Mer.

8 Andreas Hofer (1767–1810) was an innkeeper and drover who led the Tyrolean Rebellion against Napoleon, who, when Hofer was captured, gave the order, "Give him a fair trial, then shoot him."

9 Chateaubriand often refers to areas that are now part of the Netherlands and Flanders as Batavia, bearing in mind the name the ancient Romans used for the large island they settled between the Rhine and the Meuse in what is today the Dutch province of Gelderland.

10 La Fontaine, Book 3, Fable 4 (trans. Marianne Moore).

11 Chateaubriand here unfortunately shows himself to be, in the words of Henry Méchoulan, "the heir of traditional Catholic anti-Judaism." Although Napoleon had liberated the ghettos of Italy, abolished the enslavement of Jews in Malta, and paved the way for the emancipation of Jewish people throughout Western Europe, he was, as Andrew Roberts writes in his Bonaparte biography, utterly ignorant of Judaism, which—until the rabbis of France and Germany set him straight—"he seemed to believe promoted polygamy." In October 1806, Napoleon convoked a Grand Sanhedrin, nominally modeled after the tribunals composed of seventy-three judges held in ancient Israel. This new Sanhedrin, composed of both rabbis and prominent Jewish citizens, met from February to March 1807, and in April formally confirmed, among other things, that the laws of the rabbis were subordinate to the laws of France, that intermarriage between Christians and Jews was legal, and that Jews

were forbidden to engage in usury. Napoleon's intention appears to have been to promote military service among Jewish men subject to French rule and, secondarily, to encourage assimilation.

12 The Battle of Kloster Kamp took place on October 15, 1760, during the Seven Years' War.

13 Reference to the *rampjaar*, or "disaster year," that marked the beginning of the Franco-Dutch War, when the Netherlands was almost conquered by France and its allies.

14 Voltaire's *Oedipe*, Act 1, Scene 1.

15 "It is done!" The last words of Jesus on the cross, according to John 19:30.

16 After General Miollis captured the town of Mantua, he ordered a statue of Virgil erected and threw a banquet in the poet's honor.

17 Petrarch, who was crowned with laurels on the Capitoline Hill April 8, 1301.

18 A story taken from Jerome's first letter to Innocent.

19 Allusion to *Paradise Lost*, Book 2, lines 1024–1030.

20 At the time of the death of Madame de Beaumont.

21 Reference to the French conquest and colonization of Algeria (1830–1848), during which nearly one million Algerians were killed.

22 Marshal Louis-Alexandre Berthier (1753–1815), Napoleon's Minister of War and chief of staff.

23 From the *Getica*, or History of the Goths, by Jordanes, a sixth-century Eastern Roman bureaucrat of Gothic origin.

24 Allusion to a passage in Saint-Simon's *Memoirs*, in which he writes of seeing Louis XIV and Father Le Tellier, the king's confessor, "beak to beak between two candles, with nothing between them but the width of the table."

25 Charles August (1768–1810) was a Danish prince elected Crown Prince of Sweden in 1809. In May 1810, he had a stroke, fell off his horse, and died.

26 The Château de Grosbois, southeast of Paris, was owned by Moreau. Napoleon granted it to Marshal Berthier, Prince of Wagram, in 1804, at the same time he granted Moreau's town house to Bernadotte.

27 When he was adopted by King Charles XIII of Sweden, Bernadotte took the name Charles John (Karl Johan).

28 In Corneille's *Médée*, Act 1, Scene 5, Nérine asks Medea, "In such a horrible mess, what's left to you?" to which Medea replies: "Myself! Myself! I say, and that is enough!"

29 Salvian, writing about the Vandals' invasion of Roman Africa in *On the Government of God*, says they were *divino jussu ac perurgeri* ("driven onward by divine command").

30 "Emperor Alexander judged most accurately of the consequences of the Austrian match," Walter Scott writes in his biography of Napoleon, "when he said, on receiving the news, 'Then the next task will be, to drive me back to my forests'; so certain he was that Napoleon would make his intimate alliance with the Emperor Francis, the means of an attack upon Russia."

31 After the Fire of Moscow, on October 15, 1812, Napoleon is said to have signed a decree reorganizing the Comédie Française. This is also an allusion to Nero, who, according to Suetonius, sang a song in full stage regalia while Rome burned.

32 John 19:28.

33 From Adam Mickiewicz's *The Book of Polish Pilgrims* (1832).

34 From Lammenais's "Hymn to Poland," which was included as an afterword to Montalembert's French translation of *The Book of Polish Pilgrims*, published in Paris in 1833.

35 Allusion to Molière's play *Les Fourberies de Scapin* (*Scapin the Schemer*).

BOOK TWENTY-ONE

1 Palus Maeotis, or the Maeotian Swamp, refers to the swampy lands at the mouth of the Tanais River, in modern-day Rostov Oblast, and to the Sea of Azov.

2 "Human life is like a path ending in a horrible cliff. We would like to turn on our heels—but we must go! go!...We must keep walking toward the cliff...We must keep walking, keep running, through the swiftly passing years" (Bossuet, Easter Sermon, 1685).

3 Nikolay Rumyantsev (1754–1826), commonly westernized as Romanzoff, was Russia's Minister of Foreign Affairs and chancellor of the Russian Empire.

4 Jordanes.

5 Tacitus's *Annals*, Book 3, Chapter 2.

6 In Central Asia, near the Jaxartes River (today called the Syr), Alexander the Great's soldiers raised altars in honor of the conqueror's progress. The Greek soldiers, however, believed they were on the Tanais River (today the Don): a confusion Ptolemy perpetuated and Ammianus Marcellinus—whose *Rerum Gestarum* seems to be Chateaubriand's source—deepened by transferring them to the Borysthenes.

7   Central characters in Boiardo's *Orlando Innamorato* and Ariosto's *Orlando Furioso*.

8   Cybele, the ancient mother goddess, was often depicted wearing a crown of towers, as, for example, in the *Aeneid*, Book 6, lines 784–785 (trans. Robert Fitzgerald): "Cybele Mother, honored on Berecynthus, / Wearing her crown of towers, onward rides / By chariot through the towns of Phrygia."

9   Poltava, in present-day Ukraine (far south of Vyazma and Moscow), was where Peter the Great defeated Charles XII in 1709.

10 Madame de Staël, in *Ten Years' Exile*, writes: "Alexander expressed to me his regrets at not being a great general: I answered this noble modesty by saying that a sovereign was harder to find than a general."

11 The Aravaci city of Numantia, brutally besieged by the Roman general Scipio in 134–133 BCE, became a symbol of Iberian valor and independence.

12 Allusion to Jonah 3, in which Jonah is commanded to go to Nineveh and warn the populace: "Yet forty days, and Nineveh shall be overthrown."

13 Jerusalem.

14 A river of fire in the ancient Greek underworld.

15 Reference to the "Czar Bell," so large it was once used as a chapel.

16 In the last stanza of Canto 8 of the *Inferno*, approaching the inner gates of the perpetually burning infernal city of Dis, Virgil reminds Dante of the "dead writing" (*la scritta morta*) he read on the outer gates of hell—that is, the inscription that ends: "Abandon all hope, ye who enter here" (Canto 3, lines 1–9).

17 From Milton's *Brief History of Moscovia*, published posthumously in 1682.

18 When the Streltsy—a musketeer unit founded by Ivan the Terrible—rebelled for the umpteenth time in 1698, Peter the Great ordered 1,182 of them tortured and executed, and several hundred others whipped, branded, or exiled. Whether he himself beheaded anyone remains a matter of debate.

19 From Plutarch's *Life of Alexander*.

20 It's true Napoleon ordered Mortier to blow up the Kremlin, but though severely damaged, the palace was not completely destroyed—in large part "thanks to a torrential rain that dampened the fuses" (Anka Muhlstein, *Napoléon à Moscou*). Mortier died during Giuseppe Marco Fies-

chi's attempted assassination of King Louis Philippe in July 1835. Fieschi, firing from an upstairs window, killed eighteen men and wounded twenty-two others. The homemade weapon he used consisted of twentysome musket barrels set in a wooden frame and loaded with buckshot. Like other weapons devised for assassinations (for example, the one used by Chateaubriand's old schoolmate, Limoëlan, for the attempt made on Napoleon's life in 1799), Fieschi's was called a *machine infernale*.

21 A story taken from Ségur's account: "Both his legs had been broken in the engagement; he had fallen among the dead, where he remained unnoticed. The body of a horse, gutted by a shell, was at first his sanctuary; afterward, for fifty days, the muddy water of a ravine, into which he had rolled, and the putrefied flesh of the dead had served as dressing for his wounds and nourishment for the support of his languishing life. Those who say they discovered this man affirm that they saved him."

22 In March 1804, General de Caulaincourt (the Duc de Vicence) had been Bonaparte's aide-de-camp and was one of the men tasked with abducting the Duc d'Enghien from Ettenheim.

23 An inscription found on Roman tombs: "To the spirits of the dead (the Manes)."

24 An attempted coup d'état by Malet, whose plan was to take advantage of the Emperor's absence, declare him dead, and form a new provisional government. He almost succeeded.

25 Henry V was, according to the Legitimist view of things, King of France from August 2–9, 1830. Following the accession of Louis Philippe on August 9, Henry and his family went into exile.

26 Kutuzov was sixty-seven.

27 Chambray's *Histoire de l'expédition de Russie en 1812* (1833).

28 "While the savage boy was playing on the Ebro, he was taken by the ice." This is a slight distortion of Paul the Deacon's poem "*De puero, qui in glacie extinctus est*," which begins: "While the Thracian boy was playing on the Ebro, he was taken by the ice."

29 Lacépède (1756–1825) was the author of, among other books on natural history, a two-volume history of snakes.

BOOK TWENTY-TWO

1 "The carnival season [of 1813] was rather down-at-the-mouth, despite the balls inevitable in a great capital," Hortense writes in her *Memoirs*,

referring not only to the official balls of Napoleon's Court but also to private gatherings. The *salonnière* Madame de La Briche (1755–1844) was, according to Jean-Paul Clément, "ordered to reopen her salon (which had been closed all autumn) in January 1813, following a conversation in which Mathieu Molé had informed her that [Napoleon] wanted people to get back to enjoying themselves in spite of the sad news from Russia."

2 The Great Comet of 1811 was visible from Paris (and Aulnay) for almost the entire month of May and did not completely disappear from the night sky until December. The comet—which plays a central role in *War and Peace*—has often been symbolically associated with Napoleon's changing fortunes.

3 Beginning in 1802, the Senate was empowered to rule via acts, called *sénatus-consultes*, concerning all matters not addressed by the Constitution.

4 Reference to a proclamation issued by Louis XVIII on February 1, 1813.

5 "As a shadow," from the Book of Job 14:2. One of the epigraphs to the *Memoirs*.

6 Asked how he could support Napoleon's annual conscriptions, the mathematician Joseph-Louis Lagrande, author of *Théorie des fonctions analytiques*, replied: "It doesn't greatly affect the tables of mortality."

7 See Book 9, Chapter 16.

8 "Before thee, the Keeper of Orcus shook." Virgil's *Aeneid* (trans. Robert Fitzgerald), Book 8, line 296. The added comma in Chateaubriand's version means that Moreau's dog is here being addressed ("Thou, Keeper of Orcus") as though he were Cerberus, "sprawled in his gory cave / On bones partly devoured."

9 The liberal nationalist student group called the *Burschenschaft* was not formed until 1815, though many of its founding members did take part in the German Campaign of 1813.

10 Tacitus's *Germania* (trans. Alfred John Church).

11 All of these quotations come from Theodor Körner's *Lyre and Sword* (trans. C. Smith). The "Sword Song" is rumored to have been written a few hours before Körner's death in battle at the age of twenty-one.

12 Allusion to the death of Agnar, son of Ingild, mentioned in Book 2 of Saxo Grammaticus's *History of the Danes*.

13 A skald is an Old Norse bard.

14 A *mawwal* is a slow song, traditionally a lament, sung as a prelude in various Arabic traditions.

15 Adaptation of a quotation from the seventh-century BCE Greek poet Tyrtaeus, who, in the words of J. M. Edmonds, "is said to have encouraged the Lacedaemonians by his songs in their war with the Messenians."

16 There follows a quotation of Ernst Moritz Arndt's nationalist song "Des Deutschen Vaterland," which has been omitted.

17 Reference to those responsible for the September Massacres of 1792.

18 The legendary Rütli Oath, taken in an Alpine meadow in 1307, which founded the Old Swiss Confederacy.

19 The phrase comes from Tacitus's *Germania*: "The names of the gods, they call these secrets." The sentence in full, as translated by Alfred John Church, reads: "They consecrate whole woods and groves, and by the names of the gods they call these recesses [*secretum*]; divinities these, which only in contemplation and mental reverence they behold."

20 A patchwork of quotations from the end of Book 2 of Tacitus's *Annals*.

21 Jacques Clément, a Dominican monk, assassinated Henri III at Saint Cloud in 1589.

22 A confusing passage, especially because Chateaubriand gives the events out of order. On February 27, 1814, Napoleon's troops took Troyes back from the Allies, who then reoccupied the city on March 4. On March 7, Bonaparte faced Blücher at Craonne, a battle he lost, although he did force the enemy to retreat. On March 13, the Emperor traveled to Reims, where his army won a definitive victory. He is reported to have said he would "take his father-in-law [the Emperor of Austria] at Troyes" sometime between leaving Reims on March 16 and arriving at Arcis-sur-Aube a few days later.

23 Livy in Book 3 of *Ab Urbe Condita* tells the story of Verginia, a young Roman woman abducted by Appius Claudius Crassus whose death at the hands of her father leads to the restoration of the Roman Republic. Héloïse is the French nun and writer best known for her passionate correspondence with her lover and teacher, Abelard.

24 Allusion to the history of Montmartre (the Hill of Martyrs), where the first Bishop of Paris, Saint Denis, is said to have been martyred alongside Rusticus and Eleutherius in the third century CE.

25 When, in the ninth century BCE, the oracle at Delphi said the Olympic games had to be reestablished, local leaders signed a treaty that made

Elis and Olympia sacred sites. "No armed men," Sharon La Boda writes in *The International Dictionary of Historic Places* (1994), "were allowed to visit either location."

26 Eudes or Odo, Count of Paris and future King of West Francia, kept the Vikings out of the city during the siege of 885–886. Abbo Cernuus ("the Crooked") was a monk who lived through the siege and wrote a Latin poem about it, *De bellis Parisiacae*, which was possibly commissioned by Eudes.

27 From Montaigne's "On the Art of Conversation."

28 Psalm 22:15.

29 Allusion to Bossuet's funeral oration for Henrietta of England, in which it is "death," rather than misfortune, that is "prompt to fill its places."

30 Fabian Gottlieb von der Osten-Sacken (1752–1837) was a Baltic German field marshal appointed Governor of Paris by Emperor Alexander.

31 Napoleon's mother.

32 The Austrian and Russian armies were defeated at the Second Battle of Zurich in September 1799.

33 At this point, Chateaubriand quotes a dozen or so lines about a Corsican who devours Frenchmen from Chénier's poem "Promenade" (1805).

34 From Benjamin Constant's *The Spirit of Conquest and Usurpation and Their Relation to European Civilization*. See Constant's *Political Writings* (trans. Biancamaria Fontana).

35 From a letter that Paul-Louis Courier (1772–1825) wrote in May 1804.

36 "In the night of infamies, in the splendor of victories, / That man ignorant of the God who had sent him...." From Victor Hugo's ode to "Buonaparte."

37 James Mackintosh's "The Defense of Jean Peltier" (1803).

38 Playwright and Whig politician Richard Brinsley Sheridan (1751–1816).

39 Talleyrand's house on rue Saint-Florentin. In 1787, the house had been purchased by a duchess of the Infantando and retained the name the Hôtel de l'Infantando during the Empire and the early days of the Restoration.

40 Worn by members of the Holy League.

41 Taken from the May 1594 entries in Pierre L'Estoile's journals.

42 A majorat is a French title of nobility.

43 The Parcae were Nona, Decima, and Morta (aka the Fates).

44 Maubreuil claimed that Talleyrand ordered him to assassinate Napoleon on his way into exile.

45 Briareus is one of the three giants called the Hecatoncheires (offspring of Uranus and Gaia) who are fabled to have a hundred hands and fifty heads. Asmodeus is a demon prince mentioned in the Book of Tobit. To drive him away, Tobias sets fire to some spices, along with the heart and liver of a fish, "and made a smoke therewith. The which smell when the evil spirit had smelled, he fled into the utmost parts of Egypt" (Tobit 8:2–3). The idea that Asmodeus shrinks down and squeezes himself into a bottle, which must be broken in order to release him into the world, is a very old one, put forth in a number of folktales, poems, and novels, including Alain-René Lesage's *Le Diable Boiteux* (1707), which Chateaubriand would have read.

46 A republican opposed to the Orangist (royalist) party, Johan de Witt was Grand Pensionary of the Dutch Republic from 1653 until the *rampjaar* of 1672, when England, France, and multiple German states simultaneously invaded the Netherlands. The Orangists wasted no time in taking advantage of the people's unhappiness. They started a hate campaign against Johan, blaming him for failing to defend the country and finally forcing him to resign. At the same time, they imprisoned his brother Cornelis (a fellow anti-Orangist) before torturing him and sentencing him to exile. On August 20, 1672, while Johan was accompanying Cornelis out of prison in The Hague, they were set upon by the city's militia, shot, and turned over to the crowd, which tore them to pieces and ate their livers.

47 Louis Pierre Louvel (1783–1820), the fanatical Bonapartist who would, in 1820, murder the Duc de Berry.

48 *Octroyée*: i.e., royally granted or vouchsafed by the king (as opposed to passed by a majority of representatives in a republican fashion). The royal rigmarole surrounding and underlying the Charter of 1814 doomed it in the eyes of political thinkers of every stripe, from Chateaubriand to Sieyès. In June 1831 Alexis de Tocqueville, writing from Yonkers, New York, to his friend Louis de Kergorlay, would sum up the dilemma: "I cannot keep from thinking that the charter of Louis XVIII was necessarily a temporary creation; it had introduced aristocratic principles into the political laws and left in the civil laws such an active democratic principle that it was bound to destroy rather quickly the foundations of the edifice it had raised."

49 References to the Ancien Régime's Maison du Roi, in which noble attendants saw to the king's needs and desires.

50   During the late eighteenth century, the high French nobility abandoned
     their *hôtels particuliers* in the crowded Marais for new *hôtels particuliers*
     in the more spacious Faubourg Saint-Germain.

51   Allusion to Racine's *Bajazet*, Act 2, Scene 7: "I was nursed in the sera-
     glio and know its ins and outs." *Bajazet* takes place in a subterranean
     harem inside the Sultan's mazelike palace in Byzantium.

52   Thucydides's *History of the Peloponnesian War* (trans. Thomas Hobbes),
     Book 3, Chapter 38. The phrase is quoted from a speech given by the bul-
     lying populist Athenian general Cleon, whom Plutarch describes as "the
     first orator among the Athenians that pulled off his cloak and smote his
     thigh when addressing the people."

53   Napoleon required Talleyrand to marry his mistress, Catherine Grand,
     in 1802.

54   Chateaubriand takes a great deal of this paragraph directly from Ma-
     dame de Chateaubriand's notebooks.

55   Said specifically in reference to Chateaubriand.

56   Claire de Duras (1777–1828) is the author of *Ourika*, one of the first
     works of European fiction to address the inner life of a black woman
     character (a character who has been enslaved from childhood). Like
     Chateaubriand, Duras had gone into exile first in America (in 1793–94)
     and later in London (until 1808). Despite Sainte-Beuve's insinuations, it
     seems that she and Chateaubriand were not lovers but very close friends.
     In their letters they often called each other "my brother" and "my sister."
     Whether the subtitle and subtext of Duras's novella *Olivier, or the Secret*
     have to do with her less-than-platonic feelings for Chateaubriand has
     long been discussed. He admired her writing and urged her to publish
     her fiction.

57   Chateaubriand's French here alludes to a rhyming proverb: "À la Sainte-
     Mélanie, de la pluie n'en veut mie," meaning something like "On Saint
     Melanie's Day [which is celebrated in late December or early January],
     enough with the rain already."

58   The Chapelle expiatoire, dedicated to the memory of Louis XVI and
     Marie Antoinette—and loosely modeled on the Malatestiano Temple
     in Rimini—was built over the Cimetière Madeleine. "Madame la Dau-
     phine" is Marie-Thérèse (1778–1851), the eldest child of Louis and An-
     toinette.

59   At the behest of Louis XVIII, the remains of Louis XVI and Marie An-
     toinette were reinterred in the Saint-Denis basilica, home to the "royal

crypt" where almost every French monarch since Clovis (466–511) had been buried. In 1793, the corpses of the monarchs had been removed from their coffins, displayed, reburied in a mass grave, and dissolved with lime. The man "who once sat on the Bourbon throne" is Napoleon.

60 Pierre-Louis Olivier Desclozeaux (1732–1816), a royalist lawyer, lived in a house adjacent to the Cimetière Madeleine from 1789 on. He sold this house and the cemetery to Louis XVIII in January 1815, shortly before the exhumation.

61 Virgil's *Aeneid*, Book 10, lines 173–174: "three hundred / Came from the isle of Elba, rich in ore, / In exhaustible mines of the Chalybës" (trans. Robert Fitzgerald). Chateaubriand means to say iron, not steel.

62 Homer's *Odyssey*, Book 5.

63 On September 1–3, 1814, Marie Walewska (1786–1817) and her son by Napoleon, Alexandre Joseph (1810–1868), then four years old, clandestinely visited Napoleon on Elba.

64 Allusion to *Paradise Lost*, Book 4, lines 32–41:
> O thou that with surpassing Glory crowned,
> Look'st from thy sole Dominion like the God
> Of this new World; at whose sight all the Stars
> Hide their diminished heads; to thee I call,
> But with no friendly voice, and add thy name
> O Sun, to tell thee how I hate thy beams
> That bring to my remembrance from what state
> I fell, how glorious once above thy Sphere;
> Till Pride and worse Ambition threw me down
> Warring in Heaven against Heaven's matchless King.

65 Reference to the gambling game Pharoah (or Faro), in which the bank and the banker play a central role.

66 Fouché had been Napoleon's Minister of Police. Guzmán de Alfrache is the title character in a two-part moralistic picaresque novel (1599, 1604) by Mateo Alemán. Guzmán is an ordinary guy trying to make a living in sixteenth-century Spain and Italy; he works by turns as a kitchen boy, a card-sharp, a thief, a pimp, and a jester.

67 *The Green Dwarf* and *The Yellow Dwarf* were Bonapartist periodicals. "Plumes de cane" literally means "duck plumes" and refers to a coded letter published in *The Yellow Dwarf* on March 5, 1815: "I have used up ten goose plumes writing to you and still have received no reply; perhaps I would be better off with duck plumes [*plumes de cane*]," a veiled reference to

Cannes, a few miles west of Golfe-Juan, where Napoleon disembarked at the start of the Hundred Days.

68 In the late winter months of 1815, General Drouet d'Erlon and officer Lefebvre Desnouettes plotted to march on Paris from the north. Their attempt to take La Fère on March 9 failed, however; they would have been executed for treason if Napoleon had not landed at Golfe-Juan less than two weeks later.

BOOK TWENTY-THREE

1 The King's brother, the Comte d'Artois (Charles X of France).

2 Aurelius Victor's *Epitome de Caesaribus* 39.5–6: "The fact is Diocletian relinquished the imperial fasces of his own accord in Nicomedia and grew old on his own lands. It was he who, when Herculius and Galerius asked him to take back command of the empire, replied, as though warding off some sort of plague: 'If you could see the vegetables I'm growing in Salona, surely you would never think that a temptation.'"

3 Matthew 9:6.

4 Roman household god.

5 Madame de Beaumont. See Book 15, Chapter 2.

6 Much of this paragraph, like many others in the chapters on Ghent, is borrowed from Madame de Chateaubriand's memoirs.

7 It's unclear whether Chateaubriand was ever formally named acting Minister of the Interior. In a letter to his friend Fraser Frisell, Chateaubriand writes: "you know I am on the king's council, but so far I have no fixed title or position; my only orders are to speak to the king about the interior. Does this mean that if we never return to the interior, I will be charged with being minister of it?"

8 Bernadotte of Sweden, like Henri IV, had been born in Pau. There is an echo here of Voltaire's *Henriade*, Canto 1: "I sing of those heroes who reign over France / Both by right of conquest and by right of birth."

9 Lally-Tollendal's father, Thomas Arthur, Comte de Lally (1702–1766) was a French general descended from Irish Jacobites. Unjustly accused of treason for his actions as a general in India during the Seven Years' War, which was disastrous for the French, he was executed, then posthumously exonerated twelve years later by Louis XVI.

10 The lady in question is Julie Charles (1784–1817). Beautiful, tubercular, well read, she would inspire several poems in Alphonse de Lamartine's *Méditations poétiques* (1820).

11 The Dauphin here is the son of Charles X, Louis Antoine, the Duc d'Angoulême (1775–1844), who did not much care for Victor, Duc de Bellune. When Victor, who was then Minister of War and major general of the Army of Spain, arrived in Bayonne during the French invasion of Spain in 1823, the Duc d'Angoulême blamed him for failing to provide the supplies necessary for the army to maneuver their troops. Victor was subsequently forced to resign his ministry.

12 From Jean de Meun's *Roman de la Rose* (1268–1285), a continuation of the original *Roman* composed by Guillaume de Lorris earlier in the century.

13 Chateaubriand says in a genealogical essay written as an appendix to the *Memoirs* that he is distantly related to "a Breton chief named Morman or Mormoran," the ninth-century progenitor of a family whose lands lay not far from Combourg.

14 During the Second Fronde, on August 21, 1651, as his archenemy Cardinal de Retz (the coadjutor) was entering the great hall of the Palais de Justice, the Duc de la Rochefoucauld trapped him by the neck between the double doors, attempting to kill him.

15 Racine's *Les Plaideurs*, Act 3, Scene 4. When Isabelle asks Dandin how anyone can bear to watch a person suffer under torture, he replies: "It's always a good way to pass an hour or two."

16 Ancient name for the sandbanks in the Gulf of Sidra off the north African coast.

17 "Books printed on the other side of the Rhine and the Channel are a disorderly mess," Comte de Marcellus remembers Chateaubriand saying: "they are written, but they are not composed. Look at purely English or purely German tables, for that matter: you can eat there, you can certainly drink there, but *dining*? Out of the question."

18 The Order of the Golden Fleece was created in Bruges in 1429 and was awarded to Chateaubriand in 1824 by Ferdinand VII of Spain. "John of Bruges" is Jan van Eyck (1386–1440); the wording alludes to John 1:6 ("There was a man sent from God, whose name was John"), which introduces John the Baptist. The ancient territory of Batavia was more than one hundred miles northeast of Bruges, in the delta formed by the Rhine and the Meuse, but Chateaubriand's use of the word is in line with his love of ancient place-names (Armorica, Caledonia, Lusitania, etc.). He intends it to be a metonym for the greater Netherlands.

19 Mark 7:35 "And straightaway his ears were opened, and the string of his tongue was loosed, and he spake plain."

20 Pierre-Marc-Gaston de Lévis (1764–1830), whose *Maxims and Reflections* were published in 1808: "Man is bored by the good, seeks out the best, finds the bad and gives in to it, for fear of the worst."

21 Hugh Capet (d. 996) was proclaimed King of the Franks in 987. The reign of the House of Capet ended in 1328, at which point it divided into two branches: the Valois dynasty and the Bourbon dynasty.

22 The Lys ("The Lily"), whose name reminds Chateaubriand of the fleur-de-lis, is a river that runs from northeastern France to Ghent, where it flows into the river Scheldt.

23 The Zegris were a powerful family in the fifteenth-century Emirate of Granada who were said to have been responsible for brutally slaughtering their rivals, the Abencerrajes. The story was first told by Ginés Pérez de Hita in his *Historia de los bandos de los Zegríes y Abencerrajes* (1595–1619) and was later retold by Washington Irving (*Tales of the Alhambra*, 1832). Chateaubriand took up the theme in *The Last of the Abencérages*, in which the last survivor of the slaughter falls in love with the beautiful Christian Blanca, a descendant of El Cid. The Darro and the Genil are rivers that flow through Granada, and the Generalife and the Alhambra are palaces in that city.

24 Henri, Comte de Chambord, the Duc de Berry's son, was the last "legitimate" descendant to the French throne (that is, he was the last descendant of the eldest branch of the Bourbon dynasty).

25 Metonym for those faithful to the Comte d'Artois, aka *Monsieur*, later Charles X of France, who lived in the Pavillon de Marsan—part of the Louvre Palace.

26 "The faithful Marshal Soult" had declared himself a royalist after Napoleon's first abdication, then resumed being a Bonapartist the moment Napoleon returned. Exiled until 1820, he was later recalled and served as Minister of War from 1830 to 1834 under Louis Philippe.

27 1 Corinthians 9:26 "so fight I, not as one that beateth the air."

28 Exodus 24:16–17 "Now the glory of the Lord rested on Mount Sinai . . . The sight of the glory of the Lord *was* like a consuming fire on top of the mountain in the eyes of the children of Israel."

29 Fouché was born in 1763, near Nantes—hence the vaguely aristocratic "de Nantes" he added to his name. He would have liked to follow in his father's footsteps and become a slave trader, but ill health made a teacher of him. Educated by the French Oratory, a religious order, he briefly became president of his local Jacobin club before being elected Nantes's

deputy to the National Convention. In early autumn 1793, he showed himself to be one of the most enthusiastic de-Christianizers in France, forcing former priests to marry women or adopt children, and ordering the phrase "Death is an eternal sleep" inscribed on the gates of all cemeteries. When in November 1793 Lyon rose up against the revolutionary government, he traveled to the city and oversaw the execution of more than a thousand of its citizens. In addition to various other governmental appointments, Fouché was four times the minister of police (during the Directory, the Consulate, the Empire, and the Restoration). Both Robespierre and Napoleon wondered about the warp of his conscience.

30 Philippe Égalité (1747–1793) was the father of the Duc d'Orléans, later King Louis Philippe I.

31 French highwayman Louis Dominique Garthausen (1693–1721), better known by the moniker "Cartouche."

32 Talleyrand had often visited the salon of the future Louis Philippe I at the Palais-Royal.

33 Caulaincourt was Napoleon's Minister of Foreign Affairs during the Hundred Days.

34 A stew of metonyms not readily digestible. Mamluks were enslaved soldiers in the medieval Arab world and are meant to correspond, in Chateaubriand's rhetoric, with Constantinople (for him, the capital of all things Islamic). The beliefs and policies of the Jacobins were frequently called "Spartan"—i.e., pure to the point of inhumanity.

35 The Montagnards, led by Robespierre, who inaugurated the Reign of Terror.

36 In October 1468, Charles the Bold had imprisoned Louis XI in the Château de Péronne and forced him to sign a humiliating treaty. Returning to Paris, Louis was welcomed by a crowd of Parisians and their "talking birds," all shouting "Péronne." See also Book 9, Chapter 8, of the *Memoirs*.

37 Isaiah 24:20 "The earth shall reel to and fro like a drunkard, And shall totter like a hut; Its transgression shall be heavy upon it, And it will fall, and not rise again."

38 In 451 CE, the site of a major battle between the Western Roman Empire and the invading Huns, led by Attila. The exact location of the Catalaunian Plains is unclear, though it was somewhere in northeastern France, perhaps near Troyes.

39 Racine's *Phèdre*, Act 5, Scene 1: "His noble steeds, once so ardent to obey

his voice, now with mournful eyes and lowered heads, seem to consent to his sad thoughts."

40 An extremely eighteenth-century turn of phrase: Chateaubriand's sympathy for the scapegoating of Blacas (1771–1839)—the vehemently anti-republican royalist blamed for the failure of the First Restoration—led him to suppress his profound disagreement with Blacas' retrograde political ideas.

41 Ghent is thirty miles from Waterloo, but the land is very flat and was, at the time, very empty. Many others in the area also reported hearing the noise of battle.

42 John 19:23–24 "Then the soldiers, when they had crucified Jesus, took his garments, and made four parts, to every soldier a part; and also his coat: now the coat was without seam, woven from the top throughout. They said therefore among themselves, Let us not rend it, but cast lots for it, whose it shall be: that the scripture might be fulfilled, which saith, They parted my raiment among them, and for my vesture they did cast lots. These things therefore the soldiers did." Cf. Psalm 22:18 "They part my garments among them, and cast lots upon my vesture."

43 "Napoleon exaggerated the importance of his victory at Jena," writes Robert Baldick, "playing down the significance of Davoust's decisive triumph at Auerstädt on the same day (October 14, 1806)."

44 Quintus Curtius Rufus's *History of Alexander the Great* (trans. John C. Rolfe): "Darius, a king at the head of an army lately so great… fled through the places he had filled with his all but countless forces."

45 Ancient Roman spirits of the dead.

46 Jacques Antoine Manuel (1775–1827) was a lawyer, politician, and orator who opposed the restoration of the Bourbons.

47 Allusion to a remark attributed to Henri IV: *Je veux que chaque laboureur de mon royaume puisse mettre la poule au pot le dimanche*, "I desire that every laborer in my realm should be able to put a fowl in the pot on Sundays" (Edward Latham's *Famous Sayings and Their Authors*, 1906).

48 Henri I Le Balafré's response to being told that Henri III was sending men to kill him: "He is much too cowardly… He would not dare."

49 *Benna* was the Gaulish word for a four-wheeled chariot.

50 The League of Cambray was formed in 1508, ostensibly against the Turks, but in fact as a means of despoiling Venice.

51 "Thou art the man," as the prophet Nathan says to David, 2 Samuel 12:7.

52 A carmagnole was a popular jacket among the sansculottes in the 1790s. Cassius was the Roman senator who instigated the plot to assassinate Julius Caesar.

53 Jean Baptiste Machault d'Arnouville (1701–1794), a statesman who died several days after being incarcerated in the Prison des Madelonnettes.

54 Jeanne Hachette (b. 1450s, Beauvais) defended the city, commanding a regiment of women, against the Burgundians led by Charles the Bold. Her real name was Jeanne Laisné (or something along those lines), but she was nicknamed Hachette in honor of the hatchet she wielded.

55 The Constable de Montmorency (1493–1567) led the Catholic Royalists against the Huguenots in the Battle of Saint-Denis during the French Wars of Religion.

56 According to Alexander Teixeira de Mattos: "An imperial educational establishment for the daughters of members of the Legion of Honor had been founded in the buildings of the old abbey in 1809."

57 Not to be confused with Claire de Duras (who was thirty-eight at the time), this is probably a reference to her mother-in-law, Louis-Henriette-Phillipine de Noailles-Mouchy, who had served as one of Marie Antoinette's ladies in waiting.

58 In 321 BC, the Samnites fooled the Romans into marching through the narrow mountain pass called the Caudine Forks, which, according to Livy in Book 9 of *Ab Urbe Condita*, could be entered only by two narrow defiles. The Romans, having entered by one defile, found themselves blocked in by Samnite soldiers at the other.

BOOK TWENTY-FOUR

1 Thomas Aquinas, in *On Law, Morality, and Politics* (trans. Richard J. Regan): "Augustine says in his work *On Free Choice* that the natural power of judgment has certain 'rules and sources of virtue that are both true and invariable,' and we call these rules and sources of virtue *synderesis*." See also Book 2, Chapter 3 of the *Memoirs*.

2 In 1786, Louis XVI purchased over three hundred Spanish Merino sheep from his cousin, King Charles III of Spain. This flock became the basis of the experimental sheepfold called the *Bergerie royale* (subsequently renamed the *Bergerie nationale*) established at Rambouillet and tended, in Chateaubriand's words, by "anonymous guardians."

3 Allusion to medieval trials by ordeal, conducted using fire or water.

4   Tradition holds that the conqueror Timur, aka Tamburlaine, humiliated Bayezit, aka Bajazet, whom he had captured in battle, by putting him in a cage.

5   Napoleon dethroned Charles IV of Spain (1748–1819) and held him prisoner in Compiègne and Marseille for several years. Toussaint-Louverture, abducted from Haiti, died imprisoned at the Château de Joux, in the Jura Mountains.

6   Taken prisoner at the Battle of Poitiers (September 19, 1356), John II of France was brought to Edward the Black Prince, who treated him respectfully.

7   The English were the victors in the sea battle known as the Action at La Hogue, which took place in May 1692, in the middle of the Nine Years' War.

8   Isaiah 10:5–19 "O Assyrian, the rod of mine anger, and the staff in their hand is mine indignation. I will send him against an hypocritical nation, and against the people of my wrath will I give him a charge, to take the spoil, and to take the prey, and to tread them down like the mire of the streets," etc. Cf. Jonah 3.

9   Suetonius, *Lives of the Caesars* (trans. John Carew Rolfe): "Pollio Asinius thinks that [Caesar's *Commentaries*] were put together somewhat carelessly and without strict regard for truth; since in many cases Caesar was too ready to believe the accounts which others gave of their actions, and gave a perverted account of his own, either designedly or perhaps from forgetfulness; and he thinks that he intended to rewrite and revise them."

10 According to Voltaire's *Siècle de Louis XIV*, the king spoke these words after the Franco-Bavarian defeat at the Battle of Ramillies (May 23, 1706). In fact, Saint-Simon, who knew the ins and outs of Louis XIV's Court fairly well, says that, after the battle, Louis XIV wrote to Villeroi and asked him, "as a friend," to submit his resignation. Voltaire may have been borrowing from Charles V's comment after the disastrous Siege of Metz (1552): "Fortune is a woman: she loves a young king better than an old emperor."

11 Chateaubriand draws attention to the word *conservateur* (meaning conservative) to emphasize all the ways in which the historical record was not preserved, or conserved, during Napoleon's reign.

12 Ezekiel 1:15–21.

13 The Roman actor Quintus Roscius (c. 126—62 BCE), the Talma of his day.

14 Chateaubriand alludes to Béranger's sentimental Bonapartist song "Les Souvenirs du peuple," whose refrain is "Tell us about him, grandmother, / Tell us about him."

15 Probably an allusion to the work of the historian Adolphe Thiers (1797–1877).

16 *The Greek Anthology* 137 (trans. W. R. Paton).

17 A stump is a cylindrical drawing tool, usually made of tightly wound paper, used to smudge or blend pastels.

18 Tacitus's *Germania*, Chapter 14.

19 Dante's *Purgatorio*, Canto 1, lines 22–24: "Then I turned to the right, setting my mind upon the other pole, and saw four stars never seen before, except by the first people."

20 Humboldt's *Personal Narrative* (trans. Jason Wilson).

21 Éléonore, born on Île Bourbon (present-day Réunion), was Évariste de Parny's beloved; Virginie is the heroine of Bernardin de Saint-Pierre's *Paul et Virginie*.

22 From Ephraim Chambers's *Cyclopaedia*: "*Bestiarii*, among the ancient Romans, those who combated with Beasts, or were expos'd to 'em."

23 Alessandro Manzoni's "The Fifth of May" (trans. Lorna de' Lucchi):

> All these he knew; untold renown
> More glorious for the peril passed,
> Flight, then the victory at last,
> The pains of exile doffed the crown;
> Twice humbled to the very dust,
> Twice gifted with an empire's trust.
>
> He spoke: and lo, two centuries,
> Ranged face to face upon the field,
> Submissive to his voice did yield,
> As if to destiny's decrees:
> He called for silence, and then grave
> Judgment between them both he gave.

24 Matthew 4:7.

25 Virgil's *Aeneid*, Book 12, Line 830, "Sister of Jove."

26 Napoleon believed that, like his father before him, he was suffering from "cirrhosis of the pylorus," or stomach cancer, as the disease would

commonly be called today. Many contemporary scholars think he—and not his physicians, who diagnosed him with chronic hepatitis—was correct. Napoleon II (1811–1832), however, died of tuberculosis.

27 "Burning chapel." A funerary tradition probably originating with Louis X in which the royal corpse is surrounded by heraldic symbols and a huge number of candles.

28 Cromwell's death on September 3, 1658, was heralded by some of the most violent storms ever recorded in Britain and Ireland.

29 *Plumeria acutifolia*, or frangipani, which, according to Hindu, Buddhist, and Muslim traditions is associated with both burial and rebirth.

30 A translation of Chateaubriand's translation of the Vulgate, Psalm 87:16–17 (*pauper ego et aerumnosus ab adulescentia portavi furorem tuum et conturbatus sum ... tuae terrores tui oppresserunt me*). In the King James Version, this would correspond to Psalm 88:15–16.

31 In his entry on the tropicbird in his *Natural History of Birds*, Buffon writes that these long-tailed plunge-divers seem to be "harnessed to the chariot of the sun"—an observation that inspired Linnaeus to group the birds in the genus Phaethon, named for the child of Helios who was granted the right to drive the sun's chariot for a day.

32 "After his death, they all crowned themselves, and evils were multiplied upon the earth." An abbreviated quotation from the first Book of Maccabees as it appears in the Vulgate (1 Machabaeorum 1:10).

33 Chateaubriand did not recognize Louis Philippe, whom he considered a usurper. In Spain, Marie Christina of the Two Sicilies had renounced the regency in October 1840.

34 Ezekiel 37:4–5.

35 Giant in Camões's *Lusiads*. See Book 14, note 39.

36 From volume 4 of Montholon's *Mémoires pour servir à l'Histoire de France sous Napoléon* (1825).

37 Racine's *Iphigenia*, Act 1, Scene 1 (trans. John Cairncross).

38 In English in the original.

39 In 1839, the Ottoman Empire was defeated while attempting to invade Syria, their former territory, then occupied by Muhammad Ali. When European powers convened to offer support to the Ottoman Empire at the Convention of London of 1840, France was excluded because (according to Lord Palmerston, who was then the British secretary of foreign affairs) the French "positively refused" to use "coercive measures" to drive their ally Ali out of Syria. This exclusion from the convention

would seem to be what Chateaubriand means here by "our humiliation."

40 Chateaubriand's language echoes Corneille's *Pompey the Great*, Act 2, Scene 2: "His freedman Philip...collects [Pompey's] ashes in a lowly urn / And with a bit of sand he makes a tomb / For the man marked out for a fate surpassing all others." See also the allusion to Plutarch's life of Pompey in Book 18, Chapter 4.

41 The *Belle-Poule*, the name of the ship that dueled with the British frigate Arethusa in June 1778, inaugurating French intervention in the American War of Independence.

42 Scientific name of the genus to which the red-legged ham beetle (*Necrobia rufipes*) belongs; beetles of this genus are reported to have been discovered feeding on Egyptian mummies; hence the name, meaning "those who live on the dead."

43 According to a popular tradition, "the arch is so placed that on the evening of the anniversary of Napoleon's death the circle of the setting sun, when seen from the Avenue des Champs Élysées, is exactly framed within the massive masonry" (*Guide to Paris and Its Environs*, 1907). Some sources also claim the sun is framed within the masonry on August 15, Napoleon's birthday.

44 July 29, 1830, eight years before Chateaubriand visited Cannes, was the last of the "Three Glorious Days" of the July Revolution. On August 2, Charles X abdicated the French throne.

AFTERWORD

1 "Wherever I go among Christians, priests come to me and mothers bring their children, who recite my chapter on first communion to me. Then come the unhappy people who tell me the good I have had the happiness to do them. My visit to a Catholic city is announced like that of a missionary and doctor. I am moved by this double reputation. It is the only thing I like about myself. The rest of my person and fame brings me no pleasure at all" (*Memoirs from Beyond the Grave*, Book 23, Chapter 7).

2 *Memoirs*, Book 24, Chapter 17.

3 *Memoirs*, Book 1, Chapter 7.

4 Chateaubriand, *Life of Rancé*.

5 *Memoirs*, Book 31, Chapter 11.

6 *Memoirs*, Book 33, Chapter 9.

7   In 1829, Jules de Polignac, Charles X's Minister of Foreign Affairs, pro-
    posed that, if the Ottoman empire collapsed as a result of the Russo-
    Turkish War of 1829–1830, France should form an alliance with Russia
    and Prussia in order to reorganize the map of Europe. If all went accord-
    ing to Polignac's plan, Romania would have become Russian, the Neth-
    erlands Prussian, and Belgium French. Chateaubriand, in 1823, had
    similarly ambitious plans for France to join Russia's support of the
    Greeks in their war for independence from the Ottoman Empire.

8   *Memoirs*, Book 38, Chapter 2.

9   "When we conspire, when without fear," from the opéra comique *La fille
    de Madame Angot* (1872), set in Paris under the Directory.

10 After his banishment to Elba, Napoleon Bonaparte was called Father
    Violet by his supporters, who often wore the color and the flower; begin-
    ning in the 1840s, Louis-Napoléon Bonaparte—who here figures as his
    uncle's successor—was called Badinguet (for what reason no one is sure)
    by his detractors.

TITLES IN SERIES

For a complete list of titles, visit www.nyrb.com.

J.R. ACKERLEY Hindoo Holiday
J.R. ACKERLEY My Dog Tulip
J.R. ACKERLEY My Father and Myself
J.R. ACKERLEY We Think the World of You
HENRY ADAMS The Jeffersonian Transformation
RENATA ADLER Pitch Dark
RENATA ADLER Speedboat
AESCHYLUS Prometheus Bound; translated by Joel Agee
ROBERT AICKMAN Compulsory Games
LEOPOLDO ALAS His Only Son *with* Doña Berta
CÉLESTE ALBARET Monsieur Proust
DANTE ALIGHIERI The Inferno; translated by Ciaran Carson
DANTE ALIGHIERI Purgatorio; translated by D. M. Black
JEAN AMÉRY Charles Bovary, Country Doctor: Portrait of a Simple Man
KINGSLEY AMIS The Alteration
KINGSLEY AMIS Dear Illusion: Collected Stories
KINGSLEY AMIS Ending Up
KINGSLEY AMIS Girl, 20
KINGSLEY AMIS The Green Man
KINGSLEY AMIS Lucky Jim
KINGSLEY AMIS The Old Devils
KINGSLEY AMIS One Fat Englishman
KINGSLEY AMIS Take a Girl Like You
U.R. ANANTHAMURTHY Samskara: A Rite for a Dead Man
IVO ANDRIĆ Omer Pasha Latas
HANNAH ARENDT Rahel Varnhagen: The Life of a Jewish Woman
ROBERTO ARLT The Seven Madmen
WILLIAM ATTAWAY Blood on the Forge
W.H. AUDEN (EDITOR) The Living Thoughts of Kierkegaard
W.H. AUDEN W. H. Auden's Book of Light Verse
ERICH AUERBACH Dante: Poet of the Secular World
EVE BABITZ Eve's Hollywood
EVE BABITZ I Used to Be Charming: The Rest of Eve Babitz
EVE BABITZ Slow Days, Fast Company: The World, the Flesh, and L.A.
DOROTHY BAKER Cassandra at the Wedding
DOROTHY BAKER Young Man with a Horn
J.A. BAKER The Peregrine
S. JOSEPHINE BAKER Fighting for Life
HONORÉ DE BALZAC The Human Comedy: Selected Stories
HONORÉ DE BALZAC The Memoirs of Two Young Wives
HONORÉ DE BALZAC The Unknown Masterpiece *and* Gambara
POLINA BARSKOVA Living Pictures
VICKI BAUM Grand Hotel
SYBILLE BEDFORD A Favorite of the Gods *and* A Compass Error
SYBILLE BEDFORD Jigsaw
SYBILLE BEDFORD A Legacy
SYBILLE BEDFORD A Visit to Don Otavio: A Mexican Journey
MAX BEERBOHM The Prince of Minor Writers: The Selected Essays of Max Beerbohm
MAX BEERBOHM Seven Men
STEPHEN BENATAR Wish Her Safe at Home
FRANS G. BENGTSSON The Long Ships

CARL VAN VECHTEN The Tiger in the House
SALKA VIERTEL The Kindness of Strangers
ELIZABETH VON ARNIM The Enchanted April
EDWARD LEWIS WALLANT The Tenants of Moonbloom
ROBERT WALSER Berlin Stories
ROBERT WALSER Girlfriends, Ghosts, and Other Stories
ROBERT WALSER Jakob von Gunten
ROBERT WALSER Little Snow Landscape
ROBERT WALSER A Schoolboy's Diary and Other Stories
MICHAEL WALZER Political Action: A Practical Guide to Movement Politics
REX WARNER Men and Gods
SYLVIA TOWNSEND WARNER The Corner That Held Them
SYLVIA TOWNSEND WARNER Lolly Willowes
SYLVIA TOWNSEND WARNER Mr. Fortune
SYLVIA TOWNSEND WARNER Summer Will Show
JAKOB WASSERMANN My Marriage
ALEKSANDER WAT My Century
LYALL WATSON Heaven's Breath: A Natural History of the Wind
MAX WEBER Charisma and Disenchantment: The Vocation Lectures
C.V. WEDGWOOD The Thirty Years War
SIMONE WEIL On the Abolition of All Political Parties
SIMONE WEIL AND RACHEL BESPALOFF War and the Iliad
HELEN WEINZWEIG Basic Black with Pearls
GLENWAY WESCOTT Apartment in Athens
GLENWAY WESCOTT The Pilgrim Hawk
REBECCA WEST The Fountain Overflows
EDITH WHARTON Ghosts: Selected and with a Preface by the Author
EDITH WHARTON The New York Stories of Edith Wharton
KATHARINE S. WHITE Onward and Upward in the Garden
PATRICK WHITE Riders in the Chariot
T.H. WHITE The Goshawk
JOHN WILLIAMS Augustus
JOHN WILLIAMS Butcher's Crossing
JOHN WILLIAMS (EDITOR) English Renaissance Poetry: A Collection of Shorter Poems
JOHN WILLIAMS Nothing but the Night
JOHN WILLIAMS Stoner
HENRY WILLIAMSON Tarka the Otter
ANGUS WILSON Anglo-Saxon Attitudes
EDMUND WILSON Memoirs of Hecate County
RUDOLF AND MARGARET WITTKOWER Born Under Saturn
GEOFFREY WOLFF Black Sun
RICHARD WOLLHEIM Germs: A Memoir of Childhood
FRANCIS WYNDHAM The Complete Fiction
JOHN WYNDHAM Chocky
JOHN WYNDHAM The Chrysalids
BÉLA ZOMBORY-MOLDOVÁN The Burning of the World: A Memoir of 1914
STEFAN ZWEIG Beware of Pity
STEFAN ZWEIG Chess Story
STEFAN ZWEIG Confusion
STEFAN ZWEIG Journey into the Past
STEFAN ZWEIG The Post-Office Girl